ULMS 157 Introduction to HRM

Custom Publication

ULMS 157 Introduction to HRM

Custom Publication

Compiled for Frank Worthington

University of Liverpool

palgrave
macmillan

First published 2013 by
PALGRAVE MACMILLAN

Palgrave Macmillan in the UK is an imprint of Macmillan Publishers Limited,
registered in England, company number 785998, of Houndmills, Basingstoke,
Hampshire RG21 6XS.

Palgrave Macmillan in the US is a division of St Martin's Press LLC,
175 Fifth Avenue, New York, NY 10010.

Palgrave Macmillan is the global academic imprint of the above companies
and has companies and representatives throughout the world.

Palgrave® and Macmillan® are registered trademarks in the United States,
the United Kingdom, Europe and other countries.

ISBN 978–1–137–29748–8

This book is printed on paper suitable for recycling and made from fully
managed and sustained forest sources. Logging, pulping and manufacturing
processes are expected to conform to the environmental regulations of the
country of origin.

A catalogue record for this book is available from the British Library.

A catalog record for this book is available from the Library of Congress.

10 9 8 7 6 5 4 3 2 1
22 21 20 19 18 17 16 15 14 13

Printed and bound in Great Britain by
CPI Antony Rowe, Chippenham and Eastbourne

Contents

List of Figures

List of Tables

Sources

This custom publication has been compiled for use in the University of Liverpool. The chapters included are reproduced from the following works:

Chapter 1 from Thompson and McHugh: Work Organisations 2nd Edition © Paul Thompson and David McHugh 1990, 1995

Chapter 2 from Thompson and McHugh: Work Organisations 2nd Edition © Paul Thompson and David McHugh 1990, 1995

Chapter 3 from Thompson and McHugh: Work Organisations 2nd Edition © Paul Thompson and David McHugh 1990, 1995

Chapter 4 from Thompson and McHugh: Work Organisations 2nd Edition © Paul Thompson and David McHugh 1990, 1995

Chapter 5 from Blyton, Heery and Turnbull: Reassessing the Employment Relationship © Mike Reed 2010

Chapter 6 from Noon and Blyton: The Realities of Work 3rd Edition © Mike Noon and Paul Blyton 1997, 2002, 2007

Chapter 7 from Linstead, Fulop and Lilley: Management and Organization 2nd Edition © Stephen Linstead 2004, 2009

Chapter 8 from Linstead, Fulop and Lilley: Management and Organization 2nd Edition © Joanna Brewis and Stephen Linstead 2004, 2009

Chapter 9 from Noon and Blyton: The Realities of Work 3rd Edition © Mike Noon and Paul Blyton 1997, 2002, 2007

Chapter 10 from Thompson and McHugh: Work Organisations 2nd Edition © Paul Thompson and David McHugh 1990, 1995

Chapter 11 from Blyton, Heery and Turnbull: Reassessing the Employment Relationship © Robyn Thomas and Annette Davies 2010

Introduction

Customised Student Textbook
ULMS 157: Introduction to Human Resource Management

The chapters in this book are selected from a number of leading human resource textbooks published by Palgrave Macmillan Publishers. It is a customised book that the publishers have kindly brought together specifically for ULMS 157 (Introduction to Human Resource Management) students. Each chapter deals with one or more topics covered in each lecture. This book is therefore essential reading for ULMS 157 students. It provides a comprehensive introduction to the classical and contemporary people management theories and concepts that inform the study of human resource management, key orthodox and critical theoretical perspectives on the work, organizations and employee relations, and, more importantly, a clear guide to the areas of the study of human resource management theory and practices ULMS 157 students will need to demonstrate knowledge and understanding of in tutorial classes and the assessed module assignment and end of module examination.

Although this book is designed specifically for ULMS 157, it is not just an essential learning resource for this one module. It will also be very useful to students in other 1st Year, as well as in some 2nd and 3rd Year ULMS Modules.

The ULMS 157 customised module textbook therefore offers students greater value for money than a more generic introductory textbook, in that all of the content of the book relates directly to both the module learning and teaching goals and the intended overall end of module learning outcomes for students.

Dr. Frank Worthington
ULMS 157 Module Leader
(September 2012)

Introduction

Customer Student Textbook
BUMS 157: Introduction to Human Resource
Management

CHAPTER 1
Studying organisations: an introduction

As citizens of an industrial society, we tend to have a love-hate relationship with large-scale organisations. We frequently berate them for being bureaucratic, wasteful and placing us under the shadow of 'Big Brother'. Yet we take them for granted as providers of employment, public welfare, private services, and even charity or other voluntary activities. In the not-so-distant past, information, leisure, economic needs and other basic life processes were more likely to be directly and locally produced or consumed. Now, complex economic, social and political organisations provide a network of individual and social relationships through which we participate in society at local, national and global levels (Gareth Morgan, 1990).

Such organisations have therefore become a focus for academic analysis. For the time being, let us define organisations as consciously created arrangements to achieve goals by collective means. The significance of this definition will become clear later, but the important point to note is that the same paradox that affects public attitudes is often reproduced intellectually. Those very 'efficiencies' which derive from the scale and structure of organisations create conditions of domination over human liberty and democratic institutions. But even as trenchant a critic as Perrow, who notes that organisations are tools that can mobilise immense ideological and practical resources for those who control them, argues: 'If we want our material civilisation to continue as it is . . . we will have to have large scale bureaucratic enterprises in the economic, social and governmental areas. The development of industrialisation has made this the most efficient way to get the routine work of a society done' (1979: 56). This view is not necessarily shared by all commentators today. Indeed, from popular management writers to post-modernists, organisation – at least in the sense of action to create order – has become something of a dirty word. The fashion instead is for decentralisation, disorganisation and even chaos (Peters, 1989): big and bureaucratic is bad. But we are running ahead of the story.

The theory and practice of organisation has developed around bureaucracies, deriving partly from the work of Max Weber, who, at the turn of the century, was most responsible for drawing our attention to the significance of large-scale organisations. As the division of labour in society and at work became more complex and difficult to manage, the responsibility and means of co-ordination of core activities became focused on specialised units. The essence of organisation is the creation of regular, standardised behaviour and orderly structure. For Weber the characteristic

1

features of society would be complex and highly developed administrative structures governed by rules, hierarchy and experts. Most people would work for or become clients of such bureaucracies. In current discourse, such developments are linked to the wider growth of *modernism,* in which planning, calculation and a hierarchy of authority spread to most areas of social and cultural life.

Some modern writers came to believe that such an *organisation society* reached fruition in the post-1945 period (Kerr *et al.,* 1960; Bell, 1960; Prethus, 1962). The dominant themes were that private and public corporations had helped to usher in a new era where politics, ideology and conflict had been superseded by rational, scientific decision making, guided by a new, enlightened though powerful, administrative élite. Standardised mass production and consumption went hand-in-hand with central direction of the economy and state by professional managers and politicians. A special sort of person – *organisation man* – was even evoked who could be relied on to be one of the vehicles of such techniques, given that his personality and commitment was subordinated to the corporation (Whyte, 1956). As Biggart comments, Whyte was describing, 'a generation of organisational workers who had been moulded by the needs of the corporation . . . conservative, impassive little grey men. Their lives in the organisation were routine and largely unemotional' (1989: 4). The emphasis on 'man' is not accidental. An organisation society was predicated on the assumption of male corporate warrior, sustained by women at home providing the practical and emotional support.

It was pointless to desire significantly different arrangements, as all industrial societies were destined to converge into a single, similar type. The hierarchical and bureaucratic large-scale organisation, with its particular form of technology, was placed at the centre of mature industrial society. In retrospect this kind of perspective is more of an ideology masquerading as science than an accurate description of social trends. Organisation society and 'man' are part of an imagery where:

> all the major institutional landmarks of modern industrial society – the factory, the welfare state, the business corporation, representative democracy, an independent civil service, universal education and medical care – were firmly set in place and equipped to manage any new problems which were likely to emerge in the foreseeable future. Institutional fine-tuning and technical adjustment were all that was necessary to maintain social stability and economic development. (Reed, 1985: 99–100)

Grouping developments under a catch-all label of organisation society or 'complex organisations' became a means, however unintended, of stopping asking questions about how such arrangements had come into being, how they were maintained, and whether they were necessary. In particular it obliterated real differences between organisational experiences, such as being a worker in and consumer of public or private services, or being an organisation in a capitalist or non-capitalist society; and in the origins and effects of different types of technology in varied cultural settings. In other words, such frameworks obscured the social contexts and social choices made about the nature of organisations – how they are structured, managed and experienced.

With this is mind, it is better to think in terms of a variety of *organising logics* that arise out of those contexts and preferences. These may not all resemble the conventional bureaucratic way of doing things. For example, direct selling organisations (DSOs) such as Amway or Avon have been among the fastest-growing commercial organisations.

> Compared with traditional firms, DSOs appear loose and out of control. They represent an apparent management nightmare that only a thick rule book and a platoon of managers could keep together. In fact, DSOs have almost no rules and, compared with most firms, few managers. Home Interiors and Gifts, for example, with 30 000 distributors, has only thirty-five managers . . . Direct selling has a logic too, but is radically different from the logic of bureaucratic organisations . . . a conscious alternative to firms as a way to organise economic activity to make a profit, as a technique for managing labour, and as a means of earning income. (Biggart, 1989; 5–7)

This example could be seen as part of the challenge to bureaucratic organisation. However, that does not mean that there is nothing of value in the study of large-scale organisations. Whether existing organisational structures and practices are necessary and efficient, or whatever forms are dominant, it is demonstrably the case that greater power over our lives is exerted through such processes. Organisations mediate between the wider society and the individual, and joining an organisation as an employee exposes the individual to substantial direction and control. Despite the self-activity of their members, organisations as corporate bodies do have economic and political powers above and beyond those of the particular individuals that comprise them. In fact there is every indication of a concentration of those powers in a small number of organisations that is far from enlightened in its effects on us as workers or citizens.

This was a perspective raised decades ago by C. Wright Mills (1959), who dubbed those who commanded major organisations the 'power elite'. Today, takeovers and mergers continue unabated, whether the beneficiaries are tycoons such as Rupert Murdoch or faceless financial institutions. This is not one-sided. Work organisations remain crucial meeting places of contending social forces: owners, managers, professions, and workers; which generate and reflect contradiction and change. Note here that we are speaking of *work* organisations. This is not an accident. We agree with the approach taken by those such as Salaman (1979) that organisations are not a coherent category of objects capable of being studied in a distinctive way.

This is not the orthodox approach. By defining organisations as purposeful systems characterised by co-ordinated action towards an objective, Donaldson (1985: 7) can link together corporations, schools, families or neighbours fixing a fence. But though work may take place within a charity or a political party, its nature and purposes are different from those which operate under market discipline. Organisation may be necessary to ensure that co-ordinated action of any kind takes place, but actions vary enormously by the type of objective. Take Buford's account of his time among extremely well-organised football hooligans:

> Extensive preparations had gone into Manchester United's last meeting with West Ham – coaches had been hired, with complex routes into the city to evade the police, the arrival times staggered so that everyone did not appear *en masse* . . . Problems of

leadership, organisation, 'big numbers', a hierarchical command structure: the technocrat phrasing did not obscure that what Steve was describing was a civil disturbance involving several thousand people. (1991: 119–20)

Only by operating at an excessive level of generality and abstraction is it possible to treat things as diverse as scout troops and transnational companies within the same analytical framework. Salaman makes a similar point:

a genuine sociology of organisations is not assisted by the efforts of some organisation analysts to develop hypotheses about organisations in general, lumping together such diverse examples as voluntary organisations, charities and political organisations . . . It also obstructs the analysis of those structural elements which are dramatically revealed in employing organisations, but not necessarily in all forms of organisation. (1979: 33)

This is implicitly recognised in orthodox writing, which, most of the time, is not about organisations *per se*. Though comprehensive formal definitions may be retained, the overwhelming amount of writing and research is about business. Why then refer even to *work* organisations? It is certainly true that it is the profit-seeking nature of business organisations that creates their distinctive forms of management, control or other social relations. Such forms of organisation remain the structural core of advanced societies, even allowing for the decline in the proportion of those engaged in manufacturing activities. It is primarily for these two reasons that the bulk of this book is geared towards those events and experiences.

But in the end it is neither possible nor desirable to maintain a complete distinction between business and other forms of work organisation. Parts of the public sector have always operated in a market environment, and this tendency has rapidly increased in parts of the health service, local government and other public spheres in recent years. In addition, management methods or technologies may arise in a specific sector, but are frequently applied in modified forms in others. Finally, as Weber recognised, there are continuities of structure and practice deriving from the bureaucratic forms present within all large-scale organisations. For these reasons, though recognising the limitations, we prefer to retain work organisations as a broad framework. It does not mean that they are studied in isolation. Families and state structures are just two of the forces that interact with work organisations and whose links need to be examined.

Nevertheless to make a positive case for the distinctive study of work organisations does not settle who should undertake organisational analysis and how. The former question is not as bizarre as it sounds: analysis in this area has traditionally been contested by a variety of disciplines and sub-disciplines, including industrial sociology, management theory, organisational sociology and psychology, and industrial relations. This is not the place to provide detailed descriptions or historical explanations of such disciplines (see M. Rose, 1975; Hyman, 1981).

Indeed a case could be made for increasing overlaps in subject matter and conceptual frameworks. There is an increasing number of courses under the heading of organisation studies or related titles, whose primary focus is on work organisations. Though different strands will have their own more specific interests, such as motivation or skill and work satisfaction, there is a growing number of areas of overlap.

If we take management strategy, it is clear that a considerable amount of research has been done from a labour process perspective, within an industrial relations framework and by management studies itself. Similar points could be made with respect to job design, labour markets and a range of other issues. We welcome this interdisciplinary framework and its effect on organisation studies, and hope that this book reflects and encourages it.

But organisation studies cannot be said to be the sum of these and other parts. Since the 1950s a particular approach, normally labelled 'Organisation Behaviour' (OB), or sometimes 'Organisation Theory' has become dominant. It is drawn mainly from management writings and organisational psychology, but enthusiastically borrows from sociology, economics, anthropology and other areas; thus laying claim to be genuinely interdisciplinary. Although the borrowing of concepts may be eclectic, it is not random; rather it is structured by specific problematics (a network of concepts orientated towards a core idea). OB focuses on social behaviour in the enterprise, directed chiefly towards problems of motivation and the performance of individuals and groups in relation to different structures and practices. Organisation Theory is, according to Donaldson, concerned with the trivariate relationship between structure, contingency and performance; or, put another way, it is 'mainly about the analysis of different designs, and their contingencies and their outcomes' (1985: 121). When both are taken into account, the result is that: 'These writers have attempted to draw together and distil theories of how organisations function and how they should be managed. Their writings have been theoretical in the sense that they have tried to discover generalisations applicable to all organisations' (Pugh, 1971: 9). This approach is found in most American and some British textbooks and business schools. Therefore, though organisation studies has always been – by its very nature – interdisciplinary, it has often been on a narrow, management plus psychology basis. Even this 'combination' is unsatisfactory, because there is frequently little connection between the 'structural' and behavioural material. The latter is dealt with under a 'topics' approach, with separate chapters on perception or personality; often with few links with each other, with organisational life, and to the chapters on organisational design, environment or management theories that follow. A dualistic analysis is implicitly or explicitly the underpinning, which separates an analysis of the individual from that of the structural in the form of groups, society and the like.

One of the limiting factors has been the gradual split from sociology. Organisational sociology has had a less than peaceful co-existence with orthodox approaches. In the last twenty-five years there has been a shift in the study of organisations from sociology departments to business and management schools (Hinings, 1988). The orientations of OB and Organisation Theory are far narrower and more prescriptive. Donaldson (1985: 71–2, 119–20) defends this by reference to different levels of analysis. Issues of class and power, ideology and social stratification, and economic contradictions are the province of sociology. Organisation Theory concentrates on the problems of people working inside organisations. Advocates of this approach thus seek to deflect criticism of neglect of wider concerns by moving the analytical goalposts. It is impossible to study satisfactorily something like the division of labour or hierarchy of groups in a business, without an understanding of the broader social division of labour and power structure.

Some sociologists have also accepted that the split means that they are studying different objects in distinct ways. For example, Albrow argues that, 'The organisation theorist is concerned to help managers and administrators. By contrast, the sociologist is "impractical". His search is for understanding untrammelled by the needs of men of affairs' (Albrow, 1973: 412). Such a view may be in part descriptively accurate, but it has dangerous consequences. It tends to legitimise the separation between a narrow perspective which is only interdisciplinary to meet the needs of management problem-solving, and a broader analysis that neglects the dynamics of day-to-day practices in organisations. The view taken in this book is that there is a basis for a reformulated organisation studies which has a specific competence in the sphere of work organisations, retains the capacity to cross discipline boundaries, and which combines theoretical and practical emphases.

Most of the discussion so far has focused on questions concerning the parameters and scope of the study of organisations. This is not the only or main problem with the 'Organisation Theory' that Donaldson (1985) attributes to North American business and management schools. Indeed, it was dissatisfaction with the texts written from within or influenced by this tradition that led us to embark on the process of writing our own in the first place. Despite Donaldson's spirited defence, this literature continues to reproduce a taken-for-granted view of organisations with respect to their structures and processes, and notions of effectiveness and rationality. The rest of this chapter seeks to open up this discussion by examining what we have called the 'domain assumptions' of orthodox or mainstream approaches, before going on to outline some alternatives that inform the way we have attempted to understand work organisations in this book. So as to avoid the discussion getting too complex at this stage, we have not dealt with the theoretical resources that mainstream or critical approaches draw from.

Domain assumptions of mainstream approaches

This section seeks to spell out the underlying or 'domain' assumptions in mainstream organisation theory. Though there are varieties and differences, a number of dominant ways of thinking can be identified.

Organisations as goal-seekers

If organisations are consciously created instruments, then their purpose can be defined in terms of goal-seeking. This is unexceptional and, in fact, provides a means of distinguishing organisations from social institutions (for example, families) or movements (for example, feminism), which do not manifest systematic structures and processes for controlling relations between means and ends. But further definition is more controversial. Goals are seen as preferred states which organisations and their members attempt to achieve through collective and co-ordinated action: 'the planned co-ordination of the activities of a number of people for the achievement of some common, explicit purpose or goal' (Schein quoted in Mullins, 1985: 2). In this 'goal model', action and values are seen in terms of consensual collectivities. Goals are formulated, policies and objectives flow from them, and inputs in the form of activities are created, which, in turn produce outputs that allow for realisation of goals and organisational success.

Though there may be vague reference to 'environmental influences', the starting point tends to be located within, rather than outside the organisation: 'there is an assumption that the organisation has some capacity to resist environmental constraints and set its own pattern' (Benson, 1977: 5). It is true to say that obstacles and variations in these processes *are* acknowledged. Members of organisations may have goals which are contradictory to senior management; creating gaps between formal and informal, official and operative, goals and actual policies (Perrow, 1979). For example, scientific and technical workers tend to be much more committed to their job than to their company, and tensions arise between employees' desire to pursue research projects for their intrinsic value and pressure on employers to monitor and even close down those projects (Randle and Rainnie, 1994). Furthermore, sub-units of the organisation develop a life of their own, partial devolution of responsibility resulting in goal displacement (Selznick, 1949). It is management's job to ensure the best possible fit between the goals of different 'stakeholders'. Emphasis on goals does not enable distinctions between different forms of organisational activity. Various classification schemas exist based on types of goal-seeking which are beyond the scope of our argument. For a more detailed look at the issues, see Eldridge and Crombie (1974), and Clegg and Dunkerley (1980).

In search of the rational-efficient organisation

The emphasis on collective goal-seeking can only be sustained by a vision of organisations as *rational* instruments or tools; indeed this was a prime theme of Classical Management Theory, which formed the basis of modern organisational analysis. When we talk of rationality, we normally refer to the logical nature of beliefs or actions. This is an aspect of mainstream perspectives, but the basic feature concerns the development of suitable means to reach specific ends. It therefore becomes inseparable from a notion of *efficiency*. The emphasis is on rationally designed structures and practices resting on processes of calculated planning which will maximise organisational effectiveness. Some traditional theorists have described this in terms of the 'one best way' to run organisations. A more acceptable version of the rational model recognises the contingent nature of the process: 'Organisational arrangements are viewed as the outcomes of means-end decisions to bring situational circumstances and structures into alignment in order to enhance efficiency' (Bryman, 1984: 392).

Most mainstream texts continue to deny that there is one formula to fit every situation, but any serious examination of popular management writing and the associated business fads shows that the search for blueprints and formulas has not been forgotten (Pascale, 1990; Huczynski, 1993). This can be seen by the rash of books imitating the American bestseller *In Search of Excellence* (Peters and Waterman, 1982). All examine the activities of companies to find the winning formula. At the level of the individual, the equivalent is the endless exhortation to become the 'successful manager', the 'one-minute manager' and so on. Interestingly Peters and Waterman attack the 'rational model' embodied in the classical theorists such as Weber and F.W. Taylor. But their objection is actually to a particular type of rational action that is based on following rules, techniques and structural devices. They quote Selznick approvingly: 'It [the organisation] refers to an expendable tool, a rational instrument engineered to do a job . . . the transformation of an engineered, technical arrangement of building blocks into a social organism' (1982: 98). For them the key role is played by the distinctive values or culture of an organisation, for this has the effect of binding the various participants together. This is what has apparently made Eastman Kodak, McDonald's, Texas Instruments and other companies successful. The magic formula may differ, but the framework of rational action = efficiency remains the same.

Order and hierarchy

Mainstream theory is strongly influenced by ideas of organisations as cooperative social systems; self-regulating bodies, tending towards a state of equilibrium and order. This, in turn, rests partly on a notion that organisations are or should be *unitary* bodies combining the activities, values and interests of all their participants. Each part of the system plays a positive, functional role in this process, for example by generating binding social values. Thus the organisation is a system of interrelated parts or sub-units, for example departments, groups and individuals; each functioning to mobilise resources towards meeting wider goals. These parts are at the same time differentiated and interdependent, aiding processes of integration and co-ordination.

The managerial requirement to integrate potentially diverse goals and activities, could, of course, take place in a number of ways. But mainstream theory has tended to emphasise the advantages of a particular pattern of roles and responsibilities. Earlier we quoted Schein on the need for co-ordination to achieve goals. The extension of that sentence reads, 'through division of labour and function, and through a hierarchy of authority and responsibility'. Such an interpretation of the division of labour has always played a leading role in ideas of how to sustain the social solidarity necessary for the survival of the 'organism' of society or enterprise. Current managerial rhetoric is awash with terms such as 'empowering' the workforce and self-managed teams, which suggest a different way of doing things.

Managerialism

Part of management's social engineering role is to maintain the maximum degree of harmony and generate feelings of belonging in the workforce, reflecting literally the definition of organisation as 'form into an orderly whole'. Common to all versions of rational efficiency is that the logical basis of action is held to reside with the manager. In contrast, employees who restrict or oppose such action are frequently held to be acting irrationally, governed by a 'logic of sentiment', rather than one of efficiency. The more overtly managerial writers are understandably full of references to what management *should* do, and in this sense are clearly *prescriptive* in nature. For some, the role of organisational analysis is to 'help managers in organisations understand how far their behaviour can positively influence their subordinate's productivity' (W. Clay Hamner, quoted in Karmel, 1980).

Effectiveness becomes synonymous with management effectiveness, and options in debates are situated within that framework. Donaldson (1985: 86) disputes this by arguing that though both are concerned with systems effectiveness, their viewpoints are distinguishable. After all, if they were the same, there would be no point in supplying prescriptions. This is true, but the parameters are strictly circumscribed, as in the example supplied – that an organisational analyst might advise greater or less socialisation into company beliefs, with no question of the legitimacy of the beliefs themselves.

Not all mainstream writing is openly managerialist. But the underlying assumptions seldom stray too far. In the preface to a recent popular textbook (Buchanan and Huczynski, 1985), Lupton remarks that social scientists should not attach themselves to any one organisational group or its problems. But he then gives two examples of key 'puzzles'. Why and in what conditions do workgroups restrict output? What are the origins and costs of impeding technical innovation? Similarly Karmel (1980) identifies key questions. Why do people sabotage equipment? Why does the introduction of a computer make many people unhappy? Why do subordinates not obey? Alternative 'puzzles', such as why are alienating technologies designed in the first place, are conspicuous by their absence. In addition the way such problems are defined, and the recurrent use of the term *practitioners* can only refer to management practices.

A science of organisations

In terms of methodology, many mainstream writers take what Benson (1977) refers to as a 'simple positivist view'. That is, they tend towards the use of methods and a view of reality borrowed from the natural sciences. There are two particularly important features involved. First, there is great emphasis on *measurement* of organisational phenomena for example, types of structures, technologies, leadership styles, and even the fit between them. Secondly, there is an attempt to discover clear cause and effect relationships, Donaldson (1985: 84) stating the need to, 'reaffirm the commitment to valid general causal laws as the goal'. He asserts the superiority of science over lay accounts, which is hardly the point. It is a question of the nature of the scientific approach, particularly the mistaken emphasis on laws. The fact that no one can actually identify any does not seem to worry Donaldson, as this is no proof that they may not yet be discovered in the future! Inevitably under the mantle of science – whether administrative, organisational or behavioural – these generalisations are intended to apply to *all* organisations. On this basis, analysis and intervention can be used to predict and control events, and make prescriptive recommendations. Stress on technique rather than values matches the idea of organisations as technical instruments. When combined, these attitudes towards scientific intervention into the organisation itself tend to be taken for granted, rather than treated as problematic. Some criticisms have been raised alongside the exposition, but the next section opens this out more comprehensively.

An evaluation of mainstream perspectives

Mainstream perspectives are not homogeneous and there are tensions, between concepts derived from Weber, Durkheim and other key figures. There is also much of value in the body of ideas, both in terms of the issues raised and empirical work generated. Nevertheless, we can identify the outline of a number of interrelated criticisms, many of which are followed up in other chapters. *Rationality* and *efficiency* have been important themes, and no one should deny that they are legitimate aspects of organisational analysis. But in mainstream theory they are presented largely in neutral terms, as if rationality was a simple determinant of organisational structures, processes and goals. Processes are reduced to a matter of technique; devising the appropriate kind of structure, or best fit with a particular environment. A cosy picture is developed of a functional relationship between rational organisations and a rational society. This perspective removes issues of politics, power and control from organisational choices, and critical questions concerning means and ends. Donaldson (1985: 101) tries to get round this by separating the latter; 'The concern of with rational means rather than values is part of what makes such studies apolitical'. But there are as many contestable choices to be made about how to design jobs or authority structures as there are about the ends to which they are put.

A rational *model* emphasising features such as calculability is further confused with rationality or reasonableness *as such*. As Fischer and Sirriani put it: 'For the critical theorist, mainstream writers have confused the rational model of efficient administrative behaviour with organisational rationality itself . . . organisations must be conceptualised as tools for the pursuit of personal, group or class interests' (1984: 10–11). Furthermore, traditional notions underestimate the role of rationality and efficiency as ideological constructs which help to legitimise the positions, rewards and activities of dominant groups (Salaman, 1979:177–82). For example, when changes such as mergers or closures take place, they are often described in terms of *rationalisation,* as if the decision of managers or boards of directors are inevitable and the only way of doing things. It is important to acknowledge the contested nature of rationality, underpinned by the struggle for scarce organisational and social resources; and indeed, this is the direction taken by an increased range of organisational theorists (Bryman, 1984).

This is insufficiently recognised in mainstream perspectives because they are underlaid by an assumption of harmony of interests. This is reproduced in another crucial sphere, that of the division of labour. The way that tasks, functions and jobs are divided, with the consequent specialisation and hierarchies, is all too often regarded as an unproblematic, technical or functional necessity. The origins and workings of the division of labour is neglected as an issue, influenced by analyses which emphasise differentiation and interdependence. As a consequence, many deep-rooted features of organisational life – inequality, conflict, domination and subordination, manipulation – are written out of the script in favour of behavioural questions associated with efficiency or motivation. Some of these features may be seen as pathological or temporary phenomena arising from breakdowns in organisational systems, rather than a fundamental product of the structuring of the division of labour.

Notions of social harmony have also distorted an understanding of *goals.* As we saw earlier, mainstream writings have made some progress towards acknowledging goal diversity and uncertainty. This is welcome, but there are still weaknesses. Oppositional goals cannot be confined to the 'personal'. As Clegg and Dunkerley observe: 'There is no notion of rational structural sources of opposition being generated in the normal processes of organisation' (1980: 317). A sense of reification is still present, in which the organisation is treated as a thing, and the only legitimate goal-seeking collectivity. Problems cannot be avoided by the use of the 'stakeholder' model (Donaldson, 1985: 24), which postulates a spurious pluralism in which goals are held to be the result of a relatively equal trade-off between the preferences of competing, but cooperative groups (employees, managers, owners, customers). Nor is it enough for Donaldson to assert that the higher levels of management simply 'edit and select' from competing claims.

The notion that formal organisations, made up of different members, are constituted to co-ordinate wider goals as if they are a form of social contract (Albrow, 1973: 408), underestimates the extent to which dominant power groupings have set those goals and shaped the appropriate structures. In practice, co-ordination or co-operation may reflect pressure, constraint or acquiescence to power as much as shared goals. Let us take an example to illustrate the problem – the Wapping dispute. In the mid-1980s, Rupert Murdoch announced plans to move production of his press titles from Fleet Street to a new site. This was planned in secret and sprung on the workforce. The subsequent strike was used as an excuse to dismiss over 5000 workers, most of whom never got their jobs back, there is not much sign of a trade-off among stakeholders here. The power accruing from ownership gave Murdoch and his associates the means to enforce their objectives. Even those, notably journalists, who voted to accept the move, did so in a context of bribes (£2000 and BUPA membership, or threats (the sack). As one *Sunday Times* journalist wrote at the time, 'In a property-owning democracy, the price of the average citizen's soul is a little less than the cost of his or her mortgage.' But in one sense there is a pluralism in work organisations, though different from 'stakeholding'. The array of interests and interest groups that exists goes beyond a conventional management and labour dichotomy. One of the reasons that Murdoch won is that he was able to exploit divisions between journalists, mainly male printers and largely female semi-skilled workers, and white collar employees – all of whom had a history of sectional antagonism over wages, jobs and working conditions.

So, there *is* a sense in which we can refer to 'organisations' having policies or goals, but they have to be clearly recognised as frequently the property of particular individuals or groups. For example, in the late 1970s, the then Chairman of British Leyland produced the Company Plan. The extent to which it was not the product and property of the employees as a whole can be seen from subsequent events. It was put to the workforce in a ballot and rejected. Edwardes then implemented it anyway. A final broader point on this issue is important. As we saw earlier, to define or classify organisations in terms of goal-seeking distorts the differences between them. We need to differentiate between different types of goals and the wider economic and political influences upon them; and to consider how they are constructed and in whose benefit they operate. The example used earlier of direct selling companies is illustrative of alternative *organising logics* that can operate between and even within organisations. Different logics lead to the choice of particular managerial mechanisms. The scientific workers referred to earlier are subject to normative controls which attempt to mobilise commitment to the work combined with a large degree of operational autonomy. Many other white collar workers in conventional bureaucratic hierarchies are being managed through much more economistic methods, such as performance-related pay.

The failure to analyse these processes adequately underlines the extent to which organisational analysis remains consciously or implicitly management-orientated. Texts remain a curious and confusing mixture of analysis and prescription. Emphasis on a stream of advice and solutions to managers consistently undermines the generation of valid and realistic knowledge of organisational processes. Two qualifying points to this criticism need to be made: first, there *is* a need to study management as an activity; second, an openly 'management science' servicing the needs of such groups inevitably reflects existing socio-economic relations. But such an orientation is particularly dangerous to a broader organisational analysis. As Watson (T. Watson, 1980) points out, management requirements are likely to focus on short-term pragmatic relevance related to task achievement, or towards the ideological expedience of unitary and consensual views of organisational life. Theorists can become, in Baritz's (1960) words, 'servants of power', enmeshed in restrictive client relationships within the business firm. The problem is less that of the corruption arising from lucrative contracts (though it is worrying when yesterday's advocates of participation become today's advisers on union-busting) than that of knowledge and problem-solving on management terms. Thus Organisational Theory is helping to constitute a particular reality without critically analysing it, and runs the risk of reducing theory and practice to a technology of social control.

Not only does this limit the ability of analysis to be a resource for a wider range of participants, it has the negative consequence of ignoring lower-level employees except as objects or in their defined 'roles' (Salaman, 1979: 47). Limitations arise from the service role itself. Reed observes, 'organisation theory has presented management with a stock of "moral fictions" (such as "managerial effectiveness") that disguise the social reality of contemporary management practice' (1985: 95). Despite or perhaps because of that role, there are frequent complaints that official theory propagated to business students and managers is out of touch with the 'real world'.

In conclusion, we would argue that mainstream perspectives have often functioned as theories of regulation and are bound up in the purposes and practices of organisational control. This has prevented the development of 'any coherent or consensual theoretical object of the organisation' (Clegg and Dunkerley, 1980: 213). Instead organisational and societal reality has tended to be taken for granted, with emphasis on that which is prescriptive and short term. Viewing organisations as natural systems and as largely autonomous bodies has produced a limited capacity to explain historical changes and the political and economic contexts in which organisations operate. The overall objections of critical theory are summed up by Fischer and Sirriani: 'Common to all of the approaches is a concern over the conservative/elitist bias of organisational theory, a general absence of social class analysis, a failure to connect the organisation to the political economy of the larger social and historical context, a general neglect of political and bureaucratic power, and the ideological uses of scientific organisational analysis' (1984: 5).

Domain assumptions of a critical approach

Like their mainstream counterpart, critical perspectives are based on a variety of ideas and theoretical sources. The starting point is obviously critique itself: the identification of the weaknesses, limitations and ideological functions of orthodoxy. The two traditions are not always different on every point, and there are some partly overlapping objectives for some of the strands of thought, including humanisation of work processes and non-bureaucratic forms of organisation. Nevertheless through the critique an outline of a different agenda begins to emerge, with a concern for issues of power, control, domination, conflict, exploitation and legitimation. What of the more positive alternative? What do we mean by critical? Any alternative perspectives necessarily start from different guidelines and assumptions about organisations and society. Though the issues overlap, we have followed the convention of the equivalent mainstream section and divide it into parts.

Reflexivity

Critical perspectives must first of all be *reflexive*. That is they must have the capacity to reflect upon themselves, so that values, practices and knowledge are not taken for granted. Nor can we take our own experiences for granted. A useful example is provided in the novel *Nice Work*. Robyn Penrose, a university lecturer in English, is sent to shadow the managing director of a local engineering factory. She finds the noise, dirt and disorder of the foundry hard to comprehend:

> What *had* she expected? Nothing, certainly, so like the satanic mills of the early Industrial Revolution. Robyn's mental image of a modern factory had derived mainly from TV commercials and documentaries; deftly edited footage of brightly coloured machines and smoothly moving assembly lines, manned by brisk operators in clean overalls . . . The situation was bizarre, so unlike her usual environment, that there was a kind of exhilaration to be found in it, in its very discomfort and danger, such as explorers must feel, she supposed, in a remote and barbarous country. (Lodge, 1990: 121 and 130)

Despite or perhaps because of the lack of understanding, she blunders into actions that spiral out of control. In fact, our inability to experience large organisations directly in the same way – as individuals or small groups, subordinates or power holders – creates special problems for studying organisation, problems which are often resolved through the use of unsatisfactory substitutes such as metaphors – organisation are 'like' machines, garbage cans or prisons (Sandelands and Srivatsan, 1993).

We have referred previously to unproblematic conceptions of phenomena such as goals and productivity. But a key example of a problematic conception would be that of gender. Existing analyses have largely treated gender divisions as irrelevant, or in practice invisible, despite: 'the persistent fact that women's position in any organisation differs from men in the same organisations' (Woolf, 1977: 7). In this sense, orthodoxy has been as much 'male-stream' as mainstream (Mills and Tancred, 1992).

Instead of reflecting the concerns of established power-groups, organisational theory should reflect critically on and challenge existing attitudes and practices. It can draw on the distinction between practical and technical rationality identified by Habermas (1971) and subsequently espoused by many other radical writers. Technical rationality is based on the instrumental pursuit of taken-for-granted goals such as 'efficiency'. In contrast, practical rationality emphasises conscious and enlightened reflection which would clarify alternative goals and action based on the widest communication and political dialogue. These concepts are, in themselves, rooted in Weber's differentiation between a formal rationality concerned with calculable techniques and procedures, and substantive rationality which emphasises the values and the desired ends of action.

The embeddedness of organisations

A further guiding principle is the necessity to be *historical* and *contextual.* Organisational theory and practice can only be understood as something in process, otherwise the search for general propositions and instant prescriptions becomes disconnected from reality, as it has done in conventional a historical approaches (Littler, 1980: 157). It is also necessary to counter the tendency to see organisations as free-floating and autonomous; and the concentration on the micro-level of analysis, or single enterprise. This means locating organisational processes within their structural setting, examining the interaction with economic forces, political cultures and communities. To return to the gender example, it is impossible to understand the emergence and development of the sexual division of labour in organisations only from within. We have to go outside, to the family and patriarchal structures in society as a whole, in order to reflect back.

This approach means more than diffuse references to the environment. In theoretical terms, organisational issues cannot be comprehended outside of the totality constituted by capitalist society in general and the mode of production in particular (Burrell, 1980). Donaldson objects to this on the grounds that locating explanations within the wider social system denies that organisational phenomena are topics of enquiry in their own right. But no convincing argument is put forward to justify the desirability or possibility of such analytical autonomy, to say nothing of seemingly denying the validity of the work of Weber, Marx and Durkheim. Donaldson raises a more pertinent point when he argues that, 'the notion of totality is a reference to everything – nothing is left out' (1985:124). It is indeed important to avoid reducing totality to a meaningless level of generality: we do not always learn very much from general references to the effects of capitalism and patriarchy. There may not be a smooth fit between organisations and each part of the 'totality', but it is possible and necessary to show the concrete ways in which organisations are embedded in specific social, political and economic structures.

Multi-dimensionality

Explanations must not only be multi-layered, but multi-dimensional. Different modes of analysis are needed to deal with the complexities and levels of human behaviour in organisations. As we have seen, mainstream theories separate the behavioural dimension from employees' roles within the division of labour. Clearly people are constituted as individuals at the level of their identities and emotions, but that process is informed by the same 'structural' and collective phenomena that shape management strategies and job design, the broader social relations of production between capital and labour, or between the sexes.

Radical writers have long been critical of the psychological component used by mainstream theory as part of the explanation of organisational behaviour. Objections have been made to the treatment of people in organisations as 'psychologically determined entities' with abstractly and individually defined needs – for example, for self-actualisation or belongingness. This has led some critical writers firmly to reject *any* psychological orientation. Clegg and Dunkerley argue that people should be considered, 'not as subjectivities, as unique individuals or social psyches, but as the bearers of an objective structure or relations of production and reproduction which are conditioned not by psychology but by history' (1980:400). Although sharing this critique of psychological orthodoxy, we reject the view that people can be considered only as bearers of objective structures. The fact that managers and workers find themselves caught up in structural processes does not mean that they are merely passive agencies or operate solely at a group level. Any circumstances are experienced inter-subjectively, reconstructed and modified.

A purely structural analysis, even where it allows for human action and resistance, fails to get sufficiently inside those routine everyday experiences in which people react, adapt, modify, and consent to work relations. As concepts of motivation, perception and the like inadequately address the problem, some account of subjectivity and identity is necessary. Nor is the question of subjectivity significant solely at the level of the individual. A critical psychology should also identify the ways in which organisations act as 'people processors', whether through informal cultural practices or formal managerial strategies to mobilise consent.

That is not to say that it is easy to integrate the different dimensions. Our aim in this book at this stage is to establish complementarity and points of connection rather than synthesis and the solving of underlying theoretical questions. As subjectivity and psychological theories are the province of later chapters, we shall say no more at this stage.

Dialectics and contradiction

Many critical theorists (for example, Benson, 1977; Storey, 1983) utilise the notion of dialectical perspectives as a crucial means of explaining the dynamic of organisational change. In abstract terms a dialectical process refers to a movement from thesis to antithesis and synthesis and derives from Hegel and Marx. More frequently it is used to denote a reciprocal interaction, between structure and human agency or between conflicting groups. It is not always usefully employed. Gareth Morgan (1986: 266) produces a list which places 'oppositions' as varied as capital and labour, young and old and even sales and production on the same level. But a more focused emphasis on the interaction and structured antagonisms between key economic actors is valuable. We refer to 'structured' because group conflicts are shaped by contradictions – forces pulling in opposite directions – for example, between private ownership and collective social needs. These contradictions help reproduce antagonistic relations which are built into work organisation and society, and which in turn generate conflict and change.

The most direct application of dialectical pespectives to work organisations is expressed in the idea of a reciprocal relation between managerial control and worker resistance. Management control strategies are fundamentally a means of dealing with contradictions, uncertainties and crises in their socio-economic environment. New methods of control inevitably provoke and shape forms of employee resistance and sometimes counter-'strategies'. Over a period of time, management responses are likely to develop into alternative control methods, blending with and going beyond the old. For example, piecework was introduced as means for management to set targets and control through monetary incentives. But the shop floor frequently devised ways of asserting their own controls over output and earnings. In the 1970s employers in the motor industry responded by establishing new payment systems based on 'measured day rates', but still using control techniques based on work study and measurement. Over a period of time workers developed their own methods of adaptation and resistance, so the cycle continues.

This kind of perspective puts more substance into the traditional idea of an interaction between formal and informal dimensions of organisational life. However it is formulated, we can view organisations as continually having to respond to and counter *disorganisation:* a process which is underpinned by the divergent goals and interests discussed earlier in this chapter. Those who command organisations are required to mobilise a variety of resources to counter disorganisation. Although the actors themselves may not see it in these terms, we can pull together a variety of practices under the conceptual umbrellas of power, control and persuasion or consent. The factors underlying such choices and the different forms managerial and employee action take will be key and recurrent themes of this book.

Social transformation

The fact that we have argued against prescription does not mean a lack of interest in the 'practical' or the applied. We have tried to approach this in a number of ways. First, by giving an account and evaluation of up-to-date empirical research into work organisations, rather than the make-believe simulations that accompany many conventional texts. This involves critically examining as an issue in its own right the interventions made by social scientists as researchers or consultants. Second, by always analysing theories and practices together and as part of specific economic and political contexts. Showing how theories are used by managerial and other groups may sound unexceptional. But the dominant tradition has been to treat the major theories of organisation and management primarily as ideas systems and historically sequenced. The result is that most students do not get a realistic and informed view of the practicality of theory. In addition the impression is often given that theories developed in the past are outdated and 'wrong' compared to the latest favoured perspective. When these are inevitably replaced, cynicism about theory and organisational analysis is the likely result.

But alternative 'practicalities' have to go further than this and provide resources for social transformation. In this context, Benson adds a further aspect of a dialectical perspective, that of *praxis,* drawing on the previously discussed notion of practical rationality. Praxis involves developing analytical resources which go beyond reflexivity and can help members of organisations constrained by existing relations of ownership and power to reflect critically on and reconstruct their circumstances. Though some critical theorists advocate the prioritisation of 'philosophically informed armchair theorising' (Burrell, 1980: 102), we would agree with Benson's emphasis on theory as an emancipatory guide and as a means for *empowering* a wider range of organisational participants. When empowerment is used by management theorists and practioners to describe 'enabling' employees to chase more customers or do three more jobs, the term joins a long list whose rhetoric is not matched by reality.

A critical use implies no particular form of politics or intervention, but rather empowering employees to make more choices and to act more effectively to transform workplace relations. It may be argued that this reproduces a one-sided partiality that is the reverse of the management orientation of mainstream theories. There is always that danger. But the existing realities and power relations in organisations will, for the foreseeable future, enable critical theory to maintain a certain distance and intellectual independence. Furthermore, any critical theory not testing its ideas through empirical investigation or practical intervention is ultimately arid.

Finally, we should make clear that our project does not involve a rejection of the idea of organisation theory, merely a particular conception of it. It is necessary to treat mainstream theory as a series of overlapping perspectives sharing certain ideas and methods, while differing on others. Some concepts and research are useful and compatible with a critical approach, others are not. None can be considered simply as 'tools of management', or as embodying the values and interests of the dominant class. Such a view wrongly assumes that there is such a clear set of interests that can be reflected at a theoretical level. The tortuous history of organisational theory and practice in fact reveals a consistent tension between different approaches to regulation, which, in turn reflects the conflicting pressures to control *and* engage the workforce. All but the most unreflexive perspectives require some distancing from existing practices in order to act upon them in a way that will be a resource for management.

References

Albrow, M. (1973) The Study of Organizations - Objectivity or Bias?' in G. Salaman and K. Thompson (eds) *People and Organizations,* Harlow: Longman.

Bell, D. (1960) *The End of Ideology,* New York: Collier Macmillan.

Benson, J. K. (1977) 'Innovation and Crisis in Organizational Analysis', in J. K. Benson (ed.) *Organizational Analysis: Critique and Innovation,* London: Sage.

Benson, J. K. (ed.) (1977) *Organizational Analysis: Critique and Innovation,* London: Sage, Contemporary Social Science Issues, 37.

Biggart, N.W. (1989) *Charismatic Capitalism: Direct Selling Organizations in America,* London: University of Chicago Press.

Bryman, A. (1984) 'Organization Studies and the Concept of Rationality', *Journal of Management Studies,* vol. 21: 394–404.

Buchanan, D. and A. Huczynski (1985) *Organizational Behaviour: An Introductory Text,* London: Prentice-Hall International.

Burrell, G. (1980a) 'Radical Organization Theory', in D. Dunkerley and G. Salaman (eds) *The International Yearbook of Organization Studies 1979,* London: Routledge & Kegan Paul.

Clegg, S. and D. Dunkerley (1980) *Organization, Class and Control,* London: Routledge & Kegan Paul.

Donaldson, L. (1985) *In Defence of Organization Theory: A Reply to the Critics,* Cambridge: Cambridge University Press.

Eldridge, J. E. T. and A. D. Crombie (1974) *A Sociology of Organizations,* London: Allen & Unwin.

Fischer, F. and C. Sirriani (1984) *Critical Studies in Organization and Bureaucracy,* Philadelphia: Temple University Press.

Habermas, J. (1971) *Toward a Rational Society,* London: Heinemann.

Hinings, B. (1988) 'Defending Organization Theory: A British View from North America', *Organization Studies,* vol. 9, no. 1: 2–7.

Huczynski, A. A. (1993) *Management Gurus,* London: Routledge.

Karmel, B. (ed.) (1980) *Point and Counterpoint in Organizations,?* Illinois: Dryden.

Kerr, C, J. J. Dunlop, F. H. Harbison and C. A. Mayers (1960) *Industrialism and Industrial Man,* Cambridge, Mass.: Harvard University Press.

Littler, C. R. (1980) 'Internal Contract and the Transition to Modern Work Systems', in D. Dunkerley and G. Salaman (eds) *The International Yearbook of Organization Studies 1979,* London: Routledge & Kegan Paul.

Lodge, D. (1990) *Nice Work,* Harmondsworth: Penguin.

Mills, A. J. and P. Tancred (eds) (1992) *Gendering Organizational Analysis,* London: Sage.

Mills, C. W. (1959) *The Power Elite,* New York: Oxford University Press.

Morgan, Gareth (1986) *Images of Organisation,* London: Sage.

Morgan, Glenn (1990) *Organizations in Society,* London: Sage.

Pascale, R. T. (1990) *Managing on the Edge,* Harmondsworth: Penguin.

Perrow, C. (1979) *Complex Organizations: A Critical Essay,* Illinois: Scott Foreman.

Peters, T. (1989) *Thriving on Chaos,* London: Pan.

Peters, T. J. and R. H. Waterman (1982) *In Search of Excellence: Lessons from America's Best-Run Companies,* New York: Harper & Row.

Prethus, R. (1962) *The Organizational Society,* London: Macmillan.

Pugh, D.S. (ed.) (1971) *Organization Theory,* Harmondsworth: Penguin.

Randle, K. and A. Rainnie (1994) 'Control, Contradiction and Complexity in a Pharmaceutical Research Company', paper to 12th International Labour Process Conference, Aston.

Rose, M. (1975; 2nd edn 1986) *Industrial Behaviour,* Harmondsworth: Penguin.

Salaman, G. (1979) *Work Organizations: Resistance and Control,* London: Longman.

Sandelands, L. E. and V. Srivatsan (1993) 'The Problem of Experience in the Study of Organizations', *Organization Studies,* vol. 14, no. 1: 1–22.

Selznick, P. (1949) *TV A and the Grass Roots,* Berkeley, Calif.: University of California Press.

Storey, J. (1983) *Managerial Prerogative and the Question of Control,* London: Routledge & Kegan Paul.

Watson, T. (1980) 'Understanding Organizations: The Practicalities of Sociological Theory', in D. Dunkerley and G. Salaman (eds) (1980) *The International Yearbook of Organization Studies 1980,* London: Routledge & Kegan Paul.

Whyte, W.H. (1956) *The Organization Man,* New York: Simon & Shuster.

Woolf, J. (1977) 'Women in Organisations', in S. Clegg and D. Dunkerley (eds) *Critical Issues in Organisations,* London: Routledge & Kegan Paul.

CHAPTER 2
Theorising organisations

The story so far

In reviewing new writing on organisation theory at the beginning of the decade, Reed (1991: 120) commented that it was in a 'state of intellectual flux and uncertainty'. We hope in previous chapters to have captured some of the ebb and flow of such debate. But as this is an introductory text, we could not let the shadow of grand theory fall too heavily across the pages. This final chapter pulls in the other direction, though nothing too ambitious is attempted. We do not try to develop any new classificatory schema and steer clear of complex epistemological or methodological questions. Instead, the emphasis is put on examining more of the theoretical resources that underpin organisational research and analysis, reflecting back on some of the substantive issues we have dealt with elsewhere.

In those chapters, we have, of course, discussed theory, whether that be Weber's account of bureaucracy, a labour process analysis of control, or population ecology explanations of organisation–environment relations. So what's different here? Many of the theories we have looked at are specific to particular issues, such as the resource dependency theory of power. Others, such as institutional theories of convergence and diversity, have broader application but are still specific to the organisational sphere. The purpose of this chapter is to dig a little deeper and look at the resources provided by more general social science theories, sometimes labelled *paradigms*, an approach pioneered by Burrell and Morgan (1979). A paradigm is a conceptual map that draws on basic differences in the philosophy of science and social theory to enable us to see the world (and the place of organisations within it) in a distinctive way.

The world has moved on since Burrell and Morgan, whose schema never closely fitted organisational analysis (Ackroyd, 1992). But many of the underlying issues remain. For example, the most basic dividing line is how *structure* and *action* are theorised. When Marx wrote that, 'men make history, but in circumstances not of their own choosing', he was trying to express a sense of both change and constraint. Unfortunately, much of organisation theory fails to match that requirement. There is considerable determinism in which organisations and managers adapt to environments, and employees carry out goals or roles.

In the past two decades, a growing number of writers have tried to move away from this way of thinking, drawing from frameworks such as Gidden's (1984) concept of *structuration*. Structures are sets of formal and informal rules which generate common expectations and sanctions, and resources consisting of material goods and services which affect life chances. But these are not conceived of as 'external' forces, but things that people draw on in their social interactions. Structures become both the medium and outcome of that interaction. Action is conceived more precisely as *agency*. Agents deploy a range of causal powers, sometimes on behalf of others who command greater resources, sometimes to bend and break rules, but always purposeful and reflexive.

In trying to explain organisational phenomena, we cannot help drawing on an understanding of these issues, and in this book there has been an implicit approach to *theorising*. For example, trying to understand the reciprocal interaction of structure and agency informed how we view management. There is a tendency in mainstream literature, particularly of the popular variety, to see managers as free-floating individuals, always able to shape the destiny of their organisation. To conceive of managers as an agency of others, as a set of activities locked into structural constraints, goes against the grain. Yet that is the nature of the relations between ownership and control in a capitalist economy. This view, taken in the book, is often caricatured. Weir refers to 'the vulgar Marxist rhetoric of the inevitable polarisation of organisation between the two fundamental classes of bourgeoisie and proletariat. The managers are simply a muddle in the middle according to this way of thinking' (1993: 16). Or try Watson talking about the managers at ZTC, 'They were indeed interested in control, but it was control over their own circumstances . . . Managers were not seeking control on behalf of other groups' (T. Watson, 1994: 85). But such an explanation is all agency and no structure. Yes, managers are individuals with their own identities and values, struggling to make sense of their world and fight their corner within it. That makes a difference, but what they may seek and what they can do are often two different things, as his own fascinating case makes clear. Managers are an agency of control, but the interesting questions start there, because that has to be achieved in the messy reality of particular firms with particular employees, in particular economies, governed by particular parties. A sense of management as agency is not about any simple functional necessities, but, as Armstrong's recent work demonstrates, about the struggles of different professional or occupational groups to become the key core group in the workings of the enterprise. Any account of contemporary organisation must be at least *capable of* illuminating all levels, from the broader institutional constraints, through the sectional conflicts and down to real flesh and blood individuals.

In this sense, concepts such as structuration do not end debates. There has been substantial and salient criticism (Layder, 1987). It also has to be applied (Whittington, 1991b). Which structures, which agencies and in what circumstances? Nor is it the only useful principle of theorising: in Chapter 1 we outlined others which have guided our efforts in this book, including the need to be reflexive in not taking organisational processes for granted, to locate theory and practice in their historical and comparative contexts, and for explanations to be multidimensional. We have tried to utilise an approach which can explain the embeddedness of organisational action. Throughout the book we have been highly resistant to any variety of deterministic, 'one best way', or single, over-arching explanations for complex processes.

Yet clearly action is not random. The reciprocal interaction of different structures and agencies still produces specific patterns. When these patterns take on a durable, systematic form, we have referred to 'organising logics' with their own modes of rationality. Some of these are institutionally framed at national level, others have a systemic or sectoral character. None are self-contained: all are shaped by wider processes such as gender divisions and ideologies.

Social theories also have their own logic, some of which is compatible with our implicit approach, some of which is not. It is time to spell that out in greater detail than we have been able to so far.

Resources for orthodoxy

Organisation analysis has a unique relationship with a practitioner community, providing theoretical resources which range from standard academic research to simple 'how to do it' manuals. If we were to take a narrower version of management theory, it would be accurate to say that practice has unevenly drawn on two basic traditions: a rational, mechanistic one that came to the fore with Taylor and Scientific Management; and a stream of more normative, organic thinking that is particularly associated with Human Relations (Barley and Kunda, 1992). But management thinking, on the surface at least, draws lightly on theory. What are the deeper roots and means of explanation?

Weber, bureaucracy and rationality

We outlined Weber's views in some detail and his writings on bureaucracy reappear in a variety of contexts. Yet his intellectual legacy is, as we shall see, not straightforward, for it is claimed by both mainstream and critical traditions. The basis of the former claim is not difficult to identify. The current high priest of orthodoxy states that: 'Much of Organisation Theory derives from Weber's (1968) work on authority and bureaucracy' (1985: 6). If as one of its advocates asserts, mainstream theory, 'has as its central problematic the design of efficient organisations' (Hinings, 1988: 2), Weber's model of bureaucracy remains the template. Its characteristics of functional specialisation, hierarchy, depersonalisation, formal rules and the like are projected as general laws, with the arguments concerning the key contemporary and determinant variable – size, technology or any other factor.

Weber also provides orthodoxy with the theoretical sinew of rationality. Rationalisation was a theory of the transition from traditional to modern societies. For Weber, social stability was established through acceptance of authority as a form of control which people regarded as legitimate. Previous societies had been dominated by limited forms of authority based on charisma (personal qualities of leaders), or tradition (established rights and customs of dominant groups). Weber's theory went beyond economic life. Rationalisation was held to encompass processes as diverse as law, politics, religion and scientific method itself. All were becoming governed by impersonal objectives, procedures and knowledge; embodied in structures and processes which 'confronts individuals as something external to them' (Brubaker, 1984: 9). All provided a framework for coping with uncertainty. In this sense, mainstream theory draws on the idea that rational calculation makes the world more purposeful and manageable (Clegg, 1990: 32–3).

More specifically that Weber believed that the rational organisation of labour required its disciplined subordination to management and organisational goals. In this: Taylor was a resource Weber saw in his schemas for the potentially 'scientific' character of management, echoes of the themes of rationality and formal control. Paralleling his own work, Taylor saw management by 'scientific' methods as a move away from traditional authority, where owners and managers attempted to control by inefficient, personal means. Orthodoxy also sustains its conservatism through Weber's emphasis on the market embodying rationality, because it was the classic example of a disenchanted, impersonal realm dominated by the calculation of advantage, without intrusion of moral considerations (Holton and Turner, 1989: 179). Alternatives were dismissed: 'More and more the material fate of the masses depends upon the steady and correct functioning of the increasingly bureaucratic organisations of private capitalism. The idea of eliminating these organisations becomes more and more utopian' (Weber, 1984: 36).

However, Donaldson and other mainstream writers fail to acknowledge that for Weber rationalisation was a a morally and politically problematic development. Weber makes an important distinction between *formal* and *substantive* rationality. The former refers only to the calculability of techniques and procedures: 'What makes modern capitalism rational is not its ends but the unprecedented extent to which actions of its economic agents are calculated' (Sayer, 1991: 96). In contrast, the latter emphasises the values concerned with the desired ends of action. The key point is that while formal techniques are of a specific type, such values and ends inevitably differ. Thus space is opened up for recognition of contested rationalities between groups and individuals. Indeed, Weber acknowledged that the formal and substantive were always potentially in conflict, frequently making pessimistic comments about human needs being subordinated to the former. The formally rational such as the pursuit of profit by merging and 'asset stripping' companies may be substantively irrational in terms of its social consequences. In this sense, Weber does make some separation of rationality and efficiency, as there could in principle be different views of what constitutes either category. For example, workers' co-operatives and private ownership could both be regarded as efficient on the basis of different value criteria.

These kind of points form part of the basis of a defence of Weber by some writers (for example, Albrow, 1970) against the normal way his ideas are used in mainstream theory. But though this has some validity, it is not clear how significant it is. Aside from the fact that Weber is not always clear about the separation and its consequences (see Storey, 1983: 26–34), from the viewpoint of evaluating mainstream perspectives as a whole, most theorists influenced by Weber have acted as if rationality and efficiency are the same thing. As a result, they have tended to be rather uncritical of existing organisations. Reed notes, 'The causal link which he is thought to have identified between rational bureaucracy and technical efficiency provided a substantive focus and theoretical bone of contention from which a general theory of organisations, based on a systems frame of reference, could be constructed in the course of the 1950s' (1985: 17).

Weber's model of bureaucracy has of course been endlessly refined and renewed. Some *neo-Weberians* have sought to offset its simplicities by developing alternative designs within bureaucracy, such as those influenced by contingency models (Fischer and Sirriani, 1984: 9). Others have built from the distinction between formal and substantive rationality in order to uncover the neglected aspects of the functioning of bureaucratic organisations, their empirical research revealing two key processes. First, the inefficiencies arising from the following of impersonal rules, such as the displacement of the original goals by obsession with narrow interest and ritual by the office-holder. Second, the dependence of bureaucratic organisations on informal, innovative behaviour and consensual human relations. These writers, such as Blau and Gouldner, have greater affinities with social action theory, which we shall examine later.

Durkheim, human relations and social needs

The other 'founding father' of sociology to have a significant impact on organisational analysis has been Durkheim, though there is a marked contrast to Weber. Durkheim's contribution to understanding the transition to modernity centres around the significance of the *division of labour* in sustaining the social solidarity necessary for the survival of the 'organism' of society or enterprise. Writing in the late nineteenth century, he observed that the more complex division of labour in industrial, urban society was undermining traditional values and social order of a 'mechanical' kind held together by faith in a common morality. But at the same time it was laying the basis for a more effective integration of individuals in society, which was labelled 'organic solidarity'. This advanced industrial, technological division of labour was inevitably based on specialisation, hierarchy, and functional interdependence between tasks and occupations. Durkheim recognised that the new arrangements and formal structures contained sources of social disorganisation, conflict and harmful individualism; summed up in the term *anomie*. Any effective division of labour could therefore only take root and bind people together when it was sustained by new social values, by moral communities such as professional or occupational groups; and when workers had an understanding of their place within the overall scheme of production.

This kind of formulation was later interpreted through mainstream theory in terms of the permanent tension between the technical and formal needs of the organisation and the social needs of those who worked in it. It was therefore management's role not just to organise the former, but to carry out running repairs on the latter. This necessitated paying specific attention to the *informal* side of the organisation, particularly to the primary groups that people belonged to, such as work-groups. In the 1920s and 1930s this theme was taken up and popularised by Elton Mayo, who had identified problems arising from the breakdown of traditional skills and values associated with the rise of mass production. Researchers could help management to re-integrate the worker by identifying social needs and relating them to common values which led to identification with the company. Human relations analysis also drew from a Durkheimean framework . . . when it 'defined the anomic consequences of capitalism as abnormal, as a deviation from the ideal circumstances of organic solidarity' (Hamilton, 1980: 70).

Barnard (1938) extended the analysis with emphasis on how large-scale organisations could become 'co-operative social systems', based on specialised competencies and common goals. He more clearly defined the role of the executive and the specialised managerial function in terms of defining and communicating goals, and securing workforce effort. A key feature of the human relations approach is the social engineering role given to management through maintaining equilibrium and integrating the parts of the organisation. The vehicle is not formal structures of co-ordination and command, but values, informal practices and the 'logic of sentiment'. Though a subordinate aspect of organisational analysis for considerable periods, it has recently reappeared within a new socio-economic context and new management writings on corporate culture such as Peters and Waterman's *In Search of Excellence*. Attention is being focused once again on employee's social needs, the human side of the enterprise, and to creating and sustaining unity through common cultures.

Interestingly, the emphasis on *corporate* culture clashes with some central features of Durkheim's perspective which depended on the existence of professions and other intermediary groups to generate moral communities. For Durkheim, the modern individual must be equipped to question moral systems, not just to need to identify with the collective or its symbols (Dahler-Larsen, 1994: 10). In addition, Durkheim provided a critique of market rationality, which tends to foster excessive egoism and acquisitive individualism. This is just one example of a growing trend in social theory to see a different, more critical legacy from Durkheim's work (Pearce, 1989; Starkey, 1992). But, even more so than Weber, it remains the case that this is not how Durkheim has been used as a resource.

Systems theory

Mainstream organisational analysis has increasingly presented itself as divorced from broader theory. One of Donaldsons's (1985) central arguments is that organisations can be studied as an independent realm. If the outside world comes into it, it is as the 'environment', a backcloth against which it is possible specify relationships between contingencies, structure and performance. As Willmott observes, this various factors in this environment, 'must be registered and controlled if strategic adjustments are to be successfully achieved. There is minimal consideration of the relevance of social theory . . . for the study of organisations' (1990: 45). Nevertheless, Donaldson is happy to describe orthodoxy in terms of a 'functionalist-positivist' approach.

While the latter refers to the continual search for valid cause and effect knowledge, the former helps to helps sustain the orthodox focus on organisations as purposeful, interdependent systems. In doing so, the approach draws from the basic organic analogy used by Durkheim and others, in which all social systems have to adapt to the environment to survive. In such biological analogies, system parts (or sub-systems) are interconnected and each are functional to the viability of the organisation – for example, by generating binding social values. This became a theme of *functionalist* social theory (Parsons, 1951) which regards social systems as self-regulating bodies, tending towards a state of equilibrium and order. Donaldson (1985: 29) argues that there *is* movement within equilibrium, but it is a process of internal adjustment between the sub-systems, normally triggered by external change such as those in technologies or markets. Nevertheless any breakdown of order tends to be treated as pathological and the non-rational elements confined to the informal organisation.

The classical theories, including Scientific Management and Human Relations, can be conceived as *closed system* perspectives. By treating the organisation as a structure of manipulable parts that could be internally regulated, it appeared as if a rational means–ends relationship could be optimised. It was a question of re-balancing the human and technical, or formal and informal components, when one changed more rapidly than the other (R. Brown, 1992: 45). The focus on manipulating the parts, as we know, shifted to an *open systems* approach – organisations coping with uncertainty through exchange and transaction; with *contingency theory*, with its emphasis on 'designing organisations rationally so that their internal coherence and external match to their environments are both maximised' (Tsoukas, 1994c: 4), the most popular variant.

Woodward, one of the most noted contingency theorists, sums up the intellectual confidence felt by those pursuing this approach from the 1950s onwards:

> Even more important from the point of view of ultimate theory building is the fact that various schools of thought are beginning to see themselves as concerned with the study of systems . . . the starting point is the identification of a system and the subsequent questions asked are very much the same: what are the objectives and strategic parts of the system under review and how are these parts interrelated and interdependent? One result is that those concerned with the study of organisation are beginning to develop a common language, on whatever discipline their work is based, (quoted in Eldridge and Crombie, 1974: 93)

Barley and Kunda link the dominant organisational theory during this period under the heading 'systems rationalism'. Although not all its components could be described in terms of systems theory, operations research, decision-making theory and process theories of motivation shared the emphasis on controlling organisations though managing the boundaries between sub-units and the interface between inputs and outputs. In this wave of theorising 'employees were largely absent' (1992: 380), which is another way of saying that agency had been squeezed out of the picture. Individual behaviour is seen as 'determined by and reacting to structural constraints that provide organisational life with an overall stability and control' (Astley and Van de Ven, quoted in Mills and Murgatroyd, 1991: 5). The next wave was set to react against these images of orderly entities and passive people.

Critical alternatives

Social action theory

The most significant sign of a major alternative to mainstream perspectives emerged with an attack on the dominant systems theory by Silverman (1970). He brought together elements of an approach described as the *action frame of reference* or social action theory. It was not new, drawing on the phenomenological writings of Schutz

(1967) and Berger and Luckman (1967). In fact its methods can partly be traced back to Weber's conception of a social science, rather than his writings on bureaucracy. For Weber, such a science begins from interpreting social action, and the subjective meanings and purposes attached to it. This rests on a distinction between the natural and social worlds, but retains an attempt to situate individual action within material structures. Donaldson recognises another, 'interpretative' Weber and remarks that the approach works by 'gaining insights into the subjective world of actors and constructing a model of motivated actions of the typical actor in a particular social setting' (1985: 107). His complaint is merely that those who take this up ignore the 'structural', deterministic Weber.

In renewing an action perspective, Berger and Luckman popularised the concept of *social construction of reality*. Rather than conceiving of people as products of systems and institutions, they are 'actors' who create these patterns through their own meaningful activity. However, it was accepted that the products of their action – for example, organisational structures – appear to them as 'things' with an independent existence. Social construction was one of the aspects of a dialectical approach discussed earlier, and it puts a necessary stress on the possibility of change through purposeful reflection and action.

Silverman was able to apply these kind of ideas more specifically to organisations, considering them as social constructs produced and reproduced through their members' activities. This was largely neglected in systems theory, which regards organisations as part of the 'natural' world governed by 'laws' concerning their structures and effects on behaviour. Hence, as we have argued, systems theory has reified organisations and taken their basic features for granted. Silverman did not ignore structure, recognising that *roles*, as systematic patterns of expectations, were developed in the interplay between organisations and their environments. His study was largely theoretical, but others were of a more empirical nature, utilising the concept of organisations as *negotiated orders* (see Day and Day, 1977). By the early 1960s Strauss *et al.* (1963) had been analysing the negotiated order in hospitals, while other notable studies included those concerned with police and legal practices (Bittner, 1967; Cicourel, 1968), and welfare agencies (Zimmerman, 1971). A recurring theme was that controls exercised through rules in formal organisations were inevitably incomplete and unsuccessful. Any degree of effective co-ordination and co-operation is dependent on constant reworking of rules and goals, and formal and informal negotiation processes involving all participants. The subsequent customs and practices in any workplace act as a constraint on management.

The critique developed through action theory challenged the consensual and objective images of organisations that were often based on 'favoured' managerial definitions. By focusing on the realities of multiple goals and competing groups, dimensions of organisational life, such as work patterns and practices could be demystified. It shed light on why organisations do not operate as they are supposed to. This latter emphasis tied into empirical work by *neo-Weberians*, who were also concerned with the bending of bureaucratic rules through the value-systems of employees (Blau, 1955; Gouldner, 1955). Indeed, Silverman utilises some of these studies extensively. He notes, for example, how Gouldner shows that industrial relations in a gypsum mine had been based on an 'indulgency pattern': implicit rules rooted in give and take rather than formal codes. When management attempted to introduce changes which clashed with the established values and practices and reasserted formal rules, it generated grievances and strike activity.

In organisation theory as such, the action perspective made its impact through John Child's (1972) concept of strategic choice, which was directed against the environmental determinism of contingency theory. The theoretical significance is drawn out by Brown: 'This criticism emphasises "agency" as against "structure", that is the role of actors – managers, workers, or whoever – in choosing to pursue certain goals and/or follow certain lines of action albeit within constraints set by the actions of others and the context within which they are placed' (1992: 36).

Meanwhile, during the 1970s Silverman and other writers shifted the action approach in the more 'radical' direction of *ethnomethodology*. Though 'translated' as people-centred, it is actually only concerned with the production of a common-sense world and eschews any attempt at analysis of causation which would impose external categories. Nor is it concerned with the relation between ideas and interests or social and organisational structures present in the Weberian tradition. It restricts itself to accounting for the processes through which members construct their everyday life. Structures tend to be viewed at best as temporary patterns created by interpersonal action and based on available stocks of knowledge. Though some useful material on the 'organisational work' of reinterpreting these stocks of knowledge and routine practices was generated (Silverman and Jones, 1976), it soon became difficult to locate any notion of *organisation* in the traditional sense. Phenomena such as power or control, which are expressed through relatively durable structures beyond specific situations and face-to-face interactions and meanings, are simply outside its frame of reference.

Though taken to extremes in ethnomethodology, these weaknesses were inherent in action theory. In Silverman's earlier work he argued that technological and market structures were meaningful only in terms of the understandings and attachments of participants. Though structures require the involvement of actors in their reproduction, something like a product or labour market does have a structural existence partly independent from how particular individuals think or act – as anyone who has lost their job, or a fortune on the stock exchange, will testify. Concepts such as role which were used to link subjective action and structure are useful, but not substantial enough to carry the burden of explaining organisational behaviour. The more disconnected action theory became from wider concerns, the more it became 'buried in an obsessive concern for the minutiae of "everyday life" as exemplified in the intricacies of organisational routines' (Reed, 1985: 48). This is linked to a further problem limiting its capacity to act as a critical resource. Despite the emphasis on empirical studies – as we raised earlier and as Silverman has admitted – the approach is aimed at providing a *method* of analysis, rather than a theory of organisations. Nevertheless, Silverman and social action theory continues to be a focus for discussion (Hassard and Parker, 1994) and influence (Tsoukas, 1994c).

Radical structuralism

To escape the limits of an action approach, theory must move beyond how organisations and their environments are subjectively constituted to some kind of structural

explanation of the dynamics of organisational development within capitalist societies. This section examines some of the resources that can be found for that purpose by reworking and extending the concepts provided by Marx and Weber. We
use the common heading of 'radical structuralism' to signify that such theorising
begins from an account of the structural framework of organisational behaviour, but
is directed towards a critical explanation of the processes of regulation and change.

Marx and labour process theory

Marx had little to say about issues of administrative or even political organisation,
and even less about the specific question of bureaucracy. When he made observations
about bureaucracy, they were very Weberian, with references to systematic division of
labour, hierarchies of knowledge and mechanisms of formal behaviour (Sayer, 1991:
78). Nevertheless, as Goldman and Van Houten note, 'Systematic study of the sociology of organisations is almost absent in the classical and modern Marxist traditions'
(1977: 110). Those wishing to generate a discussion from Marx have had to rely on
fragments of a critique of the Prussian bureaucracy and writings on the Paris Commune of 1871 as a model of the possibility of elimination of bureaucracy through a
fully democratic administrative system (Marx, 1984). Marxist theory has tended to
focus on the dynamics and contradictions of capitalism as a whole and issues concerning the distribution of the surplus product, neglecting changes in productive processes,
organisational forms and occupational structures. Some Marxist concepts have been
influential, if often misunderstood – notably his account of the alienation of labour.
But they have remained unconnected to any systematic organisational analysis.

However, during the last twenty years Marxist-influenced theory and research has
had a profound effect on all of the disciplines concerned with work organisation.
This trend worries Donaldson (1985:127), who argues that, 'Marxism is a theory of
society therefore it cannot be a theory of organisation'. Clegg (1988: 10) makes the
apposite response that applying the same criteria to Weber would place his work on
bureaucracy outside the level appropriate to organisation theory. But there is a different point to be made. It is not the full apparatus of Marxist theory of history and
society that has been influential, but a narrower set of ideas, though still central to
his account of the working of capitalist production. That vehicle has been *labour
process theory*, set in motion by Braverman's (1974) reworking of Marx's analysis of
capitalist production (for a full account of labour process debates see P. Thompson,
1983). As the framework for an explanation of control. Here we examine the deeper
theoretical context.

Though more obviously influential in industrial sociology, labour process theory
has provided conceptual tools observable in a wide range of critical organisation writers such as Clegg, Dunkerley, Salaman, Storey and Burrell. Clegg and Dunkerley begin
Organisations, Class and Control by defining the theoretical object of organisational
analysis: 'For this volume we have proposed as such an object the concept of organisation as control of the labour process' (1980: 1). What enables such an argument to
be made? Marx may not have been interested in an understanding of organisations
per se, but he was centrally concerned with issues of work organisation and organisation of work. By this we mean a combined emphasis on work organisations as the
site of key economic processes and contradictions, and the meeting place of capital

and labour; as well as organisation of work in terms of questions including the division of labour, relations of authority and control, and the distribution of rewards.

Donaldson also rightly observed that: 'To qualify as distinctly neo-Marxian one would need to show the connection between work life in the organisation and change at the societal level' (1985). That is exactly the strength of labour process theory, which Donaldson misses because the 'Marxism' he attacks is an earlier, much more general and less successful application to the sphere of work organisation. Marx defined the form of a society and economy in a manner strongly conditioned by an understanding of work relationships. Each mode of production gives rise to class relations, which, under capitalism, are based on the sale and purchase of labour power. The partial antagonism between capital and labour as collective classes arises from the exploitation and appropriation of the surplus labour by capital based on its ownership and control of production. This is a far cry from the notion of fair exchange implied in mainstream theory. Work relations therefore cannot be analysed in general, but only as they are shaped by the demands of a specific system of production. The central characteristic of this process is the nature of labour as an active and indeterminate commodity. In other words, when it is purchased by capital, the outcomes remain mere potential. The goal of profitable production may be thwarted by workers asserting their own needs and self-organisation. In many ways this is a more sophisticated account of what industrial relations and other disciplines call the *wage-effort bargain*, the exchange of effort for reward, which has at its core of the employment relationship (Edwards and Scullion, 1982).

The above processes cannot be understood within the confines of one organisational unit. Competition between enterprises and the conflict within the employment relationship creates an accumulation process which compels capital constantly to reorganise production. Certain general features of work organisation and organisation of work tend to follow.

1. Employers need to exercise control over labour, both at the level of general directive powers and over working conditions and tasks. At the same time, it is necessary to motivate employees and gain some level of consent and co-operation. Meeting these diverse and sometimes contradictory needs is the function of management systems and agents.
2. There are constant pressures to cheapen the costs of production, notably labour. This may take place through deskilling, relocation of plant, work intensification or some other means; though subject to constraints, including worker resistance and market variations.
3. A division of labour must be structured around the above objectives, involving the design of work and division of tasks and people to give the most effective control and profitability. This is sustained by hierarchical structures and the shaping of appropriate forms of science and technology.

Let us restate this and spell out the consequences with more specific reference to organisations.

- Work organisations are distinct from other organisations and can only be properly understood within a theory of capital accumulation and labour processes.

This 'political economy' must take in relationships to institutional environments at regional, national and international level.

- 'Organisations are structures of control' (Salaman, 1981: 143). This involves more than control over uncertainty, monitoring objectives or means of getting work done. They are administrative apparatuses concerned with control over productive activity in order to maximise the surplus. Managerial agency, though inherently variable and multi-layered, develops in this context.

- In advanced capitalist societies large-scale organisations are strategic units acting as mechanisms which integrate economic, political, administrative and ideological structures (Burrell, 1980a: 99).

- Organisational structures and processes – including management and worker organisation, control and reward systems, and job design – therefore involve political issues, decisions and choices.

- Organisations do not embody any universal rationality, but rather contested rationalities arising from the partly antagonistic relation of capital and labour. Organisational change will reflect the subsequent dialectic of control and resistance.

This is not merely a question of the 'seamy side' of otherwise excellent organisations, as Gareth Morgan appears to believe (1986: 316–17). Relations of exploitation and domination are integral to capitalist and other class-divided forms of work organisation. Nevertheless, the underlying principles of the relations between organisations and capitalist society are at a very general level. They involve no laws or functional imperatives concerning *specific* forms of control, organisational structures, management strategies or job designs. Nor does reference to class necessarily incorporate particular models of consciousness or social change. All these and other matters are empirical questions to be determined by research and the unfolding of real events. The renewal of Marxist and labour process theory has generated or influenced a tremendous amount of historical and contemporary research at a more 'micro' level. This is particularly true in areas such as managerial strategies and control (Friedman, 1977; R. Edwards, 1979, Edwards and Scullion, 1982); technology, skill and work design (Wilkinson, 1983a; Child, 1985; Thompson and Bannon, 1985; Gabriel, 1988); and the sexual division of labour (Pollert, 1981; Cavendish, 1982; Westwood, 1984).

The selective and qualified use of Marx suggested here and by other theorists has inevitably led to accusations that labour process theory is no longer Marxist (Cohen, 1987). Authentic affinity with Marxism is only of concern to those who zealously guard orthodoxy and the sacred text. Even more importantly, even if the resource provided by labour process theory is valuable, there are still many gaps in explanations of key organisational processes. Some of this can no doubt be remedied by further research, but it is important to recognise the limits inherent in the perspective. It sets organisations specifically in the context of *capitalist production*, which is both its strength and weakness.

- Though the labour process is the core of productive activity, it does not encompass all aspects. Any theory of the role of organisations in capitalist society must deal with the *full circuit of capital* (Kelly, 1985; Nichols, 1986); including its realisation through the sale of commodities on the market, financial issues and the prior purchase of labour. It would be very misleading for any critical theory to proceed on the assumption that organisational processes and managerial activities were based solely on the control of labour; neglecting factors such as sales and marketing, financial controls, supply of components and product quality. Even the employment relationship, though intimately connected to the labour process, is constituted on a far wider basis (Littler, 1982). Institutions such as the state and the family, plus different cultural values and patterns in a given society, shape the distinctive character of employment relationships as can be seen by observing examples from Japan or farm work. Labour process theory is thus only a partial contribution to such analyses, though paradoxically it is in some ways ideally suited to organisation studies given that the dominant managerial theories are also overwhelmingly concerned with 'the labour problem'.

- Not all work organisations are based on commodity production, or are capitalist in character. Those in health, education or other parts of the public sector, are, at least for the moment, concerned with services for use not profit. It is possible to construct a Marxist-oriented analysis which shows the links between the various types of public and private sector within the totality of capitalist society, (Heydebrand, 1977; T. Johnson, 1972). But it remains the case that not all organisational processes or forms of work activity can be understood solely through a theory whose categories are geared to explaining capitalist production – despite distorted attempts to do so, such as Bellaby and Orribor's (1977) analysis of the health service.

- Non-profit making organisations in capitalist societies and forms of administration and enterprise in 'socialist' ones such as those in China and the former Soviet bloc countries also show evidence of bureaucracy, power hierarchies and work fragmentation: 'contemporary socialist societies appear to be at least as bureaucratic and with as much of a self-perpetuating bureaucracy as capitalist ones' (Dunkerley and Salaman, 1986: 87). This suggests that the dynamic of bureaucratisation is partly independent of capital–labour relations, and that critical theory requires concepts that enable us to focus on that problem.

This is where Weber comes in, for he has the wider account of bureaucratic rationalisation which is a necessary part of explaining these processes. For example, he perceptively predicted that state socialist systems would be *more* bureaucratic than capitalism because of the absence of countervailing power structures between the state and markets. In a command economy, the power of bureaucratised management would increase, as would the dictatorship of the official (Sayer, 1991: 145–6).

Radical Weberianism

Though defenders of orthodoxy such as Donaldson recognise a radical Weber, many critical theorists, particularly those of a Marxist persuasion, have been hostile to the Weberian tradition (Marcuse, 1971; Johnson, 1980). Their objections relate to many of the points raised earlier in the chapter. This includes the tendency to argue that there is a bureaucratic imperative obliterating organisational differences within and between societies; that there is an inherent rationality of technique; and the identification of rationality with capitalism and the market. Also, there are genuine limits to Weber's own categories – for example, the emphasis on the bureaucratic hierarchy of offices has far less relevance to shop floor employees. Nevertheless there are radical Weberian perspectives, and critical writers who aim at some kind of synthesis of key aspects of Marx and Weber's analysis of work organisations (Salaman, 1979, 1981; Littler, 1982).

They rightly point to common concerns with control and domination by management and bureaucratic élites: 'For both Marx and Weber the major elements of the structure of modern large-scale organisations stem for the efforts of those who own, manage and design the organisation, to achieve control over the members' (Salaman, 1979: 20–1). Weber recognised that control rested on the 'complete appropriation' of all the material means of production by owners. In addition, both made an attempt to explain organisational dynamics within wider social and political structures rather than as independent, isolated phenomena, subject to their own 'laws'; though clearly the analysis of structural contexts differed. Marx's account of alienated labour and Weber's emphasis on the 'iron cage of industrial labour' share a concern for the fragmented and dehumanised nature of work. Weber saw that maximum formal rationality favoured economically powerful groups and their ability to use superior resources to dictate terms and conditions in what may appear as a freely made contract or legal equality (Brubaker, 1984: 42–3). Social tensions and sectional conflicts between different interest groups was therefore inevitable.

Overlaps are less surprising than they appear. Both theorists shared a similar view of the necessity for modernity to sweep away the traditional social relations based on conceptions of natural order, personalised power and patriarchy. Capitalism was a flawed, but dynamic system compelled constantly to revolutionise production and all social spheres. The difference, as Sayer observes, was that for Marx, 'what makes modernity modern is, first and foremost, capitalism itself, (1991: 12). In contrast, for Weber, 'capitalism is but one theatre among others were the drama of rationality is played out' (1991: 134). Weber was surely right in this, but wrong in some of the ways he understood this relationship.

The central dividing line of radical Weberians from orthodox interpretations is a rejection of Weber's *fatalism* about the relations between bureaucracy and industrial societies. They do not believe that bureaucracy is necessarily universal or inevitable; but rather that it is a pervasive tendency which takes specific forms and therefore can and must be countered. Like some contemporary labour process theorists, there is more emphasis on bureaucratic control as a *management strategy* (Burawoy, 1979; Edwards, 1979; Clawson, 1980). Though not unique to any system of production, bureaucracy has to be explained through its relations with that wider formation. It's capitalist social relations that dictate the need to appropriate the means of production from workers, not some law of bureaucratic rationalisation.

However, in these discussions of syntheses and overlaps between critical perspectives, we should not lose sight of some of the more distinctive Weberian contributions. Modern states and enterprises involve complex functions, management of competing interests, and performance of problematic tasks according to observable rules and norms. Some of these processes are created by and reflect specific relations of production, as in layers of supervision whose sole function is labour control and discipline. Certain functions may be artificially expanded and new ones absorbed by bureaucrats themselves as a form of self-preservation. But, as Polan notes, bureaucratic forms are a necessary object of analysis in their own right: 'Only as a result of conceding to the bureaucracy its genuine, legitimate and distinct functions can one begin to determine the boundaries of its powers and construct political control procedures that may successfully police those boundaries' (1984: 71).

Weber's insights allow us to focus on a number of key areas. Power is frequently constructed and legitimised through 'rationalisation', particularly through the expertise associated with science and technology, and what Weber described as 'control based on knowledge'. Whereas Marx provides insights from an analysis of the consequences of the private ownership of the means of production, Weber identified the problem of concentration of power through the *means of administration*:

> The bureaucratic structure goes hand in hand with the concentration of the material means of management in the hands of the master. This concentration occurs, for instance, in a well known and typical fashion, in the development of big capitalist enterprises, which find their essential characteristics in this process. A corresponding process occurs in public organisations. (1984: 33)

Finally, work organisations operate on different levels, and in some of these, formal control procedures are important. As Littler (1982) points out, Weberian categories are especially important in understanding the employment relationship and the career structure of officials in particular. More generally, bureaucratic procedures and rules are relevant to the analysis of processes such as recruitment, reward and promotion. There is a strong case that a modified and updated Weberian analysis of bureaucracy and rationalisation remains indispensable for an understanding of contemporary work organisation. With the relevant elements derived from a Marxist tradition, they emphasise the continuity in social relations in and beyond large-scale organisations in a capitalist society. It is precisely this notion of continuity which has been under attack in the last decade.

The post-modern challenge to rationality

Post-modernism is the least cohesive of the general social theories we have examined, the term being loosely applied to an overlapping set of ideas about society and knowledge deriving from French social theorists such as Baudrillard, Lyotard and Derrida which have become increasingly influential in organisation theory in recent years (Clegg, 1990; Parker, 1992; P. Thompson, 1993; Hassard and Parker, 1993). It lays claim to be the most radical break from orthodoxy, but the orthodoxy is different from the systems and related ideas we have talked about so far. Anything with 'post' automatically specifies its opposite, so the orthodoxy must be *modernism*. This may appear puzzling – after all, existing social theories have not traditionally been defined by that label. But for Clegg (1990: 2), organisation theory is a 'creature' of modernity, while Gergen (1992: 211–12) includes almost the full range of organisational and behavioural theories in the modernist camp.

So, what is modernity? In some usages, it designates a a type of society or *epoch* (the ontological dimension); at its simplest, industrialism in which the dominant feature is the large-scale, hierarchical bureaucracy concerned with rationality and planning throughout social and economic life. Willmott sums up the argument thus: 'Its ideal is the expertly designed, perfectly ordered and controlled world in which all ambivalence and indeterminacy are attenuated, if not wholly eliminated' (1992: 70). But within such conceptions we see the seeds of another designation, modernism as a way of thinking, a way of representing knowledge about society and organisations (the epistemological dimension). Above all, it is held to be characterised by a concern for developing the 'grand narrative', a coherent story about the development of the social and natural world, revealed through the application of reason and science (Cooper and Burrell, 1988).

Post-modernists develop a dual challenge in both these dimensions of what society is and how we should look at it. Rapid social change, the shift from a society based on production to one based on information, the emergence of segmented markets dominated by more discerning consumers, and turbulent environments are said to be demanding diversity and flexibility in work organisations which are released from their bureaucratic iron cage. Though it is not their exclusive property, post-modernists concerned with the workplace embrace the notion of the post-bureaucratic organisation in which the old specialised division of labour and centralised control no longer holds sway. In turn, social theorists with a broader societal remit use this tenuous evidence of 'debureaucratisation' and 'reprofessionalisation' to sustain a broader vision of post-modernisation (Crook *et al.*, 1992).

In the sphere of knowledge and *epistemology*, post-modernists reject the tradition of grand narrative. The search for the coherent story (Braverman's theory of the degradation of the labour process in the twentieth century), or the total picture (Weber's account of the interrelated processes of rationalisation) is both pointless, because of the fragmentation of economic and cultural life; and dangerous, because it submerges diverse voices and the multiplicity of 'local' phenomena. Difference, incoherence and fluidity are preferable and more realistic because meaning cannot be fixed; it is what we make it through language which constructs rather than reflects reality. At its most extreme, this kind of thinking is seen in Baudrillard and his concept of *hyperreality*. In a media-saturated world that thrives on spectacle and encourages politicians to employ 'spin doctors' to put a twist on events as, before and after they happen, it becomes impossible to distinguish between the real and fictive. We cannot refer to distortion of reality, because there are too many realities for it to be measured against. For example, Baudrillard claimed that during the Gulf conflict it was impossible to know whether any events had taken place. This was literally a war of words in which all our information was second-hand, simulated and structured through media manipulation (for a critique see Norris, 1992).

Most post-modernists in organisation theory would not go this far, but many do embrace the view that 'truth' is a product of language games. We have Derrida's 'nothing exists outside the text', taken as the interplay of different discourses (Hassard, 1994: 9). In this context, the task of the social theorist is not to construct the authentic explanation, but to *deconstruct* texts in order to reveal the contradictions, origins, instabilities and gaps. For example, this process of re-reading may uncover the silences on gender issues in the classics of 'malestream' organisation theory (Calás and Smircich, 1992). Though such treatment is 'exposed' to public gaze, it may be regarded as inevitable, for discourse always bears the imprint of the social identity of its producers. This 'perspectivism' adds a further layer to the conception of multiple viewpoints and realities.

In our previous discussions in this book, an emphasis on the primacy of language and discourse emerged most strongly, through an examination of the ideas of Foucault and post-structuralism on power. Here, power is not a thing possessed by sovereign agents, but operates through discourses which produce knowledge and disciplinary practices that define and constrain the identities of workers, consumers and citizens. The danger is that any subject of action is lost in the interplay of discourses (Newton, 1994). But perhaps the most famous illustration in organisation theory of the abandonment of the search for the truth lying beneath the surface of social relations, is Morgan's *Images of Organisation*. Morgan does not just analyse organisational life in terms of series of metaphors – the machine, the psychic prison, the tool of domination – those images are treated as of equal validity. Despite representing contradictory 'claims', they are all 'true' in their own terms, their 'cognitive power and empirical veracity can only be assessed in terms of the purposes for which they are constructed and used . . . reality is what you make of it' (Reed, 1990b: 36). Also influential in applications of postmodern and post-structural epistemology is the shift of concern from analyses of control and rules to the construction of organisational life through cultural and symbolic resources.

There is a tension between post-modernism as epoch and epistemology. Logically, an approach which rejects narrative and totalising pictures should be hostile to or uninterested in an alternative conception of society. Indeed, there is a major gap between those theorists such as Clegg who are quite happy to use conventional tools of rational enquiry to develop accounts of post-modernity, and those who prefer the discursive 'production of organisation' to the 'organisation of production'. But the distinction is not so clear cut. Continuities and commonalities arise in at least three ways. In both dimensions there is a shared language of fragmentation and fracturing of the theoretical and practical order (Reed, 1991: 125). This imagery is taken from the origins of post-modernism as a perspective in art and culture, where eclecticism, stylistic promiscuity, paradox, and mixing of modes replaces hierarchical judgements of value and distinctions between high art and popular culture (Featherstone, 1988).

They are also linked by a rejection of the 'false promises' of rational design, the idea that knowledge should offer methodologies for defining the most rational means of controlling complex, large-scale organisations (Hassard, 1994: 4). Finally, and most importantly, there is the inconvenient and much observed fact that post-modernism is itself a meta-narrative (Boyne and Rattansi, 1990: 39–40). The need to create pictures of reality is inescapable in the illustrative and conceptual acts of theorising and there is ample evidence that writers such as Lyotard, Morgan and Baudrillard draw on post-industrialism, information society and other models that take as their starting point some kind of epochal break (P. Thompson, 1993).

In practice, then, the post-bureaucratic organisation located in the postmodern epoch is a rival narrative to those traditions deriving from Marx and Weber. The evidence for any substantial presence for such a mode of organising is either absent of misunderstood. And, though discussion of wider theoretical models such as post-industrialism is beyond our scope, there are equally sceptical critiques on offer (for example, Callinicos, 1989). Organisations may not be the 'tightly-coupled' rational machines beloved of systems theory, but when Hassard argues that, 'Above all, we should seek to explode the myth of robust structural relations through establishing the fragile character of organisational life' (1994: 16), this is merely standing orthodoxy on its head, rather then a realistic picture of the modern firm.

Just as there is considerable continuity in capitalist relations of production and in rationalisation processes, large-scale organisations are considerably more durable and able to marshal powerful resources than post-modernists allow. Power converts ambiguity into order, though the latter is not synonymous with the equilibrium of systems theory, because it is always contested and disrupted. New forms of theorising are in danger of moving so far away from rationality that they are unable to conceptualise *organisation* at all. This is not just a question of the nature of contemporary structure and agency, but the equally flawed alternative ways of seeing. As Reed comments:

> The theoretical glue once provided by an assumed epistemological commitment to rational analysis of 'organised rationality' has given way under the pressure exerted by a cacophony of voices which celebrate the reality of multiple and contested organisational rationalities which cannot be assessed or evaluated in any coherent way. (1993: 181)

It is true, as we have continually stressed in the book, that there are conflicting ends and means pursued by rival organisational actors and the diversity of organising logics and institutional settings. But contested practical rationalities need to be understood on rational grounds. How can we debate the *character* of organisational life if we cannot compare and evaluate theoretical claims or even Morgan's 'images' on rational grounds? If these remain self-contained, self-referential discourses, as Reed notes elsewhere (1991: 38), organisation theory just becomes a supermarket where metaphors or other means of representation are purchased according to preference and power.

There is an increasing and dangerous tendency in organisation theory to treat management strategy, corporate culture, Taylorism, Fordism and so on, only as discourses. Presented to us as texts, the subsequent deconstructions and re-readings are sometimes illuminating, but at the cost of being confinement to the world of inter-textuality, or parasitic dependence on other people's empirical work. The interplay of agency and structures has a real material existence. In his critique of post-modernism, Tsoukas persuasively illustrates the point:

> It is because actions are not taken and voices not uttered, in a vacuum that *not* all accounts are equally valid. No matter how much I shout at my bank manager he is not likely to lend me money if I am unemployed. This is not a figment of my imagination. Others also tell me they have had similar experience. (1992: 644)

It is because we need to understand these similarities of experience and their institutional underpinnings that some form of theoretical narrative is necessary. What we know is inherently incomplete, but we require a capacity to generate generalisable knowledge and to identify trends, if not laws; and empirical work that can help distinguish between rhetorics of the powerful and the realities of power.

There is a final challenge to rationality when post-modernism is combined with some perspectives within feminism, that argue that the dominant Weberian conceptualisation of rationality is a male one. Explanations have overlapping emphases. Some (Martin, 1990; Bologh, 1990; Putnam and Mumby, 1993) refer to the stress on instrumentalism, logic and calculability in the public realm and the exclusion of emotionality, intuitive experiences and the private realm. Others lean towards a kind of perspectivism in which masculinity is the driving force. For example, Hearn (1992) argues that it is mostly men who manage the introduction of rational method and men and masculinities that will be affected by it; while Bologh (1990: xv) addresses the ghost of Weber thus: 'Your vision, extensive and expansive as it is, is the vision from your body inscribed with your gender, your place, your time'. She shows that he had a patriarchal perspective based on ideas of mastery, control and impersonality.

The result is often projected as a distinction between male and female types of social action or rationality; the former embodied in authoritarian methods of control or hierarchical ways of decision-making, the latter in ways of organising dependent on emotional connection, nurturance, intimacy and cooperation (Ferguson, 1984; Grimshaw, 1986; Bologh, 1990). Though distinguished from any biological determination, it is still a dangerous formulation, which, as Witz and Savage (1992: 20) and Due Billing point out with reference to the work of Ferguson, is not established on any secure analytical basis. Due Billing observes that, 'There is a tendency in Ferguson's text to operate with an ideal (essentialistic) notion of "woman" and to equate femaleness with an ideology about female values' (1994: 177). The production of knowledge is a social process and an undoubtedly gendered one. Connections between masculinity, male privilege and the reproduction of organisation in the public sphere has been (Hearn, 1992) and still is (Roper, 1994) strong.

As a man of his times, Weber may well have been guilty of 'masculinism', though the stereotype of his lack of interest in the emotional may be more complicated (Albrow, 1992). More importantly, concepts and practice are distinguishable from context. Ideas of an essentially male rationality are static and deterministic, given that the overlay of rationality with masculinity is itself historically and socially produced. The fact that men have dominated women or had systematic advantages within the division of labour within bureaucracies, does not make bureaucracies male. Women as well as men can and do benefit from bureaucracy, and can pursue successful struggles within rule-governed, instrumental processes. Bureaucracy cannot just be set aside as alien practical and conceptual territory, because it is not just a discourse. Rationalisation was and is a fundamental principle of life in industrial societies and does not 'belong' to men. For example, calculable rules, whether applied to feelings, job specifications of financial reporting systems, can be initiated and operated by women as employers and managers, and experienced at the receiving end by men and women. The task of organisation theory, is surely, as Ramsay and Parker (1992) argue, to plot the *intersection* between patriarchy, rationality and bureaucracy, not to collapse each into the other.

A further 'intersection' that has been a central theme of this book is that between the sociological/structural and psychological dimensions of action. Our view has been that different modes of analysis are needed to deal with the complexities and levels of human behaviour. People are constituted as individual subjects at the level of their identities, emotions and self-directed actions. But that process is informed by the same 'structural' phenomena that shape managerial strategies or job design, such as the social relations of production between capital, labour or gender. The next section examines some of the theoretical resources we have engaged with, in a similar manner to the previous discussion.

Critical social psychologies

Mainstream theory has long included a psychological component, but has tended treat people in organisations as 'psychologically determined entities' with abstractedly and individually defined needs. In addition, the 'sciences' of organisational behaviour have managed to produce better ways of manipulating the identities and behaviour of employees, but have not succeeded in addressing the problems that make such manipulation necessary. A redefinition of the traditional agenda of organisational psychology requires that individual, group and organisational behaviour be placed in a wider context, particularly the social relations of production, and gender relations. Specifically, this would account for subjective experience, while avoiding the overutilisation of rational-cognitive explanations that focus on the individual determinants and constraints of purposive activity. Instead, we seek to maintain a focus on how subjectivity is constructed within social and organisational structures.

Given these requirements and the limitations of existing perspectives, it is understandable that we have seen the development of a variety of critical social psychologies. This label covers a multiplicity of radical viewpoints which have utilised concepts from mainstream Western social psychology, Marxist and humanist perspectives and Freudian theory. The attempts to formulate 'Marxist psychologies' (Schneider, 1975; Seve, 1978; Leonard, 1984) are of particular interest to us, because the explanation of social behaviour is located specifically in an understanding of work organisations. This production of subjectivity and consciousness in the wider social world is also explored by Henriques *et al.* (1984) through an articulation with psychoanalysis and discourse theory that attempts to move beyond both individual and social determinisms.

Social psychology has historically encompassed a wide variety of critical traditions differing mainly in their concerns for internal critique of methodology and content as opposed to critique of the sociocultural relations of the knowledge they produce (Wexler, 1983). From work such as that of Moscovici (1972), Gergen (1973) and Rosnow (1981), we gain a focus on the methodological limitations of social psychology and its lack of relevance to social issues. These are essentially calls for reform which, in their understanding of human social relations in terms of relatively fixed characteristics and roles, follow the liberal tradition of social emancipation through individual transformation. Alternatively, we have the vein of critique characterised by Armistead (1974), Archibald (1978) and Larsen (1980), which focuses on examining radical alternatives within social psychology. Although not always consistent with each other, these critiques do maintain a perspective on the often repressive nature of socially organised relationships. Appealing to both humanist and Marxist theory, they are concerned with social transformations leading towards human emancipation and, like the more conventional methodological critique, they also appeal to internal procedural reform. Being essentially theoretical critiques, their focus is outside the specific contradictions of social existence, tending to enshrine critique as a principle in itself.

The tradition of the Frankfurt School – for example, in the work of Horkheimer, Adorno, Marcuse and latterly Habermas – examines the role of ideologies in the production of our knowledge of the social contexts in which we exist. This provides a self-reflexive critique of how social psychology operates both to uphold the current social order and to work against the possibility of a socially transforming discipline. The image produced is of an instrumentalised culture where psychology, in servicing and refining control procedures, acts to blind individuals to their capacities and lock them into dependence on commodity relations by presenting these as the inevitable 'natural order'. According to Van Strien, the conceptual framework developed by the Frankfurt School is of importance in moves towards an emancipatory social science, as it: 'puts science directly at the service of Man's consciousness of his own possibilities, interests and values' (1982: 18). However, as critique based on radical alternatives, it does have a tendency to be, 'broadcast without a specific audience at the receiving end'. Criticism is again elevated as an emancipatory practice in itself, without linking it to the everyday experience of those whom it was assumed to benefit.

Such problems continue to be reproduced within the tradition, for example in Steffy and Grimes' critique of personnel/organisational psychology introduced. This is itself essentially based on analysis of validation procedures through the Critical Theory of Foucault and Habermas. They claim that the *technical rationality* constructed by procedures validating theory and practice produce ideologically distorted perceptions and communications that are: 'sponsored by dominant groups to stabilise and legitimise their control and domination' (1992: 195). Their answer is to introduce new emphases on validity practices that are not bounded by technical rationality. Claims to valid action need to be sustained by social consensus and undistorted communications, on the basis that rational debate can undermine purely technical reasoning.

The problem is that the prescriptions they put forward do not differ greatly from those already used in conventional personnel and occupational psychology. At one point they recommend MBO, the precursor of goal-setting, as a 'participatory technique'. The necessary corollary to the new validation procedures, that the training of both 'social scientists and management students be multi-disciplinary, perhaps at the expense of specialisation' though laudable, is perhaps none too realistic at present. On this basis it would appear that however desirable and probably necessary, a psychology based on this tradition of Critical Theory will probably not provide a great deal of competition to current practices in terms of their influence on and role in HRM strategies.

Social action

As in our previous discussion, social action theory is also a resource, in this case because of the stress on the intersubjective nature of social behaviour as a form of negotiated order. The useful contribution of social action theories is first in the methodological emphasis that they maintain in rooting their work in accounts of subjective experience; and secondly, in the linking of accounts of how subjectivity is constructed to structures of control, culture and ideology in organisations. In relation to organisational psychology they represent that part of the domain of analysis characterised by subjective, partly rational action processes based on phenomenological, social constructionist models. They provide a link to the ethnomethodological tradition in sociology and to symbolic interactionism, which has been influential in both sociology and social psychology.

Symbolic interactionism, following from Mead (1934), has long been the area where an interface between sociological and socio-psychological conceptions of identity has existed. The construction of identity and the social milieu within which individual identity exists is, in this model, dependent on interaction with others and through others with the self. Subjectivity, then, is mainly a product of intersubjective processes and is constructed through the negotiation of social rules and conventions. The social production of subjectivity, though acknowledged, is addressed through an understanding of how the formal and informal processes of culture and ideology impinge upon individual functioning. This phenomenological emphasis on situated meaning in the construction of subjectivity is a necessary methodological focus in providing a reflexive account of organisational behaviour and informs much of our account of the securing and reproduction of identity. What it lacks is the framework for understanding the social order which conditions action inside the organisation. Indeed, neither critical social psychologies nor social action theories present consistent theories of either subjectivity or its structural location. To expand on this theme, we turn to consider further the relations between Marxism and psychology.

Marxism, psychology and beyond

As we said earlier, Marxist contributions to psychology have been underdeveloped. In a broad sense, their understandings of subjectivity at work, whether described as psychologies or not, begin with the concept of alienation: the estrangement of creative capacities that means that 'work is external to the worker, that it is not part of his nature, and that, consequently, he does not fulfil himself in his work but denies himself (Marx, 1963: 124–5). The reference to a 'human nature' is not to an eternal set of values or behaviours such as aggression or jealousy beloved of reactionary thinkers, but rather to certain characteristics which distinguish man's species-being, such as the capacity for purposeful and reflective action.

Utilising a Marxist framework, we can grasp that alienation is given specific and concrete form by its location in the capitalist labour process. When the worker no longer owns or controls the products of labour, individual needs and capacities are subordinated to the requirements of capital accumulation, with the psychological consequence that the worker feels a stranger in his or her work. Alienated labour deepens with the further development of capitalism, as new forms of science, technology and management are used to incorporate skills and knowledge. This ties in with the analysis of Braverman (1974), particularly the emphasis on the separation of conception and execution. Volpert, Hacker and other German organisational psychologists have produced some useful specific concepts in this area, particularly those of action regulation and the partialisation of action (Resch *et al.*, 1984). These integrate models of the cognitive structuring and regulation of work with the context-bound restriction of labour in fragmented and alienated activities. Management still need to engage the subjectivity and tacit skills of the workforce at some level to ensure profitable production; for example, through quality circles. But as a tendency running through management's structuring of work, alienation is a valuable point which confirms Marx's general analysis. Linked to the concept of alienation is that of *commodity fetishism*. The socially constructed relations between labour and capital embodied in the organisation of production and exchange, are experienced as an alien power and as the natural order of things. This is then reinforced by the dominant ideologies which proclaim, for example, that the operation of the market is determined by laws of supply and demand that are beyond human planning and control.

The problem with constructing a critical psychology from Marxism, however, is that there are no adequate tools for understanding how alienated social relations are subjectively experienced and acted on by the individual. Marxism tends to deal with individuals only as bearers of economic categories such as labour and capital, and many social scientists influenced by Marxism have explicitly rejected any psychological explanation, as we showed with reference to Clegg and Dunkerley's earlier work (1980). It is certainly necessary to have an account of the material structures which shape our experiences and personalities. But this does not mean that people are simply 'bearers' or that attitudes and behaviour can be 'read-off' from material circumstances (Leonard, 1984: 25). A purely structural analysis, even where it allows for human action and resistance, fails to get sufficiently inside those routine everyday experiences in which people react, adapt, modify and consent to work relations.

In their analysis of the Insco case, Knights and Collinson recognise that Marxist and labour process literature tend to produce critiques of social structures and institutions which take as given the behavioural practices which reproduce our concerns with identity. Such structures are both consequences of and give rise to the behavioural routines through which we generate secure identities for ourselves. Without accounts of identity, then, analysis of how structures and the power relations and strategies through which they are maintained will always be incomplete.

The absence of this social psychology from labour process theory means that it is unable to recognise how individuals, such as the men and women in our case study, seek security through controlling and/or subordinating themselves to others. (Knights and Collinson, 1986: 171). The absence of such tools of analysis helps explain why Marxists have had a tendency to try a forced marriage with Freudianism in order to borrow ideas, such as that of the unconscious and the dynamic model of personality (Schneider, 1975; Deleuze and Guattari, 1977); which was for some an attempt to reconcile the irreconcilable (O'Neill, 1985). Furthermore, if individuals do not recognise their common class interests within these categories, they are deemed to be suffering false consciousness. This concept denies the validity of what people think or feel merely because it does not correspond to a set of imputed interests they are supposed to have.

The only modes of reaction allowed are habituation to the demands of capitalist production or collectively to resist and seek to transform society (Leonard, 1984:

164, 206). Although we do not doubt either the existence or desirability of various forms of worker resistance, there are a far greater number of responses to alienated work. As Willmott (1989) observes, wage labour does not always destroy or deny the subjectivity of employees. The worker has an identity as labour, and indeed other identities such as gender and ethnicity. He or she may become attached to and seek to develop the valued aspects, such as the skilled image of the craft worker or the service to the community of the nurse. These processes are not unambiguously positive. Attachment to routines can diminish creative capacities. A popular story at Ford Halewood was of the man who left Ford to work at a sweet factory where he had to divide up the reds and blues, but left because he could not stand the decision-making (Beynon, 1975: 109). Identity projects can also be dominated by anxieties and constrained within the range of known possibilities, such as the aggressive salesman or feminine secretary. The search for a secure identity or sense of solid self can be self-defeating, either because the individual occupies a range of range of positions which pulls identity in different directions (Henriques *et al.*, 1984), or because the identity, like commodities, becomes fetishised (Willmott, 1989); treated as a thing to which there is no alternative. This may lead individuals to a self-defeating project of continual re-investment in the search for security, which in turn reproduces the very institutions which constrained their experiences in the first place. But, at the same time, such perspectives can over-state trends of this kind. Employee's pursuit of identity, whether occupational, class or gender, has always been tied to formal and informal self-organisation in the labour process. Not only does this generate positive meaning and attachments, the 'misbehaviour' is a continual problem for management (Thompson and Ackroyd, 1995).

New thoughts?

While the mainstream agenda in OB continues with its traditional concerns, labour process theory and critical organisational psychology have grasped the nettle of subjectivity with some enthusiasm. This has been boosted by the previously-discussed rise of the post-modern challenge and its meta-spirals of reflexive discourse. As Burrell (1994: 2) argues, we are moving from 'old thinking' in OB (and organisation theory in general) with its mechanistic emphasis on social engineering, to 'new thinking' characterised by *reflective action* and themes of 'openness, ambiguity, meaning and interpretation, narrative understanding, self-reflection, enactment and self-organisation'. These themes are not ubiquitously present, nor are they necessarily treated in a consistent manner, but this is entirely in tune with the post-modern predilection in art, literature, music and architecture, that has quite justly raised appropriation to the status of creativity. We shall not repeat earlier critical comments on the mode of analysis, but reflect on a more practical aspect. The humanistic sentiments of such work (see, for example, Vargish, 1994) echo Van Strien's argument that to develop emancipatory projects, mainstream social science can be, 'ransacked for their practical experience and theories of practice' (1982: 24). In this sense, such new thinking parallels our own attempt to tie together some of the common themes in OB through situating the concept of identity within structures of organisational domination and exploitation. The difference lies perhaps in the appeal of the new thinking to achieve change through the self-transformation of managers into a more humane and self-reflexive species. New thinking explores the theatre, values and projects of organisational life but with a focus on the experiences of professionals, managers and executives.

These developments seem to reflect the genesis of a critically informed social action theory of management – one that does not trade in the prescription of the mainstream agenda, but rather in narratives of practice, cautionary tales of where managers can go wrong. The question to be answered is whether managers will or even can transform themselves through such reflexiveness, at present there being no real signs that humanistic values are impinging on bottom-line definitions of organisational effectiveness, the ongoing rhetoric of empowerment not excepted.

This is not to say that the values inherent in 'new thinking' are not welcome, and indeed they provide a crucial route for the incorporation of issues of subjectivity into OB. Other routes are developing the themes of subjectivity and identity, albeit with the more prosaic aims of reforming the discipline rather than the subject or the client, as exemplified in Hosking and Morley's (1991) cognitive/political psychology of organising and Hollway's (1991) proposals on a movement towards a work psychology reflexive of the relations of knowledge, power and practice. The focus on management found almost everywhere today produces an appearance that the workforce is steadily becoming unreachable as a subject of study, except perhaps in case studies of organisational 'success'. This is especially true of attempts to research what Corbett (1994: 5) calls the 'dark side' of OB in issues such as, 'drug use, unethical behaviour, the secret workings of organisational cabals and violent behaviour'. Corporate discourses envision these as irrational and irrelevant to the construction of corporate harmony, regardless of their role in the everyday experience and identity work of organisational participants. It remains the role of critical organisation theory to get beneath these surface appearances of organisational life.

In using identity as a linking concept, we are in no way claiming that it is the complete answer to understanding issues connected to the 'subjective factor'; rather, that it is one means of taking our understanding further. Nor do we claim that it is possible at this stage to use identity or any other means to produce an integrated critical social psychology. Unfortunately, in redefining the agenda, there is no new and improved magical ingredient which will wash away all the contradictions between these perspectives and provide us with a realistic, emancipatory paradigm with which to proceed. What we have tried to do in Part Two of this book is to use the discussion of identity and subjectivity to address issues that arise in and across mainstream and critical theories and research, reassessing and integrating material within some consistent focus. The approach taken, though focusing mainly on the experiential level, is, we believe, compatible with the structural framework deriving from the perspectives informed by labour process and Weberian concepts in Part One.

Theory, knowledge and practice

Paradigm diversity or closure?

In this chapter we have tried to set out the main general resources available for theorising about work organisations. Our own prime resources have been labour process theory, radical Weberianism and elements of critical social psychology. It would be difficult to argue that these and other components of a critical approach could, or even should, be synthesised into a coherent explanation of work organisations. However, despite differences and sometimes flatly opposed explanations, they can be drawn on as a resource for understanding the complexity of issues involved. In part, this is because there is some common ground. Referring to action theory and the more radical structuralist perspectives, Dunkerley and Salaman observe: 'Both seek to undermine the notion of inevitability in organisational structure; both seek to insert active human beings and groups and their values and interests into the complex processes which give rise to organisational structures' (1986: 93). Complementarity is often more feasible than synthesis – for example in that the labour process and Weberian analyses illuminate power and control through the discussion of means of production, and of administration.

This rather pragmatic view of theorising will be opposed by those who believe that theories can and must operate from within hermetically sealed boxes. For one of the assumptions made by Burrell and Morgan (1979) about the paradigms with which we began this chapter is that they were incommensurable. In other words, their basic differences about knowledge and the world were so basic that theory could only be developed within each framework, which would then do battle with the others. As paradigms frame and define relevant interpretation, 'any observations that do not seem to fit in particular approach belong in some other paradigm' (Ackroyd, 1994: 278). Ackroyd is rightly sceptical about the origins and consequences of the mentality of paradigm closure. Yet it is difficult for paradigms to 'speak' to one another, when they not only make different 'reality assumptions', but develop highly distinctive 'languages' of their own. It is, in fact, one of life's little ironies that many of those who believe most strongly in the constitutive power of language cannot write a sentence that can be understood without a dictionary, a gin and tonic and a great deal of patience! The problem of theoretical communication is compounded by the very different national traditions in organisation theory, as accounts of the past and present in North America (Aldrich, 1992) and Francophone analysis (Chanlat, 1994) reveal.

In some ways, intellectual fashion has moved on from closure. If anything, in these post-modern times, paradigm diversity is the (dis)order of the day. Gareth Morgan has certainly shifted his stance in this way, and now talks about the need to 'harness the possibilities which they offer' (1990: 27). A more concrete version of the same thing is offered by Hassard (1991) who reinterprets the same empirical data through the paradigmatic 'eyes' of each of Burrell and Morgan's original quartet. This is certainly an interesting exercise, but as Parker and McHugh (1991) observed of this effort, the ability to hop between languages is not the same as demonstrating its analytical usefulness. Proclaiming the value of multiple paradigms is really closure by any other name, for each speaks from behind its own walls. The post-modern relativist twist that everything is of equal value merely adds to the problem and is open to the same objections that were raised by Reed to Morgan's use of metaphors: that we end up with taking products down from the shelf instead of rigorous debate and research.

For it is, nevertheless, essential for theories and theorists to engage one another. This may not be as difficult as it appears. As Ackroyd (1992, 1994) reminds us, a lot of the best research is not led by a commitment to paradigms, or is stimulated by 'boundary exchanges' between them. It is possible to have reservations about the strategic exchange theory of Watson (1994) or the discourse analysis of Pringle (1989) but still find exciting and revealing accounts of managerial and secretarial work. Sometimes it is necessary to get behind the different languages and explore whether writers are saying substantively similar things. Other differences can be put down to level of analysis. It is perfectly legitimate to have a more structural or a more micro emphasis of management or some other aspect of organisational life. The key is not to close off analytically the possibilities of 'seeing' the other dimension.

Of course, sharp theoretical disagreements will remain, not so much because of different paradigms, but because rival claims are being made about organisations and society. Ultimately the key problem is not paradigm, but reality incommensurability. Organisations cannot be at the same becoming more and less bureaucratic. Theorising must always remain dynamic and open enough to recognise changes. The 'theoretical' tensions between agency and structure, in part, reflect permanent tensions in practice between co-operativeness and individualism, or normative and economic controls. That is why good theorising is dependent on good research. It will never by enough for theory to be triggered by texts. This seems a useful point to move towards a broader consideration of the uses of knowledge.

Management and theory

If we examine the interaction between theories and practices, no mechanical and few direct relationships can be found. As with the approach to theorising by academics, organisational theories are a *resource* for practitioners, mostly, of course, for employers and managers. Taylor and Mayo, for example, were great synthesisers of ideas and practices in a way that management found useful, not just as a guide to action but as a way of clarifying and legitimating their role. Yet theorists, and Taylor was a prime case, frequently rail against companies that do not swallow their whole package but rather apply them selectively. As Chandler (1977: 277) observes, 'No factory owner . . . adopted the system without modifying it'. This should come as no surprise. Employers and managers are pragmatists and, with some exceptions such as the Quaker-owned companies in the UK, seldom show any intrinsic interest in ideas in themselves but rather for their 'use value'; or, as one senior manager is quoted in Gowler and Legge (1983: 213): 'There's no good ideas until there's cash in the till'.

This is one of the main reasons why, as Watson (1986: 2) correctly notes, there will never be a full and generally acceptable organisational or management theory. But it is not merely a case of a plurality of competing perspectives. The *partiality* of such theories is inherent in their use in control and legitimation processes. It is in the nature of theories of and for management that they give incomplete pictures. The perspectives and accompanying prescriptions only address aspects of the basic contradictions in capitalist work organisation. Therefore, at one level both theorists and practitioners respond within a continuum that has Taylor's minimum interaction model at one end and varieties of human relations at the other. Employers, of course, would like it both ways. Bendix gives an example of a management journal in 1910 calling for 'absolute authority as well as the willing co-operation of the workers' (1956: 272).

To some extent, they can do this by *combining* theories and practices within the continuum. That human relations did not challenge Taylorism on its own terrain of job design and structures, but rather sought to deal with its negative effects and blind spots. That story of combination to deal with different dimensions of organisational experience is repeated through every period and sector. It is, of course, the case that management is not only trying to deal with the contradictory aspects of utilising human labour. Variations in strategy and practice reflect broader problems, such as harmonising different functions and sites of decision-making. But the resultant difficulties in managing the contradictions are similar – different routes to partial success and failure, as Hyman noted.

It would be wrong to give the impression that the choice and use of theories is solely an internal matter. This would reinforce the erroneous view that organisational theories as an historical sequence of 'models of man', the new naturally replacing the old as grateful managers learn to recognise the more sophisticated account of human needs and behaviour. Selectivity is also conditioned by *circumstances*, involving a number of key 'macro' and 'micro' dimensions. At the broadest level, organisational theories interact with the political economy of broad phases of capital accumulation. Taylorism and classical management perspectives emerged at a time when the scale and complexity of organisations and of markets were undergoing a fundamental change. The globalisation of markets and intensified competition, particularly from Japan, has stimulated major shifts in management thinking in the more recent period.

Yet there were so many misconceptions surrounding 'Japanisation' that it is difficult to disagree with the view that it is a bad abstraction (Dicken and Savage, 1987: 2), which conflates unrelated and non-essential factors behind an inappropriate racial tag. As Marchington and Parker comment, 'there must be some doubt as to whether there is anything inherently Japanese about the practices employed' (1987: 28). They point to the kind of British companies that have a history of consensual, paternalistic management and encouragement of enterprise unionism. But we would put it another way. Japanisation, like other sets of management ideas and practices, is a resource which is drawn on selectively. So the Japanese experience can be seen either as confirmation of the need to retain managerial prerogatives or for the expansion of worker participation, or indeed as both (Streek, 1987: 295). Even unions can draw on those aspects which are perceived as egalitarian, such as single-status conditions. Interestingly, Wickens is bitingly critical of faddist managers, who 'have only an idealised, often out-of-date, sanitised version of Japanese-style management based on constantly recycled versions of the human resource and other management techniques of some of Japan's larger companies' (1987: 37).

To return to more general themes, ideological conditions are also influential, as evidenced by the spillover of entrepreneurial values from the political to the managerial sphere. At a micro-level, the choices made by particular companies reflect even more complex factors. In particular, the *sector*, with its specific product market and labour market, technological framework and political context, is a vital consideration. Each country, too, has its own unique configuration of intellectual, social and economic conditions mediating the form and content of organisational change. But just as there are global markets for products, so there are increasingly for ideas. This process is enhanced by the spread of pop-management and 'airport lounge' books, as the success of the excellence genre is testament to. Unfortunately, it reinforces the tendency for academics to form alliances with sections of management around particular perspectives or techniques as solve-all solutions. So much ideological investment is made in the process that the chosen vehicle can seldom meet the burden placed on it. Hence burn-out, cynicism and later fortunate loss of memory – until, that is, a new solution comes along! But why do managers so often become locked in this fatal embrace? This is an under-developed area (Huczynski, 1993; Thompson and O'Connell Davidson, 1994), but part of the explanation is that, as an interest group, management requires a means of defining and expanding its activities. Referring to the recent spread of interest in corporate culture, Thackray comments, 'Culture is particularly seductive because it appears to open up a new frontier of managerial activism' (1986: 86). This option is particularly attractive to the personnel or human resource teams of large corporations, reminding us that the adoption of theories and practices is also likely to be affected by the internal fissures within the managerial labour process. With the demise of the great practitioner-theorists such as Taylor and Fayol, and the growth of more specialised academic production, management is also in a more *dependent* position.

But the attraction is also a reflection of the fact that the meaning of management is inseparable from the management of meaning (Gowler and Legge, 1983). Organisational theories become part of a language and a subculture through which management tries to understand itself and legitimate its activities to others, even when those ideological resources are used in a contradictory and rhetorical way. The essence of these points is that regardless of the social influences, organisational and management theory has a level of autonomy and its own rhythm of development. Regardless of the cycles of interest in ideas and imitations of the fashion cycle, they have their own very real effects. And as they are grappling with genuine problems, it is possible to draw positive lessons, even for those of us who want to take the process of organisational change much further.

Learning from past and present

There is a danger in any book that focuses on critique of theoretical and practical orthodoxy, of simply knocking everything down. To paraphrase Gouldner's comment for other purposes, critical social scientists have too often been morticians who bury people's hopes, and this has been further added to by the post-modern abandonment of belief in the possibilities of progress through any type of rational design. We believe that it is important for critical theory not just to proclaim the limits of existing organisational forms and practices. Those constraints arising from dominant relations of wealth, power and control are real enough, as observation of the very partial progress of QWL programmes or employee participation illustrates. But solely 'negative learning' implies an *essence* to work organisation under capitalism which denies it any significance. For instance, the *Work Relations Group* led by the noted American radical scholar Jeremy Brecher (1978: 20) argues that the history of such research 'exposes the shallow conceptions of "job enrichment", "workers' control" and the like as window dressing which leaves untouched the essential tyranny of the capitalist labour process'. Certainly many aspects of work reorganisation have been and still are based on increasing the intensity of labour, tightening controls and marginalising sections of the workforce. But when Marx wrote that the logic of competition between companies compels them constantly to revolutionise the means of production, he was recognising that by its very nature capitalism is a dynamic system.

The search for profitability involves innovations in technology, coordination of resources and utilisation of people's skills and knowledge that offer positive lessons relevant to any more democratic and egalitarian social order at work. This is not the same as the orthodox Marxist view, expressed by the founders of the Soviet Union, that a socialist society simply 'adds on' the techniques of capitalist work organisation to new property relations. Those techniques rather have to be added to, rethought and resituated in a new context of a fully democratic economy. For job enrichment or teamworking, however flawed, are also indicators of the great potential of human labour to create more efficient and satisfying forms of work. To argue that all this is mere superficial window dressing is to fly in the face of the reality that we all find some work situations more creative and rewarding than others. Furthermore, there appears in some spheres to be a lot more to learn about innovative forms of work organisation from capitalism than from existing and past state socialist societies.

A further reason for not regarding the worlds of today and tomorrow as wholly sealed off from one another is that there is much to learn from the existing practices of employees. As Brecher rightly says, there is a massive 'hidden history of the workplace' which needs to be recognised and uncovered. That history is based on the self-organisation of workers trying to resist and transform work relations. Admittedly that was easier to see when craft labour was dominant and many workers genuinely felt that they could run the factories better than their bosses. Old-style movements for workers' control are no longer feasible in a world of transnationals, global production and semi-skilled labour. But there remains a wealth of untapped experience and knowledge in employees' informal job-controls and patterns of organisation.

Though measures such as TQM are back-handed compliments from employers, little is learnt because workers' self-activity is seldom given institutional form. Discussions of alternative forms of organisation often depend on examples such as producer co-operatives. Such initiatives have grown rapidly in recent years, partly as a response to the economic recession and restructuring. As collectivist and democratic forms of management and ownership, co-operatives constitute an important experience, despite their critics from left to right who predict inevitable degeneration into traditional structures (Cornforth, 1988). But the fact remains that they are relatively marginal in the economy. With a few well-known exceptions such as the large-scale Mondragon movement in Spain, most are small, labour-intensive and self-financed and they flourish in areas of the market where there is little competition from mainstream organisations (Rothschild and Allen Whitt, 1986). Alternatives within the mainstream economy are few indeed and those that have taken place, such as the UK Lucas workers' alternative plan, have had to bear a heavy burden as exemplar and hope for the future (Collective Design Project, 1986). This initiative arose as a strategic means of local trade union organisation to provide a positive alternative to dependence on making armaments, based on production that was both socially useful and economically viable, and technology that was human-centred. Predictably, though highly praised by all and sundry, it did not get very far with management. But the emphasis on alternative technologies has perhaps had a more lasting impact and is tied into further design work done by the Control Systems Centre at UMIST (Corbett, 1985b). Such initiatives illustrate one of our central points, that positive connections can be made between the kind of theoretical critiques of technological determinism and deskilling made by labour-process and other writers, and practical initiatives in new forms of work design.

We would also do well not to forget that the mainstream world of large-scale organisations includes the public sector. Such services in the UK, notably those in local government, have been given a rough ride in recent years, both with respect to their funding and sharp attacks on their efficiency. Some of the criticisms have been well deserved. Much local authority service provision has been characterised by over-centralisation, a lack of flexibility in meeting diverse consumer demands and poor managerial direction in setting and attaining goals. But the innovative organisational response, mainly from Labour local authorities, has been neglected (Goss and Parston, 1989). All these examples illustrate the need and potential for organisational theorists to broaden their conception of practitioners and extend contacts and collaboration to broader groups of clients, including those in the voluntary and public sectors, and to trade union and other employee organisations. Nevertheless, practice without theory is blind and such activity has to be underwritten by more extensive analytical work directed towards developing new thinking on renewing existing and extending alternative organisational forms. Rationality, for all its flaws, is not dead.

References

Ackroyd, S. (1992) 'Paradigms Lost: Paradise Gained? Notes on the Discovery of Meta-Theory in Organizational Analysis', in M. Reed and M. Hughes (eds) *Rethinking Organization: New Directions in Organization and Analysis*, London: Sage.

Ackroyd, S. (1994) 'Recreating Common Ground: Elements for Post-Paradigmatic Theories of Organization, in J. Hassard and M. Parker (eds) *Towards a New Theory of Organizations*, London: Routledge.

Albrow, M. (1970) *Bureaucracy*, London: Pall Mall.

Albrow, M. (1992) 'Sine Ira et Studio – or Do Organizations Have Feelings?' *Organization Studies*, vol. 13, no. 3: 313–29.

Aldrich, H. E. (1992) 'Incommensurable Paradigms? Vital Signs from Three Perspectives', in M. Reed and M. Hughes (eds) *Rethinking Organization: New Directions in Organization and Analysis*, London: Sage.

Archibald, W. P. (1978) *Social Psychology as Political Economy*, Toronto: McGraw-Hill Ryerson.

Armistead, N. (1974) *Reconstructing Social Psychology*, Baltimore: Penguin.

Barley, S.R. and G. Kunda (1992) 'Design and Devotion: Surges of Rational and Normative Ideologies of Control in Managerial Discourse', *Administrative Science Quarterly*, vol. 37: 363–99.

Barnard, C. (1938) *The Functions of the Executive*, Cambridge, Mass: Harvard University Press.

Bellaby, P. and P. Orribor (1977) 'The Growth of Trade Union Consciousness Among General Hospital Nurses', *Sociological Review*, vol. 25.

Bendix, R. (1956) *Work and Authority in Industry*, New York: Harper & Row.

Berger, P. L. and T. Luckman (1967) *The Social Construction of Reality*, London: Allen Lane.

Beynon, H. (1975) *Working for Ford*, Wakefield: E.P. Publishing.

Bittner, E. (1967) 'The Police on Skid Row: A Study of Peace Keeping', *American Sociological Review*, vol. 32, no. 5: 699–715.

Blau, P. M. (1955) *The Dynamics of Bureaucracy*, Chicago: University of Chicago Press.

Bologh, R. (1990) *Love or Greatness: Max Weber and Masculine Thinking – A Feminist Inquiry*, London: Unwin Hyman.

Braverman, H. (1974) *Labor and Monopoly Capital: The Degradation of Work in the Twentieth Century*, New York: Monthly Review Press.

Brecher, J. (1978) 'Uncovering the Hidden History of the American Workplace', *Review of Radical Political Economics*, vol. 10, no. 4, Winta.

Brown, R. (1992) *Understanding Organizations: Theoretical Perspectives in Industrial Sociology*, London: Routledge.

Burawoy, M. (1979) *Manufacturing Consent: Changes in the Labour Process Under Monopoly Capitalism*, Chicago: University of Chicago Press.

Burrell, G. (1980a) 'Radical Organization Theory', in D. Dunkerley and G. Salaman (eds) *The International Yearbook of Organization Studies 1979*, London: Routledge & Kegan Paul.

Burrell, G. (1994) Foreword to H. Tsoukas (ed.) (1994d) *New Thinking in Organizational Behaviour*, London: Butterworth & Heinemann.

Burrell, G. and G. Morgan (1979) *Sociological Paradigms and Organizational Analysis*, London: Heinemann.

Calas M. and L. Smircich (1992) 'Rewriting Gender into Organization Theorising: Directions from Feminist Perspectives', in M. Reed and M. Hughes (eds) *Rethinking Organization: New Directions in Organization Analysis*, London: Sage.

Callinicos, A. (1989) *Against Postmodernism: A Marxist Critique*, Cambridge: Polity.

Cavendish, R. (1982) *Women on the Line*, London: Routledge & Kegan Paul.

Chandler, A.D. (1977) *The Visible Hand*, Cambridge Mass.: Harvard University Press.

Chanlat, J-F. (1994) 'Francophone Organizational Analysis (1950–1990): An Overview', *Organization Studies*, vol. 15, no. 1: 47–80.

Child, J. (1972) 'Organization Structure, Environment and Performance: the Role of Strategic Choice', *Sociology*, vol. 6, no. 1: 1–22.

Child, J. (1985) 'Managerial Strategies, New Technology and the Labour Process', in D. Knights, H. Wilmott and D. Collinson (eds) *Job Redesign: Critical Perspectives on the Labour Process*, London: Gower.

Cicourel, A. V. (1968) *The Social Organization of Social Justice*, New York: Free Press.

Clawson, D. (1980) *Bureaucracy and the Labour Process: The Transformation of US Industry, 1860–1920*, New York: Monthly Review Press.

Clegg, S. (1988) The Good, the Bad and the Ugly[7], *Organisation Studies*, vol. 9, no. 1:7–13.

Clegg, S. (1990) *Modern Organizations: Organization Studies in the Postmodern World*, London: Sage.

Clegg, S. and D. Dunkerley (1980) *Organization, Class and Control*, London: Routledge & Kegan Paul.

Cohen, Sheila (1987) 'A Labour Process to Nowhere?' *New Left Review*, 107: 34–50.

Collective Design Project (eds) (1986) *Very Nice Work if You Can Get It: The Socially Useful Production Debate*, Nottingham: Spokesman.

Cooper, R. and G. Burrell (1988) 'Modernism, Postmodernism and Organizational Analysis: An Introduction', *Organization Studies*, vol. 9, no. 2: 91–112.

Corbett, J.M. (1985b) 'Prospective Work Design of a Human-Centred CNC Lathe', *Behaviour and Information Technology*, vol. 14, no. 1: 201–14.

Corbett, J. M. (1994) *Critical Cases in Organisational Behaviour*, London: Macmillan.

Cornforth, C. (1988) 'Patterns of Cooperative Management: Revising the Degeneration Thesis', paper to a Conference on: *New Forms of Ownership and Management*, Cardiff Business School.

Crook, S., J. Paluski and M. Waters (1992) *Postmodernization*, London: Sage.

Dahler-Larsen, P. (1994) 'Corporate Culture and Morality: Durkheim-Inspired Reflections on the Limits of Corporate Culture', *Journal of Management Studies*, vol. 31, no. 1: 1–18.

Day, R.A. and J.V. Day (1977) 'A Review of the Current State of Negotiated Order Theory: An Appreciation and a Critique', *Sociological Quarterly*, 18 (Winter), 126–42.

Deleuze, G. and F. Guattari (1977) *AntiOedipus: Capitalism and Schizophrenia*, New York: Viking.

Dicken, P. and M. Savage (1987) The Japanisation of British Industry?: Instances from a High Growth Area', *Industrial Relations Journal*, Spring 1988, vol. 19, no. 1.

Donaldson, L. (1985) *In Defence of Organization Theory: A Reply to the Critics,* Cambridge: Cambridge University Press.

Due Billing, Y. (1994) 'Gender and Bureaucracies – A Critique of Ferguson's "The Feminist Case Against Bureaucracy[7], vol. 1, no. 4: 173–93.

Dunkerley, D. and G. Salaman (1986) 'Organizations and Bureaucracy', in M. Haralambos (ed.) *Developments in Sociology,* vol. 2, Ormskirk: Causeway Press.

Edwards, R. (1979) *Contested Terrain: The Transformation of the Workplace in the Twentieth Century,* London: Heinemann.

Edwards, P. K and H. Scullion (1982) *The Social Organization of Industrial Conflict: Control and Resistance in the Workplace,* Oxford, Basil Blackwell.

Eldridge, J. E. T. and A. D. Crombie (1974) *A Sociology of Organizations,* London: Allen & Unwin.

Featherstone, M. (1988) Tn Pursuit of the Postmodern: An Introduction', in *Theory, Culture and Society,* vol. 5: 195–215.

Ferguson, K. (1984) *The Feminist Case Against Bureaucracy,* Philadelphia: Temple University Press.

Fischer, F. and C. Sirriani (1984) *Critical Studies in Organization and Bureaucracy,* Philadelphia: Temple University Press.

Friedman, A. (1977) *Industry and Labour: Class Struggle at Work Monopoly Capitalism,* London: Macmillan.

Gabriel, Y. (1988) *Working Lives in Catering,* London: Routledge. Zimmerman, D. (1971) The Practicalities of Rule Use', in J. Douglas (ed.) *Understanding Everyday Life,* London: Routledge & Kegan Paul.

Gergen, K. J. (1973) 'Social Psychology as History', *Journal of Personality and Psychologyt,* vol. 26, no. 2: 309–20.

Gergen, K. (1992) Organization Theory in the Postmodern Era', in M. Reed and M. Hughes (eds) *Rethinking Organization: Mew Directions in Organization and Analysis,* London: Sage.

Giddens, A. (1984) *The Constitution of Society,* Cambridge: Polity Press.

Goss, S. and G. Parston (1989) *Public Management for New Times,* London: Labour Coordinating Committee.

Gouldner, A. (1955) *Wildcat Strike,* London: Routledge & Kegan Paul.

Gowler, D. and K. Legge (1983) The Meaning of Management and the Management of Meaning: A View From Social Anthropology', in M.J. Earl (ed.) *Perspectives on Management: A Multidisciplinary Analysis,* Oxford: Oxford University Press.

Grimshaw, J. (1986) *Feminist Philosophers,* Brighton: Wheatsheaf.

Hamilton, P. (1980) 'Social Theory and the Problematic Concept of Work', in G. Esland and G. Salaman (eds) *The Politics of Work and Occupations,* Milton Keynes: Open University Press.

Hassard, J. (1991) 'Multiple Paradigms and Organizational Analysis: A Case Study', *Organization Studies,* vol. 12, no. 2: 275–99.

Hassard, J. (1994) 'Postmodern Organizational Analysis: Towards a Conceptual Framework', *Journal of Management Studies,* vol. 31, no. 3: 1–22.

Hassard, J. and M. Parker (eds) (1994) *Towards a New Theory of Organizations,* London: Routledge.

Hearn, J. (1992) *Men in the Public Eye,* London: Routledge.

Henriques, J. *et al.* (1984) *Changing the Subject: Psychology, Social Regulation and Subjectivity,* London: Methuen.

Heydebrand, W. (1977) 'Organisational Contradictions in Public Bureaucracies: Toward a Marxian Theory of Organisations', in J. K. Benson (ed.) *Organisational Analysis: Critique and Innovation,* London: Sage Contemporary Social Science Issues 37.

Hinings, B. (1988) 'Defending Organization Theory: A British View from North America', *Organization Studies,* vol. 9, no. 1: 2–7.

Hollway, W. (1991) *Work Psychology and Organisational Behaviour: Managing the Individual at Work,* London: Sage.

Holton, R.J. and B.S. Turner (1989) *Max Weber on Economy and Society,* London: Routledge.

Hosking, D. and I. Morley (1991) *A Social Psychology of Organising: People, processes and Contexts,* Hemel Hempstead: Harvester Wheatsheaf.

Huczynski, A. A. (1993) *Management Gurus,* London: Routledge.

Johnson, T. (1972) *Professions and Power,* London: Macmillan.

Johnson, T. (1980) 'Work and Power;, in G. Esland and G. Salaman (eds) *The Politics of Work and Occupations,* Milton Keynes: Open University Press.

Kelly, J. E. (1985) 'Management's Redesign of Work', in D. Knights, H. Willmott and D. Collinson (eds) *Job Redesign: Critical Perspectives on the Labour Process,* Aldershot: Gower.

Knights, D. and D. Collinson (1987) 'Shop Floor Culture and the Problem of Managerial Control', in J. McGoldrick (ed.) *Business Case File in Behavioural Science,* London: Van Nostrand.

Larsen, K. S. (1980) *Social Psychology: Crisis or Failure?,* Monmouth, Oregon: Institute for Theoretical History.

Layder, D. (1987) 'Key Issues in Structuration Theory: Some Critical Remarks', *Current Perspectives in Social Theory,* vol. 8: 25–46.

Leonard, P. (1984) *Personality and Ideology: Towards a Materialist Understanding of the Individual,* London: Macmillan.

Littler, C. R. (1982) *The Development of the Labour Process in Capitalist Societies,* London: Heinemann.

Marchington, M. and P. Parker (1987) 'Japanisation: a Lack of Chemical Reaction?' paper presented at Conference on: *Japanisation of British Industry,* UWIST.

Marcuse, H. (1971) 'Industrialisation and Capitalism', in O. Stammer (ed.), *Max Weber and Sociology Today,* Oxford: Blackwell.

Marx, K. (1963) *Early Writings,* trans. T. B. Bottomore, London: Penguin.

Marx, K. (1984) 'The Spirit of Bureaucracy and Beyond Bureaucracy: The Paris Commune', in F. Fischer and C. Sirriani (eds) *Critical Studies in Organization and Bureaucracy,* Philadelphia: Temple University Press.

Martin, J. (1990) 'Deconstructing Organisational Taboos: The Suppression of Gender Conflict in Organisations', *Organisational Science,* vol. 1: 1–21.

Mead, G.H. (1934) *Mind, Self and Society,* Chicago: Chicago University Press.

Mills. A.J. and S.J. Murgatroyd (1991) *Organizational Rules,: a Framework for Understanding Organizations,* Milton Keynes: Open University Press.

Morgan, Gareth (1986) *Images of Organisation,* London: Sage.

Morgan, Gareth (1990) 'Paradigm Diversity in Organizational Research', in J. Hassard and D. Pym (eds) *The Theory and Philosophy of Organizations,* London: Routledge.

Moscovici, S. (1972) 'Society and Theory in Social Psychology', in J. Israel and H. Tajfel (eds). Moscovici, S. and M. Zavalloni (1969) The Group as a Polarizer of Attitudes', *Journal of Personality and Social Psychology,* 12: 125–35.

Newton, T. (1994) 'Resocialising the Subject? A Re-Reading of Grey's "Career as a Project of the Self', *Sociology,* 28.2, Working Paper Series, Department of Business Studies, University of Edinburgh.

Nichols, T. (1986) *The British Worker Question,* London: Routledge & Kegan Paul.

Norris, C. (1992) *Uncritical Theory: Postmodernism, Intellectuals and the Gulf War,* London: Lawrence & Wishart.

O'Neill, N. (1985) 'Marxism and Psychology', in M. Shaw (ed.) *Marxist Sociology Revisited,* London: Macmillan.

Parker, M. and G. McHugh (1991) 'Five Texts in Search of An Author: A Response to John Hassard's "Multiple Paradigms and Organizational Analysis: A Case Study"', *Organization Studies,* vol. 12, no. 3: 451–6.

Parker, M. (1992) 'Post-Modern Organizations or Post-Modern Organization Theory?' *Organisation Studies,* vol. 13, no. 1: 1–17.

Parsons, T. (1951) *The Social System,* New York: Collier Macmillan.

Pearce, F. (1989) *The Radical Durkheim,* London: Unwin Hyman.

Polan, A.J. (1984) *Lenin and the End of Politics,* London: Methuen.

Pollert, A. (1981) *Girls, Wives, Factory Lives,* London: Macmillan.

Pringle, R. (1989) *Secretaries Talk: Sexuality, Power and Work,* London: Verso.

Putnam, L.L. and D.K. Mumby (1993) 'Organizations, Emotion and the Myth of Rationality', in S. Fineman (ed.) *Emotion in Organisations,* London: Sage.

Ramsay, K. and M. Parker (1992) 'Gender, Bureaucracy and Organizational Culture', in A. Witz and M. Savage (eds) *Gender and Bureaucracy,* Oxford: Blackwell.

Reed, M. (1990b) 'From Paradigm to Images: The Paradigm Warrior Turns Post-Modernist Guru', *Personnel Review,* vol. 19, no. 3: 35–40.

Reed, M (1991) 'Scripting Scenarios for a New Organization Theory and Practice', *Work, Employment and Society,* vol. 5.no. 1: 119–32.

Reed, M. (1993) 'Organizations and Modernity: Continuity and Discontinuity in Organization Theory', in J. Hassard and M. Parker (eds) *Postmodernism and Organizations,* London: Sage.

Resch, M., W. Hacker, K. Leitner and T. Krogoll (1984) 'Regulation Requirements and Regulation Barriers: Two Aspects of Industrial Work', in M. Thomas (ed.) *Design of Work in Automated Manufacturing Systems,* Oxford: Pergamon.

Roper, M. (1994) *Masculinity and the British Organization Man Since 1945,* Oxford: Oxford University Press.

Rosnow, R.L. (1981) Paradigms in Transition: The Methodology of Social Enquiry, New York, Oxford University Press.

Rothschild, J. and J. Allen Whitt (1986) *The Co-operative Workplace: Potentials and Dilemmas or Organizational Democracy and Participation,* Cambridge: Cambridge University Press.

Salaman, G. (1981) *Class and the Corporation,* London: Fontana.

Sayer (1984) 'A "Modern" Industry in a "Mature" Region: the Remaking of Management-Labour Relations', working paper, Urban and Regional Studies, University of Sussex.

Sayer, D. (1991) *Capitalism and Modernity: An Excursus on Marx and Weber,* London: Routledge.

Schneider, M. (1975) *Neurosis and Civilisation: A Marxist/Freudian Synthesis,* New York: Seabury.

Schutz, A. (1967) *The Phenomenology of the Social World,* Evanston: North WesternUniversity Press.

Silverman, D. (1970) *The Theory of Organizations,* London: Heinemann.

Silverman, D. and J. Jones (1976) *Organizational Work: The Language of Grading and the Grading of Language,* London: Macmillan.

Starkey, K. (1992) 'Durkheim and Organizational Analysis: Two Legacies', *Organization Studies,* vol. 13, no. 4: 627–42.

Steffy, B. D. and A. J. Grimes (1992) 'Personnel/Organization Psychology: A Critique of the Discipline', in M. Alvesson and H. Willmott (eds) *Critical Management Studies,* London: Sage.

Storey, J. (1983) *Managerial Prerogative and the Question of Control,* London: Routledge & Kegan Paul.

Strauss, A., L. Schatzman, D. Ehrlich, R. Bucher and M. Sabshim (1963) "The Hospital and its Negotiated Order', in E. Friedson (ed.) *The Hospital in Modern Society,* New York: Macmillan.

Streek, W. (1987) The Uncertainties of Management in the Management of Uncertainty: Employers, Labour Relations and Industrial Adjustment in the 1980s', *Work Employment and Society,* vol. 1, no. 3: 281–308.

Thackray, J. (1986) 'The Corporate Culture Rage', *Management Today,* Feb.: 67–70.

Thompson, P. and E. Bannon (1985) *Working the System: The Shop Floor and New Technology,* London: Pluto.

Thompson, P. (1993) 'Postmodernism: Fatal Distraction', in J. Hassard and M. Parker (eds) *Postmodernism and Organisations,* London: Sage.

Thompson, P. and J. O'Connell Davidson (1994) The Continuity of Discontinuity: Management Rhetoric in Turbulent Times', *Personnel Review,* August.

Thompson, P. and S. Ackroyd (1995) 'AH Quiet on the Workplace Front: A Critique of Recent Trends in British Industrial Sociology', forthcoming.

Tsoukas, H. (1992) 'Postmodernism, Reflexive Rationalism and Organizational Studies: A Reply to Martin Parker', *Organization Studies,* vol. 13, no. 4, 643–49.

Tsoukas, H. (1994c) 'From Social Engineering to Reflective Action in Organizational Behaviour', in H. Tsoukas (ed.) *New Thinking in Organizational Behaviour,* London: Butterworth & Heinemann.

Van Strien, P.J. (1982) 'In Search of an Emancipatory Social Psychology' in P. Stringer, (ed.) *Confronting Social Issues: Applications of Social Psychology,* vol. 2, London: Academic Press.

Vargish, T. (1994) 'The Value of Humanities in Executive Development', in H. Tsoukas, (ed.) *New Thinking in Organizational Behaviour*, London: Butterworth & Heinemann.

Watson, T. (1986) *Management, Organization and Employment Strategy: New Directions in Theory and Practice*, London: Routledge & Kegan Paul.

Watson, T. (1994) *In Search of Management: Culture, Chaos and Control in Managerial Work*, London: Routledge.

Weber, M. (1968) *Economy and Society*, New York: Bedminster Press.

Weber, M. (1984) 'Bureaucracy, in F. Fischer and C. Sirriani (eds) *Critical Studies in Organization and Bureaucracy*, Philadelphia: Temple University Press.

Weir, D. (1993) 'Why Isn't There any Good Management Research?' *British Academy of Management Newsletter*, no. 15, June.

Westwood, S. (1984) *All Day, Every Day: Factory and Family in the Making of Women's Lives*, London: Pluto.

Wexler, P. (1983) *Critical Social Psychology*, Boston: Routledge & Kegan Paul.

Whittington, R. (1991b) 'Putting Giddens into Action: Evolving Accounts of Managerial Agency', paper for *Conference: Towards a New Theory of Organizations*, University of Keele.

Wickens, P.D. (1987) *The Road to Nissan*, London: Macmillan.

Willmott, H. (1989) 'Subjectivity and the Dialectics of Praxis: Opening up the Core of Labour Process Analysis', in D. Knights and H. Willmott (eds) *Labour Process Theory*, London: Macmillan.

Willmott, H. (1990) 'Beyond Paradigmatic Closure in Organizational Enquiry', in J. Hassard and D. Pym (eds) *The Theory and Philosophy of Organizations*, London: Routledge.

Witz, A. and M. Savage (1992) The Gender of Organizations', in A. Witz and M. Savage (eds) *Gender and Bureaucracy*, Oxford: Blackwell.

CHAPTER 3
The emergence of large-scale organisations

Organising the new work forms

The aim of this chapter is to locate and explain the formation of the large-scale industrial bureaucracies that have been the primary object of analysis of the subject of organisation studies. Our time frame focuses on the crucial period at the beginning of the twentieth century, but moves backwards and forwards in order to understand the process of emergence of such organisations as the foundation of business development.

By the beginning of the twentieth century business organisations were beginning to be, 'transformed from chaotic and ad-hoc factories to rationalised, well-ordered manufacturing settings' (Goldman and Van Houten, 1980: 108). This was not just a product of growth, merger and technological innovation. It was also a question of *management*. Though the trend was in its infancy, firms were beginning to move away from particularist and uneven practices, towards the beginnings of an industrial bureaucracy. Indeed the two were intimately connected, given that the increasing scale of work organisation meant that it was no longer possible to rely on personal or unspecified forms of direction. Changes involved systematising and stabilising both the practices of management and the organisation of the labour process. Job hierarchies; new patterns of work supervision, measurement and reward; as well as greater specialisation and detailed division of labour, became more characteristic of organisational life. It is important to trace the genesis and development of this industrial bureaucracy, reflecting on the theoretical issues through the work of Weber, Taylor and others. Mainstream writings largely lack this kind of historical and comparative character. Moreover, they tend to treat managerial and organisational theories as ideologies with universal effects.

Theories of management are not 'invented' and applied. Rather they form a resource through which both academics and practitioners try to understand and act. How that happens will depend on different social contexts and the histories that have shaped them. Of course, we do not have the space to provide a detailed business history that captures all events, variations and issues across societies. The aim is to give a broad picture that locates ideas in context and that focuses particularly on employment and labour process questions. In this chapter that picture is predominantly of USA and British circumstances. Nevertheless, in the final section we shall discuss how specific that experience is and compare it briefly to the formation of large-scale organisation in some other national contexts.

The rise of the factory system

Work processes prior to the factory system were not characterised by an extensive division of labour, nor by directly imposed coercive authority. In handicraft and domestic production, small producers were typically involved in independent commodity production, often based on the family structure. They owned their own means of production, worked according to their own patterns, and sold the goods at markets. Some trades or crafts were organised through the guild system. This combined employer and employee, normally within the framework and traditional authority of apprentice, journeyman and master. Neither system was flexible enough to be an adequate basis for responding to the needs of an emergent market economy. Industrialisation and the new capitalist production relations developed from a variety of organisational structures, including artisan production, co-operatives, centralised manufacture and the putting-out system (Berg, 1985). We want to focus mainly on the last.

Though the site of the work remained the 'cottage', workers continued to retain their own tools and capacity to organise their own work, and there was little division of labour. A relationship of wage labour was established, merchants supplied the raw materials and owned the finished product. Some historians see the putting-out system as a phase of *proto-industrialisation*. Rural workers were the ideal labour force, as they were worked for less than their urban equivalents and were too isolated to organise against the merchant's pricing. New markets, sources of capital accumulation and training grounds for entrepreneurial skills also constituted important features. Berg rightly notes that this 'phase' was not universal, took different regional and other forms and had varied outcomes. But the point of transition from cottage to workshop and then factory raises crucial *organisational* issues.

Mainstream theory commonly asserts that the new and more complex forms of organisation, with the associated detailed division of labour and hierarchies, developed largely because they were *technically* required by the scale of production, technology and related factors. A number of writers, notably Marglin (1974) and Clawson (1980) have used specific historical evidence on the factory system to challenge this general explanation. It is directed at helping to explain why workers were deprived of control of process and product through the centralised organisation of the factory system. A common response is to argue that the impetus was the necessity to shift from hand production to power-driven machinery located in a central source. In addition, there was the benefits of division of labour, pointed to in Adam Smith's famous pin factory example.

Both Marglin and Clawson show that bringing workers together in workshops and later in the factory – for example in the weaving and spinning trades – did not necessarily involve power-driven machinery or any other technical innovation. In fact, contrary to technological determinist arguments, 'organisational change precedes, both historically and analytically, the technological revolution which is the foundation of modern industry' (Clawson, 1980: 57). The issue of the division of labour is more complicated. Marglin does not argue that it, or hierarchy, were brought into being by capitalist organisation of work. But a distinction is made between the specialisation of occupation and function that is present in any social division of labour, and the particular forms of specialisation involved in the putting-out system and then in the factory. The minute division of work was not necessarily more efficient; rather it provided a role for the capitalist to play in organising production and to take a greater portion of the rewards: 'The social function of hierarchical work organisation is not technical efficiency, but accumulation' (Marglin, 1974: 62).

Given the time lapse, the evidence on this question is inevitably patchy. What, however, is beyond doubt is that though the new framework provided an impetus for technical innovation, efficiency and technical superiority were not the only, or even primary, reasons for the rise of factory organisation. The putting-out system allowed workers a great deal of control over their hours, rhythm, intensity and quality of work. Furthermore, there was a high level of embezzlement of raw materials, as workers sought to secure a fairer return for their labour. Historians have provided a large body of evidence that the workshop and the factory were utilised as a means of discipline and control in order to facilitate capital accumulation (Pollard, 1965; E. P. Thompson, 1967; Landes, 1969). Coercive authority could be more easily applied, including systems of fines, supervision (for instance the overlooker system in textiles), the paraphernalia of bells and clocks, and incentive payments. The employer could dictate the *general* terms of work, time and space; including the division of labour, overall organisational layout and design, rules governing movement, shouting, singing and other forms of disobedience. Doray gives numerous examples of French factory regulations, including fines for faulty work, writing on walls or entering the factory through the wrong door. He does, however, point out that when applied to the labour process, regulations were not particularly detailed: 'They asserted, in repetitive fashion, the principle of the employer's authority over an unspecified range of activities' (1988: 27–8). It is not surprising that many workers bitterly resisted entry to the factory and the associated forms of discipline. In those early periods, employers were frequently forced to resort to groups such as convicts, paupers and child labour.

To break such resistance, new work habits had to be created appropriate to the discipline of labour time and cash nexus at the heart of the wage relation. Employers' concern with the moral issues of sexuality, drink, bad language and theft was directed less by fidelity to religious doctrine than to the *behavioural* characteristics – obedience, punctuality, responsibility and performance – linked to capitalist rationality and its new forms of organisational culture. As Clegg and Dunkerley observe, the triumph of the formal factory organisation was strongly determined by its 'moral machinery' (1980: 62). This term was used by the economist Andrew Ure, noted for his pertinent advice to employers. He and other such advisers, were, however, clear that neither the division of labour nor work values were sufficient for the purpose of achieving the goal of creating 'factory hands'. *Mechanisation* was necessary to destroy old work habits and to tie the worker to the 'unvarying regularity of the machine'.

Marx showed how workers were able to use the employer's continuing dependence on their handicraft skills and knowledge as a weapon of resistance. In turn, Ure recognised that the unity of capital and science was necessary to try to reduce skills to dexterities, to create a technical framework independent of the producers, and to reduce labour costs by *intensifying* work rather than the limited option of raising hours. Marglin's notion of the factory as a social control device independent of technology is therefore incomplete (Clawson, 1980: 54). Without these kinds of development, the formal control developed in the factory could not have been adequately realised. It is always necessary to resist the temptation to describe these processes of organisational change in finished rather than relative terms. Employer control remained at a very general level and still had to be accommodated to high levels of worker skill, knowledge and self-organisation. Work was still often labour intensive and there was little or no bureaucratic or management structures. To explain the further development of large-scale organisation we need to focus more closely on the evolution of forms of control.

Modes of control in the transition to bureaucratic organisation

There were a number of obstacles to the development of a more bureaucratic work organisation during the nineteenth century. Even a more mature factory system rested on control structures that were inimical to moves in that direction. As Littler (1982: 69) argues, British industry presented a spectrum of modes of control that, despite differences, were fundamentally non-bureaucratic in nature. Using a range of evidence, three basic modes can be distinguished.

Entrepreneurial or simple control In early factories at the beginning of the nineteenth century, owners could exercise a large degree of power and control personally. Referring to the famous foundry owner, Bendix observes, 'Boulton maintained a personal relationship with his workers, knew their names and their families, and relied upon this relationship to ensure the discipline and work performance needed in his enterprise' (1956: 57). Exercise of authority under entrepreneurial control was therefore simple and direct, and sustained frequently by legal coercion and harsh market conditions. Even at this stage, however, it was not always possible to exert control personally. Foremen could be utilised, but also, 'an important preliminary solution to the control dilemmas of divided authority was to rely on family ties' (Rueschemeyer, 1986: 57). At the required minimal level of co-ordination, the family or close friends of the entrepreneur proved sufficient. Middle managers were virtually absent; in fact, many employers were hostile and suspicious about the idea of a separate 'class' of managers.

Of course this situation could not survive a growth in the size and complexity of operations. Littler (1982) notes that the familial framework was rapidly discarded under such conditions, particularly in the USA. Nevertheless, some writers argue that direct and often despotic entrepreneurial authority remained at the centre of what Richard Edwards (1979) describes as *simple control*. There are important qualifications to be made to the model of entrepreneurial or simple control, particularly Edward's version. It is extremely doubtful whether it was representative of the economy until the end of the nineteenth century as he claims, rather than confined to a minority of firms (Littler, 1982: 64). In addition, though despotic authority was certainly a pervasive influence, it often had to accommodate to the power of other figures in the enterprise, such as craft workers. Hence the image of the all-seeing, all-knowing employer underestimates the struggles at the frontier of control in the workplace. There is also considerable evidence that a more significant mode of control involved contracting arrangements.

Contracting One of the main reasons why management was so slow to develop was the tendency of employers to delegate responsibility for work organisation to sub-contractors, around whom the employment relationship was constructed. We are concerned here with the internal contractor rather than the independent sub-contractor who was involved, for example, in outwork trades such as clothing and boots and shoes. Evidence from historians such as Pollard (1965) on the UK, and more recently Clawson (1980) on the USA, shows that internal contracting was in extensive use in a range of industries, including textiles, iron and steel, mining and transport. What did the organisation of work consist of?

> The inside contractor made an agreement with the general superintendent or owners of a company to make a part of their product and receive a certain price for each completed unit. . . . Inside contractors had complete charge of production in their area, hiring their own employees and supervising the work process . . . were employees of the company, and in most cases they received a day wage from the company as well. (Clawson, 1980: 71)

They accumulated considerable status and power, both in the community through patronage, and in the workplace through their high income. In some cases this meant a social position and standard of living higher than company officials, and a capacity actually to pass on much of the detailed work delegated to them by the employer to assistants!

Nevertheless the intended advantages to employers were clear. Responsibility, risks and costs could be partly shifted on to contractors, thus creating greater flexibility in circumstances where managerial skills and knowledge of work operations were limited. In effect contracting functioned as a means of transition through a period of growing enterprise complexity and scale. It was certainly hierarchical, but not bureaucratic in the sense of centralised authority, rules and record-keeping. Yet it proved capable of handling expanded output and technical innovation (Clawson, 1980). It did not encompass all industries or all labour within the firm. Newer industries such as service and process industries and railways were based on direct employment relations (Littler, 1982: 68).

Craft control Contracting is often seen as overlapping with the 'helper system', in which skilled workers were assisted by a small number of less-skilled operatives. In some cases craft workers hired and paid them, thus reproducing contractual relations. However, the scale of operations was small, with often just one helper; the practices were exercised by craft workers normally within a trade union framework; and the system operated often in conjunction with foremen. In fact the helper system is the basis for a model of craft control utilised by writers such as Stone (1973) and Montgomery (1976), in which skilled workers had the power to plan and direct immediate work processes. It is important not to exaggerate this 'partnership in production', for we are talking about a system of worker-directed job controls. But though not the equivalent of employer systems, such controls had a significant capacity to resist and constrain employer authority. This was put succinctly by F. W. Taylor in 1911 about his experience in the steel industry:

> As was usual then, and in fact is still usual in most shops in this country, the shop was really run by the workmen, and not the bosses. The workmen together had carefully planned just how fast each job should be done, and they had set a pace for each machine throughout the shop, which was limited to about one-third of a good day's work [that is, the maximum possible]. Every new workman who came into the shop was told at once by the other men exactly how much of each kind of work he was to do, and unless he obeyed these instructions he was sure before long to be driven out of the place by the men. (1947: 128)

This was somewhat exaggerated in order to prove the need for Taylor's scientific management system, and particularly neglected the role and powers of the foremen. Though this varied from industry to industry, there was a far more extensive range of powers and functions than foremen hold today. The foreman's empire included substantial influence over both the manner and timing of production and the cost and quality of work, and responsibility for employees – often including hiring and firing. They operated under similar delegated authority to inside contractors, and enjoyed parallel status within and outside work. But that role must be seen within the framework of craft controls. The foreman would sometimes be a master of his trade or chief skilled worker, and would have to share or at least accommodate to the powers of craft workers and contractors.

Decay and decline of traditional controls

Despite the variety of control relationships, each in its own way functioned as a constraint to management and bureaucracy. The shift further in this direction in the last quarter of the nineteenth century must again be seen not merely in terms of gradual evolution and advance of technique. There were social contradictions as well as inefficiencies in traditional methods. Simple control is a clear case. During the period in question, the size and complexity of industrial firms increased considerably. During the last third of the century the average plant in the USA more than doubled in size and by 1900 there were 443 with more than 1000 wage earners (Nelson, 1975: 4). The impetus for change included mergers, concentration of resources, technical innovation, and shifts away from local and regional markets. This leap was particularly marked in the USA, given its late entry onto the industrial stage, and the relative freedom of business from social reform traditions and strong union organisation.

Such processes inevitably affected existing social relations, being characterised by an increasing separation of entrepreneurs and top managers from the daily activities of the workforce. Organisationally the crucial issue was a growing gap between the structures and expertise of management, and a more extensive division of labour, with its requirements for new forms of control and co-ordination. For capital, the solution had to go beyond the employment of more managers, towards transforming the structures of managerial activity itself.

Problems associated with internal contract had more to do with contradictions than straightforward inefficiencies. According to Clawson, these were in two major areas. The very fact that the company had entered into subcontract arrangements meant that it was difficult to evaluate such activities. Contractors therefore used that power to keep employers as much in the dark as possible, aided by the fact that companies seldom kept many formal records. In addition to the income, the consequent social position of contractors was a problem, in that it was difficult for employers to motivate their own officials, who often felt inferior in power, status and rewards to the larger contractors. Craft job controls were also a serious obstacle to employers taking full advantage of mechanisation and expanded but more competitive markets. As Stone notes of the steel industry:

> At the same time that their labour costs as a percentage were rising, the labour system also prevented employers from increasing their productivity through reorganising or mechanising their operations. The workers controlled the plants and decided how the work was to be done. Employers had no way to speed up the workers, nor could they introduce new machinery that eliminated or redefined jobs. (1973: 26)

This again may be a somewhat exaggerated description, but it helps to explain why both contracting and craft arrangements came under increasing attack. Employers began to abolish internal contracting in order to shift income to the company and to create a hierarchy under their own control and acceptable to their own officials (Clawson, 1980: 119). Companies often tried to convert some of the contractors into foremen, but many preferred to quit. The power of craft workers was also increasingly challenged in the 1880s. A minority of firms tried to formulate a system of co-partnership, in the UK and France based largely on profit-sharing schemes geared explicitly to ensuring loyalty to the company (Brannen, 1983; Doray, 1988). There were other head-on clashes in the 1890s, including those between the Amalgamated Society of Engineers and their employers in the UK, and major conflicts in the US steel industry, such as the Homestead strike of 1892 (Stone, 1973).

Employers began to assert their general right to run production as they saw fit. This took a particularly virulent form in the USA with its weaker unions, as manifested in the 'open shop' campaign run by some employers. The predominant measures used by capital there and elsewhere to challenge and change existing modes of control, were, however, less dramatic. An important area was to modify the role of *supervisory labour*. This often involved breaking up the foremen's empire, with a shift away from traditional functions such as hire and fire and work organisation, towards the narrower but vital sphere of task supervision and discipline. As Littler (1982) shows, this was accompanied by considerable sub-division of the foreman's role. Examples include supervisory labour carrying out quality control, rate fixers, and 'feed and speed' functions. A further interrelated change was in *payment systems*, which became more centrally determined; undermining the bargaining role played by foremen and contractors. In addition, piecework and bonus arrangements spread rapidly.

Significantly, the new systems required some formal standards of effort and labour management record keeping. Payment through the office indicated a move towards a more direct employment relationship. It should, however, be noted at this stage in the battle for control of output, that management techniques were generally not sophisticated enough to include time study or job analysis, and were constrained by workers' initiative and knowledge. Companies frequently had to rely on the cruder measures of rate cutting and employment of 'rate-busters' to prove to the workforce that quotas could be increased.

We have already noted that such changes required an increase in *record-keeping*, given the need to specify objectives and keep track of results. The administrative aspects of a management system thus began to be set in place, including that of simple cost accounting. In some companies simple organisation manuals began to appear, complete with management principles and charts (R. Edwards, 1979: 30). Technological changes accompanied administrative ones, further increases in the detailed division of labour and mechanisation were facilitated by the greater knowledge of productive processes that capital was gaining. Not only was greater output achieved, but the capacity of employers to dispense with skilled workers and exert greater controls over labour generally through standardised procedures was enhanced. As one employer remarked, 'I want machines so simple that any fool could run them' (quoted in Goldman and Van Houten, 1980: 116). Engineering principles orientated towards treating workers as simple costs of production were therefore becoming more important than personal and direct controls.

Of course these developments were part of a broader process of the creation of the modern business enterprise. Chandler (1962, 1977) stresses that viability was only achieved when the 'visible hand of management' rivalled or replaced the market as a means of co-ordinating the flow of materials through enterprise and economy. In other words, a managerial hierarchy was able to supervise a large number of operating units and to co-ordinate, monitor and plan their activities. The path to the new forms of enterprise began in the USA with the railroads and the need to manage their vast regional operations, but gradually spread to other sectors, as modern big business in the decades before 1917 was able to integrate mass distribution and mass production. In this context, some firms developed from the internal growth of small single-unit firms who developed national and global networks, others from mergers. The new consolidated, multi-departmental enterprises centralised the administration of production and research facilities, and established vertical integration, attempting to control supplies and markets. Though the convergence between the growth strategies of firms and their new structures was not to reach its climax until after the First World War, with the development of multi-divisional, multinational enterprises, a salaried managerial class was fast rising in numbers and power (Supple, 1991: 501–2).

Management as a conscious and specialist activity was enhanced by the spread of associations and journals dealing with management methods (Clawson, 1980: 167–8). Entrepreneurial ideologies were complemented or challenged by more professional concerns with the 'labour problem'; and direct recruitment from colleges grew, though specialist technical training was still relatively limited. In addition a growing army of clerical, technical and administrative employees was necessitated by new payment systems, record-keeping and mechanisation; as well as the other growth functions of purchasing, sales and finance. It was not just a case of management hierarchy: by the turn of the century the workforce was subject to structures of what Richard Edwards (1979) refers to as *hierarchical control*. As other writers put it, 'differential job statuses and wages for workers were an integral component of the hierarchical nature of the

industrial pyramid' (Goldman and Van Houten, 1980: 122). Job ladders and individu-
ated reward systems were also a means of compensating for the growing homogenisa-
tion of labour by artificially dividing the workforce (Stone, 1973).

It must be stressed that these measures were experimental and varied in nature.
Different countries and even sectors had their own unique characteristics and influences which added to the incoherence of transition processes (Littler, 1982), a process
we shall return to in the final section of the chapter. Finally, though there was a great
advance in managerial organisation compared to the earlier period, even in the USA it
was still very much in its infancy. There was still little systematic and long-term planning, and as for work organisation, management 'was unable to make the qualitative
leap to a different system because it had no alternative conception of how production
should be organised' (Clawson, 1980: 168). That situation was soon to change.

Classical theories and the bureaucratisation of production

Taylorism and systematic management

The major means of change was through the work of Frederick Taylor and his
'scientific management' system. Not that Taylorism was unique or totally new: only
time and motion study could genuinely be put in that category. A trend towards
systematic management was already identifiable, as we have seen with instances of
more formal management methods, cost accounting, standardisation of work, and
use of less-skilled workers. Nyland (1988: 56) comments that, 'The "systematisers"
were a diverse group of engineers, accountants and works managers who argued
that US firms had grown to a size where the internal functioning of the enterprise
was becoming increasingly chaotic and wasteful'.

When Taylor proclaimed his new system as a 'science', some British engineers
described it as common sense masquerading under a high-sounding title (Geoff
Brown, 1977: 158). Understandable though the reaction was, it missed the point.
Taylor was not just in the right place at the right time, he played a crucial role in
theorising and *popularising* the new ideas. Furthermore, it was intimately connected
to a body of practice, with Taylor 'Napoleon of the war against craft production'
(Clawson, 1980: 202). Taylorism was therefore the most conscious part of the sys-
tematisation of management, and of the regulation and control of production.

Such developments met the needs of capital in that period (M. Rose, 1975: 58).
This was particularly the case in the USA, where larger corporations were developing
higher levels of product and labour specialisation to cope with rising demand
(Littler, 1982). A shift away from skilled labour towards unskilled immigrant workers was taking place, but still within the context of a relatively high-wage economy.
This required new forms of co-ordination, integration and control; and methods
of keeping down labour costs. The orientation of larger firms towards professional
managers, engineers and consultants additionally provided a supportive framework for the rise of Taylorism. Engineers were central figures and carried out wide-
ranging activities, including extensive refinements in accounting procedure (Nelson,
1975: 50). In the 1890s Taylor began to publicise his ideas about time study and

piece rates, mainly through the American Society of Mechanical Engineers, and gathered round him a group of enthusiastic adherents.

His own work was first carried out at the Midvale Steel Works (owned by a friend of the family), in a variety of 'detective' roles ranging from unskilled labourer, machinist, clerk, gang boss, foreman, master mechanic, chief draughtsman and chief engineer. Experiments were also carried out in a small number of other firms in old and new industries. It was not just in the USA that such initiatives took place: by the time of the First World War one per cent of French as well as US firms had introduced schemes, often in new sectors such as electrical manufacturing and automobiles (Fridenson, 1978) and there were similar initiatives on a smaller scale in other European countries. In Britain, a minority of firms experienced the arrival of works engineers, rate-fixers, progress men, operations inspectors, work hustlers and other representatives of the growing army of non-producers (G. Brown, 1977: 149–52).

Principles Many discussions of Taylorism in organisational texts discuss its defining principles around the idea of the employee as 'economic man' and are thus able to treat it as a failed theory of motivation. This is a far cry from the real basis of Taylor's ideas, which were concerned with the control of the labour process. Taylor was adamant that his system was a total package – one best way of organising work. Though affecting the activities of management and workers, the ideas were developed directly out of his obsession with combating the kind of worker's control of output – labelled 'soldiering' – observed at the steel works. He distinguished between natural and systematic soldiering: the former referring to the tendency to want to take it easy, the latter to practices deliberately geared to maximising rewards and job security. To solve the 'labour problem' a number of basic management principles were advanced:

1. The development of a science for each element of work
2. Scientific selection and training of workers
3. Co-operation between management and workers to ensure that the work is done according to the science
4. Equal division of work and responsibility between management and workers, each side doing what they are best fitted for.

These sound rather bland, but their significance can only be understood when set against Taylor's description of inefficient practices. Included under this were 'rule of thumb' methods of deciding on the nature of work tasks; workers choosing their own methods of work and training; and worker's knowledge being the basis of productive technique. He was particularly critical of management by initiative and incentive, when workers were given inducements to use their skills and know-how in the most economical way, without strict managerial determination of tasks.

Scientific management started from the belief that management had to reverse existing power relations in production: 'The management assume, for instance, the burden of gathering together all of the traditional knowledge which in the past has been possessed by the workmen and then of classifying, tabulating, and reducing this knowledge to rules, laws and formulae' (Taylor, 1947: 36). The continual concern with rules and laws in Taylor's writings show why it can be located firmly within a process of bureaucratisation of production. As Braverman (1974: 119) makes clear, it can also be seen as a control system based on the monopolisation of knowledge by management and its use to specify each step of the labour process. This 'separation of conception and execution' is clearly echoed in Taylor's comments such as: 'all possible brain work should be removed from the shop floor and centred in the planning and lay-out department' (quoted in Braverman, 1974: 113).

Other aspects of the above principles are not so prominent. Take selection: Taylor's search for workers who would follow his instructions to the letter is legendary. His tutelage of Schmidt, picked for his strength and stupidity, was repeated elsewhere, such as the selection of Pinnell – 'the hardest working man' in a railway factory – by time and motion men on behalf of British management (G. Brown, 1977: 156–7). When even his time in the lavatory was recorded and only measured after breakfast when his energy was greatest, it was little wonder that Pinnell came to wish he was dead. But despite the interest of some of Taylor's followers, explicit techniques to place the right worker in the right job remained an underdeveloped part of scientific management.

What about the previously-mentioned emphasis placed by OB on Taylorism as the model of 'economic man'? This is largely misleading. Like most of his contemporaries interested in management reform, Taylor *did* believe that workers were motivated by the pursuit of rational self-interest and that incentive wages – in the form of a differential piece-rate system – were the solution to most labour problems. The tendency to restrict output, however, was seen as an unnecessary product of the absence of any scientific authority for work standards. Management could ensure co-operation on the basis of a consensus established by objective work measurement. Economic incentives could be used to overcome the hostility of workers to giving up traditional job controls. This exchange proved to be a limited and fragile basis for co-operation and certainly did not ever eliminate restriction of output. But an instrumental view of human labour was a far cry from a complex theory of motivation. Taylor was far more concerned with breaking the power of the work-group and removing the basis for collective bargaining through individualistic payment systems (Littler, 1982: 55).

Ideology and practice The consequences of the operation of such principles were explicitly recognised by Taylor. There would be a need for: extensive work measurement to predetermine tasks; the employment of cheaper, deskilled and substitutable labour in more fragmented jobs; a large increase in the number of non-productive employees to enforce, monitor and record new work arrangements; and functional foremanship that subdivided traditional responsibilities and involved reporting to the all-powerful planning department. It would, of course, be foolish to believe that all of this came to pass smoothly. In fact, there are a number of writers who believe that Taylorism was a 'practical failure' and was not widely implemented due largely to worker resistance and employer suspicions (Palmer, 1975; R. Edwards, 1979; Goldman and Van Houten, 1980). This is often complemented by arguments that its significance is as a management *ideology* which was itself later discredited (M. Rose, 1975; Burawoy, 1979).

What is the balance of these two processes? We should certainly not underestimate the ideological purposes. Taylor himself emphasised the pressing need for a 'complete mental revolution' in the attitudes of the two parties. Whatever success was achieved can largely be attributed to the stress on the *scientific* character of the system, which trades on the predominantly uncritical attitudes to knowledge under such a mantle. Its technical orientation was of particular appeal and use to engineers in their struggle to establish themselves as the core management group in US industry (Armstrong, 1984). But there was a potential appeal to workers and unions from the same source; 'Under scientific management arbitrary power, arbitrary dictation, ceases; and every single subject, large and small, becomes the question for scientific investigation, for reduction to law' (Taylor, 1947: 211). The theoretical separation of authority from hierarchy was an attempt to construct some level of consent in the employment relation; and, with the increased productivity and wages from the system, was to be the basis for the co-operation promised in Taylor's principles.

In practice it never quite worked like this. As an ideology of science it strengthened management by providing, 'the technocratic rationale for authority in formal organisations' (Kouzmin, 1980: 68). It was also flawed and contradictory in nature. It is strange that a science of management had to be based on knowledge and skills appropriated from workers. Of course it never was a science, but rather a control system, and has tended to be seen as a set of techniques to be countered and contested by generations of shop stewards. In one of his weaker moments, Taylor even admitted the stopwatch had an element of 'guesswork'.

Most of the misunderstandings concerning the practical success of Taylorism stem from confusion about what *criteria* to employ. Many of those who see it as a failure are viewing Taylorism as a coherent and total package. This is understandable given that it coincides with Taylor's own views and his tendency to withdraw co-operation when companies refused to follow all the complexities of the schemes. But it is wrong. We need to redefine the criteria in two ways. First, as already indicated, we must consider it as part of a broader movement of systematic management that was implemented in a variety of forms. Second, it was also implemented in a selective manner: 'employers looked upon scientific management exactly as Taylor insisted that they should not: as an arsenal of devices designed to simplify and improve the management of labour' (Bendix, 1956: 286). All the elements were juggled about by companies according to their needs and prejudices. A close analysis of the early literature on Taylor firms' by Nelson (1975: 68–78) showed that none fully represented the principles set out in *Shop Management*. References to time study can be found in every firm, and planning departments were widespread. But incentive payment schemes were patchy and employers found that functional foremanship embodied too many layers of responsibility.

Once these factors have been acknowledged, we can recognise a widespread, if uneven, diffusion of key aspects of Taylorist practices in industrial societies in the 1920s and 1930s (G. Brown, 1977; Clawson, 1980; Littler, 1982; Nyland, 1988). Taylor's death in 1915 opened the door to a variety of consultants to introduce further versions of scientific management. Some were short-cut emulators, other were Taylor's disciples such as Gantt, and the Gilbreths with their extension of Taylor's early emphasis on the study of fatigue and their advances in the use of cameras to record and time movements. This factor and changes in the external environment guaranteed that scientific management did not spread in pure form.

In current managerial and sociological literature Taylorism always appears as a dynamic duo with *Fordism*. Links there certainly were. Henry Ford's innovations in technical control through the flow assembly line extended Taylorist principles such as job fragmentation and allowed for a greater level of intensity of labour through speed-up of the line and other measures (Littler, 1982: 56–7). In addition, the scale of Ford's operations and his willingness to introduce the 'five dollar day' as a means of combating labour turnover, enabled another of Taylor's principles – high wages for high productivity – to be realised. Ford's plants did not use the apparatus of Taylorite time and motion study, but the management nevertheless collected a considerable amount of information on tasks, so that, for example, they had enough information to produce 7800 individual job-profile sheets (Doray, 1988: 96). This reinforces a crucial point, that we must not fetishise Taylorism at the expense of the broader trend towards 'scientific' management. The managerial regime at Ford had its own innovations in labour utilisation, stretching the semi-skilled labour by a permanent process of de-manning and flexibility: a mode of operation that challenges the stereotype of rigid machinery, products and labour under mass production (Williams *et al.*, 1992b).

Meanwhile, in Europe, the most extensive implementation of neo-Taylorite schemes came through the *Bedeaux system*. Charles Bedeaux was a French full-time management consultant whose schemes were based on his 'discovery' of a universal measure for all work, given the name 'B unit'. He aggressively sold them as a cheap and quick method that did not need to have major consequences for existing management structures. Like the Gilbreths, he entered the unexplored territory of fatigue through basing the measurement on the proportions of work and rest required for completing a task. Though he had considerable international success, Bedeaux had his greatest impact in Britain, where employers used the circumstances of the 1930s depression to install the system and utilise it for the purposes of rate-cutting and speed-up (G. Brown, 1977; Littler, 1982). This example illustrates the way that scientific management varied in both form and timing between and within countries. Whereas Britain's late adoption differed from the US and French models, other economies such as Germany and Sweden followed distinctive paths; for example, combining rationalisation measures with greater use of psychological testing (Fridenson, 1978). Contrary to some recent studies, Taylorism did influence the organisation of work in Japan, but 'was used as a vehicle for job analysis and standardised procedures rather than as a comprehensive control system' (Littler, 1982: 156–7). Aspects of the latter, notably the separation of thinking and doing, as well as individual output norms, did not fit into preexisting patterns of fluid job boundaries, work teams and the power of foremen over production planning.

Lack of uniformity was undoubtedly influenced by the pattern of resistance from a variety of groups. There has been well-documented resistance from craft and non-craft workers, using every method from strikes to informal disruption (Nadworthy, 1955; Brown, 1977; Montgomery, 1976). Workers were particularly opposed to effects such as deskilling and speed-up, because, as one put it, he 'never knew a rate to be raised after a time study' (quoted in Baritz, 1960: 98). But the plain fact is that resistance did not succeed in stopping the long-term diffusion of scientific management, though it certainly delayed and mediated it. This is often put down to the gradual shift in union attitudes from opposition to reluctant accommodation and occasional enthusiastic co-operation. There is a great deal of truth in this assessment, though some unions had always had a conciliatory attitude, and the behaviour of official structures should not be confused with rank-and-file members who continued resistance. Indeed, the very institutionalisation of scientific management guarantees that it is accompanied by a low-intensity war at shopfloor level.

Changes of this kind were influenced by later progressive Taylorites who lacked his hostility to trade unions and were prepared to give them an institutionalised role in work study and bonus schemes. Scientific management could also be given an progressive aura by its association with planning, Nyland (1988) showing that some of its adherents advocated the extension of the system to the whole society constraining the role of markets. He also correctly points to the neglect of Taylorism's wider capacity to improve work efficiency in the spheres of scheduling, stores management and purchasing and plant lay-out. Though whether this is enough to commend Taylorism despite the control dimension is more arguable.

Supervisory and managerial resistance also continued to be a considerable constraint both in the USA and Britain (Nelson, 1975: 75–6; Littler, 1982: 181–2). New schemes tended not only to change traditional roles, but to erode decision-making powers. Employers and managers often found it hard wholly to embrace Taylorism. Taylor was often bitterly critical of their competence. It challenged their traditional judgement, discretion and powers, to say nothing of straining their patience through contract stipulations that the company must do as exactly as he told them. The high costs, disrupted routines and social antagonisms meant that failure was more often linked to managerial opposition than that of workers.

Given the evidence, the problem of Taylorism is not *whether* it was introduced, but *how*, and what its *limits* were as a control system. We shall return to the former later, but with respect to the latter, right from the start many employers realised that Taylor's neglect of 'the human factor' and of what Friedman (1977) calls 'the positive aspects of labour' such as know-how and goodwill, made it impossible to use on its own. We shall return to the combination with psychological methods later, but even as a means of bureaucratisation of production, Taylorism was insufficient.

Weber and administrative theories of management

For some writers, the concept of bureaucratisation of production is a problematic one. Braverman (1974: 120) objects that it endorses the mistaken view that such work arrangements are endemic to large-scale organisation rather than a product of capitalist social relations. Our argument in this book is that bureaucratisation *is* a universal tendency, but can only be understood through the specific forms it takes in different modes of production or more specific business systems. But there is a different point at stake. Braverman's influential theory of the labour process is constructed on the implicit assumption that what we have been describing as bureaucratisation could be fully represented by Taylorism. However, what Taylorism provided was a system of detailed control over work, aided by a set of bureaucratic rules, and Clawson (1980: 248) argues that this is in contrast to Weber's stress on the remote and impersonal qualities of bureaucracy.

We shall return to this question later. For now it is sufficient to observe that Taylorism had far less to say about the *employment relationship*: 'those structural conditions which surround the appointment, promotion and dismissal of individuals'

(Littler, 1982: 37). Scientific management was meant to be able to be applied at any given level of task or technology, but it 'left management in the position of having a set of principles laying down how to make its workforce more productive, whilst possessing no body of knowledge that specifically applied from supervisory levels upward in the organisational hierarchy' (Clegg and Dunkerley, 1980: 99). This was particularly important in the context of the previously observed growth of middle management – middle managers were monitoring the performance of the operating units under their command, but were not subject to systematic evaluation themselves. It is Weber and other theorists of formal management and administration who can give us a greater understanding of developments of this nature. The emphasis here is on *understanding*: Weber was not a theorist-practitioner like Taylor, and the ideas discussed below were not immediately implemented in organisations.

In common with most other writers, we do not intend to list all the complex features of bureaucracy that Weber includes as defining characteristics, but instead to group them under two headings:

The employment relationship   The office is a vocation and a full-time undertaking. Officials are selected on a basis of technical qualification, education and expertise. There is separation of office and office-holder: it is not his or her property and the employee does not possess the means of administration. Thorough and expert training is part of the conditions of employment.

A career structure is provided based on the organisational hierarchy. Tenure is for life, with fixed salary, pension rights and appropriate social status. Officials are appointed by higher authority, not externally elected, and promotions are similarly regulated, for example, through seniority.

Work structures and relations   There is a hierarchy of offices, with continuous and regulated activity within a fully ordered system of super and subordination. Within the chain of command, there is a division of labour based on defined responsibilities, rights and duties. Calculable rules and regulations, impersonal modes of conduct and a common control system govern the conduct of work. Written documentation are the basis of management of the office.

From these characteristics it is understandable that some may question their links to the *bureaucratisation of production*. After all, the impetus for Weber's analysis came primarily from the organisation of the state and the regulation of administrative employees. The historical context is also important for an understanding of the significance of measures such as full-time work as a vocation. In the period under consideration, it was still important to break away from patrimonial, charismatic and other relations, whereby people could be placed in position through inheritance and similar 'private' attributes. The emphasis on calculable rules and regulations may also seem a bit abstract. But both examples highlight that the ideal type of bureaucracy is linked to Weber's wider theory of *rationalisation*.

We discussed the problematic character of the idea of rationality, but rationalisation is held to be the key modernising characteristic for the development of industrial societies. Authority in industrial societies was rational because it was formal and based on precise and predictable rules, calculation and accounting. For these reasons the bureaucratic organisation and administration best permitted the development of appropriate attitudes, structures and practices in public and private sectors. In this context, bureaucracies are a specific type of rational-legal authority: officials work within a framework in which command and task are based on authority derived from impersonal rules. But Weber's theories are not as separate from production as they may appear. He made it clear that they referred to bureaucratic *management* as well as administration. The Weberian 'causal chain' (Collins, 1986: 21–9) links the concept of rationality explicitly to the emergence of capitalist enterprise and markets. These were held to be rational because of their capacity for calculability, predictability and routinisation – through production, distribution, accounting and market pricing mechanisms. Preconditions for this 'rationalised' capitalism started from the complete private appropriation of the means of production, which Weber said must be unhampered by 'irrational obstacles' such as workers' rights to participate in management. In addition, there was the need for common management, free labour under the compulsion of the 'whip of hunger', mass markets, minimal trade restrictions and institutional, legal support from the bureaucratic state.

Weber also argued that large, capitalist enterprises were becoming 'unequalled modes of strict bureaucratic organisation' (Weber, 1984: 32). He was aware and approving of the role played by scientific management in this process. It was 'completely' the ideal vehicle for the necessary imposition of military discipline in the factory, given its capacity for dehumanisation and conditioning of work performance. Techniques such as Taylor's 'shop cards', which specified the daily routines of employees, were ideal vehicles of bureaucratisation. What is more, Taylor saw management by 'scientific' methods as a move away from traditional authority where owners and managers attempted to control by inefficient personal means. On reflection, it is therefore possible to see that Weber's schema is not only compatible with Taylorism, but also that the practices he describes can reinforce systems of work control. Formal structures of management enhance centralisation of power, and hierarchical organisation aids functional specialisation, task fragmentation and labour discipline, while emphasis on predictable performance minimises the discretion of employees.

But, as Littler (1982) argues, it is in the sphere of the employment relationship that Weber adds something new. The career structure linked to the bureaucratic hierarchy strengthens a commitment to the organisation absent from Taylorism. A specific form of bureaucratic motivation is also sustained by the identification of job security, status, rewards and performance to organisational structure. Employees may react against the bureaucratisation of control embodied in rules prescribing the way a task is performed, but welcome rules governing selection, training and promotion within the employment relationship. Nor is it necessarily confined to office administration. Some modern radical theorists argue that employers are increasingly turning to strategies of bureaucratic control for the shop floor. Edward's research on companies such as Polaroid, IBM and General Electric points to two crucial features of the strategy. There is a finely graded stratification and division of the workforce; the hierarchical structures devised to divide and conquer, tending to 'break up the homogeneity of the firm's workforce, creating many seemingly separate strata, lines of work, and focuses for job identity' (R. Edwards, 1979: 133). In addition, impersonal rules form the basis of company policy. Detailed and specified criteria for job descriptions and performance are monitored by supervisors, rather than work tasks being directly enforced. The stress is on positive incentives in performance, not negative sanctions. Taken together with the job security and 'career' structure through job hierarchies, long-term identification with the company can be built.

Hence, contrary to Clawson's view, impersonality and 'remoteness' can be an effective control mechanism. This kind of use of Weberian categories as explanatory tools indicates their continuing relevance, but also their limitations. Clearly bureaucratic structures have no universal rationality. Rather they are in part consciously constructed by employers for specific purposes that cannot be reduced to 'efficiency'. A further qualification needs to be made in relation to the *legitimacy* arising from bureaucratic systems. Undoubtedly they can generate loyalty and commitment. But the position of shop floor workers is not comparable to the higher officials of a public organisation such as the civil service, which provides long-term security and stable career structures with a minimum conflict of interests. Private companies are seldom able to match those kind of conditions, and the centrality of the wage-effort bargain will always tend to introduce uncertainty and conflict into the employment relationship.

Insights derived from Weberian theory have been applied in Britain and the USA from the late 1940s. But companies were able to draw on parallel developments in classical management theory in the inter-war period. Other theorists of formal organisation, were, like Weber, concerned to tackle the administration of the whole enterprise. By far the most significant was Fayol, a Frenchman who shared the engineering and management background of Taylor. 'Fayolism' inspired, amongst other things, the reorganisation of railway and engineering companies, and department stores in France (Fridenson, 1978); and translation of his short text enabled wider influence. His main concern was to establish the validity of studying and training management itself, not just the management of others. Emphasis was put on formulating general features of management, first in the form of five elements; planning, organising, commanding, co-ordination and control – then through fourteen principles. The themes contained in the latter echo and extend Taylor and Weber; including division of work, stability of tenure, authority of command and subordination of the individual interest to the general (for the full list see Pugh, 1963: 66). One principle, that of unity of command, differed sharply from Taylor's belief in functional authority.

The basis of the approach in Fayol and other similar theorists such as Gullick and Urwick was orientated to rationalising management structures, often through centralisation and specified spans of control; emphasis on the managerial role in setting and securing goals; and planning for the optimal use of resources. Modern management came to take many of these things for granted, which led some to invest Fayol's theorising with a high status and lasting effect. In fact his work was more of a practical guide with simple 'plan-ahead proverbs' (Perrow, 1979: 70) akin to today's numerous management handbooks. Later writers are more likely to prefer the judgement of Clegg and Dunkerley that 'the "principles" are neither universally empirically applicable, nor theoretically coherent' (1980: 103).

What matters more than flawed, hand-me-down principles is that classical theories were engaging with real changes in economy and enterprise. When Chandler began to use the railroad as his blueprint for large-scale organisation, his emphasis was on the emergence of organisational charts, hierarchies of office and functional authority. This can be linked to a wider and related argument from Williamson (1975: 1981) that organisations emerge in the form of hierarchies when markets fail. Or to be more precise, when it is more efficient to internalise transactions – for labour, components, services and so on – within multi-divisional or vertically-integrated firms, than to have them mediated by and through the market. Because markets become increasingly complex, prices and other indicators cannot give complete information which allows individuals to cost transactions accurately. This uncertainty and complexity can often be better handled through organisations constituted as bureaucratic hierarchies, because they can monitor behaviour, establish rules and procedures and provide better information and control.

So, to return to Chandler (1977): by 1918, the 'visible hand' that had brought the vertically integrated bureaucracies into existence was extended to defining the role and specific tasks of top management within general offices. The context was a further centralisation of administration, often within new multi-divisional structures such as those at General Motors. This process included uniform accounting and statistical controls that allowed senior administrators to evaluate managerial performance and exercise long-range planning. In Chandler's later work (1990), he emphasises that investment in production and distribution that facilitated economies of scale is combined with further investment in managerial skills that lead to economies of scope and enhanced organisational capabilities. Supple comments,

> From these viewpoints, the modern industrial firm is crucially characterised by expansion overseas, by product diversification, and (most significantly) by administrative complexity – that is, by the growth in the number of its operating units, each carrying out a different economic function and all co-ordinated by a management hierarchy. (1991: 504–5)

This focus on organisational design, strategy and structure, is valuable, but partial. The neglect of the informal dimensions of organisational life by classical theories left gaps that had to be filled.

Social science and industry: a courtship

'Increasingly the men who manage and direct industry, find themselves incapable of effectively controlling their organisations'. This is how Baritz (1960: 3) begins his brilliant account of the historical uses of social science in US industry. Managers had, by the early part of the twentieth century, already drawn on the expertise of people such as Taylor and other consultants. But there had been little sign of embracing the emergent social sciences. This began to change in the period after the First World War when some major US corporations began financing industrial psychology and endowing business schools as part of a process of research and experimentation. Moves towards co-operation with social scientists arose from the same process as links with Taylorism; the vulnerability of management to the appeal of planning and science.

Enter the human factor

The instrumental attitudes of employers to any theories perceived to be of immediate use can be seen in the favourable attitude adopted towards the battery of
tests and measurements offered to fit people to jobs. This kind of intervention represented a version of Taylor's 'scientific selection of the worker' by other means.
In fact the *Bulletin of the Taylor Society* carried articles discussing issues of human
personality and arguing that newly recruited workers should be tested for personality, character and temperament. In 1915, an article about one factory noted
that:

> A system of cards was used, one side of each card contained information about
> the worker's identity, parents, ethnic origins and previous employment; the other
> contained a certain amount of medico-psychological information ('anaemic, 'non-
> chalant') and notes on the individual's degree of motivation and way of life ('father
> out of work', 'mother agreed to take care of child', etc.). This was followed by his
> medical record (doctor, optician, dentist) and by basic health advice on the need
> for rest and fresh air. (Doray, 1988: 188)

Far from being different academic species, it is arguable that the human relations
current partly derived from a form of Taylorist revisionism. Nevertheless the battle
cry of 'neglect of the human factor' was directed against the costs of scientific management in terms of resistance and disenchantment. The simple appeal and apparent applicability of the variety of tests convinced a growing minority of employers.
Problems arose when naive enthusiasm and unrealistic expectations quickly ran up
against the crude nature and limited results arising from the techniques. By the mid-
1920s, and in changed economic circumstances, the tests had been abandoned by
most companies (Baritz, 1960: 71).

Accounts of the development of British industrial psychology (M. Rose, 1975: 65–
87; G. Brown, 1977: 213–28) show it to be more sober, centralised, less consultancy-
based and affecting even fewer firms. It took a particular interest – derived from
experiences of the Industrial Fatigue Research Board during the war – in monotony.
Fatigue was, as we have seen, an issue which also concerned the scientific management movement, linked as it was to the need for the successful measurement of
work. Common interests and client relations again meant, as in the USA, 'a large
proportion of their problems had to be taken over from the scientific managers'
(M. Rose, 1975: 86). But despite sharing some common assumptions about efficiency, productivity and work organisation, British researchers established a distance
from Taylorism.

Myers perceptively noted the hostility generated among workers by scientific
management through its attack on skills, and the effects of speedup and time and
motion study. He made attacks on the notion of 'one best way', rightly pointing
to the greater complexity of behaviour and industrial conditions. This critique
was linked to a more sympathetic consideration of the need to convince the trade
unions of the validity of social science interventions, and to win more generally
the consent of the workforce. The relatively progressive stance of British industrial
psychologists is further illustrated by their alliance with a small group of employers centred on the Quaker families such as Rowntree, who shared their enthusiasm

for 'scientific planning' and dislike for the harsher aspects of Taylorism. When those companies began to utilise psychologists, however, there was still considerable suspicion and resistance from employees; particularly when they were introduced at the same time as scientific management methods (G. Brown, 1977: 216). The Quaker tapestry firm, Lee's, divided the managerial responsibility for 'psychology' and Taylorist 'mechanics' between the owner's two sons (Johnson and Moore, 1986). Most British employers, however, still preferred to cut costs simply by squeezing wages and exploiting favourable market circumstances.

But industrial psychology was not as isolated a phenomenon as it appeared. In the USA particularly it was part of a wider period of experimentation involving human relations and Taylorist management, as employers chose within and between the new techniques. Richard Edwards (1979: 102) gives an interesting example of the Bancroft textile company employing a consultant to introduce welfare work in 1902, and Taylor's follower Gantt to reorganise production in 1905! *Welfarism* was a significant part of that context. A paternalistic concern for the well-being of employees in return for loyalty and hard work, had a long pedigree in some companies. Company towns were one manifestation, as employers provided houses, schools, stores, sanitation and lighting in order to attract an adequate labour force. But the rhetoric had shifted from older themes of community and improving the working man to themes of entitlements and better working conditions (Barley and Kunda, 1992: 372).

Welfare work was also present in conventional circumstances. An increasing number of firms began to employ welfare secretaries whose role ranged from encouraging a 'proper moral atmosphere' to the provision of social and medical facilities. This interest was not philanthropic – 'Capital will not invest in sentiment', as one leading employer put it (quoted in Nelson, 1975: 104). It arose from attempts to grapple with the recruitment and motivation problems deriving from the increasing size of the labour force and a new industrial relations situation shaped by declining loyalty and rising unrest. There was a parallel development in the growth of employment or personnel departments as a means of dealing 'scientifically' with such issues – again showing an overlap with Taylorism. In the USA and Britain professional personnel bodies grew from the seeds of welfare work.

But in the latter country, welfarism was strongly connected to the study of fatigue in the laboratory of wartime factories. As in the USA, British welfarism was described by one of its leading members as combining 'pity and profit' (quoted in G. Brown, 1977: 185). Lee's issued 'partnership certificates' to employees who had shown a genuine interest in the company. Many workers, particularly the women who were its prime object, saw its motivation as directed primarily towards profit, given the emphasis on improving conditions for the sole purpose of maximising output. After the war, changing economic circumstances saw the decline of welfare initiatives. But in the USA, to a greater extent than Britain, there was a broader framework of 'welfare capitalism'. Companies such as General Electric, International Harvester and US Steel continued policies of off-the-job benefits in the form of insurance, health, pensions, social clubs, profit-sharing schemes and other measures (R. Edwards, 1979: 91–7).

But the process took many different forms. Take Ford, for example. The company had only limited social provision, but it had social control potential. The 'Sociological Department' had investigators who were empowered to visit homes to check on absentees and monitor an employee's family, values and habits. But this social control mechanism did not exist in the abstract. To act as a counterweight to the assembly line and associated problems of labour turnover and unionisation, Ford had profit-sharing schemes and the famed five dollar day. The department could therefore ascertain the 'fitness' of workers for these generous rewards!

In a period in which space was opened up for employers by defeated industrial militancy and repression of socialist organising, welfarism in the USA also had close ties to the development of company unions. This was different from the kind of enterprise unions initiated more recently by Japanese employers. The former arose primarily from wartime attempts to institute limited forms of worker representation, such as works councils. After the war many large companies, often utilising their new personnel departments, were quick to consolidate this trend by initiating company unions as a focus for formal grievance procedures, thus alleviating the need for independent union representation (Edwards, 1979: 106). There was some success in delaying or undermining unionism, and employers learnt some important lessons on the importance of controlled employee involvement and formal procedures. But, as in Britain, little survived the economic changes associated with the growing depression and sharpening social polarisation. Company unionism and welfarism did not provide an adequate means of pursuing the collective interests of workers, while at the same time they became a financial burden for employers without solving any of their fundamental control problems inside the factory.

Hawthorne and beyond

The Hawthorne studies occupy a pivotal place in organisational theory. Begun in the mid-1920s, the research was carried out in the large Hawthorne plant employing 29 000 workers making electrical appliances for Bell as a subsidiary of American Telegraph and Telephone (AT&T). Management regarded themselves as progressive, but this was with regard to a willingness to experiment rather than their general attitudes, for they were strongly anti-union. The significance of Hawthorne is not because of the results of the research as such, for both its findings and methods are widely regarded as highly questionable (Carey, 1967; Silver, 1987). Rather, it reflects two factors: first, the sustained nature of the intervention itself, combining psychologists, sociologists and anthropologists. In this way the courtship between social science and industry became something of a formal engagement; second, the interpretation of the results became the core of *human relations* theory and subsequent managerial practices. This was partly due to the propagandising work of Elton Mayo (1946), despite the fact that he did not join the team properly until 1928 and was much more peripheral than those who actually wrote up the detailed research, such as Roethlisberger and Dickson (1964) and, to a lesser extent, Whitehead (1938).

Let us retrace these steps briefly. Early experiments centred on varying the lighting for two small test groups of women workers. The purpose was to identify conditions affecting worker performance. Unfortunately no firm conclusions could be drawn, as productivity increased under every level of illumination and even for the control group that was not being subjected to any changes at all! At the time this caused great puzzlement, but it was later theorised that the real change had been the segregation of a small group, which blossomed under special attention and treatment. Thus the 'Hawthorne Effect' was born, through which it was recognised that the research intervention itself is an independent variable in its effects on human behaviour. Initially the puzzlement led to a further stage of experiments on groups of women selected for their degree of friendship with one another. Again the emphasis was on manipulation of environmental variables, this time of a greater variety: rest pauses, length of working day, group bonus schemes and so on. Observers, initially placed in a test room, were gradually encouraged to act like supervisors and become more friendly with the group. Until 1929, in almost all cases output rose, with the only consistent factor again being the effects of creating a special group with its identity strengthened by the replacement of two 'un-cooperative' members. However, worker interest in experiments declined and output fell with the onset of the depression. Furthermore, additional experiments with two other groups to test further the effects of incentives and rest pauses had inconclusive results, both experiments being discontinued amidst some discord.

All this confusion might appear to be grounds for giving up. But a more positive line was taken that a constant factor was the significance of employee attitudes and the influence of supervisory techniques upon them. The successful experiments were those that allowed the individuals to coalesce into a group, though it is difficult to imagine how the special conditions could be transferred.

> Right now I couldn't ask for anything better than I have. I just can't explain what it is but I sure like it in the test room . . . I think we work for the most wonderful man in the Western Electric Company. We have no boss. Mr._simply waits on us . . . We have privileges that a lot of the other girls don't have. We are allowed to go down and lie on the couch when we are tired or don't feel good, and the matron was told not to say anything to us. Of course, none of us have done that yet because we always feel pretty good and we have rest periods and can do anything we want to in those ten minutes. (Roethlisberger and Dickson, 1964: 144)

Attitudes are not simply created by interaction with management. Employee preoccupations arise from a variety of sources, so further means were found of identifying them. Even while the above experiments were going on, the company and researchers had initiated an interviewing programme to explore the relations between employee morale and supervision. 'Counsellors' were trained by researchers to play the role of the observers in the illumination phase. Over a long period of time a variety of formal and more open-ended techniques of interviewing were used as a means of gaining information and of detecting, diverting and redirecting dissatisfactions. The counsellor was told by the company, 'to watch constantly for signs of unrest and to try to assuage the tension of the worker by discussion before the unrest became active' (quoted in Fischer and Sirriani, 1984: 182). Employee complaints were treated as unreliable due to their vagueness (hot, cold, damp, smoky or dusty were apparently inferior to 'the temperature in the room was 67°F'); or because they really revealed some personal, external disturbance. Even when told of grievances, management did not act on them. Aside from letting off steam, the process could also be used to adjust employees to the work situation and screen out effective counsellors as management material.

A final phase of research linked together the concern with employee attitudes and the earlier focus on the group. The famed 'bank wiring room' experiments were based on an existing work-group carrying out wiring, soldering and inspecting tasks with a supposedly unobtrusive observer present. What was 'discovered' on the face of it was no different from Taylor's observations in the steel industry: the work-group systematically controlled and restricted output on the basis of their own conception of a fair day's work and enforced group norms on any fellow workers who deviated by overproducing (rate-busters) or underworking (chisellers). The interpretation and reaction was, however, sharply different. Despite the restrictions, cliques and hostilities, a more accommodating picture of group identities was endorsed. Instead of suppressing the group and attempting to individualise its members, human relations is concerned to cultivate its sentiments and switch its loyalties to management. Roethlisberger and Dickson note, 'It is as well to recognise that informal organisation is not "bad", as they are sometimes assumed to be' (1964: 559). As it is fruitless to try to destroy it, management's task is to achieve a greater harmony between the informal and formal organisation. This can be done through controlled participation, effective communication and socially skilled, humane supervision. Referring to the experience of one of the Hawthorne experimental groups, Mayo commented that, 'Before every change of program, the group is consulted. Their comments are listened to and discussed; sometimes their objections are allowed to negative a suggestion. The group undoubtedly develops a sense of participation in the critical determination and becomes something of a social unit' (quoted in Baritz, 1960: 88–9).

As an alternative managerial *tactic* this makes a lot of sense, indeed a minority of British employers were reaching similar conclusions (G. Brown, 1977: 243). Today, it is applied in a new and more sophisticated way in current Japanese management techniques. The problem arises from how Mayo and the human relations tradition theorised their understanding of Hawthorne. They were determined to fashion a general theory of behaviour in organisations. Later management theorists have dubbed a key element of this approach 'social man' (Schein, 1965). For Mayo, this started from a critique of the so-called 'rabble hypothesis' he attributed to economists and management theorists such as Taylor; in which individuals act solely according to rational self-interest. In contrast, 'social man' proceeds from the assumption that the major human need is for social solidarity which can be satisfied through group association. Naturally, this plays down the role of economic incentives. Such associations are seen to create social routines which substitute for logical and individual self-interest. Mayo preferred the term 'non-logical' to 'irrational', but the essential message is clear: workers act according to sentiments and emotions.

Contrary to some accounts, he did not believe that management was by definition and contrast rational, for all individuals were held to be governed by the same abstract instincts and needs. Rather managers and administrators could *become* rational, precisely because they can free themselves from social routines and the accompanying emotional involvements. This is an extremely curious notion, as any analysis of management shows that it has *its own* routines and 'illogicalities'. But it indicates the uncritical attitude of human relation's writers towards the economic elites. Interestingly the new theorists of corporate culture manage to maintain the emphasis on emotions, symbolism and 'irrationality' without separating management and workforce in the same way.

It must also be said that the empirical basis for Mayo's assertions in the Hawthorne experience is very shaky. Group solidarity was carefully engineered through the selection and treatment of those workers involved, even to the point of replacing 'un-cooperative' workers. Even this did not sustain co-operative activity. Mayo interpreted restriction of output as a combination of group sentiments and lack of trust in management. But there are alternative and simpler explanations: 'Restriction of output by voluntary norms was a rational response by primarily economically orientated agents to the increasingly likely prospect of unemployment' (Clegg and Dunkerley, 1980: 131). Environmental influences on employee attitudes were recognised, but it was held that the consequences could be dealt with and 'adjusted' inside the enterprise.

The denial of economic factors led to some absurd psychologisms. Mayo used the curious term 'pessimistic reveries' to account for industrial unrest of any kind. Put another way, strikes and other actions that restrict output are obsessive preoccupations and signs of maladjustment, even to the point of identifying industrial unrest with mental breakdown and casting trade union leaders as psychological deviants! Not surprisingly, unions very rarely get mentioned in Mayo's writings. That did not stop later followers. The psychologist McMurry argued that not only were unions unnecessary when management acted fairly, but that workers joined unions not to protect their jobs and improve pay, but because of unconscious cravings to improve the emotional situation at work (Baritz, 1960: 175).

It would, however, be misleading to view human relations theory through its excesses. To add to 'social man', a second highly influential level of theorisation emphasised the essentially co-operative nature of the enterprise. In fact, the two were linked, as Mayo continually referred to the supposed eager desire of workers for co-operative activity. It is easy to dismiss this kind of analysis, particularly given the capacity of human relations researchers systematically to ignore or re-interpret conflictual processes. But they *had* identified significant changes in the socio-economic sphere that brought the issue of co-operation to the fore. They pointed to the disparity between the attention paid to technical efficiency and economic functions, and the absence of 'the development of skills and techniques for securing co-operation' (Roethlisberger and Dickson, 1964: 552). The need to improve the latter was especially important because, as Mayo recognised, the balance between technical and social skills had been disrupted as workers' traditional forms of craft socialisation and identity had been undermined by mechanisation and the assembly line.

Emphasis is therefore put on the role of management to use the formal organisation to intervene in the *informal,* so as to create and sustain consent. Only in this context can we understand what appears to be the superficial solutions of human relations practices, with their prescriptions of 'democratic' supervision, good communications, teamwork and socially skilled leadership. Mayo's 'lifelong obsession with social harmony' (M. Rose, 1975: 115), was not based merely on his distorted empirical observations, but was underwritten by an organic model of society in which equilibrium and stability are the natural order of things, while structural divisions and conflicts are pathological. Mayo was worried about the 'extensive maladjustment of our times' as a period of rapid change undermined values and atomised individuals. The task was to recreate a sense of community inside the workplace, a call we are again hearing from advocates of corporate culture.

During the same period, Chester Barnard, the President of the New Jersey Bell Telephone Company, was developing an even heavier emphasis on the basis for human co-operation, that was to have a major impact on later mainstream theorists (Perrow, 1979). Co-operation necessary to the survival of society could be most clearly observed in organisations. Unequal power and resources were irrelevant against the 'fact' that individuals voluntarily entered and submitted themselves to a common goal unachievable without collective effort. Organisations were rational and individuals were not. But, like Mayo, his virtual deification of the formal organisation still reserved the key role for management. The rationality of the 'non-personal' organisation was in practice again located with the executive elite, who, as decision-makers, had responsibility for what Peters and Waterman, in praising Barnard, describe as 'managing the values of the organisation' (1982: 26). For co-ordination was still required to *make* a system, particularly as a sense of common purpose was not always present amongst the 'lower participants'. Barnard therefore reinforced the emphasis, not just on co-operation, but on the balance of formal and informal. As Perrow points out, this is the most extreme identification with the formal organisation, devoid of any concern for the negative effects of power and domination, or even the stress in human relations theory on sympathetic supervision and controlled participation.

Consolidating human relations

Recognising the significance of co-operative activity was an advance, but it was wrong to transfer the analysis from the work-group to the organisation as a whole. The fundamental contradiction at the heart of human relations theory and of Barnard is that co-operation, even of the 'spontaneous' kind, has to be created. Reed refers to an intellectual schizophrenia whereby, 'a theoretical framework is forced to reconcile the contradictions generated by a metaphysic that assumes collective moral consensus as a social given and at the same time advocates the adoption of techniques whereby this may be engineered' (1985: 6). There is therefore a wide consensus among the critics we have discussed that the significance of the tradition is to be located in its *ideological appeal* M. Rose (1975: 124) puts this most succinctly in his memorable comment that Mayoism is the twentieth century's most seductive managerial ideology in which social scientists and managers fashioned each other in their own image.

There is a great deal of accuracy in the view that one of its major functions was to legitimate the power and authority of both emergent professional 'classes' of managers and industrial consultants. The problem is that such an analysis can slip into giving the impression that human relations was a gigantic, if dangerous, con-trick with no purchase on reality. In part the reverse is true, for it only makes sense as a reaction to and means of shaping new realities. The depth of economic and political crisis meant that, by the 1930s corporate America felt under siege' (Neimark and Tinker, 1986: 25). Congress had passed corporatist legislation allowing companies greater control over markets and pricing in return for acceptance of codes governing minimum wages and maximum hours, plus guarantees of union membership and collective bargaining rights. In addition, the country was experiencing a huge strike wave of sit-down strikes and factory occupations. Large corporations bitterly resisted the 'New Deal' institutions and the union organising drive. But the more perceptive of them, also realised that, 'the crisis generated critical problems of social control and legitimation for management' (Boreham, 1980: 25). A second front was opened, drawing extensively on the human relations package of better communication, democratic leadership, cooperation and social integration. This went hand-in-hand with early versions of the managerial revolution thesis, General Motors claiming that the organisation was a community of stakeholders for which management was a trustee.

The success of strikes and union organising drives only consolidated a recognition of the importance of consent and attention to employee attitudes in the more general writings of human relations theorists, such as T. N. Whitehead in his *Leadership in a Free Society* (1936). Despite the weakness of the tradition in Britain, Whitehead's book was well received in progressive management circles worried about the changing position of business in a more democratic community. Human relations was able to provide greater legitimation of management authority than Taylor, because it went beyond the narrow confines of 'science' and formal organisation to address issues more in tune with the times. But it would not have made the same impact merely as a body of ideas. It had to help generate new *practices*.

Though it was still confined to a minority of even the largest employers throughout the 1930s, Bendix, Baritz and other researchers show that an increasing number of firms such as General Electric, General Motors and Procter and Gamble, developed programmes influenced by human relations theory. The Hawthorne researchers had put considerable emphasis on 'personnel work' in its broadest sense of 'adequate diagnosis and understanding of the actual human situations – both individual and group – within the factory' (Roethlisberger and Dickson, 1964: 591). With this background, greater consideration was given in many large companies to the training of managers and supervisors in the arts of intensive communication, social skills, and non-authoritarian leadership that would motivate as well as command. Personnel departments grew further, alongside more use of attitude surveys. General Motors managed to combine them neatly with spying on union activists, by employing Pinkerton detectives to carry out the tests! As previously, the war acted as a spur, large companies and the state finding the use of tests an invaluable means of dealing with the problems associated with the sudden employment of thousands of new workers. Despite a sustained attack by more critical academics, the diverse applications and effects of human relations theorus had established a bridgehead for the social sciences in industry, and, by the 1940s the movement had gained substantial institutional support (Barley and Kunda, 1992: 374).

Conclusion and evaluation

Back to the future?

This chapter is not intended as a history lesson. We have already referred to the danger of linear models which conceive of management theory and practice as self-contained models and eras swept away by over-hyped 'revolutions' in thinking and doing. Rather our concern has been to show how organisational theories draw from and allow us to explore the real emergence of complex, large-scale industrial organisations. Future chapters will discuss how this relationship has evolved, but in this final section, we want to provide some links between the two by briefly considering the practical and theoretical legacies left by the two major traditions of scientific management and human relations.

It is easier to start with what we have just left. The 1950s saw the relationship between social science and industry blossom still further, facilitated both by the development of OB and related disciplines in business schools specialising in the human side of the enterprise, and the training of middle and senior executives in leadership and management development (Barley and Kunda, 1992: 375). Rhetorical claims, however, foundered on a failure to demonstrate an exact and direct relationship between theory and practice. Perrow, for example, has written sceptically of the 'thirty year history of the effort to link morale and leadership to productivity' (1979: 97). Nor were the practices or solutions necessarily any less superficial than Hawthorne. Bendix (1956: 326–7) remarks that the National Association of Manufacturer's new-found attachment to 'two-way communication' was based on the assumption that employers relayed *facts* to the workforce to promote cooperation, whereas what workers say is *information* which management can use to 'eliminate misunderstandings'.

Despite the re-rise of harder managerial 'sciences' such as operations research and systems analysis, human relations approaches did not disappear. The body of research and to a lesser extent practical intervention moved on to new topics such as leadership styles and group dynamics. Whatever limits there may have been to its ideas and results, the human relations current continued to provide, in Bendix's words, a *vocabulary of motivation*. This term is particularly appropriate, given that the primary theoretical means of grappling with the 'human factor' moved onto the terrain associated with more sophisticated behavioural science techniques and issues centred on motivation and the school of psychology consolidated around figures such as Maslow, McGregor and Herzberg, who explored the full implications for management of responding to all members of organisations as a human resources. But the earlier human relations tradition, which had laid dormant and often abused for its naïvety suddenly became fashionable again in the 1980s. In particular, the influence of Japanese management techniques, with their emphasis on teamwork, workgroups and corporate cultures, brought human relations back into focus.

The legacy of Taylorism has been more disputed. Long reviled for its apparent barbarity and economism, scientific management was brought out of the broom cupboard by the radical theorist Braverman (1974). The argument that Taylorism constituted *the* means of managerial control in the twentieth century has been shown to be exaggerated, but there is plenty of evidence that key elements of the system have been updated and extended. Ossie Jone's (1994) entertaining account of life as a work study engineer in the 1970s and 1980s shows how the traditional techniques of method and time study were superseded by a system known as Simplified Pre-Determined Motion Time Study (SPMTS). This is merely one of a long line of innovations throughout the century. SPMTS was favoured by the engineers and would have delighted Taylor, in that it promised the illusion of the removal of the 'subjective' element of rating from work measurement. Such developments may not convince all the sceptics, given that they admittedly focus on a narrow, if well-known feature of scientific management. More convincing is the rise of the latest US management fix, business re-engineering or core process redesign, whose tools – activity value analysis, time compression management and so on – and ethos are clearly rooted in Taylorism and classical theories (Thackray, 1993). But we should not get contemporary developments out of proportion. The lesson of *this* chapter remains. Taylorism and other management theories are not packages, and, given the separable nature of their elements, any practical legacy will be diverse and uneven. Furthermore, the history of large-scale organisations shows that managers combine elements of different approaches according to perceived need and fashion. The respective traditions embody a permanent tension between different approaches to the management of work organisation. Although this is frequently described in mainstream writing as technical and human organisation and the need to integrate the two, it may be thought of more accurately in terms of competing control systems. For example, in their historical survey of US managerial discourse, Barley and Kunda (1992) distinguish between rational (for example, scientific management, systems theories) and normative (for example, human relations, organisational culture) ideologies of control. Rather than one simply displacing another, there are successive and alternate waves paralleling broad cycles of economic expansion and contraction. Impressive as their schema is, like most organisational theory, it is derived from US experience. To round off this chapter, we want to make some brief qualifications to this tendency.

Beyond the American model

We have, during this chapter, pointed to a number of sources of variation in the way that Taylorism and the human relations tradition developed across and within various units – sectors, countries, companies – shaped by the requirements of cultural and other forms of adaptation and pressures of resistance from key actors. However, this framework still tends to assume models that arise and are adapted to at given stages along a single line of development. Chandler's accotint of the rise of the 'modern' integrated business enterprise can be used to illustrate the general argument. He does give a historically-informed explanation of the emergence of the phenomena. In general terms the USA was a seed-bed for managerial capitalism primarily because of the size and the nature of the domestic market (Chandler, 1977: 498–500). It was not only faster growing than other nations, but more open and less class-divided. This encouraged the techniques and technologies of mass production and distribution. In contrast, domestic markets in Western Europe were smaller and with slower growth. This limited the same kind of developments and kept greater reliance on middlemen to handle goods. Even where integrated enterprises did appear, they often remained small enough to be dominated by owner-managers. This kind of reasoning allows Chandler to evaluate other national experiences against this standard. British entrepreneurs are said to have failed to invest in manufacturing, marketing and management in key capital-intensive industries. As a consequence this 'personal capitalism', dependent on atomistic economic organisation such as the single-plant family firms in industries such as cotton and steel, was a pale version of its US counterpart: 'neglecting investment in administrative capabilities and research, dogged by short-termism, preoccupied with family and personal management, prejudiced against salaried managers, determined to ensure a steady income stream rather than to maximise growth and profits in the long run' (Supple, 1991: 511).

This account of stunted organisational capabilities makes an attractive link to *institutionalist* explanations for Britain's declining economic performance. Such frameworks point to factors which shaped industrial development: entrenched employee job controls; the separation of the banking system from the finance of industry; and educational provision that failed to provide adequately trained managerial and technical staff. As a result, managerial structures and expertise were underdeveloped and 'the British only adapted patchwork improvements to their existing organisational and productive structure' (Elbaum and Lazonick, 1986: 7). Echoes of such explanations can be found today in critics of short-termism and institutional failure in Britain's political economy, such as Will Hutton's influential *Guardian* columns. But the remit is much broader than Chandler's 'internal history' of business enterprise. In emphasising the role of educational, state, legal and other institutions, such writers can demonstrate variations in industrial development.

It can also be argued that given the similarities between financial and industrial systems the UK and the USA, Chandler's model of management and enterprise is even less likely to apply to other European countries. Modern American, or perhaps Anglo–Saxon, conceptions of management are built on assumptions of the superiority of a *general science* of co-ordination and control, a profession of management above particular specialisms and functions (Fores *et al.*, 1992). In comparison, the Franco–German tradition draws on quite different sources. For example, Rueschemeyer (1986) notes the significance of public administration as a bureaucratic model for private enterprise in Germany, while the French state has developed vocationally-orientated higher education to produce generations of technocrats for the private and public sector. Germany and a number of other countries also have a tradition of engineering-based technical competence as the base for industrial progress.

If the form and content of large-scale organisations is socially constructed, Supple's comments on Chandler have more general application: 'What his assumptions make it difficult to do, however, is to generalise his results to a rounded and substantial exploration of the interrelationships and evolution of economic systems generally' (1991: 510). Beyond Europe, this lesson is even more pertinent. Japan has received considerable academic attention for its distinctive forms of ownership and management. For example, in the influential corporate form of *keiretsu*, units are part of vertically organised enterprise groups clustered around a dominant company or companies. Interlinked shareholdings involving subcontractors and banks establish stability and mutual interest in the long-term success of the group, the joint risk-taking and access to capital avoiding the short-termism associated with the Anglo–Saxon model (G. Henderson, 1993: 38–9). Crucially, this risk-taking is also shared with the *state*, as in the well-known example of co-ordination of economic development through the Ministry of International Trade and Industry (MITI).

Such involvement is frequently a characteristic feature of *late industrialisation*. In Japan the commercial class was marginal to early industrialisation and the state was the primary agent in mobilising capital and mediating market forces (Littler, 1982). But the primary example of state-sponsored development is in Korea. Conglomerate enterprise groups, known as *chaebol*, are both directed and disciplined by the state through financial controls, subsidies and incentives. For example, following the bankruptcy of the leading cement producer in the 1970s, the South Korean government transferred its production facilities to another chaebol (Amsden, 1992: 15). This pattern has been repeated continually in the immensely successful restructuring process that has made the country into one of the fastest growing in the world. But the state is not the only manager of the industrialisation process. As Amsden (1992: 9) shows, 'Salaried engineers are a key figure in late industrialisation because they are the gatekeepers of foreign technology transfers'. With Korean firms choosing specialised engineers over administrators, we have a further example of different forms of enterprise management within managerial capitalism. Family ownership is a key dimension of South Korea's corporate structures and familism has been a further characteristic of some East Asian economies, particularly Taiwan and Hong Kong. Family business, particularly among overseas Chinese, operates according to particular lineage and inheritance rules, which, in turn, shape how businesses grow, given that a wider sharing of trust is constrained by the familial form. More importantly for our purposes, the forms of co-ordination and direction of the enterprise are necessarily distinctive: 'there is strong patrimonial and personalistic direct control, rather than on the more impersonalised, formalised and standardised control of the rational-bureaucratic model which we are familiar with from the West' (Clegg, 1990: 164).

Despite the success of the East Asian economies, we are not suggesting that these factors are the only or even main path to success. After all, there are substantial differences between those economies, as well as common contrasts to 'Western' models, highlighting the need for a comparative analysis of management structures and practices (Whitley, 1992a). In other words, the example demonstrates our final theme, that socially constructed organisational diversities are the proper object of analysis for organisational theory. This is not a minor point. Measuring organisations and change against a single, linear standard rears its misleading head again later, this time with Japanese management replacing the American model. One of the recurring weaknesses that underpin this kind of thinking is an absence of or inadequate means to conceptualise organisations in their environments.

References

Amsden, A.H. (1992) *Asia's Next Giant: South Korea and Late Industrialisation,* Oxford: Oxford University Press.

Armstrong, P. (1984) 'Competition between the Organizational Professions and the Evolution of Management Control Strategies', in K. Thompson (ed.) *Work, Employment and Unemployment,* Milton Keynes: Open University Press.

Barley, S.R. and G. Kunda (1992) 'Design and Devotion: Surges of Rational and Normative Ideologies of Control in Managerial Discourse', *Administrative Science Quarterly,* vol. 37: 363–99.

Bendix, R. (1956) *Work and Authority in Industry,* New York: Harper & Row.

Berg, M. (1985) *The Age of Manufactures,* London: Fontana.

Boreham, P. (1980) The Dialectic of Theory and Control: Capitalist Crisis and the Organization of Labour', in D. Dunkerely and G. Salaman (eds) *The International Yearbook of Organization Studies 1980,* London: Routledge & Kegan Paul.

Brannen, P. (1983) *Authority and Participation in Industry,* London: Batsford.

Braverman, H. (1974) *Labor and Monopoly Capital: The Degradation of Work in the Twentieth Century,* New York: Monthly Review Press.

Brown, G. (1977) *Sabotage,* Nottingham: Spokesman. Brown, H. (1980) 'Work Groups', in G. Salaman and K. Thompson, (eds) *People and Organizations,* Harlow: Longman.

Burawoy, M. (1979) *Manufacturing Consent: Changes in the Labour Process Under Monopoly Capitalism,* Chicago: University of Chicago Press.

Carey, A. (1967) The Hawthorne Studies: A Radical Criticism', *American Sociological Review,* 32: 403–16.

Chandler, A. (1962) *Strategy and Structure: Chapters in the History of the Industrial Enterprise,* Cambridge, Mass.: MIT Press.

Chandler, A.D. (1977) *The Visible Hand,* Cambridge Mass.: Harvard University Press.

Chandler, A. D. (1990) *Scale and Scope: the Dynamics of Industrial Capitalism,* Cambridge, Mass.: Harvard University Press.

Clawson, D. (1980) *Bureaucracy and the Labour Process: The Transformation of US Industry, 1860–1920,* New York: Monthly Review Press.

Clegg, S. and D. Dunkerley (1980) *Organization, Class and Control,* London: Routledge & Kegan Paul.

Clegg, S. (1990) *Modern Organizations: Organization Studies in the Postmodern World,* London: Sage.

Collins, R. (1986) *Weberian Sociological Theory,* Cambridge University Press.

Dickson (1964; 2nd edn) Management and the Worker, New York: John Wiley.

Doray, B. (1988) *A Rational Madness: From Taylorism to Fordism,* London: Free Association Books.

Edwards, R. (1979) *Contested Terrain: The Transformation of the Workplace in the Twentieth Century,* London: Heinemann.

Elbaum, B. and W. Lazonick (eds) (1986) *The Decline of the British Economy,* Oxford: Clarendon.

Fischer, F. and C. Sirriani (1984) *Critical Studies in Organization and Bureaucracy,* Philadelphia: Temple University Press.

Fores, M., I. Glover and P. Lawrence (1992) 'Management Thought, the American Legacy and the Future of European Labour Processes in 1992', paper to 10th International Labour Process Conference, Aston.

Fridenson, P. (1978) 'Corporate Policy, Rationalisation and the Labour Force-French Experiences in International Comparison, 1900–29', paper presented at Nuffield Deskilling Conference.

Friedman, A. (1977) *Industry and Labour: Class Struggle at Work Monopoly Capitalism,* London: Macmillan.

Goldman, P. and D.R. Van Houten (1977)'Managerial Strategies and the Worker: A Marxist Analysis of Bureaucracy', in J.K. Benson (ed.) *Organizational Analysis: Critique and Innovation,* London: Sage.

Goldman, P. and D. R. Van Houten (1980) 'Uncertainty, Conflict and Labor Relations in the Modern Firm 1: Productivity and Capitalism's Human Face', *Economic and Industrial Democracy,* vol. 1: 65–98.

Henderson, J. (1993) 'Industrial Policy for Britain: Lessons from the Easf, *Renewal,* vol. 1, no. 2: 32–42.

Johnson, A. and K. Moore (1986) *The Tapestry Makers: Life and Work at Lee's Tapestry Works,* Birkenhead: Merseyside Docklands Community Project.

Jones, O. (1994) 'Professionalism and Work Study: An Alternative Perspective on Subjectivity and the Labour Process', paper to 12th International Labour Process Conference, Aston.

Kouzmin, A. (1980) 'Control in Organizational Analysis: the Lost Polities', in D. Dunkerley, and G. Salaman (eds) *The International Yearbook of Organization Studies 1979,* London: Routledge & Kegan Paul.

Landes, D.S. (1969) *The Unbound Prometheus,* Cambridge: Cambridge University Press.

Littler, C. R. (1982) *The Development of the Labour Process in Capitalist Societies,* London: Heinemann.

Marglin, S. A. (1974) 'What do Bosses Do? The Origins and Functions of Hierarchy in Capitalist Production', *Review of Radical Political Economics,* 6: 60–102.

Mayo, E. (1946) *Humon Problems of an Industrial Civilisation,* New York: Macmillan.

Montgomery, D. (1976) 'Workers' Control of Machine Production in the Nineteenth Century', *Labor History,* vol. 17, no. 4: 486–509.

Nadworthy, M. (1955) *Scientific Managment and the Unions,* Cambridge: Mass.: Harvard University Press.

Neimark, M. and T. Tinker (1986) 'On Rediscovering Marx: Dissolving Agency Structure in Dialectical Unity', paper to 4th International Labour Process Conference, Aston.

Nelson, D. (1975) *Managers and Workers: Origins of the New Factory System in the United States 1880–1920,* Madison: University of Wisconsin Press.

Nyland, C. (1988) 'Scientific Management and Planning', *Capital and Class,* no. 33: 55–83.

Perrow, C. (1979) *Complex Organizations: A Critical Essay,* Illinois: Scott Foreman.

Peters, T. J. and R. H. Waterman (1982) *In Search of Excellence: Lessons from America's Best-Run Companies,* New York: Harper & Row.

Pollard, S. (1965) *The Genesis of Modern Management,* London: Edward Arnold.

Roethlisberger, F.G., and W.J. Dickson (1964; 2nd edn) Management and the Worker, New York: John Wiley.

Rose, M. (1975; 2nd edn 1986) *Industrial Behaviour,* Harmondsworth: Penguin.

Rueschemeyer, D. (1986) *Power and the Division of Labour,* London: Polity Press.

Schein, E.H. (1965) *Organizational Psychology,* 1st edn, Englewood Cliffs, NJ: Prentice-Hall (also 1980, 3rd. edn).

Silver, J. (1987) 'The Ideology of Excellence: Management and NeoConservatism', *Studies in Political Economy,* 24, Autumn, 105–29.

Stone, K. (1973) The Origins of Job Structures in the Steel Industry', *Radical America,* vol. 7, no. 6.

Supple, B. (1991) 'Scale and Scope: Alfred Chandler and the Dynamics of Industrial Capitalism', *Economic History Review,* vol. xliv, no. 3: 500–14.

Taylor, F.W. (1947) *Scientific Management,* New York: Harper & Row.

Thackray, J. (1993) 'Fads, Fixes and Fictions', *Management Today,* June.

Thompson, E. P. (1967) Time, Work Discipline and Industrial Capitalism', *Past and Present,* 38: 55–97.

Van Houten (1980) 'Uncertainty, Conflict and Labor Relations in the Modern Firm 1: Productivity and Capitalism's Human Face', *Economic and Industrial Democracy,* vol. 1: 65–98.

Weber, M. (1984) 'Bureaucracy[7], in F. Fischer and C. Sirriani (eds) *Critical Studies in Organization and Bureaucracy,* Philadelphia: Temple University Press.

Whitehead, T.N. (1936) *Leadership in a Free Society,* Cambridge, Mass.: Harvard University Press.

Whitehead, T.N. (1938) *The Industrial Worker,* London: Oxford University Press.

Whitley, R. (ed.) (1992a) *Business Systems in East Asia,* London: Sage.

Williams, K., C. Haslam, J. Williams and T. Cutler (1992b) Ford-v-"Fordism": The Beginning of Mass Production', *Work, Employment and Society,* vol. 6, no. 1: 517–48.

CHAPTER 4
Management and control

We saw in Chapter 2 that the first quarter of the twentieth century marked the emergence of professional management as social force, specialist occupational category and set of distinct work practices. This development was integral to changes in the organisation of capitalist production, with the modern bureaucratic enterprise increasingly based on the joint stock company, often in the new multi-divisional form, with its separation of ownership and management. In this type of structure, middle managers headed autonomous divisions which integrated production and distribution by co-ordinating flows from suppliers to consumers in the more clearly defined markets (Chandler, 1977). Such divisions administered their functional activities through specialist departments. All this encouraged the professionalisation of management and the rapid spread of administrative techniques. Management thought became intimately linked to the appearance of a distinct occupational grouping, organisational theory being used as a resource to understand the complexities of the large-scale organisation and management's role within it.

A key theme underlying the contradictory and partial organisational prescriptions, strategies and tactics was the belief in principles and even 'laws' concerning the nature of managerial activities and functions. As John Child observes:

> Management's claim to professionalism, for instance, was only plausible if it could be shown to possess some uniform and generalised body of knowledge upon which its practioners could draw. The so-called 'principles of management' could be presented as a theoretical base upon which the subject of 'management' rested. (1969: 225).

Much of this development was during the inter-war period of 'classical' writers such as Fayol, Taylor and Barnard. As we saw, Fayol was the most concerned to elaborate common characteristics of management. These consisted of *planning* general lines of action and forecasting; *organising* human and material resources within appropriate structures; *commanding* the *activities* of personnel for optimum return; *coordination* of varied activities; and *control* to ensure consistency with rules and command. These were situated within a detailed set of principles reflecting the division of labour and hierarchy of the bureaucratic enterprise, tempered by equitable treatment and personal responsibility. One of the effects of this way of thinking was to define managerial functions by a process of abstraction from specific activities into a conception of *general* management (Armstrong, 1987a). Managerial work would differ not in kind but only in the proportion which is actually 'managerial'. This would have a profound influence on management thought, spreading the idea that knowledge, skills and experience are common and transferable.

Meanwhile, in Britain, Mary Parker Follett was producing prescriptions for a science of behaviour informed by the concerns of the human relations tradition. Management could learn this science because it was derived from situational laws governed by the needs of the system. As such, management could represent and integrate all interests through its capacity to apply optimal solutions through depersonalised authority. Classical writings have now been superseded in the post-war period by a body of more detailed studies of management. Indeed, the study of organisation has become synonymous with that of management. In the Anglo-American tradition of organisation theory, management studies has emerged as an 'intellectual field' sustained by an extensive network of educational and training institutions (Whitley, 1984). The more confident asserted the viability of a management or administrative science whose methods and knowledge could support rational activities and decision-making. A post-war generation of 'new systematisers' (Barley and Kunda, 1992: 377) ranged from those who developed techniques of Operations Research such as Critical Path Method and Program Evaluation and Review Technique, to contingency theorists with their attempts to specify causal relations between environmental and structure variables, and motivational schemas based on rational calculation. Employees were either absent or objects to be acted on through the new systems. The new ground rules drew on 'hard' knowledge that could be learnt by managers in general rather than functional specialists. Such an approach competed with the influence of human relations perspectives, with their notion of training managers to learn how to exercise social and leadership skills.

This chapter aims to examine such claims through an analysis of the nature of management. It will argue that though both traditional and recent research offer important insights, the perspectives are partial and flawed. In particular they neglect important dimensions such as power and control, confirming the diagnosis of mainstream perspectives, as well as the divisions and contradictions embedded in the managerial labour process itself. Of course power and control are not just adjuncts to a discussion of management. This chapter set out the central debates about control and power in organisation in their own right.

The nature of management

The modern literature (for example, Drucker, 1955; Stewart, 1967; Mintzberg, 1973; Kotter, 1982) shares the central concern of the classical writers to identify common functions and criteria for effectiveness. There has been an even greater emphasis on the individual as a unit of analysis, a problematic of 'what do managers do?' (Hales, 1986). The answer given is a positive one. Drucker starts his well-known text by saying that 'The manager is the dynamic, life-giving element in every business . . . the only effective advantage an enterprise has in a competitive economy' (1955: 13). Texts continually invoke as examples captains of industry such as

Lee Iaocca, the ex-Chrysler boss. In this elevated role, the manager is presented almost as a free-floating centre of power. Organisations are still frequently treated as closed systems, with the assumption that 'it was largely within management's own powers to fashion behaviour and relationships as might best suit their own purposes' (J. Child, 1969: 168). Paradoxically, by focusing on the individual, management can be analysed as if it was homogeneous, leading to the conception of the 'universal manager' carrying out a generalised set of functions standing above any specific context (Mintzberg, 1973).

Theorists could agonise about whether management was science, art, magic or politics (T. Watson, 1986: 29), but all options rest on the analytical and practical skills of 'successful managers'. The constant struggle for competency is further linked to the assumption that management *effectiveness* is tangible and identifiable (Hales, 1986: 88). To this end anything can be quantified and learned. The focus of course changes. It may, for instance, be the fashionable qualities of managerial excellence (see Hitt *et al.*, 1986: 1011).

These various assumptions underwrite the more fundamental view of management practices as a neutral resource, the central task of which is deciding what should be done and getting other people to do it. In this view, which we describe as *technicist,* managers can embody and carry out the central mission of the organisation and secure its desired objectives. This links back to the idea discussed in Chapter 1 of managers as the guardians of organisations being rational tools to secure goals. By conceiving of the ends as unitary and the means as objectively rational, the socially-constructed, political character of organisational arrangements is removed (Berkeley Thomas, 1993: 37).

Managers are also seen as functionally necessary in a deeper sense. The functions are 'indispensable' and are ones which 'no one but the manager can perform' (Drucker, 1977: 39). As Willmott observes (1984: 350), this view confuses the general process of management of resources with the role of managers empowered to command others within specific institutional frameworks. Put another way, it wrongly assumes that, 'the management function must, of necessity, reside with a particular category of agents who manage or administer other agents' (Hales, 1988: 5). In particular circumstances, work teams or worker co-operatives can equally be said to be carrying out managerial functions.

Organisational theories seldom acknowledge the wider context in which managerial work is undertaken. Whitely argues that it is better to attempt to, 'specify general features of managerial tasks in terms of their functions in the organisation and change of economic enterprises as interdependent units of resource co-ordination and control, rather than identifying the characteristics of all jobs by "managers"' (1984: 343). Elsewhere, the wider theory of a 'managerial revolution' was being articulated. Part of the idea of an 'organisation society', the theory rested on a particular interpretation of changes in the nature of the large corporation. As the dominant form, joint stock companies were held to be characterised by a separation of ownership and control, share dispersal and a corresponding rise in the importance of a professional managerial elite who run the new corporations. Although the growing significance of management is indisputable, many adherents of the theory (Berle and Means, 1935) took the new corporate system to be a 'purely neutral technocracy', with managers with different backgrounds and experiences exercising social responsibilities. Tougher versions (Burnham, 1945) envisaged a managerially planned and controlled society beyond the workplace, with management becoming the dominant class of all industrial societies.

The managerial revolution thesis had a wider significance for social theory, often influenced by systems thinking (Reed, 1984: 278). At its core was the view that capitalism as a system based on individual private ownership was being supplanted by a post-capitalist society in which old political disputes about ownership were irrelevant (Dahrendorf, 1959). But these theoretical developments enabled management writers such as Drucker to assert that 'we no longer talk of "capital" and "labour", we talk of "management" and "labour"' (1955: 13). Some scepticism was expressed by senior managers who referred to 'claptrap' about social responsibilities, reminding their colleagues that they remained the servant of their employers (J. Child, 1969: 152–3). Managerial capitalism had extended its tentacles. But we should remember the qualifications made in Chapter 2 about the culturally-loaded nature of such theory and practice. Organisational life in Germany and other countries was not dominated by the search for a profession of management: 'Continentals appreciate the specialist nature of most executive jobs: they do not see why specialists should be described as "managers", nor are they notable for having occupational groups which call themselves "professionals". European business does not seem to have suffered through the lack of either idea' (Fores and Glover, 1976: 104).

Managers as leaders and decision-makers

Having set out the basic assumptions of mainstream approaches, it is useful to highlight some of the further dimensions of research which shape the broader view of management activities. From the 1950s onwards considerable attention has been paid to the interrelations between management, leadership and decision-making. Textbooks are normally quick to point out that all leaders are not managers and not all managers have or even need leadership abilities. Indeed there is a modest subliterature on leadership qualities as such; for example on whether successful leaders all have or need particular personality traits. We are concerned, however, with the way in which leadership studies frequently merge with those of management by virtue of a focus on effective management *styles*. In fact most texts not only use the terms 'management' and 'leadership styles' interchangeably, they refer to the same research.

A common starting point is often McGregor's (1960) famous theory of X and Y assumptions that management have about people. The former leans towards Taylorist notions of employees who dislike work and initiative, and therefore have to be directed and coerced; while the latter accepts that they have self-direction and self-control if they are committed to organisational goals and are involved in decision-making. People need whipping versus people are better at whipping themselves, as someone once mischievously put it. McGregor's theory is clearly part of the human relations tradition and follows through the perceived results of the Hawthorne studies in terms of the beneficial effects of participatory leadership and sympathetic supervision. A variety of subsequent studies developed categories based on a comparison between democratic and autocratic management or leadership styles. The dominant message is that democratic leadership is better, both for increasing morale and productivity, and for improving the quality of decisions. How democratic it is remains open to question. Most new styles have always left management command structures intact. Nichols and Beynon quote one manager at 'Chemco': 'Democratic leadership is the only way. But you'll know that won't you. Psychologists have proved it with children' (1977: 123). Those evaluating the results of such styles have also been sceptical, with Perrow noting that 'the history of research in this area is one of progressive disenchantment with the above theses' (1979: 98).

Some of the studies are careful to allow for combinations of styles or particular styles in appropriate circumstances. In addition, Fiedler's (1967) research offers a thoroughgoing contingency approach in which effectiveness is linked specifically to organisational context. By developing a 'least preferred co-worker scale', the suit-ability of a task or relationship orientated leader was shown to be dependent on the degree to which the task is structured, the leader's position power, and the relations between leaders and led. But even this has a relatively limited notion of the con-text of management practices, and rests on individualistic and small-scale scenarios. The literature on leadership and management styles has failed to integrate a deeper analysis of how management strategies develop and their interrelationship with the political economy of the firm and society. We shall return to this question later.

A crucial part of leadership is decision-making, Simon (1960) regarding the lat-ter as synonymous with management. It is therefore not surprising that this has been another focus for researchers. For example, organisations have been analysed as decision-making systems, while Mintzberg (1973) has used 'decisional roles' as one category of classification of management activities and functions. Traditional approaches tend to start from a *rational choice* model which having assumed consist-ency of goals, requires the setting out of decision-making alternatives and assess-ment of likely outcomes. Once again the emphasis is on skills and techniques to aid the optimal or 'one best' decision. Assessments must take into account the technical and human requirements, one text recommending a balance of the skills of Captain Kirk and Mr Spock from Starship Enterprise!

Social scientists can help managers to design appropriate centralised or decentral-ised structures; identify stages in the process, such as generation, evaluation, choice, implementation and follow-through; and ensure an awareness of the behavioural dimensions of decision-making in groups. This may include specific techniques, the best known of which is brainstorming. Another important area is access to informa-tion and the design of management information systems. One of the purposes is to separate routine, 'programmed' decisions and enhance the ability of management to concentrate on strategic decisions (Stewart, 1970). The above emphasis reinforces a technicist view of management processes and activities. It further neglects the ine-qualities in access to information which structure decision processes, which are fre-quently legitimated by reference to technical expertise (J. Child, 1973). The *politics* of decision-making is also highlighted by Pettigrew (1973), who points to the hierar-chy of powers shaped by the control of resources.

Researchers are aware, however, of limits to rationality. March and Simon (1958) introduce the concept of 'intended rationality', recognising that there are consider-able constraints to the capacity to access and evaluate a full range of options. The existing structures of specialisation and hierarchy in organisations, as well as the routine practices identified in a Weberian analysis, will limit the content and flow of information and set agendas for decision-making. As a result, organisational participants are boundedly rational, have to work with simplified models of reality and there is 'limited search' and 'satisficing' rather than optimal choices. Cyert and March (1963) point to similar processes such as 'uncertainty absorption', whereby in order to maintain stability of operations, rules and processes are geared to short-run decisions and frequent reviews. What emerges are policies and decisions by 'incremental comparison'; not a rational science, but a 'science' of muddling through (Lindblom, 1959).

Management practices: a new realism?

Demarcating the boundaries of rationality helped to extend the study of management. But discussion of the core issue of defining and classifying activities moved on to a more detailed 'realism'. Fores and Glover argue that, 'observation shows that [this] classical view is largely a convenient fiction. . . In reality, executive work is complex, confusing to the outsider, and rarely predictable (1976: 194). What 'observations' are they talking about? By getting a large and varied group of managers to fill in diaries, Stewart (1967) drew up classifications based on how they spent their *time*. This produced emissaries, writers, discussers, troubleshooters and committee men. A later study (1976) focused on patterns of contact – this time identifying hub, peer-dependent, man-management and solo. In contrast, Mintzberg (1973) confined himself to five chief executives and classified ten roles under three headings: under *interpersonal* come figurehead, leader and liaison; under *informational* – monitor, disseminator and spokesman; and under *decisional* come entrepreneurial, disturbance-handler, resource allocator and negotiator. We would agree with Hales' observation that many of the categories used in these and other studies are largely interchangeable, for example leader/figurehead/spokesman. New terms such as 'network building' and 'setting agendas' correspond in substance to old favourites such as 'planning'. He produces a composite list from six of the best-known studies, which 'exhibit striking parallels with the supposedly outdated "classical principles of management"' (1986: 95). In addition, some of the variations merely reflect managerial *ideologies,* with modern writers in a more democratic era preferring to describe command as motivation (Mullins, 1985: 121).

Nevertheless, it remains the case that the new empirical studies do partly break with traditional approaches and those found in popular management books. Once the complication of producing labels and lists is set aside, more realistic insights are available. We have already referred to Cyert and March's findings on the short-term incrementalism in the sphere of decision-making. But the significant breakthroughs are aided by a willingness to use a greater variety of research methods than those used in broad-brush analyses of managerial functions. Structured or unstructured observation methods, time-budget studies and self-report questionnaires can capture a greater sense of fluidity and processual factors (Horne and Lupton, 1965; Stewart, 1967, 1976; Mintzberg, 1973; Kotter, 1982; Burns, 1982).

Such studies reveal that the image of the reflective strategist, thinker and planner is a myth. An alternative picture is indicated through the language of realism. Though there are variations between the studies, management practices are said to

Table 4.1 Managerial functions

(1) Acting as a figurehead and leader of an organisational unit
(2) Liaison: the formation and maintenance of contacts
(3) Monitoring, filtering and disseminating information
(4) Allocating resources
(5) Handling disturbances and maintaining work flows
(6) Negotiating
(7) Innovating
(8) Planning
(9) Controlling and directing subordinates.

Source: Colin P. Hales, 'What Do Managers Do?: A Critical Review', *Journal of Management Studies*, 23: 95.

be opportunistic, habitual, tactical, reactive, frenetic, ad-hoc, brief, fragmented, and concerned with fixing. This arises primarily because the manager has to adapt to continued uncertainties, limited information and contradictory pressures, not least on time and energy. As a result, routines are shaped by short-time spans, the domination of face-to-face interaction and lateral communication in gathering and using information. For Mintzberg, this actually corresponds to managerial preferences for use of informal structures, gossip and speculation.

Nor are such activities necessarily bad for effectiveness and efficiency. Though energy can be dissipated in conflict and power struggles between cliques, Kotter (1982) points out that patterns do emerge based on establishing and maintaining *networks* vital for co-operation and a flow of information. Finally, though the focus is on the internal world of the organisation, the new realism is not incompatible with an analysis of environmental pressures. Loveridge's (1982) study of manufacturing companies in the Midlands showed that marketing and financial pressures, plus the need to accommodate to the power of workforce job controls, led in the direction of federal structures and short-term reactive policies and a concern with implementation rather than planning.

The realist challenge to the idea of the scientific and rational character of management is useful and widely accepted. It has not, however, established unchallenged intellectual domination. Not only do textbooks remain influenced by prescriptions from Fayol, but preoccupations with *new* lists of functions can still be described as variations on a classical theme. Indeed, the actual choice of new lists is extensive. Many pop management writers recycle a limited number of activities under new and more exotic titles, including that of jungle fighter and gamesman. Lists are merely the outward form of a belief in a transferable and common *essence* of management. Partly in response to the excesses of claims about new forms of organisation and management, influential voices are calling for a return to that 'essence', though it is redefined as the pursuit of rhetoric, identity and robust action (Eccles and Nohria, 1992). Nor is this impetus purely theoretical. Recent years have seen the rise of a competence movement, primarily in the USA and the UK, which aims to specify a common currency of occupational standards and to develop managers with the aid of behavioural and task measurements (Burgoyne, 1993).

There are also inherent limits and even drawbacks. It is, as Hales (1988) notes, an *internal* critique, and at the heart of the problem is the fact that it is at the *empirical* level only. Realism can show us that management is not what it is made out to be. Instead it portrays the activities of managers, 'as a quite arbitrary set of roles with little suggestion as to why they are as they are' (Armstrong, 1986: 19). The pervasive image of ad-hocery and muddling through seems to deny both purpose and coherence. Hales (1986) rightly observes that by focusing on individual jobs, rather than on management as a process, behaviour is unsituated and neglects the institutional context and functions. This is worsened by the tendency of behavioural analysis to concentrate on observable activities in a non-problematical way. For all its limitations, responsibilities and functions were the focus of classical theory, and many of the criticisms levelled at it have been attacks on a straw man (Berkeley Thomas, 1993: 51). In this sense, 'realism' marks a retreat from a broader framework of analysis. Understanding managerial work requires questions to be asked not just about what managers do, but about what they have to ensure others do. In other words, an emphasis on the *control* of particular organisational units in the labour process, though Hales later qualifies this by referring to control as one phase of the management process (1988: 5). The next part of this chapter will look in more detail at the relationships between management and control. Many of the issues raised by the realist critique are returned to when we assess perspectives on control strategy.

Control

There is not a great deal to say about the treatment of control in mainstream writing. Given the assumption of goal consensus, the issue is often simply ignored or trivialised. When it *is* discussed explicitly in standard textbooks, the chapters devoted to it are sometimes of a rather bizarre nature in almost omitting any reference to conflicts between groups. The talk is of technical inputs and outputs in a self-adjusting system, performance standards and feedback mechanisms. Control is reduced to a *monitoring* device, with management's fole being to check progress, ensure that actions occur as planned and to correct any deviation. It is also seen in a unitary way: 'controlled performance' with an assumption of goal-consensus. Some writers (Lawlor, 1976) put an emphasis on people desiring control – for example, getting enjoyment from dependence on higher authority. Resistance is smuggled in occasionally when discussing the *behavioural* implications as people 'react' to control processes, requiring management to adjust strategies accordingly.

We do accept that not all control processes arise from or are structured by antagonistic interests. Stock inventories and financial budgeting are necessary and not always conflictual features of any system of work organisation. A written job description may under certain conditions actually allow employees to assert power or control. But most control processes remain difficult to separate from the social relations of work, even when they appear to be neutral. This was the important conclusion of Blau and Schoenherr (1971), who used the concept of *insidious* controls to highlight the way in which management can utilise impersonal and unobtrusive means. Examples include selective recruitment of staff whose sense of professionalism or expertise enable them to work without direct controls; use of resource allocation as a financial discipline; and controls embodied in technology. Thus even those staff who exercise considerable work autonomy, such as those in higher education, have a series of indirect constraints over their actions. This kind of research is one of the few bridgeheads into the much wider body of work on control from a radical perspective.

Radical perspectives

Radical writers on organisation and management frequently *begin* from an analysis of control relations. The first radical text to make a major impact on organisation theory began by defining the theoretical rationale of organisational analysis: 'For this volume we have proposed as such an object the concept of organisation as control of the labour process' (Clegg and Dunkerley, 1980: 1). This framework derived from Marx's analysis of the capitalist labour process, which was updated and revitalised by Braverman (1974) and a range of other 'labour process' theorists discussed below.

All societies have labour processes, but under capitalism the labour process has specific characteristics. The most significant is what Marx referred to as the transformation of labour power into labour. In other words, when capital purchases labour it has only a potential or capacity to work. To ensure profitable production capital must organise the conditions under which labour operates to its own advantage. But workers pursue their own interests for job security, higher rewards and satisfying work, developing their own counter-organisation through informal job controls, restriction of output and the like.

To resolve this problem, and because they are under competitive pressure from other firms to cut costs and raise productivity, employers seek to control the conditions under which work takes place. Control is not an end in itself, but a means to transform the capacity to work established by the wage relation, into profitable production. It is a term, summarising a set of mechanisms and practices that regulate the labour process (P. K. Edwards, 1990). Richard Edwards (1979: 18) distinguishes three elements in any system of control:

1. direction and specification of work tasks;
2. evaluation, monitoring and assessment of performance;
3. the apparatus of discipline and reward to elicit co-operation and compliance.

Such elements may, however, be best described as *detailed* control, in that they are normally connected to immediate work processes; whereas *general* control refers to management's capacity to subordinate labour to its direction of the production process as a whole. This distinction made by P. K. Edwards (1990) and other writers is of significance in that it allows for recognition of tremendous variations in how detailed control is exercised. Such a model can even allow for employers giving workers significant discretion over tasks, as in semi-autonomous work groups, *if* it maintains the employers' overall control. Control is also not absolute, but, at least at the immediate level, a contested relationship. Conflict is built into the wage-effort bargain, with even mainstream writers recognising that an employment contract outlining required performance runs up against employees with their own goals and wants.

What about the role of management in this process? Claims of independent actors carrying out a neutral role are disputed by evidence concerning the top strata of management (Zeitlin, 1974). By their motivation, social background and connections, rewards and share-holdings in corporations, most managers are part of the capitalist class. Although this is a useful corrective, this 'sociological' analysis is not the crucial point. For example, a number of entrepreneurs, such as Alan Sugar of Amstrad, are from a traditional working-class background. But what matters is the structural location and functions in the organisation. If anything, entrepreneurs from this background tend to identify even more closely with their new role.

Proceeding from an analysis of process and functions, radical theorists (Carchedi, 1977; R. Edwards, 1979) argue that management performs a *dual* function in the enterprise. Managerial practices are a necessary means of *Coordinating* diverse activities and services, particularly as production becomes a more collective process. However, they also bear the imprint of the antagonistic social relations within the capitalist labour process. These require management to carry out functions of *control* and surveillance, exercising hierarchical authority over workers separated from the means of production. Though it is not always clear that it is possible to distinguish between a 'neutral' co-ordination and an 'antagonistic' control, managers do act as agents carrying out the 'global functions' of capital, functions which, were delegated as part of the bureaucratisation of production. The idea of agency conjures up rather crude images of conspiracies and empty vessels: 'In the capitalist system, the principal function of management is to exploit labour power to the maximum in order to secure profits for the owners of capital' (Berkeley Thomas, 1993: 61). But the generality 'to the maximum' is meaningless. There are only specific and diverse means through which the requirements of capital are brought about, in which management takes an active rather than a predetermined role.

Radical analyses often get tangled up in attempts to designate managers to precise class positions. This theme does not concern us here (though see Johnston, 1986 for a critical account). What is important is that we have available a framework for understanding management practices which provides an alternative to the dominant combination of behavioural and managerial revolution theories. The fact, for example, that executives of a large corporation have the formal status of employees is, as Braverman observes, merely the form given to the domination of capital in modern society:

> Their formal attribute of being part of the same payroll as the production workers, clerks and porters of the corporation no more robs them of the powers of decision and command over the others in the enterprise than does the fact that the general, like the private, wears the military uniform, or the pope and the cardinal pronounce the same liturgy as the parish priest. (1974: 405)

Instead of the separation of ownership and control, radical writers distinguish between *real* or economic ownership and agents holding actual *possession* (De Vroey, 1975; Carchedi, 1977). Managerial agents are governed by the external constraints imposed by the dynamics of competition and capital accumulation, with profitability remaining the crucial criteria through which the successful management work is judged. If anything, this is enhanced by property ownership and related forms of control becoming increasingly depersonalised with the rise of finance, pension funds and other institutional shareholders. Individual enterprises become 'simply units in a structure of intercorporate relations' (J. Scott, 1985: 142), the division of ownership and possession resulting in greater vulnerability for managers who know they may be removed from office (Holland, 1975).

A structural analysis does not imply that the growth of new forms of managerial labour is irrelevant. The heterogeneity of management has increased with the sheer extent and diversity of delegated functions and the competing groups, such as accountants and engineers, who lay claim to them. Within an increasingly complex hierarchy, middle and lower-level managers occupy 'contradictory class locations' (E. O. Wright, 1976) carrying out functions as agents of capital *and* as salaried employees. They are likely to exercise 'partial' possession; operational rather than allocative control, to use the language of organisational analysis (Carter, 1985: 122). We shall return to the significance of these divisions later.

Management strategies

Radical perspectives have been conditioned by Braverman's (1974) argument that the twentieth century has seen the tightening of managerial control, primarily through the application of Taylorist and scientific management strategies. Detailed evidence is provided of the extension of such methods from simple to complex production and their use in the transformation of clerical labour. When allied to managerial shaping of science and technology through mechanisation and automation, work design and organisation continue to embody key Taylorist principles such as task fragmentation and the separation of conception and execution. Braverman provided an important corrective to the widespread view that Taylorism was a failed system, superseded by more sophisticated behavioural theories to be used for motivational and job design tools (see M. Rose, 1975).

But it is widely recognised that Braverman overestimated the dominance of Taylorist strategies and practices, and underestimated the varied and uneven implementation, influenced by worker hostility, management suspicion and appropriateness to given environments. If Taylorism is taken to be part of a broader movement towards 'scientific' management focused on fragmentation of tasks and their subjection to increasing job measurement and evaluation, as well as the structuring of work processes so that skills and planning activities are located off the factory and office floor, then particular elements remain a highly significant component of control strategies, though seldom on their own.

Precisely because Braverman confused a particular system of control with management control in general, the question of *strategy* was put firmly on the agenda because of the resulting debate on alternatives. This is not to say that issues of strategy had no place in the existing organisational literature. How Chandler (1962) regarded strategy, defined as long-term planning and resource allocation to carry out goals, as the characteristic feature of the modern multi-divisional firm. But control over employees was not dealt with systematically. Strategy has also been increasingly part of the agenda of the business policy and corporate management literature (Steiner and Miner, 1978). Radical perspectives differ from both in avoiding the prescriptive search for the 'best way'; remaining free to analyse what management *does*, rather than what it *should* do.

What of the alternative strategies raised in the labour process debate? Some of the best-known contributions have already been discussed in previous chapters. Richard Edward's (1979) model is based on historically successive dominant modes of control which reflect worker resistance and changing socio-economic conditions. A nineteenth-century system of *simple* or *personal* control by employers exercising direct authority gave way to more complex *structural* forms with the transition from small business, competitive capitalism to corporate monopolies. The first of these forms was *technical* control typified by the use of the assembly line which can pace and direct the labour process. The contradiction for management is that it created a common work experience and basis for unified shop floor opposition. In contrast, a system of *bureaucratic* control embedded in the social and organisational structure of the firm rather than in personal authority, offers management a means of re-dividing the workforce and tying it to impersonal rules and regulations. With his co-thinkers among radical economists (R. Edwards *et al.*, 1975; Gordon *et al.*, 1982), Edwards has also argued that employers consciously create *segmented* labour markets as a response to economic crises and as a divide and rule strategy, particularly using gender and race.

In contrast, Friedman (1977) rightly eschews the notion of stages, preferring to set out ideal types or strategic poles of responsible autonomy and direct control which run parallel throughout the history of capitalism. Each strategy generates its own inflexibilities in areas such as hiring and firing and task specification. The choice of strategy is governed by variations in the stability of labour and product markets, mediated by the interplay of worker resistance and managerial pressure. There is, however, an element of common ground in the belief that there has been a gradual historical tendency towards more consensual, integrative strategies, internal markets, institutionalised rules and in some cases, work humanisation schemes. This is also the view of the other major control theorist, Burawoy (1979, 1985). He periodises the development of capitalist work organisation in terms of the transition from *despotic* to *hegemonic* regimes. The former involved relations of dependence and coercion that did not prove viable for capital or labour. Workers sought collective representation and social protection from the state. Capital also had an interest in state regulation of conflict and a minimal social wage that would boost purchasing power. The shift to hegemonic regimes was also based on an internal state in the workplace that provided an 'industrial citizenship', using grievance machinery and regulated bargaining that minimised possible resistance and class solidarity.

This kind of judgement of long-term trends has not looked quite so accurate in a period where many companies have used the recession to restructure the workplace. Whereas some writers (see MacInnes, 1987) doubt whether the basic features of industrial and employment relations have significantly changed, there is certainly considerable evidence that in Britain and the USA many employers are consciously reconstituting employment practices in a harsher and more authoritarian way. In the USA (Parker, 1985) there have been aggressive de-unionisation campaigns and 'concession-bargaining' which forces workers to renegotiate worse pay and conditions. Although Britain's deeply-rooted union tradition largely prevents extensive de-unionisation and concession-bargaining, there has been a strong emphasis, particularly in the newer industries, on single-union and 'no-strike' deals; reduced demarcation and increased flexibility; more direct management communication with the shop floor, by-passing shop stewards; as well as new human resource initiatives such as quality circles (Morgan and Sayer, 1984.

Events of this nature have led Burawoy to define the new dominant factory regime as one of *hegemonic despotism*. This is not a return to arbitrary tyranny, but the apparently 'rational' power of a capital that is mobile across the globe, over the workforce. (1985: 150). But regardless of the pervasiveness of such trends, new conceptual categories of this nature merely illustrate the fundamental problem of the control theories we have been examining. Alternative strategies have been put on the map, but too often within what has been described as the 'panacea fallacy' (Littler and Salaman, 1982) or 'monism' (Storey, 1985). That is, the idea that capital always seeks and finds definitive and comprehensive modes of control as the solution to its problems. Admittedly, this is somewhat less true of Friedman, who in his own defence argues that responsible autonomy and direct control have in-built contradictions and are, 'two directions towards which managers can move, rather than two predefined states between which managers choose' (1987: 3). But there is still a sense of a search for all-embracing categories, which have their parallels in behavioural theory, such as Etzioni's (1961) structures of compliance, or Schein's (1965) linear models of economic, social and complex man.

Nevertheless, the control debate has sparked off an extensive and useful amount of empirical work within the parameters of labour process theory. Early case studies tended to focus on reaffirmation of theses of deskilling and tighter controls (Zimbalist, 1979), or critiques of them highlighting moderating factors such as markets and worker resistance (Wood, 1982). More recent efforts have been concerned to establish trends in their own right. Studies dealing with the introduction of new technology have stressed that deskilling and direct control represent only one aspect of a range of management strategies. We have already discussed the variations shown in Wilkinson's study. John Child's (1985) research shows even more clearly how ideas of strategy can be used, whilst recognising variations in goals and environments. He identified a variety of strategies, including elimination of direct labour, sub-contracting, polyvalence or multi-tasking and job degradation. These were connected to an even wider set of influences, including those of national economic cycles, government policy and the culture of organisations.

Some research has tried to apply models to specific industries, but without any claims for universality. A good example is the use by Murray and Wickham (1985) of Richard Edwards's theory of bureaucratic control. They studied two Irish electronics factories employing mainly female semi-skilled workers, showing that direction, discipline and evaluation are all carried out according to explicit rules rather than direct controls. Supervisors do not monitor production performance and enforce discipline. This is left to inspectors on the basis of statistical records that can identify the operators responsible. Supervisors, however, are central to processes of evaluating the social character of the 'good worker' in order to facilitate promotion through the internal labour market. The elaborate and artificial hierarchy created at the plants meant that one-third of workers had been promoted from the basic assembly grade, thus confirming Edward's view that employees are given positive material reasons for complying with bureaucratic rules.

Other studies have focused on specific strategies and processes of control such as recruitment policies (Fevre, 1986; Maguire, 1986; Winstanley, 1986) which are neglected in an exclusive focus on the labour process. The most extensive research has been carried out on *gender*. Socially-defined notions of femininity as a form of control have been observed in multi-nationals operating in the Third World (Pearson, 1986). Plant management consciously exploits cultures of passivity and subordination by combining an image of the company as a patriarchal family system with the manager as father figure, with Western-style beauty competitions and classes (Grossman, 1979). In the West, Grieco and Whipp's overview argues that 'managerial strategies of control make use of and enhance the sexual divisions in society' (1986: 136). Studies of office and factory workers (Glenn and Feldberg, 1979; Pollert, 1981; West wood, 1984; Bradley, 1986) show that management use womens' marginality to work, arising from the family, to frame their labour control policies. Strategies of paternalism and restrictive controls on supervision and piece-rates are frequent, though not always successful or uncontested.

In reflecting on the above debates, a degree of common ground emerges. Product and labour markets, worker resistance and a range of other external and internal factors are recognised as moderating control strategies and shaping power relations in the frontier of control between capital and labour. The variations in strategy that result are not random, but reflect the fundamental tension we have talked of between managements' need to control and discipline, while engaging workers' commitment and cooperation. Strategies therefore contain inherent contradictions (Storey, 1985; Hyman, 1987). These are enhanced by the difficulty of harmonising the different managerial functions, sites of intervention and decision-making, that include technology, social organisation of labour and relations with the representative bodies of employees. Hyman notes that, 'there is no "one best way" of managing these contradictions, only different routes to partial failure' (1987: 30). Management of large organisations is therefore likely to try combinations of control strategies and practices, appropriate to particular environments or sections of the workforce. As one of us has remarked elsewhere:

> The most consistent weakness of existing theory has been to counterpoise one form of control to another . . . No one has convincingly demonstrated that a particular form of control is necessary or inevitable for capitalism to function successfully. (P. Thompson, 1989: 151)

Questioning the idea of control strategies

The above 'consensus' does not satisfy those within and outside the radical perspective who are critical of the explanatory power of concepts of management control strategy. For some, the problem with a Marxist-influenced agenda is that, like more orthodox accounts, it wrongly assumes high levels of rationality, this time applied to top management (Bryman, 1984: 401). Others go beyond the previously-noted criticism of 'panacea fallacies' to object to the treatment of management as omniscient, omnipotent and monolithic. Based on her study of chemical plants, Harris mocks the image of managers who have the attributes of deity and 'papal innerrancy' when dealing with workers, commenting that radical writers assume that senior management 'always know what is in capital's interests and unfailingly order things so that they work together for its greater good' (1987: 70). There are conflicts within management reflecting contending interests groups and the difficulty of carrying out integrative functions. Nor is it always possible to draw a neat dividing line between workers and managers, given that managers are also wage labourers subject to controls. The distortions in such analyses are held to derive from a wider determinism and functionalism in which 'managers are regarded as unproblematic agents of capital who dispatch their 'global functions' in a rationalistic manner' (Storey, 1985: 195).

Capital's interests are not given and management practices cannot be 'read-off from them. Assumptions of a 'tight-coupling' underestimate the diversity and complexity of such practices, and the significance for decision-making processes within the enterprise. It is also the case that in addition to the responsibilities that managers have to the control apparatus of the enterprise, they need to control their own personal identities and make sense of their own work in the employing organisation. Managerial work therefore has a 'double control' aspect in which there is a strategic exchange between individuals and organisations (T. Watson, 1994). The consequence of the above critiques is the belief that too few insights are generated into what 'flesh and blood' managers actually do.

At a general level many of these criticisms would be accepted across a wide spectrum. But some would carry it much further:' 'current uses of the terms "strategy" and "control" are somewhat misleading guides both to actual management conduct and to the causes of particular outcomes in work organisation and industrial relations' (Rose and Jones, 1985: 82). We can break this down into two issues: do identifiable management strategies exist? and are practices centred on controlling workers? Those who argue against the idea of coherent strategies with a fixity of purpose believe that management activities are more likely to be piecemeal, uncoordinated and fragmented, with at best a striving for logical incrementalism. Management is concerned primarily with 'keeping the show on the road' (Tomlinson, 1982: 128), corresponding with the 'realist' views discussed earlier.

Supportive research exists in areas such as work reorganisation schemes (Rose and Jones, 1985) and new technology and skills in engineering (Campbell and Currie, 1987). Any strategic capacity is held to be inevitably undermined by a plethora of sites of decision-making; varied objectives among different management specialists and interest groups; the need to smooth over diverse and contradictory practices; and the requirement of sustaining a consensual accommodation with employee organisations. The result is an unpredictable variety of managerial intentions characterised by a 'plant particularism' (Rose and Jones, 1985: 96), and control structures as merely 'temporary outcomes' (Storey, 1985). Campbell and Currie plump for the idea of 'negotiated preferences' and there is a general orientation towards explanations based on *practices* rather than strategy.

Some of these differences may reflect the sector being researched. For example, engineering is well known for its 'seat-of-the-pants' approach to management, whereas other sectors such as food or chemicals are noted for a more strategic approach. Nevertheless, this kind of approach is confirmed by some writers on industrial relations (Purcell and Sissons, 1983), who note the problems created by the absence of management strategies towards their own employees, particularly of strategies that are integrated into overall business objectives. Instead there is a continued dominance of reactive and opportunistic practices directed towards immediate problem-solving (Thurley and Wood, 1983: 209). What *kind* of strategy is said to be absent is not always made explicit. But the basic model used is similar to that popularised by Chandler, which, like many other adaptations to the business sphere, is strongly influenced by military experience and terminology (Shaw, 1990). That is, detailed and co-ordinated plans of campaign in which conscious, long-term planning based on corporate goals is supported by appropriate courses of action and allocation of resources. This can be seen in the business policy debate (Steiner and Miner, 1978) in which the burgeoning number of MBA students are warned of the negative consequences of the absence of corporate strategy.

But conceptions of management strategy in the above frameworks are in themselves problematic. A stereotyped polarity is set up between a conception of objective rationality which implies perfect foresight, choice and follow-through, and a bounded rationality of constrained choice in complex realities. Complaining that discourses of strategy are primarily about shoring up the power of senior managers and consultants, Knights and Morgan reject the concept altogether: 'Nothing new is really added by talking the discourse of strategy; on the contrary, a limit is put on our understanding of the special phenomenon because we are forcing action into a particular rationalistic and individualistic framework' (1990: 480). But the mistake is actually made by the critics. It is they who force action into a conceptual straitjacket. By adopting a straw man of 'strong' strategy, they have set criteria for strategy so stringently that it becomes impossible to meet them (J. Child, 1985).

Although it is wrong to attribute rational intent to management, it is equally mistaken to assume that strategy has to be seen as always consistent, systematic and without contradiction. Strategies may not always be effectively followed through at the implementation stage, as with the introduction of new technology. They may not constitute a coherent package for the whole operation of a company, perhaps manifesting a disjuncture between job design plans and employee relations. Coherence is an important variable, but it has to be set against the knowledge of inevitable contradictions and the likelihood of 'loose-coupling' between planning and practices. Strategies are likely to be accompanied by bargaining within management and with the workforce, so making the end result uncertain. As Friedman rightly notes, 'Irrationality, inconsistency, lack of system certainly exist and must be allowed for; however, a more useful concept to introduce is failure' (1987: 294). Even where changes are introduced without clear intent, they can establish the preconditions for subsequent strategy (Hyman, 1987: 47).

Managers frequently act on the world with poor information, but they can and do act strategically. It is only necessary for researchers to show a degree of intent or planning, and to infer a logic over a period of time from the frequency and pattern of action, or from 'emergent outcomes' (Hales, 1988: 12). The same criteria apply to the activities of workers. Groups such as printers or doctors do not always behave in a fully conscious or coherent manner. But observation reveals a clear pattern of operation of occupational and job controls, and strategies of closure aimed at excluding competitors, often women (Cockburn, 1983; Witz, 1986). The latter point reinforces research on households that shows that strategies emerge from 'bottom-up', day-to-day activities; a weaker, but still legitimate sense of strategy that relies on social scientists observing and analysing predictable patterns (Wallace, 1993).

Of course, the capacity for strategy is not random. Certain external conditions are likely to push management in that direction. Streek (1987) puts forward a persuasive case that economic crisis and rapidly changing market environments have created a 'general strategic problem' whose core element is the need for *flexibility*. However, the very nature of uncertainty and varied conditions in sectors and countries produces different strategic responses. For example, countries such as West Germany and Austria, with traditions of tripartite state, union and employer bargaining, have seen moves towards flexibility that retains a strong union role and corporatist regulation of wages and labour markets. Streek's analysis not only builds in an explanation of such variations, it provides a framework for understanding the general conditions under which strategies develop. At times of crisis and readjustment, 'the variety of strategies and structures within the collectivity of firms is bound to increase at least until a new standard of "best practice" has been established' (1987: 284). This is not the case at all times. More stable environments produce routinisation of decisions, with management practices governed by tactical accommodations rather than strategic thinking. Britain in the 1950s is a case in point. Economic expansion and new markets, combined with labour shortages, created conditions for the growth of powerful shop steward structures and localised bargaining. Industrial relations were characterised by short-term considerations and 'fire-fighting' which became a dangerous liability for employers as conditions changed in the next decade.

The second strand of critique questions whether the centrality given to control of labour is actually reflective of managerial behaviour. It is argued that we cannot view management strategies and tactics from the vantage point of the labour process, but must consider the role of product and labour markets, and technologies. Control proceeds in a complex cycle from planning to implementation, involving groups such as accountants and industrial engineers. Analysis should focus on the 'multiple constituents' of management expertise beyond the confrontation of capital and labour in the control of the labour process' (Miller and O'Leary, 1987: 10). Such a critique can be presented in a 'Marxist' form. Accumulation and costs of production are what matters to capital and its agents, not control. If anything, managers are dominated by problems of the *outcomes* of the labour process, including sales, marketing, supply and cash flow. Kelly uses the concept of the full circuit of capital to argue that we must be concerned not only with the *extraction* of surplus value through controlling the labour process, but its *realisation* through the sale of commodities, as well as the prior *purchase* of labour. On these grounds, 'there is no sound reason for privileging any moment in the circuit' (J. E. Kelly, 1985: 32).

Iin their research into the Imperial Tobacco Group in the 1970s Morgan and Hooper use a similar framework to distinguish between three circuits of capital: *industrial* capital refers to that used in the management and design of the production process itself; *commercial* refers to the sphere of buying and selling and therefore functions such as marketing, advertising; and *banking* refers to the process of capital used in lending and borrowing, governed by accountancy and financial controls. These distinctions are used to argue that radical theories of the labour process have often lost sight of the role of capital and ownership because of the emphasis on management control. The case study shows a series of strategies pursued simultaneously, representing the particular circuits. To break out of a static tobacco market, top management prioritised commercial and banking strategies, rather than developing existing labour processes. In particular, companies such as Imperial were drawn into investments in the share and gilts markets. These proved successful, but when the resultant money was invested in production they had disastrous results. Firms are thus conceptualised as 'sites of a complex integration of circuits of capital' (1987: 623), which management must integrate and control.

Other writers question whether control can be regarded as the factor which distinguishes between a dominant management and subordinate labour. Management has non-control functions and characteristics of employees, whereas workers exercise job controls and may be involved in the regulation of others (Melling, 1982: 249). At a more theoretical level, Cressey and MacInnes (1980) observe that workers have an interest in the viability of their own units of capital as well as in resisting subordination, matching capital's dual relationship with labour as a commodity and as a source of co-operation necessary for profitable production. Some mainstream writers use their own research into the chemical industry (Harris, 1987) and the chemicals, engineering and biscuit industries – for example, (Buchanan, 1986) – to argue that workers basically accept managerial authority, give commitment and effort willingly, and have convergent interests with management, thus negating any preoccupation with control. This is likely to be linked to a rejection of 'zero-sum' conceptions of power in which one side necessarily gains at the expense of the other (Harris, 1987: *77)*. Even some radical writers believe that capital and management are not necessarily dominant, with unions having considerably more power, even in a recession, than is usually acknowledged (J. E. Kelly, 1985: 49; M. Rose and Jones, 1985: 101).

It is certainly true that, as Hyman observes: 'If most orthodox literature on business strategy ignores or marginalises the conflict between capital and labour, most Marxist literature perceives nothing else' (1987: 34). This has a curious parallel with the virtual total emphasis in organisation behaviour on 'man-management'. So, the full circuit of capital is a very useful and necessary concept for understanding the capitalist enterprise. Furthermore, change and crisis often arise from disarticulation of the moments of the circuit (J. E. Kelly, 1985), as we saw in the Imperial example. Such concepts can be combined with more orthodox accounts of the changing pattern of *corporate control* that plot how large firms seek to solve their competitive problems by reshaping structures and forms of intervention in the market (Fligstein, 1990). Such 'modes of control' have included vertical and horizontal integration; the multi-divisional form; and more recently, financial means of integrating diverse portfolios built up through acquisition.

However, these perspectives do not invalidate a specific emphasis on relations of control between capital and labour. This is not just another process equivalent to marketing or financial accounting. The management of workers and work remains at the heart of the enterprise and indeed of economic reproduction as a whole. But such an orientation need have no marginalising effect on the analysis of other social relations. As P. K. Edwards (1987) observes, the problem of 'privileging' one part of the circuit arises only if the analysis assumes that this one part determines what happens in the others.

Nor are we saying that control is normally the *goal* of management; but rather that it is a *means* embodied in strategies and techniques. It is true that management strategies are not always developed with labour's role in mind. But it is ultimately difficult to separate a concern with 'outcomes' such as product quality or financial targets from acting on labour in some way. Strategies towards markets or technologies will often be constrained or moderated by labour policies and the practices of workers (Friedman, 1987). In addition, as John Child notes: 'strategies which are unspecific towards the labour process may still have relevance for it' (1985: 110). An example is the introduction of new technology, which much research shows is frequently used as a means of more general work reorganisation.

On the issue of the existence of co-operation and common interests, we would wholly concur. In fact, we would go further. As one of us has observed: 'Workers do not always need to be overtly controlled. They may effectively "control" themselves' (P. Thompson, 1989: 153). Participation in routine practices to create interest or increase rewards can generate *consent* to existing structures of control and power, as Burawoy's (1979) famous studies of production 'games' indicate. What is puzzling is why some writers insist on co-operative and consensual processes being counterposed to those of control and conflict. It is increasingly recognised that all have to be theorised as different products of the contradictory relations within the enterprise. Not only do consent and control coexist, 'the mobilisation of consent' forms an increasingly central part of management–employee relations strategies in the newer sectors influenced by Japanese practices.

We also accept that workers exercise controls, but it would be a serious mistake to regard these controls as *equivalent* to those of management. This would fail to distinguish between *types* of control, particularly between the general and detailed dimensions referred to earlier in the chapter. At the general level of direction of production, managerial dominance is guaranteed by their stewardship of the crucial organisational resources. This is not 'zero-sum' because it cannot be 'added up'. Clearly, however, control of immediate work processes is largely zero-sum, in that if workers control a given item, then management cannot also do so (P. K. Edwards, 1990).

Bringing the threads together: management as a labour process

What is required is a structural analysis that can account for both the constraints on and complexities of managerial behaviour: a perspective that is neither deterministic or voluntaristic. *One* way forward begins from a remark made by Braverman, that 'Management has become administration, which is a labour process conducted for the purpose of control within the corporation, and conducted moreover as a labour process exactly analogous to the process of production' (1974: 267). An offshoot is that the alienating conditions attached to the purchase and sale of labour become part of the managerial apparatus itself. Though little more than an aside, it has been utilised by a number of writers, notably Teulings (1986), to produce an analysis of management's role in the administrative apparatus of industrial organisations. The very fact that management is a 'global agent' carrying out the delegated functions of capital, means that it is part of a collective labour process at corporate level. As we have previously indicated, this delegation in part reflects the transfer of functions such as co-ordination from the market to management and administration.

Table 4.2 Institutionalisation of distinctive management functions at separate levels of management

	Function	Levels
I	the ownership function	institutional management
	— accumulation of capital	— creation and preservation of
II	the administrative function	legitimations
		strategic management
	— Allocation of investments	— development of objectives
III	the innovative function	structuring management
	— product market development	— new combinations of production factors
IV	the production function	operational management
	— control of the direct labour	— direction and co-ordination of direct
	process	labour

Source: W. M. Teulings, 'Managerial Labour Processes in Organised Capitalism', *Managing the Labour Process,* D. Knights and H. Willmott (eds), Gower, 1986.

As that role has evolved, it has also become *differentiated*. So, for example, large administrative divisions are, in the case of accounting; 'producing nothing but elaborate mechanisms of control associated with the realisation of capital and its enlargement' (T. Johnson, 1980: 355). But it is not only a case of the emergence of specialised functions and departments.

Differentiation also takes place in terms of *levels*. Teulings puts forward a model based on the existence of four distinct management functions: ownership, administrative, innovative, and production (see Table 4.2). Two major consequences of the new division of labour follow. First, though the power of the administrative machinery of which management is a part has increased, the power of *individual* managers tends to diminish, due to the rationalisation and routinisation of their activities. With the development of more complex managerial structures, new techniques have been introduced to integrate, monitor and control middle and lower management (Carter, 1985: 98).

> Years ago there might be five hundred fellas but you would only have one boss. Now everyone has a chief . . . You can't discuss the job with them, everything is ticked in little boxes now. The boss is scared because if they don't treat everyone in a standard way they are afraid the other bosses will report them. (Plessey engineer, quoted in Thompson and Bannon, 1985: 170)

Hale's analysis of management divisions of labour qualifies Teulings by showing that some management functions – those that the latter designates as operational – have their origins in the labour process rather than the market, and that there is not an exact correspondence between functions and levels. Those divisions are vertically fractionalised so that 'there is a differentiation within the performance of management work in terms of the extent to which agents are involved in the decision-making process' (Hales, 1988: 10). As Watson (1994) shows in his account of a major UK telecommunications firm, even senior plant-level managers will frequently find themselves frustrated by centralised control in companies that takes place at the cost their strategic inputs orientated towards long-term viability, from. Many will be subordinated to senior management through merely providing information from which decisions are made.

Managers managing other managers takes place in different forms in the modern corporation, whether it be multi-divisional structures, holding companies or conglomerates, where varying forms of decentralisation go hand-in-hand with increased accountability and monitoring. At a micro-level, techniques such as management by objectives are still important, though presented as a form of control and motivation arising from the *objective* demands of the task (Drucker, 1955), which reproduces an aspect of the relationship workers have with 'scientific management'. In other cases, managers become more literally victims of their own devices (Storey, 1983: 93), as shown in studies such as Nichols and Beynon (1977) on the chemical industry. The latter additionally note the flattening out of career structures and exposure to redundancy, characteristic of many managers. We know from other evidence (V. Smith, 1990) that middle managers in particular are becoming prime victims of organisational restructuring. Even the detailed studies of management functions discussed earlier in the chapter, have the purpose of restructuring and rationalisation. Both Mintzberg (1973) and Drucker (1979) favour using techniques to split-off routine activities from senior layers, introducing separation of conception and execution within management itself. This can now be further aided by computer technology and information systems.

The second consequence of changes in the managerial labour process is the growth of structural conflicts and imbalances between the different levels and functions. Teulings argues that each level of management tends to follow a rational logic of its own, enhancing the potential for defence of specific group interests – for example, between production-orientated operational management and the strata concerned with innovation in product markets. Such tendencies are worsened by the absence, or limits to, formal mechanisms to resolve or bargain conflicts. Instead they are likely to be dealt with at the operational level, leading to a disproportionate emphasis on changing the practices of shop floor workers.

One effect not discussed by Teulings is on managerial *ideologies*. The legitimatory content in management thought has traditionally been directed towards two objectives: convincing non-management groups who challenged managerial goals and activities; and sustaining common aspirations (J. Child, 1969: 228–9). This becomes more problematic with the development of competing claims to fashion management theories and practices. Such competition cannot be wholly understood within the kind of framework which talks of levels. It neglects the role of what Armstrong calls *interprofessional competition* (1984, 1986, 1987b). It has long been recognised that professional groups pursue market strategies based on claims to exclusivity of knowledge and monopolies over a set of practices (T. Johnson, 1972; H. Brown, 1980). But the examples and models have mostly come from the older and 'social' professions such as law and medicine, with professions active in business have seldom figuring as prominently.

One of the reasons for the neglect is that the sociology of the professions has emphasised the traditional 'role conflict' between professional autonomy and the bureaucratic principles of work organisation (Child, 1982; Rueschemeyer, 1986). Radical writers interpret these trends in terms of the conflict between acting for capital, and increasingly taking on the characteristics of employees. Some refer to the growth of a new professional-managerial class (Ehrenreich and Ehrenreich, 1979), with others preferring to talk of the proletarianisation of the 'middle layers' (Braverman, 1974). Though some insights can be gained from such perspectives, a primary focus on issues of class location is limited. Armstrong's model allows us to focus on the specific role of the professions in the managerial labour process.

However, Armstrong is critical of the latter concept. He agrees that lower management has been subject to greater controls and its own version of the separation of conception and execution, but he is concerned that attention is drawn away from the basic contradiction between labour and capital, legitimising the existence of any form of unproductive activity by referring to it as a labour process in its own right. But as long as the connections to the dominant capital–labour contradiction are maintained, we see no reason why the concept cannot be usefully employed. Armstrong prefers to talk of struggles for control within capital, reflecting the, 'tensions and contradictions within the agency relationship' (1989: 312). In other words, employers and senior managers are inescapably dependent on other agencies to secure corporate goals and policies.

So, in practice, management functions for capital are moderated by competition between occupational groups. Each profession has a core of specialist knowledge and activities which can form the basis of advancement through a 'collective mobility project'. But the core can only be effectively used if it is sufficiently indeterminate to prevent parts being detached, or routinised. Whereas the general point might apply to all professions, those active in *business* have to face rival claims over the carrying out of control functions. For example, drawing on the work of Layton (1969), Armstrong (1986: 26) argues that scientific management's techniques and justification for the control of labour through the 'planning department' was an expression of an ideology of engineering. Industrial engineering rests on the design of operating procedures which monitor and control labour costs (Storey, 1983: 275). But the attempt to place engineers at the apex of the firm through the diffusion of such techniques has clearly not been fully achieved, given that engineers do not predominate in the higher levels of management. At the heart of the 'failure' lies the difficulty of maintaining a monopoly over control practices which could be carried out by others.

To make matters worse, British development has taken place based on a definition of management hostile to engineering. This is because of a combination of finance and marketing as favoured specialisms, and the tendency to define management as a set of general functions and skills divorced from productive expertise (see earlier in this chapter). One commentator noted that a result has been, 'a whole generation of MBA students who will not go near a manufacturing strategy . . . They want to be in at the gin-and-tonic end with the financial strategy' (quoted in Armstrong, 1987b: 428). Other professions have gained because of the popular belief that the education of engineers does not equip them for dealing with people and money. As a potential agency they therefore experience difficulty in establishing the vital commodity of 'trust' with those in positions of power. It is therefore not surprising that many engineers seek a route out of production into senior management through courses such as MBAs. The consequent low status of engineering identified in the Finneston Report and by Child *et al.* (1983) is, however, as we have seen, a peculiarly Anglo–American phenomenon. In contrast, West German management is dominated by professional engineers, due in part to the historical relevance of engineering techniques and technical education to competition with British and other manufacturing goods, and to access to training in financial techniques.

In the case of accounting and other financial specialisms, there has been a dramatic rise from the days of poorly paid clerks and book-keeping tasks. Some of the factors involved include the development of *management* accounting as a cost control technique in the industrial restructuring during and after the depression of the mid-1920s. In the USA, the control function of management accounting can be clearly identified in the following definition from the National Association of Accountants:

> the process of identification, measurement, accumulation, analysis, preparation, interpretation, and communication of financial information used by management to plan, evaluate and control within an organisation and to ensure appropriate use and accountability for its resources, (quoted in Wardell, 1986: 28)

Other factors include, once again, the need for co-ordination and control over middle managers in multi-divisional companies; and the legal requirements for control through auditing. The cohesiveness of an accounting elite in business has been facilitated by the acceptance of an inevitable 'horizontal fissure' in the profession. This has allowed a range of routine tasks to be delegated to 'accounting technicians' (T. Johnson, 1980; Glover *et al.*, 1991), thus maintaining indeterminacy and monopoly over core practices. Accountants have also undertaken an aggressive campaign to encroach on the spheres of other professions through such measures as manpower audits and human resource accounting (Armstrong, 1986: 32). Though only a minority are closer to real power, the spread of a 'financial rationality' means that British boardrooms are increasingly dominated by those with a background in banking or accountancy, within a 'managerial culture which is often preoccupied with accounting measures and procedures' (Armstrong, 1988).

Such developments have begun to threaten the power of the *personnel* function, a segment of management which had also enjoyed a major long-term growth. From the days of its origins in company welfare workers, the Institute of Personnel Managers now has more than 20000 members. Throughout that development personnel professionals have had a continual struggle to convince business power-holders that they could move from welfare to general management functions. They consolidated a hold over administrative functions such as interviewing and record-keeping, as well as expanding into the newer areas of staff development and determination of wage rates and incentives (Carter, 1985: 102). In a partnership of mutual convenience, the behavioural sciences have helped develop a mystique that, 'the personnel manager is probably the only specialist in the organisation whose role can be distinguished by the virtually exclusive concern with the management of human assets' (Mullins, 1985: 129). But the problematic of 'dealing with people' has inherent limits in establishing a monopoly of knowledge or practice, particularly when its 'behavioural nostrums' are routinely taught to the full range of business students (Fowler, 1985). It is therefore unsurprising that surveys (Daniel and Millward, 1983) have reported a lack of qualified and trained personnel staff in many companies. Fortunately for the profession other factors have been working in their favour, notably the spate of employee legislation and codes of practice in the 1960s and 1970s, and the recommendations of the Donovan Report (1968) that firms should central-ise and formalise their bargaining procedures. Both measures allowed personnel to extend and monopolise spheres of expertise, as well exercise greater authority over lower line managers (Armstrong, 1986: 37).

But deregulation of labour markets, decentralisation of bargaining and scrapping of aspects of employment law, have given a further twist to the ratchet of inter-professional competition by eroding or redistributing established personnel func-tions. This is complicated by the rise of Human Resource Management (HRM). On the surface it seems positive – after all, personnel managers have long trumpeted the importance of treating human resources as an organisation's greatest asset rather than as a cost to be minimised. HRM can then be seen as an upmarket version of personnel with a tactical name change (Torrington, 1989). This is perhaps the 'soft' version of HRM, with the harder versions stressing the integration of the manage-ment of human resources into core business strategy and practice (Guest, 1989; Storey, 1989). The significance of the latter is that it enables, perhaps necessitates, other managerial groups, particularly line managers, to take HRM 'on-board'.

Whether it is *in fact* becoming more strategic or more effective is open to dispute (Guest, 1990), but the perception of greater centrality has sparked off a struggle by managers across a variety of functions to absorb the rhetoric and responsibilities of HRM (Poole and Mansfield, 1992). The efforts of traditional practioners to defend and carve out new territories was not helped by a widely reported study from a team at the London School of Economics that produced headlines of 'Personnel officers are a waste of time says new study' (*Independent on Sunday*, 15 May 1994). Perhaps, like other professional groups, personnel is heading for a split: 'a polarised profes-sion consisting of a mass of "clerks of works", performing routine administrative work for a newly self-confident line management, whilst a few elite "architects" of strategic human – resources policy continue to operate at the corporate headquar-ters level' (Armstrong, 1988: 25).

The kind of analysis in this section usefully adds to an understanding of the com-plex levels and functions within the managerial labour process. As Whitely (1984) argues, there is limited standardisation across managerial tasks and this helps to explain the lack of progress in establishing management *as such* as a profession. The growth of MBAs and other qualifications suggests attempts to develop certification of skills and knowledge, as well as a career route. But they can best be seen as a form of individual credentialism and filter into higher-paid jobs, and not necessarily a convincing one, with some employers showing considerable scepticism (Oliver, 1993). The jibe 'masters of bugger all' may be unfair, but it reflects historic tensions between generalism and specialism, as well as a feeling that the content of many courses is pitched above business requirements and the realities of middle manage-ment work. It may be that employers, at least in the UK, will turn towards a more practical competency-based certification through the Management Charter Initiative or other aspects of the National Council for Vocational Qualifications.

A focus on competing agencies and professions also emphasises the specific his-torical bases and differences in the development of management theories and prac-tices; particularly between different national traditions, though we have little space to elaborate on them here. The discussion also embodies the general purpose of this chapter, that of developing a structural analysis of management that recognises the contradictory sources of influence over activity. Hence it becomes possible to utilise a conception of agency that accepts considerable variation in management practices, as well as enabling us to understand the rise of new groups competing for influence. For example, business consultants, research and development engineers and IT analysts are using their knowledge to challenge the existing expert division of labour (Reed, 1992a).

Of course, this is far from the last word on these issues. For example, Chapter 11 attempts to develop an understanding of the individual and subjective orientations of managers compatible with the framework outlined here. But for now, we move to the related theme of power.

Reference

Armstrong, P. (1986) 'Management Control Strategies and InterProfessional Competition: the Cases of Accountancy and Personnel Management', in D. Knights and H. Willmott (eds) *Managing the Labour Process*, Aldershot: Gower.

Armstrong, P. (1987a) The Divorce of Productive and Unproductive Management, paper to 5th International Labour Process Conference, Aston.

Armstrong, P. (1987b) 'Engineers, Management and Trust', Work, Employment and Society, vol. 1, no. 4: 421–40.

Armstrong, P. (1988) 'The Personnel Profession in the Age of Management Accountancy', Personnel Review, vol. 17, no. 1: 25–31.

Armstrong, P. (1989) Management, Labour Process and Agency', *Work, Employment and Society*, vol. 3, no. 3: 307–22.

Barley, S.R. and G. Kunda (1992) 'Design and Devotion: Surges of Rational and Normative Ideologies of Control in Managerial Discourse', *Administrative Science Quarterly*, vol. 37: 363–99.

Berkeley Thomas, A. (1993) *Controversies in Management*, London: Routledge.

Berle, A. A. and G.C. Means (1935) *The Modern Corporation and Private Property*, New York: Macmillan.

Blau, P.M. and R. A. Schoenherr (1971) *The Structure of Organizations*, New York: Basic Books.

Bradley, H. (1986) 'Work, Home and the Restructuring of Jobs', in K. Purcell *et ah* (eds) *The Changing Experience of Employment, Restructuring and Recession*, London: Macmillan.

Braverman, H. (1974) *Labor and Monopoly Capital: The Degradation of Work in the Twentieth Century*, New York: Monthly Review Press.

Brown, H. (1980) 'Work Groups', in G. Salaman and K. Thompson, (eds) *People and Organizations*, Harlow: Longman.

Bryman, A. (1984) 'Organization Studies and the Concept of Rationality', *Journal of Management Studies*, vol. 21: 394–404.

Buchanan, D. (1986) 'Management Objectives in Technical Change', in D. Knights and H. Willmott (eds) *Managing the Labour Process*, Aldershot: Gower.

Burawoy, M. (1979) *Manufacturing Consent: Changes in the Labour Process Under Monopoly Capitalism*, Chicago: University of Chicago Press.

Burawoy, M. (1985) *The Politics of Production*, London: Verso.

Burgoyne, J.G. (1993) 'The Competence Movement: Issues, Stakeholders and Prospects', *Personnel Review*, vol. 22, no. 6: 6–13.

Burnham, J. (1945) *The Managerial Revolution*, Harmondsworth: Penguin.

Burns, T. (1982) *A Comparative Study of Administrative Structure and Organizational Processes in Selected Areas of the National Health Service* (SSRC Report, HRP 6725) London: Social Science Research Council.

Campbell, A. and B. Currie (1987) 'Skills and Strategies in Design Engineering', paper presented to 5th International Labour Process, UMIST.

Carchedi, G. (1977) *On the Economic Identification of the Middle Classes,* London: Routledge & Kegan Paul.

Carter, R. (1985) *Capitalism, Class Conflict and the New Middle Class,* London: Routledge & Kegan Paul.

Chandler, A. (1962) *Strategy and Structure: Chapters in the History of the Industrial Enterprise,* Cambridge, Mass.: MIT Press.

Chandler, A.D. (1977) *The Visible Hand,* Cambridge Mass.: Harvard University Press.

Child, J. (1969) *British Management Thought,* London: Allen & Unwin.

Child, J. (1973) (ed.) *Man and Organization,* London: Allen & Unwin.

Child, J. (1982) 'Professionals in the Corporate World', in D. Dunkerley and G. Salaman (eds) *The International Yearbook of Organisation Studies 1981,* London: Routledge & Kegan Paul.

Child, J. (1985) 'Managerial Strategies, New Technology and the Labour Process', in D. Knights, H. Wilmott and D. Collinson (eds) *Job Redesign: Critical Perspectives on the Labour Process,* London: Gower.

Child, J. *et al.* (1983) 'Professionalism and Work Organization: a Reply to Kevin McCormack', *Sociology,* vol. 20, no. 4: 607–14.

Clegg, S. and D. Dunkerley (1980) *Organization, Class and Control,* London: Routledge & Kegan Paul.

Cockburn, C. (1983) *Brothers: Male Dominance and Technological Change,* London: Pluto Press.

Cressey, P. and J. MacInnes (1980) 'Voting for Ford: Industrial Democracy and the Control of Labour', *Capital and Class,* no. 11: 5–37.

Cyert, R.M. and J.G. March (1963) *A Behavioural Theory of the Firm,* Englewood Cliffs, NJ: Prentice-Hall.

Dahrendorf, R. (1959) *Class and Class Conflict in Industrial Society,* London: Routledge & Kegan Paul.

Daniel, W. W. and N. Millward (1983) *Workplace Industrial Relations in Britain,* London: Heinemann.

De Vroey, M. (1975) 'The Separation of Ownership and Control in Large Corporations', *Review of Radical Political Economics,* vol. 7, no. 2: 1–10.

Drucker, P. (1955) *The Practice of Management,* New York: Harper & Row.

Drucker, P. (1977) *People and Performance,* London: Heinemann.

Drucker, P. (1979) *Management,* London: Pan.

Eccles, R.G. and N. Nohria (1992) *Beyond the Hype: Rediscovering the Essence of Management,* Boston, Mass.: Harvard Business School Press.

Edwards, P.K. (1990) 'Understanding Conflict in the Labour Process: The Logic and Autonomy of Struggle', in D. Knights and H. Willmott (1989) *Labour Process Theory,* London: Macmillan.

Edwards, R. (1979) *Contested Terrain: The Transformation of the Workplace in the Twentieth Century,* London: Heinemann.

Edwards, R., M. Reich and D.M. Gordon (1975) *Labour Market Segmentation,* Lexington, Mass.: D.C. Heath.

Ehrenreich, B. and J. Ehrenreich (1979) The Professional-Managerial Class', in P. Walker (ed.), *Between Labour and Capital,* Brighton, Harvester.

Etzioni, A. (1961) *A Comparative Analysis of Complex Organizations,* New York: Free Press.

Fevre, R. (1986) 'Contract Work in the Recession', in J. Purcell, S. Wood, A. Watson and S. Allen (eds) *The Changing Experience of Employment, Restructuring and Recession,* London: Macmillan.

Fiedler, F.E. (1967) *A Theory of Leadership Effectiveness,* New York: McGraw-Hill.

Fligstein, N. (1990) *The Transformation of Corporate Control,* Cambridge, Mass.: Harvard University Press.

Fores, M. and I. Glover (1976) 'The Real Work of Executives', *Management Today,* Sep.

Fowler, A. (1985) 'Getting into Organizational Restructuring', *Personnel Management,* vol. 17, no. 2: 24–7.

Friedman, A. (1977) *Industry and Labour: Class Struggle at Work Monopoly Capitalism,* London: Macmillan.

Friedman, A. (1987) 'The Means of Management Control and Labour Process Theory: A Critical Note on Storey', *Sociology,* vol. 21, no. 2: 287–94.

Glenn, E.K. and R.L. Feldberg (1979) 'Proletarianising Office Work', in A. Zimbalist (ed.) *Case Studies on the Labour Process*, New York: Monthly Review Press.

Gordon, D.M., R. Edwards and M. Reich (1982) *Segmented Work, Divided Workers*, Cambridge: Cambridge University Press.

Grossman, R. (1979) 'Women's Place in the Integrated Circuit[7], *Radical America*, vol. 14, no. 1: 29–48.

Guest, D.E. (1989) 'Personnel and HRM: Can You Tell the Difference?' *Personnel Management*, Jan.: 48–51.

Guest, D. E. (1990) 'Human Resource Management and the American Dream', *Journal of Management Studies*, vol. 27, no. 4: 377–97.

Hales, C. P. (1986) What do Managers Do? A Critical Review of the Evidence', *Journal of Management Studies*, vol. 23, no. 1: 88–115.

Hales, C.P. (1988) 'Management Processes, Management Divisions of Labour and Managerial Work: Towards a Synthesis', paper presented to 6th International Labour Process Conference, Aston.

Harris, R. (1987) *Power and Powerlessness in Industry: An Analysis of the Social Relations of Production*, London: Tavistock.

Hitt, M. A. *et al.* (1986) *Management Concepts and Effective Practice*, St. Paul, Minn.: West Publishing.

Holland, S. (1975) *The Socialist Challenge*, London: Quartet.

Horne, J. H. and T. Lupton (1965) 'The Work Activities of Middle Managers', *Journal of Management Studies*, vol. 2, no. 1: 14–33.

Hyman, R. (1987) 'Strategy or Structure: Capital, Labour and Control', *Work, Employment and Society*, vol. 1, no. 1: 25–55.

Johnson, T. (1972) *Professions and Power*, London: Macmillan.

Johnson, T. (1980) 'Work and Power;, in G. Esland and G. Salaman (eds) *The Politics of Work and Occupations*, Milton Keynes: Open University Press.

Johnston, L. (1986) *Marxism, Class Analysis and Socialist Pluralism*, London: Allen & Unwin.

Kelly, J. E. (1985) 'Management's Redesign of Work', in D. Knights, H. Willmott and D. Collinson (eds) *Job Redesign: Critical Perspectives on the Labour Process*, Aldershot: Gower.

Kotter, J. (1982) *The General Manager*, New York: Free Press.

Lawlor, E.E. (1976) 'Control Systems in Organizations', in H.D. Dunnette (ed.) *Handbook of Industrial and Organizational Psychology*, Chicago: Rand McNally Publishing.

Layton, E. T. (1969) 'Science, Business and the American Engineer', in R. Perruci and J. E. Gersth (eds) *The Engineer and the Social System*, New York: John Wiley.

Lindblom, C.E. (1959) 'The Science of Muddling Through', *Public Administration Review*, vol. 19: 79–88.

Littler, C. R. and G. Salaman (1982) 'Bravermania and Beyond', *Sociology*, vol. 16, no. 2: 25–69.

Loveridge, R. (1982) 'Business Strategy and Community Culture', in D. Dunkerley and G. Salaman (eds) *The International Yearbook of Organization Studies 1981*, London: Routledge & Kegan Paul.

MacInnes, J. (1987) *Thatcherism at Work*, Milton Keynes: Open University Press.

Maguire, M. (1986) 'Recruitment as a Means of Control', in K. Purcell, S. Wood, A. Watson and S. Allen (eds) *The Changing Experience of Employment, Restructuring and Recession*, London: Macmillan.

March J. G. and H. A. Simon (1958) *Organizations*, New York: John Wiley.

McGregor, D. (1960) *The Human Side of the Enterprise*, New York: Harper & Row.

Melling, J. (1982) 'Men in the Middle or Men on the Margin?' in D. Dunkerley and G. Salaman (eds) *The International Yearbook of Organisation Studies 1981*, London: Routledge & Kegan Paul.

Miller, P. and T. O'Leary (1987) 'The Entrepreneurial Order, paper presented to 5th International Labour Process Conference, UMIST.

Mintzberg, H. (1973) *The Nature of Managerial Work*, New York: Harper & Row.

Morgan, K. and A. Sayer (1984) 'A "Modern" Industry in a "Mature" Region: the Remaking of Management-Labour Relations', working paper, Urban and Regional Studies, University of Sussex.

Murray, P. and J. Wickham (1985) 'Women Workers and Bureaucratic Control in Irish Electronic Factories', in H. Newby, (ed.) *Restructuring Capital, Reorganisation in Industrial Society,* London: Macmillan.

Oliver, J. (1993) 'A Degree of Uncertainty', *Management Today,* Jun.

Parker, M. (1985) *Inside the Circle: A Union Guide to QWL,* Boston: Labor Notes.

Pearson, R. (1986) 'Female Workers in the First and Third Worlds: the "Greening" of Women's Labour', in J. Purcell, S. Wood, A. Watson and S. Allen (eds) *The Changing Experience of Employment, Restructuring and Recession,* London: Macmillan.

Pettigrew, A. (1973) *The Politics of Organizational Decisionmaking,* London: Tavistock.

Pollert, A. (1981) *Girls, Wives, Factory Lives,* London: Macmillan.

Poole, M. and R. Mansfield (1992) 'Managers' Attitudes to Human Resource Management', in P. Blyton and P. Turnbull (eds) *Reassessing Human Resource Management,* London: Sage.

Purcell, J. and K. Sissons (1983) 'A Strategy for Management Control in Industrial Relations', in J. Purcell and R. Smith (eds) *The Control of Work,* London: Macmillan.

Reed, M. (1984) 'Management as a Social Practice', *Journal of Management Studies,* vol. 21, no. 3: 273–85.

Reed, M. (1992a) 'Experts, Professions and Organizations in Late Modernity', paper to Employment Research Unit Conference, Cardiff Business School.

Rose, M. (1975; 2nd edn 1986) *Industrial Behaviour,* Harmondsworth: Penguin.

Rose, M. and B. Jones (1985) 'Managerial Strategy and Trade Union Responses in Work Reorganization Schemes at Establishment Level', in D. Knights, H. Willmott, D. Collinson (eds) *Job Redesign: Critical Perspectives on the Labour Process,* London: Gower.

Rueschemeyer, D. (1986) *Power and the Division of Labour,* London: Polity Press.

Schein, E.H. (1965) *Organizational Psychology,* 1st edn, Englewood Cliffs, NJ: Prentice-Hall (also 1980, 3rd. edn).

Scott, J. (1985) 'Ownership, Management and Strategic Control', in K. Elliot and P. Lawrence (eds) *Introducing Management,* Harmondsworth: Penguin.

Shaw, M. (1990) 'Strategy and Social Process: Military Context and Sociological Analysis', *Sociology,* vol. 24, no. 3: 465–73.

Simon, H. A. (1960) *Administrative Behaviour,* New York: Macmillan.

Smith, V. (1990) *Managing in the Corporate Interest: Control and Resistance in an American Bank,* Berkeley, Calif.: University of California Press.

Steiner, T. and B. Miner (1978) *Management Polio/ and Strategy,* West Drayton: Collier-Macmillan.

Stewart, E. (1967) *The Reality of Management,* London: Pan.

Stewart, E. (1970) *The Reality of Organizations,* London: Macmillan.

Stewart, E. (1976) *Contrasts in Management,* Maidenhead: McGraw-Hill.

Storey, J. (1983) *Managerial Prerogative and the Question of Control,* London: Routledge & Kegan Paul.

Storey, J. (1985) The Means of Management Control', *Sociology,* vol. 19, no. 2:193–211.

Streek, W. (1987) The Uncertainties of Management in the Management of Uncertainty: Employers, Labour Relations and Industrial Adjustment in the 1980s', *Work, Employment and Society,* vol. 1, no. 3: 281–308.

Teulings, A. (1986) 'Managerial Labour Processes in Organised Capitalism; the Power of Corporate Management and the Powerlessness of the Manager', in D. Knights and H. Willmott (eds) *Managing the Labour Process,* Aldershot: Gower.

Thompson, P. (1989) *The Nature of Work: An Introduction to Debates on the Labour Process,* London: Macmillan.

Thompson, P. and E. Bannon (1985) *Working the System: The Shop Floor and New Technology,* London: Pluto.

Thurley, K. and S. Wood (1983) *Industrial Relations and Management Strategy,* Cambridge: Cambridge University Press.

Tomlinson, J. (1982) *The Unequal Struggle? British Socialism and the Capitalist Enterprise,* London: Methuen.

Torrington, D. (1989) 'Human Resource Management and the Personnel Function', in J. Storey, (ed.) *New Perspectives on Human Resource Management,* London: Routledge.

Wallace, C. (1993) 'Reflections on the Concept of "Strategy"', in D. Morgan and L. Stanley (eds) *Debates in Sociology,* Manchester: Manchester University Press.

Wardell, M. (1986) 'Labor and the Labor Process', paper at ASTON-UMIST Labour Process Conference.

Watson, T. (1986) *Management, Organization and Employment Strategy: New Directions in Theory and Practice,* London: Routledge & Kegan Paul.

Watson, T. (1994) *In Search of Management: Culture, Chaos and Control in Managerial Work,* London: Routledge.

Westwood, S. (1984) *All Day, Every Day: Factory and Family in the Making of Women's Lives,* London: Pluto.

Whitley, R. (1984) 'The Fragmented State of Management Studies', *Journal of Management Studies* vol. 21, no. 3: 331–48.

Willmott, H. (1984) 'Images and Ideals of Managerial Work', *Journal of Management Studies,* vol. 21, no. 3: 349–68.

Winstanley, D. (1986) 'Recruitment Strategies as a Means of Control of Technological Labour', paper at ASTON-UMIST Labour Process Conference.

Witz, A. (1986) 'Patriarchy and the Labour Market: Occupational Controls and the Medical Division of Labour', in D. Knights and H. Willmott (eds).

Wood, S. (ed.) (1982) *The Degradation of Work: Skill, Deskilling and the Labour Process,* London: Hutchinson.

Wright, E.O. (1976) 'Contradictory Class Locations', *New Left Review,* no. 98.

Zeitlin, M. (1974) 'Corporate Ownership and Control: the Large Corporation and the Capitalist Class, *American Journal of Sociology,* vol. 79, no. 5: 1073–119.

Zimbalist, A. (ed.) (1979) *Case Studies on the Labour Process,* New York: Monthly Review Press.

CHAPTER 5

Control in contemporary work organizations

Mike Reed

Control relations are fundamental to the organization of work processes within any socio-economic order. This is in part due to the technical need for co-ordinating mechanisms that, at least in theory, will ensure that work gets done in ways that are appropriate to the organization's requirements (Berry et al., 1995). But it is also due to the political need for forms of regulation and surveillance that manage the conflicts that necessarily pervade the work organization. Work is a 'contested terrain' in which the 'frontier of control' within and between work groups is a dynamic process subject to the complex and shifting power relations in which these groups are embedded (Edwards, 1979; Fox, 1971; Goodrich, 1975; Thompson, 1989). Thus, any particular form or regime of workplace control is located within a wider political economy of power relations within which its distinctive organizational logic and architecture will emerge and take on a not insignificant degree of institutional continuity and resilience (Burawoy, 1985). Organizational control, therefore, is viewed in this chapter as consisting of *a complex and dynamic configuration of mechanisms and practices through which the regulation and monitoring of work performance is contested by groups or 'corporate agents' (Archer, 2000, 2003) embedded in institutionalized power relations.*

The key institutionalized power relation in which organizational control mechanisms and practices are located is the employment relationship because it is an enduring and ubiquitous institution of all advanced capitalist political economies. As such, 'organizational control' is always embedded within a wider set of 'social control' relations and mechanisms geared to the maintenance of social order (Innes, 2003). They interact with each other in highly complex ways to form dynamic patterns of power relations between the major 'corporate agents' within advanced capitalist societies who have the organizational capacities to shape institutional outcomes.

Consequently, the control logics and forms that become established within work organizations emerge out of the interplay between the constraints and opportunities made available by prevailing power structures and the ways in which these are creatively exploited by employers and employees in pursuit of their collective interests and values. Organizational control regimes emerge from the attempts of certain groups to design and impose certain principles and mechanisms of 'regulative surveillance' on other groups who are engaged with them in struggles to dominate the process through which resources are allocated and the distributional outcomes which it reproduces. As corporate agents, groups will possess and deploy varying organizational capacities required to engage in power struggles over the mechanisms through which control can be secured, maintained and challenged. In this respect, control systems within work organizations are necessarily dynamic entities that develop in ways that are indelibly shaped by ongoing power struggles within the workplace and the wider economy and polity in which it is located (Elger and Smith, 2005). Thus, the degree of internal consistency that the former achieve is limited by the extremely broad range of stakeholder interests and values which they have to accommodate and regulate.

The chapter will review and evaluate the thesis that a form of organizational control has been in the process of developing since the late 1980s that signifies a radical transformation in the way through which effective 'regulative surveillance' over work had been achieved for most of the twentieth century. *This 'new control logic' is seen to combine electronic surveillance, cultural engineering and political management to form a hybridized control regime that fundamentally breaks with the core features of the conventional, 'neo-Weberian' control model/regime* (Reed, 1999; Sewell, 2001, 2005; Thompson and Warhurst, 1998). By recombining more advanced information and communication technologies with indirect and implicit cultural and political management techniques, organizational elites are now able, it is argued, to implement modes of regulative surveillance that dispense with much of the, relatively inefficient and ineffective, control infrastructure on which the orthodox model/regime relied (Castells, 2000; Sennett, 2006; van Dijk, 1999). Control has become leaner, internalized, flexible and mobile within advanced capitalist societies and business corporations that operate in globalized political economies characterized by extreme instability and uncertainty. The major focus of control has moved away from the design and monitoring of standardized work tasks towards the management of highly complex informational, human and material 'flows' that are inherently resistant to the orthodox control technologies embedded in bureaucratic hierarchies. In their place, a new morphology of 'network-based' control forms has emerged in which hybridized control regimes, selectively combining principles and elements drawn from complementary and competing control logics, are fast becoming the norm – both in the private and public sectors of all advanced capitalist political economies (Clegg et al., 2006). Some economic sectors and institutional fields – such as informatics, pharmaceuticals and the creative industries – may be more advanced and radical in restructuring their control regimes than others – such as mass catering, clothing manufacture and retailing. But the underlying 'direction of travel', it is contended by many influential researchers and commentators (Castells, 2000; Barker, 1999; Davidow and Malone, 1993; Heckscher and Donellon, 1994; Kanter, 1990), is driving towards a hybridized form of 'network control' that will come to dominate increasing areas of socio-economic life in the twenty-first century.

The next section of the chapter will review the key features of the orthodox, neo-Weberian control model/regime and its putative strengths and weaknesses under prevailing socio-economic conditions. This will be followed by a consideration of research on organizational control that has given much greater emphasis to the cultural forms through which regulative surveillance over work is achieved. In turn, this will lead into a review of more recent work on contemporary organizational surveillance and discipline that draws extensively on Foucault's analysis of 'capillary power and control' in modern societies (Burrell, 2006; Foucault, 1976a, b, 2003). The latter refers to more finely grained, horizontal or web-like forms of control that go about their business in much less transparently coercive and authoritarian ways than more orthodox control regimes. Research on 'therapeutic' or 'disciplinary' forms of control has provided both theoretical and empirical inspiration for those researchers who have identified the key features of the new control model/regime as it has emerged in response to much more subtle forms of regulative surveillance focused on issues such as commitment, emotion, identity and mobility. It also resonates with the analyses of those researchers who, rather more ambitiously and perhaps unwisely, have attempted to construct prognoses of the generic forms of organizational control that will become dominant in twenty-first century capitalist economies and societies as they attempt to cope with the extreme discontinuities and uncertainties endemic in global geo-political systems and structures. A concluding section will provide an overview discussion and assessment of the key themes and debates elaborated in previous sections.

Neo-Weberian control

Much of the history of work and work organization during the twentieth century can be viewed as the gradual emergence, development and refinement of a control model/ regime that most closely approximated to the core structural and cultural elements of rational bureaucratic administration as identified by the German sociologist, Max Weber (Beniger, 1986; Child, 2005; Clegg, 1990; Edwards, 1979; Heckscher and Donellon, 1994; Jacques, 1996; McAuley et al., 2007; Morgan, 1990; Perrow, 1986; Reed, 1999; Thompson, 1989). This control model/regime takes the primary features of bureaucratic control – functional specialization, process standardization and hierarchical co-ordination – and builds relatively unobtrusive and indirect, but vital, 'secondary control mechanisms' on to these core structural elements. In this way, more sophisticated processes of cognitive and normative control can be 'grafted on' to the primary structural control mechanisms that bureaucratic organization relies on to achieve effective behavioural regulation within the workplace through formalized rule systems and standardized operating procedures (Perrow, 1986: 119–56). As a result, neo-Weberian control is seen to facilitate the development of a much more integrated and continuous form of regulative surveillance than is possible under the more direct and fragmented forms of workplace control practised and legitimated by Taylor's Scientific Management and Fordist mass production regimes (Littler, 1985). The latter generate highly personalized, diffuse and often relatively confrontational forms of supervision over work performance, while the former permits a much more remote, depersonalized, well-integrated and unobtrusive form of regulative surveillance to emerge.

Within a 'neo-Weberian' control regime, employees are more likely to submit voluntarily to control instruments – such as rule systems – focused on the cognitive and normative processes through which basic 'behavioural premises and patterns' are set. Of course, to some extent, this focus on the need for primary structural control mechanisms to be complemented by more subtle and unobtrusive secondary control mechanisms – that frame the tacit assumptions and premises on which work behaviour is routinely based – anticipates the much greater emphasis that Foucauldian scholars and researchers give to internalized discipline and self-surveillance at work (Barker, 1999; Burrell, 2006; McKinlay and Starkey, 1998; Townley, 1994, 1999, 2004, 2008). But the neo-Weberian control model also speaks to the growing emphasis on informal workplace control mechanisms – such as Burawoy's (1979) study of 'shop-floor games' and Knights et al.'s (1985) anthology on the micro-politics of technological and organizational change – that has emerged from over three decades of workplace research carried out within the labour process tradition, beginning with the publication of Braverman's (1974) classic study.

Throughout the 1980s and 1990s, the labour process tradition intellectually energized research on and debate over the inherent complexity of organizational control regimes that mediated between political economy and work designs within advanced capitalist economies (Knights and Willmott, 1990; Knights et al., 1985; Thompson, 1989). By focusing on the dynamic combinations of structural, technological and ideological mechanisms through which management struggle to sustain control in the face of endemic worker resistance, in all its multifarious forms, labour process research illuminated the multi-dimensional nature of regulative surveillance at 'the organizational coalface' (Burawoy, 1985; Child, 1985; Littler and Salaman, 1982; Reed, 1989, 1990; Salaman, 1979). Yet, it could not shake off the criticism that its 'realist' ontology and 'objectivist' methodology sustained a form of analysis that 'drastically underestimates the knowledgeability and capability of workers faced with a range of management imperatives. . . . What is lacking is an adequate discussion of the reactions of the workers, as themselves knowledgeable and capable agents, to the technical division of labour and Taylorism' (Giddens, 1982: 40). Thus, an emerging critique of labour process studies of organizational control that crystallized around the theme of the 'missing subject' (Casey, 1995; Knights and Willmott, 1985, 1989, 1990) identified a substantive concern and a theoretical-cum-methodological problem that would increasingly resonate with the 'cultural turn' in studies of work organizations and control regimes in the 1990s. A sustained analytical and empirical focus on 'worker subjectivity', including the subjectivity of managerial, technical and professional workers, was maintained within labour process research on changing control regimes over a period of two decades or more. But the latter found itself under continual pressure to develop a 'sociology of management knowledge' that provided a more coherent exposition of how new control theories and techniques come to be fabricated, implemented and revised. For many researchers and commentators (Reed, 1989, 1990; Watson, 1994; Whitley, 1984; Whittington, 1994; Willmott, 1987), this search for a 'sociology of management knowledge' that would enable us to better understand the complexities of 'control in practice' would only be feasible if the more deterministic predilections of a quasi-Marxist labour process tradition were to be succeeded by a neo-Weberian control model in which managerial and worker agency played a central role. In this way, it was argued, Weber's analytical interests in the structural architecture through which bureaucratic control is formally realized – through functional specialization, process standardization and hierarchical co-ordination – could be complemented by a substantive interest in the managerial agency through which these control mechanisms become operationalized.

Thus, both Weber and Braverman, starting from very different ideological and methodological premises, were seen to be guilty of presenting highly abstract analyses of organizational control that needed to be substantially revised in the light of empirical findings and theoretical developments focused on 'real world control strategies and practices'. Consequently, the growing emphasis on 'worker subjectivity and agency' throughout the 1980s stimulated the emergence of approaches in which corporate culture and organizational symbolism were to take a much more centre stage role in the understanding of control within work organizations. These approaches would reject the highly rationalistic and deterministic assumptions on which both neo-Weberian theory and labour process analysis had reportedly rested (Turner, 1990). In their place, the former would offer conceptions of 'organizational control' in which themes such as identity, emotion, insecurity and ethnicity would play a much more central substantive and theoretical role than they had ever enjoyed within the once dominant neo-Weberian and neo-Marxist approaches (Casey, 1995, 2002; Collinson, 2003).

Cultural control

From the mid-1980s onwards, the increasing emphasis on culturally based forms of organizational control – in which symbolically mediated modes of regulation, monitoring and disciplining at work became the major concern – was embedded within a wider 'cultural turn' in the study of work organizations (Martin, 2002; Martin and Frost, 1996; Reed, 2005). In part, the latter signalled an intellectual movement in support of general theoretical approaches – such as social phenomenology, postmodernism, post-structuralism and neo-institutionalism – that attached fundamental importance to the status of 'work organizations' as socially constructed entities. The latter had no existence or meaning apart from that given to them by, and continually reconfirmed through, the cultural processes and practices that made them possible in the first place (Alvesson, 2002; Hassard and Parker, 1993; Parker, 2000; Smircich, 1983, 1985; Westwood and Linstead, 2001). But it also reflected the growing influence of particular research methodologies and tools – such as discourse analysis, institutional ethnography, organizational sensemaking and actor-network theory and analysis – that derived intellectual inspiration from these wider theoretical movements. These new and innovative approaches aspired to provide interpretive studies of control processes grounded in detailed understandings of the linguistic, symbolic and discursive practices through which they were generated and reproduced (Alvesson and Karreman, 2000; Grant et al., 1998, 2004; Law and Hassard, 1999; Phillips and Hardy, 2002; Smith, 2005; Thompson, 2003; Weick, 1995).

Taken as a complete package, these general theoretical approaches and the specific research programmes and practices that they promote hold out the promise of a revitalized cultural sociology of organizational control (Du Gay and Pryke, 2002; Ray and Sayer, 1999). The latter would equip researchers to identify precise patterns of compliance and commitment within the workplace that are seen to emerge out of delicate and ambiguous negotiations as to meaningful collective interpretations and the modes of social intervention that they sanction. Instead of viewing control relations as institutionalized social entities that exert a considerable degree of continuous structural constraint over the interpretive options available to social actors and the courses of social interaction potentially flowing from them, cultural researchers, who prioritize the symbolic, linguistic and discursive antecedents of control relations, re-assert the latter's essentially open, contingent and transitory nature.

For cultural researchers, 'control' is, by its very nature, open to multiple linguistic and discursive interpretations as to its meaning, status and relevance within shifting organizational settings. These interpretations defy the lazy imposition of pre-determined theoretical categories relating to 'political economy' or 'social structure' or 'labour market' on the part of the analyst – who is then presumed to have privileged access to a level and degree of understanding unavailable to the actors involved in that situation. Thus, for these cultural researchers, our theoretical understanding of control processes within work organizations is necessarily parasitic upon the primary understandings and accounts of them constructed by those who make and remake them (Smith, 2005). As cultural researchers, our central role is to explicate the narrative storylines that organizational members construct and communicate about their understanding of control practices in their everyday organizational lives. If the cultural researcher wishes to re-interpret these narrative storylines through a wider theoretical lens, then this must be done with extreme care and humility typical of the 'reflexive researcher' in order that the complex iterative relationship between 'theoretical' and 'everyday' forms of understanding may be properly maintained and appreciated (Smith, 2005).

But the turn towards control as an inherently reflexive cultural process and practice, rather than an objectified material artefact and entity, also signalled a growing interest in forms of organizational control in which the 'management of meanings' was coming to dominate both academic research and public debate about 'the future of work' (Casey, 1995; Handy, 1984; Keat and Abercrombie, 1991; Leadbeater and Lloyd, 1987; Pettigrew and Fenton, 2000).

As advanced capitalist political economies began to undergo a conceptual metamorphosis into 'knowledge economies', the focus of research attention in the study of organizational control turned towards the 'knowledge-intensive-organizations' which were now seen to constitute the leading edge of dramatic innovations in control regimes and their supporting cultural technologies (Alvesson, 2004; Child, 2005; Thrift, 1999, 2005). These were typically forms of work organization in which relatively large numbers of professional, managerial and technical workers were employed. They also required even more complex forms of regulative surveillance attuned to the self-managed working environments in which such categories of 'expert labour' were used to performing their highly complex and ambiguous work tasks (Fincham, 2009; Reed, 1996; Robertson and Swan, 2003). Within 'knowledge-intensive-organizations', the focus for managerial control strategies and practices was seen to be moving even further away from the external imposition of standardized and formalized routines towards the 'the manufacture of commitment and consent' through the manipulation of corporate cultures that contained components of paternalistic ideology, team-based working, competitive individualism, performance management and professional work ethics (Alvesson, 2004; Alvesson and Willmott, 2002; Barley and Kunda, 1992; Casey, 1995; Courpasson, 2000; Karreman and Alvesson, 2004; Kunda, 1992; Robertson and Swan, 2003, 2004;

Thompson and Warhurst, 2001). Selected elements of this culturally based control regime were also seen to be emerging in relation to certain categories of lower-level employees who were formally outside the 'core employment group' of professional, managerial and technical staff but whose skills and expertise are regarded as critical to the success of high quality, high performance work regimes in which the quality of 'customer service' is the overriding concern (Barker, 1999; Ezzamel and Willmott, 1998; Frenkel et al., 1999; Knights and McCabe, 2003; Korczynski, 2003; Sewell, 1998; Sturdy and Fineman, 2001).

Over a period of time, this growing body of work – focusing on organizational control as a socio-cultural process in which employers and managers strive to shape, if not transform, the subjective understandings that employees have of their work roles and their wider significance for the corporation's long-term viability – sensitized researchers to the endemic resistance of workplace cultures to managerial manipulation (Ackroyd and Thompson, 1999; Albrow, 1997; Fineman, 1993; Kunda, 1992; Pettigrew, 1985; Martin, 1992, 2005; Morgan and Sturdy, 2000; Strati, 2000). As Knights and McCabe (2003: 79) have, more recently, reflected, 'management deployed the discourse of re-engineering and culture change to signify a shift away from bureaucratic, hierarchical control and towards autonomy, responsibility, and self-discipline. For us, re-engineering signifies a change toward a process-based, rather than a functional, approach to the organization of work'. However, as Knights and McCabe's research – in organizational settings as diverse as call centres, automobile manufacture and financial services – also demonstrates, these cultural re-engineering programmes could not disguise *the political reality of management's continued preoccupation with long-term profitability and the constraints that this unavoidably imposed on culture change initiatives within the workplace.* It also highlighted the fact that whereas the repackaging of previously isolated and relatively mundane culture change techniques and experiments – such as total quality management, business process engineering and project team working – was relatively new and innovative, they still contained structurally embedded tensions and contradictions that inevitably generated unintended consequences that severely limited their longer-term impact. Pre-existing structural inequalities in power and authority, between and within various managerial, professional, technical and operational groups, continued to exert a disproportional impact on the effects that such cultural re-engineering strategies and programmes had on institutionalized control relations. This did not mean to say that they had no long-term impact on organizational control regimes but that their effects were mediated by a complex range of structural factors that are often underestimated, if not ignored, by researchers who tend to overplay the theoretical importance and practical influence of culturally based forms of explanation (Westwood and Linstead, 2001).

Indeed, by the second half of the 1990s something of a theoretical and political backlash was beginning to be expressed on the part of more mainstream organizational control researchers who felt that the 'cultural turn' had itself 'spun out of control' in ways that were having a deleterious effect on their capacity to identify long-term continuities in control strategies and forms (Ackroyd and Thompson, 1995; Reed, 1999, 2005; Thompson and McHugh, 1995). The pre-occupation with culturally based forms of control – in both private and, especially, public sector work organizations (Ferlie et al., 1996; Newman, 2001; Pollitt, 1993) – seemed to be generating a form of discursive reductionism or determinism in which an obsession with linguistic practices and symbolic forms marginalized, if not excluded, any concern with the underlying socio-material conditions in which they are grounded and which indelibly influence their organizational impact.

Also, 'the cultural turn' seemed to be supporting the promulgation of highly contentious generalizations about the growing influence of various 'cultural control narratives' – such as 'the culture of the customer' (Du Gay, 1996; Du Gay and Salaman, 1992) or 'emotional labour' (Fineman, 1996; Fineman and Sturdy, 1999; Hochschild, 1983) – which, at the very least, were in need of conceptual clarification and empirical specification (Fournier and Grey, 1999; Korczynski, 2003). Thus, the overwhelming emphasis given to the role of discursive practices in shaping control strategies and relations came to be seen as counterproductive for many mainstream researchers. This was the case insofar as it analytically marginalized the key link between structural movements in the wider political economy of contemporary capitalism and changing forms and patterns of control at the level of capitalist work organization. It also encouraged the widespread adoption of an underlying conception of expert or 'knowledge work' in which more orthodox – that is, materially and structurally based – forms of control were seen to be 'genetically incapable' of being effectively mobilized and implemented (Thompson and Ackroyd, 2005). In turn, this tended to reinforce modes of analysis that seemed to be fixated with putative 'paradigm shifts' in control regimes where there is assumed to be system-wide transformations in control logics and patterns. As a result, the critics argued, these modes of, culturally based, analysis were ill-equipped to accommodate the emerging social and organizational reality of complex combinations of hybridized control systems that displayed much greater continuity with the neo-Weberian control model/ regime than could ever be envisaged by more 'epochal-type' analysis (Thompson and Warhurst, 1998).

Nevertheless, 'the cultural turn' imprinted itself on the study of organizational control logics and regimes in ways that were to influence the field up until the present time. This was particularly the case as increasing numbers of researchers and commentators within the field began to draw on the work of the French philosopher/historian of ideas and organizational practices, Michele Foucault, for intellectual inspiration and insight into the increasing importance of 'capillary power and control' in modern societies and organizations.

Capillary control

As Burrell (2006) has recently noted, there has been something of an ideological and theoretical polarization in relation to how Foucault's work has been received and assimilated into mainstream studies of work organization. There is no doubting the theoretical and methodological impact of his work on the study of organizations over the last couple of decades or so. But the ways in which it has been evaluated has attracted a diversity of interpretive interventions. For some, Foucault is the unthreatening pluralist whose core ideas and claims can be incorporated into more orthodox approaches towards the sociology of work without too much fuss and disruption (Grint, 1991; McKinlay and Starkey, 1998). For others, his work has provided vital intellectual inspiration for an expanding body of post-modern/ post-structuralist theorizing about new forms of disciplinary surveillance and control within contemporary work organizations that fundamentally questions, indeed radically undermines, the philosophical foundations, theoretical coherence and knowledge claims associated with more mainstream approaches such as labour process theory and neo-Weberian institutional theory (Clegg et al., 2006; Knights, 2009; Sewell, 2001, 2005; Willmott, 2005). For a third group of interlocutors, the distinctions, indeed divisions, between Foucault and, say, Marx and Weber have been grossly overemphasized such that the materialist ontological foundations and structural analytical sensitizers of Foucault's work on the historical development of micro-level organizational control technologies and practices have been illegitimately obscured and marginalized (Marsden, 1999; Pearce and Woodiwiss, 2001; Rawlinson et al., 2002). As a result, this third interpretation contends Foucault's potential contribution to our understanding of the internal dynamics and contextual embedding of organizational control technologies has remained a largely untapped resource that is still awaiting its full exploitation.

Whatever interpretive gloss we put on Foucault's work and its implications for research on emerging control regimes in contemporary work organizations, we can identify three, interrelated, areas in which his work has been extensively and productively drawn upon to provide new insights into changing control relations and the endemic contradictions and tensions that they embody.

First, it entails a decisive break with theoretical approaches to the study of organizational control that continue to overemphasize the significance of vertical control systems at the expense of horizontal, 'web-like' or multi-stranded capillary forms of control that do not conform to the institutional logic of bureaucratic rationality and authority. In this respect, Foucault and his followers are much more interested in the informal, internalized forms of disciplinary control that are evident, for example, in team-working- or peer-review-based quality management systems than in more formalized regulatory control institutions such as collective bargaining (Foucault, 2003; McKinlay and Starkey, 1998). These forms of 'disciplinary control' seem to become even more significant where new information and communication technologies provide 'certain information about subordinate behaviour while eliminating the necessity for face-to-face engagement. They can transmit the presence of the omnipresent observer and so induce compliance without the messy, conflict-prone exertions of reciprocal relations' (Zuboff, 1988: 323).

Second, the attention that Foucault and those who have followed him – sometimes labelled as the 'governmentalists' (Dean, 1999; Miller and Rose, 2008; Rose, 1989, 1999) – give to the more complex, 'bottom-up' or network-based forms of control that have emerged in contemporary neoliberal political economies and societies is seen to be contextualized by the development of new forms of 'governmentality' within the workplace. The latter are thought to embody new ways of thinking about and practicing 'governance' – that is, the actual conduct of governing – in an era when established forms of highly centralized 'command and control' systems typical of large-scale corporate bureaucracies can no longer cope with the complexity and instability inherent in global capitalism (Castells, 2000; Thompson, 2003; van Dijk, 1999).

Finally, each of these innovations in control – that is the increasing significance of workplace capillary control within network-based forms of governance – seems to suggest the more widespread diffusion of *hybridized forms of organizational control*. The latter usually combine competing design principles and operational processes within much more loosely integrated and informally co-ordinated control regimes that radically depart from the core axioms and overarching rationale of the neo-Weberian model. As a result, the state is afforded much less theoretical and empirical significance in accounting for changing control regimes because it is no longer able, or prepared, to take on the range of responsibility and detailed accountability entailed in the notion of 'sovereign power'. Indeed, 'the state' is seen to be increasingly differentiated and fragmented into more specialized and diverse political agencies than can no longer be contained within centralized 'command and control' systems (Cerny, 2005). This 'dispersed state' may be called upon to intervene in situations that potentially threaten the underlying cohesion and stability of the established socio-economic order – such as the recent financial crisis and current economic recession. But this is unlikely to lead to the reconstruction of the 'sovereign state', with all its panoply of centralized command and control systems, because the process of structural hybridization has simply gone too far for such a reversion to the neo-Weberian form to be politically and organizationally feasible.

Following the example that Foucault set in *Discipline and Punish* (1976) and in other publications, such as *The Birth of the Clinic* (1976) and *Society must be Defended* (2003), the overriding focus for the 'governmentalists' has been the practical technologies through which modern organizations, and their administrative, professional and managerial elites have designed and implemented control regimes that have the socio-psychological internalization of work discipline at their very core. Throughout the work of those researchers and scholars who have followed Foucault's lead, there is a sustained analytical focus on *how continuous control* of workplace mentalities, practices and relations is realized through the fabrication and application of *seemingly mundane techniques and systems* such as timetables/schedules, delegated supervision, team-working, performance benchmarking, individualized staff selection and appraisal, spatial segregation and enclosure and remote monitoring (Barker, 1993, 1999; Clegg et al., 2006; Frenkel et al., 1999; Garrahan and Stewart, 1992; Reed, 1999; Sewell, 1998, 2001, 2005; Sewell and Wilkinson, 1992; Sturdy and Fleming, 2003; Taylor et al., 2002; Tomaney, 1994). While much of this kind of research has been concerned with relatively standardized and rationalized work in factories, call centres and mass consumption outlets, attention has also been directed at higher level, 'knowledge work and organizations' in which expert labour of various kinds – managerial, technical and professional – is subject to similar, if somewhat more elaborate and indirect, control techniques that combine cultural, technological and organizational mechanisms (Courpasson, 2000; Deem et al., 2007; Grey, 1994; Robertson and Swan, 2003, 2004; Townley, 1994). Within this research setting, theoretical and empirical attention shifts towards the discursive construction of workers as 'disciplined subjects' and the panoply of symbolic and cultural processes through which occupational and organizational identities are selectively managed (Alvesson and Robertson, 2006; Alvesson and Willmott, 2002; Casey, 1995; Collinson, 2003; Jacques, 1996; Kondo, 1990). Indeed, it is this point that the detailed focus on the mundane control practices and techniques through which everyday regulative surveillance within the workplace is routinely achieved gives way to wider questions about new forms of 'governmentality' and 'governance' at work that are implicit within Foucault's ideal typical model of 'panopticon control' (Dean, 1999; Edwards, 2006; Miller and Rose, 2008; Zuboff, 1988).

Sewell (2001, 2005), among others (Barker, 1999; Burrell, 1988; Clegg et al., 2006; Townley, 1994, 1999, 2004), has argued that Foucault's forensic analysis of 'panopticon control' – that is, the detailed, intrusive, continuous and remote surveillance and disciplining of behaviour typical of the modern prison – provides an analytically and interpretively powerful metaphor for understanding the control regimes emerging across modern organizations. Based on Bentham's ideal typical model (Edwards, 2006) of the organizing principles that should inform the architectural design and administrative operation of the modern prison, Foucault's concept of 'panopticon' facilitates a deeper understanding of the cultural and discursive control mechanisms that shape everyday organizational life. This is so to the extent that it gives us insight into the complex 'micro-circuits and techniques of control' within contemporary organizations that are much more difficult to pin down and contest than the externally imposed and structurally fixed control logic and technology inherent in orthodox neo-Weberian control. 'Panopticon control' is more opaque, pervasive and insidious because it subjects individuals and groups within work organizations to mundane techniques of appraisal, categorization, treatment, enumeration and segmentation that are extremely difficult to identify, much less contest and resist, because they have become accepted as 'normal' and 'taken-for-granted'. As Sewell (2001: 191) argues, 'never before in the workplace have we been subjected to such a degree of enumeration and classification through the application of surveillance and performance measurement, undertaken by superiors and peers alike . . . However, these are not presented as instruments of power and control. Rather, they constitute a reformatory therapy enacted through behavioural normalization'. Once these normalizing and disciplining techniques are brought together and eventually integrated within a general regime of surveillance that facilitates the continuous monitoring of all movements and flows within the work organization, then we have a form of 'generative discipline and control' as 'a potent, creative and powerful social force, difficult for us to resist' (Barker, 1999: 42).

In practice, this may take some considerable time to come to fruition and the degree of overall integration achieved between the various control techniques may be more unstable and fragile than the theoretical, ideal typical, model of 'panopticon control' suggests (Edwards, 2006). Additionally, the extent to which certain employees willingly participate in such disciplinary control regimes – because they derive material advantage from their involvement and/or their values and beliefs predispose them to identify with the regulatory norms that such regimes inculcate – should not be underestimated. Nevertheless, the 'governmentalists' are convinced that Foucault's analysis of 'panopticon control' precisely and systemically identifies the complex combination of discursive, technical and organizational mechanisms and practices through which contemporary control systems 'become manifest in actual day-to-day organizational activity as a method for doing good work in the organization' (Barker, 1999: 42). Within modern work organizations, control becomes 'embedded in the various means whereby we "shape" ourselves. Through this process, we necessarily surrender some of our autonomy to the will of the organization . . . many organizational disciplines undoubtedly are overt and tangible . . . most times, however, disciplines work beyond the perception of an organization's members . . . we surrender our autonomy in a number of ways that appear to us as natural occurrences' (Barker, 1999: 42–3).

As already indicated, 'panopticon control' seems particularly well-suited to contemporary forms of 'governmentality' and 'governance' that demand much more flexible, adaptable, mobile and sophisticated control systems than those typically associated with neo-Weberian control regimes – within both the private and public sectors of most modern capitalist political economies (Barney, 2004; Castells, 2000; Ezzamel and Reed 2008; Farrell and Morris, 2003; Newman, 2001; Stalder, 2006; Thompson, 2003). Thus, contemporary debates around the type of control regime most closely associated with the 'post-bureaucratic organization' (Child and McGrath, 2001; Heckscher and Donnellon, 1994; Pettigrew and Fenton, 2000; Reed, 2005, 2010 forthcoming) seem to indicate that network-based, 'stakeholder' or 'participative' forms of governance, operating within and between different levels of socio-political decision-making (Crouch, 2005; Ezzamel and Reed, 2008), require dynamic combinations of control mechanisms and processes that cannot be accommodated within the linear design logic on which neo-Weberian control is premised. Standardization, formalization and centralization of control processes and relations are increasingly seen to be at odds with intensifying ideological demands for devolved and dispersed forms of political, economic and social organization that are responsive to the need to do something about the 'democratic deficits' inherent in modern capitalist societies and workplaces. They are also seen to be increasingly inconsistent with the much more elaborate, indeed 'seductive', control systems required in knowledge-intensive organizations which require their employees to exercise much higher levels of decision-making autonomy and discretion than is usually the case in conventional bureaucratic structures (Alvesson, 2004; McKinlay, 2005; Sewell, 2005).

Thus, new forms of governance at work can be seen as a response to intensifying political demands for forms of organizational democracy that give employees, customers, clients and citizens a substantial role on the co-production and co-evaluation of public services (Clarke et al., 2007). They also reflect escalating economic demands for forms of organizational management that are sensitive to the need for 'high trust/low control' employment systems in which core 'knowledge workers' will only fully exercise their specialist expertise if they are convinced that they are properly recognized and protected by the corporate culture. Consequently, the organizational capacity of orthodox control regimes to meet these demands and expectations is seriously in doubt because they lack the openness, transparency and flexibility associated with network-based forms of political and economic governance (Ezzamel and Reed, 2008).

However, 'governmentalists' remain pessimistic about the potential of these new forms of governmentality and governance to achieve anything approaching the political ideal of 'participative democracy' in contemporary organizational forms or practices within the workplace or beyond. Indeed, they see 'panopticon control' as symptomatic of the increasing ideological domination and discursive pervasiveness of a form of neoliberal doctrine and practice in which rationalities and programmes of government are shaped by 'indirect mechanisms and techniques' linked to the new and dispersed centres of power emerging in advanced liberal economies and democracies (Miller and Rose, 2008). At the core of these 'indirect mechanisms and techniques' of government lie *new practices and relations for calculating* how individuals, groups and organizations are to be administered and controlled in ways that are consistent with a new ethic of individual choice and personal responsibility under the unstable and uncertain conditions inherent in advanced liberal economies and democracies. Within this unstable and changing context, a plethora of expert techniques and skills are required to develop, apply and legitimate the new mechanisms and practices through which organizational control can, potentially at least, be realized at work, at play, at home and in public life. As Miller and Rose (2008: 24) describe the current situation:

> 'Advanced liberal rule depends upon expertise in a different way, and connects experts differently into technologies of rule. It seeks to de-governmentalize the state and to de-statize practices of government, to detach the substantive authority of expertise from the apparatuses of political rule, relocating experts within a market governed by the rationalities of competition, accountability and consumer demand. It seeks to govern not through "society", but through the regulated choices of individual citizens, now construed as subjects of choices and aspirations to self-actualization and self-fulfilment . . . . As an autonomizing and pluralizing formula of rule, this form of rule is dependent upon the proliferation of little regulatory instances across a territory and their multiplication, at a "molecular" level, through the interstices of our present experience. It is dependent, too, upon a particular relation between political subjects and expertise, in which the injunctions of the experts merge with our own projects for self-mastery and the enhancement of our lives'.
>
> (Miller and Rose 2008: 24)

At the level of the work organization, this regime of advanced liberal rule leads to a proliferation of control technologies that are increasingly difficult to combine, much less integrate, into cohesive 'control regimes'. The latter seem to oscillate, often wildly, between the desire of organizational elites to re-assert control as a route to securing compliance and to delegate control as a means to achieving commitment and trust from employees. However, the increasingly dispersed, fragmented and disconnected levels of institutional governance, within contemporary capitalist political economies and societies, also makes it increasingly difficult for macro-level political managers and micro-level organizational administrators to co-ordinate effectively their control strategies and practices in ways that sustain coherent narratives of change and innovation (Crouch, 2005; Thompson, 2003; Whitley, 1999, 2003). The proliferation and elaboration of 'post-bureaucratic' intra-organizational control regimes (Johnson et al., 2009) – whether through more sophisticated cultural mechanisms and information technologies or through simpler, even cruder, modes of coercive imposition and punishment or through, rather tentative and fragile, combinations of both the 'old' and 'new' – seems to generate an underlying process of 'hybridization' in which control management becomes even more precarious and contingent.

Control hybrids

Control hybrids have been an increasingly influential theme in research on organizational control over the last decade or so. This is so for a number of reasons. First, the process of hybridization – that is, the socio-political processes through which organizations develop more complex, multi-dimensional and multi-level control systems based on combinations of components drawn from a diverse range of institutional logics and forms that often conflict with each other – raises fundamental questions about the dynamics of organizational change and innovation in an increasingly 'hyper-competitive' and 'uncontrollable' environments (Castells, 2000; Clegg et al., 2006; Ferlie et al., 1996; Pettigrew and Fenton, 2000). Second, the increasing prevalence and significance of hybrid control regimes also prompts difficult debates over the theoretical frameworks, models and methodologies that organizational researchers and analysts need to understand and explain these, relatively new and innovative, organizational forms and practices. Much of mainstream organizational theorizing and analysis is based on typologically based forms of classification and categorization, premised on clear, coherent and consistent 'logics of differentiation and identification', which may no longer pertain in the radically unstable and uncertain global world in which we now live. Finally, the putative move towards hybrid control logics and forms provokes serious and difficult questions about 'the distribution of power and privileges within organizational boundaries . . . a hybrid is not a smooth organizational combination of contradictory principles but a new creation, a singular model capable of challenging the very nature of bureaucracies' (Clegg et al., 2006: 333).

As complex, intermediary organizational forms based on contradictory, and often competing if not conflicting, logics, control hybrids can be seen as a response to intensifying levels of socio-economic, political and cultural complexity and instability within the wider environment. They are also 'condemned' to struggle with the deep-seated discontinuities and disruptions that the latter inevitably generates. In this respect, hybridization can be interpreted as an organizational strategy for attempting to manage the deepening structural inequalities, political divisions and cultural contestations that advanced 'informational capitalism' (Castells, 2000) necessarily throws up and reproduces. Insofar as they are expected to juggle with the competing demands of market rationality, political expediency, social inclusivity, administrative conformity and legal integrity, contemporary work organizations, and their managerial elites, are forced to come to terms with an unmanageable range and diversity of social values and interests – while also managing to maintain their own power base and legitimacy. Hybridization, potentially at least, offers an organizational means for 'managing the unmanageable' insofar as it facilitates the segmentation, containment and regulation of fundamental economic, political and cultural conflicts – what Weber called the 'warring gods' – that cannot, in any meaningful or practical sense, be effectively eradicated.

Considered in this light, the increasing prevalence and relevance of control hybrids within contemporary work organizations might be interpreted as a new solution to an old problem – that is, the evolution of pluralistic organizational forms that offer real prospects for achieving the incremental resolution of deep-seated conflicts through the expansion of more transparent forms of 'communicative rationality' in which closed circuits of decision-making are opened up to wider participation (Ray and Reed, 1994). At the same time, control hybrids may also offer increasingly hard-pressed and insecure organizational elites a viable strategy for sustaining their power and legitimacy within a socio-historical context when traditional cultural sources of political legitimacy, such as bureaucratic rationality and authority, seem obsolete. This is achieved through a more broadly based and inclusive systems of oligarchic rule – in which middle-tier and lower-level elite groups, closer to the 'chaotic messiness' of operational control, are more coherently aligned with strategic decision-making circles and circuits – combined with more substantial decentralization and delegation of the practical conduct of governance than is usually the case within conventional bureaucratic hierarchies (Clegg et al., 2006).

Practical organizational examples of hybrid control forms can be identified across the full spectrum of contemporary private and public sector corporations – from 'high performance work systems', 'flexible labour markets', 'knowledge-creating companies' and 'network production and distribution systems' (Applebaum et al., 2006, Grimshaw et al., 2005; Nohria and Berkley, 1994; Nonaka and Takeuchi, 1995; Peck, 1996) within the former to 'multi-agency partnerships', 'primary care networks', 'foundation hospitals' and 'public–private partnerships' within the latter (Ferlie et al., 1996; Massey and Pyper, 2005; McLaughlin et al., 2002; Miller, 2005; Newman, 2001). All of these organizational forms involve significant dispersal and delegation of control in order to stimulate enhanced participation by and accountability to 'citizen consumers' (Clarke et al., 2007) in ways that facilitate the co-production and co-evolution of the new governance structures and systems which they will require. But, at the same time, they are overlaid by 'panopticon-style' systems of surveillance and discipline – such as auditing regimes, performance management technologies, market-testing reviews and individualized behavioural competence assessments – that are designed and tested by middle-tier, professional experts, deployed by lower-level operational managers and legitimated by policy-making elites as strategically vital to the organization's survival in a hyper-competitive global market. In turn, 'softer', culturally and discursively based, control techniques are also extensively and intensively deployed as mechanisms geared to anticipating and containing the inevitable resistance, in all its manifest variety, which these, relatively new and innovative, control systems will face (Courpasson, 2000; Thrift, 2005).

In these respects, structural contradictions and the socio-political tensions that they inevitably generate are built into the very design principles and mechanisms on which control hybrids are developed. Hence, instability, fragmentation, disputation and ambiguity are necessary, rather than contingent, features of control hybrids insofar as they reflect and mediate, in their institutional form and operational logic, the situational conditions and contexts within which they emerged and from which they take their cultural legitimacy and political authority. Thus, the 'structural and cultural inheritances' (Archer, 2000, 2003) that control hybrids draw upon for their political authority and cultural legitimacy entail capacities and constraints that simultaneously empower and limit their ability to shape the socio-historical contexts in which they are embedded and the material conditions under which they operate. Domination – that is, institutionalized structures of power relations – remains highly concentrated around a relatively small and cohesive set of strategic elites or oligarchs that 'strive to build a democratic plurality of actors while reinforcing, unobtrusively, the power of the inner circle' (Clegg et al., 2006: 338). A much wider range of social, political and economic interests are accommodated within this, still highly concentrated, power structure, through various forms of control dispersal, delegation and devolution to a more inclusive range of stakeholders than would usually be the case under mono-organizational forms – such as 'command and control' systems. Yet, the structural backbone of hybrid control forms, underpinning the combinations of diverse elements from which they are constructed and maintained, is provided by the substantial power inequalities between strategic elites, who determine 'the rules of the game' that will indelibly shape how such hybrids are designed and function, and subordinate groups who are required to follow, and ideally internalize, these rules. While the inclination of subordinate groups to follow elite-determined 'rules of the game' will be highly variable, and their capacity to resist, subvert and avoid such rules will be highly contingent, hybrid control forms are likely to remain just as much 'contested terrains' as their organizational predecessors and the 'structural and cultural inheritances' that they, in turn, were bequeathed by their organizational forebears.

Discussion and conclusion

Previous exposition and evaluation in this chapter clearly indicates that more recent analyses of changing forms of organizational control have been intellectually dominated by, broadly speaking, Foucauldian analytical perspectives and models that highlight the 'delicate mechanisms' through which workplace discipline and surveillance are routinely achieved within modern societies. Indeed, they have closely followed Foucault's (2003: 30) injunction to make an ascending analysis of control which 'begins with its infinitesimal mechanisms, which have their own history, their own trajectory, their own techniques and tactics, and then look how these mechanisms of power, which have their solidity and, in a sense, their own technology, have been and are invested, colonized, used, inflected, transformed, displaced, extended and so on by increasingly general mechanisms and forms of overall domination'. This dedicated focus on the 'micromechanics of control', and the material operations, technical instrumentation and expert knowledge through which they are mobilized, has provided crucial intellectual sustenance to contemporary researchers who are intent on mapping the mundane techniques through which organizational discipline can be achieved in particular settings. They are primarily interested in *'how' control works* in a wide range of localized organizational contexts and, tentatively, exploring the wider implications of these analyses of 'practical control' for more generalized forms of domination in modern societies. The fact that organizational control always works imperfectly should not obscure the reality of contemporary control regimes that recombine selected elements of both 'old' and 'new' technologies of regulative surveillance in ways that mark a distinct shift in the art and practice of governance in advanced liberal societies.

There is little doubt that these 'localized and ascending' analyses of changing organizational control regimes, once they are connected to more generalized and globalized forms of power and domination – as is the case in the work of the 'governmentalists' discussed in an earlier section of this chapter – have been highly productive for the study of work and work organizations. They have made us more sensitive to the 'micromechanics of control', in all their contemporary complexity, and their problematic intersections with macro-level domination structures and elite control strategies that have been the major research interest for succeeding genera-tions of Marxist and Weberian scholars in the sociology of work and organization studies. In addition, this work on the 'micromechanics of control' has helped us to better understand the internal dynamics and external trajectories of emerging con-trol hybrids as they struggle to manage and contain the conflicting imperatives – for commitment and compliance, for participation and regulation, for quality and effi-ciency, for individualism and collectivism and for dispersal and concentration – that initially created them and now sustains them within highly unstable and threaten-ing geo-political environments.

In these respects, this increasingly influential body of work on control hybrids seems to resonate very powerfully with wider debates over transformations in contemporary political economies where the putative shift towards 'post-bureaucratic' or 'network-based' state structures – within which power and control become much more widely dispersed and elongated than under conventional hierarchical structures – dovetails with intensifying political demands for greater 'democratization' within the workplace and its radical implications for intra-organizational control regimes (Castells, 2000; Mulgan, 1997; Reed, 2005; Thompson, 2003). Yet, previous discussion within this chapter also indicates that it would be a fundamental error to assume that the increas-ing prevalence and importance of micro-level hybridized control regimes necessarily entails the widespread dilution of concentrated hierarchical power and control – that is, structures of domination that provide ruling minorities located within the top com-mand positions of political, economic and cultural hierarchies (Scott, 2001, 2008) with the institutional capacity to shape the strategic mechanisms through which intermedi-ate and lower level control is secured.

Previous discussion also indicates that the growing significance of 'soft power and control' – that is culturally and discursively based rather than materially and structurally based forms of power and control (Clegg et al., 2006; Lukes, 2005; Nye, 2004) – within hybridized control regimes should not be taken to imply that 'hard power and control' are, in effect, redundant. *It is the, increasingly complex, combina-tions of 'hard' and 'soft' control within contemporary work organizations and within the wider structures of domination in which they are embedded that provides the analytical key to explaining the dynamics and trajectories of change in contemporary control regimes* (Perrow, 2002, 2008). In this respect, concentrations of elite power and control, embedded within and supported by structures of domination, remain far more resil-ient and significant than many theorists of the hybridized control regimes emerg-ing under the conditions presented by 'informational capitalism' have assumed. As Harrison (1994: 171–88) has argued in relation to the increasing reliance of capital-ist corporations on networked production systems in which a core of powerful, elite firms dominate a wider ring of subordinate producers and suppliers:

'the evolving global system of joint ventures, supply chains, and strategic alli-ances in no sense constitutes a reversal – let alone a negation – of the 200-year-old tendency towards *concentrated control* within industrial capitalism, even if the actual production activity is increasingly being decentralized and dispersed . . . . downsiz-ing, outsourcing, and mass layoffs are creating fear and insecurity among a large and growing fraction of the population. In the brave new world of lean production, there are winners, but there are also a growing number of losers. Such is the *dualistic* nature of networked production systems; what I call the dark side of flexibility'.

Relocated within this wider political economy – in which concentrated elite firm power and dualistic labour market structures and employment management strategies remain dominant – the move towards hybrid control regimes at the level of capitalist work organization can now be interpreted as part of a wider attempt, on the part of corporate elites, to shift the economic burden of radical corporate restructuring and related organizational change on to those least able to protect themselves from its consequences (Thompson, 2003). Thus, the move towards intra-organizational control hybrids, across both the private and public sectors within advanced capitalist political economies and societies, can now be seen as *a key component of a continuing bureaucratization of the employment relationship in which concentrated strategic control by political and economic elites is, however tentatively and tendentiously, more effectively aligned with dispersed forms of operational control at the local level.* The continuing bureaucratization of the capitalist employment relationship entails the development of more elaborate 'secondary control mechanisms' (referred to earlier on in this chapter) in which employees, particularly 'knowledge workers', are discursively reconstructed as 'disciplined subjects' that internalize, at least to some degree, the more extensive normative requirements of their working lives under the new, hybridized intra-organizational control regimes that networked capitalism generates. Pressures to develop an infrastructure of more elaborate 'secondary control mechanisms', at least for those who remain in employment and especially for those that are assigned 'core' status, are likely to become even more pronounced in conditions of globalized economic recession. Increasing differentiation, if not polarization, between what Castells (2000) calls the 'core workforce' and the 'generic disposable workforce' predisposes management towards more hybridized intra-organizational control regimes leading 'workers to experience multiple sources of loyalty, identity and commitment, as well as feelings of insecurity and destabilization' (Grimshaw et al., 2005: 29). In turn, limited improvements in worker empowerment and autonomy made possible under control hybridization may be threatened by the much tighter product and labour market conditions that economic recession imposes (Hyman, 2006). This is particularly the case for those professional occupational groups and knowledge workers worst hit by the employment impact of economic recession and its deleterious effects on their labour market power and organizational status (Percival, 2009). Much depends, as always, on where employees are structurally located within the power and control hierarchies that continue to shape network-based forms of organizing and the political skill with which they deploy whatever room for manoeuvre this positioning affords to them.

This re-interpretation of the shift towards hybrid control – as a further elaboration, rather than reversal, of bureaucratization by extension of the 'secondary control mechanisms' that certain key groups of employees experience – is entirely consistent with the analyses that researchers, such as Thompson (2003) and Clegg et al. (2006), have recently formulated of the much more fragmented and disconnected, yet concentrated and streamlined, power structures through which advanced capitalist political economies are currently managed. Thus, the more extensive reliance on intra-organizational control regimes based on the deployment of 'soft power' and inter-organizational governance structures that are much more market-based and decentralized than those characteristic of neo-corporatist style industrial/managerial capitalism can be seen as two sides of the same political coin – that is, an attempt on the part of coalitions of top-level elite groups, operating under the chronic instabilities and uncertainties endemic to advanced 'informational capitalism', to delegate operational control to middle/lower-level elites much more substantially than ever before while retaining strategic control at the centre. This *dualistic control strategy* may have worked, in a fashion, for much of the neoliberal dominated 1980s and 1990s during which the economic, political and cultural costs of radical institutional and organizational restructuring were, largely, borne by traditional blue-collar groups located in the primary and manufacturing sectors of the economy. Whether or not it can survive the latest global financial crisis of 'fast capitalism' (Dale and Burrell 2008; Grey, 2009; Sennett, 2006; Thrift, 2005) is a moot point, given that it is the 'high value end' of the manufacturing and service sectors – in which 'knowledge intensive-firms' and their 'knowledge workers' are most prominent – where the employment consequences of the latest 'shake-out' are likely to be most dramatic and where the underlying cultural legitimacy of new control regimes are likely to be most severely tested. For those within the 'core group' that remain in employment, the material and cultural advantages that they derive from a dualistic control strategy and the hybridized control regimes that it engenders may be considerable. But this is likely to be of little consolation to those 'generic workers' or 'knowledge workers' who are regarded as 'surplus to requirements' within a much harsher economic climate in which work organizations and their managers can no longer afford the luxury of hoarding and protecting relatively scarce expert labour from the vicissitudes of a global economic downturn.

References

Ackroyd, S. and Thompson, P. (1999). *Organizational Misbehaviour*. London: Sage.

Albrow, M. (1997). *Do Organizations Have Feelings?* London: Routledge.

Alvesson, M. (2002). *Understanding Organizational Culture*. London: Sage.

Alvesson, M. (2004). *Knowledge Work and Knowledge-Intensive Firms*. Oxford: Oxford University Press.

Alvesson, M. and Karreman, D. (2000). 'Varieties of Discourse: On the Study of Organization through Discourse'. *Human Relations*, 53 (9): 1125–49.

Alvesson, M. and Willmott, H. (2002). 'Identity Regulation as Organizational Control: Producing the Appropriate Individual'. *Journal of Management Studies*, 39 (5): 619–44.

Alvesson, M. and Robertson, M. (2003). 'The Best and the Brightest: The Construction, Significance and Effects of Elite Identities in Consulting Firms'. *Organization*, 13 (2): 195–224.

Applebaum, E., Bailey, T., Berg, P. and Kalleberg, A. L. (2000). *Manufacturing Advantage: Why High Performance Work Systems Pay Off*. Ithaca. New York: ILR Press.

Archer, M. (2000). *Being Human: The Problem of Agency*. Cambridge: Cambridge University Press.

Archer, M. (2003). *Structure, Agency and the Internal Conversation*. Cambridge: Cambridge University Press.

Barker, J. R. (1993). 'Tightening the Iron Cage: Concertive Control in Self-Managing Teams'. *Administrative Science Quarterly*, 38: 408–37.

Barker, J. R. (1999). *The Discipline of Teamwork: Participation and Concertive Control*. Thousand Oaks, California: Sage Publications.

Barley, S. R. and Kunda, G. (1992). 'Design and Devotion: Surges of Rational and Normative Ideologies of Control in Managerial Discourse'. *Administrative Science Quarterly*, 41: 404–41.

Barney, D. (2004). *The Network Society*. Cambridge: Polity Press.

Beniger, J. R. (1986). *The Control Revolution: Technological and Economic Origins of the Information Society*. Cambridge. Mass: Harvard University Press.

Berry, A. J., Broadbent, J. and Otley, D. (1995). *Management Control: Theories, Issues and Practices*. London: Macmillan.

Braverman, H. (1974). *Labour and Monopoly Capital: The Degradation of Work in the Twentieth Century*. New York: Monthly Review Press.

Burawoy, M. (1979). *Manufacturing Consent: Changes in the Labour Process Under Monopoly Capitalism*. Chicago: University of Chicago Press.

Burawoy, M. (1985). *The Politics of Production*. London: Verso.

Burrell, G. (1988). 'Modernism, Post Modernism and Organizational Analysis 2: The Contribution of Michel Foucault'. *Organization Studies*, 9 (2): 221–35.

Burrell, G. (2006). 'Foucauldian and Postmodern Thought and the Analysis of Work' in M. Korczynski, R. Hodson and P. Edwards (eds). *Social Theory at Work*. Oxford: Oxford University Press, 155–81.

Casey, C. (1995). *Work, Self and Society: After Industrialism*. London: Routledge.

Casey, C. (2002). *Critical Analysis of Organizations: Theory, Practice, Revitalization*. London: Sage.

Castells, M. (2000). *The Rise of Network Society*. Second Edition. Oxford: Blackwell.

Cerney, P. (2005). The *Changing Architecture of Politics*. London: Sage.

Child, J. (1985). 'Managerial Strategies, New Technology, and the Labour Process' in D. Knights, H. Willmott and D. Collinson (eds). *Job Redesign: Critical Perspectives on the Labour Process*. Aldershot: Gower, 107–41.

Child, J. (2005). *Organization*. Oxford: Blackwell.

Child, J. and McGrath, R. (2001). 'Organizations Unfettered: Organizational Form in an Information-Intensive Economy'. *Academy of Management Journal*, 44 (6): 43–76.

Clarke, J., Newman, J., Smith, N., Wilder, E. and Westmarland, L. (2007). *Creating Citizen-Consumers*. London: Sage.

Clegg, S. (1990). *Modern Organizations: Organization Studies in the Post-Modern World*. London: Sage.

Clegg, S. R. Courpasson, D. and Phillips, N. (2006). *Power and Organizations*. London: Sage.

Collinson, D. (2003). 'Identities and Insecurities: Selves at Work'. *Organization*, 10 (3): 527–47.

Courpasson, D. (2000). 'Managerial Strategies of Domination: Power in Soft Bureaucracies'. *Organization Studies*, 21 (1): 142–61.

Crouch, C. (2005). *Capitalist Diversity and Change: Recombinant Governance and Institutional Entrepreneurs*. Oxford: Oxford University Press.

Dale, K. and Burrell,G. (2008). *The Spaces of Organisation and the Organisation of Space*. London: Palgrave Macmillan.

Davidow, W. and Malone, M. (1993). *The Virtual Corporation: Structuring and Revitalizing the Organization for the 21st Century*. New York: Harper Collins.

Dean, M. (1999). *Governmentality: Power and Rule in Modern Society*. London: Sage.

Deem, R., Hillyard, S. and Reed, M. (2007). *Knowledge, Higher Education and the New Managerialism*. Oxford: Oxford University Press.

Du Gay, P. (1996). *Consumption and Identity at Work*. London: Sage.

Du Gay, P. and Salaman, G. (1992). 'The Cult(ure) of the Customer'. *Journal of Management Studies*, 29 (5): 615–34.

Du Gay, P. and Pryke, M. (eds) (2002). *Cultural Economy*. London: Sage.

Edwards, R. (1979). *Contested Terrain: The Transformation of the Workplace in the Twentieth Century*. London: Heinemann.

Edwards, P. (2006). 'Power and Ideology in the Workplace: Going Beyond even the Second Version of the Three-Dimensional View'. *Work, Employment and Society*, 20 (3): 571–81.

Elger, T. and Smith, C. (2005). *Assembling Work: Remaking Factory Regimes in Japanese Multinationals in Britain*. Oxford: Oxford University Press.

Ezzamel, M. and Willmott, H. (1998). 'Accounting for Teamwork: A Critical Study of Group-Based Systems of Organizational Control'. *Administrative Science Quarterly*, 43: 333–67.

Ezzamel, M. and Reed, M. (2008). 'Governance: A Code of Many Colours'. *Human Relations*, 61 (5): 597–615.

Farrell, C. and Morris, J. (2003). 'The Neo-Bureaucratic State: Professionals, Managers and Professional Managers in Schools, General Practices and Social Work'. *Organization*, 10 (1): 129–56.

Ferlie, E., Pettigrew, A., Ashburner, L. and Fitzgerald, L. (1996). *The New Public Management in Action*. Oxford: Oxford University Press.

Fincham, R. (2009). 'A New(ish) Model of Professional Work' Unpublished paper, 24th Employment Relations Unit (ERU) Annual Conference, 3/4th September, Cardiff Business School.

Fineman, S. (ed.) (1993). *Emotion in Organizations*. London: Sage.

Fineman, S. (1996). 'Emotion and Organizing' in S. R. Clegg, C. Hardy and W. Nord (eds). *Handbook of Organization Studies*. London: Sage, 543–64.

Fineman, S. and Sturdy, A. (1999). 'The Emotions of Control'. *Human Relations*, 52 (5): 631–63.

Fournier, V. and Grey, C. (1999). 'Too Much, Too Little, and Too Often: A Critique of Du Gay's Analysis of Enterprise'. *Organization*, 6 (1): 107–28.

Foucault, M. (1976a). *The Birth of the Clinic*. London: Tavistock Publications Ltd.

Foucault, M. (1976b). *Discipline and Punish: The Birth of the Prison*. Harmondsworth: Allen Lane.

Foucault, M. (2003). *Society Must be Defended*. London: Allen and Lane.

Fox, A. (1971). *A Sociology of Work in Industry*. Collier Macmillan.

Frenkel, S., Korczynski, M., Shire, K. A. and Tam, M. (1999). *On the Frontline of Work in the Information Economy*. Ithaca and London: Cornell University Press.

Garrahan, P. and Stewart, P. (1992). The *Nissan Enigma: Flexibility at Work in a Local Economy*. London: Cassell.

Giddens, A. (1982). 'Power, the Dialectic of Control and Class Structuration' in A. Giddens and G. Mackenzie (eds). *Social Class and the Division of Labour*. Cambridge: Cambridge University Press, 29–45.

Goodrich, C. L. (1975). *The Frontier of Control: A Study in British Workshop Politics*. London: Pluto Press.

Grant, D., Keenoy, T. and Oswick, C. (eds) (1998). *Discourse and Organization*. London: Sage.

Grant, D., Hardy, C., Oswick, C. and Putnam, L. (eds) (2004). *The Sage Handbook of Organizational Discourse*. London: Sage.

Grey, C. (1994). 'Career as a Project of the Self and Labour Process Discipline'. *Sociology*, 28: 479–98.

Grey, C. (2009). *A Very Short, Fairly Interesting and Reasonably Cheap Book about Studying Organizations*. Second Edition. London: Sage.

Grimshaw, D., Marchington, M., Rubery, J. and Willmottt, H. (eds) (2005). *Fragmenting Work: Blurring Organizational Boundaries and Disordering Hierarchies*. Oxford: Oxford University Press.

Grint, K. (1991). *The Sociology of Work in Industry*. Cambridge: Polity Press.

Handy, C. B. (1984). *The Future of Work*. Oxford: Blackwell.

Harrison, B. (1994). *Lean and Mean*. London: The Guilford Press.

Hassard, J. and Parker, M. (eds) (1993). *Posttmodernism and Organizations*. London: Sage.

Heckscher, C. and Donnellon, A. (eds) (1994*). The Post-Bureaucratic Organization: New Perspectives on Organizational Change*. London: Sage.

Hochschild, A. R. (1983). *The Managed Heart*. Berkeley: University of California Press.

Hyman, J. (2006). 'The Remaking of Work: Empowerment or Degradation?' in G. Wood

and P. James (eds). *Institutions, Production, and Working Life*. Oxford: Oxford University Press, 185–202.

Innes, M. (2003). *Understanding Social Control: Deviance, Crime and Social Order*. Berkshire: Open University Press.

Jacques, R. (1996). *Manufacturing the Employee: Management Knowledge from the 19th to 21st Centuries*. Thousand Oaks CA: Sage.

Johnson, P., Wood, G., Brewster, C. and Brookes, M. (2009). 'The Rise of Post-Bureaucracy: Theorists' Fancy or Organizational Praxis?'. *International Sociology*, 24 (1): 37–61.

Kanter, R. M. (1990). *When Giants Learn to Dance*. London: Unwin Hyman.

Karreman, D. and Alvesson, M. (2004). 'Cages in Tandem: Management Control, Social Identity, and Identification in a Knowledge-Intensive Firm'. *Organization*, 11 (1): 149–74.

Keat, R. and Abercrombie, N. (eds) (1991). *Enterprise Culture*. London: Routledge.

Knights, D. (2009). 'Power at Work in Organizations' in M. Alvesson, T. Bridgman and H. Willmott (eds), *The Oxford Handbook of Critical Management Studies*, Oxford: Oxford University Press, 144–165.

Knights, D. and Willmott, H. (1985). 'Power and Identity in Theory and Practice'. *Sociological Review*, 33 (1): 22–46.

Knights, D. and Willmott, H. (1989). 'Power and Subjectivity at Work: From Degradation to Subjugation in Social Relations'. *Sociology*, 23 (4): 535–58.

Knights, D. and Willmott, H (eds) (1990). *Labour Process Theory*. London: Macmillan.

Knights, D. and McCabe, D. (2003). *Organization and Innovation: Guru Schemes and American Dreams*. Berkshire: Open University Press.

Knights, D., Willmott, H. and Collinson, D. (eds) (1985). *Job Redesign: Critical Perspectives on the Labour Process*. Aldershot. Gower.

Kondo, D. K. (1990). Crafting Selves: Power, Gender, and Discourses of Identity in a Japanese Workplace. Chicago: University of Chicago Press.

Korczynski, M. (2003). 'Communities of Coping: Collective Emotional Labour in Service Work'. *Organization*, 10 (1): 55–79.

Kunda, G. (1992). *Engineering Culture: Control and Commitment in a High-Tech Corporation*. Philadelphia: Temple University Press.

Law, J. and Hassard, J. (eds) (1999). *Actor Network Theory and After*. Oxford: Blackwell.

Leadbeater, C. and Lloyd, J. (1987). *In Search of Work*. Harmondsworth: Penguin.

Littler, C. R. (1985). *The Development of the Labour Process in Capitalist Societies*. London: Heinemann.

Littler, C. R. and Salaman, G. (1982). 'Bravermania and Beyond'. *Sociology*, 16 (2): 251–69.

Lukes, S. (2005). *Power: A Radical View*. Second Edition. London: Macmillan.

Marsden, R. (1999). *The Nature of Capital*. London: Routledge.

Martin, J. (1992). *Cultures in Organizations; Three Perspectives*. Oxford: Oxford University Press.

Martin, J. (2002). *Organizational Culture: Mapping the Terrain*. Thousand Oakes. CA: Sage Publications.

Martin, J. and Frost, P. (1996). 'The Organizational Culture War Games: A Struggle for Intellectual Dominance' in S. R. Clegg, C. Hardy and W. R. Nord (eds). *Handbook of Organization Studies*. London: Sage, 599–621.

Massey, A. and Pyper, R. (2005). *Public Management and Modernization in Britain*. Basingstoke: Palgrave Macmillan.

McAuley, J., Duberley, J. and Johnson, P. (2007). *Organization Theory: Challenges and Perspectives*. Englewood Cliffs. NJ: Prentice Hall.

McKinlay, A. (2005). 'Knowledge Management' in S. Ackroyd, R. Batt, P. Thompson and P. Tolbert (eds). *The Oxford Handbook of Work and Organization*. Oxford: Oxford University Press.

McKinlay, A. and Starkey, K. (eds) (1998). *Foucault, Management and Organization Theory*. London: Sage.

McLaughlin, K., Osborne, S. and Ferlie, E. (eds) (2002). *New Public Management: Current Trends and Future Prospects*. London: Routledge.

Miller, D. (2005). 'What is Best "Value"? Bureaucracy, Virtualism and Local Governance' in P. Du Gay (ed.). *The Values of Bureaucracy*. Oxford: Oxford University Press, 233–54.

Miller, P. and Rose, N. (2008). *Governing the Present: Administering Economic, Social and Personal Life*. Cambridge: Polity.

Morgan, G. (1990). *Organizations in Society*. Basingstoke: Macmillan.

Morgan, G. and Sturdy, A. (2000). *Beyond Organizational Change: Structure, Discourse and Power in UK Financial Services*. Basingstoke: Macmillan.

Mulgan, G. (1997). *Connexity: How to Live in a Connected World*. Boston. Mass: Harvard Business School Press.

Newman, J. (2001). *Modernizing Governance: New Labour, Policy and Society*. London: Sage.

Nohria, N. and Berkley, J. D. (1994). 'The Virtual Organization: Bureaucracy, Technology and the Implosion of Control' in C. Hecksher and A. Donnellon (eds). *The Post-Bureaucratic Organization: New Perspectives on Organizational Change*. Thousand Oakes. CA: Sage, 108–28.

Nonaka, I. and Takeuchi, H. (1995). *The Knowledge-Creating Company: How Japanese Companies Create the Dynamics of Innovation*. Oxford: Oxford University Press.

Nye, J. S. (2004). *Soft Power: The Means to Success in World Politics*. New York: Public Affairs.

Parker, M. (2000). *Organizational Culture and Identity*. London: Sage.

Pearce, F. and Woodiwiss, T. (2001). 'Reading Foucault as a Realist' in J. Lopez and G. Potter (eds). *After Postmodernism: An Introduction to Critical Realism*. London: The Athlone Press, 51–62.

Peck, J. (1996). *Workplace: The Social Regulation of Labour Markets*. London: The Guilford Press.

Percival, J. (2009). 'Architect Job Losses Sore as Crunch Hits Construction'. *The Guardian*. Friday 20th March, p. 13.

Perrow, C. (1986). *Complex Organizations: A Critical Essay*. Third Edition. New York: Random House.

Perrow, C. (2002). *Organizing America: Wealth, Power, and the Origins of Corporate Capitalism*. Princeton: Princeton University Press.

Perrow, C. (2008). 'Conservative Radicalism'. *Organization*, 15 (6): 915–21.

Pettigrew, A. M. (1985). *The Awakening Giant: Continuity and Change in ICI*. Oxford: Blackwell.

Pettigrew, A. M. and Fenton, E. M. (2000). *The Innovating Organization*. London: Sage.

Phillips, N. and Hardy, C. (2002). *Discourse Analysis: Investigating Processes of Social Construction*. Newbury Park, CA: Sage.

Pollittt, C. (1993). *Managerialism and the Public Services*. Second Edition. Oxford: Blackwell.

Rawlinson, M., Carter, C. and McKinlay, A. (eds) (2002). 'Themed Section on Foucault, Management and History'. *Organization*, 9 (4): 515–56.

Ray, L. and Sayer, A. (1999). *Culture and Economy: After the Cultural Turn*. London: Sage.

Ray, L. J. and Reed, M. (eds) (1994). *Organizing Modernity: New Perspectives on Work, Organization and Society*. London: Routledge.

Reed, M. (1989). *The Sociology of Management*. London: Harvester.

Reed, M. (1990). 'The Labour Process Perspective on Management Organization: A Critique and Reformulation' in J. Hassard and D. Pym (eds). *The Theory and Philosophy of Organizations: Critical Issues and New Perspectives*. London: Routledge, 63–82.

Reed, M. (1996). 'Organizational Theorizing: A Historically Contested Terrain' in S. R. Clegg, C. Hardy and W. R. Nord (eds). *Handbook of Organization Studies*. London: Sage, 31–56.

Reed, M. (1999). 'From the "Cage" to the "Gaze"? The Dynamics of Organizational Control in Late Modernity' in G. Morgan and L. Engwall (eds). *Regulation and Organizations: International Perspectives*. London: Routledge, 17–49.

Reed, M. (2005). 'Beyond the iron Cage? Bureaucracy and Democracy in the Knowledge Economy and Society' in P. Du Gay (ed.). *The Values of Bureaucracy*. Oxford: Oxford University Press, 115–40.

Reed, M. (2010 forthcoming). 'The Post-Bureaucratic Organization and the Control Revolution' in M. Harris (ed.). *Managing Modernity*. Oxford: Oxford University Press.

Robertson, M. and Swan, J. (2003). 'Control – What Control? Culture and Ambiguity Within a Knowledge – Intensive Firm'. *Journal of Management Studies*, 40 (4): 831–58.

Robertson, M. and Swan, J. (2004). 'Going Public: The Emergence and Effects of Soft Bureaucracy within a Knowledge-Intensive Firm'. *Organization*, 11 (1): 123–48.

Rose, N. (1989). *Governing the Soul: The Shaping of the Private Self*. London: Routledge.

Rose, N. (1999). *Powers of Freedom*. Cambridge: Cambridge University Press.

Salaman, G. (1979). *Work Organizations: Resistance and Control*. London: Longman.

Scott, J. (2001). *Power*. Cambridge: Polity.

Scott, J. (2008). 'Modes of Power and the Re-conceptualization of Elites' in M. Savage and K. Williams (eds). *Remembering Elites*. Oxford: Blackwell, 27–43.

Sennett, R. (2006). *The Culture of the New Capitalism*. New Haven: Yale University Press.

Sewell, G. (1998). 'The Discipline of Teams: The Control of Team-Based Industrial Work through Electronic and Peer Surveillance'. *Administrative Science Quarterly*, 41: 397–429.

Sewell, G. (2001). 'The Prison-House of Language: the Penitential Discourse of Organizational Power' in R. Westwood. and S. Linstead (eds). *The Language of Organization*. London: Sage, 176–98.

Sewell, G. (2005). 'Nice Work? Re-thinking Managerial Control in an Era of Knowledge Work'. *Organization*, 12 (5): 685–704.

Sewell, G. and Wilkinson, B. (1992). 'Someone to Watch Over Me: Surveillance, Discipline and Just-in-Time Labour Processes'. *Sociology*, 26: 271–89.

Smircich, L. (1983). 'Concepts of Culture and Organizational Analysis'. *Administrative Science Quarterly*, 28: 339–59.

Smircich, L. (1985). 'Is the Concept of Culture a Paradigm for Understanding Organizations and Ourselves?' in P. Frost, L. Moore, M. Louis, C. Lundberg and J. Martin (eds). *Organizational Culture*. Beverly Hills. CA: Sage, 55–72.

Smith, D. (2005). *Institutional Ethnography: A Sociology for People*. New York: Rowan and Littlefield.

Stalder, F. (2006). *Manuel Castells: The Theory of the Network Society*. Cambridge: Polity.

Strati, A. (2000). *Theory and Methods in Organization Studies*. London: Sage.

Sturdy, A. J. and Fineman, S. (2001). 'Struggles for Control of Affect' in A. J. Sturdy, I. Grugulis and H. Willmott (eds). *Customer Service: Empowerment and Entrapment*. Basingstoke: Palgrave.

Taylor, P., Mulvey, G., Hyman, J. and Bain, P. (2002). 'Work Organization, Control and the Experience of Wok in Call Centres'. *Work, Employment and Society*, 16 (1): 133–50.

Thompson, G. (2003). *Between Hierarchies and Markets: The Logic and Limits of Network Forms of Organization*. Oxford: Oxford University Press.

Thompson, P. (1989). *The Nature of Work: An Introduction to Debates on the Labour Process*. London: Macmillan.

Thompson, P. (2003). 'Disconnected Capitalism: Or Why Employers Can't Keep their Side of the Bargain'. *Work, Employment and Society*, 17 (2): 359–78.

Thompson, P. and Ackroyd, S. (1995). 'All Quiet on the Workplace Front: A Critique of Recent Trends in British Industrial Sociology'. *Sociology*, 29 (4): 610–33.

Thompson, P. and Warhurst, C. (eds) (1998). *Workplaces of the Future*. Basingstoke: MacMillan.

Thompson, P. and Ackroyd, S. (2005). 'A Little Knowledge is Still a Dangerous Thing: Some Comments on the Indeterminacy of Graham Sewell'. *Organization*, 12 (5): 705–10.

Thompson, P. and McHugh, D. (2005). *Work Organization: A Critical Introduction*. Third Edition. London: Macmillan.

Thrift, N. (1999). 'The Rise of Soft Capitalism'. *Cultural Values*, 1: 29–57.

Thrift, N. (2005). *Knowing Capitalism*. London: Sage.

Tomaney, J. (1994). 'A New Paradigm of Work Organization and Technology' in A. Amin (ed.). *Post-Fordism: A Reader*. Oxford: Blackwell, 157–94.

Townley, B. (1994). *Reframing Human Resource Management: Power, Ethics and the Subject at Work*. London: Sage.

Townley, B. (1999). 'Performance Appraisal and Practical Reason'. *Journal of Management Studies*, 36: 287–306.

Townley, B. (2004). 'Managerial Technologies, Ethics and Management'. *Journal of Management Studies*, 41: 415–45.

Townley, N. (2008). *Reason's Neglect: Rationality and Organizing*. Oxford: Oxford University Press.

Turner, B. (1990). 'The Rise of Organizational Symbolism' in J. Hassard and D. Pym (eds). *The Theory and Philosophy of Organizations: Critical Issues and New Perspectives*. London: Routledge, 83–96.

Van Dijk, J. (1999). *The Network Society*. London: Sage.

Watson, T. J. (1994). *In Search of Management: Culture, Chaos and Control in Managerial Work*. London: Routledge.

Weick, K. (1995). *Sensemaking in Organizations*. Thousand Oaks CA: Sage Publications.

Westwood, R. and Linstead, S. (eds) (2001). *The Language of Organization*. London. Sage.

Whittingon, R. (1994). 'Sociological Pluralism, Institutions and Managerial Agency' in J. Hassard and M. Parker (eds). *Towards a New Theory of Organizations*. London: Routledge, 53–74.

Whitley, R. (1984). 'The Fragmented State of Management Studies: Reasons and Consequences'. *Journal of Management Studies*, 21 (3): 331–48.

Whitley, R. (1999). *Divergent Capitalisms: The Social Structuring and Change of Business Systems.* Oxford: Oxford University Press.

Whitley, R. (2003). 'From the Search for Universal Correlations to the Institutional Structuring of Economic Organizations and Change: The Development and Future of Organization Studies'. *Organization,* 10 (3): 481–501.

Willmott, H. (1987). 'Studying Managerial Work: A Critique and a Proposal'. *Journal of Management Studies.* 24: 249–70.

Willmott, H. (2005). 'Theorizing Contemporary Control: Some Post-Structuralist Responses to Some Critical Realist Questions'. *Organization,* 12 (5): 747–80.

Zuboff, S. (1988). *In the Age of the Smart Machine: The Future of Work and Power.* Oxford: Heinemann.

KEY CONCEPTS

alienation	making out
estrangement	control versus consent
forced labour	workplace fiddles
voluntary labour	joking at work
false consciousness	sabotage
powerlessness	whistle-blowing
meaninglessness	escaping
isolation	consent and resistance
self-estrangement	interpreting workplace behaviour

CHAPTER AIM

To explore how employees survive the alienating tendencies at work by developing various coping strategies.

LEARNING OUTCOMES

After reading and understanding the material in this chapter you will be able to:

1. Describe how alienation results from the four types of estrangement originally identified by Marx.
2. Explain and assess Blauner's version of alienation.
3. Describe the concept of 'making out' and evaluate its role in creating consent within the workplace.
4. Classify various types of workplace fiddles and evaluate why they occur within the workplace.
5. Explain four functions of joking at work.
6. Describe and interpret the importance of workplace sabotage.
7. Explain the concept of escaping within a workplace context.
8. Assess whether the five survival strategies should be interpreted as forms of consent or resistance.

Introduction

This chapter, perhaps more than any other in the book, illustrates the importance of viewing work as a rich and varied domain of human activity. It is concerned with the ways in which employees get through their working day: how they survive the boredom, tedium, monotony, drudgery and powerlessness that characterise many jobs. In examining this issue, it is necessary to cover a wide range of concepts and research evidence. At the same time, there is one central principle around which the discussion is organised: the notion that in order to 'survive' work, people are obliged to become resourceful and creative in developing strategies that allow them to assert some control over, and construct meanings for, the work activities they are directed by managers to undertake.

In the analysis that follows, we are seeking to access the domain of the informal activities in work that are normally hidden from the gaze of the outsider. It is the domain where the subjective experiences of individuals are collectively constructed and reconstructed to create shared understandings and develop norms that guide and pattern behaviour. Yet it is also a regulated world where the structural constraints imposed by power holders (especially managers) limit the actions of individuals and workgroups. The result is a curious mixture of consent and resistance to work.

The analysis begins with a discussion of the extent to which work produces conditions of alienation for employees. This is followed by an examination of the way that alienating tendencies may be countered through various creative strategies by employees. From an assessment of the empirical research on informal work behaviour, five survival strategies are explored: 'making out', fiddling, joking, sabotaging and escaping. Finally, there is an assessment of whether these strategies can be construed as forms of workplace consent or resistance, or both.

Learning outcome 1: Describe how alienation results from the four types of estrangement originally identified by Marx

---

Alienation – an objective state or a subjective experience?

The word 'alienation' is freely used in the media (especially in serious late night television talk shows and Sunday newspapers) and arises in everyday conversation. Yet alienation remains one of the most contested terms in the academic study of work. In fact, in attempting to define and explain 'alienation' fully it would be possible to write a whole chapter on the concept. Here we have restricted the discussion to outlining two different perspectives on alienation. The first views alienation as an objective state, and builds on concepts originally defined by Karl Marx, while the second introduces elements of subjectivity into the analysis of alienation, and stems from a study by Robert Blauner.

Alienation as an objective state

Marx argues that alienation is an intrinsic part of the capitalist labour process, and therefore is an unavoidable objective state in which all workers find themselves.

It manifests itself because in selling their labour power, employees are relinquishing the right to control their own labour, thus discretion over how and when work should be undertaken becomes the prerogative of employers. This subordination of employees to their employer (or to managers who are acting on behalf of the employer, and sometimes referred to as the 'agents of capital') makes the activity of work a degrading and dehumanising activity.

> [Under capitalism] all the means for developing production are transformed into means of domination over and exploitation of the producer; that they mutilate the worker into a fragment of a human being, degrade him to become a mere appurtenance, make his work such a torment that its essential meaning is destroyed.
>
> (Marx, 1930: 713, quoted in Fox, 1974: 224)

As a result of this relationship, according to Marx, employees experience four types of estrangement:

- self-estrangement
- estrangement from the product of their labour
- estrangement from their species being
- estrangement from others.

Each of these are described in more detail below, and you can see how they are linked together by looking at the top half of the flowchart in Figure 6.1.

- *Self-estrangement.* Work ought to be a source of satisfaction in its own right, but under capitalism work is merely the means for people to acquire money to satisfy their needs outside working hours. In other words, people only find extrinsic meaning in work. As a consequence, employees experience a sense of 'self-estrangement' because while they are in work undertaking the activities as instructed by their managers, they cannot be themselves. They are separated from their true selves; they experience a sense of alienation. To get a better idea of how vividly Marx expressed this, see Excerpt 6.1. Also see Cox (1998).
- *Estrangement from the product of one's labour.* The output (the product or object) of one's labour is the physical expression of the effort that has been undertaken and the skills that have been used – a process Marx labels 'objectification'. However, the product of a person's labour is not owned by the employee; it becomes the property of the capitalist (the process of expropriation). As a consequence, the dispossessed employees see the product of their labour as something that is distant and separated from themselves. They become estranged from the product of their labour – in other words, the product becomes an alien object. Or, as Marx expresses it:

> The *alienation* of the worker in his product means not only that his labour becomes an object, an *external* existence, but that it exists *outside him,* independently, as something alien to him, and that it becomes a power on its own confronting him; it means that the life which he has conferred on the object confronts him as something hostile and alien.
>
> (Marx, 1969: 97, emphasis in original)

- *Estrangement from one's species being.* The alienation caused by self-estrangement and estrangement from the product has wider repercussions for humankind. Marx argues that through work people express their creativity, produce the means of their own existence and hence realise their humanity. This free, creative endeavour is the very purpose of life, but under capitalism work becomes coercion: forced labour. This means that people become estranged from their very nature; they are left alienated from their 'species being'.

- *Estrangement from others.* Because of their estrangement from their essential nature, people are left estranged from each other. Marx's argument here stems from a belief that human beings are distinct from animals because of their self-awareness. Thus a person can understand the world through his/her own actions and behaviour, and by appreciating the role and behaviour of others, in relation to him or herself. However, the three previous forms of estrangement combine to create conditions in which the unique qualities of humankind are diminished. Under forced labour, people are owned and controlled. They experience this directly and also recognise this estrangement in other people. Consequently, they are both estranged from their own humanity and from others.

Excerpt 6.1

Self-estrangement under the capitalist labour process

[The worker] does not affirm himself but denies himself, does not feel content but unhappy, does not develop freely his physical and mental energy but mortifies his body and ruins his mind. The worker therefore only feels himself outside his work, and in his work feels outside himself. He is at home when he is not working, and when he is working he is not at home. His labour is therefore not voluntary, but coerced; it is *forced labour*. It is therefore not the satisfaction of a need; it is merely a *means* to satisfy needs external to it. Its alien character emerges clearly in the fact that as soon as no physical or other compulsion exists, labour is shunned like the plague. External labour, labour in which man alienates himself, is a labour of self-sacrifice, of mortification. Lastly, the external character of labour for the worker appears in the fact that it is not his own, but someone else's that it does not belong to him, that in it he belongs, not to himself, but to another. Just as in religion the spontaneous activity of the human imagination, of the human brain and the human heart, operates independently of the individual – that is, operates on him as an alien, divine or diabolical activity – in the same way the worker's activity is not his spontaneous activity. It belongs to another; it is the loss of his self.

Source: Marx (1969: 99–100) (emphasis in original).

Figure 6.1 summarises this discussion by mapping the relationships between the various concepts in Marx's theory of the labour process and alienation. The top half of the flowchart shows how each of the concepts is linked and leads to alienation at work.

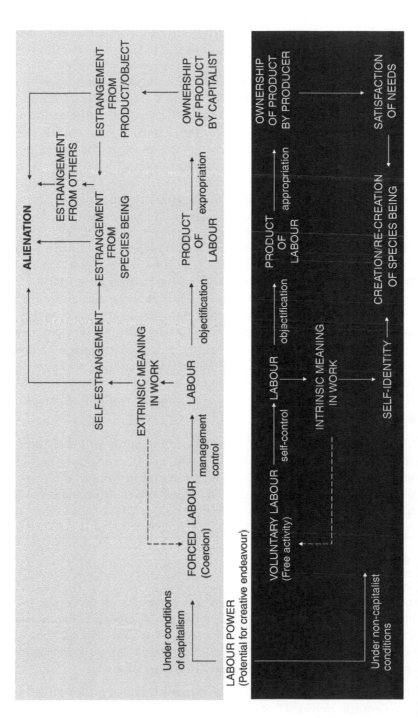

Figure 6.1 Marx's theory of the labour process and alienation

Non-alienating conditions

The bottom half of the flowchart in Figure 6.1 suggests how under noncapitalist conditions the problem of alienation might be avoided. If each of the components are compared with their equivalents in the top half of the diagram, it is clear that while there are similarities, the difference is that the person undertaking the work remains in control of both his/her labour and the product of his/her labour. The consequence of self-control over one's labour is that a person is more likely to derive intrinsic meaning from the work being undertaken, rather than only seeing it as a means of getting money. In turn, this might mean that people's self-esteem and feelings of worth are enhanced – therefore it contributes to their self-identity. Similarly, control over the product of their labour (appropriation rather then expropriation) means that the outcome of people's endeavour and effort of work remains in their possession, and they can choose how to use this to satisfy their needs. Overall, there is no alienation because the four features of estrangement do not occur.

The concept of false consciousness

For Marx, the condition of alienation was an objective state under which all employees within capitalist relations suffered. In many ways, this places the concept of alienation beyond empirical investigation because it matters little whether people feel or say they are alienated since the assumption is that the structures of capitalism determine the objective state of alienation. In other words, subjectivity is not part of the analysis, and Marxists are likely to argue that people who claim to be satisfied and fulfilled at work are merely expressing a 'false consciousness': a failure to appreciate the objective reality of their position of subordination and exploitation. Moreover, the Marxist approach to alienation is linked to the work ethic because it rests on the fundamental assumption that, in an ideal world, work ought to be intrinsically rewarding. As Anthony (1977: 141) points out:

> For Marx, alienation represents an imperfection in the purity of the ideal of work, which is the only activity that gives man his identity. The essential paradox of alienation is that it is a pathological state of affairs produced in work as the result of an over-emphasis on a work ethic and on work-based values. It becomes possible to speak of man alienated by his work only when he is asked to take work very seriously.

Exercise 6.1

What do you think?
The bottom half of the flowchart in Figure 6.1 is idealistic. Indeed, you might argue that it is unrealistic given that the capitalist labour process is the dominant form of work organisation. However, there might be workers around the world who, although often operating within conditions of capitalism, experience some of the elements illustrated by the bottom half of the flow chart.

1. To explore this idea, take each of the occupations below and assess their work using the concepts provided in the flow-chart:
   • a farmer in a small community in a developing country

- a freelance photographer
- a full-time housewife/househusband
- an Internet entrepreneur
- a prostitute
- a shopkeeper (self-employed)
- employees in a workers' cooperative
- a drug dealer
- an artist (painter, sculptor etc.).

2. You have probably found evidence of non-alienation in some of these occupations, but how might a Marxist use the concept of 'false consciousness' to suggest your analysis is inadequate?

Learning outcome 2: Explain and assess Blauner's version of alienation

---

Alienation as a subjective experience

An alternative way of looking at alienation is to start from two assumptions that differ from those suggested by Marx.

Assumption 1: alienation is not inevitable under capitalism.
Assumption 2: work has different meanings for different people.

Both of these assumptions suggest that it is inadequate to view alienation as an objective condition (the same for all employees under capitalism), but that instead, alienation should be considered a subjective experience (differing from situation to situation, and person to person). One of the most notable attempts to explore the concept in this manner has been undertaken by Blauner (1964). He begins from the proposition that 'alienation is a general syndrome made up of a number of different *objective conditions and subjective feelings-states* which emerge from certain relationships between workers and the sociotechnical settings of employment' (Blauner, 1964: 15, emphasis added). He argues that alienation should be divided into four dimensions, each of which can be investigated for different workers to enable a profile of alienation to be drawn up.

Blauner's four dimensions are summarised in Table 6.1. To illustrate how these dimensions can be used to assess work, we have selected two jobs to compare, nursery assistants and car-park attendants. To undertake such an analysis properly we should be assessing the views of people who actually do these jobs, but for illustrative purposes we will have to rely on some general assumptions. In terms of the dimension of powerlessness, both nursery assistants and car-park attendants are likely to have little control over their conditions of employment, but they might differ in terms of their experiences of control over the work process.

The car-park attendant's work will be paced by the arrival and departure of customers, and he or she is likely to be doing the same repetitive tasks all day long. The nursery assistant's pace of work will fluctuate with the demands of the children, but he or she will be able to have some influence over this, for example by distracting them onto different tasks. Nursery assistants will also be able to have some control over

Table 6.1 Blauner's four dimensions of alienation

Conditions of alienation	Definition	Possible indicators/measures of alienation	Corresponding conditions of freedom non-alienation
1 Powerlessness	Employees are controlled and manipulated by others or by an impersonal system (such as technology) and cannot change or modify this domination	• Extent of control over the conditions of employment • Extent of control over the immediate work process: – pace of work – method of work	Autonomy (empowerment)
2 Meaninglessness	Employees lack understanding of the whole work process and lack a sense of how their own work contributes to the whole	• Length of work cycle • Range and variety of tasks • Completeness of task	Purposefulness
3 Isolation	Employees experience no sense of belonging in the work situation and are unable or unwilling to identify with the organisation and its goals	• Type and extent of social interaction – formal – informal	Belonging
4 Self-estrangement	Employees gain no sense of identity or personal fulfilment from work, and this detachment means that work is not considered a worthwhile activity in its own right	• Instrumental attitudes • 'Clock-watching' • Expressions of boredom	Self-expression

Source: summarised from Blauner (1964: 15–35).

the approach they take to the work (albeit within prescribed guidelines). In terms of the second dimension of meaninglessness, the short-cycle, repetitive tasks of car-park attendants may give a sense of achievement, although the lack of range and variety ultimately make the work dull. Nursery assistants have a greater range and variety of tasks, with longer work cycles and far less predictability in the work. Potentially this makes the work more meaningful, but also vulnerable to more frustrating experiences.

In terms of isolation, both jobs involve contact with others, but whereas the interactions between car-park attendants and their customers are brief and formal, nursery assistants will experience extended periods of highly informal interaction with children, as well as interaction with other members of the nursery staff (both formal and informal) and parents (mainly formal). Finally, in terms of self-estrangement, nursery assistants are likely to experience a greater sense of fulfilment than car-park attendants. Of course there will be boring aspects to the job, and sometimes the time will drag, but the variety and unpredictability might compensate for this. Car-park attendants are likely to find activities to distract themselves from the work – reading the newspaper, listening to the radio and so forth – because it is not fulfilling in its own right.

Overall, therefore, it is likely that on average a nursery assistant will feel alienation less than the car-park attendant, although because much of this assessment depends on the subjective experiences of particular individuals in these roles. It would be logically possible to find some nursery assistants who express attitudes that reflect a sense of powerlessness, meaninglessness, isolation and self-estrangement, and car park attendants whose work gives them a sense of autonomy, purposefulness, belonging and self-expression. Indeed, it is the subjective aspect to Blauner's theory that distinguishes it from that of Marx.

Even though Blauner acknowledges the subjectivity of alienation, like Marx, he also considers that there are objective conditions which tend to produce alienation. Rather than generalise about the capitalist system as a whole, Blauner differentiates *between* capitalist enterprises according to their technology, and generalises from this:

> There is ... no simple answer to the question: Is the factory worker of today an alienated worker? Inherent in the techniques of modern manufacturing and the principles of bureaucratic industrial organization are general alienating tendencies. But in some cases the distinctive technology, division of labor, economic structure, and social organization – in other words, the factors that differentiate individual industries – intensify these general tendencies, producing a high degree of alienation; in other cases they minimize and counteract them, resulting instead in control, meaning, and integration.
>
> (Blauner, 1964: 166–7)

Ultimately, this leads Blauner to a position of technological determinism: he suggests that greater automation will free workers from the drudgery of assembly lines and machine minding and will result in decreasing alienation for employees (Blauner, 1964: 182–3). This is an optimistic projection that suggests the problem of alienation will be resolved within the capitalist framework – a position which, was vehemently challenged by Braverman (1974) and subsequent labour process theorists.

Criticisms of Blauner's work

Blauner has been criticised for trivialising Marx's notion of alienation 'by conceptualising it in subjective terms' (Watson, 1987: 107). However, while there are numerous points of criticism that can be levelled at Blauner's work (not least the degree of thoroughness of the empirical data upon which he based his conclusions; see Eldridge, 1971), the problem of being 'overly subjective' is not one of them. Certainly Blauner is accepting the importance of subjectivity because the implication of his thesis is that different employees will have different alienation profiles. But Blauner seems far more interested in using this to generalise about occupational groups, and in particular to assess whether certain types of production technologies led to greater alienation than others. In fact, as his analysis progresses, subjectivity disappears from the discussion. If his thesis was truly examining subjectivity, then his focus would be on individual employees, rather than occupational groups. Moreover, he would probably be more concerned with exploring whether employees doing similar jobs experience the dimensions of alienation differently, and the extent to which this leads to individual, rather than collective profiles of alienation.

Yet in spite of these criticisms, Blauner's biggest contribution is to reclaim the concept of alienation from Marxist theorists. In reinterpreting the concept and breaking it down into the four separate dimensions, he provides components of alienation which are potentially variable in their intensity and also measurable (or more accurately, comparable). This shifts alienation from being an absolute to a relative concept, and allows the theoretical possibility of (objective) conditions of alienation producing (subjective) feelings of non-alienation, as well as (objective) non-alienating conditions leading to (subjective) feelings of being alienated. In other words, allowing subjectivity into the discussion of alienation helps to interpret the complexities and dynamics of employee behaviour and orientations to work. Furthermore, it obliges the observer to recognise that there can be multiple meanings and interpretations of behaviour, even though there may be (shared) structural constraints within the work setting.

Exercise 6.2

What do you think?

1. Use Blauner's four dimensions of alienation described in Table 6.1 to analyse each of the jobs listed below:
   - supermarket checkout operator
   - lawyer
   - assembly line worker in a factory producing electronic circuit boards
   - teacher.
   (If you prefer, you could use examples of jobs you have done yourself or that you are familiar with.)
2. What are the difficulties or drawbacks in applying Blauner's four dimensions to particular jobs?

To sum up

So far we have considered two approaches to alienation. The first, based on the original ideas of Marx, views alienation as an objective condition of all work under capitalism. The second, illustrated through the work of Blauner, suggests that alienation varies between occupations, and to this extent is experienced subjectively by employees. Although these approaches differ, they both recognise that employees can find themselves in situations of alienation. Therefore the remainder of this chapter is concerned with exploring the question of how (if at all) employees attempt to combat alienating tendencies at work.

Surviving alienation

Our central proposition is that employees develop coping strategies which combat alienation through informal processes and action. In other words, employees take charge of their own destinies by inventing methods of coping that lie outside the formal influence of management. These methods also provide opportunities for employees to counter the prevailing values and beliefs of managers with their own interpretations of the tasks, rules and social interactions that take place at work. In some instances these strategies are collectively negotiated and undertaken by groups of employees; in other instances they represent individual attempts to survive. As we shall see, the meanings and behaviours are dynamic rather than fixed, plural rather than unitary, and creative rather than mundane.

The five main survival strategies that employees engage in are listed below, and in the sections that follow, each is explored in more detail.

- making out
- fiddling
- joking
- sabotage
- escaping.

Learning outcome 3: Describe the concept of 'making out' and evaluate its role in creating consent within the workplace

---

Making out

The notion of 'making out' is usually associated with the research undertaken by Michael Burawoy (1979). Like many of the empirical studies discussed in this chapter, Burawoy's method of data collection was based on getting close to the subject under study. It involved participating in the work process in order to experience directly the workplace dynamics and develop an understanding of the meaning and significance of social interaction.

With the permission of management, Burawoy began work as an employee in the machine shop of an engine plant which was a division of a multinational company in the United States. From this position of participant observer, Burawoy witnessed an elaborate system of informal behaviour by employees that acted to regulate the work process and ensured that targets were met, yet provided the opportunity for the workers to reassert some control over their working day. He argues that these unofficial shopfloor activities can be seen as a series of games employees play. These are games concerned with beating the system, finding the angles, working out the dodges or discovering the loopholes – in other words, 'making out'.

> The game of making out provides a framework for evaluating the productive activities and the social relations that arise out of the organization of work. We can look upon making out, therefore, as comprising a sequence of stages – of encounters between machine operators and the social or non-social objects that regulate the conditions of work. The rules of the game are experienced as a set of externally imposed relationships. The art of making out is to manipulate those relationships with the purpose of advancing as quickly as possible from one stage to the next.
>
> (Burawoy, 1979: 51)

Burawoy builds on the pioneering work of Roy (1952, 1953, 1955) to explore how the practice of making out is typically concerned with ways that employees get around the formal rules and regulations laid down by management. At its simplest, making out can be interpreted as the means through which employees secure themselves higher earnings by creatively manipulating the incentive systems (primarily piece-rate payment schemes). However, Burawoy's research led him to argue that economic gain is not the sole motivator for making out. Rather, he suggests (1979: 85) that a range of interlinking motives are at play:

- the reduction of fatigue
- the desire to pass time
- the relief of boredom
- the social and psychological rewards of making out on a tough job
- the social stigma and frustration of failing to 'make out' on an easy job.

He describes the informal rules and practices that he and his co-workers engaged in as they joined the game of making out. Yet, in so doing they were adapting to the alienating tendencies in the work; they were manipulating the management's rules for their own ends, but they were not fundamentally *challenging* the rules or undermining management's prerogative to set the rules. In fact, through playing the game of making out they were *consenting* to the formal rules and structures imposed by management.

> The issue is: which is logically and empirically prior, playing the game or the legitimacy of the rules? Here I am not arguing that playing the games rests on a broad consensus; on the contrary, consent rests upon – is constructed through – playing the game. The game does not reflect an underlying harmony of interests; on the contrary, it is responsible for and generates that harmony .... The game becomes an end in itself, overshadowing, masking, and even inverting the conditions out of which it emerges.
>
> (Burawoy, 1979: 81–2)

Excerpt 6.2

Making out among refuse collectors

McIntosh and Broderick (1996) evaluate the impact of compulsory competitive tendering (CCT) on the work of a local authority cleansing department. In addition to identifying changes in the organisation of work, they note the impact on the ability of the refuse collectors to 'make out' through a system of 'totting':

> Totting involved sifting through bags and bins in search of 'valuables' or 'sellables' which were then either kept or sold – many refuse collectors regularly took part in car boot sales. The pooling of lead and copper and returned bottles was also an important source of extra income .... Management were often willing to turn a blind eye and saw much of these activities as rewards for doing such a low-status job .... Such activities have not gone completely but the opportunity to tear open bags (a number of households were often identified as being sources of 'tot') has been drastically circumscribed due to the pressures of the workload.
>
> (McIntosh and Broderick, 1996: 424)

In addition, some of the social aspects of the work that made the job bearable have been affected by work intensification, as these quotes from drivers illustrate:

> We had regular people who gave us tea and biscuits, butchers would give us sausages and a bit of meat for doing little jobs for them. Most of that is gone now, we don't have time to stop and do odd jobs. (p. 424)

> We used to have time to chat to the old folks and stop a couple of times a day for tea round people's houses. We used to have customer care. Now you are lucky if you see anyone, let alone talk to them. (p. 425)

Manufacturing consent

Theorists such as Crozier (1964), Mayo (1933) and Roethlisberger and Dickson (1966) have argued that games undermine management objectives because they are the expression of a counter-control by the shopfloor. But Burawoy concludes that far from representing a threat to capitalism, games 'manufacture consent' towards the existing social relations of production and help secure the creation of surplus value. By challenging the periphery of the rules, the core of those rules – to produce for the employer – goes uncontested. In this way Burawoy shifts the focus of analysis away from control towards consent. He argues that the labour process under advanced capitalism should not be seen solely in terms of management's control over employees, but must also be viewed as a means through which employees are persuaded to consent to their own subordination, thereby cooperating with management's overall objectives (Burawoy, 1985: 126). This counter-balancing of control with consent helps to address some of the criticisms levelled at Braverman's (1974) analysis of the labour process, which dwelt upon the centrality of the labour control objectives of management.

Control vs. consent

The tensions between control and consent have been subsequently brought into sharper focus by Hyman (1987). Table 6.2 illustrates the contradictions embedded in the labour process which emerge from Hyman's discussion (1987: 39–43). The argument starts from the premise that management is faced with two competing pressures. On the one hand, there is a need to control and direct employees to ensure that production and performance targets are met. On the other hand, there is a requirement to enlist the skill and cooperation of employees in meeting those targets. These competing pressures lead to four key contradictions.

- *Contradiction 1.* Management must simultaneously limit and harness discretion: limit the discretion which employees might apply against management's interests and harness those aspects of their discretion which aid profitable production.

  For even though capital owns (and therefore has the right to 'control'), both means of production and the worker, in practice capital must surrender the means of production to the 'control' of the workers for their actual use in the

Table 6.2 Fundamental contradictions in managing the labour process

	Control		Consent
Management aim:	To secure employee compliance	vs	To enlist employee cooperation
Contradiction 1:	Limiting discretion	vs	Harnessing discretion
Contradiction 2:	Close supervision (direct control) (low trust)	vs	Employee autonomy (responsible autonomy) (high trust)
Contradiction 3:	Disposable labour (numerical flexibility)	vs	Dependable labour (commitment)
Contradiction 4:	Cohesive workforce	vs	Collective solidarity

Source: based on Hyman (1987: 39–43).

production process. All adequate analysis of the contradictory relationship of labour to capital in the workplace depends on grasping this point.

(Cressey and MacInnes, 1980: 14)

- *Contradiction 2.* Management must impose systems of close supervision to ensure that their objectives are complied with, yet also provide the space and freedom for employees to exercise creative discretion. Friedman (1977b) argues that managers are therefore faced with a choice between two broad supervision strategies of either trying to establish 'direct control' (involving the simplification of work and close supervision) or 'responsible autonomy' (wider discretion over how work is completed, with consequently less supervision).These strategies do not resolve the contradiction – not least because they are mutually exclusive. Direct control might be the best way to guarantee compliance, but at the cost of commitment; responsible autonomy may enlist commitment, but does not guarantee compliance with management wishes. Some managers might recognise the possibility of placing a different emphasis on control or consent depending on the group of employees: responsible autonomy for highly skilled, core employees in scarce supply but direct control over low-skilled, peripheral workers who are easily replaced. But even responsible autonomy might need to be moderated with some direct control given that 'there are few (if any) workers whose voluntary commitment requires no external reinforcement' (Hyman, 1987: 42).

  More cynically, however, it might be argued that responsible autonomy is a ploy by managers to disguise their dependency on the workforce. By emphasising autonomy, empowerment, discretion and an absence of close supervision, they can engage in a more subtle attempt to obscure the exploitative nature of the labour process, and particularly the commodity status of labour.
- *Contradiction 3.* Management requires labour to be both disposable and dependable. If labour power is considered a commodity, employees can be hired or fired according to the changing requirements of the business (reflecting seasonal, weekly or even daily fluctuations in demand). Managers can therefore seek to maximise the disposability of labour. However, operating a hire-and-fire policy is likely to both undermine the commitment of employees to the organisation, and alert those workers whose skills are in scarce supply, or who are strategically placed, to their centrality to the success of the organisation. Conversely, to implement policies of dependability (such as employment security and the

development of an internal labour market) acts to reduce the ability of managers to adapt the labour force to match fluctuations in demand. Indeed, this trade-off between commitment and flexibility has become one of the central problems for contemporary human resource management (for fuller discussion see Noon, 1992: 23–4).

- *Contradiction 4.* Management recognises the need to create a cooperative, cohesive workforce for the benefit of profitable production, but the problem for management is that such a cohesive workforce may develop a collective solidarity that could be used against management's interests. In other words, the workforce cohesion necessary to meet management objectives potentially also provides the conditions for collective solidarity, which may lead workers to challenge those objectives. In a similar way, policies aimed at individualising the workforce and controlling the individual worker (through, for example, performance related pay, appraisal and promotion) potentially undermine the basis of cooperation between employees that management invariably requires to meet performance targets.

Overall, Burawoy's proposition that, within the workplace 'coercion must be supplemented by the organisation of consent' (1979: 27) helps to synthesise the above contradictions embedded in the capitalist labour process. Essentially, the contradictions reflect the fundamental differences of interest between employers and employees. It is in the employer's interest to secure as much surplus value as possible from the labours of their employees, while it is in the employees' interest to limit the exploitation and extract full payment for their effort. Consequently, employers and managers seek to obscure the appropriation of surplus value, and it is precisely because the game of making out aids this process of obscuring the exploitation that managers are generally content to go along with it. It is only when making out becomes counter-productive that managers seek to suppress it.

> The participation [of workers] in games has the effect of concealing relations of production while co-ordinating the interests of workers and management.... It is through their common interest in the preservation of work games that the interests of workers and shop management are co-ordinated. The workers are interested in the relative satisfactions games can offer while management, from supervisors to departmental superintendents, is concerned with securing co-operation and surplus.... The *day-to-day adaptations of workers create their own ideological effects that become focal elements in the operation of capitalist control.*
>
> (Burawoy, 1985: 38–9, emphasis in original)

Criticisms of Burawoy

While Burawoy's analysis is persuasive and helps to explain why alienating work is endured more often than it is challenged, two important criticisms can be levelled at his thesis.

- *Burawoy's analysis ignores gender.* The workplace he studied was composed entirely of men, so he had no opportunity to explore the importance and effect of gender on the social organisation of production. It could be argued that gender could have an important impact upon several of the features that Burawoy characterised as being critical to the manufacture of consent: the shopfloor culture encouraging competition, game playing as an end in itself, the structure of work, the social hierarchy and workgroup dynamics (for a fuller discussion, see Davies, 1990). Of course a similar point may be made about ethnicity and other ways in which employees are stratified.

- *Burawoy overstates the role of consent.* Burawoy's eagerness to explain consent blinds him to the possibility that there remains a subversive element in some of the making out he describes. While being incorporated into the system, the employees are still challenging it through constantly subverting the capitalist control of the labour process by continually inventing new ways of making out. As Clawson and Fantasia (1983: 676) comment:

> Over and over again, Burawoy takes some feature of the workplace which had generally been identified as evidence of workers' progressive potential, and argues that it actually serves to reinforce the system. He does not seem to understand that a phenomenon can do both things at the same time, that something can be itself and its opposite. In other words, Burawoy's Marxist argument lacks a dialectical analysis.

To sum up

Burawoy argues that employees creatively find time and space to pursue their own objectives within the broad rules set by managers. This process of making out provides them with both extrinsic and intrinsic rewards, thereby creating an incentive to perpetuate the behaviour and consent to the regime established by management. Managers tolerate the making out activities of employees because such activities help to obscure the ultimately exploitative nature of the capitalist labour process. However, critics have suggested that Burawoy too readily interprets employee behaviour as consent and disregards the extent to which many of the behaviours represent a form of resistance, through informal actions which subvert management's intentions.

This last point needs further emphasis because it has important implications for the analysis in the rest of the chapter. What seems to have happened is that in presenting a case for the importance of consent on the shopfloor, Burawoy has allowed the role of resistance to slip from view. Making out is not just about consent: it may also represent a form of resistance. In other words, in considering making out as a survival strategy, we should be aware of its dual impact. Moreover, this is a cautionary note to bear in mind as we turn to the next survival strategy: workplace fiddling.

Learning outcome 4: Classify various types of workplace fiddles and evaluate why they occur within the workplace

Fiddling

In one way or another, everyone is on the fiddle. It might take a direct form, such as stealing supplies from the workplace (stationery, building materials, produce, and so forth) or artificially inflating expense claims. It can also be indirect, such as doing repairs to personal items using the company's equipment and materials, making personal phone calls and 'cyberloafing', which means using the Internet for personal reasons, such as emails, surfing, playing computer games, downloading music, paying bills, shopping online and even engaging in cybersex (Lim, 2002). In addition, employees will fiddle time from the organisation. Even in highly regulated environments with tight monitoring there are opportunities to fiddle the system. For example, Townsend (2005) describes how employees in an Australian call centre have learned how to manipulate the call monitoring system to provide extra rest breaks. A call centre operator explains:

> We can take a call, and if they [customers] need to pay a bill then we transfer them into the computer interactive system 'cardgate'. What we can do is hit transfer but we don't release the button. So then we are on mute while the customer does the interactive computer processes. And that really gives you three or four minutes. Sometimes I go and have a cup of tea or maybe go to the toilet, every now and then I go out for a cigarette. The best part is that the cardgate system does not hang up when the caller is finished if we remain on transfer. I can sit there for 20 minutes if I want to but I don't push my luck, 10 minutes for a cigarette is plenty. And a call of that length isn't unusual so it won't stick out in your stats. You have to think these things through, the last thing I want to do is get caught by being greedy.
>
> (Townsend, 2005: 56)

The list of fiddles at work is as extensive and varied as human ingenuity, and for many it represents an important additional (albeit covert) element in their total rewards, and an important way of altering the balance of the effort–reward bargain.

Researchers have unearthed the fiddles that are endemic in particular occupations (see for example Ditton, 1977), but it is Mars (1982) who has perhaps gone furthest in analysing the practice and significance of workplace fiddles. It is useful to summarise his work briefly here, for it reveals not only the relationship between forms of fiddling and the occupational structure, but also illustrates how for many, the motive for fiddling goes far beyond any anticipated financial benefit. Indeed the frequently small financial gain would often not seem to justify the risks involved unless other contributory factors are influencing the decision to fiddle.

Mars (1982) has developed a typology of fiddling and linked this to distinctive characteristics of different occupations. He uses two dimensions to categorise jobs: first, whether the jobs are subject to extensive rules and close supervision, and second, whether the jobs involve group activity and are characterised by strong workgroup controls. The presence or absence of these characteristics translates into four different occupational categories, each of which provide different opportunities for fiddling. He labels those people who choose to exploit this opportunity to fiddle as 'hawks', 'donkeys', 'wolves' and 'vultures' – each label denoting the characteristics of the way they fiddle, as explained below.

- *Hawks*: People who work as individuals rather than as part of a group and also are not subject to close supervision; examples include journalists, entrepreneurial managers, waiters and taxi drivers. Someone owning and operating a small business would also fit into this category.

- *Donkeys*: People in jobs that are highly constrained by rules and who work in relative isolation from others – such as shop assistants and many assembly line workers.
- *Wolves*: People who 'work – and steal – in packs' (Mars, 1982: 2), with groups operating according to clearly defined rules, controls and hierarchies governing their fiddling activity. Examples here might include airport baggage handlers and dock gangs.
- *Vultures*: People who need the support of a group in order to fiddle, but who act alone. Mars includes such occupations as travelling salespeople and bread roundspeople in this category where group support may be needed to collude with a fiddle (for example, the delivery drivers who share the knowledge about which places they can deliver short to, where checks are unlikely to be carried out, and where to sell the extra goods afterwards).

In drawing such distinctions, Mars usefully points to the different opportunities and constraints for fiddling that characterise different jobs. It reveals that fiddling of one form or another is possible in (and endemic to) almost all occupations. Thus, for a large part of the workforce, the rewards from their job comprise not only the visible element (their wage or salary, paid holidays, pension, and so on) but also an invisible element, reflecting fiddled goods and/or fiddled time. Even in jobs which at first sight appear very highly constrained by close supervision and/or detailed rules governing behaviour, fiddling still takes place. Moreover, it occurs even when penalties are severe and where the possible amounts to be fiddled are small in comparison to the gravity of the sanctions applicable if the person is caught.

This leads to the conclusion that any financial benefit from fiddling at work is only one motive, and, for many people, not necessarily the most important one. For some, fiddling provides the only interest in an otherwise monotonous work day – a survival strategy. Indeed, the risk element of getting caught may add a frisson of excitement. For others, fiddling may be an expression of frustration or resentment, 'a way of hitting out at the boss, the company, the system or the state' (Mars, 1982: 23).

Excerpt 6.3

Fiddling at the supermarket
One of the common fiddles amongst shopfloor employees at a large UK supermarket chain is 'grazing'. This is when shelf stackers consume some of the products while they work, for example, crisps, sweets, biscuits and pieces of fruit. This grazing activity is particularly prevalent during the night shift when there are no customers around and fewer managers. In the words of one store manager:

> Grazing is frowned upon but it is difficult to catch the culprits. We know it is occurring because we find empty packets hidden at the back of shelves. During the summer months strawberries are a particular attraction for grazers. We frequently find a pile of strawberry stalks and a half-empty carton of cream.

Another problem the store has is with van drivers who deliver the orders that customers place through the Internet shopping service. The store manager explained:

> We find that van drivers will regularly stop for breaks when they are on their deliveries. They are not supposed to because they are given proper scheduled breaks as part of their shift. They ought to do the deliveries as efficiently as possible, and then return to the store. We also know that some of them do private errands for friends and family on their rounds – picking things up and dropping them off at other houses.
>
> Worst of all is when the drivers cut corners in giving good customer service. They are supposed to spend time with the customer explaining whether any items have been substituted and checking whether these are acceptable. If they don't do this, then the customer might ring the store to complain about the item when they unpack their shopping. We will then have to refund them for the item and collect it, or else give the customer the item free of charge.

Why managers tolerate fiddling

Although the types, motives and outcomes of worker-initiated fiddles are many and varied, this picture is made even more complex when management's approach to fiddling is taken into account. It is sometimes assumed that workers engage in fiddling in spite of the best endeavours by management to prevent it, but managers frequently 'turn a blind eye' to fiddling activity, provided that it does not rise above a certain level, or does not involve fiddling a third party (for example, the customer). A survey of 813 UK managers conducted by *Management Today* (2000) revealed that 50 per cent were aware of fiddling in their workplace, but only four in ten would be prepared to take action to stop it occurring. This toleration varies according to the type of fiddle involved, as Figure 6.2 illustrates.

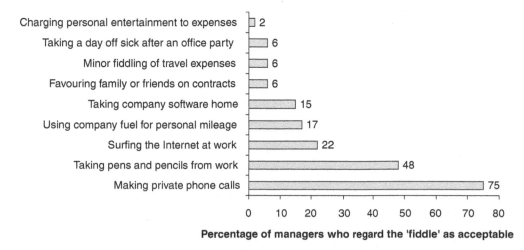

Percentage of managers who regard the 'fiddle' as acceptable

Figure 6.2   Acceptability of workplace fiddles

There are several possible motives for managers to collude with fiddling:

- It might reflect management's awareness of the near-impossibility of stamping out fiddling entirely, and if one form of fiddling is suppressed, another is likely to develop to take its place.
- It might help management maintain a cooperative workforce – if all fiddling was heavily policed by management this might increase workforce discontent and reduce the degree of worker consent to other management objectives.
- It might enable management to pay lower wages. The availability of fiddles to those working in hotels and restaurants, for example – ranging from not declaring income from tips to the tax authorities, to fiddles related to the food and drink served – helps to subsidise low wages. Similarly, among Ditton's (1977: 17) bread salespeople (generally low-paid and working long hours), morale was sustained by sales supervisors indicating a 'solution' to the threat of the salespeople having to make up shortages in takings: over-charging customers.
- It might be because managers themselves are also involved in fiddling, either for their own monetary gain or to protect their position. Mars (1982: 68), for example, recounts the case of a supermarket where, to balance stocks against stock records, checkout operators were asked by managers to fiddle the customers. More recently, a study by D'Abate (2005) based on interviews with 30 middle managers located in a variety of industries in North America revealed that a large amount of company time and resource was spent on conducting their personal affairs in business hours. The list includes making personal appointments, organising personal time, paying bills, participating in betting syndicates, reading, daydreaming and even watching television. The most widely reported behaviours were personal phone calls, having conversations about non-work issues and surfing the Internet.

To sum up

Although a covert activity, fiddling of one form or another appears to be an integral element of most occupations. In terms of a 'survival strategy', fiddling normally involves breaking the rules, whereas making out involves working within the rules. But the distinction is not always clear cut. However, for most people involved in some form of fiddling at work, the monetary value of the fiddling is likely to be small – so much so that the efforts required to prevent it are often not seen to be worthwhile. Fiddling can yield additional income, but also represents a source of social and psychological gain to individuals responding to aspects of their job, those in authority over them, their co-workers and/or their customers.

Exercise 6.3

What do you think?
Read Excerpt 6.3 about 'fiddling at the supermarket', then answer the following questions.

1. Using Mars' typology, into which category would you put (a) the shelf-stackers and (b) the van drivers?

2. Evaluate each of the fiddles at the supermaket. Are some more detrimental to the organisation than others? Are some more acceptable than others? Explain your answers.
3. Put yourself in the position of the employees. How might they justify their fiddling?
4. What advice would you give the store manager about dealing with these fiddles?

Learning outcome 5: Explain four functions of joking at work

Joking

The most disappointing aspect of examining the role of humour in work organisations is that when the humour is taken out of the context in which it emerged, it usually ceases to be funny. It is rather like having to explain a joke – it ruins it. Consequently, at the risk of ruining some good jokes, this section explores the significance of humour at work. It is important to begin the analysis by acknowledging the pioneering work of the anthropologist Radcliffe-Brown (1952), who identified the significance of the 'joking relationship' between people.

> What is meant by the term 'joking relationship' is a relationship between two persons in which one is by custom permitted, and in some instances, required to tease or to make fun of the other, who, in turn, is required to take no offence... The joking relationship is a peculiar combination of friendliness and antagonism. The behaviour is such that in any other social context it would express and arouse hostility, but it is not meant seriously and must not be taken seriously. There is a pretence of hostility and real friendliness. To put it another way, the relation is one of permitted disrespect.
>
> (Radcliffe-Brown, 1952: 90–1)

Subsequent studies of joking and humour have argued that these activities are a natural part of work organisations and also perform four important functions:

- Joking maintains social order and releases tension.
- Joking challenges authority.
- Joking forges group identities.
- Joking alleviates monotony and makes work tolerable.

Each of these is explained in the following sections.

Joking maintains social order and releases tension

A primary function of the joking relationship is the prevention or reduction of antagonism; typically it develops between people who are required to be in close contact for long periods of time, yet who have some divergence of interests. Not surprisingly, therefore, the concept can be applied to work settings where teasing and banter are part of the daily routine of organisational life. For example, Bradney (1957) used the concept of the joking relationship to explain how sales staff in a large department store regulated their interpersonal relations. She argued that joking helped to mitigate the intrinsic antagonisms caused by the formal work roles and structures:

> There is clearly a divergence of interests among sales assistants ... as a result of their formal relationship. Each wants to increase her own sales – to earn both a better living and the approval of her employer – and is in competition with the others to do this. There is also every likelihood of hostility and conflict between them when they interrupt and hinder each other just at a time when this interferes most with selling.
>
> (Bradney, 1957: 183)

The 'joking relationship' provides the employees with an informal structure through which differences of interest and status are negotiated through playful insults and teasing ('permitted disrespect') rather than with open hostility. Bradney concludes:

> By means of a tradition of joking behaviour between its members, which is quite unknown to the management, this store is able to avoid considerable tension and disagreement that would be likely to occur as a result of the difficulties inherent in its formal structure. In so doing it gives the employees a source of positive enjoyment in carrying out their routine activities and incidentally, by means of this, renews their energy to cope even more adequately with their routine problems.
>
> (Bradney, 1957: 186–7)

To take another example, Spradley and Mann (1975) used participant observation to explore the working lives of waitresses, and demonstrate how humour reinforces the gender division of labour within the cocktail bar they studied. The waitresses worked closely with the male bartenders, and strong bonds developed between them. Yet there was a clear status differential, with the waitresses in a subordinate position. Waitresses quickly learned that the needs of the bartenders came first because they had the power to make the waitresses' work comfortable or difficult. The joking relationship between the barmen and the waitresses was one means by which any conflict caused by this power imbalance was mediated. The bartenders would use humour to assert their status, cover their own mistakes and to reprimand a waitress. On the other hand, the waitresses employed humour to assert themselves, particularly as a response to feelings of unfairness and powerlessness. Thus, conclude Spradley and Mann:

> Anger and frustration are dissipated and feelings of inequality felt by the waitresses are deflected .... It creates a buffer between the waitress and bartender in potential conflict situations and provides a means for handling inadequate role performances that occur in full public view .... But the joking relationship also maintains the status inequality of female waitresses and reinforces masculine values. By providing a kind of 'safety valve' for the frustrations created for women in this small society, joking behaviour insures that the role of female waitresses remains unchanged.
>
> (Spradley and Mann, 1975: 100)

To take a more extreme example, Sanders (2004) reports how humour helped prostitutes to cope with the negative emotions that surface in their work; in particular it provided a means of dealing with the disgust they might feel towards a client. In the words of one of the prostitutes:

> There are some men who are so smelly and not nice to be round. So we have to laugh to get through the whole thing. I could tell you so many situations where we have laughed and laughed our way through a service, not with the clients but at the clients. When you are laughing it doesn't feel like such a daunting job when we have a giggle about the clients.
>
> (Sanders, 2004: 283)

This suggests that humour plays an important role in enabling an employee to cope with the inevitable frustrations, tensions and even degradations of working life. As a form of safety valve, it allows an individual to let off steam, without challenging the power structures and inequalities that have led to the frustration in the first instance (Wilson, 1979). Spradley and Mann's (1975) waitresses enjoyed moments where they asserted themselves through humour, but the gendered power structure remained intact. Similarly Boland and Hoffman (1983), in a study of a small machine shop, noted how the machinists would frequently put cartoon-like drawings into the steel drums containing the finished pieces for the quality inspectors at the customer's plant. The jokes poked fun at the competence of the inspectors and management, compared with the skill and judgement of employees in the machine shop.

Joking challenges authority

Joking at work is a way of challenging authority structures. In other words, jokes are an expression of the informal triumphing over the formal (Douglas, 1975). This raises the question whether humour may be construed as a subversive activity at work. Empirical studies of humour in fact reveal very few examples where humour is used in a subversive manner. One such example can be found in Westwood's (1984) study of a clothing factory. As participant observer, she cites a 'prank' that resulted in the end-of-day buzzer being set off ten minutes early and the women fleeing the building with glee, fully aware that it was not the official leaving time:

> The next day management instituted an investigation into what was termed 'the incident'. The shopfloor was absolutely delighted that their speedy exodus had caused such obvious pain to management. Everyone who was asked about it shook their heads wisely, at once 'agreeing' with management's view that this was a very serious matter, while keeping quiet about the identity of the buzzer-pusher.
>
> (Westwood, 1984: 91)

The use of humour by employees to undermine authority through ridiculing managers or organisational processes is considered by some commentators to be clear evidence of humour being a strategy of resistance (Ackroyd and Thompson, 1999; Collinson, 2002). It certainly has such potential, but incidents of clear resistance tend to be less strategic than opportunistic. There are some exceptions: for example Rodrigues and Collinson's (1995) study of a Brazilian newspaper and Taylor and Bain's (2003) studies of Scottish call centres show how humour can be used to coordinate an oppositional culture among employees and provide a forceful weapon in collective organisation. To illustrate the collective acts of resistance, consider the quotes below from two employees interviewed by Taylor and Bain (2003: 1502–3).

> When you were nominally following the rules, you would do so in such a way as to be subversive. The dress code changed and we were told, 'You have to wear a shirt and tie.' So we got word round, 'Tomorrow, wear shirts and ties that make us look as unprofessional as possible.' I wore a tie about four or five inches wide, illustrating the history and future of the motor car in glorious Technicolor, along with a purple-checked shirt. Everybody dressed like this and there was nothing managers could do.

> One night a manager ... was showing new starts round, and he passed the mission statement, which was prominently displayed on a wall. Suddenly, he remembered he had ten people in tow and he hadn't pointed it out to them. So he led them back and started reading it when, spontaneously, about ten of us stood up and saluted him, singing 'The Star Spangled Banner'. And, of course, these new starts got the message that there was no respect for either management or company.

Taylor and Bain (2003: 1506) conclude that in this organisation:

> The [trade union] activists were instrumental in their use of humour, clear in the knowledge that it helped make them and the union popular and served to weaken managerial authority and legitimacy. Subversive satire was allied to a wider collective purpose.

Although there are instances such as these where humour acts as a rallying point for collective organisation against management authority, what is striking from broader case evidence is the extent to which humour is highly regulated and ritualised by the workgroups. Far from subverting authority, humour tends merely to issue mild challenges, which seem more about preserving the status quo than overturning it. Indeed, it could be argued that jokes provide an outlet for the expression of frustration and discontent which might otherwise build up unchecked, and eventually become channelled into activities that have more serious consequences for the organisation (see the discussion on sabotage below).

Joking forges group identities

It is also apparent from the examples cited so far that humour seems to be playing a role in establishing a shared group identity. This occurs through a process of social regulation whereby the members of a work setting use humour as one of a range of cultural devices to establish group norms and perpetuate the group's existing dominant values. Humour thereby reinforces the existing social structure, and is performing a boundary function (Linstead, 1985b: 744) by protecting the group from outsiders. For example, in a vivid description of the role of humour among engineering workers in a vehicle plant, Collinson (1988) reveals how the supervisors and white-collar staff became the butt of jokes for the engineers: jokes which explicitly denigrated them as being stupid, manipulative and effeminate, and hence different from the hard-working, proudly masculine 'fellas' on the shopfloor.

Newcomers and deviants were also controlled by humour. For example, the apprentices were subjected to initiations which range from embarrassing (being sent for a 'long stand') to the degrading: 'Pancake Tuesday is always celebrated by "greasing the bollocks" of the apprentices with emulsion then "locking them in the shit-house, bollock naked" (Collinson, 1988: 189). These practical jokes 'not only instructed new members on how to act and react, but also constituted a test of the willingness of initiates to be part of the male group and to accept its rules' (ibid: 188). It was all about bringing people into line; for example, Collinson was told in reference to a lad who entered the company with 'diplomas galore':

> They had a French letter on his back by ten o'clock. They had him singing and dancing in the loo with the pretext of practising for a pantomime ... we soon brought him round to our way of thinking.
>
> (Collinson, 1988: 189)

In some instances this can have a pernicious effect, with employees feeling excluded or victimised. In particular it can become a form of harassment, creating severe difficulties for women in male-dominated environments (see for example Jenkins, Martinez Lucio and Noon, 2002) or ethnic minorities (Excerpt 6.4).

In Collinson's study, humour was also used by the engineers to control their colleagues who were considered not to be working hard enough under the collective bonus scheme. Humour was a way of bringing co-workers into line in order to maximise earnings. The effect of all this was eloquently summed up by the engineer who commented that:

> The men are the gaffers now. They watch each other like hawks. The nature of the blokes is such that they turn on each other... You're more worried about what the men think than the gaffers .... I'm just as bad if there's someone not working.
>
> (Collinson, 1988: 197)

Excerpt 6.4

Just light-hearted banter and horseplay?
A broker at a London firm sued his former employers for racial discrimination and unfair dismissal. He claimed that he was subjected to anti-Semitic abuse, including the names 'Yiddo' and 'Jew boy'. He also objected to the way a Jewish skull-cap was placed on top of the office television whenever a Jewish person was giving the financial bulletins. On one occasion he was told to put on a Nazi uniform (hired by the company) as punishment for turning up late. He refused to put on the costume, not least because his grandmother had died in Auschwitz.

The company claims that the culture of the office meant that 'banter' was a way of relieving stress in such a high-pressured job. They said that it was applied to everyone, and that the broker himself had engaged in it, calling his manager a 'big-nosed tosser', his colleague a 'fat Jock' and non-Jewish people in the office 'Yoks' (Yiddish slang for gentiles). Furthermore they said there was a 'bad taste costume' ritual whereby brokers who arrived late had to dress up in humiliating outfits hired by the company: for example, a Welsh broker had to wear a Bo Peep costume.

Source: Based on reports in *Guardian*, 'Skull cap used by "race jokers"', 1 February 2001, and *The Times*, 'Brokers "used racial abuse to relieve stress"', 1 February 2001.

Joking alleviates monotony and makes work tolerable
Conformity and compliance at work can also be encouraged by humour in another way: by obscuring the monotony of the work process. This is vividly demonstrated by Roy's (1960) participant observation as a machine operator in a factory. When Roy first joined the factory he became acutely aware of how tedious the work was, but as he became embroiled in the jokes and pranks on the shopfloor, he found himself distracted from the boredom. Many of the jokes became predictable daily events – 'banana time', 'peach time', 'window time' and so on – and these rituals suppressed some of the drudgery of the 12-hour working day by punctuating it with moments of humour. Indeed, it was only after a serious argument had broken out, causing the social cohesion of the workgroup to break up and all interaction to be 'strictly business', that Roy was reminded of the tedium of the work process and began to experience fatigue. In other words, it was humour that provided a means of coping with the boredom and the hard work.

Humour allows people to distance themselves from the unpleasant and boring aspects of work (Cohen and Taylor, 1976: 34), as exemplified by the engineering worker from Collinson's study (1988: 185) who commented that, 'Some days it feels like a fortnight .... I had to stop myself getting bored so I increased the number of pranks at work.' Or the women in Westwood's study (1984) who used jokes, often related to sex, to spice up the drudgery of the day. A favourite joke of some of the women in the factory she studied was to:

> Draw lewd pictures of penises and naked men and women, give them captions and send them around the units hoping that they would embarrass some of the other women and provoke a response... Written jokes were passed around and sniggered at through the working day. It all added excitement and 'a bit of a laff' to the factory days. Sex, of course, was a crucial ingredient and always managed to spice up the end of the day.
>
> (Westwood, 1984: 91)

From this point of view, the practical joking and the repartee revealed by the studies cited above are merely examples of employees taking a break from work by indulging in a pleasurable activity. To think about this and the other functions of joking, attempt Exercise 6.4.

Exercise 6.4

What do you think?
Using your knowledge of the four functions of joking, interpret the events described in Excerpt 6.4.

Now choose an example of the use of humour from your own work experience (past or present). Which of the four functions most adequately explains the motivations of those involved?

To sum up

A difficulty in generalising about the significance of humour in work organisations is assessing the impact of subjectivity. The meaning of 'a joke' is negotiated by the participants of a setting, but its significance may vary from individual to individual. The same humorous incident can be perceived in various ways, and may have alternative meanings for different participants. However, irrespective of the specific interpretation an individual puts on a humorous event, the empirical evidence suggests a common theme: joking at work plays an important regulatory function by providing a means of expression that assists group cohesion and deflects attention from the dehumanising aspects of work. On occasion it is used to challenge authority, but rarely does it undermine the existing power hierarchy. In this way joking is a vital factor in obscuring the social relations of production, and suppressing the alienating tendencies of work.

Learning outcome 6: Describe and interpret the importance of workplace sabotage

---

Sabotage

The notion of sabotage often conjures up the image of people engaged in wilful acts of destruction, as retribution for some felt injustice: from the Luddites in the 1820s who destroyed the machinery that was progressively replacing their jobs, to the more contemporary examples of the sacked accounts clerk whose last act is to reformat the computer's hard disk, erasing all the payroll information. Or the newspaper sub-editor whose anger with management led him to reword a news story so that the initial letter of each paragraph formed the word 'bollocks' when read vertically. However, studies suggest that this popular image of sabotage fails to account for the complexity and subtlety of motivation and method (for example Dubois, 1979; Edwards and Scullion, 1982; Taylor and Walton, 1971).

In particular, Linstead (1985a) identifies two key problems in the analysis of sabotage. First there is the difficulty of trying to interpret the action, especially whether it represents an intentional, malicious attempt to destroy or disrupt the work process or the product. Second, there is the problem of whether or not to designate the action as rational behaviour. Should all acts of sabotage be attributed to a logical cause, even in the absence of a specific declaration of intent? Both of these problems highlight the need for specific contextual information before it is possible to understand the meanings and motives of sabotage behaviour.

These problems make any generalisation about sabotage fraught with difficulties, not least the danger of understating the importance of the subjective experience of the supposed saboteur. Nevertheless, it is possible to classify acts of sabotage into two broad categories (loosely based on Taylor and Walton, 1971).

- A temporary expression of frustration with the work process, rules, managers, co-workers, or indeed any aspect of the organisation. In such circumstances sabotage is likely to be the wilful malicious act of a frustrated individual. The anger is placated and the tension dissipated through, for example, kicking the photocopier or being intentionally rude to a customer. Although undesirable in the eyes of management, the consequences of such sabotage are transient and generally offer no serious threat to the functioning of the organisation. Such incidents may even be seen as tolerable and necessary expressions of dissent which act as a kind of safety valve.

- An attempt to assert control over the work process, thus presenting a direct challenge to authority, and consequently far more serious for management. In some circumstances such sabotage may be expressed as individual action (for example, halting a machine by, quite literally, 'putting a spanner in the works'); in others, a meaningful challenge can only be orchestrated through collective action (for example, customs officers at an airport 'working to rule' by checking every passenger, thus causing enormous disruptions).

As with the case of humour, acts of sabotage may simultaneously have different meanings for different people involved, so in practice there is far more complexity than this simple typology might suggest.

A further problem is that in practice many acts of sabotage do not easily fit these categories, but are located in a grey area between the two. Consider the following example cited by two of the first academics to consider the significance of sabotage at work, Taylor and Walton (1971: 228):

> When 600 shipyard workers employed on the new Cunarder Q.E.2 finished on schedule they were promptly sacked by John Brown's, the contractors involved. With what looked like a conciliatory gesture they were invited to a party in the ship's luxurious new bar, which was specially opened for the occasion. The men became drunk, damaged several cabins, and smashed the Royal Suite to pieces.

One interpretation might be that this was a rational act of reasserting control by a group of workers reflecting their alienation from the product of their labour. Another interpretation: the frustration of the sacking, linked to the indignity of being invited to 'celebrate' this, unleashed a temporary destructive urge. Then again, perhaps the men were just so drunk that they lost any sense of rational intent and would have gone on the rampage irrespective of where they were drinking. All three interpretations might be correct. Indeed, each might be applicable to different workers: the behaviour may have been the same, but the reasons behind it may have differed. If questioned, the workers might have attributed different meanings and significance to their behaviour – provided, of course, they could remember the incident once they had sobered up.

Virtuous sabotage? The case of whistleblowing

There might be instances where the supposed sabotage is perpetrated by those who believe they have a duty to bring out into the open malpractice or misconduct occurring within the organisation. This is usually called 'whistleblowing'. The bad publicity that ensues is clearly disadvantageous for the organisation, but are whistleblowers really saboteurs? If they believe they are performing a public service by the disclosure of information about an unlawful or unethical practice, they have virtuous rather than malicious motives. For example:

> Joy Cawthorne resigned as an instructor at an outdoor activity centre in protest over its safety standards. Subsequently, she gave evidence against her former

employer after four children died in a canoeing accident in Lyme Bay. The managing director was convicted of manslaughter and sentenced to three years' imprisonment.

(Lewis, 1997: 6)

An alternative interpretation is that a whistleblower is an aggrieved or disgruntled employee seeking revenge on the organisation. This means he/she is acting with malicious intent, so whistleblowing constitutes a form of sabotage. While this might be the case in some instances, it is also clear that whistleblowing is costly for an individual's career. He or she often faces harassment or retaliation (Micelli and Near, 1992), gets sidelined in career terms, loses his/her job and finds it difficult to get alternative employment (Alford, 2001). For example, Glazer and Glazer (1989) found that over two-thirds of the 64 whistleblowers they interviewed had become unemployed as a result. So according to Perry (1998: 240–1), 'whistle blowing might well be classified as a form of occupational suicide – or perhaps accidental career death'.

Unintentional sabotage?

Analysing sabotage becomes even more confusing because some actions may have destructive or damaging results without there being any malevolence in the minds of the perpetrators. Indeed, there are numerous instances when attempts to adjust the work process to achieve productivity targets, and thus 'make out', carry the risk of potential negative long-term consequences. For example, Taylor and Walton (1971: 232) cite the practice in aircraft assembly of using an instrument called a 'tap' which allows the wing bolts to be more easily inserted but potentially weakens the overall structure. Using the tap is strictly prohibited by factory rules, yet its use continues covertly because without it production cannot function effectively. So should the workers who use 'taps' be described as saboteurs? Or are they merely irresponsible workers?

In the following example there is little evidence of malicious intent behind the worker's actions; he is easing the work, making out as best he can within the rules set by management:

The engines passed the [worker] rapidly on a conveyor. His instructions were to test all the nuts and if he found one or two loose to tighten them, but if three or more were loose he was not expected to have time to tighten that many. In such cases he marked the engine with chalk and it was later set aside from the conveyor and given special attention. The superintendent found that the number of engines so set aside reached an annoying total in the day's work. He made several unsuccessful attempts to locate the trouble. Finally, by carefully watching all the men on the conveyor line, he discovered that the [worker] was unscrewing a *third* nut whenever he found two already loose. It was easier to loosen *one* nut than to tighten two.

(Mathewson, 1931: 238, emphasis in original, cited in Hodson, 1991: 281)

In the next two examples, the employee's behaviour in each case reflects a frustration with the conditions of work imposed by management; the first incident takes place in a brewery, and the second in a wire manufacturing company. Read them and then attempt Exercise 6.5.

> One of the young male workers [in the brewery] took a bottle in his hand and made a throwing motion with it. Later, on break, I asked him what he was throwing at. He replied that he was not throwing at anything in particular... He said that he didn't want to do any damage, that he was just bored and that it would be fun to lob bottles out like grenades and watch them crash and blow up .... He added, 'It's so dull out there I'd just like to make something happen, to have something interesting to do or see.'
>
> (Molstad, 1986: 231)

> [Bobby] was originally called to make a small adjustment on the depth of the machine's applicator. It was a simple adjustment accomplished by loosening a single screw. In a normally equipped shop it would have been a five-minute job, but Bobby could not find the proper screwdriver. We searched all the toolboxes, but the screwdrivers were either too large or had been ground at the ends. Bobby asked Carroll [the boss] if he could buy a screwdriver at the hardware store down the street. Carroll refused and told him to grind one of the ones we had. Bobby tried, but ended up stripping the screwhead so badly that nothing could get it out. Then Carroll came to the floor and in typical fashion chewed Bobby out in front of everybody. After Carroll left, Bobby brought the applicator over to the bench and used a ten-pound copper mallet to smash a machine part that cost hundreds of dollars to replace.
>
> (Juravich, 1985: 135–6)

Exercise 6.5

What do you think?
Using your knowledge of sabotage, interpret the incidents in the brewery and the wire manufacturer.

There are occasions where the consequence of an act of sabotage is separated in time and space from the saboteur. For example, devising and intentionally spreading computer viruses is a malicious act of sabotage, yet the perpetrators may have no specific organisational target for their actions. Their motives seem to be the challenge of creating something that frequently destroys the work of others, but the consequences of their actions may never be known to the perpetrators, as they remain unaware of how extensively and to whom the virus spreads.

To sum up

In trying to generalise about sabotage, as in the case of joking, we are faced with the difficulty of interpreting the behaviour of individuals and understanding the meanings that they attribute to it. It is impossible to interpret all acts that have destructive consequences as being planned, rational behaviour with malicious intent. Indeed, stupidity, thoughtlessness and irrationality may better explain the behaviour in some circumstances. However, while making out, joking and to some extent fiddling are widely tolerated by management, sabotage is not. It is viewed as a negative activity, perhaps because it presents a direct challenge to authority, and carries a more easily quantifiable cost: the damage and loss of production, customers and so on. Nevertheless, consistent with the other forms of informal behaviour, sabotage can also be interpreted as a way in which employees (individually and collectively) respond to alienating tendencies at work.

Learning outcome 7: Explain the concept of escaping within a workplace context

---

Escaping

The term 'escape' can be applied in two ways that are relevant for our present discussion.

- *Physical escape*: by quitting the job (temporarily through absence, or permanently through exiting the organisation). This is relatively easy to identify as it can be represented in job turnover figures and levels of absence. A high labour turnover indicates some dissatisfaction with the job, although sources of this dissatisfaction may be diverse and difficult to pinpoint: pay, conditions, job content, promotion opportunities, superordinates, co-workers, recognition, equity or some combination of these. Similarly, voluntary absence (taking a day off) is used by a significant proportion of people as a temporary respite from the pressures and frustrations contained within many work settings.
- *Mental escape*: by withdrawing into one's own thoughts. This is more complex to analyse because it is harder to detect and can take a variety of forms. One way of coping with boredom, for example, is to retreat from conscious activity into the realms of daydream. The work is performed in an automaton-like fashion, relying on internalised routines which act to free the person to concentrate on thoughts outside of work. In this sense, the person can 'escape' into a world of his/her own. Indeed, this can be the only way of coping for some service sector workers (such as flight attendants) who are obliged to maintain a cheerful façade for hours on end.

Physical and mental withdrawal are not mutually exclusive categories. For example, Deery, Iverson and Walsh's (2002) analysis of call centre work reveals how the combined effects of monotonous, low-discretion work, close monitoring by management and intense interpersonal interaction (sometimes with abusive customers) takes its toll on employee well-being. The coping strategy of emotionally exhausted employees was both absence (physical withdrawal) and a less helpful, depersonalised approach to customers (mental withdrawal).

More generally, employees might combine the two forms of escape by mentally distancing themselves from their work tasks and daydreaming about how to escape from their particular job: perhaps by gaining qualifications at night school, securing a small-business grant or playing the lottery. For instance, in her analysis of the monotonous work on the shopfloor of a manufacturer of healthcare products, where the layout of machinery inhibited conversation and radios were banned by management, Pass (2005: 14) comments:

> One male worker explained that the only way to get through the day was to become 'robotic', allowing your mind to escape whilst your body continued maintaining the speed of the line. After 5 years of working in the Blow-Moulding department, checking bottles all day, he said he frequently spent his time mentally winning the lottery.

Employees might realise the futility of dreaming of their own escape, so engage in the stoic tolerance of their particular work circumstances in the hope that this will secure a better future for daughters and sons. As Westwood (1984: 235) observes from her study of hosiery workers:

> [The] women wanted their daughters to have the opportunity to pursue education and training as a means to a life which would be more autonomous. There was a strong sense from the women that they did not want their daughters to be undervalued or wasted in the way they had been.

A similar attitude is evident among male workers, particularly for their sons. To take an example from Collinson's (1992: 185) study of engineering workers:

> [Alf, 30 years old] feels imprisoned on the shopfloor with little possibility of promotion .... Investing in the self-sacrificing role of parental breadwinner, Alf holds on to a belief in 'personal success' and dignity .... He insists, 'I've not done too bad, I keep me family. But it's too late for me. I've been telling the lad I want him to do better than I've done. He'll have every opportunity I didn't have. I'm probably more ambitious for the kids than I am for me. If I could give them my ambition, I'd consider myself a success then. Some, if they got a lad in here [the factory] would think it were a success, me, I'd consider it a failure.'

These views represent a type of deferred gratification or success by proxy, and bring together the two parts of escaping: the mental escape of oneself through dreaming of, and planning for, the physical escape of one's offspring from similar future conditions of boredom and oppression.

The instances of withdrawal contained in these examples reflect a way of coping with work that accommodates the prevailing circumstances that face employees – a coping strategy based on resigned acceptance of the status quo. While it is likely that such employees would display neither a very high commitment to the organisation nor an enthusiasm for their work, it does not automatically follow that they would perform their tasks inefficiently or carelessly. Indeed it may be a means of coping with the repetitive and boring work that characterises low-skilled, routine jobs.

A related form of mental escape is cynicism, whereby employees distance themselves from the values of the organisation, and express this disbelief, but continue to remain in the organisation and do the job effectively. Fleming and Spicer (2003) argue that this 'disidentification' with the values of their employer allows workers to distance themselves from the organisation and thereby prevents them from directly challenging the norms and values. In other words the employees engage physically with the tasks and conform with the rules, but are not engaged with the values and beliefs represented through the organisational culture – so they are working at a 'cynical distance'. To illustrate their point, Fleming and Spicer (2003: 166) give the following hypothetical example:

> Instead of a McDonald's worker identifying with the values enshrined in the training programmes (quality, team work, cleanliness, efficiency and so on), she may be extremely cynical toward the company and see through to more base managerial motives (perhaps wearing a 'McShit' tee-shirt under her uniform in a clandestine fashion). Crucially, however, she performs as an efficient member of the team nevertheless .... Even though our cynical McDonald's employee has transgressive tastes in clothing that dis-identify with her employer, she acts as if she believes in the prescribed values of the organization and it is at this level that cultural power is operating in its most potent form.

The cynicism might also be a collective act, whereby employees share their disbelief in the values of the organisation, mock it and yet remain loyal. For instance, Fleming's account of working in a call centre in Australia reveals how the employees felt patronised by the management culture. For instance, Fleming (2005: 1481) describes the exchange between a group of employees who were discussing some of the training material they were meant to take home to work on:

> *Jane*: Yeah, you get a handbook and it says [*in a childish American tone*] 'What are the 3Fs?' and you think [*in the same sarcastic tone*] 'Oh, gee, would they be the 3Fs I saw on the other page?' It's very much an adult/child relationship they are trying to instigate here.
> *Mark*: [*in a sarcastically immature voice*] I keep mine with me on my desk all the time. I might just forget the 3Fs so I can never be without it.
> *Jane*: [*in a fatherly voice*] What about your recognition certificate, son – have you got that?
> Mark: Of course!
> *Jane*: [*back to her own voice*] I don't. I lost mine [*laughs*].

Fleming and Spicer (2003) see cynicism as a form of resistance to management, because it reveals that employees have not internalised the values; moreover, it might form the basis of a counter-culture within the workplace (Fleming, 2005). However, cynicism allows employees to distance themselves from the values of the company, and therefore not directly challenge the management or leave the organisation. In our typology this can be described as a form of mental escape, and it could be interpreted as consenting to the organisational norms rather than resisting them.

To sum up

Physical escape presents a problem for management either in the form of the need to address absence or revise recruitment and retention policies – in this sense it represents a challenge. Mental escape does not necessarily present a problem for management: unlike making out, fiddling, joking, sabotage and physical escape, the mental escape from work does not raise an alternative discourse, and in this sense offers no challenge. It is the most passive of the informal behaviours explored, yet, more poignantly than any of the others, suggests accommodation with the various aspects of estrangement that constitute alienation.

Learning outcome 8: Assess whether the five survival strategies should be interpreted as forms of consent or resistance

Conclusion – surviving by consent and resistance

The discussion has highlighted five principal strategies that employees can adopt to deal with the alienating tendencies of work: making out, fiddling, joking, sabotage and escaping. It is clear that these represent 'unofficial' or 'informal' behaviours at work: they demonstrate the importance of looking below the surface into the depths of the workplace where other, complex patterns of action and meaning can be found. To explore this domain, it is necessary to use research methods that get close to the subject, either through direct involvement (participant observation, sometimes covert) or detailed case-study analysis (semi-structured interviews and close observation). Such methods were employed by all the researchers cited in this chapter, and their subsequent analyses have helped to illuminate a side of work previously shaded by management rhetoric. In other words, alternative behaviours are being enacted on a daily basis by employees in a bid to survive the worst aspects of their working days.

But caution needs to be exercised: to explain work as 'a struggle for survival' may be melodramatic. Moreover, to characterise the five survival strategies as always problematic for management is, as has been noted already, an untenable proposition. What seems to be occurring is that each of the strategies can represent (and be interpreted as) consent or resistance to management. This warrants some explanation, so to assist in this, Table 6.3 summarises the different behaviours that could be interpreted as representing consent or resistance for each of the five survival strategies.

The problem of different interpretations

Table 6.3 is designed to show how each of the survival strategies could be interpreted in different ways:

- There can be different interpretations of *different* survival strategies. For example, some people might consider making out, joking and escaping as forms of consent, while viewing fiddling and sabotage as forms of resistance.
- There can be different interpretations of the *same* survival strategy. For example, some people might see making out as a form of consent, while others would view it as a form of resistance.

Table 6.3 Interpretation of the five survival strategies

Survival strategy	Interpreted as a form of consent	Interpreted as a form of resistance
Making out	Acts of 'game playing' within the organisation's rules, which result in mutual benefit for employees and managers	Acts that undermine management control by bending the rules to satisfy the self-interest of employees
Fiddling	'Deserved' perks that help subsidise wages and confer status on employees	Theft that affects profitability and undermines the integrity of everyone in the organisation
Joking	Forms of group self-regulation that preserve the status quo and provide a way of letting off steam	Challenges to management authority that undermine the status and policies of managers and make them appear foolish
Sabotage	(a) Expressions of frustration or irresponsible behaviour (letting off steam) (b) Well-meaning actions that have unintended negative consequences	(a) Malicious acts against property and people, intended to 'get even' with the organisation (b) Well-meaning actions intended to 'expose' the organisation (whistleblowing)
Escaping	Acts of withdrawal that result in employees accepting the status quo, even though they disagree with management policy or objectives	Acts that result in withdrawal of goodwill or mental and physical effort, thereby reducing organisational performance and undermining management objectives

- There can be different interpretations from situation to situation. In other words, a particular piece of behaviour associated with a survival strategy might be considered a form of consent in one situation but a form of resistance in another, because of the different circumstances that surround it.

To illustrate how there might legitimately be different interpretations, consider the following example. A builder employed on a new housing development has taken a few bags of cement. He might consider this a permissible 'perk', but the site manager might interpret it as theft from the company (a sackable offence). On the other hand, the builder might be stealing the cement to 'get back at' his employer, while the site manager simply turns a blind eye, believing it to be a way of circumventing demands for better pay. So the same fiddling behaviour might represent an expression of either consent or resistance (by the builder); equally, it may be interpreted (by the site manager) as either an expression of resistance (therefore a problem) or consent (no

---

Exercise 6.6

What do you think?

If you currently have a part-time job (or have taken a vacation job in the past) think about the various strategies that you and your work colleagues have used to get through the working day:

1. Provide examples for each of the five strategies: making out, fiddling, joking, sabotage and escaping.
2. Take each example in turn and decide whether it should be viewed as a form of consent or resistance. Justify your decision.

problem). Furthermore, the interpretations by the builder and site manager might coincide or differ, thus potentially adding greater complexity to the situation.

Interpretation is complex

Even where a particular behaviour seems clearly to fall into one category or the other, there are frequently alternative interpretations. Take, for example, the escape strategy of absence from work. It has been noted how regularly taking days off is generally seen as unacceptable by management and is often viewed with disdain by fellow employees (especially those with a strong work ethic). However, suppose a secretary was absent from the office the first Monday in every month in order to take an elderly parent to the hospital for a regular check-up. Should these extra 12 days unofficial paid leave be construed as resistance; or might such regular absences enhance the secretary's consent to managerial authority when in work? Similarly, are all jokes innocuous ways of coping by letting off steam, or might the pointed humorous comments aimed at the supervisor slowly erode the latter's status and authority? Even sabotage poses problems of interpretation: for instance, does the photocopier fail to work because it has been kicked by an employee, or does an employee kick the photocopier because it fails to work?

Once again, a complex picture emerges which requires the analysis of work to incorporate a plurality of interpretations, experiences and behaviours. It forces us to question unreflective, supposedly 'common sense' understandings that frequently litter management textbooks and the popular press. The foregoing analysis puts us in a position to challenge the dogmatic viewpoints of those who state that all rule-bending is problematic, all fiddling is costly, all sabotage is destructive, all joking is fun, or all absence is simply laziness.

References

Ackroyd, S. and Thompson, P. (1999) *Organizational Misbehaviour,* London: Sage.

Alford, C. F. (2001) *Whistleblowers: Broken Lives and Organizational Power,* Ithaca, NY: Cornell University Press.

Anthony, P. D. (1977) *The Ideology of Work,* London: Tavistock.

Blauner, R. (1964) *Alienation and Freedom,* Chicago: University of Chicago Press.

Boland, R. J. and Hoffman, R. (1983) 'Humor in a machine shop', in L. Pondy, P. Frost, G. Morgan and T. Dandridge (eds), *Organizational Symbolism,* Greenwich, Conn.: JAI Press: 187–98.

Bradney, P. (1957) 'The joking relationship in industry', *Human Relations,* 10 (2): 179–87.

Braverman, H. (1974) *Labor and Monopoly Capital,* New York: Monthly Review Press.

Burawoy, M. (1979) *Manufacturing Consent,* Chicago: University of Chicago Press.

Burawoy, M. (1985) *The Politics of Production,* London: Verso.

Clawson, D. and Fantasia, R. (1983) 'Beyond Burawoy: the dialectics of conflict and consent on the shop floor', *Theory and Society,* 12: 671–80.

Cohen, S. and Taylor, L. (1976) *Escape Attempts,* Harmondsworth: Penguin.

Collinson, D. (1988) '"Engineering humour": masculinity, joking and conflict in shop–floor relations', *Organization Studies,* 9 (2): 181–99.

Collinson, D. (1992) *Managing the Shopfloor,* Berlin: de Gruyter.

Collinson, D. L. (2002) 'Managing humour', *Journal of Management Studies,* 39 (3): 269–88.

Cox, J. (1998) 'An introduction to Marx's theory of alienation', *International Socialism Journal,* 79: 41–62.

Cressey, P. and MacInnes, J. (1980) 'Voting for Ford: industrial democracy and the control of labour', *Capital and Class*, 11: 5–33.

Crozier, M. (1964) *The Bureaucratic Phenomenon*, London: Tavistock.

D'Abate, C. P. (2005) 'Working hard or hardly working: a study of individuals engaging in personal business on the job', *Human Relations*, 58 (8): 1009–32.

Davies, S. (1990) 'Inserting gender into Burawoy's theory of the labour process', *Work, Employment and Society*, 4 (3): 391–406.

Deery, S., Iverson, R. and Walsh, J. (2002) 'Work relationships in telephone call centres: understanding emotional exhaustion and employee withdrawal', *Journal of Management Studies*, 39 (4): 471–96.

Ditton, J. (1977) *Part-Time Crime: An Ethnography of Fiddling and Pilferage*, London: Macmillan.

Douglas, M. (1975) *Implicit Meanings: Essays in Anthropology*, London: Routledge and Kegan Paul.

Dubois, P. (1979) *Sabotage in Industry*, Harmondsworth: Pelican.

Edwards, P. K. and Scullion, H. (1982) *The Social Organisation of Industrial Conflict*, Oxford: Blackwell.

Eldridge, J. E. T. (1971) *Sociology and Industrial Life*, Middlesex: Nelson.

Fleming, P. (2005) 'Kindergarten cop: paternalism and resistance in a high–commitment workplace', *Journal of Management Studies*, 42 (7): 1469–89.

Fleming, P. and Spicer, A. (2003) 'Working at a cynical distance: implications for power, subjectivity and resistance', *Organisation* 10 (1): 157–79.

Fox, A. (1974) *Beyond Contract*, London: Faber and Faber.

Friedman, A. (1977b) 'Responsible autonomy versus direct control over the labour process', *Capital and Class*, 1 (Spring): 43–57.

Fuchs, V. (1968) *The Service Economy*, New York: Basic Books.

Glazer, M. P. and Glazer, P. M. (1989) *The Whistleblowers*, New York: Basic Books.

Hodson, R. (1991) 'Workplace behaviors', *Work and Occupations*, 18 (3): 271–90.

Hyman, R. (1987) 'Strategy or structure? capital, labour and control', *Work, Employment and Society*, 1 (1): 25–55.

Jenkins, S., Martinez Lucio, M. and Noon, M. (2002) 'Return to gender: an analysis of women's disadvantage in postal work', *Gender, Work and Organization*, 9 (1): 81–104.

Juravich, T. (1985) *Chaos on the Shop Floor*, Philadelphia: Temple University Press.

Lewis, D. (1997) 'Whistleblowing at work: ingredients for an effective procedure', *Human Resource Management Journal*, 7 (4): 5–11.

Lim, V. K. G. (2002) 'The IT way of loafing on the job: cyberloafing, neutralizing and organizational justice', *Journal of Organizational Behavior*, 23: 675–94.

Linstead, S. (1985a) 'Breaking the "purity rule": industrial sabotage and the symbolic process', *Personnel Review*, 14 (3): 12–19.

Linstead, S. (1985b) 'Jokers wild: the importance of humour in the maintenance of organizational culture', *Sociological Review*, 33 (4): 741–67.

Management Today and KPMG Forensic Accounting (2000) *Business Ethics Survey*, October.

Mars, G. (1982) *Cheats at Work: An Anthropology of Workplace Crime*, London: Allen and Unwin.

Marx, K. (1969) 'Alienated labour', in T. Burns (ed.), *Industrial Man: Selected Readings*, Harmondsworth: Penguin: 95–109.

Mayo, E. (1933) *The Human Problems of an Industrial Civilisation*, New York: Macmillan.

McIntosh, I. and Broderick, J. (1996) 'Neither one thing nor the other: compulsory competitive tendering and Southburg cleansing services', *Work, Employment and Society*, 10 (3): 413–30.

Micelli, Z. and Near, J. (1992) *Blowing the Whistle*, New York: Lexington Books.

Molstad, C. (1986) 'Choosing and coping with boring work', *Urban Life*, 15 (2): 215–36.

Noon, M. (1992) 'HRM: a map, model or theory', in P. Blyton and P. Turnbull (eds), *Reassessing Human Resource Management*, London: Sage: 16–32.

Pass, S. (2005) *'Playing the Game': An Employee Perspective of High Performance Work Systems*, paper presented to British Universities Industrial Relations Association conference 2005.

Perry, N. (1998) 'Indecent exposures: theorizing whistleblowing', *Organization Studies*, 19 (2): 235–57.

Radcliffe-Brown, A. R. (1952) *Structure and Function in Primitive Society,* London: Cohen and West.

Rodrigues, S. and Collinson, D. (1995) 'Having fun? Humour as resistance in Brazil', *Organization Studies,* 16 (5): 739–68.

Roethlisberger, F. J. and Dickson, W. J. (1966) *Management and the Worker,* Cambridge, Mass.: Harvard University Press.

Roy, D. (1952) 'Efficiency and "the fix": informal inter-group relations in a piecework machine shop', *American Journal of Sociology,* 57: 255–66.

Roy, D. (1953) 'Work satisfaction and social reward in quota achievement: an analysis of piecework incentive', *American Sociological Review,* 18: 507–14.

Roy, D. (1955) 'Quota restriction and goldbricking in a machine shop', *American Journal of Sociology,* 60: 427–42.

Roy, D. (1960) 'Banana time: job satisfaction and informal interaction', *Human Organization,* 18: 156–68.

Sanders, T. (2004) 'Controllable laughter: managing sex work through humour', *Work, Employment and Society,* 38 (2): 273–91.

Spradley, J. P. and Mann, B. J. (1975) *The Cocktail Waitress: Women's Work in a Man's World,* New York: Wiley.

Taylor, L. and Walton, P. (1971) 'Industrial sabotage: motives and meanings', in S. Cohen (ed.), *Images of Deviance,* Harmondsworth: Penguin: 219–45.

Taylor, P. and Bain, P. (2003) '"Subterranean worksick blues": humour as subversion in two call centres', *Organization Studies,* 24 (9): 1487–509.

Townsend, K. (2005) Electronic surveillance and cohesive teams: room for resistance in an Australian call centre? *New Technology, Work and Employment,* 20(1): 47–59.

Watson, T. J. (1987) *Sociology, Work and Industry,* 2nd edn, London: Routledge and Kegan Paul.

Westwood, S. (1984) *All Day Every Day,* London: Pluto.

Wilson, C. P. (1979) *Jokes: Form, Content, Use and Function,* London: Academic Press.

CHAPTER 7

Managing culture

Stephen Linstead

QUESTIONS ABOUT CULTURE

1. What is organizational culture? What is it good for?
2. Are companies with strong cultures always successful?
3. What are the dysfunctions of culture?
4. What are subcultures, and are they healthy?
5. How is organizational culture related to national culture?

CASE STUDY   Culture at Company T

Company T is a Canadian automobile assembly plant employing some 1300 people. In response to increased foreign competition, the corporation decided to implement a participative management programme focused on quality. In 1980, the plant hired consultants to help implement a quality of working life (QWL) programme. The union refused to participate, but approved a participative management programme and the plant management decided to go ahead.

The plant was functionally organized, with a plant manager, assistant plant manager and six department managers, including industrial relations, controller, quality, operations, manufacturing engineering and materials. The plant ran two shifts a day and in addition to the operations manager, there were 2 production managers (one responsible for each shift), 8 superintendents, 22 general supervisors, 7 utility supervisors and 66 foremen, each of whom supervised up to 50 hourly workers.

As a result of problems encountered in the implementation of the QWL programme after two years, it became clear that while both consultants and managers had originally engaged in a process with social and technical redesign goals, the real challenge was one of cultural change and personal transformation. They were up against a distinctive and extremely strong company culture, whose assumptions were working a kind of sea change with their interventions, distorting their purpose and twisting their outcomes.

Aggression: 2 × 4 management

The culture of Company T was distinctive even by the estimation of company members. It positively sanctioned an aggressive macho management style, termed '2 × 4 management', which consisted of reprimands in the form of intensive verbal abuse ('yelling and screaming'), dramatic confrontations, and generally, figuratively, 'beating up' on offenders. Extreme examples of this behaviour had become myth in the organization and perpetrators were spoken of as something of folk heroes:

In the old days here, there used to be a lot of grandstanding, but a lot of it was for show. I can remember one day, 'X' came out onto the floor and he saw a piece that he did not like, and he started jumping up and down on it and he bashed it all in and yelling and screaming and then he said, 'Now throw it out, because it is not good for anything' and when he turned around, he winked at me. It was a show, it was fun, it was a game. It was just like a John Wayne movie, as soon as the movie was over with, they became human again.

The perception was that those who were good at 2 × 4 management got promoted at Company T:

If your boss catches you out, catches something wrong with the product in your area, you can respond in one of two ways. You can say, 'OK, I'll find out what's wrong', or you can say, 'God damn it, it's John Smith. I'm going to call him in here and chew him out.' The second way looks much better, more glory in it.

This macho style was seen by many as being quite anachronistic, as representing a culture very distinct from the 'larger' culture in which managers spent their family, civic and recreational lives. Some experienced embarrassment when describing their work environment to their friends and families:

My brother, who is an accountant, says he cannot believe this place, that it is like a game instead of a workplace, but he thinks everything about this place is ridiculous.

And even the worst 2 × 4 managers were recognized as being quite different away from work:

Mind you, he was a fine fellow outside. He used to tell me that he kept his leopard skin suit in the guard house and would put it on when he came in. In the past, if you wanted to get ahead, you had to do a little more of the 2 × 4. The idea was, if you did not beat, you got beaten.

Managers referred to the company culture as a jungle, the workers as 'animals', the extreme 2 × 4 type managers as 'monsters', and yet, while many expressed aversion to the harsh style, others found it tough, 'honest' and hence, appealing:

I prefer the straightforward approach. I don't like the foul language. But I do not think people listen to you if you are a nice guy. I don't think people listen to [the assistant plant manager] as much as they used to. People are scared of someone who chews them out.

Competitiveness: 'shiftitus' and empire building

If the tough macho management style was one of the salient values underlying the Company T culture, the other was an intense competitiveness which manifested itself in two forms of behaviour: competition between shifts ('shiftitus') and lack of cooperation between functions ('empire building'). Both these forms of competition were highly valued. 'Shiftitus', with its disease-like connotations, was defined by one manager as 'we do not like to see the other shift run as well as we do'. It was intense in Company T. As mentioned earlier, there were two shifts, A and B. The two shifts were constantly compared and invited to compete in order to encourage people to work hard. At times, however, it got out of hand:

> It is a big game, to get the other guy. There is a lot of resentment and competition. We base everything on results and so people will resort to things like counting back on the line [including items made on the production line but not packed or despatched as shift output] to get a better count for their shift. Sometimes the foreman will lock up his tools so that the other people on the next shift will not get them. We have to do process books, to make sure things like tools and materials are exchanged, otherwise people start breaking into each other's lockers. Rivalry is good but you have to keep the lid on.

Despite the recognized damage and waste incurred by the competition, it had some defenders. These fell into two categories. There were those who felt that, in general, it was healthy because it fostered 'good, clean competition'. Others felt that it was part of the fun of working at Company T. It was a macho, competitive, street-fighting world:

> I knew everything about the machines in my area and I used to turn up the speed on the line for brief periods of time so that my boys could produce more units than the other shift. Sometimes the foreman from the other shift would sneak in early to make sure I was not going on overtime. But I just knew to regulate the line and get things done faster and I had everyone behind me, my boys loved to do it that way. They loved to shove it in their [the other shift's] face.

Similarly, functional loyalty was very strong in Company T. This was sometimes referred to as 'empire building' and permeated all levels of the organization from the operating committee down:

> It is really incredible how one unit pits itself against another in this place. It is as if there is a wall at the end of each unit, and anything that passes through that wall is no longer a problem for that unit. People pass things along because there is always pressure, there is always pressure to deliver the numbers. Despite all the lip service about quality being most important, if you do not get the numbers, you get nothing.

Lying, cheating and stealing culture

While the two values of 2×4 management and competitiveness formed the basis of the company culture, pursuit of these values on the individual level was commonly recognized as resulting in a set of interconnected assumptions about behaviour which was widely recognized as dysfunctional. On an individual level, the 2×4 management led to considerable fear of being exposed and humiliated and forced people into a secretive, self-defensive, mode termed 'covering ass':

> I've had it solid, with that 2×4 style – it nullifies you. You just start covering ass and playing your cards close to the vest. You collect a lot of excuses and you are ready to hand them out if anything comes up. So the problems never get solved.

The competitiveness, on the other hand, meant that functions and shifts worked actively to pass the buck, passing poor quality products from one department to another, failing to take responsibility for product defects, and rushing faulty products out the door in an effort to 'beat' the other production shift in a race for numbers. This activity was known in the culture as 'shipping shit':

> The biggest problem around here is that there is no trust, no one wants to get blamed for anything. So say the sealer goes bad and you know how to fix it, but you do not fix it; what you do is to call maintenance or to call industrial engineering. That way they get stuck with the problem and you do not get chewed up for it. It could be that it was your fault, that your guys screwed up the gun, but you try to cover that up and get it pinned on maintenance and engineering. For example, if you had a big hole, it might be something you could fix, but if you fixed it too many times, then it would become your responsibility, you would pick up the job and you can't hold that job.

The need to hide personal and functional problems and failures, fuelled by the desire to be competitive and to win, combined with the fear of retaliation resulted in tacit acceptance of all kinds of rule breaking which managers in Company T called 'lying, cheating and stealing'. Essentially, these terms referred to the concealing of information, parts and personnel which was viewed as a 'survival tactic':

> This culture [lying, cheating and stealing] is still important, this is how they survive. If someone gets on their back, they say 'we know how to fix that: lie, cheat and steal'. There is not real progress there. There is a recognition that it is a problem, but to tell you the truth I think [the assistant plant manager] does it as well. He lies, cheats and steals to get the plant manager off his ass.

'Lying, cheating and stealing' also involved concealing (stockpiling) parts, hiding personnel (giving them fictitious jobs to do so that they won't be transferred) and falsifying reports concerning injuries, defects and manpower:

> The book records say that we have a million dollars of obsolete material. But before the last launch, we shipped it out and it turned out to be 2 million dollars worth. There are kitties all over the place. Foremen squirrel things away that they think they need. Foremen get hit over the head all the time for scrap, so it is better to hide it away and call it lost stock. I think I would do the same thing. But it makes for a lot of waste in the system.
>
> Another example is, if you are running rough on certain parts of the line and defects come up, someone will stamp it off so that it does not show up as a loss for our department. That is dangerous; it is just bad for the company. We are more concerned about covering ass than quality or quantity. We would rather run with one man less than we need to do the job properly. We expect the repairmen to pick up the slack. If the repair does not get it, it goes out and the warranty gets it.

Again, as with competition and the macho style, lying, cheating and stealing, while felt by some to be dysfunctional, were seen by others as simple flexibility, with the goal of getting the job done. This perspective is not unusual and often forms an important aspect of the informal value system of organizations:

> We all fight to keep down costs, but ... costs are still way out of control. But you know, it is mostly the new supervisors whose budgets are way over. If they understood the old system better, they maybe would lie, cheat and steal a little and would be better off. Old supervisors who know the ropes, his budget will always be under ... lying, cheating and stealing is a system which has worked. Everyone watched what they spent and they stayed on their toes ... Most seasoned supervisors can keep it within limits.

Finally, of course, there were those who perceived the lying, cheating and stealing as part of the fun of Company T culture. It represented a kind of freedom to wheel and deal, to live by your wits. It was perceived as a game with its own challenges and satisfactions, a healthy environment for those that survived. Part of the difficulty in introducing change was that many managers liked the excitement and the subterfuge. They had survived in Company T because they were good at playing a game and holding a job which required considerable skill, knowledge and personal toughness.

Source: Adapted from Frances Westley (1990) 'The eye of the needle: Cultural and personal transformation in a traditional organization', *Human Relations* 43(3): 273–93. Reprinted by permission of Sage Publications Ltd. Copyright © The Tavistock Institute 1990.

QUESTIONS ABOUT THE CASE

1. Does Company T have a shared culture?
2. Is Company T a 'strong' culture?
3. What are the problems of the culture?
4. Do you think the company can be changed?

Introduction

Organizational culture has become an essential element in our understanding of organizations. There is an interrelatedness between this and other concepts such as leadership, organizational structure, motivation, power and strategy. The rise of the popularity of the organizational culture concept in the 1970s and 1980s, promising as it did to secure employee commitment, coincided with the relative decline in both the popularity of and broader research interest in the field of motivation. Although culture was often presented as the 'answer' to the problems of failing companies, Peter Anthony (1994: 6), in discussing one of the few longitudinal studies of organizational change, notes that 'the attempt to change corporate culture was accompanied by complex political processes and structural adjustment' and later comments 'the case for culture cannot win: if change is confined to culture it will not work, if accompanied by structural change it cannot be isolated as crucial to success' (Anthony 1994: 15). More recently, there has been a growing recognition that it is impossible to extricate culture as a 'variable' from other elements of the organizational context. Nevertheless, one of the main reasons for the rise in interest in organizational culture was to understand how it impacts on organizational change: for a time it was seen as the hidden obstacle to success.

The growing concern with the economic ascendancy of Japanese companies and the need to dismantle the crumbling industrial bureaucracies of the West at the end of the 1970s fuelled the dramatic rise of the organizational culture or 'excellence' literature (see Pascale and Athos 1980; Deal and Kennedy 1982; Peters and Waterman 1982). Old structures and the old-fashioned values associated with them needed to be replaced, but with what? Thomas Peters and Robert Waterman and Terrence Deal and Allen Kennedy were in no doubt that 'strong' cultures were the key to prosperity. The suggestion was simple, timely, flattering and inspiring in its concern with success, and comforting in its implication that for a company to become successful it simply had to change its core values (Guest 1992; Anthony 1994: 16).

Unfortunately, most of the major culture changes of the 1980s were accompanied by major downsizing or divestment and depended significantly on size and growth strategies. This is not to deny that culture is an important dimension of organization, although it does seem to be easier to argue for culture as a barrier to change (Johnson 1992) than as a guarantor of success. Steven Feldman (1996) argues that culture is neither one thing nor the other, and is simultaneously both an obstacle to change and a ground for creative development – it forms the *context* for action. Frances Westley (1990), as we have seen above, provides an example of a culture with which no one was happy but to which almost everyone subscribed, in an organization that was committed to conflict, violent and abusive management and internal competition. Company T, as Westley calls it, was proud of its '2 × 4' management, which dealt with people verbally as though they were hitting them with a 2 × 4 inch plank of wood; 'shiftitus' where shifts doing the same job would strive to better each other to the extent of damaging overall performance; and 'lying, cheating and stealing', which was basically do or say anything to make yourself and your group look good and everyone else look bad. The people who worked in this system did not like it: nevertheless it was powerful and they felt unable to change it. As a culture it was just as 'strong' and pervasive as McDonald's or IBM but worked against organizational effectiveness.

The origins of organizational culture

The idea of culture in relation to organizations has a long but tortuous history (Chan and Clegg 2002). The initiatives of nineteenth-century work reformers such as Robert Owen, mentioned in the Introduction to this book, were foundational in setting an agenda for industrial organization in cultural as much as organizational terms, and ethical Quaker capitalists such as Joseph Rowntree and Edward Cadbury saw their mission in sociocultural as well as business terms. Even F.W. Taylor's scientific management had important cultural objectives, which threatened the subcultural influences of both organized labour and management. After the 1920s, at least, it was overtly recognized from the Hawthorne Studies that the social dimensions of work are important elements of effectiveness and the Studies also identified the critical function of the supervisor or shop-floor leadership. But it was Elliott Jaques (1952) who perhaps first coined the term 'culture' specifically in relation to work organization in *The Changing Culture of a Factory*, which was part of a series of accounts of participatory management in the Glacier Metal Company, although structure (that is, size and design of the organization), reward systems and the use of hierarchy (that is, different layers of authority from top management to shop-floor supervisors) were also important to the success of the project.

During subsequent years, organizational psychologists such as Chris Argyris (1964) were beginning to note the importance of the subconscious dimensions of organization and its psychological health. In the 1950s Alvin Gouldner, an American sociologist, also identified the importance of the implicit dimensions of working life that were taken for granted, in two books, *Wildcat Strike* (1955) and *Patterns of Industrial Bureaucracy* (1954). In the former he tells the story of a gypsum mine in which the local managers had been accustomed to letting the men have little favours – borrowing equipment, leaving early, taking breaks and so on – in return for working committedly when necessary. The mine was taken over by new management from outside the area – 'cosmopolitans' – who did not understand the implicit system of concessions and obligations (which Gouldner called the 'indulgency pattern') and immediately tightened up discipline and rules. The workforce did not like this and performance dropped, culminating in a 'wildcat strike' when one of the workforce was dismissed for an infringement which had been customarily overlooked as normal practice under the old regime.

Another related development in the 1960s was the discovery of *negotiated order theory*, which was based on work done in psychiatric hospitals by Anselm Strauss and his colleagues (1963). What Strauss et al. argued was that hospitals are composed of different groups or 'congeries' of professionals and non-professionals. Each of these groups has an interest in how, for example, a patient is managed, treated by drugs, given occupational therapy or cared for on the ward, and each has an influence over how the actual treatment happens in practice (think of a time you may have spent in hospital: did you prefer it when one doctor saw you rather than another? When one shift of nursing staff was working rather than another? How about the cleaners or voluntary workers? How did the presence and behaviour of the other patients affect your treatment? Did you ever notice any tensions between groups of staff?). Strauss et al. argued that each of these groups had a view about what made their job easier, what should be their responsibility and into what decisions they should have an input; each also had a view about what was morally and ethically desirable behaviour. In addition, individuals within groups developed relationships with particular patients and shared these perceptions over time, individuals have careers and even patients can have 'sick careers', and there were always issues of power and resource allocation in the background. Strauss et al. argued that the way things were done was constantly shifting and realigned from time to time; there were implicit rules as well as explicit ones, and groups customarily negotiated the order of how things happened, consciously and unconsciously. A good film to watch that relates to negotiated order, power and culture is *One Flew Over the Cuckoo's Nest* (1975) starring Jack Nicholson and directed by Milos Forman.

Around the same time, Harold Garfinkel (1984 [1967]) was developing *ethnomethodology*, a form of sociology which concentrated on the ways in which people make sense of their social situations, that stressed the importance of unspoken rules, talk, common sense and the taken-for-granted aspects of social life. The idea of membership was also important to Garfinkel, and particularly the things people had to learn to become a 'member' of a social group. Much of Garfinkel's work over-lapped with the work of anthropologists, who customarily studied exotic societies, and in 1971 Barry Turner (who was influenced by the work of Garfinkel and the banker-philosopher Alfred Schütz, on whose work Garfinkel based many of his ideas) published *Exploring the Industrial Sub-Culture*, the first book to bring the two disciplines together in looking at the way stories, rites, rituals and humour shaped behaviour in organizations. Turner's book did not have immediate impact but is now recognized as having been pioneering.

Related to the emphasis of this work on the non-obvious, and the importance of the implicit and taken-for-granted in forming our experience of organizations, some social psychologists involved in organizational change, who called themselves organizational development (OD) specialists, began to recognize the significance of the unsaid as a barrier to transformation. They often argued that their work was to bring out the unconscious obstacles to organizational change, as a form of cultural intervention. So ideas of culture, in relation to organization and organizational change, had been around for quite a while before the 'excellence' literature picked them up, but in contrast to that literature they emphasized the implicit and unconscious elements of experience and the processes of sense-making and meaning-making rather than the content of communication and the explicitly expressed values.

Jim Olila (1995) argued that in the tradition of the study of the non-obvious, anthropologists who study organizations are interested in the tensions that people experience as a series of 'gaps' in their organizational experience. Not exactly creating a definition of culture, he suggested that in practical terms cultural *tension* as the object of investigation could be seen as 'gaps'. These gaps he described as:

- *the ideal/real culture gap* (the tension between what ought to be done and what actually takes place)
- *the formal/informal culture gap* (the tension between the official, often written description of who, what, why and when in an organization versus the unofficial, unwritten, yet frequently the most comfortable, traditional or successful ways of getting things done by those who are deemed best, most fun or most compatible for the job or task regardless of their official position, title or duties)
- *the overt/covert culture gap* (the tension between known and publicly acknowledged ways of thinking, feeling and doing and those known ways which are never spoken about, the shadowed or occluded areas of the culture)
- *the conscious/unconscious gap* (the tension between ways of thinking, feeling and doing in which we are aware we participate and those in which we engage but are not aware are taking place).

He also argued that this approach recognizes the complexity of everyday life: rather than having single identities, loyalties and experiencing the same reality, we all have multiple identities, loyalties and experiences of reality, and the exciting thing about investigating organizational cultures is teasing out this tissue of differences and seeing how it works, doesn't work, or can work better. In a management sense, we are talking about the management of diversity.

Charles Hampden-Turner (1990) also draws on anthropological sources and argues similarly that culture is a response to human *dilemmas,* a means of problem solving. Human beings are faced with alternatives in living their lives in a very fundamental way: how to develop communities; how or whether to cultivate the land; whether to be dominating or cooperative as a society; how to arrange for procreation and the succession of the race; how to manage time and adapt to the climate; whether to be individualistic or group-oriented. Some of these things, through mutual interaction over time, become shared and common; others become more elaborated and differentiated, a result of the difference that Olila identifies. In organizational terms, these dilemmas become formulated in such terms as 'the need to adapt the organization to a changing environment' versus 'the need to integrate members of the organization internally'; or 'the need for periodic change' versus 'the need to preserve key continuities'. Culture is what evolves to bridge these gaps.

Defining culture

Myriad attempts have been made to define culture, but this does not necessarily mean that the concept is elusive – on the contrary, the manifestations of culture are often very concrete in buildings and behaviours. Andrew Brown (1998) gives a list of what he calls definitions of culture, but in actuality, taken out of the context of the pieces of which they were originally part, most of them are just partial *descriptions* of culture, and all of them make some sense (see Exhibit 7.1). Brown also attempts to classify these into a rather crude structured hierarchy, but this is a confused and confusing exercise, as is his account of the development of theories of culture.

A useful collection of definitions can also be found in Martin (2002: 57–8) and Alvesson (2002) is also helpful in identifying the scope of the culture concept. Paul Bate (1994: 20) seeks to examine what other writers have tried to define culture as, and he also comes up with a wide variety of types of definition. But his approach is both more subtle and theoretically alert than is Brown's. What Bate argues is that culture and strategy are not just related, or similar, but that strategy is itself a cultural phenomenon (an outcome of cultural processes) and culture is strategic (a way of dealing with problems so that living becomes easier). Applied to organizations, this does not mean that the culture of a company and its strategy will be seamless and supportive, but that work needs to take place in both areas simultaneously if either is to change. The issue of the relation between culture and strategy. However, given Peter Anthony's argument that every organizational culture change process tends to take place at the same time as a structural change, so its effects are hard to measure, it is little wonder that the many attempts to isolate and measure 'culture' as a variable (from the early 'climate' studies onward) have tended to founder. This empirical confusion has given rise to some theoretical confusion as well, as can be seen in Exhibit 7.2. Here Drennan (1992) identifies causal factors that determine culture, but of these several are structural factors, and some are environmental. Items 1 and 6 might be components of *corporate* culture, but only item 12 would be considered to be part of *organizational* culture. Culture is not, as in Drennan's functionalist approach, about the content of causal chains; on the contrary it is about how factors that may or may not occur within causal chains are interpreted and become meaningful in the context of social action by members of the organization.

Exhibit 7.1

Some definitions of organizational culture

- The culture of the factory is its customary and traditional way of thinking and doing things, which is shared to a greater or lesser degree by all its members, and which new members must learn, and at least partially accept, in order to be accepted into service in the firm. Culture in this sense covers a wide range of behaviour: the methods of production; job skills and technical knowledge; attitudes towards discipline and punishment; the customs and habits of managerial behaviour; the objectives of the concern; its way of doing business; the methods of payment; the values placed on different types of work; beliefs in democratic living and joint consultation; and the less conscious conventions and taboos (Jaques 1952: 251).

- The culture of an organization refers to the unique configuration of norms, values, beliefs, ways of behaving and so on that characterize the manner in which groups and individuals combine to get things done. The distinctiveness of a particular organization is intimately bound up with its history and the character-building effects of past decisions and past leaders. It is manifested in the folklore, mores and the ideology to which members defer, as well as in the strategic choices made by the organization as a whole (Eldridge and Crombie 1974: 89).

- A set of understandings or meanings shared by a group of people. The meanings are largely tacit among members, clearly relevant to the particular group and distinctive to the group. Meanings are passed on to new group members (Louis 1980).

- Culture is a pattern of beliefs and expectations shared by the organization's members. These beliefs and expectations produce norms that powerfully shape the behaviour of individuals and groups in the organization (Schwartz and Davis 1981: 33).

- Organizational culture is not just another piece of the puzzle, it is the puzzle. From our point of view, a culture is not something an organization has; a culture is something an organization is (Pacanowsky and O'Donnell-Trujillo 1982: 126).

- A pattern of basic assumptions – invented, discovered or developed by a given group as it learns to cope with its problems of external adaptation and internal integration – that has worked well enough to be considered valid and, therefore, to be taught to new members as the correct way to perceive, think and feel in relation to those problems (Schein 1985: 9).

- The shared beliefs that top managers in a company have about how they should manage themselves and other employees, and how they should conduct their business(es). These beliefs are often invisible to top managers but have a major impact on their thoughts and actions (Lorsch 1986: 95).

- Culture is 'how things are done around here'. It is what is typical of the organization, the habits, prevailing attitudes and grown-up pattern of accepted and expected behaviour (Drennan 1992: 3).

Source: Adapted from Andrew Brown (1998) *Organizational Culture*, London: Financial Times/Prentice Hall, p. 6.

EXHIBIT 7.2

The sources of an organization's culture

According to David Drennan the twelve key causal factors which shape a company's culture are:

1. Influence of a dominant leader
2. Company history and tradition
3. Technology, products and services
4. The industry and its competition
5. Customers
6. Company expectations
7. Information and control systems
8. Legislation and company environment
9. Procedures and policies
10. Rewards systems and measurement
11. Organization and resources
12. Goals, values and beliefs

Source: Andrew Brown (1998) *Organizational Culture*, London: Financial Times/Prentice Hall, p. 42. Adapted from D. Drennan (1992) *Transforming Company Culture*, London: McGraw-Hill.

The question then remains: Is the nature of an organization's culture a factor for success? Despite the views of managers and consultants, research has been unable to demonstrate it, although there does seem to be some evidence that it has impact in particular combinations of factors, including economic climate, and that it can be a *barrier* to success (Barney 1986).

Culture is a means of finding a way to resolve differences and of helping people work together, often through symbols that work effectively without our having to think about them (see also Johnson 1992). We 'know' what things mean, without having to be too specific – in other words, symbols work best as an umbrella which is sufficiently general to contain a diversity of orientations (like the national flag of a country: the Union Jack of the UK actually combines elements of the national flags of England, Scotland and Northern Ireland within it) rather than having a great deal of specificity. Ed Young (1989) and Stephen Linstead and Robert Grafton Small (1992) also argue that rather than culture being an exclusive expression of shared values, where it is most strongly expressed it is an attempt to contain potentially divisive difference and conflict. In short, if we all think the same we do not need to express it, we tend to accept it. In fact, we are not even aware that we do all think the same, because we accept our views as reality and don't positively choose to accept or reject alternatives as we don't recognize alternatives as such. Jorge Luis Borges (1962:181) cites the (apparently mistaken) observation by the historian Edward Gibbon in his *History of the Decline and Fall of the Roman Empire*, where he observed that there is a complete absence of camels in the text of the Qur'an. For Borges this is the most convincing indication of the text's authenticity, the one feature that indicates that the Qur'an was written by an Arab. A Westerner trying to write a Middle Eastern document would think that camels were an important symbol of authenticity and would remark on them repeatedly; an Arab who saw them constantly however, would take them for granted and think them not worthy of remark. This raises a major question about 'strong' visible cultures – to what unspoken problems are they a response, and what conflicts are being avoided or suppressed? Paradoxically perhaps where cultures are most visible is where we should expect the deepest conflict and divergence of opinions.

Of course, organizational culture still relates in many ways to a system of shared meaning held by members that distinguishes the organization from other organizations, but this may not always be easy to articulate for the members. In fact, the concept of 'culture' relates to something that most of us can recognize from our experience of organizations, but is rather elusive when we attempt to define it. For Deal and Kennedy (1982) and Peters and Waterman (1982), culture is 'the way we do things around here' or 'the rules of the game for getting along in the organization'. For Linda Smircich (1983), culture is 'not something an organization has, but something an organization is'. In other words, an organization is a place where cultural processes happen, but it is also an outcome of those processes working in society. The organization itself is both a product and a producer of culture. This dual dimension is often missed by the more managerialist of commentators who seem to see culture as an object. But we can go further to suggest that cultural processes do not operate in a unified way – they are fragmentary, incomplete, contradictory, disrupted and neither stop nor start when we want them to. Although culture cannot be completely controlled, it can still be open to some manipulation.

Edgar Schein (1985) defines culture as 'the deeper level of basic assumptions and beliefs that are shared by members of an organization, that operate unconsciously, and that define in a basic, "taken-for-granted" fashion, an organization's view of itself and its environment'. Schein has a model that identifies three levels of culture (as described in Figure 7.1). The three levels are composed of: *artefacts and creations* (objects, buildings, uniforms, technology and so on); underpinned by *values* that are not visible, but of which we are or can be made aware; and *basic assumptions,* which are taken for granted, invisible, preconscious and hard to access. Furthermore, he argues that the culture reveals itself when it is most stressed, when presented with problems and challenges, rather than in its routine, which is similar to Hampden-Turner's dilemma-centred view of culture. This has an important consequence: to observe what a culture does when faced by problems, you have to be there, you cannot rely on questionnaires. Further, if culture is unconscious, it cannot be easily articulated. Questionnaires can therefore only access the known, visible and pretty unremarkable aspects of culture. Nevertheless, many 'culture investigations', both academic and commercial, rely on such instruments. Whatever it is that these instruments elicit, Schein and others (especially social anthropologists) would argue, it is not culture.

Linstead and Grafton Small (1992: 333) argue that a distinction can be made between 'corporate culture' and 'organizational culture'. The former is:

> devised by management and transmitted, marketed, sold or imposed on the rest of the organization, with both internal and external images yet also including action and belief – the rites, rituals, stories and values which are offered to

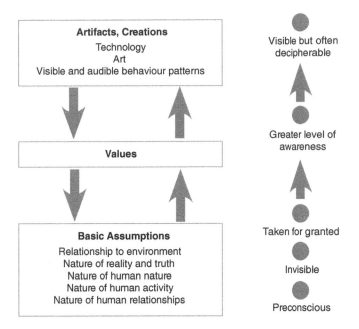

Figure 7.1 Schein's three levels of culture

Source: Edgar Schein (1985) *Organizational Culture and Leadership*, p. 14. Copyright © Edgar Schein 1985. Reprinted by permission of John Wiley & Sons, Inc.

Personalization can extend to some unusual workplaces

Source: Photo © Garance Maréchal

organizational members as part of the seductive process of achieving membership and gaining commitment.

The latter, however, is that which 'grows or emerges within the organization and which emphasizes the creativity of organizational members as culture-makers, perhaps resisting the dominant culture'. In other words, the organizational culture may consist of subcultures, and it may be fragmented, but it will be the outcome of cultural processes which take place wherever human beings attempt to achieve a collective understanding of their everyday world by making it meaningful.

Joanne Martin (2002: 111–14) notes that there are distinctions that need to be made between the related concepts of organizational culture – organizational climate, organizational identity and organizational image (Ashkanasy et al. 2000). *Organizational climate* (Denison 1990) tends to take a psychological approach to the measurement of content themes (beliefs, values, basic assumptions) or informal practices (behavioural norms) while neglecting the cultural and symbolic forms – stories, physical arrangements, rituals, jargon – that are the core of organizational culture research. Climate studies therefore tend to take a narrow approach to cultural issues, and, insofar as they assume consistency of culture and climate, assume that the manifestations of culture in symbolic forms would be consistent with and predicted by the key measures upon which they concentrate their attention. Many culture researchers would disagree, and would argue that the distinction between the two lies in how they define meaning and what phenomena they consider to be significantly meaningful. *Organizational identity* (Hatch and Schultz 1997) refers broadly to what members perceive, feel and think about their organization and is thus less broad than culture. *Organizational image* is what the organizations audiences – customers, shareholders, regulators, key publics – believe to be its values and beliefs and their own values and beliefs about the company. These images are projected outward and may then be absorbed back into the company's meaning system to affect its identity, that is, who we are and who we think we are is always in interaction with who others think we are. In this chapter, we will concentrate on the idea of culture only, but there will inevitably be points at which questions of image overlap.

Basic dimensions of culture

Organizational cultures, viewed as a whole, may vary along different dimensions. Brown (1998: 58) argues that the key dimensions are *transparency/opaqueness* and *simplicity/complexity* (see Figure 7.2). The first dimension relates to whether the culture is easily understood in terms of clarity, whether things are what they appear to be, whether the 'ropes' and rules of the culture are immediately accessible or whether they need to be discerned through experience and insight. This varies according to how tightly or loosely coupled the various elements of the culture are, and whether the *actual* culture corresponds to the *espoused* culture. The simplicity/complexity dimension refers to the quantity of cultural artefacts, beliefs and assumptions; the diversity of such items; and the number of embedded subcultures and their relationships to the dominant culture. Where a culture is both complex and opaque, it will take a newcomer considerably more time to learn how to 'fit in'.

Another commonly mentioned measure of organizational culture is strength or weakness. Brown adapts a formulation by Payne (1990) which regards strength as a production of the interaction of the widespread distribution of beliefs, or strength of consensus, and the intensity with which beliefs are held, or strength of feeling. These dimensions are illustrated in a range of organizations from supermarkets to religious organizations as shown in Figure 7.3. Taken in combination with the

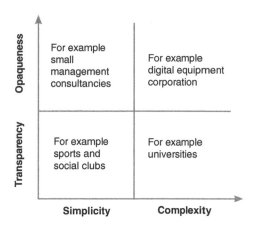

Figure 7.2 Culture and socialization

Source: Andrew Brown (1998) *Organizational Culture,* London: Financial Times/Prentice Hall, p. 59.

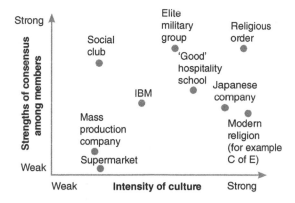

Figure 7.3 Examples of strong and weak cultures

Source: Andrew Brown (1998) *Organizational Culture,* London: Financial Times/Prentice Hall, p. 76. Adapted from Roy Payne (1990) 'The Concepts of Culture and Climate', *Working Paper 202*, Manchester Business School.

dimensions of transparency/opacity and simplicity/complexity, the textural variety of cultures is readily apparent, although such schematic treatments of culture inevitably sacrifice subtlety and detail for the ability to contain a broad picture of cultural possibilities.

Strong cultures

Despite the variations to be observed in cultural strength, the literature has not been obsessed with cultural processes but with 'strong cultures' and how they can be created. Traditional control processes in organizations tend to operate through direct orders or programmes and procedures. Cultural control strategies tend, however, to operate by generating the consent of the workforce through the diffusion and popularization of either the culture of the senior management, or a culture which senior management popularize without actually sharing (Bate 1994: 39). The values and norms are first disseminated; then there may be some denial and censorship of alternative or oppositional views; finally there will be some attempt to define and limit the parameters of what is able to be discussed, and eventually people will internalize this and just avoid certain topics and lines of critique (Kirkbride 1983: 238). Interestingly, people tend to leave organizations when this happens. However, control is increasingly being exercised over sensory, aesthetic and emotional responses – people are being told what to feel as well as what to think, and these feelings are played on by culture manipulators. Omar Aktouf (1996), in Exhibit 7.3, outlines some of the characteristics which managers seek to disseminate among the brewery workers he studied.

Exhibit 7.3

Supervisory culture in Algiers and Montreal: Managers' views

The good employee (who has the potential to become a foreman) is:

- submissive: ever consenting, obedient and disciplined;
- punctual: doesn't lose a half-minute of production time;
- serious: 'doesn't talk', totally absorbed in his task;
- malleable: lets himself be 'formed', acquires the 'right' bent;
- ambitious: 'wants it', 'works his guts out' to succeed, gives 'his maximum'.

Foremen should (in order of importance):

- achieve their assigned objectives: quotas are first and foremost, everything else comes 'after';
- set an example: particularly concerning the points listed above;
- be 'firm': never yield on any issue, do not be 'soft', output before all else;
- be a policeman with 'velvet gloves': supervise and obtain productivity without problems;
- 'have a grip': able to boss the men, be inflexible and uncompromising;
- not 'try to please': 'to please' the employees is 'playing their game';
- know how to be tough: 'deal severely with', 'sanction' and 'make an example of offenders to avoid shirking' on the part of the employees;
- be 'able to solve his own problems': 'to show initiative';
- but all the same, know how to 'communicate' while 'maintaining discipline' and 'not going further than he's asked'.

Formal criteria for the evaluation of foremen in Montreal:

- Production per line
- Production per machine
- Production per job
- Number of breakdowns
- Number of conflicts.

Source: Omar Aktouf (1996) 'Competence, symbolic activity and promotability', in Stephen Linstead, Robert Grafton Small and Paul Jeffcutt (eds) *Understanding Management*, London: Sage, pp. 66–77.

Strong cultures are intended to engender commitment, dedication and devotion, enthusiasm, passion and even love in employees. And they can work: at least they can have great impact. If employees 'feel' for the company, if it touches them in some way, they will follow its leaders anywhere because they value, even idolize, everything it stands for. Or so the argument runs. Arlie Russell Hochschild's book *The Managed Heart* (1983) looks at the issue of emotional labour, where employees are required to manage their selves sufficiently to generate a display of emotion for the benefit of the company. Flight attendants are required to 'smile from the inside' and debt collectors have to project the sort of self-image that would make debtors pay their bills. Hochschild argues that human feeling has been commercialized, manipulated for competitive advantage. Companies expect their employees artificially to generate sincere feelings. The job of the leader then is not just the management of meaning (Smircich and Morgan 1982), but also the management of feeling (Bate 1994; Hancock and Tyler 2001: 125–49).

Employees, as Deal and Kennedy (1982) argue, are uncertain about not only what to think in the modern world, but also what to feel, and whether they are worthy to be in that world. Companies with strong cultures offer to fill these mental and emotional gaps; 'think this', 'feel this' and act accordingly and you will be worthy, they say (Schwartz 1990). Dedicate yourself to the company, constantly go the extra mile, love its products and services – Ray Kroc of McDonald's constantly urged his employees to love the beauty of a burger, an aesthetic that still escapes many of us in the age of *Super Size Me* – and success is virtually ensured.

Bate (1994) goes on to look at how order is maintained in strong cultures. He identifies six processes:

1. *Taking care of people* – making them feel safe, valued, comfortable and secure, fully employed and protected. But it also means, as Deal and Kennedy (1982: 56) put it, 'not permitting them to fail'. This is sometimes known as 'tough love'.
2. *Giving people their head* – people are given freedom, responsibility and considerable autonomy in how the task is achieved. But this freedom depends entirely on whether they 'deliver'. It requires the employee to take the corporate mission personally, to literally take it to heart. This is referred to as 'loose-tight' control (Peters and Waterman 1982: 318).
3. *Having fun* – criticism and resistance to control can be disarmed by encouraging an atmosphere of playfulness and a sense of fun. In many companies with strong cultures, joking is common, parties frequent, fancy dress, pranks and humorous gifts and spoof awards habitual. Everyone joins in; affection, loyalty and community are developed; having a good time and laughing at oneself are encouraged, while questioning the point of the event is discouraged. Not that employees do not see through the hokum – they acknowledge it *and* value it for its playfulness, its non-seriousness. In this way, criticism is neutralized (Willmott 1991: 10).
4. *Giving personal gifts* – companies can reward employees with personal gifts direct from the CEO after good performance. Scandinavian Airline Systems (SAS) in Sweden did this in 1982 with Jan Carlzon, the managing director, himself sending each employee a gold watch after a year in which the company returned to profitability (Carlzon 1987: 113). The range of gifts, being direct and personal,

is supposed to have more impact than a mere monetary bonus. Bate argues that this affects the individual cognitively, that is, accepting the gift from the leader is tantamount to accepting the leaders definition of the corporate mission, and emotionally, as such a gift can physically trigger positive emotions about the company which can be recalled for a long period.

5. *Spelling it out* – the vagueness of feelings is always grounded in specific rules which define standards. Even if these rules are informal and implicit, violation of them can be serious to the point of termination.

6. *Getting heavy* – strong cultures, in short, need their 'bastards' to make them stick (Deal and Kennedy 1982: 56). Making visible public examples of people – one executive at National Cash Register (NCR) in the USA returned from lunch to find his desk and chair on the pavement and in flames – reminds everyone what the rules are and who has the power.

Finally, not only do strong cultures have to manage the positive, softer emotions like love and affection, but fear, anger and jealousy can be powerfully manipulated too. They might not produce the apparent degree of unity behind the corporate mission or the sense of dedication and loyalty that the celebratory cultures do, but they are deeply ingrained and hard to dislodge. Both types of culture 'trap' people. Company T is an example of such a culture, as were many of the big engineering-based industrial bureaucracies that dominated Western smokestack industry for most of the twentieth century. Some of these companies have become dramatically smaller since the 1980s, but little seems to have changed in their cultures. Organizations with strong cultures not only seek complete loyalty and compliance from members but also try to become the dominant basis for a member's identity. Some regard these organizations as 'greedy institutions' that make extraordinary demands on individuals (Flam 1993: 62). Nevertheless, as Thompson and McHugh (2002: 207) note, because the vast majority of organizations have varieties of weak culture, and strong cultures remain comparatively rare, we should be cautious in employing approaches which may lead to 'underestimating both the fragility of corporate culture and the creative appropriation, modification and resistance to such programmes'.

Cultural heterogeneity

Organizational cultures, even when they do represent a common perception held by the organization's members, or a system of shared meaning, are not uniform cultures. Large organizations, like British Airways, might have one dominant culture expressing the core values of the corporation, which in a very general way are shared by most of the organizations members. They also have sets of subcultures typically, but not exclusively, defined by department designations and geographical separation (see Parker 2000 for a thorough discussion of the importance of subcultures supported by empirical evidence). However, as Hampden-Turner (1990) argues, the corporate response to tension between subcultures, as in that between the service elements and the operational elements in British Airways (BA), is what shapes the culture itself. His approach to culture seeks to identify key dilemmas. In BA, despite the undoubted success of the airline in turning itself round from public loss maker to private profit maker, there were divergences between the rhetoric of the corporate culture and its professed values, and what people reported as the reality. These tensions persisted throughout the next decade and a half, and as Brewis (2007) summarizes, a succession of CEOs struggled to understand and ultimately failed to resolve this tension – with consequences for the airlines performance. Aktouf (1996), in his ethnographic study of breweries in Algiers and Montreal, noted the same thing at an empirical level. There was a strongly articulated idealized view by the managers as to what their criteria for promoting supervisors were, as we saw in Exhibit 7.3, yet the workers' more realistic view of what was actually necessary to get promoted diverged strongly from this, as we see in Exhibit 7.4.

EXHIBIT 7.4

Supervisory culture in Algiers and Montreal: The workers' view

The workers' profile of an ideal foreman:
- 'competent', firstly;
- has confidence in us, doesn't feel obliged to be incessantly on the workers' backs;
- we can trust him, isn't 'two-faced';
- a man of his word, dignified, a 'true example';
- talks to the employees, listens, 'has a heart';
- 'respects' the employees, treats them like 'people';
- is fair;
- is not 'tense' (obsessed with output, and who transfers obsession to everybody).

The profile of the typical real foreman:
- 'Most of the guys are chosen [to become foremen] not because they're competent hard workers, but because they're "two-faced" or "hard-headed"; these are guys who climb over the backs of their colleagues, I don't like that.'
- 'They don't know anything, don't do anything except try to catch you out just to shame you! Those are the types that are encouraged.'
- 'Good or bad, they're all the same. A dog doesn't eat dog, so they close ranks against us.'
- 'There are some here who only want to crush you – crush you with work and filth.'
- 'They never stop pushing. One might think they're only here to make trouble.'
- 'One time I injured my hand, blood was pissing out of me, and all the boss was interested in was that I fill out a report before going to the hospital! And they come around every year to shake your hand!

Source: Omar Aktouf (1996) 'Competence, symbolic activity and promotability', in Stephen Linstead, Robert Grafton Small and Paul Jeffcutt (eds) *Understanding Management*, London: Sage, pp. 66–77.

Some commentators have attempted to identify basic types of culture found in organizations. These typologies are necessarily crude and general, but may neverthe-less have value in broadly characterizing organizations. Perhaps the earliest such attempt was by Roger Harrison (1972) and later developed by Charles Handy (1993: Chapter 7). Harrison uses dimensions of centralization and formalization to iden-tify four cultures – *role culture, task culture, power culture* and *atomistic culture* (which Handy calls *a person* culture) as shown in Figure 7.4. *Formalization* refers to the extent to which rules, policies and procedures dominate organizational activities, while *centralization* refers to how much power and authority is concentrated at the top levels of an organization. Centralization is most evident in terms of what types of decision are allowed at various levels of an organization, particularly in authoriz-ing and giving rewards to employees.

Ironically Harrisons dimensions are in fact structural dimensions rather than cognitive or behavioural ones and are certainly not symbolic ones! However, what he is saying is that there are typical sets of behaviours, and associated mindsets, that tend to go along with particular structures, examples being project teams, big bureaucracies, small entrepreneurial companies or chambers of lawyers. Andrew Kakabadse, Ron Ludlow and Susan Vinnicombe (1988: 225–37) took the same framework but looked at what they called *power levers,* that is, the characteristic and different types of influence which work best in each culture. Again, in this example, culture is difficult to separate from power and structure. Their framework is described in Table 7.1.

Another typology was also attempted by Deal and Kennedy (1982) as shown in Figure 7.5. They related the amount of risk involved in the core activities of the company to the speed of feedback from the environment on the consequences of those activities to categorize four main cultural types.

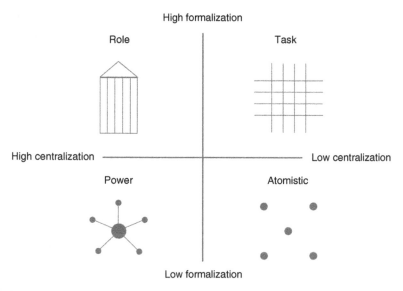

Figure 7.4 Culture quadrant by Roger Harrison

Deal and Kennedys cultures are characterized as follows:

- *The tough-guy macho culture:* A world of individualists who regularly take high risks and get quick feedback on whether their actions were right or wrong.
- *The work hard, play hard culture:* Fun and action are the rule here, and employees take few risks, all with quick feedback; to succeed, the culture encourages them to maintain a high level of low-risk activity.
- *The bet-your-company culture:* Cultures with big-stakes decisions, where years pass before employees know whether decisions have paid off. A high-risk, slow-feedback environment.
- *The process culture:* A world of little or no feedback where employees find it hard to measure what they do; instead they concentrate on how it's done. We have another name for this culture when the processes get out of control – bureaucracy!

In Deal and Kennedy's scheme, the major influencing factor on the culture seems to be the task of the organization, coupled with the financial consequences of its operations. But feedback about task performance also affects the identity of employees, their sense of who they are in these companies. Collectively, groups develop patterns of behaviour which may become ritualistic; symbols and symbolic behaviours (or meanings associated with particular behaviours) which are peculiar to them; their own language and jargon; and stories, legends and traditions. These features help to establish meanings and beliefs and they are transmitted – as culture is a communicative phenomenon – through formal and informal socialization processes. The formal processes emphasized in much of the culture literature include:

- education and training
- selection and appraisal
- role modelling by superiors and peers
- leadership.

Culture and leadership

In particular, leaders can exert a powerful influence on the culture of their organization, especially if they are the founder. Organizations are replete with stories and myths about founders, and significant leaders who came after the founder. Leaders can shape the culture of their organizations by:

- what they pay attention to and notice
- their reactions to problems and crises
- role modelling, coaching, mentoring and teaching
- their criteria for selection, reward, promotion and punishment/sanction
- their influence on organizational structure and policy.

This is in general reinforced, or may be undermined, by its consistency of fit with:

- mechanisms of control in the organization (for example meetings, budgets, peer surveillance)

Table 7.1 Relationships between power-related behaviours and cultures

Types of power lever	Power culture	Role culture	Task culture	Person culture
Reward levers	Rewards offered for supporting key power figures	Rewards offered for following existing rules, regulations and procedures	Rewards for high task performance, project leadership and so on	Acceptance by peers
Coercive levers	Mistakes, misdemeanours and actions punished if they threaten key power figures	Punishment for working outside role requirements or breaking rules, procedures or communication patterns	Focuses on low task performances or differences of expert opinion. Rejection from elite group or cancellation of project possible	Threatened by/with group expulsion
Legitimate levers	Rules and regulations can be broken by key power figures	Behaviour in keeping with defined authority, relationships, rules, procedures, job outlines and descriptions	Problem-solving ability through technical expertise. Senior management can be challenged on technical grounds	Behaviour according to needs of individuals in situation. Loyalty to those with whom one interacts, with allegiance to organization as a whole
Personal levers	Strong, decisive, uncompromising, charismatic behaviour. Manipulation by leaders. Low support for those who are not key power figures	Personal power from perceived rightful issuing, observance and interpretation of rules, procedures and allocation of work. Personal support offered only to fulfil role requirements	Status and charisma derived from problem-solving skills	Personal power through sharing and partnership. Personal growth, developing supportive environment
Expert levers	Knowledge and performance standards based not on professional criteria but on influence over others – political	Working solely within one's specialist role – not crossing boundaries or disturbing existing role structure	Constant skills development to solve new and more complex problems. Driving standards higher	Behaviour and work standards developed by group members at any one time. Individuals expected to adhere to current informal standards
Information levers	Information valued only if it helps achieve personal ends	Information flows according to role prescriptives and established patterns and procedures	Driving to acquire and share new information for better problem solving	Any relevant information to be shared among the group
Connection levers	Making numerous contacts and connections is vital, within and without the organization. Generates a closed shop culture	Contacts and connections only required to fulfil role demands according to regulations – e.g. health and safety advisers	Extensive network of experts inside and outside the organization. Loyalty to experts (profession, discipline) rather than organization	A personal sympathetic/emotional link with others. Satisfy a need to be with people one likes

Source: Adapted from Andrew Kakabadse, Ron Ludlow and Susan Vinnicombe (1988) *Working in Organizations*, Aldershot: Penguin, pp. 228, 229, 232, 234.

Bet-your-company High risk Slow feedback e.g. Oil company	**Tough-guy macho** High risk Fast feedback e.g. Film company
Process Low risk Slow feedback e.g. Insurance company	**Work hard, play hard** Low risk Fast feedback e.g. Restaurant

Amount of risk (left axis)

Speed of feedback (bottom axis)

Figure 7.5 Simple quadrant by Deal and Kennedy

Source: Adapted from the model of a simple quadrant from T.E. Deal and A.A. Kennedy *Corporate Cultures: The Rites and Rituals of Corporate Life* (Penguin books 1988). Copyright © Terence E. Deal, Allan A. Kennedy 1988.

- organizational structure (for example size of sub-units, levels of hierarchy, number of sites, distance of divisions from headquarters)
- organizational systems (for example types of production technology, operating procedures)
- formal statements (for example policies, reports, manuals, press releases).

We might think of the leader's actions (the first list) as the reality and the more formal arrangements (the second list) as the rhetoric or the difference between doing and saying. Sometimes bringing policy and practice into alignment is referred to as the need to 'walk the talk', which is not always easy to achieve. The study by Aktouf cited earlier revealed a glaring dichotomy, as he says:

> the organization (that is, its members) does the utmost to maintain an official discourse, and then acts in direct opposition to that discourse. When asked about the reasons for the systematic promotions of foremen whose behaviour and attitude are a blatant contradiction of the organizations official position, managers inevitably answer that it was 'because the workers did not want to be promoted'!

When companies are small and the leaders can be visible and lead by example, the influence they can have over the development of their companies can be much more directly felt than when they are CEOs of large multidivisional companies. Communication then becomes critical, but it is often seen as being one-way, the problem being defined as spreading the CEO's word to get people to follow, rather than increasing upward and lateral flows of communication to improve sharing, if shared meaning is really what culture is about. Two examples of this are illustrated below.

In 1988, at a management development seminar held at the Basingstoke Hilton in the UK, the arrival of the company's human resources director was preceded by a flurry of activity to present a well-ordered reception. He had masterminded the company's much vaunted and very successful culture change over the previous three years. The great man arrived, his acolytes running before him to announce his coming. The conference room was hushed. 'Now,' he began, 'the first thing I'd like to see is you all holding up your mission cards!' A forest of small cards rustled across the room as hands were raised in the apparent expression of a common faith. Within a year, the company and the great man parted abruptly at the chief executive's instigation.

On another occasion, at the end of a management development course, managers gathered at the company's country house management development centre. The chief executive was to arrive en route to the airport to take a flight to the Far East. He would interrupt his progress to present awards to the assembled managers. The morning was spent in preparation, scripting, the preparation of the ceremonials, the formal dressing, the arrangement of the setting, the rehearsal of the presentations, the preparation of the appropriate frame of mind. The great man arrived. His limousine pulled up outside the centre and course participants, tutors and staff of the centre alike mentally came to attention. His hand was raised, the signal given and the ceremony began. The course participants went forward one at a time to shake hands with the incarnate author of their corporate performance. It was a dignified and solemn moment. He exchanged a few words with each of the managers in turn and many commented afterwards that he seemed 'quite human'. The performance completed, he gestured his valediction. A chauffeur ushered him to his waiting car, to the airport and to other incarnations, other performances.

Source: Adapted from Heather Höpfl (1996) 'Authority and the pursuit of order in organizational performance', in Paul Jeffcutt, Robert Grafton Small and Stephen Linstead (eds) *Organization and Theatre*, special issue of *Studies in Cultures, Organizations, and Societies* **2**(1): 73–4.

The above quite empty incidents demonstrate how difficult it is for the CEO to change anything so 'deep' as culture with the customary methods in use. Much of the culture literature recognizes that meaning and common-sense understanding are the bedrock of culture, and that they are transmitted in some circumstances by stories, myths, rites and rituals. But primarily they are imparted by experience, especially shared experience, and the everyday occurrence of events which may be weakly and metaphorically described as rites, or storytelling. These rites have the advantage of being living and organic, changing and developing, rather than having the dead quality of the contrived stories which most companies now construct or stage-manage about their senior managers. For example, Michael Levin, the consultant who helped BA to change its culture in the 1980s, tells this story of the first day of the relaunched Super Shuttle service from London to Manchester, which provided hot breakfasts and newspapers for the first time:

We then had 96 people lined up in front of the BA desks. I was frantic. We were not clearing them fast enough. I tried to get some four-stripers [supervisors] to help but they said 'We are four-stripers, we can't do that'. But then I happened to see out of the corner of my eye that one of the managers was helping. Guess who it was – Marshall [the CEO]. They were in horror, they were aghast. (Young, D. 1989: 3)

While one might wonder what the CEO was doing at the check-in desks, and who on earth had trained him to use the computer system, it makes a good story. BA modelled its changes on those at SAS, which had been described in the bestselling book *Moments of Truth* by Jan Carlzon (1987), its managing director. In the book, Carlzon tells an almost identical story of himself helping with the baggage on a flight, saying that he did it to emphasize to the workers that everyone at every level is responsible to the customer and if necessary should help out. BA and Marshall must have not only copied this example, with the slight change to check-in desks, but also contrived it, as Marshall had no skills and no experience in the airline industry, so, if he was not to make things worse, he must have been trained beforehand. If the incident ever happened, of course (other than Levin, neither the author nor his colleagues in several years of working and researching in BA were ever able to find anyone who actually witnessed the incident). Ironically, in June 1997, while BA was negotiating with the unions on a pay cuts and redundancy package, it was revealed that it was training its managers to operate flights and check-in procedures in preparation for a strike. It was widely felt that BA engineered the strike to break the union, and it completely backfired on management and the high-profile CEO Bob Ayling, who no doubt was planning a similar publicity stunt himself. However, by the time of the strike he was so unpopular with the customers he would have found it difficult to show his face in the check-in area. BA subsequently tried strenuously to rebuild both its public image and its culture, by reaffirming the importance of people with mixed success – and Ayling was forced to step down in 2000. In 2001 the British foot and mouth crisis was followed by 9/11, resulting in 7000 redundancies, with a further 5800 the following year. Although wining service awards in 2002, industrial action in 2003 and staff shortages in 2004 led to further disastrous impacts on service, and in 2008 the airline, already rated Europe's worst for lost luggage and second-worst for delayed bags, cancelled 200 flights and lost 15,000 bags due to problems at the new Terminal 5 at London's Heathrow (Walsh 1997; Brewis 2007; Bloomberg News 2008).

Additionally, no matter how hard the CEO might try to motivate with corporate symbolism and ritual and the issuing of mission statement cards to everyone, even if the message is successfully bought by the shop floor, the level where culture hits a problem is the level where organizational politics is most keenly felt. Sometimes this is in senior management, sometimes at supervisory level, as in this short example.

Sometimes, workers find that managerial politics gets in the way of their motivation to perform well in accordance with the 'mission' of the organization. Meeting production targets and delivering a quality product or service often conflict, and 'culture' is supposed to resolve these kinds of dilemmas. In a bakery in the north of England, where the workers in question were making mince pies for the early Christmas market, the workforce frequently showed considerable concern for their product's quality. They would often fail to pack pies which they considered to be substandard. Once a pie was made, the policy according to supervision was 'pack as much as we can get away with, although quality control had other ideas. When confused about what to pack and what not to pack, and finding the criterion of whether they would like to purchase the goods themselves in such a condition of no help, and caught between supervision and quality control, they resorted to the management for arbitration. 'Who pays your wages?' said Jack (the production manager), 'me or quality?' The workers, in some puzzlement, replied that they thought it was the company.

It was very difficult for workers in this organization, with an understanding of the organization's mission and what the customer (who could easily be themselves) would want, to find that these considerations were overridden by internecine warfare between the plant manager and quality control. This is also difficult for CEOs to understand and hear about: people generally will not tell them; it will not appear as a response in a survey; and generally employees will be reluctant to reveal it to inquirers. Middle managers also experience difficulties with corporate culture initiatives, according to Anthony (1994: 64–77), because top management often engineers its culture change with staged performances, such as we have discussed, with the only real objective being to improve financial performance, not to change values. But it sells it to middle managers as the great new initiative, and expects them to sell it to supervision and the shop floor. Supervision and the shop-floor workers have, of course, seen it all before and are typically cynical. They go along with change for a while but expect that top management will eventually show its 'true colours' with dismissals, redundancies, savage cuts, disciplinary measures or just plain heart-lessness. Eventually this might happen, especially if top management never believed in the 'new order', but got its efficiency gains. The shop floor expected to be sold out and they were, and the middle managers who believed in and worked for the new cultural changes often feel deeply betrayed and cheated. It is now quite common to find managers still working long hours effectively but who claim to have lower morale than ever. They work because of their professionalism, they say not because of their 'commitment'.

Symbolic action

Jeffrey Pfeffer (1981) introduced the distinction between symbolic management and substantive management in the early 1980s, to distinguish between those acts of a manager that were done deliberately to carry extra meaning, and those that were part of the normal run of things. This distinction has been widely propagated, mostly by writers who have little understanding of the symbolic process. The corollary of this is that managers often believe that anything can become symbolic, but just because they think it ought to be does not make it symbolic. Neither does it make it inevitable that if it does become symbolic, the managers preferred meaning will be the one that is taken (Feldman 1996). Of course, if you are the CEO and have the power, you are more likely to be able to make your meaning stick, at least in public. The stories about Marshall and Carlzon above were of 'symbolic' management, yet there is little evidence as to how these stories were received, although they were widely retold. But they were powerful images, and as such would be likely to circulate and have impact. Jack's rebuttal of the workers on the quality issue (see Box above) was no less symbolic, and delivered a powerful message to those involved, but it was not a memorable image.

Sometimes humour will be used to undermine the intended symbolic message. Acting symbolically is more a matter of acting publicly, in ways that give off powerful images which can easily be associated with the other more content-laden messages that are being given out. Ralph Halpern, for example, former chairman of the UK Burton Group, a menswear manufacturer and retailer, always wore the group's clothes and insisted from the start that the companies' employees would 'wear the strategy' – actually wear the clothes which they were selling to the public. This gave a powerful message to the employees. Some years later, when the 50-something Halpern, now Sir Ralph, was exposed for having an affair with an 18-year-old topless model, she revealed that he still insisted that she wear the group's products during their erotic assignations (luckily the group had by that time diversified into sexy lingerie!). The shareholders found this consistency symbolically reassuring, perhaps additionally consoled by his reported demands for sex 'up to five times a night'. Four days after his exposure they voted him Britain's best CEO remuneration package of £2 million p.a. and called him 'the greatest Englishman since Churchill'. Halpern was clearly no novice in the art of symbolic management as Gerry Johnson (1989: 547) points out. Back in 1977 when the Burton Group was in crisis, he obtained a reduction in capacity, which could have just as easily been obtained by closing several small plants, by closing the main headquarters plant in Leeds. He did this because the headquarters 'castle' symbolized the stability and complacency he wanted to challenge, and closing it down signalled that manufacturing was not the heart of the company, giving a much-needed boost to the retail section. The Burton turnaround was spectacular, with it becoming Britain's most profitable retailing group less than 10 years after posting a £13 million loss.

So although the idea of symbolic management is theoretically flawed and practically difficult to control, acts with strong symbolic associations and high image quality do seem to have an impact upon and help to change people's minds about a company, often without their knowing it, because symbols are effective, to the extent that they mean something without the 'reader' having to think about it. Some companies then fall into the trap of contriving images and events and symbolic performances, while others do not. The example below illustrates one extended metaphor that in the end had the opposite effect to what was intended.

CASE EXAMPLE   What were you doing the day the war ended?

The British Airways UK Sales Conference: September 1989

The following account of a piece of organizational theatre was provided by a participant. It demonstrates how meanings are invested in performance and what happens when the performance becomes insupportable.

That autumn the airline business was buoyant. The company was achieving most of its revenue targets and people in the sales department were charged with anticipation. Every September, all members of the sales department, some three hundred people, are invited to participate in the annual sales conference and this particular year everyone felt they really had something to celebrate.

The location and theme of the conference is always a fairly well kept secret. This adds to the general air of expectancy. Stories and anecdotes concerning previous conferences were rife. Rumours, predictions and theories about who, where and what were put forward by just about everybody in the weeks before the event.

The suspense was eased yet stimulated by the arrival of 'The Invitation'. The location was Gatwick or rather a four star hotel very close to it. The theme was announced as, 'What were you doing the day the War ended?' The Invitation itself came from the Allied HQ and was printed in a 1940s style. All those attending the conference were requested to dress in the attire which they felt best fitted in with the theme of the conference.

The conference itself started on a warm Saturday afternoon in September. It was to run through to Monday morning. A large majority of the participants had requested a day off for the Monday aware that alcohol and sheer exhaustion would necessitate at least 18 hours sleep after a 'good sales conference'.

The next thing to do was to hire a costume. This turned out to be quite costly despite sales teams using the same fancy dress hire shop and getting a bulk order discount. The cost of hiring the costumes, £35 for the weekend (washing, if necessary, was extra) promised to be well worth it. The first opportunity to 'dress up' came on Sunday morning. The scene at breakfast was extraordinary. Italian generals ate cornflakes with women from the French Resistance. An American five-star general with foot long epaulettes on each shoulder politely ordered bacon, sausage and tomato. The Field Sales Manager, Adolf Hitler, swapped jokes with two young London evacuees who were fully kitted out with gas masks and name labels. The feeling of excitement continued as everyone boarded coaches taking them to the venue for the main conference seminar. Here an introduction to the proceedings was given by the Field Marshal, General Manager UK Sales. His role was to explain the campaign strategy, to identify the location of enemy action. He prowled up and down, pointing with his swagger stick to the battle lines drawn up on a wall chart.

And so the day went on. All the presentations contained innumerable references to war. The evacuees, French Resistance, Gestapo, American Generals, the Home Guard and the Medical Corps all listened dutifully. Lunchtime continued with the war-time theme. Wooden trestle tables, benches, masking tape crosses on the windows and a catering company's idea of what 1940s army rations might have been kept 'the troops' in the mood. Indeed, all the day's events were planned to keep people 'in the mood' but by 4.30 in the afternoon the proceedings began to drag. The novelty of being dressed as a Japanese Admiral or a Desert Rat began to wear off. The team from Northern England Sales who were all dressed as clowns began to have trouble with their face make-up. The Japanese Admiral finally discarded his heavy overcoat with a sigh of relief.

The presentations ran on. The event should have finished by 6.00 p.m. but it was 6.30 p.m. when the Field Marshal rose to give his final address. It was too late. He was confronted by a weary and lacklustre assembly of ridiculously overdressed, tired and irritated individuals who had had enough of the 'performance'. As their leader tried to rouse them with exhortations to future performance targets, their own performance and participation had become unbearable. They had thrown off their roles and the props which supported them.

Source: Heather Höpfl (1996) 'Authority and the pursuit of order in organizational performance', in Paul Jeffcutt, Robert Grafton Small and Stephen Linstead (eds) *Organization and Theatre*, special issue of *Studies in Cultures, Organizations, and Societies* **2**(1): 74–5.

Culture and control

One of the earliest writers to publish a sociological critique of organizational culture, utilizing the work of Durkheim, Carol Axtell Ray (1986) argues that in the early years of the twentieth century scientific management and associated techniques established what Weber (1964) termed 'bureaucratic control'. In essence, the manipulation of rewards established, or rather bought, the workers' loyalty which led to the organization's ultimate objective, increased productivity. After the impact of the Hawthorne Studies, recognition of the social needs of the workforce was increasingly taken into account. In this model of humanistic control, it was the provision of a satisfying task or work group life that produced worker loyalty, which in turn led to increased productivity. In more recent times, culture control has been achieved. By a manipulation of culture, including myth and ritual, the workforce comes to love the firm and its goals and, as a result, we find increased productivity. Of course, reality is rather more complex than this, but the critique does have substance. For some commentators, cultural management is just the latest control strategy, a direct descendant of Taylorism, except that human control replaces technical control (see Boje and Winsor 1993: 66–7.

In a similar vein, Smith and Wilkinson (1996) offer an unusual account of what they call a totalitarian culture. Sherwoods, the company they studied, is a progressive, non-hierarchical company, a very successful part of a hugely successful multinational. Pursuing 'furious interaction, and 'knocking the corners off politics' with a religious fervour that places everyone, even top management, in an open-plan office, they produce a self-policing conformity. Managers can be demoted by their subordinates if they are not performing, and they are paid well in excess of the industry norms in order to keep them – the 'golden handcuffs'. Smith and Wilkinson raise some disturbing questions about how conflict is apparently obliterated in this company, arguing that Sherwoods takes on a nightmarish quality 'because tight control coexists with a high degree of autonomy and an almost citizen status for members. If there is an analogy with penal institutions, it is the open prison'(1996: 131).

CASE EXAMPLE   Sherwoods

The central feature of this organization is that it is both an open system and yet achieves unusually complete control. There is little scope for privacy. Managers have been active in bringing this about. 'We are our own policemen.' They are not passive 'cogs in a machine'. The family who own the company would not want them to behave mechanically. Anti-bureaucratic, relatively undifferentiated, this organization is not an organization. Yet its reach is very complete. This degree of control is exceptional: the institutionalization of cooperation; the exorcism of politics through the 'cleansing' effect of 'free speech'; job rotation between functions for managers – 'safer promotions'; and through keeping the characteristics of new recruits within known and agreed parameters – the 'sheep dip'. Sherwoods is a somewhat totalitarian system not in a fascist, violent sense, but because, except for research scientists who work in a separate building, it is total. It is full of methods for creating consent. Several of its officers reported that when they first came, they thought Sherwoods 'a bit funny', but they can 'see it as natural now'.

This lack of privacy precludes serious dissent. Criticism is encouraged, but only within bounds. Excepting the unchallenged, strategic rules of ROTA (the accounting system – return on total assets), open management and FAN (social responsibility, lobbying and supplier control policy – friends and neighbours), day-to-day restrictions are set by the evolving collective conscience of the organization itself. Control is not imposed by officers. Control does not have a specific location. 'Everybody is at the heart of things', but everybody also has several others within their gaze, and everybody is clearly observed by others. Everybody is central both as a necessary agent and in terms of the encircling attention of co-agents.

Attentiveness is probably the best approximation of the way Sherwoods works. In any organization there are dividing lines and points of censure. But few would devote the attention that Sherwoods gives to happy 'separations', nor the obsessive degree of quality control, for which Sherwoods is well known. In this attentive organization, members are also held to attention. They are their own policemen.

Source: Adapted from Steve Smith and Barry Wilkinson (1996) 'No doors on offices, no secrets: We are our own policemen. Capitalism without conflict?', in Stephen Linstead, Robert Grafton Small and Paul Jeffcutt (eds) *Understanding Management*, London: Sage, pp. 130–44. Reprinted by permission of Sage Publications Ltd. Copyright © Sage Publications 1996.

Drawing on these critiques and examples, we can pick up two lines of critique which are essentially postmodern – that culture can be seen either in terms of *surveillance,* where control is exercised through a combination of vertical and horizontal peer observation and self-discipline, which was the case in Enron (Swartz and Watkins 2003), a view which will be explored further in Chapter 7 on Organizational Control and Chapter 11 in relation to teams, or *seduction,* where people 'buy into' a version of their organization, which is in fact a fantasy, a blueprint copy of a supposedly successful original that never existed, which also occurred in Enron. In fact, while not being as extreme as Enron, many companies nowadays maintain cultural control through a combination of both these strategies, as can be illustrated in Disneyland or McDonald's, where fantasy images of the company are used to sell the product. Surface pleasantry is vital, but behind the smile are two very Tayloristic and disciplinarian corporations (see Ritzer 1990/2003, 1999; Van Maanen 1991; Boje 1995; Bryman 2004).

Exhibit 7.5

The comedy of winners

Enron liked to close its meetings with humor, and this year was no exception. A videotaped skit began to roll purporting to show how Enron innovated. It opened with a tired cleaning woman emptying a trash can in the office of an overworked young associate. 'Gee,' she tells him. 'you guys should find something to do with all this paper you throw away!' The junior associate slumped over his desk from the rigors of his eighty hour work week, suddenly sits bolt upright. Cut to the next morning. He dashes to the head of Enron's trading group and breathlessly shares his idea: Enron should create the market for trading recycled paper and pulp. 'It's huge!' he promises, spreading his arms wide.

As soon as the associate leaves, the head trader, who was cool to the idea, leaps from his chair and speeds to the office of the head of the Wholesale trading group, played by Greg Whatley, the real head of Wholesale trading. The head trader starts to sell Whatley on *his* idea of creating a paper trading business. 'It's a very inefficient market,' he stresses. 'We can make a killing!'

Whatley, a man well known for his aggressive style, grabs the trader by the lapels, puts a finger to his lips and pulls him into a restroom, the only place, everyone in the audience knows, that Enron's hidden cameras and listening devices can't go. Whatley peeks under every stall. Then he listens intently to the pitch again. 'We should develop the business plan and go to Skilling [then COO],' he says. 'Get cracking.'

But Whatley and the trader have not been careful enough. A low-level employee has overheard their conversation through an air-conditioning vent. While the executives dither, he races back to his desk and makes a phone call. Jeff Skilling's secretary answers and gives him an appointment to discuss *his* idea – for creating a market in paper and pulp. The low-level employee is played by David Cox, who in real life went from a minor job running Enron's graphics department to creating the company's paper and pulp trading division. He was now, true to form, another Enron multimillionaire.

The audience applauded wildly when the skit ended – sure, the culture at Enron was treacherous, but that was the point. Enron hired the best and the brightest: so fighting your way to the top was tougher. But once you got there, you knew – it was incontestable, incontrovertible – that you were a winner.

Source: Extracted from Mimi Swartz with Sherron Watkins (2003) *Power Failure: The Inside Story of the Collapse of Enron*, New York: Doubleday, pp. 13–14.

The move from bureaucratic to symbolic control is in fact difficult for most organizations, but particularly those in which there are concentrations of professionals, such as hospitals, universities and other areas of public service. A number of studies have drawn attention to how public sector employees tend to have stronger union affiliations, strong client-based relations, weak identification with the employing organization, stronger identification with professional bodies and peers, considerable expert power, and are more likely to be oriented to ethical as opposed to commercial values (Sinclair 1991: 326–7). In recent cases, such as Enron (beautifully illustrated in the film *The Smartest Guys in the Room*) a group of professionals within an organization may develop unethical values (see Exhibits 7.5 and 7.6 for aspects of how culture can reinforce such values regardless of the manager's personal attitude towards them (Swartz and Watkins 2003)). Research from which these observations are made supports the view that professional public sector employees, such as clinicians, nurses, academics, welfare workers and engineers, are less likely to tolerate management-imposed constraints, will treat the organization as a means to an end and as a place to do the work they have chosen as a vocation or career. These professionals tend to strive for high levels of autonomy or freedom and generally have high expectations of achieving intrinsic self-fulfilment without strong identification with the organizations in which they work. Strong beliefs about public service, dedication or almost a 'calling' to the job, especially where there are heavily client-based relations, such as with clinicians, strengthens the view that strong subcultures or multicultures flourish in these types of organizations (Eastman and Fulop 1997, citing Sinclair 1991 and Bovens 1992). As Amanda Sinclair comments, control through a dominant culture, especially one based on private sector models, such as McDonalds, might not be an appropriate management approach to integrate, accommodate or exploit the differences in organizations with strong multicultures (1991: 328–9). Moreover, many public sector organizations are recognized as having a range of governance or control structures, including collegial, bureaucratic and professional ones – the typical *knowledge organization* with a high concentration of experts – that defy one all-embracing culture (Sinclair 1991: 328, citing Benveniste 1987).

Exhibit 7.6

Winners and losers in the 'World's Best Company'

Sherron Watkins went to the Enron Corporation's November management conference in the year 2000 determined she wouldn't be taken for a loser. The year before, at her first such meeting after being promoted to vice president she had blown it. Booked into the Hill Country Hyatt and Resort for three days of corporate team building she had opted, in the recreational hours for the company-sponsored salsa-making class. At affairs such as these where Enron took over the entire hotel and offered an array of afternoon networking and socializing activities, it was to important to pick one that advanced your career. A smart, ambitious employee would never sign up for the afternoon of fly fishing, for instance, because you couldn't lose the smell of fish in time for the evening cocktail party, and because you could wind up wasting your afternoon with guys who worked in the once crucial but now irrelevant pipeline division. That left, as career-building activities, skeet shooting, the road rally tennis, golf, facials, pedicures, outlet shopping and antiquing in a nearby Hill Country town.

To understand the loaded nature of the choices you had to understand the loaded nature of life at Enron. Salsa making, for instance, had turned out to be a disaster. One of the small hotel conference rooms had been converted into a kitchen for the occasion; Sherron had entered straight from her facial without makeup, without combing her hair and she was chopping jalapeños with three pipeline guys – middle-aged men shaped like bumpy Bosc pears – when the then COO, soon to be CEO, Jeff Skilling, had walked in. Or rather, he'd poked his head into the room, narrowed his eyes, and raised his peaked nose, as if to test the air. It had not pleased him. At just that moment he'd caught sight of her. 'Uh, hi, Sherron,' Skilling had said, and then whoosh, he was gone. In his wake Sherron found herself enveloped in that uniquely Enronian sense of dread: she knew she'd been caught with a bunch of losers, far, far away from Skilling's winning team.

Once, the pipeline guys had mattered but that was long ago. In the 1980s Enron was one of the largest pipeline companies in North America, moving natural gas from the Gulf Coast to the East Coast, the West Coast, the Midwest and beyond. But as Jeff Skilling's influence over CEO Ken Lay grew, Enron changed identities several times. It always positioned itself as the company of vision but it supplemented its base. In the late 1980s and early 1990s Enron revolutionized the way natural gas was bought and sold by operating more like a finance company than a gas company. In the mid-1990s, Enron started selling and trading power, battling across the country to deregulate entrenched electric utilities.

Lately, with the boom in dot.com and high-tech companies, Enron was vigorously morphing into an Internet-telecommunications conglomerate. Enron Online, the company's online trading platform was already the largest e-commerce site in the world and now 'broadband' was the new buzzword inside the company. Enron was gearing up to trade space available on high-speed telephone lanes in order to deliver movies and more into private homes over its Enron Intelligent Network, a new and improved Internet. It was poised to dominate AT&T and all the other behemoths.

This corporate shape shifting made Enron seem to Wall Street less like an IBM or an Exxon and more like the poster child for the new economy, a business so fast paced, so protean, and so forward looking that it could change its stripes, virtually overnight, to suit the Zeitgeist. So if you wanted to get ahead at Enron, you had to be able to change too.

- Does Enron have a 'strong' culture?
- Is it possible to have a culture of change?
- How does Enron's culture affect individual identity?

Source: Adapted from Mimi Swartz with Sherron Watkins (2003) *Power Failure: The Inside Story of the Collapse of Enron*, New York: Doubleday, pp. 1–3.

In many organizations there might also be different operational demands that encourage a 'culture' that is not easily brought under any group or individual's control. Members of the University of California, Berkeley have for some years been studying organizations that they describe as 'high-reliability organizations'. They have studied aircraft carriers, nuclear power plants, air traffic control systems and the operation of large electric power grids – organizations all likely to be involved in major crises, needing rapid response capacities and even having to deal with major catastrophes (Pool 1997: 44). In high-reliability organizations there is no one permanent structure or pattern of activity, in the sense that some groups operate bureaucratically and in a hierarchical manner, others in a professional and collegial way (as described above), while others operate in an emergency mode. The high-reliability organizations, or the ones that seem to outperform others in their industry, have the capacity to have everyone switch between these modes of operating,

National culture – or kitsch?
Source: Photo © Chris Poulson

depending on the situation. At any one time, all members might be operating in an emergency or crisis mode for a period of time. Communication in these organizations is intense, frequent and encouraged, as is the practice of challenging rules and procedures or looking for what can go wrong before it happens. Mistakes are not punished when someone is trying to do the 'right' thing. An inbuilt tolerance or expectation of ambiguity and uncertainty in management practices is the norm, which the researchers noted was one of the most unsettling aspects of these organizations. Often managers and employees alike struggle with this ambiguity because they believe that a well-functioning organization always knows what it is doing next and how (Pool 1997: 44–5). To sustain 'high reliability' literally means working with and encouraging multicultures as the basis of encouraging a 'culture' of learning (see also Pauchant and Mitroff 1988).

The cultural relativity of management

Another reason why values might be difficult to change could be the extent to which they are connected to wider cultural values which support them. Workforce diversity is increasingly a worldwide phenomenon, and besides the multicultural composition of a workforce based in a single country, many companies coordinate operations based in several countries, manufacturing and assembling products across different locations. Parochial attitudes and ethnocentric views persist in developed, less-developed and underdeveloped economies, even when a society is multicultural in its composition. Whether these biases translate into a predominantly monolingual society or an intolerance towards other cultural norms, it can prevent a country or organization from taking full advantage of the new global opportunities in faster growing regions like China, India and the Asia-Pacific. That companies need to 'Think Global: Act Local', or practise globalization in the new world markets, has

214

become something of a cliché (see Torrington 1994). However, some writers have examined the consequences of the developing global–local dilemma (Humes 1993) and found that despite the visionary rhetoric, the practice itself is anything but simple. Hari Bedi (1991) provides an insightful analysis of globalization from the practising Asian managers point of view, critiquing the extension of Western practices (ersatz capitalism) into other cultures, which themselves have long histories of civilization and their own complex social arrangements and values.

However, as Edward Hall (1959) argues, cultures are communicated by more languages than simply the verbal. Consider the following questions:

1. You arrive for a meeting with a business client at the scheduled time of 10:00. By 10:45 the client is still not ready to see you. What do you think?
2. You arrive for a meeting with an agent whose performance is likely to be very important to your operations. The agent s office is small, crowded and cluttered and in a seedy part of town. How is your confidence affected?
3. You arrive at the offices of a major supplier who has told you how well the business is doing. However, the managing director's office is almost bare, with simple furniture and little decoration. Do you still believe the company is doing well?
4. Your company asks you to review the restaurant of a friend as a venue for entertaining clients. The food is awful. Your friend tells you that he really needs the business and is relying on you for a good review. What do you do?
5. You have clinched the deal and shaken hands on it, but when you try to set a date to meet and sign formal contracts, the other party is reluctant to commit. What do you do?

Each of these situations would normally be interpreted as a warning signal in Australia, Canada, the UK or the USA. But they would be interpreted quite differently in other cultures, such as South America, East Africa or Japan (where the Western haste to do business is often a disadvantage); the Middle East (where a crowded office is a good sign that the agent is busy and in touch with the action); Japan (where minimalist furnishing is a sign of great discernment and can even be more expensive than opulence); various parts of Southeast Asia, the Middle East and South America where personal relationships incur obligations (that is, you would give the good public review but tell the friend in private that the food required improvement – and they would take the responsibility of not making you a liar on their behalf); and parts of Asia and Africa where a 'gentleman's agreement' is considered more binding than a written contract (where personal obligation, being based on moral principles, is more powerful than the technicalities of legal compulsion). Hall identifies five non-verbal languages which communicate information to us without anyone speaking, and they correspond to each of the five questions above: time, space, things, relationships and agreements. Hall's point is that we all have a characteristic way of 'reading' these things according to our cultural background, and we do this without thinking. When we go into other cultures, however, we may be making the wrong reading, and we need to be on our guard against this.

Two other early macro-frameworks were also developed to help identify the differences in cross-cultural understanding. Robert Westwood (1992) gives a useful outline of the theory behind the concept of culture, including the framework developed by Kluckhohn and Strodtbeck (1961; see also Adler 1991). These two frameworks identify five basic orientations or core dimensions of culture as responses to questions which all societies must answer:

1. What is the essence of human nature?
2. How do/should people relate to their environment?
3. What is the basic time orientation of people?
4. What state of being and action are people basically predisposed to?
5. What is the basis for a relationship between people?

The frameworks then identify three states of possible cultural responses – positive, negative and neutral – which are tabulated horizontally against the five vertical dimensions, as shown in Table 7.2. Although the columns in Table 7.2 may be vertically related, the orientations may also vary horizontally between questions. In other words, because you believe that people are basically evil does not necessarily mean that you think they are subservient to nature – a negative response to one item does not automatically entail a negative response to all. So, any culture may not necessarily have all its scores in one column, and may have items of value in all three as part of its basic cultural matrix. Understanding this cultural underpinning can often help to make inexplicable actions – like the Arab car mechanic who refuses to commit to a time for having your car repaired – explicable (Arab cultures would score in column 1 in Table 7.2 across the dimensions of 'time', 'being' and 'relationships', a common phrase being *'inshallah'* or 'if Allah wills'). Having respect for the past, they value traditional obligations highly and lineal obligations can at any time take precedence over work-related ones. This also poses problems for the introduction of quality initiatives which require the statement in advance of performance standards, service standards and benchmarks. We also gave the example where many management fads were difficult to copy in Asia and one reason for this was the strong basis of family ties in businesses (that is, scoring in column 1 on 'relationships').

A series of much cited studies and commentaries by Geert Hofstede (1980, 1991, 1998, 1999, 2001; Hofstede et al. 1990; Hofstede and Peterson 2000) saw the development of an influential but controversial framework of cultural differentiation along four continuums, to which Hofstede and Michael Bond (1988) added a fifth:

- *Individualism–collectivism* (is it more important to stand out as an individual, or to be established as a member of a group?)
- *Power distance* (tall societies with the very poor and very rich, and authority structures in which those in authority do not respond to the wishes of those below, are distinct from those egalitarian societies in which many voices are heard and taken into account)
- *Uncertainty avoidance* (the need for certainty, risk avoidance, caution)
- *Masculinity-femininity* (quantity, measurement, regulation and order as against quality of life, caring, concern with feelings and expression)
- *Long-term-short-term orientation* (Confucian dynamism – the ability to pursue long-term and general goals as against short-term gain and advantage).

These dimensions, when related to each other, produced cultural maps of the world which enabled countries to be located relative to each other. This classification has not been without its critics and controversies. Cultural assumptions are

Table 7.2 Dimensions of basic cultural assumptions

Core dimensions	Cultural assumptions		
	1	2	3
What is the essence of human nature?	People are basically evil	People are a mixture of good and evil	People are basically good
How do/should people relate to the environment?	People are subservient to nature	People are in harmony with nature	People should be masters of nature
What is the basic time orientation of people?	To the past	To the present	To the future
What state of being and action are people basically predisposed to?	The desirable state is simply to 'be'; to act spontaneously and without long-term expectations	People should act and strive towards their own self-development and actualization	People should act so as to achieve measurable accomplishments
What is the basis for a relationship between people?	Lineal – orientation is towards the group – is based on family ties; continuance of family line is a prime goal	Collateral – orientation towards a group – less emphasis on blood-ties. Continuance through time	Individual – the individual person is the focus. Individual interests take precedence over group interests

Source: Robert Westwood (1992) *Organizational Behaviour*, Hong Kong: Longmans, p. 43, adapted from Kluckhohn and Strodtbeck (1961).

very deep, and are expressed in a variety of ways, of which verbal language is just one. Learning to read the other non-verbal languages of culture is an important skill, which international managers of the future must acquire.

For Hofstede, these five continuums are the assumptions, shared meanings and relativities which underpin social and organizational life in different national cultures and inevitably shape behaviour. In terms of the power distance dimension, we would appreciate power differently, for example, according to whether we lived in a society in which a few people had wealth and influence and many people had little wealth and no influence, such as India, or whether we lived in a society in which most people had a good standard of living and a chance to participate in decision making, such as Sweden. Similarly, our view of knowledge, in terms of what we may know and how we may know it, could vary: high power distance societies often restrict the flow of information from the few to the many, regarding most people as not worthy of knowledge; while low power distance societies are more open and communicative about a variety of matters, regarding most people as having great ability to learn and improve themselves. So the concepts of organizational learning and the learning organization are likely to be highly culturally relative: in Hong Kong, for example, it has often been difficult for researchers to gain access to a sufficient range of companies to gather significant evidence. Cultural differences, especially as argued by Hofstede (1980, 1991), are associated with these forms of power and knowledge and traditional justifications such as membership of certain clans or castes, religious rituals, veneration of ancestors and so on, and are often used to maintain the exclusion of the many from access to knowledge and power. Patriarchs in societies who encourage headship not leadership do not want their employees to learn too much. Similarly, in certain collective cultures with high power distance, where members of certain family groups or tribes have job security, such as parts of the Middle East, there is often little incentive for managers to develop themselves, and initiatives such as total quality management (TQM) have had great difficulty in getting a foothold. Many of the concepts that Western businesses use to talk about 'competitiveness', 'efficiency' and 'profitability' are technique-driven and ignore the harder aspects of culture, both national and organizational (Negandhi 1986).

These cultural substructures have expressive forms in social and organizational institutions like the education system, the property system or the tax system, and are represented in language and symbol. Thinking again of institutions in terms of the power distance idea, high power distance societies would tend to have an elitist education system for the children of the wealthy, whereas more egalitarian societies would tend to provide education for all those who were able to benefit. Political systems would usually offer at best a restricted participation in high power distance societies and would more often be dictatorships, even if paternal ones. Low power distance societies would tend to have more participatory, democratic systems. In terms of specific practices and behaviours, high power distance societies would have more rules of exclusion restricting individual freedom, more initiation rituals and more taboos, while low power distance societies would have rules conferring individual rights and guaranteeing access to information. Privately, individuals in high power distance societies would tend to have more topics that they would discuss in open conversation, such as religion or politics, whereas in low power distance societies these would often be the subject of popular debate and satirical humour.

Non-verbal artefacts (things, objects, social and organizational arrangements) can carry cultural meaning as well as verbal ones. Hierarchy, as a structure, is a highly significant symbol of life in high power distance societies, and in some societies such as Japan it is necessary for a person to know the exact social level of another before he or she can determine the correct way to address that person. Position in the hierarchy here carries privilege and respect and requires others to act in a deferential way. In low power distance societies, such as the USA and the UK, hierarchy is regarded more loosely, and in terms of function in the organization not in terms of personal worth, and is less meaningful. To be the managing director of a company in Hong Kong is far more socially significant than being the managing director of a similar company in Huddersfield, Houston, Helsinki or Hyderabad. Societies where place, time, body language, buildings, dress, property and other non-verbal symbols are regarded as important are known as 'high-context societies', where the primary focus is on who is speaking rather than the content, and many Asian and Middle Eastern societies fit this description. Western societies, where what people say tends to be taken at face value, are known as 'low-context societies', and here the focus is on *what* is being said rather than on who said it. In a high-context culture, criticism of a speech is seen as criticism of the speaker and as disrespectful; in a low-context culture it is seen as criticism of the words only, and no disrespect is implied. It is very difficult for low-status managers from a low-context culture, where they may have been used to speaking freely in front of the managing director and having their opinions listened to, to move into a high-context culture where they will find themselves ignored and will run the risk of giving great offence to the senior managers there.

Nonetheless, the notion that a unified, homogeneous national culture can adequately explain all or even most patterns of behaviour at the organizational level is highly problematic, and many of the findings of Hofstede's own research and similar research following his approach have been contradictory. Many studies do not differentiate between national and organizational culture and often treat organizational culture as homogeneous because it exists in a particular country (Tayeb 1988: 41). Even though perceptions of power are heavily influenced by wider cultural influences, Monir Tayeb suggests that such things as education, age and the seniority of a manager are also likely to affect perceptions of power and these demographics might explain differences found in organizations in similar cultures. National culture does impact strongly at the organizational level in areas such as autonomy and freedom, economic rewards, job expectations and management approaches (Tayeb 1988: Chapters 8 and 9). Attitudes, values and norms relating to autonomy and freedom influence expectations about delegation and hence authority within organizations as well as devolution or the decentralization of such things as decision making. Thus, as previously stated, the extent to which participatory and democratic practices are possible in organizations is largely culture-specific. As a result, many management approaches are, according to Tayeb, also strongly related to the national culture. Thus, whether or not egalitarian and democratic management approaches, as opposed to inegalitarian, paternalistic and autocratic ones, are considered appropriate in an organization is largely a by-product of national culture and extremely difficult to change. Formalization, or the degree to which people accept rules, policies and procedures, is also determined to a large extent by national culture and thus impacts more directly on organizational culture. Values relating to privacy and independence of the individual over the group are the key determinants of how much formalization is tolerated in workplaces.

A range of other societal factors, such as the labour market composition (for example level of skills, levels of employment, degree of unionization, extent of casual versus full-time employees), the industrial relations system (laws covering employment and work conditions, conciliation and arbitration of disputes and union and employer rights) and the class system of a country (for example how wealth and opportunities for social mobility are distributed) also affect how organizations operate and the cultures within them. These are often referred to as institutional factors. Commitment and trust of employees by management, for example, are two particularly important aspects of organizations that can also be heavily influenced by such things as the labour market and industrial relations systems within countries (Tayeb 1988: Chapters 8 and 9). Other national factors, such as the economic system (for example capitalist, socialist, mixed economy, closed economy), systems of government (for example elected, dictatorship) and the legal system (for example nature of civil and commercial law) also affect certain work practices and the cultures of organizations. Both the social and national factors are embedded in national cultures, but they are often more easily changed or manipulated than widely held attitudes and values (see Fulop 1992: 361–9; Schwartz and Sagie 2000). For many years Japanese companies offered such things as lifetime employment, which many observers attributed to something paternal or clan-like in the culture of Japan, and hence its organizations. Yet when hard economic times arose these practices were quickly questioned and ceased in many large companies (Fulop 1992: 367).

At the organizational level, a number of other factors sometimes called 'contingency variables' also influence both the type of organizational structure and culture that might emerge. Thus the size of an organization might mean that larger organizations tend to be more bureaucratic and therefore centralized, no matter where they might be located. The markets that organizations enter are likely to influence how they practise management; for example, many Japanese 'transplant' companies in the car industry have had to modify their management practices to operate in countries such as Australia, the USA and the UK. Technologies can also influence how organizations develop their management practices, for example certain computer technologies, mass production and assembly methods produce similar problems across a range of countries irrespective of national culture. It is no surprise to realize that core aspects of scientific management were adopted in many parts of the world – Guillén (2006) even argues that its principles were influential in the development of modernist architecture and maps that development across several countries. The form of ownership of the company or business (for example limited liability shareholders versus owner-managers) can affect the degree of centralization and hierarchy in organizations, probably more than national culture (Tayeb 1988: Chapters 8 and 9).

The neglect of these considerations has been part of growing criticism of Hofstede's work. The cross-cultural psychologist Harry Triandis (1993) makes the point that Hofstede does not attempt to integrate his work with any of the growing number of studies in the broader social science literature, developing only his own agenda, and unnecessarily polarizes his value pairs, when in reality 'two can coexist and are simply emphasized more or less' varying situationally – we can all behave individualistically or collectively, rigidly or flexibly, opportunistically or far-sightedly, trustingly or suspiciously and so on (Triandis 199: 42). Shalom Schwartz (1992: 2–3), for example, found that the organizational levels and national level of culture tended to be dynamic and closely integrated rather than stable and independent as in Hofstede's research. Schwartz (1992) also points out, as have others, that the 'normative ideals' of a culture cannot be inferred from a statistical average of individual responses, and furthermore that unless the value set investigated is comprehensive, significant values that interrelate with the values studied could be ignored, distorting the whole picture (see also Schwartz 1999, 2004, 2006). Schwartz's research on human values generated seven dimensions rather than the five of Hofstede, and he considered them to be quite different (Schwartz 1994: 116). Further, Hofstede did not check for equivalence of meaning of terms and concepts across contexts, which renders his comparisons 'virtually meaningless' (Schwartz 1994: 94). Trompenaars and Hampden-Turner, although working in the shadow of Hofstede and seeking to build an even larger database with similar assumptions, nevertheless argue that similarly positive or negative responses can frequently be found in compared countries but for very different reasons, and these differences are important (Hampden-Turner and Trompenaars 1993; Trompenaars and Hampden-Turner 1998; for critical appraisals see French et al. 2001; Jacob 2005).

Hofstede's most recent and most virulent critic, Brendan McSweeney (2002a, 2002b) takes him ferociously to task for his methodology; for the deterministic way in which he defines national culture as distinct from organizational and occupational cultures while nevertheless being implicit, core, systematically causal, territorially unique and relatively uniformly shared; and for neglecting other possible explanations for the phenomena he identified, such as other (non-national) cultural causes like ethnicity or gender; non-cultural causes, such as political changes, economic circumstances or even civil wars; and national heterogeneity. Hofstede's (2002) replies are somewhat evasive, but do indicate that Hofstede has both expressed some caution about the nature and use of the constructs while accumulating validation evidence from a considerable number of studies by, and in some cases with, others. McSweeney (2002b) maintains that the problems are with *both the analysis and the validation procedures* because 'fallacious assumptions necessarily lead to inaccurate empirical descriptions regardless of the quantity of data and statistical manipulation used' (McSweeney 2002a: 112). Peter Smith (2002) acknowledges the substantial scholarship behind Hofstede's contribution, including his willingness to engage his critics, but identifies several significant continuing general and specific criticisms of Hofstede's extrapolating move from identifying certain work-related values and goals to the cultural characteristics of societies, noting in particular Hofstede's unwillingness to entertain that 'increasing social change may require us to study not just how societies hold together, but also how they fragment' (Smith 2002: 129).

The criticisms are summarized in a thorough and balanced way by Magala (2005 Chapter 2, section 3 ff.). Magala (2005: 73) notes that Hofstede has two major concerns underpinning his work – the first is *the problems of multicultural workforces* in globally operating corporations, the second, *political instability* in the face of persistent inequalities and conflicts. Nation states are controversially given a privileged status in Hofstedes thinking because they provide the prefabricated building blocks of identity through the management of cultural heritage. The processes of socialization into particular identities are carried out through large and small institutions and organizations. This owes much to the conservative thinking of influential mid-twentieth-century American sociologist Talcott Parsons. Much of Hofstede's subsequent research preserves this demographic imperialism – regardless of how arbitrary the historical origins of particular geo-political boundaries might be – and its structural-functionalist ideology (McSweeney 2002a). Yet Hofstede's Cold War theory has both implicit and explicit exceptions: it was never intended to apply to the Warsaw Pact countries, for example, where the national cultures of such countries as Poland, Hungary, Czechoslovakia, Bulgaria and Romania were repressed by a totalitarian political system with an integrated military arm and institutional, occupational and organizational arrangements were standardized and imposed (Magala 2005: 76). Yugoslavia, conveniently treated as a homogeneous culture by Hofstede and well known for its participatory organizational forms, was not recognized in terms of its historical background as a fragile compromise solution after the First World War to the Balkan problem that resulted from the disintegration of the Austro-Hungarian Empire. Its violent fragmentation in the 1990s indicated how profound the cultural differences contained under a military dictatorship could be (Schwartz and Bardi 1997, 2000; Schwartz et al. 2000; McSweeney 2002a: 110–11). Hofstede (2001: 464–5) does caution researchers that his methodology is effective for some levels of culture but not all, that subcultural influences based on age, gender, class and specific organizational features elude it, and that detecting differences within cultures requires different methods. His view is that these elements are minor variations – but this is a typical assumption of neocolonial thought and severely contested by postcolonial commentators (Banerjee and Linstead 2001; Smircich and Calás 2006). Magala (2005: 77–85) identifies the characteristics of the criticisms of Hofstede:

- *In-built Western bias*
  Despite Hofstede's own critique of Western theories of motivation and leadership, his original four-dimensional model showed a discernible Western European bias

that he later tried to correct by adding a fifth dimension from Chinese research. However, subsequent studies were predominantly carried out by Western or Western-trained researchers who were insensitive to dimensions of other cultures that remained 'tacit' – knowledge was either ignored or reconstructed within the existing model. Magala (2005: 77) gives the example of 'shame' versus 'guilt' typologies of societies (common for example in contrasting Japan with the West) that were disregarded as being a variant manifestation of 'high-context' versus 'low-context' cultures. Somewhat weakly given his broader claims, Hofstede (2001: 465) argues against the charge of 'sophisticated stereotyping', that his instrument only measures differences between the cultures of a large multinational (IBM), and that other instruments and qualitative methods should be used to detect 'the essence of cultural differences in other populations'. But as Magala notes, the problem of Eurocentrism is not just Hofstede's, and most cross-cultural studies tend to reproduce the view that the rest of the world is a source of raw material (data) for the West's (and North's) 'ideas factory'. The ideas themselves are developed from generalizations from Western social research and disregard any indigenous social inquiry. There is also an inherent universalist ideological bias, that the continuation of the enlightened modernization of the less- or underdeveloped world requires both parliamentary democracy and free-market capitalism. As postcolonial theorists have pointed out, this tends to extend the injuries of 'empire' beyond colonial rule and by other means and occludes alternative models – justifying them with a circular reliance on its own 'science' (Banerjee and Linstead 2001; 2004; 2006).

- *In-built static and conservative nature of the dimensional model*
  The culture of one organization may be a weave of subcultures or multicultures, overcrossed by a variety of external cultural, social, national and contingency factors. Culture, structure and strategy are not separate 'variables', as some theorists might wish to argue, but rather need to be seen as inseparable and treated holistically as suggested by Bate (1994) and Anthony (1994). Because culture is not an 'independent' variable, you cannot change structure or strategy without affecting culture. This is particularly so at the organizational level, but at any level culture does change over time (Roberts and Boyacigiller 1984; Lytle et al. 1995). Even Hofstede's own research shows changes occurring among certain dimensions but does not understand them as signs of major change (Smith 2002: 111–12). Hofstede's model is leaden-footed in this because he bases his assumptions of how cultural identity is formed on a Parsonian functionalist model that sees the factories of socialization as being family, school, workplace and the political sphere. Not only is the whole area covered by media and cultural studies, and the sociology of consumption, ignored, but the smooth functioning of institutions and bureaucracies under the umbrella of the nation state is assumed – an assumption that flies in the face of contemporary research on identity across several disciplines (Giddens 1991; Castells 1997; Bauman 2004; Hatch and Schultz 2004; Pullen and Linstead 2005; Pullen 2006). The nuclear family as an institution is not simply different across cultures, it has changed dramatically in the past 50 years, in the West in particular. Communications technologies with the Internet and mobile phones in particular have given young people access to a far wider range of social networks than previously possible, workplaces are far more multicultural and multiethnic, organizations

are constantly re-engineering themselves, and the concept of shifting and multiple identities has emerged as a characteristic of postmodern society. Identities are not necessarily consistent any more – if they ever were – and their relation to culture is complex (Beech and McInnes 2005). Exhibit 7.7 offers a humorous real example of postmodern identity-play in a pub football team. This is not to say that *everything* changes or is unstable, but Hofstede's whole approach – concepts, theory, method, analysis, practice – is firmly rooted in a modernist style of thinking and finds contemporary post-industrial social dynamics problematic.

E X H I B I T 7.7

Identity and culture: What's in a name?

Lynam Athletic, named after the dapper sports presenter Des, had a terrible first season. They finished bottom of the lowest division in the South Birmingham Sunday League. So they decided to act.

First, they transferred to the Coronation League – the thinking being that with more teams in the Coronation's lowest division they had less chance of finishing bottom again. Next, they sought assistance from the professionals. The self-proclaimed 'worst team in the Midlands' entered the Carling Pub Football awards in the Team Most In Need of Help' category and for the first time they tasted triumph.

The prize was a training session with the Plymouth Argyle manager, Ian Holloway – a man known for getting the best out of underperformers. Holloway asked why Athletic needed help. Well, they said, they weren't awful footballers exactly, but they just couldn't do it as a team and were tired of losing by scores of up to 13–0.

Holloway told them this was already promising. 'Most teams think they're really great and are arrogant,' he said 'so you lot knowing you're crap is great. It means we can start from somewhere.

But as Holloway said, this was only the start. Lynam Athletic decided to take serious collective action. If Lynam Athletic were going to be winners, they needed a new identity. So, one by one, they changed their names by deed poll. Darren Yeomans became Thierry Henry [Barcelona and France], Kevin Alban became Cristiano Ronaldo [Manchester United and Portugal], Majid Ali became Ronaldinho [Barcelona and Brazil]. Out went Jon Barber Paul Blears, Dan Branch, Darryl Brown, Marc Clifton, Connor Edgcumbe, Ian Flatt, Chris Gray, Pete Hall, Nick Hall, Neil Kimpton, Andrew Mullan, Jon Robins and Ben White. In came Jamie Carragher [Liverpool and England], Dani Alves [Sevilla and Brazil], Cafu [AC Milan and Brazil], Michael Essien [Chelsea and France], Ruud van Nistelrooy [Real Madrid and Holland], Steven Gerrard [Liverpool and England], John Terry [Chelsea and England captain] Lionel Messi [Barcelona and Argentina], Kaka [AC Milan and Brazil], Iker Casillas [Real Madrid and Spain], Fabio Cannavaro [Real Madrid and Italy], Hernán Crespo [Inter Milan and Argentina], Petr Cech [Chelsea and Czech Republic] and Wayne Rooney [Manchester United and England]. A team of world-beaters.

Iphone Alves to see how he's coping with life as a sporting superstar.

'Hello, is that Dani?'

'No, it's Paul.' He stops. 'Oops, yes, it's Dani. It's hard to remember.' He giggles. 'My girlfriend keeps asking me why everyone's calling me Dani.'

Why did they decide to change their names? 'It was all a bit of a laugh really. Thierry Henry came up with the idea after a match.'

Henry says: 'We wanted to strike fear into the opposition and we certainly weren't going to do that with our football skills.' He realizes there is work to be done – Van Nistelrooy smokes 20 a day and Gerrard rarely plays sober.

In the week, Henry, Terry, Kaka and Messi work for a games development company but on Sunday they will play their first game as the all-stars. How does Alves feel their opponents, Coldland, will react? They'll probably think we reckon we're good, calling ourselves these names. We expect they'll kick us a lot. Lucky I play at the back.'

The deed poll commits Athletic's players to using their new name at all times and on all formal documents. They believe it will be worth it.

My phone rings. 'Hi, it's Michael Essien, I heard you wanted to talk to me.' Essien, in a gentle Brummie brogue, says his mates didn't give all this a great deal of thought. For example, he's just discovered that he'll need a new passport. 'But it's no problem. I've no immediate plans and we won't be playing in Europe this season.'

Essien is convinced the name change will improve his game. And that's not all. 'I think it's going to make a big impact with the ladies.'

In terms of motivation and self-belief, it makes a kind of sense. But one thing puzzles me. I call Alves, a driving instructor by day, and tell him I have a personal question. 'Go on,' he says.

Why on earth did you choose the relatively un-celebrated Dani Alves? 'Well,' he says, 'we chose our names according to the position we play, and we decided they had to have played in the Champions League to qualify The only right-backs I could think of were Dani Alves and Gary Neville [Manchester United and England] … and who wants to be Gary Neville?'

Source: Adapted from Simon Hattenstone 'Big names make Lynam Athletic a des res' *Guardian* Wednesday 26 September 2007 (http://sport.guardian.co.uk/columnists/story/0,,2177280,00.html).

- *In-built methodological bias*

  Apart from the fact that Hofstede has criticized the Western bias of concepts such as motivation and leadership in organization studies, his own work almost inevitably displays some aspects of such a bias. This is inevitable when a cluster of concepts are condensed into a small number of 'master' concepts. An attitude survey can be contested as an appropriate (simplistic) tool for the investigation of culture, in that it cannot access the taken-for-granted or sub-conscious aspects of culture that it prioritizes; the reliability of its respondents can be challenged; its ability to recognize and discriminate between organizational, professional, occupational and national cultures can be disputed; and because of its tendency to 'zip-up' subdimensions. On this last point, Magala (2005: 82) notes that a construct like Uncertainty Avoidance actually contains three *themes* – the *closure of the individual mind* (open to new ideas or conservative of old ones?), *the question of freedom* (does one embrace ambiguity as an occasion to be creative, or try to avoid having to take the initiative?) and *the question of organizational culture* (is my action structured and constrained by rules, or do I have flexibility in how I operate?). Furthermore, there is the problem *of perspective* – are respondents avoiding uncertainty in means (how things are done) but being flexible about goals (what is done), or flexible about the means of achieving stable goals? Difference on this issue leads Hofstede to rate the Greeks (flexible of means, certain of goals) as the least uncertainty-avoiding nation while House makes it the Swiss (certain of means, adaptable on goals). Furthermore, are respondents themselves able to distinguish sufficiently between *reality* (what they do) and *desirability* (what they think should be done). An old question but an important one given the evidence that Hofstede (Hofstede et al. 1990) himself generated in a study of Dutch and German organizations, where differences between organizational sub-units were attributable to *practices,* while at individual and cultural levels they were attributable to *values.*

Differences in approach therefore make a difference. The most recent significant study has been the GLOBE (Global Leadership and Organizational Behaviour Effectiveness) project by House et al. (2004) who found they had to 'unpack' or 'unzip' some of Hofstede's dimensions into:

- Future orientation
- Gender equality
- Assertiveness
- Humane orientation
- In-group collectivism
- Institutional collectivism
- Performance orientation
- Power distance
- Uncertainty avoidance.

But House's team found that on seven out of nine dimensions there was a negative correlation between values and practices. The assumption behind much of the culture literature, certainly in Hofstede and most obviously in Schein's (1985) culture model, is that values and beliefs shape action, which is their expression. However, values may emerge from the observation of pragmatic action, whether positive (this should be the case in future) or negative (that should not happen again). More practically oriented cultures will display little difference between practice and values; more abstract, aspirational or principled cultures will display potentially considerable difference from time to time. The relationship, House argues, can be complex – although he seems to argue for a managerial form of value practice engineering, which we have critiqued earlier in this chapter. Nevertheless, the modest critique of this approach signals a characteristic of all critical approaches to cultural issues related to organizations, whether heterodox economics, cultural sociology, political history, or critical psychology – the need to unpack assumptions, to trace influences carefully, and to deconstruct the object of investigation.

Gender and culture

Talk is an important part of culture. Therefore, if men and women communicate differently we might anticipate differences in the kinds of cultures which develop where one or the other is dominant. We might also expect that the way people are customarily required to communicate will make it easier for one or the other gender to become successful in that culture. Men and women have never been viewed as, or treated as, equals in the workplace. Jobs have been differentiated and even whole occupations, especially those in service industries, have been designated 'women's work'. Fewer than 20 per cent of all managerial posts are held by women, and at more senior levels this falls to 10 per cent. Men are often seen to be rational, calculating and resilient whereas women are seen as being emotional, changeable and lacking resolution. This forms the background to what men and women do in any real organization, but Deborah Tannen (1990) indicates that men and women actually talk differently and thus communicate different things when they speak. As Tannen (1990) argues, women tend to learn styles of speaking which make them appear less confident and self-assured than they really are, and as a result they lose out on those organizational issues, like promotion, that depend on appearing confident. Women tend to say 'we' rather than 'I' when discussing work, and as a result get less credit for what they do. They tend to boast less and ask more questions, which can often make them seem less sure of themselves. Women downplay their certainty while men minimize their doubts. Men are more likely to save their own face in a problem situation. Above all, powerful people, which usually means men, are more likely to reward people with similar language styles to their own.

To give another example: a New York psychiatrist in the mid-1980s joined one of the earliest Internet chat groups in order to try to develop a new way of counselling and helping people. He chose as his name 'Doctor', which he had not fully realized was gender-neutral. One day he was chatting in a side room with a woman and he realized that she had thought that he too was female. He was astonished by the richness and openness of the communication that he was receiving and assumed that this was the way women talked to each other. As a result, he created a false identity for himself as a woman, an easy thing to do on the Internet. He was able to build some very loyal friendships in this way and helped many people, but he wearied of the strain of constantly having to be someone else, and so he joined the

Table 7.3 Gherardi's classification of women's cultural positioning

| Male positioning | Women's reciprocal positioning | | |
	Accepted	Contested	Imposed
Friendly	*The guest* A cooperative position	*The holidaymaker* A mismatched position	*The newcomer* An open-ended position
Hostile	*The marginal* A stigmatized position	*The snake in the grass* A contested position	*The intruder* A unilaterally imposed position

Source: Silvia Gherardi (1995) *Gender, Symbolism and Organizational Cultures,* London: Sage, p. 109. Reprinted by permission of Sage Publications Ltd. Copyright © Sage Publications 1995.

group under his own identity, his female alter ego introducing him as a great guy and a lovely person, a fine doctor and so on. He hoped that he would build relationships with all his friends and the female alter ego could disappear from the picture. Unfortunately, none of his friends from his other identity could get along with him when he was being himself, and they found him stiff and a bit cold! As a man, he could not communicate in the same way – they did not expect it and were unreceptive to it – and they did not communicate with him in the same manner either (Stone 1995: 63–87).

So what you say and how you say it are different depending on your gender, and this may both open and close doors to you depending on your gender's position within the organization's culture. Of course an organization that only rewards one communicative style is losing its ability to hear a wide range of information and increase the flexibility of its actions, but it does not stop there. As Silvia Gherardi (1995) notes, organizations tend to write stories for their participants, with gendered roles for women to play. She identifies six discursive positions that were offered to or imposed on women in her studies, in which men were basically either friendly or hostile and women's positions were either accepted, contested or imposed (see Table 7.3). Women could be accepted in a friendly manner, as a guest, treated pleasantly, but politely circumscribed and not allowed to be a 'real' member of the culture like the men were. Gherardi's respondent Giovanna tells us:

> I felt as if I was a guest. Just as a guest is placed at the head of a table, treated politely, and never allowed to wash the dishes, so I was surrounded by a web of polite but invisible restraints. I began to suspect something when I saw the other women when they arrived and were, so to speak, 'integrated'. For example, I almost never go into the production department to talk with the workers. My older male colleagues go because they like it. They go and see their friends, and then they pretend that they are protecting me from the 'uncouthness of the working class'. So I find myself constantly on the phone dealing with the editorial office, the commercial office, the administration. I'm almost always in the office. *It's as if I'm at home and they're always out.* It's true that they are better at what they do, and I'm better at what I do, or we women are, but constantly being their guest is getting me down. (Gherardi 1995: 110–11, emphasis added)

We might recall the argument of Marta Calás and Linda Smircich in Chapter 2 on how women are being used to domesticate the workforce and free up males for international assignments, apparently because of women's greater interpersonal and caring skills. It is part of the permanent guest role that women are being asked to play. However, things could be more unpleasant if the males were hostile. Gherardi's respondent Fiorella tells of her experience of being marginalized:

> I felt I'd become invisible, I thought I was transparent. There's no point in recounting individual episodes or blaming things on hostility. Formally, everything was as it should be, and they treated me politely, like gentlemen, but I counted for nothing. I discovered this little by little and it was tough admitting it to myself. What had I got to complain about? The situations were quite clear, the solutions were reasonable, indeed they were the only ones feasible.

Everything was already decided and all I had to do was agree and implement. There was no need to open my mouth at meetings. I realized I had been pushed to one side even though my expertise was publicly praised. (Gherardi 1995: 112)

These kinds of examples show how limited by organizational culture the equal opportunities and positive discrimination approaches can be. Nothing was done wrong in either of these situations and the men were reasonable, polite and even gentlemanly. However, the women were 'second-class citizens' and powerless.

In Gherardi's other examples, the positions are more uncomfortable. If the woman is in the *holidaymaker* position, then everyone else is just waiting for her to move on, nothing really changes, and they all make contingency plans behind her back; if seen as a *snake in the grass,* then they plot to get rid of her and make her fail; if seen as a *newcomer,* then they reserve judgement, for long periods of time, are anxious and make it hard to get commitments to projects and participation in processes; and if seen as an *intruder,* she will be constantly openly challenged. Many of these categories could apply to men in some situations, but the question is clearly one of degree; women start off by being *other,* whereas men at the very least receive the benefit of the doubt and the 'testing' of a new male appointee is not likely to last for years but to be resolved fairly quickly. The feeling of being trapped by invisible nets is a typical indicator that the problem is cultural, and making these invisible nets visible is difficult, particularly when the 'nets' are often constructed and enacted by those with the power to change the situation.

Conclusion

Despite the fact that it is difficult to define, the idea of culture captures some dimensions of human social organizing that other strictly psychological, socio-logical or economic approaches cannot adequately address. It is about interaction, sharedness, distinctiveness, similarity and difference, meaning and significance, signs and symbols, rituals and tokens, leadership, common sense and the taken-for-granted. It is also about problem solving, thinking strategically, devising and operating within structures and, perhaps surprisingly, change. It is not entirely separable from these activities, and is affected by power relations, gender, ethnic-ity, time and place. In the late 1970s and the 1980s the main concern of studies of culture was with creating new cultures of excellence in performance; in the late 1980s and the 1990s the concern developed into changing cultures which were a drag on performance and perception of the environment. In first decade of the new century, the focus has shifted as a result of such cases as Enron to address how and whether cultures that are excellent in terms of performance can also excel mor-ally. Culture has so many facets that as research on culture and the application of ideas of managing culture are put into practice, new emphases continually emerge. Although it became something of a fad in the 1980s, as this chapter has shown, culture has a firm basis in a range of underlying theories across disciplines and remains one of the most important concepts we have in management and organi-zation theory.

Let us now revisit our questions on culture at the beginning of the chapter.

Answers to questions about culture

1. **What is organizational culture? What is it good for?** Organizational culture is a complex phenomenon, usually related to shared values and shared meanings in an organization, but also related to common ways of dealing with, or ignoring, commonly experienced problems. It is a form of common sense, an outcome of cultural processes at work in a particular setting. The benefits of paying attention to culture are that it focuses on people but in particular on the symbolic significance of almost every aspect of organizational life. It emphasizes shared meanings, even if implicit, and alerts us to the influencing potential of values, beliefs, ideology, language, norms, ceremonies, rituals, myths and stories. It constructs leaders as shapers of meaning. It also emphasizes the importance of communication and learning, and the importance of how others perceive us; and it alerts us to the fact that organizational environments are also socially constructed.

2. **Are companies with strong cultures always successful?** No! Strong cultures can be a barrier to change if they are negative cultures, but, even so, with the happiest, most creative culture there are still other factors that can frustrate performance, such as the economic climate and competitive situation, that are out of the organization's control.

3. **What are the dysfunctions of culture?** Culture tends to select and socialize people who are alike, and so often there is a lack of diversity and critical thinking in strong cultures, and the tendency to stick to old recipes even when things change. There can be a focus on the emotional and non-rational, to the extent that simple but important technicalities, like structural arrangements, inventory control or quantitative analysis of the market, can be neglected.

4. **What are subcultures and are they healthy?** Subcultures are groups of people who are part of a wider group, subscribing to the overall culture but with some distinctly different values of their own. Large companies will certainly have many of these; sometimes they will be associated with functions – marketing, maintenance and so on – or with professions – engineering, legal, accounting. But they can occur even in small companies and may not be related to any company features. They can be a source of creativity or division and destructive conflict, depending on the nature of their values and how they differ from those of the rest of the company.

5. **How is organizational culture related to national culture?** Organizational culture is often influenced by the background culture in which it is located, sometimes explicitly. Indeed, in the 1990s BA removed the British flag from the tail-planes of its jets and replaced it with a variety of different ethnic tailplane designs to reflect the diversity of its business and its increasingly global culture, or at least give that impression. There are several underlying assumptions about the world, which are characteristic of different national cultures and affect the ways in which people habitually think and orient them towards particular organizational preferences. However, these assumptions are not intractable, although it should not be assumed that they can be easily changed or set aside. Culture is a complex concept and other variables such as national and contingency ones need to be considered when trying to make sense of organizational cultures and subcultures.

REVISITING THE CASE STUDY

Let us take a look at the questions we raised on the case study in the light of our discussion.

1. Does company T have a shared culture?

The answer here is broadly 'yes'. Although many people declare themselves unhappy with it, because of the 'sink or swim' nature of the culture, they go along with it and play the game. One feature of culture is that if a culture is shared this does not mean it is shared equally; not everyone will believe in it to the same extent, some may be enthusiastic, some may hate it, some just comply. The culture, however, is not one which unites them behind a collective objective – the shared culture is a divisive one of every shift/department for itself.

2. Is company T a 'strong' culture?

The answer here is again 'yes'. It is not a positive one in the sense that the literature talks about companies like McDonald's, Hewlett-Packard, Marks & Spencer and Ben and Jerry's, of which commitment, dedication and love of the company are hallmarks, and few people seem to be having fun, but it is one which quickly sanctions those who are not part of it. You suffer if you do not play the game. It is also very explicit and dramatic, but the performances are not formally staged on occasions; people do the 'staging' on an everyday basis, which suggests that the behaviour is habitual and ingrained and will consequently be hard to shift.

3. What are the problems of the culture?

Well first of all, it is divisive and defensive. It sets sections up against each other and produces senseless internal competition. Managers try to look good and cover up problems, and no one is working towards a mutual goal or goals. The lying, cheating and stealing means that the organization has systems and procedures that do not work and those new managers who try to follow them end up failing. The organization is not getting the information it needs passed up the hierarchy and as a result it cannot be a learning organization. Development will be difficult, if not impossible. At an individual level, the 2×4 culture makes people anxious, perhaps bitter, but certainly risk averse. Fear is the worst climate for creativity and problem solving. In addition, although there is no evidence on the gender balance of the company, it would appear to have a masculinist culture, which would affect the potential benefits to be gained from a greater diversity of approaches.

4. Can the company be changed?

Well, any culture can be changed given time. The consultants in this case worked with key managers at an interpersonal level, exploring with them the problems they were facing and the effects of the culture, and tried to get them to change their behaviour. This was not always easy for them – people who have been 'beaten up' every day have a tendency to miss the beatings when they stop and crave the structure that the old ways gave them. Additionally, any change produces a period of mourning for the old way before the new behaviour is internalized, and so plenty of support and reinforcement is necessary. However, managers involved in this type of individual change can provide mutual support for each other. It is also essential in opening up channels of communication. At the right time, top-down support will also be an important reinforcement, especially if changes in structure and procedure are complementary to and require changes in behaviour. So change will be difficult, but it is possible, given effort across a range of mutually supporting areas.

References

Adler, N. (1991) *International Dimensions of Organizational Behaviour,* Boston, MA: PWS-Kent.

Aktouf, O. (1996) 'Competence, symbolic activity and promotability', in Linstead, S., Grafton Small, R. and Jeffcutt, P. (eds) *Understanding Management,* London: Sage.

Alvesson, M. (2002) *Understanding Organizational Culture,* London: Sage.

Anthony, P. (1994) *Managing Culture,* Buckingham: Open University Press.

Argyris, C. (1964) *Integrating the Individual and the Organization,* New York: John Wiley.

Ashkanasy, N.M., Wilderom, C.P.M. and Peterson, M.F. (2000) *Handbook of Organizational Culture and Climate,* Thousand Oaks, CA: Sage.

Banerjee, S.B. and Linstead, S.A. (2001) 'Globalization, multiculturalism and other fictions: Colonialism for the new millennium?', *Organization* 8(4): 683–722.

Banerjee, S.B. and Linstead, S.A. (2004) 'Masking subversion: Neocolonial embeddedness in anthropological accounts of indigenous management', *Human Relations* 57(2): 221–47.

Banerjee, S.B. and Linstead, S.A. (2006) 'Make that sixty-seven: A rejoinder to Whiteman and Cooper's "Sixty-six ways to get it wrong"', *Human Relations* 59(3): 429–42.

Barney, J. (1986) 'Organizational culture: Can it be a source of sustained competitive advantage?', *Academy of Management Review* 2(3): 656–65.

Bate, S.P. (1994) *Strategies for Cultural Change,* London: Butterworth Heinemann.

Bauman, Z. (2004) *Identity,* Cambridge: Polity.

Bedi, H. (1991) *Understanding the Asian Manager,* Sydney, NSW: Allen & Unwin.

Beech, N. and McInnes, P. (2005) 'Now where was I? Questioning assumptions of consistent identity', in Pullen, A. and Linstead, S. (eds) *Organization and Identity,* London: Routledge.

Benveniste, G. (1987) *Professionalizing the Organization,* San Francisco, CA: Jossey-Bass.

Bloomberg News (2008) 'British Airways' Terminal 5 problems at Heathrow spill over to 4th day', *International Herald Tribune,* 30 March http://iht.com/articles/2008/03/30/business/30heathrow.php (accessed 1 April 2008).

Boje, D.M. (1995) 'Stories of the storytelling organization: A postmodern analysis of Disney as "Tamara-Land"', *Academy of Management Journal* 38(4): 997–1035.

Boje, D.M. and Winsor, R.D. (1993) 'The resurrection of Taylorism: Total quality management's hidden agenda', *Journal of Organizational Change Management* 6(4): 57–70.

Borges, J-L (1962) 'Pierre Menard, author of the Quixote' in Irby, J.E and Yates, D.A (ed. and trans.) *Labyrinths: Selected Stories and Other Writings,* New York: New Directions Publishing Corporation.

Bovens, M. (1992) 'Conflicting loyalties: Ethical pluralism in administrative life', paper presented at the *First International Productivity Network Conference,* 21–24 July, Canberra, Australia.

Brewis, J. (2007) 'Culture', in Knights, D. and Willmott, H. (eds) *Introducing Organizational Behaviour and Management,* London: Thomson.

Brown, A. (1998) *Organizational Culture* (2nd edn), London: Financial Times/Pitman.

Bryman, A. (2004) *The Disneyization of Society,* London: Sage.

Carlzon, J. (1987) *Moments of Truth,* New York: Harper & Row.

Castells, M. (1997) *The Power of Identity,* Oxford: Blackwell.

Chan, A. and Clegg, S. (2002) 'History, culture and organization studies', *Culture and Organization* 8(4): 259–73.

Deal, T.E. and Kennedy, A.A. (1982) *Corporate Cultures: The Rites and Rituals of Corporate Life,* New York: Addison-Wesley.

Deal, T.E. and Kennedy, A.A. (1988) *Corporate Cultures: The Rites and Rituals of Corporate Life,* London: Penguin.

Denison, D. (1990) *Corporate Culture and Organizational Effectiveness,* New York: John Wiley.

Drennan, D. (1992) *Transforming Company Culture,* London: McGraw-Hill.

Eastman, C. and Fulop, L. (1997) 'Management for clinicians or the case of "bringing the mountain to Mohammed"', *International Journal of Production Economics* 52: 15–30.

Eldridge, J.E.T. and Crombie, A.D. (1974) *A Sociology of Organizations,* London: Allen & Unwin.

Feldman, S. (1996) 'Management in context: Culture and organizational change', in Linstead, S., Grafton Small, R. and Jeffcutt, P. (eds) *Understanding Management,* London: Sage.

Flam, H. (1993) 'Fear, loyalty and greedy organizations', in Fineman, S. (ed.) *Emotion in Organizations,* London: Sage.

French, W., Zeiss, H. and Georg Scherer, A.G. (2001) 'Intercultural discourse ethics: Testing Trompenaars' and Hampden-Turner's conclusions about Americans and the French', *Journal of Business Ethics* 34: 145–59.

Fulop, L. (1992) 'Management in the international context', in Fulop, L., Frith, F. and Hayward, H. (eds) *Management for Australian Business: A Critical Text,* Melbourne: Macmillan.

Garfinkel, H. (1984 [1967]) *Studies in Ethnomethodology,* Cambridge: Polity Press.

Gherardi, S. (1995) *Gender, Symbolism and Organizational Cultures,* London: Sage.

Giddens, A. (1991) *Modernity and Self-Identity,* Cambridge: Polity.

Gouldner, A. (1954) *Patterns of Industrial Bureaucracy,* New York: The Free Press.

Gouldner, A. (1955) *Wildcat Strike,* London: Routledge & Kegan Paul.

Guest, D. (1992) 'Right enough to be dangerously wrong: An analysis of the "In Search of Excellence" phenomenon', in Salaman, G. (ed.) *Human Resource Strategies,* London: Sage.

Guillén, M. (2006) *The Taylorized Beauty of the Mechanical: Scientific Management and the Rise of Modernist Architecture,* Princeton, NJ: Princeton University Press.

Hall, E. (1959) *The Silent Language,* New York: Doubleday.

Hampden-Turner, C. (1990) *Corporate Culture: From Vicious to Virtuous Circles,* London: Economist Books/Hutchinson.

Hampden-Turner, C. and Trompenaars, A. (1993) *The Seven Cultures of Capitalism,* New York: Currency Doubleday.

Hancock, P. and Tyler, M. (2001) *Work, Postmodernism and Organization,* London: Sage.

Handy, C. (1993) *Understanding Organizations,* London: Penguin.

Harrison, R. (1972) 'How to describe your organization', *Harvard Business Review* 50(3): 119–28.

Hatch, M.J. and Schultz, M. (1997) 'Relations between organizational culture, identity and image', *European Journal of Marketing* 31: 356–65.

Hatch, M.J. and Schultz, M. (2004) *Organizational Identity: A Reader,* Oxford: Oxford University Press. Hochschild, A.R. (1983) *The Managed Heart,* Berkeley, CA: University of California Press.

Hofstede, G. (1980/2001) *Culture's Consequences: International Differences in Work-Related Values,* London: Sage.

Hofstede, G. (1991) *Cultures and Organizations: Software of the Mind,* London: Harper Collins.

Hofstede, G. (1998) 'Attitudes, values and organizational culture: Disentangling the concepts', *Organization Studies* 19(3): 477–92.

Hofstede, G. (1999) 'The universal and the specific in 21st-century global management', *Organizational Dynamics,* (summer): 34–43.

Hofstede, G. (2002) 'Dimensions do not exist: A reply to Brendan McSweeney', *Human Relations* 55(11): 1355–61.

Hofstede, G. and Bond, M.H. (1988) 'The Confucian connection: From cultural roots to economic growth', *Organizational Dynamics* 16(4): 4–21.

Hofstede, G. and Peterson, M.F. (2000) 'National values and organizational practices', in Ashkanasy, N.M., Wilderom, C.P.M. and Peterson, M.F. (eds) *Handbook of Organizational Culture and Climate,* London: Sage.

Hofstede, G., Neuijen, B., Ohayv, D. and Sanders, G. (1990) 'Measuring organizational cultures: A qualitative and quantitative study across twenty cases', *Administrative Science Quarterly* 35: 286–316.

Höpfl, H. (1996) 'Authority and the pursuit of order in organizational performance', in Jeffcutt, P., Grafton Small, R. and Linstead, S. (eds) *Organization and Theatre,* special issue of *Studies in Cultures, Organizations, and Societies* 2(1): 67–80.

House, R.J., Hanges, P., Mansour, J., Dorfman, P. and Gupta, V. (2004) *Culture, Leadership and Organizations: The GLOBE Study of 62 Societies,* Thousand Oaks, CA: Sage.

Humes, S. (1993) *Managing the Multinational: Confronting the Global–Local Dilemma,* New York: Prentice Hall.

Jacob, N. (2005) 'Cross-cultural investigations: Emerging concepts', *Journal of Organizational Change Management* 18(5): 514–28.

Jaques, E. (1952) *The Changing Culture of a Factory,* New York: Dryden Press.

Johnson, G. (1989) 'The Burton Group (B)', in Johnson, G. and Scholes, K. (eds) *Exploring Corporate Strategy,* London: Prentice Hall.

Johnson, G. (1992) 'Managing strategic change: Strategy, culture and action', *Long Range Planning* 25(1): 28–36.

Kakabadse, A., Ludlow, R. and Vinnicombe, S. (1988) *Working in Organizations,* London: Penguin.

Kirkbride, P.S. (1983) 'Power in the workplace', unpublished PhD thesis, University of Bath, UK.

Kluckhohn, F.R. and Strodtbeck, F.L. (1961) *Variations in Value Orientations,* Evanston, IL: Row, Peterson.

Linstead, SA. and Grafton Small, R. (1992) 'On reading organizational culture', *Organization Studies* 13(3): 331–55.

Lorsch, J. (1986) 'Managing culture: The invisible barrier to strategic change', *California Management Review* 28(2): 95–109.

Louis, M.R. (1980) 'Organizations as culture-bearing milieux', in Pondy, L.R., Frost, P.J., Morgan, G. and Dandridge, T.C. (eds) *Organizational Symbolism,* Greenwich, CT: JAI Press.

Lytle, A.L., Brett, J.M., Barsness, Z., Tinsley, C.H., and Janssens, M., (1995) 'A paradigm for quantitative cross-cultural research in organizational behavior', in B.M. Staw and L.L. Cummings (eds) *Research in Organizational Behavior,* vol. 17, pp. 167–214.

Magala, S. (2005) *Cross-cultural Competence,* London: Routledge.

Martin, J. (2002) *Organizational Culture: Mapping the Terrain,* Thousand Oaks, CA: Sage.

McSweeney, B. (2002a) 'Hofstede's model of national cultural differences and their consequences: A triumph of faith, a failure of analysis', *Human Relations* 55(1): 89–118.

McSweeney, B. (2002b) 'The essentials of scholarship: A reply to Geert Hofstede', *Human Relations* 55(11): 1163–72.

Negandhi, A.R. (1986) 'Three decades of cross-cultural management research,' in Clegg, S.R., Dunphy, D.C. and Redding, S.G. (eds) *The Enterprise and Management in South-East Asia,* Hong Kong: Centre for Asian Studies, University of Hong Kong.

Olila, J. (1995) 'Corporate anthropology and organizational change', unpublished working paper, Erasmus University, Rotterdam.

Pacanowsky, M.E. and O'Donnell-Trujillo, N. (1982) 'Communication and organizational culture', *The Western Journal of Speech and Communication* 46(spring): 115–30.

Parker, M. (2000) *Organizational Culture and Identity,* London: Sage.

Pascale, R.T. and Athos, A.G. (1980) *The Art of Japanese Management,* London: Penguin.

Pauchant, T. and Mitroff, I. (1988) 'Crisis prone versus crisis avoiding organizations: Is your company's culture its own worst enemy in creating crisis?', *Industrial Crisis Quarterly* 2: 53–63.

Payne, R. (1990) *The Concepts of Culture and Climate,* Working Paper 202, Manchester Business School.

Peters, T. and Waterman, R.H. (1982) *In Search of Excellence,* New York: Harper & Row.

Pfeffer, J. (1981) 'Management as symbolic action: The creation and maintenance of organizational paradigms', in Cummings, L.L. and Staw, B. (eds) *Research in Organizational Behaviour* 3(1): 1–52.

Pool, R. (1997) 'When failure is not an option', *Technology Review* July: 38–45.

Pullen, A. (2006) *Managing Identity,* London: Palgrave Macmillan.

Pullen, A. and Linstead S. (2005) *Organization and Identity* London: Routledge.

Ray, C.A. (1986) 'Corporate culture: The last frontier of control?', *Journal of Management Studies* 23(3): 287–98.

Ritzer, G. (1990/2003) *The McDonaldization of Society,* Thousand Oaks, CA: Pine Forge Press. Ritzer, G. (1999) *Enchanting a Disenchanted World: Revolutionizing the Means of Consumption,* Thousand Oaks, CA: Pine Forge Press.

Roberts, K.H. and Boyacigiller, N. (1984) 'Cross national organizational research: The grasp of the blind men', in L.L. Cummings and B.M. Staw (eds) *Research in Organizational Behavior,* vol. 6, Greenwich, CT: JAI Press, pp. 455–88.

Schein, E. (1985) *Organizational Culture and Leadership,* San Francisco, CA: Jossey-Bass.

Schwartz, H. (1990) *Narcissistic Process and Corporate Decay,* New York: NYU Press.

Schwartz, H. and Davis, S.M. (1981) 'Matching corporate culture and business strategy', *Organizational Dynamics* 10: 30–48.

Schwartz, S.H. (1992) 'Universals in the content and structure of values: Theoretical advances and empirical tests in 20 countries', in Zanna, M. (ed.) *Advances in Experimental Social Psychology,* vol. 25, New York: Academic Press, pp. 1–65.

Schwartz, S.H. (1994) 'Beyond individualism/collectivism: New cultural dimensions of values', in Kim, U., Triandis, H.C., Kagitcibasi, C., Choi, S-C. and Yoon, G. (eds) *Individualism and Collectivism: Theory, Methods and Applications,* London: Sage, pp. 85–119.

Schwartz, S.H. (1999) 'Cultural value differences: Some implications for work', *Applied Psychology: An International Review,* 48: 23–47.

Schwartz, S.H. (2004) 'Mapping and interpreting cultural differences around the world', in Vinken, H., Soeters, J. and Ester, P. (eds) *Comparing Cultures, Dimensions of Culture in a Comparative Perspective,* Leiden, The Netherlands: Brill.

Schwartz, S.H. (2006) 'Value orientations: Measurement, antecedents and consequences across nations', in Jowell, R., Roberts, C., Fitzgerald, R. and Eva, G. (eds) *Measuring Attitudes Cross-nationally: Lessons from the European Social Survey,* London: Sage.

Schwartz, S.H. and Bardi, A. (1997) 'Influences of adaptation to communist rule on value priorities in Eastern Europe', *Political Psychology* 18: 385–410.

Schwartz, S.H. and Bardi, A. (2000) 'Moral dialogue across cultures: An empirical perspective', in E.W. Lehman (ed.) *Autonomy and order: A communitarian anthology.* Lanham, MD: Rowman & Littlefield.

Schwartz, S.H., Bardi, A. and Bianchi, G. (2000) 'Value adaptation to the imposition and collapse of Communist regimes in Eastern Europe', in Renshon, S.A. and Duckitt, J. (eds) *Political Psychology: Cultural and Cross Cultural Perspectives,* London: Macmillan – now Palgrave Macmillan, pp. 217–37.

Schwartz , S.H. and Sagie, G. (2000) 'Value consensus and importance: A cross-national study', *Journal of Cross-Cultural Psychology* 31(4): 465–97.

Sinclair, A. (1991) 'After excellence: Models of organisational culture for the public sector', *Australian Journal of Public Administration* 50(3): 321–32.

Smircich, L. (1983) 'Concepts of culture and organizational analysis', *Administrative Science Quarterly,* 28(3): 339–58.

Smircich, L. and Calás, M. (2006) 'From the woman's point of view ten years later: Towards a feminist organization studies', in Clegg, S., Hardy C., Lawrence, T. and Nord, W. *Handbook of Organization Studies,* London: Sage, pp. 284–346.

Smircich, L. and Morgan, G. (1982) 'Leadership: The management of meaning', *Journal of Applied Behavioural Science* 18(2): 257–73.

Smith, P.B. (2002) 'Culture's consequences: Something old and something new', *Human Relations* 55(1): 119–35.

Smith, S. and Wilkinson, B. (1996) 'No doors on offices, no secrets: We are our own policemen: Capitalism without conflict?', in Linstead, S., Grafton Small, R. and Jeffcutt, P. (eds) *Understanding Management,* London: Sage.

Stone, A.R. (1995) *The War of Desire and Technology at the Close of the Mechanical Age,* Boston, MA: MIT Press.

Strauss, A., Schatzman, L., Ehrlich, D., Bucher, R. and Sabshin, M. (1963) 'The hospital and its negotiated order', in Friedson, E. (ed.) *The Hospital in Modern Society,* New York: Macmillan.

Swartz, M. and Watkins, S. (2003) *Power Failure: The Inside Story of the Collapse of Enron,* New York: Doubleday.

Tannen, D. (1990) *You Just Don't Understand: Men and Women in Conversation,* New York: William Morrow.

Tayeb, M.H. (1988) *Organisations and National Culture,* London: Sage.

Thompson, P. and McHugh, D. (2002) *Work Organisations: A Critical Introduction,* London: Palgrave Macmillan.

Torrington, D. (1994) *International Human Resource Management,* New York: Prentice Hall.

Triandis, H.C. (1993) 'Review of cultures and organizations: Software of the mind', *Administrative*
Science Quarterly, 38(2): 132–4.

Triandis H.C. (1994) *Culture and social behavior,* New York, NY: McGraw-Hill.

Trompenaars, F. and Hampden-Turner, C. (1998) *Riding the Waves of Culture: Understanding Cultural Diversity in Global Business* (2nd edn), New York: McGraw-Hill.

Turner, B.A. (1971) *Exploring the Industrial Sub-Culture,* London: Macmillan – now Palgrave Macmillan.

Van Maanen, J. (1991) 'The smile factory: Work at Disneyland', in Frost, P., Moore, L.F., Louis, M.R., Lundberg, C.C. and Martin, J. (eds) *Reframing Organizational Culture,* Newbury Park, CA: Sage.

Walsh, J. (1997) 'BA hopes to clear air with top-flight moves', *People Management 23(October):* 11.

Weber, M. (1964) *The Theory of Social Economic Organizations,* London: Heinemann.

Westley, F.R. (1990) 'The eye of the needle: Cultural and personal transformation in a traditional organization', *Human Relations* 43(3): 273–93.

Westwood, R. (1992) *Organizational Behaviour,* Hong Kong: Longmans.

Willmott, H. (1991) 'Strength is ignorance; slavery is freedom: Managing culture in modern organizations', *Journal of Management Studies* 30(4): 515–52.

Young, D. (1989) 'British Airways: Putting the customer first', unpublished paper, Ashridge Strategic Management Centre, Ashridge Management College, UK.

Young, E. (1989) 'On the Naming of the Rose: Interests and multiple meanings as elements of organizational culture', *Organization Studies* 10(2): 187–206.

CHAPTER 8
Gender and management

Joanna Brewis and Stephen Linstead

QUESTIONS ABOUT GENDER

1. What is expected of managers in modern Western organizations? What should be expected? How does this relate to gender?
2. To what extent has management theory made room for gender?
3. Is gender a profit issue or a moral issue?
4. Are you more likely to attain a management position if you are male?
5. Are men and women concentrated in different occupations?
6. What is positive discrimination?
7. Are women equal to or different from men?
8. Is globalization creating more opportunities for women or perpetuating their subordination?
9. Does being male or female make a difference to the way you manage?
10. Do men experience gender-related problems too?
11. Would a 'feminization' of organizations represent a desirable alternative?
12. What is the relationship between gender and management?

CASE STUDY   TransCorp

Matthew looked at his watch as he locked his car and began to hurry across the car park. 7.15,' he thought, 'I really should have got in earlier today.' Slightly breathless, he pushed open the doors of TransCorp, pausing only briefly to nod to the caretaker, and ran up the stairs to his office two steps at a time. The office looked less than welcoming – desk positioned strategically to face the door, filing cabinets gleaming, the only personal touch a small cactus on his window sill – as he removed his jacket and sat down at his PC. It seemed only minutes later that there was a knock at the door and his boss David entered. He began immediately: 'Matt, there's a problem on the floor. Some of the morning shift haven't arrived yet and you know we've got a rush on with that order for InterMotor. Can you go down there and wait for the latecomers? They need talking to. We really need to get this sorted out today – they've been goofing off down there recently and it's not good enough.'

Without further ado, David left. Matthew stared at his screen, willing himself to descend to the shop floor and reprimand the stragglers. He did not enjoy this particular aspect of his work, but in his position as deputy production manager he knew it was his responsibility. Sighing, he donned his jacket once again and made his way down to the floor.

Half an hour later, Matthew returned to the office, feeling wrung out and upset. There had been the predictable angry scenes on the floor, with staff complaining that the revised shift start times were inconvenient for them and that it was not fair to expect them to come to work an hour earlier than usual. He had had to reiterate that it was only a temporary measure, the order was important and the staff had to arrive on time so as to be able to meet their targets. However, secretly he sympathized with them. He was also growing increasingly tired of the long hours expected of him, the way he had to behave towards his staff, a style set by David and his other seniors, and the continual effort he had to make to suppress his own emotions, which surfaced particularly when he was feeling tired – and he certainly was today. It was now 8 a.m. and Matthew reflected that people working for other companies, in other positions, were only now commuting to work, knowing when they arrived they could leave at 5 p.m. or 6 at the latest. He himself faced at least another twelve hours, and that was only if the remainder of the day's production went according to TransCorp's carefully laid plans. Otherwise he could be at work until midnight or later.

Matthew spent the rest of the morning, in between dealing with constant calls from the floor and interruptions at the door, drafting a plan for the plant's summer shutdown. This year was going to be especially difficult, as machinery needed to be replaced and moved around the floor as well as the usual repairs and maintenance being carried out, and budgets had been cut to the extent that only a very limited number of personnel could be retained during the two weeks when the plant was officially shut. Because of the considerable overtime available, he was only relieved that the responsibility for deciding who these staff were to be belonged to Human Resources and not his own department. David had made it clear to Matthew that his plan needed to be as radical as possible – the minimum possible number of staff working the maximum possible number of hours. It was 2.30 p.m. before he looked at his watch and realized that he had not eaten or drunk anything at all that day. At this point, his phone shrilled again – his partner Sarah wanting to know if he could get home by 7.30 that evening to look after the children, as she wanted to attend her evening class. He told her that it would be impossible, they began to argue and he eventually hung up the phone cursing her. 'She just doesn't understand,' he told himself. 'Here I am struggling to keep it all together at work, in a crucial period for the company, and all she can do is complain about how I'm never at home.'

Later that day, some time towards 7 p.m., Matthew walked down to the snack machine at the end of his corridor and began to punch in his request, when Julie, a production colleague, appeared from her own office, looking furious. She began to reel off her own list of complaints:

> You'll never guess what that git of a boss of yours has just said to me. 'Nice legs, Jules!' Can you believe it? God knows, they look at me like I've just landed from Mars if I turn up in trousers and then I have to put up with that kind of rubbish when I wear a skirt. And even then they expect me to walk, talk and behave like a man. I hate this place sometimes.

Matthew remembered Julie's outburst when he was driving home. He thought to himself that while he found his job exciting and challenging on the whole and it gave him immense satisfaction when an order was completed to the correct standards and went out by the deadline, there were times when he really resented having to be 'one of the boys' and join in with the sexist jokes and chat. When he arrived home he found Sarah in bed, lights extinguished all over the house and a note on the kitchen table telling him how furious she was. He wearily walked upstairs, undressed and got gingerly into bed beside her, only managing to set the alarm for 5.30 a.m. before falling into an exhausted sleep.

QUESTIONS ABOUT THE CASE

1. What are your impressions of TransCorp as an organization?
2. What does the description of Matthew's day tell you about what it means and how it feels to manage in TransCorp? What do you think is expected of managers in this organization?
3. Given Matthew's feelings about his work, does it seem to suit his preferred managerial style?
4. What does this suggest about Matthew's view of himself as a manager and/or as a man?
5. What are the consequences of Matthew's behaviour as a manager:

   [a] for him as an individual?

   [b] for his staff?

   [c] for Sarah and his children?
6. Julie tells Matthew that she is disgusted by the comment that David makes about her legs. What other problems might you expect a female manager in TransCorp to encounter?

Introduction

Gender is a powerful principle in the organization of our lives. An individuals identity as either male or female, possessing masculine or feminine qualities, makes a difference to the way in which he or she experiences his or her social world. It is therefore significant to consider the influence of gender when examining what managers do and how they do it.

Although this was not historically the case, there is now a large body of organizational literature which insists that gender is taken into account when examining managerial work. Within this body of work we can identify several competing perspectives on gender, although it is also true to say that some (for example liberal feminism, diversity) are much better represented than others (for example radical feminism). In this chapter we discuss five of these perspectives – the *liberal feminist, radical feminist, diversity, gender in management and gendering management* approaches. The key characteristics of each are summarized in Table 8.1.

Table 8.1 Perspectives on gender

Perspective	Key concepts	Typical writers
Liberal feminism	Women not naturally inferior to men Importance of social justice/equality Vertical segregation (glass ceiling) Horizontal segregation Long agenda of equality of opportunity	*Historical:* Mary Astell Mary Wollstonecraft Hannah Woolley *Comtemporary:* Marilyn Davidson and Cary Cooper Betty Friedan Rosabeth Moss Kanter Barbara White
Radical feminism	Women naturally superior to men Importance of social emancipation/change Radical reversal/inversion of contemporary social structures Separatism	Mary Daly Shulamith Firestone Susan Griffin Kate Millet Valerie Solonas
Diversity	Diversity, including gender difference, should be recognized in organizations Individualist focus Improve productivity through a widening of organizational access and participation Strong business case MOSAIC	Patricia Arredondo Rajvinder Kandola and Johanna Fullerton Stella Nkomo R. Roosevelt Thomas
Gender *in* management	Management relational Women and men socialized differently, manage differently Male transactional versus female transformational leadership Transformational leadership most effective in current socioeconomic climate Globalization of gender	Beverly Alimo-Metcalfe Helen Brown Marta Calás and Linda Smircich Sally Helgesen Judy Rosener
Gender*ing* management	Interaction of management and gender Foucauldian – gender identity produced by discourse Masculinist organizational discourse sustains masculine managerial identity Successful managers (whether male or female) therefore masculine Problems of this emphasis on masculinity	Mats Alvesson and Yvonne Due Billing David Collinson and Margaret Collinson Silvia Gherardi Deborah Kerfoot and David Knights Stephen Whitehead Amanda Sinclair

Where the first three approaches place different emphases on the impact of gender on management *practice,* the gender *in* management and the gender*ing* management approaches insist on introducing the concept of gender into management *theory.* This reveals the extremely significant neglect of gender in the foundational theories of management, and inspires us to take a look at how some of the main theories about management and organization have failed to take gender issues into account – especially classical management theory, human relations theory and the work of Abraham Maslow on motivation. In fact, in contrast to commentators such as Fiona Wilson (1996) and Frances Tomlinson, Anne Brockbank and Joanne Traves (1997), we find that these theories were not gender *blind,* but on the contrary very gender *aware* in their active efforts to *suppress gender difference.* Later theories, on the other hand, which built on their predecessors, did in fact fail to take gender into account more by omission than commission. We then look in further detail at the more contemporary attempts to bring gender and management together, two of which fall under the gender in management heading – these are the *feminine in management* approach and the *gender globalization* approach. Finally, after identifying certain key problems with these viewpoints, we outline the characteristics of our preferred alternative, building on the gendering management approach and focusing on management *processes;* that is, regarding gender as fluid, and carefully examining the ways in which gender and management interact and *mutually* shape each other.

Liberal feminism

Liberal feminism can be traced back to eighteenth-century writers such as Mary Wollstonecraft (1970 [1792]) and further. It argues that men and women are equal in all important respects and, more specifically, that women are as capable as men of the reasoned behaviour required in the modern workplace. An important strand of the liberal feminist literature identifies the existence of a 'glass ceiling' in modern organizations. This refers to an invisible, implicit but impenetrable attitudinal barrier which prevents women from reaching senior management positions. Marilyn Davidson and Cary Cooper (1992), for example, claim that women find it difficult to break through this ceiling because of the ways in which they are viewed and view themselves in both wider society and individual organizations. In a similar vein, Richard Anker (1997: 325) points to the common preconception that women are assumed to be less than happy supervising others and more comfortable taking orders – and the resultant belief that they are unsuitable for management and supervisory work. Moreover, Davidson (1997) has augmented her analysis of the glass ceiling by publishing her findings from research into the problems and challenges faced by black and ethnic minority women managers. According to her argument, this group of managers faces a double bind – of gender and race – when seeking career development. Davidson suggests that this double bind manifests itself as a 'concrete ceiling', which is not only more difficult to pass through but also blocks these women's view of the top jobs, thus sapping their motivation to achieve them. More recently, Linda Hite (2007), reporting on interviews with Hispanic women managers, makes similar points. These include her argument that 'Challenges [facing these women] range from the discomfort of being among the few and finding limited resources in place to assist your transition to the more insidious practice of discrimination.' She also points out that, in the US, 38.6 per cent of managers and professionals are white women, 30.6 per cent are African-American and only 22.4 per cent Hispanic.

While the *attitudinal* ceiling militating against upward career mobility is a demonstrable barrier to women's progression in many occupations, the constraints that they face in building careers may have more dimensions. Many occupations are *segmented* by gender at the point of entry rather than level of progression, to the extent that women don't have realistic options in taking up certain occupations or professions, and are customarily channelled into others. Women are also regarded as less geographically mobile than men, largely due to their continuing role as primary caregivers with regard to both children and elderly family (Wajcman 1998). This may also affect their availability for work at certain times of the day, or school year, and may of course result in career breaks for childrearing. This constitutes a *spatio-temporal* career barrier, which may be compounded for women from ethnic minority backgrounds that make different community demands. Rather than a glass ceiling, and far from it being shattered, many women continue to be imprisoned by a *'glass cube'*.

Work like that of Davidson and Cooper, and Anker claims that the historically influential definition of women as somehow irrevocably feminine, congenitally subordinate, emotional and irrational, and therefore ill-equipped for work at the top of the organizational 'tree', results in vertical segregation – the situation in organizations where men predominate in the ranks of the most senior. This phenomenon is neatly illustrated by the UK Equal Opportunities Commission[1] report *Sex and Power* (2007). It begins by suggesting that 'If we hope to shatter the glass ceiling, we would need to find the nearly 6,000 women "missing" from more than 33,000 top positions of power in Britain today.' (Equal Opportunities Commission 2007: 1). To illustrate this claim more substantively, the report cites figures including the fact that only 10 per cent of the directors of FTSE 100 companies – an index listing the top one hundred publicly quoted companies in the UK in terms of market share,

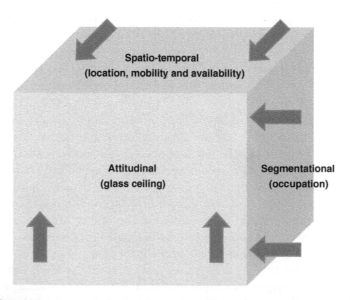

Figure 8.1 The glass cube – continuing barriers to women's career development

including Vodafone, Barclays, Ryanair, Lloyds TSB, Avis Europe and JJB Sports – are female. The total of 'missing' women here is some 448.

Likewise, only 20 per cent of British Members of Parliament are women, and when we include ethnic minority women (evoking Davidson's concrete ceiling) this figure falls to a minute 0.3 per cent. A Fawcett Society report published in early June 2007 notes that there have only ever been three black female MPs, and that an Asian woman has yet to be elected into the House of Commons. The Society estimates that at the current rate of 'progress' it will take over 300 years before Parliament is in fact representative of the number of ethnic minority women in the British population *(Metro.co.uk* accessed 10 June 2007). And ethnic minority women fare no better in the job market at large – while only 11 per cent of UK-based managers or senior officials are white women, the equivalent figure is 6 per cent for Pakistani women and 9 per cent of Black Caribbean women (Equal Opportunities Commission 2007: 9). The UK also comes off badly in comparison to other countries in that it lies 59th in a global league table of women's parliamentary representation – behind Rwanda, Afghanistan and Iraq (Equal Opportunities Commission 2007: 7).

These data are important in many ways, but in particular because of the obvious influence that Members of Parliament have over the running of the country and the shaping of future policy. Quelch (2000) makes the somewhat acerbic observation that those running the FTSE companies probably have *more* impact on the life of the average British citizen than many government ministers. The Equal Opportunities Commission (EOC) (2007: 3) also points out that 'progress on women's representation across a wide range of professions and sectors is painfully slow, and in some cases has gone into reverse'. In the British armed forces, for example, there are now only two women of senior rank, representing a 50 per cent drop since 2006. Relatedly, we can also note data concerning gender differentials in promotion. In a meta-review of various studies, Grimshaw and Rubery (2007: 69) single out findings including the greater emphasis that might be placed on employment *stability* as opposed to *qualifications* for women in this regard, the fact that women are often paid less than men following the same promotion and that women very often don't have access to the requisite training and development to secure promotions or may be considered unsuitable by their seniors due to perceptions of their domestic responsibilities – as we suggested with the 'glass cube'.

Furthermore, even in European countries with a better reputation than the UK for forward thinking regarding gender equality, such as Sweden, 'In most high level jobs, male over-representation is very strong. Only about 10–15 per cent of higher middle and senior managers and seven per cent of all professors are women.' (Alvesson and Billing 1997: 4). In Finland, which also has a generally progressive image, 'managerial labour markets continue to be vertically segregated according to gender' (Tienari 1999: 6). Elsewhere in Europe, in the Czech Republic for example, patterns of vertical segregation are similar: Rosemary Crompton (1997: 139) suggests that women here 'predominate ... in lower-level occupations'. Indeed Crompton concludes that, in banking in particular and despite the general expansion in employment positions following privatization of this sector after the 'velvet revolution', Czech women seem to be stuck at the level of middle management and experience considerable difficulty ascending to the most senior jobs. This, she says, mirrors the situation in the same industry in the West (Crompton 1997: 140). Indeed, banking might be more widely seen as an example of men 'riding the glass elevator' (Williams 1995, cited in Teigen 1999: 103): although it is dominated overall by women, it is men who fill most of the senior management positions. So men benefit from what Williams refers to as their 'token' status in this occupation, whereas the same is scarcely true of women in male-dominated jobs. Indeed Janne Tienari (1999: 3) suggests that, even where women are relatively successful in achieving senior positions in the banking industry, such as in France, this occurs because the women involved are willing to work full time, even if they have young families, and take the minimum time off for maternity leave and similar benefits, if indeed they choose to have children at all. Female managers in French banking adopt an approach to work which could be argued to emphasize their 'sameness' with their male colleagues, but which probably involves 'personal difficulties and sacrifice'.

Relatedly, Claire Brown and Liz Jones (2004), in an assessment of why men achieve more senior positions in Australian nursing than their female counterparts despite being in the definite minority in this profession, conclude that one factor is men's greater geographical mobility – which recalls our argument about spatio-temporal movement as part of the three dimensional 'glass cube'. However the most important factor explaining men's greater seniority was the substantial likelihood that they had worked continuously, on a full-time basis, since their original registration – unlike their female counterparts who had tended to take career breaks to give birth to and care for children.

The available figures about women in management are often contradictory. Fiona Wilson (2003: 18) claims that numbers of women at management level – especially the most senior levels – are *falling* both in the USA and the UK, whereas Mats Alvesson and Yvonne Due Billing (1997: 3) suggest that in most Western countries they are increasing, albeit at a somewhat gradual pace. Still, as Alvesson and Billing assert elsewhere:

> Of course, statistics are always unreliable and frequently say more about norms of classification than about reality 'out there', but it is still clear that men have close to a monopoly on the most senior positions and greatly outnumber women in middle-level managerial jobs in virtually every country. (2000: 145)

Calás and Smircich (2006: 284) make a similar point, arguing that 'no single indicator shows that the economic conditions of women in the world, as a whole, are at parity with the conditions of men' regardless of how statistics are manipulated (Gastelaars 2002). Worldwide the proportion of women working has risen to over 40 per cent but there is no improvement in equality in terms of 'real socio-economic empowerment for women, an equitable distribution of household responsibilities, equal pay for work of equal value, and gender balance across all occupations'. (ILO March 2004: 1, cited in Calás and Smircich 2006: 284). Women still constitute 60 per cent of the working poor and in the US earn 74 per cent of the dollar rewards acquired by men (Calás and Smircich 2006: 284–5). However, it would be wrong to underestimate the radical changes that have taken place in the gender composition of the workplace in recent years. Data from the London Chamber of Commerce, for instance, indicate that 450,000 professional jobs were created in the UK between 1981 and 1996 and that 69 per cent of these vacancies were filled by women (McDowell 2001: 351; Charles 2002: 26). And there are positive long-term changes afoot more generally, as Table 8.2 illustrates.

Table 8.2 Changes in British women's employment, 1970s–2006

	1970s	2006
	%	%
Employment rates	60	70
Numbers of professionals	10	40
Hourly pay gap (full-time) between men and women	29	17
Numbers of MPs	4.3	20

Source: Equal Opportunities Commission (2006: 1).

Equally, the number of women in the UK working for money is now higher than the number of those who do not, and since 1979 British women's paid employment has increased at an approximately similar level to the decline in men's employment (McDowell 2001: 351; Bristow 2002: 16).

But despite the fact that there are some positive indications as regards women's progression into employment in general and management and the professions in particular, liberal feminism also points to the substantial evidence suggesting that they are perceived to be more or less suited to particular *occupations* on the basis of their gender. Richard Anker (1997: 325) offers a helpful summary of these employment-related clichés which describe women as having: caring natures; skills in domestic work; greater manual dexterity; greater honesty; a more attractive appearance; less physical strength; less ability in science and maths; less motivation to travel; more motivation to work at home; less willingness to face danger or to employ force; more docility; less willingness to join trade unions; more tolerance of mundane and repetitive work; more acceptance of lower wages; and less need for income. Illustrating the operation of these clichés in the labour market is also fairly straightforward. In the UK, for example, Labour Force Survey statistics for 2005 (cited in Equal Opportunities Commission 2006: 23–4; and Grimshaw and Rubery 2007: 102) show that only 1.3 per cent of bricklayers, 0.4 per cent of carpenters and joiners, 5.2 per cent of civil and structural engineers, 17 per cent of software engineers and 7.8 per cent of quantity surveyors are female, as against 81 per cent of administrators and secretaries, 69 per cent of sales and customer service personnel, 95 per cent of receptionists, 74 per cent of waitresses and 73 per cent of kitchen and catering assistants.

We can also consider Rachel Woodward and Patricia Winter's (2006: 46) discussion of areas of the British Army which remain closed to women altogether. These represent 30 per cent of the available occupations in this branch of the armed forces and include 'the infantry, the Royal Armoured Corps and Household Cavalry, the RAF Regiment and the Royal General Marines Service'. Indeed, as Woodward and Winter also suggest, up until April 1998, women were barred from a full *53 per cent* of Army jobs. And in terms of workplace occupational segregation elsewhere, Rosemary Crompton points out that, in the Czech Republic, women doctors are overrepresented in 'the more caring aspects of medicine' such as paediatrics, neona-tology and general practice (1997: 139, 145). Sweden also displays a high level of horizontal segregation, such that only 'Fourteen per cent of all employed women and

13 per cent of all employed men work in occupations with an equal sex distribution' (Fransson and Thörnqvist 2006: 607).

The evidence regarding mothers who engage in paid employment is also instructive in this regard, and bears out the persistence of gender stereotypes around division of labour in the home as in the workplace. As Hughes (2002: 113) suggests, 'Paid work and education become additions to the seemingly intransigent nature of women's responsibilities for domestic care'. That is to say, the available data indicate that men are not taking on responsibilities in the home – for housework and child-care – in proportion to the hours that their partners work *outside* the home. Thus women are increasingly working what is known as the 'double day'. We should also note the longstanding and persistent controversy about 'working mothers' and the effect that this has on these women's reliability as employees and their children's development (Charles 2002: 72; Hughes 2002: 63, following Kaplan 1992). Furthermore, other studies suggest most of us in the UK still believe that mothers should not work outside the home if their children are not yet in school, and that they should put their family responsibilities above anything else (Charles 2002: 49, 70–1). There are also data indicating a general preference amongst British mothers for part-time, flexible (and also lower paid) work, or indeed to quit work altogether following childbirth (Elliott 2003; Elliott and Chittenden 2003).[2]

Relatedly, Christine Everingham, Deborah Stevenson and Penny Warner-Smith (2007), drawing on data from research with Australian women who came of age either prior to or during the resurgence of the women's movement (which they date as 1970–1984), argue that the younger women in their cohort are actually resentful of feminism to some degree as they perceive it as *limiting* their life choices. More specifically, Everingham et al. suggest that things have not simply improved for women, in that although their 'liberation is taken for granted', in general they are still much more likely to make use of organizational work–life balance measures than men to 'organize their paid work around the perceived needs of their children'. Further, this inevitably disadvantages mothers as compared to their childless counterparts, since they 'have *no* choice but to take up poorly paid, flexible work options because they have no other way of managing both family and work commitments'. Many women then, the authors aver, reject the notion that they have more alternatives available to them than their predecessors, because they cannot afford to be full-time mothers and retain any measure of independence from men, even if they want to – the rhetoric of choice which lies behind contemporary Western neo-liberalism notwithstanding.

Likewise, Ning Tang and Christine Cousins (2005: 542) comment that part-time work is 'almost the only form of employment' for British and Dutch mothers alike. They argue with reference to both countries that 'Female part-time work would appear to be a response to the expectation that full-time workers work long hours, the long working hours of their partners and a lack of institutional support for combining work and the family' (ibid.). Tang and Cousins do nonetheless suggest that Sweden is the most egalitarian country of the eight European nations they studied with regard to domestic division of labour – echoing points we made earlier about this country's progressive image. As Clarissa Kugelberg (2006: 153) indicates, Swedish fathers have had the same rights as mothers to parental leave since the mid-1970s plus, in practice, 'mothers share with their partners the responsibility for supporting the family and fathers are taking an increasing part in parental work'.

However, according to Tang and Cousins (2005: 543), this 'greater aspiration to balance family and working life and for men to participate more in childcare and domestic tasks' also produces higher levels of work–life *im*balance for Swedish men and women alike, while Kugelberg (2006: 169) argues that the measures relating to parental leave and associated practices around flexible working patterns are 'used largely by mothers and thus associated with motherhood, not fatherhood'.

Linda Hite (2007) adds race and ethnicity to the work–life balance equation. For example, based on her research, she avers that 'strong cultural expectations regarding marriage and motherhood add another dimension and can complicate choices for Hispanic women who are striving for career success while maintaining their cultural heritage'. Also germane in this regard, and demonstrating how work–life imbalance in the 'developed' world might impact on those in 'developing' countries, is Arlie Russell Hochschild's (2003 [2000]) discussion of the 'global care chain: a series of personal links between people across the globe based on the paid or unpaid work of caring'. An example might be a woman in the 'developing' world caring for her siblings because her mother is caring for the children of a nanny who has left the country for a first world nation. The nanny is employed to look after yet another woman's children, because this last mother works full time outside the home – as do, say, 65 per cent of US women with children of six and under.[3] And, as Hochschild also points out, 'Much of the research on women in the United States and Europe focuses on a chainless, two-person picture of "work–family balance" without considering the childcare worker and the emotional ecology of which he or she is a part.' She goes on to suggest that this 'emotional ecology' includes potential transference of feelings by the immigrant carer from their own children to their new charges or, alternatively, persistent and intense anguish caused by familial separation. Hochschild also refers to data from migration studies which suggest that the number of women moving from country to country is liable to increase, and that many of those who go abroad to care for others' children are not only mothers themselves but also educated to a high level.

Relatedly, in the public sector in post-Communist Poland, Alison Stenning and Jane Hardy (2005) argue that reforms have hit women workers hardest, bringing 'worsening pay, conditions and opportunities and ... an increase in both their work-related and domestic responsibilities', the last because marketization in health and education has meant fewer nursery places and reduced hospital in-patient stays, translating into additional burdens on the family unit as well as greater pressure at work. Tang and Cousins (2005: 545–6) make similar observations about women's employment outside the home in Bulgaria, the Czech Republic, Hungary, Romania and Slovenia following the fall of Communism. They do point out that robust parental leave mechanisms still exist in Romania and the Czech Republic, in contrast to many Western Europe nations, but that this in itself may disadvantage working mothers as many privatized companies are unable to afford 'extended maternity and parental leave'. Further, the 'double day' of paid *and* domestic labour referred to above is alive and well for many working women in these former Communist countries – with the exception of Slovenia (aka the 'Sweden of the South').

Horizontal segregation also occurs at managerial levels. Evidence suggests that certain management functions represent 'female ghettos', in the sense that they are less well paid than other functions; they are less well regarded and less likely to be represented at board level than other functions; and they are overpopulated by women. One particularly pertinent example is human resource management, an area which, we would suggest, is again assumed to require a specific kind of people-related skills base, to demand sensitivity, intuition and a certain gentleness. In the UK in 2005, for instance, 58 per cent of human resource managers were women, but only 21 per cent of ICT managers. Against these data we should also remember that women made up some 34 per cent of managers and senior officials across the board (Equal Opportunities Commission 2006: 24). So female managers, we could argue, tend to be located in staff or support management functions per se as opposed to what might be seen as the 'front line' or 'battle zone' of line management (Tienari 1999: 1).

Additional findings regarding horizontal segregation in particular can be found in Walby's (2007) report on the gendered future of work in the UK. She suggests, for example, that two consecutive reports from the University of Warwick offered very different estimates of whether or not women would benefit from the widely predicted increase in the number of jobs available per se. The 2004 estimate covers 2002–2012 and suggests that 75 per cent of the new jobs created during this period will be taken by women. The 2006 estimate, covering 2004–2014, identifies the same figure as a much more conservative 50 per cent. The 2006 predictions for change by sector also effectively leave the gender status quo untouched – so, for example, jobs in education and health are set to rise from 23.9 per cent to 24.3 per cent of the workforce, while the concomitant rise in numbers of women in these sectors is from 67.2 per cent to 70 per cent. And predictions for increased numbers of management, professional and technical jobs show these rising from 44 per cent of men in such occupations in 2004 to 48 per cent in 2014, while the same figures for women are 38 per cent and 43 per cent. As Walby (2007: 11) suggests 'Even after the projected changes, women are much more likely than men to be in the lowest level occupations and less likely to be in the highest level occupations'.

Her final conclusion is twofold. First is an optimistic scenario where 'Women and men are integrated in a high skill, high productivity economy' (2007: 27). This is facilitated by women receiving higher levels of education, sex discrimination at work being on the decline and organizations becoming more family-friendly, as well as the general expansion of the UK economy 'especially in areas where women are currently employed' (ibid.). The other much more negative potential outcome is that 'Women continue to be situated in low paid, segregated occupations in a divided economy' (ibid.), as driven by continued horizontal segregation, poorly remunerated and low-skilled employment and inflexible employment practices. As Walby also avers, the latter scenario becomes all the more likely if UK businesses' response to global competition is to cut costs as opposed to strategies which seek instead to add value to goods and services.

Such compelling evidence of persistent horizontal and vertical segregation compels liberal feminists to demand that steps be taken to address gendered inequality of opportunity in the workplace. They demand that gender be managed in organizations in such a way as to minimize any differences between the employment chances available to men and those available to women. Thus they espouse what is often described as the long agenda of equal opportunities. A short agenda, as defined by David Goss (1994: 158), focuses solely on staying within the parameters established by anti-discrimination law (for example the Sex Discrimination Act in the UK). As Exhibits 8.1 and 8.2 demonstrate, however, this legislation is frequently insufficient to provide for genuine equality between working men and women – in this instance in the area of pay in particular.

A long agenda of equality of opportunity, on the other hand, aims at what is known as 'equal share'; that is, allowing women the same level of access to and participation within every level and area of the organization. The long agenda implies a more concerted attack on gendered inequalities, and often incorporates so-called positive discrimination, which deliberately favours women over men in an effort to 'level the [organizational] playing field' (Goss 1994: 160). Measures might include: equal opportunities policies; gender sensitization training; family-friendly provisions like flexitime, job share or subsidized workplace crèches to accommodate domestic responsibilities;[4] tracking of recruitment, retention, promotion and job movement rates to identify any problem areas; performance management systems that reward those managers who achieve equal opportunities objectives in terms of recruitment, development and promotion, and penalize those who do not; succession planning; feeder groups at local educational institutions; and group-based selection processes to minimize bias. Some employers may even choose to introduce quota systems, mentors, and management and leadership training especially for women to build confidence, although these approaches have to be carefully managed so that they don't in fact break the existing legislation by discriminating against men – as the all-women Labour Party shortlist of prospective general election candidates was ruled to do by the European Court in 1996 (Whitehead 1999: 23, 30–n2).

It is now nearly four decades since the Equal Pay Act (1970) was passed in Britain. This legislation requires that men and women working for the same employer and doing the same or similar work be paid the same wages. However, Annual Survey of Hours and Earnings (ASHE) and New Earnings Survey (NES) figures for 2006 suggest that women full-timers currently earn only *86.7 per cent* of their male counterparts' hourly pay. For women working part-time this falls to *59.8 per cent*. Being employed in a male-only private sector workplace is also likely to add some *6 per cent* to one's pay, whereas working in a women-only environment would *decrease* the same pay by *7 per cent*. In the public sector the same figures are + *7 per cent* and – *9 per cent* respectively. We can also point to findings that suggest the 'unexplained' gap between men and women's pay – in other words, what is *not* accounted for by a human capital argument which identifies differences in these group's capabilities and qualifications – is often significantly bigger than the 'explained' gap. Moreover, this unequal treatment tends to worsen as women get older, whether they have taken career breaks to raise children or not.

Elsewhere in the EU the situation is similar, such that equal pay law has been in effect in Sweden, for example, since 1980 but women's wages were still only *92 per cent* of men's in 2002. Sweden, like the UK, has the concept of equal pay for work of equal value but it is 2001 amendments to the Equal Opportunities Act which look likely to have the most impact on this persistent inequality. That is to say, all Swedish employers of more than ten people are now required to annually record differences between men and women's wages and interpret these to suggest whether any differences are in fact justifiable. This process is overseen by the Equal Opportunities Ombudsman *(sic)*. Across the EU more generally, women earn on average *74 per cent* of men's wages, based on data from 2000.

EXHIBIT 8.1

Pay inequalities in sport and the arts

The slow pace of change in this regard is especially well illustrated by the case of the internationally renowned Wimbledon tennis tournament, which only announced equal prize money for men and women in February 2007. In the 2006 tournament, then, Roger Federer earned £655,000 as men's singles champion, compared to £625,000 for his female counterpart Amelie Mauresmo. The gender differential had long been defended by the All England Club on the basis that men play best of five sets tennis, whereas the women's equivalent is best of three. However, as three-time men's singles victor John McEnroe points out:

> The old argument is that the guys are out there playing best of five, which is true. But I've seen a lot of three-hour movies which weren't as good as the one-and-a-half hour movies, so that doesn't automatically mean if you are out there for longer that you deserve more money.

Significantly, British legislation only requires that a woman do *equivalent work or work of equal value* to a male colleague to be able to claim the same remuneration as him, at least since the passing of the Equal Pay Regulations in 1983. However, the public sector workers' union Unison and the Equality and Human Rights Commission are both solidly behind the fight to narrow the earnings differential. This has also emerged as a key issue from the government's Listening to Women initiative. The Industrial Society, moreover, has publicly challenged the existing legislation, describing the procedures for bringing a claim of unequal pay as cumbersome and difficult to follow: it also urges employees to discuss their salaries openly so that gender-based pay differentials are more easily exposed.

This may also be music to the ears of female arts workers in Britain. Findings from an *ArtsProfessional* (2006) survey indicate that the gender pay gap in this sector is still *19 per cent* – nearly 6 per cent *higher* than the national average. Comparison between men and women at a senior level does reduce the overall gap to *5 per cent plus,* but this figure is misleading in the sense that a combination of vertical and horizontal segregation in the sector serves to further disadvantage female workers. In other words, only 25 per cent of the full-time jobs in British arts are held by men, but more than half of these individuals say they occupy a senior role, compared to less than a quarter of women. What we see here, then, is a situation comparable to those in banking and nursing, where men are in the minority overall, but in the majority when it comes to senior positions – and the salaries that come with them. *ArtsProfessional* refers to this as 'the reinforced glass ceiling'.

Sources: Based on *ArtsProfessional* (2006) 'Salary survey: discrimination writ large', 132(23 October): 11. Available at: http://www.artsprofessional.co.uk (accessed 12 June 2007); Susanne Fransson and Christer Thörnqvist, (2006) 'Some notes on workplace equality renewal in the Swedish labour market', *Gender, Work and Organization* 13(6): 606–20; Damian Grimshaw and Jill Rubery (2007) *Undervaluing Women's Work, Working Paper Series* (53), Manchester: Equal Opportunities Commission; Heather Joshi, Gerry Makepeace and Peter Dolton (2007) 'More or less unequal? Evidence on the pay of men and women from the British Birth Cohort Studies', *Gender, Work and Organization* 14(1): 37–55; Mark Hodgkinson (2007) 'McEnroe backs Wimbledon's sexual equality', *Telegraph. co.uk*, 22 February. Available at: http://www.telegraph.co.uk (accessed 12 June 2007); Geoffrey Mortlake (2007) 'No thanks necessary for getting you girls the big moolah', *Observer*, 25 February. Available at: http://www.guardian.co.uk (accessed 12 June 2007).

EXHIBIT 8.2

Similar job, more responsibility, different gender

Kate Bornstein describes leaving a job at an American IBM subsidiary for a post at Ford Aerospace following her gender reassignment surgery. The jobs were similar, except for the fact that the Ford position in fact carried more responsibility, but Bornstein took a 30 per cent pay cut when she moved to Ford. As she points out, 'The only thing that had changed in my life was the gender I was presenting'. At IBM she had been hired as a man, at Ford as a woman.

Deirdre McCloskey would certainly understand Bornstein's predicament. Born Donald, McCloskey is an American economist and historian who, as she puts it, 'crossed' genders between 1994 and 1997. Since beginning to live as a woman she says her fellow academics have in the main been warmly accepting – indeed she was elected President of the US Economic History Association in 1997. However, McCloskey also writes that:

I notice already, without claiming expertise, that a woman's life in the academy is different. Admittedly my perspective is a trifle peculiar just yet. The first time I was chatting in a group of male economists as the only woman and made a point which was ignored, a point commended warmly a few minutes later when Harvey made it, I thought, ' *Wonderful:* they're treating me like a woman!' The thrill I can tell you has faded.

Sources: Based on Kate Bornstein (1998), *My Gender Workbook: How to Become a Real Man, a Real Woman, the Real You, or Something Else Entirely*, New York and London: Routledge, p. 152; Deirdre N. McCloskey (2000) *Crossing: A Memoir*, Chicago: University of Chicago Press, p. 264.

The case for gender sensitization training in particular can be made by reference to prevailing stereotypes which tend to delay the progress of women into senior management positions, even where equal opportunity policies and legislation are in place. Amanda Sinclair (1998) firstly identifies what she calls the 'pipeline effect' stereotype; that is, the belief that over time more women are obtaining degrees, gaining access to businesses and acquiring relevant experience, so that all we have to do now is wait for them to progress into management, having made sure that enough are coming in at entry level and providing the right kind of training and development.[5] She also points to the stereotype which suggests that women don't make it into management because there is a lack of suitable candidates for the positions falling vacant, which therefore constructs women as undereducated, less committed, insufficiently mobile and ill-equipped to stand the organizational 'heat'. This second argument has it that the problem lies with women, and that it is one which no amount of equal opportunities labour will change (Sinclair 1998: 18–24). Moreover, although much of the available evidence actually contradicts such beliefs – suggesting that women in reality are more committed to career, organization and staff, and harder

Gender stereotypes in Ibiza
Source: Photo © Garance Marechal

working than their male colleagues, or at least that there is very little difference between the genders in this regard (see, for example, White 1995; Wilson 2003: 23–26) – both stereotypes were found to be alive and well among male and female managers in British retailing I (Tomlinson et al. 1997: 224–5).

Rosie Cunningham, Anita Lord and Lesa Delaney (1999) also argue that the attitudes of senior managers are central to making sure that equal opportunities initiatives endure. In particular, they claim that restructuring in the British Civil Service has had a detrimental impact on gains that its women have made in areas such as breaking through the glass ceiling, in the main because the Next Steps project, established in 1988 to improve service and increase efficiency, has led to a fragmentation of the organization into semi-autonomous agencies. This in turn has created greater autonomy for those managers who might not be sympathetic to the equal opportunities cause. The specific agency that Cunningham et al. examined had several laudable initiatives in place, yet greater managerial freedom as a result of Next Steps had also increased workload and concomitantly reduced individual managers' desire to promote equal opportunities. Budget constraints on the new agencies also meant less commitment to 'intangibles' of this kind. Less central control translated into less accountability, for example in terms of equal opportunities monitoring. Moreover, the marketization of the Civil Service saw it having to compete to retain its contracts and, as a result, equal opportunity initiatives like flexiwork and job share were often seen as being at odds with the need to keep costs as low as possible when submitting contractual bids.

In sum, the main impetus behind liberal feminist arguments is social justice, the moral case for equality of opportunity, organizationally and elsewhere. As Sally Holtermann (1995: 105) argues, if employers choose to pursue the long agenda:

> Employees gain the benefits of increased equality of opportunity for men and women in the workplace (and at home). All family members gain from an easing of the strain of juggling work and caring responsibilities, and some children will gain the social and development benefits of quality childcare facilities.

However, as Holtermann (1995: 104–5) also points out, there are distinctive advantages in business-related, quantitative terms to those employers who choose to adopt an equal opportunities stance. For example, corporate image should be enhanced, employee productivity may rise and labour relations improve as a result of greater respect for the employer, and cost savings may also be generated by greater retention of female labour and lower absence rates. Holtermann notes, in addition, that other employers benefit from efforts in this area, for example from an enlarged pool of skilled and experienced labour, and that national productivity may rise, thus benefiting the country as a whole. Nonetheless, she asserts that there are certain dangers in promoting this business case – not least because equality of opportunity may become seen not 'primarily as a matter of social justice, desirable in its own right, but merely as something that can be pursued if, and only if, it coincides with the employing organization's own self-interest' (Holtermann 1995: 110–11).

Radical feminism

The liberal feminist stance can be compared to the particular radical feminist position taken, for example, by Susan Griffin (1980) and Mary Daly (1984a, 1984b). This suggests that women are in fact naturally different from men – that they possess certain characteristics which render them closer to nature, closer to their passions and emotions, more intuitive and instinctive – and that they are therefore *superior*. Radical feminism may, as a result, advocate that women be deliberately introduced into the higher echelons of management so as to counterbalance the narrow masculinist thinking evident at these levels. This kind of thinking produces supposedly rational outcomes such as nuclear weapons. These are, their supporters would have it, intended as deterrents, as guarantors of continued peace. However, if such weapons are used, as they were by the US in August 1945 on Hiroshima and Nagasaki, they make for the long-term erosion of genetic health and the environment across a huge geographical area, quite apart from their immediate capacity for annihilation. It is this kind of objection which radical feminists identify women as uniquely equipped to make (see, for example, the discussion of the women's peace movement in McNeil 1987: 40–56).

In a slightly different vein, but one which also extols the virtues of women over men, the Australian Master Builders Association (AMBA) claimed that, now technological change has removed much of the heavy labour from the industry, women are to be preferred for construction jobs over men because they are highly motivated, diligent, conscientious, neater, cleaner, better communicators and good negotiators. Thus, say the AMBA, women construction workers will improve standards, management practices, safety records and customer relations (Vincent 1998). Other writers in the radical feminist tradition, however, would see the entry of women into traditionally male fields as a form of collaboration with the enemy. They advocate instead a form of separatism where women live and work separately from men, so as to allow them to run their lives according to feminine principles. An example is the tendency for women-only organizations to be flatter in structure and more cooperative in ethos than those employing both men and women (Oerton 1996). The extreme separatist case is made by Valerie Solonas (1983), who calls for women to destroy men altogether as otherwise, she counsels, they can never achieve genuine freedom.

However, Sarah Oerton (1996) also suggests that women-only organizations face pronounced viability problems, given that they tend to attract fewer customers and resources than their mixed-sex counterparts. This is not simply, Oerton argues, because these organizations are categorized as inefficient, utopian, downmarket, radically left wing and operating in the 'wholefood ... [and] woolly jumpers' sectors of the economy (1996: 30). She points out the widespread assumption that those working in such organizations must also be feminists, lesbians, and therefore man-haters who are beyond heterosexual control. The consequent threat constructed around these women is effectively neutralized via their economic marginalization. This, as Oerton also states, happens regardless of the sexuality of the people involved (and in some cases regardless of their political orientation).

Diversity

Again in contrast to the equal opportunities stance, of which organizational liberal feminism forms an important strand, there is also a large body of work around the need to manage what has become known as *diversity* in the workplace – to be responsible for and sensitive to the different types of individual who make up an organization. Anna Lorbiecki and Gavin Jack (2000: S18) suggest that diversity management is now 'common practice' in the US and is increasingly being implemented in the UK and Canada. This interest in diversity has arguably received a considerable fillip from the current furore around *globalization*. There are many definitions of this phenomenon, but the one offered by Barbara Parker is useful for our purposes here:

> [the] increased permeability of traditional boundaries of almost every kind, including physical borders such as time and space, nation-states and economies, industries and organizations and less tangible borders such as cultural norms or assumptions about 'how we do things around here'. (Parker 1998: 6–7)

These economic, sociocultural, political and technological developments mean that people are generally moving more freely across the surface of the globe, and they translate into increasingly diverse workforces in many organizations worldwide. The department in which one of the authors works (in a university located in England's East Midlands) is a case in point – at the time of writing, its various employees hailed from countries as diverse as China, Poland, England, Russia, Mexico, Belgium, New Zealand, Germany, Canada, Italy, the Czech Republic, France and Scotland. Moreover, with labour shortages of the order of 75 million workers predicted for the European Union in years to come, it seems that such movements, leading to more diversity within member states' workforces, are set to continue – this despite current controversies about immigration in the same geographical region.

Gender is an important topic in diversity, as are race, ethnicity, class, (dis)ability and HIV status, as well as other issues less prominent in the equal opportunities literature, such as personality, value systems, working style, religion, lifestyle, education level and so on. As Patricia Arredondo points out, the idea of managing diversity refers to:

> a strategic organizational approach to workforce diversity development, organizational culture change, and empowerment of the workforce. It represents a shift away from the activities and assumptions defined by affirmative action [an equal opportunities tactic involving positive discrimination] to management practices

that are inclusive, reflecting the workforce diversity and its potential. Ideally it is a pragmatic approach, in which participants anticipate and plan for change, do not fear human differences or perceive them as a threat, and view the workplace as a forum for individuals' growth and change in skills and performance *with direct cost benefits to the organization.* (Arredondo 1996: 17, cited in Lorbiecki and Jack 2000, S19, emphasis added)

EXHIBIT 8.3

Problems with equal opportunities approaches

- Those who are the recipients of supposedly preferential treatment being stigmatized.
- The development of a culture of tokenism, within which 'getting the numbers right' – that is to say, achieving a target number of disadvantaged employees – is the main issue.
- An 'assimilation' or 'melting pot' culture being established where differences are minimized and not developed to their full potential and where individuals are expected to fit into a predetermined mould, the consequences of which are seen to be a 'play it safe' approach to work and a reluctance to be creative or to take the initiative.
- Targeting the disadvantaged on a permanent basis rather than making efforts to ensure that an organization naturally encourages equality of opportunity for *all*.
- The outdated idea that organizations still need to focus on recruiting the disadvantaged, rather than ensuring that they are present at all levels of the organization.
- The incorrect assumption that overt and blatant prejudice is still an issue in organizations.
- The creation of poor role models for aspiring members of disadvantaged groups; and so on.

Sources: Based on Rajvinder Kandola and Johanna Fullerton (1998), *Managing the Mosaic: Diversity in Action,* London: Institute of Personnel and Development; and R. Roosevelt Thomas, Jr (1991), *Beyond Race and Gender: Unleashing the Power of Your Workforce by Managing Diversity,* New York: AMACOM.

The main issue for proponents of diversity management is that managers need to empower *all staff* to realize their full potential – with 'all staff' explicitly including white men. In fact, Kandola and Fullerton and US writer R. Roosevelt Thomas argue that equal opportunity approaches such as liberal feminism are aimed only at the disadvantaged and therefore potentially create problems in organizations. Exhibit 8.3 outlines some of the key difficulties which diversity writers associate with claims for equal employment opportunity. As a result of these identified deficiencies of equal opportunity approaches, the managing diversity camp suggests that an alternative is to focus on individual development needs, to allow all members of the organization the opportunity to develop as they need to in order to become fully productive employees. Kandola and Fullerton (1998), for example, propose MOSAIC as the paradigm for managing diversity. Exhibit 8.4 outlines key components of the MOSAIC approach. Of course many of these techniques can also be identified as forming part of the long agenda of equality of opportunity, described earlier. The difference is that diversity initiatives supposedly target *everyone* within an organiza- tion, as opposed to focusing simply on less well-represented groups such as women or people of colour.

According to Lorbiecki and Jack (2000: S20–1), although the US diversity initi- ative initially gained momentum as a result of late 1980 and early 1990 claims about changing workforce demographics and the consequent need for employers to turn their attention to 'non-traditional' sources of labour, a more political turn in the literature occurred when it became clear that diversity connected with prevail- ing New Right standpoints and their emphasis on the individual. That is, diversity began to be seen as an alternative to affirmative action, a new and more appealing way for employers to demonstrate their social and moral commitments. Diversity, quite simply, was easier to market to American and, by this stage, European employ- ers. It then took on a third dimension – that of economics – when writers began to counsel that diversity was the only means of ensuring corporate survival, preserving company image and enhancing the bottom line. The highly variegated global mar- ket, such commentators claimed, simply could not be served by 'eight white guys at the top of the organization making decisions for 40,000 people around the world' *(Sloan Management Review* 1995: 16, cited in Lorbiecki and Jack 2000: S21).

Exhibit 8.4

Managing diversity via the MOSAIC acronym

Mission and value — A set of values which supports and justifies diversity management and encourages the expression of differences.

Objective and fair processes — All organizational processes (for example recruitment) must be regularly audited in order to ensure that they are fair to *everyone*.

Skilled workforce — Managers and workforce alike must be skilled in 'fairness and awareness' – they must understand the principles of diversity management, know why it is important and work to ensure that diversity is respected. Managers should adopt an approach of continuous development of self and others, asking for feedback on their own performance and continually working to improve that performance, as well as ensuring that others' progress is not left to chance.

Active flexibility — This also needs to be implemented, not only in the organization of work (for example flexi-time), but also in benefits. A 'cafeteria' of benefits can enable each employee to choose the benefits that most suit them. For example, if an individual does not have children, they will not have need of an organizational crèche, but may be keen to own company shares.

Individual focus — Individual employees are the focus of diversity management, *not* groups of employees such as women.

Culture that empowers   The culture must be empowering, encouraging employees to experiment with ways of respecting and managing diversity themselves.

Source: Based on Rajvinder Kandola and Johanna Fullerton (1998), *Managing the Mosaic: Diversity in Action,* London: Institute of Personnel and Development, pp. 144–66.

CASE EXAMPLE   Managing diversity in the workplace: Corning USA

When James Houghton took over as chief executive officer of Corning in 1983, he apparently made diversity management a key principle. This was primarily because Houghton had identified that turnover rates for women and blacks were higher than for white men, with the consequence that Corning's investment in these groups in terms of recruitment and selection costs, and training and development, was being wasted. He also felt that the make-up of Corning's workforce should become more reflective of its customer base, so as to ensure better consumer relations. To address these issues, Houghton firstly implemented two quality improvement teams – one for blacks and one for women. Awareness training was made mandatory throughout the organization so as to identify which unconscious organizational values were working against these groups. One issue identified as a result of this training was the importance that the Corning culture placed on working late and the way in which this disadvantaged women, who were more likely than men to have pressing domestic responsibilities. There was also a general improvement in communication about diversity – for example, the publication of stories in the company newspaper about Corning's diverse workforce and successful organizational projects involving diverse groups of people. Further, career planning was introduced for everyone. Corning also began to offer educational grants in exchange for students working summers at a plant within the corporation. Many of the participants in this programme then came to work for the organization upon graduating. Corning's summer internship programme also expanded, with a particular emphasis on offering places to women and blacks, and, finally, contacts with university groups such as the Society of Women Engineers were instigated. Significantly, given the overall thrust of the managing diversity argument, while James Houghton acknowledges the social and moral benefits of the approach that he has implemented, he also states that: It simply makes good business sense' (Houghton, cited in Thomas 1990: 110).

Source: Adapted and reprinted by permission of *Harvard Business Review.* From 'From affirmative action to affirming diversity' by R. Roosevelt Thomas, March/April 1990, p. 110. Copyright © 1990 by Harvard Business School of Publishing Corporation. All rights reserved.

AUTHORS' NOTE: Ironically, in 1997, Dow Corning, a Corning subsidiary, was forced to pay several million dollars in damages to thousands of women who had been damaged by its faulty silicone breast implants. The alleged cause was that the product was insufficiently tested; that is, women did not take sufficient part in its development and their needs were not properly monitored.

Nonetheless, and in contrast to the liberal feminist and radical feminist projects, because the main objective of diversity is to improve business performance, such projects arguably have little moral or social strength (Lorbiecki and Jack 2000: S21). Any such benefits could even be regarded as incidental. As a consequence, a company pragmatically following gender-sensitive policies as a result of diversity initiatives to increase productivity might find itself following research and development or marketing practices which ignore and ultimately damage the interests of women – as Dow Corning did with the breast implant scandal. Rachel Woodward and Patricia Winters (2006) discussion of the shift from a focus on equal opportunities to one on diversity in the British Army since the late 1990s or so is also instructive here. This they suggest came about as a result of similar developments in the private sector, as well as a recognition of the business case for diversity management outlined above. It takes the form, Woodward and Winter argue, of 'recognizing and working with difference, rather than either providing special treatment for one group, or arguing that those differences themselves do not exist'. However, when it comes, for example, to arguments around whether women should be excluded from 'direct combat positions' – the front line, in other words – the 2001 statement on The Wider Employment of Women in Ground Combat makes it very clear that gender difference in this context is understood as essential, innate, given. Thus, although a minute proportion of women could (the Army concedes) pass the physically demanding assessment procedure for recruitment to an infantry post, their continuing exclusion is not on this basis. Instead it is because, as the statement itself suggests:

> We have no way of knowing whether mixed gender teams can develop the bonds of unconditional trust, loyalty and mutual support that must be strong enough to survive the test of close combat. Nor can we tell what will be the impact o[n] the other members of the team if a member of the opposite sex is killed or maimed. (Ministry of Defence n.d., cited in Woodward and Winter 2006: 56–7)

Thus women are being excluded here qua women – they are *not* men and thus pose an inevitable threat to cohesion within combat units.

Also in this vein, David Thomas and Robin Ely (1996) suggest that approaches to managing diversity in practice fall into two main categories, one of which (the 'learning paradigm') is much more far-reaching than the other ('access legitimacy'). These approaches are summarized in Exhibit 8.5. It would scarcely be controversial to argue that those organizations fitting within the learning paradigm are likely to be few and far between. Fully developed diversity, it seems, is a difficult goal to achieve, although Thomas and Ely (1996: 89) also warn that simply seeing its benefits in business terms (the access legitimacy approach) may prevent problems such as racism, sexism, homophobia and sexual harassment being addressed as part of any such initiative.

The three approaches to gender and management which we have examined so far identify gender as properly having a certain kind of impact on management *practice*. Liberal feminism, for example, argues that managers should make every effort to minimize gendered differences in terms and conditions, whereas radical feminism suggests that differences between men and women should be recognized, either so as to make the most of women's 'special contribution' to organizations, or via some form of economic separatism. Diversity, on the other hand, counsels that, although gender difference needs to be recognized, celebrated and exploited in organizations, it should receive no more attention than any other kind of difference.

EXHIBIT 8.5

Two approaches to managing diversity

Access legitimacy	Learning paradigm
Accepts and celebrates differences and emphasizes equality for everyone.	Differences to be incorporated at *all* organizational levels but equality for everyone is also stressed.
Main aim is to ensure that external market (customers) matches internal market (workforce), so emphasis is on hiring staff of an appropriate gender, ethnic and cultural mix.	Changes market, products, strategies and organizational culture – for example, the legal firm Deway-Levin, after recruiting a female Hispanic lawyer, changed the type of case that it pursued.
Benefits include the hiring of minority groups who were previously disadvantaged in the labour market.	Seeks to learn from its diverse staff group and to develop their capabilities, which may uncover unforeseen opportunities.
More of a marketing/PR strategy, no real attention given to developing capacities which the diverse workforce might have.	Organization may change its core business or identify new business possibilities.
Global companies might use this approach to interact with external markets and difference cultures.	
No strategies in place to incorporate differences across the board so may remain dominated at management level by white, Anglo-Saxon men.	

Source: Adapted from David A. Thomas and Robin J. Ely (1996), 'Making differences matter: A new paradigm for managing diversity', *Harvard Business Review*, (September–October): 79–90.

However, there is another way to conceive of the relationship between gender and management which involves introducing the concept of gender into management theory, and understanding how gender affects the way managers think and act. With this in mind, we now move to consider the theory of managerial work, which attempts to conceptualize what management is (and, more often than not, what it should be), with particular attention to the presence and positioning of gender within that analysis. It quickly becomes apparent from our discussion that such theorizing has traditionally either sought to deny the significance of gender for an understanding of managers and managing, or has simply not taken it into account. It fails to recognize the relationship between management and gender: first, because it makes little or no room for any analysis of the actual individuals who occupy the management role, treating management as an abstract set of functions, principles or processes; and, second, because it fails to recognize gender as a significant variable in organizational life even in the face of overwhelming empirical evidence. Indeed, it has been widely suggested that mainstream management theory is actually more accurately labelled 'malestream'. Management in this kind of theory is typically presented as genderless, either because it consists solely of a collection of functions (classical management theory) or because it can be explained as a more or less appropriate relationship to one's workforce (theories of human relations or management 'style'). However, management is an inescapably embodied and therefore also a gendered experience, an experience which is different for men and women whether they are the managers or the managed. The omission of gender by mainstream/malestream theories of management means that such theories cannot account for the complexity of the management experience; they cannot capture how it feels and what it means to manage (or indeed to be managed) in a modern organization. We assert, therefore, that gender and management connect with each other in significant and highly visible ways and go on to review two bodies of work presenting exactly this argument.

Nevertheless, at this juncture it is also important that we remember the point made by Chris Grey (1995) and Mats Alvesson and Yvonne Due Billing (1997), who warn against *over*gendering management theory. As Alvesson and Billing have it:

> Any perspective runs the risk of being used in a one-eyed fashion, reducing all phenomena to issues of men and women or masculinity and femininity. Gender over-sensitivity ... means not considering or too quickly disregarding other aspects or possible interpretations. It means an over-privileging of gender and a neglect of alternative standpoints. (1997: 12)

So the 'gender' lens *is not* the only way to look at management, any more than the lenses of structure, functions, culture or quality are. It does not reveal any ultimate or privileged truth about management, although it is an important, and practically useful, means of understanding how management gets 'done' in modern organizations. This caveat established, the discussion which follows concerns the ways in which gender has been constructed in management and organization theory.

Classical management theory

For classical management theory, as exemplified in the work of Frederick Winslow Taylor (1947 [1911]), Henri Fayol (1949 [1916]) and Colonel Lyndall Urwick (1969 [1937]) in the early twentieth century, management consists simply of the execution of a series of functions. It is these functions, suggest such theorists, which ensure the smooth and effective running of the organization. Management here is presented as a depersonalized activity: it is manag*ement* that is the focus rather than the real-life process or performance of manag*ing* (Hayward 1992: 186–8). The emphasis is on formal, structured principles of design and administration to suit all organizations, everywhere. Urwick, for example, claims that the study of the human experience of organizing can yield up principles which can govern any form of human organization. For him, regardless of the organization's type (it could be a local church, hospital, government agency, army regiment, supermarket, newspaper, whatever), purpose, people (manual workers, knowledge workers, men or women) or the political and social theory behind its creation (capitalism or socialism, say), these principles were technical and universal: they applied to all managerial situations (Urwick 1969 [1937]: 49). An excellent example of the supposedly global character of the principles put forward by the classical management theorists is the fact that Lenin was keen to apply the four key tenets of Taylor's capitalist scientific management methods in Communist Russia. However, it is worth noting at this stage that commentators did not agree with each other on what the 'universal' principles were, and that many of these writers have sought variously to retain, restate, narrow or refute original formulations such as those offered by Fayol, as discussed below (Hales 2001: 2). Nonetheless, such tensions notwithstanding, the belief in universality held firm for several decades.

As we might expect from its insistence on formality, there is also an overall emphasis within classical management theory on the application of science to the study of management, in order – through observation, hypothesis development and experimentation – to arrive at the 'one best way' to manage. Fayol (1949 [1916]), for instance, on the basis of his own management experience, suggested that management (which he referred to as administration) consisted of:

- *organizing* (dividing tasks to be done between workers, and ensuring that this division of labour is efficient and effective)
- *coordinating* (overseeing division of labour in terms of ensuring that the parts support each other)
- *controlling* (monitoring the activities of workers within the division of labour, including discipline if necessary)
- *purveyance* (forecasting and planning future workforce activity).

In a similar vein, Taylor's (1947 [1911]) key ideas were, first, that every individual's labour should be designed using a scientific analysis of that work. Furthermore, Taylor stated that managers must coordinate their workers' activities in order that tasks to be done are in fact completed. He also believed in a strict separation of conception and execution. That is, Taylor stated that managers should manage and workers work: he counselled that workers should not themselves have any control over the way in which they work or over what they do. Fourth, scientific management does not ignore the fact that individuals have different abilities – far from it. Taylor was at pains to point out that not everyone was capable of working in a scientifically determined 'one best way', and that individuals needed to be carefully selected according to their ability to work hard and in accordance with instructions. He also emphasized that rates were to be negotiated with individuals only and not with the collective or group, although, as Chris Nyland (1989) has pointed out, Taylor came to embrace the necessity, and arguably the positive features, of collective bargaining with trade unions in his later years. Similarly, he was aware that there were women in the workforce. In fact a review of the role of women in scientific management by Sue Ainslie Clark and Edith Wyatt was welcomed by Taylor. The recent republication of this review includes correspondence between Taylor and Wyatt, who later gave very supportive evidence to a US congressional committee addressing scientific management (Nyland 2000). Moreover, although within this approach the gender of managers has no relationship to the way that they *should* manage, Taylor implicitly acknowledged that in reality, and in most circumstances, it will have some relationship to the way that they *do* manage. This is why he argued that the principles of scientific management need to be fully enunciated and understood. Scientific management would, it can be inferred, thereby enable women and men to overcome any differences in their 'innate' styles of managing and manage in the most efficient way.

Yet, despite Taylor's awareness of and interest in the effects of scientific management on women, including his suggestion that they should be given two days off a month with no questions asked, the implication being that this was to accommodate the menstrual cycle, for him individual or gender characteristics were not the *defining* features of either work or management. Other underlying and objectively observable principles determined what work and management were, and could be measured. Here, then, the main emphasis is on the manager as a functionary, as an individual who works for the benefit of the whole organization – and therefore of all those within it (the last assumption is especially apparent in Taylor's work) – but who has no especial identity or contribution which is unique to him or her *individually* as far as the organization is concerned. Management for Taylor and his fellow classical management theorists was *normative:* any managerial work on relationships was just a matter of aligning people with the correct abstract principles *(norms),* adherence to which was the overall function of management. Difference and diversity were not just to be ignored, they were to be *suppressed* and rationality, traditionally regarded as a male/masculine trait, was to dominate in the workplace (Linstead 2000).

Max Weber, whose theory of bureaucracy was as theoretically influential as were Taylor's recommendations for practice, had a similar view of the association between women and emotion and the need to banish emotion (and consequently women) from the organizational stage in favour of objective institutional rationality (Bologh 1990: 28–9; Burrell 1997: 244). Similarly, as Michael Roper avers with regard to Lyndall Urwick:

> The effort involved in maintaining the space for his work within [his] domestic context was replicated in the very content of his writing at this time, which … reached more than ever towards a vision of the organization in which personal demands were contained. (Roper 2001: 193 – also see Brewis 2005: 503)

Urwick himself struggled to balance work (at the International Management Institute in Geneva) and home life – wife Joan, his two children and his mother – and this might well be reflected in a body of work recording his compulsion 'to bleach organizations of "personalities"' (Roper 2001: 190). Here again, the key management principle of *sine ira et studio* ('without hatred or passion') is writ large, which in itself implicitly signals a masculine organization.

But it was in the reform of office work, and particularly through the efforts of Frank and Lilian Gilbreth (see, for example, Gilbreth 1911), that the labour process became most obviously gendered, where (rational) men managed (emotional) women and order was maintained thereby – as immortalized in the film *Cheaper by the Dozen.* Here the Gilbreths' insistence on the routinization of the workplace was extended into the home and even the womb (they had 12 children), and the story turned into an ironic romp about the way they reputedly lived family life according to work study principles. The 'one best way' to do things was gently 'sent up'. However, despite some glimpses of gender in the principles put forward by classical management theory, it is also true to say that it was never directly addressed as an issue for managers, or for the managed.

Human relations theory

What is sometimes viewed as a 'softer' turn in management and organization theory, away from the emphasis on measurement and timing in classical management, was primarily associated with the Hawthorne Studies, and their development under the influence of Elton Mayo. It is also associated with the later theoretical influence of Abraham Maslow and his theory of the hierarchy of human needs. Both Mayo and Maslow conducted research in which women played a significant part, yet subsequently produced theories which ignored gender as a factor. The reasons for this are different in each case, but had a considerable effect on later studies.

The Hawthorne Studies were initiated in 1924 by managers of the Hawthorne Plant of the Western Electric Company in Chicago. They had originally been ergonomic studies of the effects of the physical surroundings of work on productivity – especially that of lighting. After all, as an electricity producer, Western had an obvious interest in demonstrating that using more electricity could increase companies' profits – an approach which is currently being rediscovered as managing your customers' value-added. There had been clinical studies of fatigue and monotony since the First World War, and the methodologies used by Hawthorne were an extension of these. The apocryphal account of how Mayo, an Australian philosopher/ psychologist working at Harvard University, came to be involved has it that the managers involved in the early days of the studies had no idea how to interpret the data and asked him to help them with their analysis because of similar workplace studies he had conducted and his connections with the prestigious Rockefeller Foundation. In actual fact, the managers had plenty of ideas – what they wanted was an expert to help *mediate* their interpretations. Mayo, however, had ideas of his own and when he eventually came to write on the studies he treated the data rather selectively and as a platform for his own theories (Mayo 1945, 1960 [1933]; Trahair 1984; Gillespie 1991).

One of these theories was based on the fact that as a young man he had had bad experiences of political demagogues in Adelaide who had swayed the local unions and caused considerable industrial and social unrest and political damage. Mayo was, as a result, deeply mistrustful of collective sentiment. He had also failed twice, in Adelaide and Edinburgh, to become a doctor of medicine, and had subsequently channelled his energies into psychology, particularly counselling and psychiatry. As a consequence, Mayo's approach to organizations was to treat their problems as symptoms of a malaise which might be collective, but was probably individual. Its source, he felt, was the disruption of traditional community occasioned by urban concentration: for Mayo, work organizations therefore had to fulfil some of the functions of community for their members in order to prevent tensions manifesting themselves in lowered output, absenteeism, fatigue, boredom, sickness and what he called 'pessimistic reveries'. A third factor might be added, which was that Mayo had never fitted neatly into any particular academic discipline himself – he also read widely, if not always wisely, in many genres. This emerged in his methodology as multidisciplinarity: one of the most distinctive features of the Hawthorne Studies was the inclusion of psychologists, social anthropologists, statisticians and representatives from a range of other disciplines in the research programme.

Mayo liked to build 'big picture' social arguments, and his perspective was not too dissimilar from Taylor's, as critical commentators like Harry Braverman (1974) have pointed out. Yet it is still remarkable that, although the empirical phase of the Hawthorne experiments was conducted on two groups, one of which was entirely male and the other entirely female, this gender segregation was not treated as an object of analysis. The female group was initially coerced into taking part in the experiments and was separated from the main body of the shop floor by being put in a separate room, with a male supervisor. They were closely supervised and monitored, involved in the distribution of activities and the organization of work, given incentives and manipulated in other ways, and were also medically monitored for changes in their condition which might lead to fatigue. Such was the intrusiveness of the management in fact that two of the workers who had become difficult and vocal in their argumentation for improvements in conditions were removed from the group against their will.

In discussing the accounts of the experiments, Richard Gillespie (1991: 204) points out that both Mayo (1945, 1960 [1933]) and later Fritz Roethlisberger and William Dickson (1939) ignored the possibility of collective action by workers. The only dimension that mattered was the individual, and any economic arguments – even where, as with the male group in the bank wiring room, these seemed to have considerable merit – were regarded as 'simply an unconvincing rationalization of behaviour actually driven by sentiments' (Gillespie 1991: 204). This is despite the fact that output by the women increased and output by the men decreased! As Jeff Hearn and Wendy Parkin (1994) point out, the absence of gender and sexuality from this consideration of 'human relations', 'interpersonal relations' and 'emotional relations' calls into question what these terms can possibly mean. They argue that gaps like these are in fact attempts by male theorists not just to reorganize social relations, but to incorporate gendered and sexual relations into organizational analysis in a non-gendered and asexual way (Wilson 1996: 829). However, this was not 'gender *blindness*', as Wilson (1996) and Tomlinson et al. (1997: 219) argue, but a conscious and active *suppression* of gender difference, arising from an intellectual commitment to abstract generalizations, disembodied reasoning and a basically Freudian view which saw women, despite their surface differences, essentially as men without penises (Linstead 2000).

Maslow's hierarchy of needs

Another theorist whose work, although not directly related to organizations, was incorporated into the human relations approach was the psychologist Abraham Maslow. Maslow had similar views about the fundamental nature of human beings to those of Mayo, and his theory of motivation is said to treat men and women as if gender were inconsequential. Maslow argued that human beings are 'driven' by needs which can be classified according to a hierarchy, ranging from basic physiological survival at the bottom, through safety/security, social/affiliative and esteem/recognition, to self-actualization at the top. For Maslow, self-actualization was the ultimate need, but his critics assert that, although his studies of self-actualizing people included women, his definition of self-actualization itself reflects stereotypically *male* experiences and traits (Kasten 1972; Cullen 1994; Wilson 1996). Thus, self-actualization becomes an expression of the male self which *denies* relatedness rather than the female self which *defines* itself in relation to others (Chodorow 1989). Maslow, it is claimed, also privileged the notion of a need hierarchy rather than seeing these needs as webs of interrelated emotional and physical needs (Gilligan 1982; Wilson 1996).

Interestingly, Maslow's starting point for the hierarchy was in fact research on captive primates with regard to dominance behaviour. Human behaviour was at the time (the 1930s) widely held to be predominantly determined by sex (Freud) or dominance/power (Adler). Maslow focused on the latter issue and worked with primates at first in order to develop a basic understanding of dominance behaviour. Nonetheless (and quite apart from the questionable value of extrapolating conclusions based on animal behaviour to human behaviour), his research was deeply flawed. This is particularly evident in the fact that, as later field studies demonstrated, apes behave differently in their wild communities, where social skills rather than physiological traits are more important in the emergence of certain apes in dominant roles, from the way they do in an experimental setting (Cullen 1997). Moreover, recent work has indicated that the reproductive strategies of female primates are far more complex than was hitherto assumed. Females will deliberately mate during their most fertile period with males outside their community, thus adding variety to the gene pool, while continuing to mate with males from the tribe during infertile periods. Hidden subversive behaviour, then, seems to have greater consequence than more obvious dominance behaviour (Weiss 1997).

Based on this somewhat problematic study, then, Maslow concluded that the apes which were less aggressive and most relaxed about their dominance (and consequently most *worthy* of their positions) had greater confidence in themselves. He carried this idea through into his research on sexuality, which focused on women and what he called 'dominance-feeling' (later 'self-esteem'), which was an essential underpinning for self-actualization. However, when giving examples of self-actualizers, he came up with a sample which was predominantly male. This has been variously held to be a result of restricted opportunities for women in society at the time (Friedan 1963: 310), or a consequence of the fact that the ways in which Maslow believed women self-actualized (for example motherhood) are not publicly recognized (Maslow 1954: 92; Cullen 1994: 130). But the gender bias in the hierarchy actually came from the aforementioned conflation of dominance behaviour with self-esteem, which led Maslow to conclude that high-dominance women, who displayed more masculine traits, had more in common with high-dominance men than low-dominance women. He therefore suggested that any gender distinction could be *dropped altogether* as it was so misleading (Maslow 1939: 18; Cullen 1994: 134).

As is also the case with Taylor, Mayo and others, then, Maslow here is not unaware of gender, but instead chooses to deny observable differences between men and women for theoretical reasons. As Cullen points out, his low-dominance women had many qualities which were indicative of high self-esteem if viewed from a more relational perspective, but for Maslow they could not be self-actualizers. The high-dominance women, we would add, conversely displayed many behaviours which could be regarded as narcissistic or self-centred. Furthermore, we already know from Dallas Cullen's work that Maslow's primate research was notable for its methodological problems, and she (1994: 134–5) makes the same observation of his later studies. Especially disturbing is his 1963 assertion that, on the basis of his knowledge of high-dominance women, and in contrast to men, 'women generally were not destroyed by being raped because fear makes women more feminine and rape represents a woman's desirability and power since the rapist has an erection' (Lowry 1982: 90, cited in Cullen 1994: 136). Yet the hierarchy built on flawed primate research and even more flawed sexuality research, and displaying a very significant gender bias, has been so influential in management and organization theory as to have been regarded as a 'classic among classics' (Matteson and Ivancevich 1989: 369, cited in Cullen 1994: 127). Moreover, as Brewis et al. (2006: 18) suggest, following a range of contemporary OB (organizational behaviour) textbook writers, 'the influence of Maslow's sixty year old theory is visible in a wide range of contemporary management techniques or approaches, including TQM, BPR, empowerment and self-managing teams'.

Later management theories

It is true to say that later management theories do become more sophisticated in their greater recognition of the fundamentally *relational* nature of the management task (Wilson 1996), paying greater attention to the fact that managing not only involves the persuasion and co-option of others, but also itself evolves as an activity in response to the outcomes of these negotiations. The developing relationship between workforce and management, leaders and followers, emerges as important. Such theories also recognize that management is a process rather than a function, it involves undertaking the task of mana*ging*, there are various different ways to manage and some of these are more appropriate or effective in certain circumstances than others. So these theories retain the emphasis on organizational efficiency and effectiveness which is characteristic of classical management and human relations theory, but also emphasize that management is relational, stylistic and processual. Much of this work has concentrated on leadership styles, and often blurs the boundary between leadership and management.

However, all these more relational (and more recent) theories – here we would include the work of theorists such as Fred Fiedler (1967, 1974), Robert House (1971) and Paul Hersey and Kenneth Blanchard (1996), fuller details of which are presented in Chapter 10 – can also be criticized for their gender blindness. Indeed we would claim here that this *is* a blindness rather than a suppression, because none of these theorists seem to be following such a grand social mission or theoretical plan as Taylor, Mayo or Maslow. They are arguably mere technicians when considered alongside the pervasive influence of these giants. Although managing in this later work is more modestly acknowledged to be temporally located, there is greater emphasis on the *relationship* between the manager and the workers than on the specific characteristics, background and extrinsic factors (for example gender) which affect the *individual* involved in managing. The manager is a shadowy figure, someone who remains anonymous, a non-reflective practitioner who simply needs to choose or be assigned to manage in suitable ways in specific situations. There is no discussion of what we referred to earlier as the 'embodied' experience of managing, how it feels and what it means to be a manager, and therefore no discussion of the individual manager's gender. But if we continually speak and write about management as a series of functions, principles, processes, relationships and/or styles, we cannot begin to understand how it is practised in different contexts or why.

Gender in management

Despite this absence of gender from mainstream/malestream management theory, some organizational analysts have sought to establish the interrelation between gender and management. That is, they consider the embodied nature of managerial work, management as performed by gendered subjects, by individuals who identify as male or female, and the consequences that this may have for organizational and managerial practice. In other words, how male and female managers *actually* manage becomes the focus. This work tends to retain the relational theorists' emphasis on management as process and the differences between managerial styles, as well as often relying on the classical management theory notion of a 'one best way' to manage as regards organizational effectiveness – if perhaps seeking to reverse it. However, the real contribution of this more contemporary theory is arguably its acknowledgement that it *matters what kind of person* is doing the managing.

This *gender in management* approach argues that, because men and women are socialized differently, they manage differently. Researchers in this area have therefore concentrated on identifying the key characteristics of 'masculine' and 'feminine' managerial styles. Judy Rosener (1990, 1997), for example, argues for an emphasis on the *feminine in management* because feminine styles, she claims, are most effective in the current socioeconomic climate. Critics of the feminine in management school, however, adopt *a gender globalization* approach, which insists that specific management styles are relatively insignificant except that they facilitate the globalization of masculinized organization (for example Calás and Smircich 1995). Women are introduced into the domestic workforce as having the most appropriate managerial styles because this allows males to strut the international stage and be more globally mobile. Let us look more closely at these approaches.

The feminine in management approach

Judy Rosener's (1990) research asked male and female managers to describe their own managerial style. She discovered that male managers, by their own account at least, adopted what she refers to as a *transactional* leadership style. This style uses the principle of exchange in managing – giving rewards or punishment for work done well or badly. Rosener's male respondents also said that they relied a good deal on their positional authority – the status conferred upon them by the organization – in order to manage others. Women, on the other hand, reportedly used a style that Rosener calls *transformational* leadership. This places the emphasis on motivating staff by: persuading them to commit to group/organizational goals; encouraging them to participate in decision making; managing through personal qualities rather

Childcare at work
Source: Photo © istockphoto

than by using one's position; and trying to make staff feel good about themselves (for other, slightly different definitions of transactional and transformational leadership). Rosener attributes these differences between men and women to gender socialization in early childhood. She also has it that the feminine model of leadership is likely to be more apposite and more successful in economically turbulent times than the command-and-control style preferred by her male respondents. Rosener's more recent work continues to extol the virtues of women managers. *America's Competitive Secret: Women Managers* (1997), for example, argues that the key to maintaining US corporate success and ability to compete in global markets is having women in senior positions in organizations, because their management style increases productivity, innovation and thereby profits through women's aptitude for ambiguity and their willingness to empower others.

Sally Helgesen (1995) echoes Rosener's sentiments, firstly in her suggestion that gendered management styles develop as a result of differential socialization, and that women are consequently better at developing creativity, cooperation and intuition in others than men. She goes on to emphasize their preference for managing via relationships as opposed to hierarchical position, to claim that they listen and empathize much more than their male counterparts and to assert that feminine leadership 'principles' are becoming more influential because they simply suit today's public realm better than the 'warrior values' espoused by men. Helen Brown's suggestion that *women-only* organizations tend to be characterized by flat structures with diffused leadership (as also claimed by Sarah Oerton) is relevant here too, especially given her argument that women have the right social skills to create and manage such non-hierarchical organizations (Brown 1992, cited in Gherardi 1995: 91).

Indeed similar evidence emerges from at least two meta-reviews of the literature on management styles and gender. Alice Hendrickson Eagly and Blair T. Johnson

(1990) reviewed a total of 370 studies using varying methods, concluding that the evidence does point overall to women adopting a more democratic and people-centred approach to managing others, and men tending to be more autocratic and task/production oriented, although these gender differences, apart from democracy versus autocracy, were found to be strongest in *artificial* environments such as laboratories or assessment centres. Studies undertaken in *real* workplaces did not indicate such pronounced differences. Ellen Fagenson (1993, cited in Alvesson and Billing 2000: 147–8) also summarizes the available research and suggests that women err towards the transformational, web-based, interdependent style of leadership, instead of using their status as men would tend to do.

Taking a rather different approach to the exploration of gender and management style, the British researcher Beverley Alimo-Metcalfe theorizes that the way in which decisions are made in organizations about managerial selection and promotion is at least part of the reason why there are relatively few women in senior management positions. Given that men make up the majority of those involved in formulating choices of this kind, she focuses on discovering whether men and women see leadership qualities differently, so as to be able to ascertain if, 'by excluding a significant or matched proportion of women from this sample, one is likely to end up with male-biased criteria of leadership qualities' (Alimo-Metcalfe 1995: 4). In fact, from Alimo-Metcalfe's research, it appears that male and female managers *do* define effective management differently. Her female managers perceived an effective manager to be someone who relates to others as equals and is sensitive and aware of the effects that they have on others. Alimo-Metcalfe's male managers, on the other hand, valued influence and self-confidence as being particularly important among managerial interpersonal skills. Furthermore, the women spoke positively of a supportive working style which empowers and builds teams, whereas the men placed the emphasis on drive, direction and transmitting a clear purpose to staff.

Alimo-Metcalfe borrows from Rosener in designating these differences of style as transformational and transactional. She then proposes that transformational qualities are undervalued when managerial assessment takes place because, as we already know, it is men who dominate in these situations, and it is also men who would tend to favour transactional characteristics, as displayed by other men, across the board. Moreover, this general preference for promoting men is evident despite the fact that much of the available research, as we have seen, emphasizes the importance and relevance of the transformational leadership approach in a complex and diverse world, and the fact that quality management and leadership is deemed to be central to our collective success and well-being in the future (Rosenbach and Taylor, cited in Alimo-Metcalfe 1995: 8). In sum, then, Alimo-Metcalfe's conclusions – that men and women managers value different kinds of managerial style, and the style valued by women may be more apposite in today's organizational world, whatever the stance taken by those who select for and promote to managerial positions – are very similar to those emerging from the research undertaken by Rosener, Helgesen and others.

Joyce Fletcher (2003 [2002]), on the other hand, argues against Helgesen in particular in suggesting that the decline of the heroic, individualistic, masculine-oriented leader has been – in the words of her title – 'greatly exaggerated'. As far as she is concerned, the concomitant 'female advantage' argument is therefore deficient.

Fletcher avers that the gendering of these leadership styles derives from 'something commonly called the "separate spheres" phenomenon' – in other words, the bifurcation that we in the West tend to assume between the public and private spheres of work, the gendering associated with this bifurcation and the discursive elevation of public over private. She then goes on to point out that arguments claiming the apparent rise and rise of 'post-heroic leadership' as *the* contemporary avatar for business effectiveness 'violate some basic principles and beliefs – about gender, power, individual achievement, and even work and family – that we, as a society, hold dear'. This she says helps us to understand why these new models of leadership are not more in evidence in workplaces (despite a substantial level of agreement that they work) and why more women aren't breaking through the glass ceiling – a subject also dealt with by Alimo-Metcalfe in a slightly different way, as we have seen. Fletcher adds that 'because these relational actions are associated with the domestic sphere they are unlikely to be seen as requiring skill of any sort, but instead ... are likely to be attributed to one's natural inclination or personality'. This also means that men who practise this new mode of leadership are much more likely to be rewarded because it is not understood as something that men 'naturally do'. And in any case behaviour which 'needs others' – as this relational, transformational, post-heroic model does – goes against deeply ingrained Western beliefs about the importance of individual achievement.

Sarah Rutherford (2001) in studying a large airline, found that business function, not gender, was the largest single influence on managerial style. Even in times of great change men are able to hold on to the most powerful positions in organizations, and the feminization of management, contra Rosener and pro Calás and Smircich, has neither increased the numbers of women in senior managerial ranks nor produced a more feminine style of management. The convergence of patriarchal and business interests perpetuates male power, allows stereotypes to continue to militate against women's advancement, and enables men, through adopting some more feminine communication skills, to outflank women's advancement.

Finally, although Mats Alvesson and Yvonne Due Billing (1997: Chapter 6) point out that there are two 'camps' of researchers in the gender in management school – one asserting that there are *no* significant differences between the genders in this regard – they also suggest that the 'differences' camp has come to the fore in recent years, despite the fact that 'the majority of the academic empirical work supports the no-or-little-difference thesis'.[6] This may very well be because of the pervasiveness of gender stereotypes in contemporary society, such that in general we find it easier to accept that men and women are much more different than they are similar.

Gender globalization

While also belonging to the gender in management school, a radical critique of the feminine in management approach came from Marta Calás and Linda Smircich (1995, 2004). They argued that this approach combines with the emphasis on globalization to perpetuate the second-class status of women in the workforce. At the risk of oversimplifying their subtle original argument, they pointed out that, as globalization takes an increasing hold, American male managers are forced to become 'global managers' and spend long periods of time overseas. As a result, there is a need for them to be replaced back on the 'home front'. Couple this to the argument that the new flexible organizations, which employ team-based workers and expect high commitment from their members, need softer, more relational, 'feminine' skills rather than the controlling and hard-driving style of traditional management (a viewpoint also espoused by the feminine in management theorists), and the result is a greater 'domestication' of US home industry, women becoming the 'reserve army' of labour, while the global scene becomes more of a 'battlefield'. Women are brought into the workforce and increasingly into management positions to care for the home-based workforce, while the promotable males are sent overseas to grow and develop the business – to go to war with the competition in the global marketplace, or develop strategy in the rarefied air of the boardroom. As we have already seen, men are after all much less encumbered with domestic duties and childcare and so are generally more mobile, women's 'special' interpersonal skills notwithstanding. Women may also be socially constructed as less willing to undertake occupations which necessitate considerable travel, indeed as more motivated to work at home per se – that is, actually in the domestic environment (Anker 1997: 325).

Nick Forster, writing on the subject of those women who *do* achieve international careers, echoed Calás and Smircich in his claim that 'they still represent only a tiny proportion of the total worldwide expatriate population' (Forster 1999: 79), despite the fact that women appear to be just as keen as men on working overseas and are as successful as their male counterparts when they are given the chance to do so. Nonetheless, their selection is much less likely due to assumptions about their domestic commitments. They also face adaptation difficulties in more patriarchal cultures like those of the Middle East or Asia and often do not receive any organizational support for their partners if they choose to travel as well. In fact, of Forster's own sample of British managers and professionals on international assignments (IAs), 89 per cent of the women were single, compared to only 27 per cent of the men. Moreover, Forster's data suggest that the women involved on IAs were more junior than the men, such that there is a glass ceiling in the international context just as there is domestically, and that women were less likely to be given significant projects to oversee. He finishes by arguing that 'if companies are really committed to turning the dual mantras of 'internationalization' and 'equal opportunities' into strategic and HRM realities, then many will have to take a critical look at their current expatriate management policies' (1999: 89), not least because of the competitive realities of attracting and utilizing the best human resource, regardless of gender. Other writers agree with Calás and Smircich and Forster that the building blocks of the international order are gendered, and the personal is not only political but also international (see, for example, Enloe 1990, 1993; Walby 1997: 185–7).

The changing role that women are playing in the economy (which, it should be noted, is also highly variable across the global market – see, for example, Brewis and Linstead 2000: 248) is therefore inextricably connected to global developments which the feminine in management approach tends to ignore. What is also of relevance is the way in which Calás and Smircich in their 1995 paper particularly make an implicit connection between women and the transformational approach to management, and men and the transactional approach, as do the feminine in management researchers. But in reassessing the original paper Calás and Smircich (2004: 476–7) felt that the feminine in management idea had been 'incorporated instrumentally into the managerial "toolkit"', and any critical potential it had has been silenced by the resurgence of more 'manly' discourses. The deployment of white women did, as they predicted, remove opportunities for ethnic minorities, but it did not present any great career advantages for those women – globalization, they observe, benefits the 'selected few, *both* at home and abroad'. The feminine in management imagery served to naturalize the broader exploitation of labour under globalization through increasing lower paid service jobs (work is a labour of love) and increasing hours worked (a woman's work is never done).

Assessing the gender in management argument

The varying cases made by Rosener, Helgesen, Alimo-Metcalfe, Calás and Smircich and others, then, seem to rest on the assumption that women are socialized to manage in certain ways and therefore to value a particular kind of managerial approach. However, although these studies represent an advance on traditional management theory in acknowledging the importance of gender, we suggest they do not take sufficient cognizance of important processes *within* the organization – they place too much emphasis on life 'outside the factory gates'. It is implied that male and female managers arrive at work fully socialized, that the workplace itself has little effect on the ways in which they behave. Thus gender in management researchers perhaps fail to recognize the *interplay* of gender and management, the ways in which gender works to shape managerial work *and vice versa*. Rather, they seem to adhere to an 'add gender and stir' approach.

In criticizing Judy Rosener in particular, Cynthia Fuchs Epstein *(Harvard Business Review* 1991: 151), for example, places more emphasis on work context than pre-work gender socialization in shaping individuals' behaviour at work. Epstein also cites her research among lawyers and her own experience as demonstrating that women frequently engage in 'combative', 'punitive' and 'authoritarian' (that is, 'masculine') behaviour. *In*-work variables, then, such as the size and culture of the organization, should not be underplayed as influencing and in turn being influenced by management style. Additionally, age, class and ethnic differences as non-work variables *apart* from gender may also shape/interact with managerial behaviour. Gender, as Jane Mansbridge *(Harvard Business Review* 1991: 154–6) avers, is perhaps perceived as being too 'sexy' in contemporary management theorizing, attracting so much analytical attention that the exploration of other important factors which influence the way management is done are neglected. We have of course already heard very similar arguments from Mats Alvesson and Yvonne Due Billing and Chris Grey. Moreover, women managers' preference for the transformational style of leadership, if it exists at all, may actually be a function of *those whom they manage*. Allan Cohen argues that Rosener, for example, overlooks the fact that many of her female managers were responsible for professionals who may well not have taken kindly to a more directive managerial approach. Like Epstein, he also criticizes her for overestimating the influence of pre-work gender socialization (Cohen, *Harvard Business Review* 1991: 158).

And it is important that we do not overplay the *differences* between men and women's socialization per se. The socializing of women to work outside the home does not occur in a context separate to the one in which men are socialized. Neither does their socialization into the essentially private world of caring and nurturing. Women do not learn to be women in isolation from men and then bring these values into the workplace – they are socialized in interaction with men (Gherardi 1995: 91). And if we overemphasize gender differences in management theorizing, asks Silvia Gherardi, how can we then account for those men who prefer to work within a more democratic organizational framework and manage in more democratic ways – like the 52 per cent of male managers who said they preferred to use teamwork and a participative management style when surveyed by the British Institute of Management (Vine 1997)? Gherardi suggests that some accounts of gender and managerial work overvalorize the 'either/or' of the gender framework, and points instead to the concept of *dual presence,* as developed by Italian feminists in the 1970s. This represents the mindset of women at this time who self-identified in a 'cross-wise' manner. These women saw themselves as subverting *but not abandoning* conventional feminine role models by operating in *many* arenas *across* the social spectrum. They did not allow the world to be symbolically divided up into 'men's business' and 'women's business' – they continually transgressed, did things they were not supposed to do and caused men's and women's activities to merge until the gender divide, at the level of action at least, became more fluid (Gherardi 1995: 94–5). In a similar vein, Mats Alvesson and Yvonne Due Billing, in their critique of the feminine in management literature in particular, agree with Gherardi that it makes 'no distinctions ... between different groups of women (or men) or historical and culturally different settings' (2000: 148) and Judy White's (1995) research into female executives concludes that these women were more different in their approach to leadership than they were similar. She suggests that these differences derived from their varying ages, experiences and expectations.

Other key problems with approaches which connect gender and management style include the fact that their conclusions might be seen only to reinforce the stereotypical recruitment patterns which are already apparent in management practice. We already know that management functions like human resources are female ghettos, and that women predominate in such areas because they are widely understood to have particularly well-developed people skills, to be more intuitive, more sympathetic and more effective communicators than men. Such gender-based segregation at work limits women's opportunities in management, as well as those of their male counterparts, who may be considered insufficiently masculine if they undertake positions which are seen to fall under the heading of 'women's work': indeed they may experience difficulties in gaining access to these kinds of jobs per se. By way of contrast, Epstein argues that:

> Women ought to be in management because they are intelligent, adaptable, practical, and efficient – *and* because they are capable of compassion, as are other human beings ... men also can (and do) express [humanitarian values] if they are not made to feel embarrassed about showing them. And those categories of toughness and drive that many men are made to feel comfortable with should be prized in women who wish to express them when they are appropriate. The category is 'people', not 'men and women'. (Epstein, *Harvard Business Review* 1991: 151, emphasis added)

Relatedly, Amanda Sinclair argues against 'comparative studies of female versus male leaders, which only [serve] to further entrench the dominant assumptions and norms of leadership against which women are measured' (2005: 5). In addition, and as Diane Meehan (1999: 39) notes:

> In many ways, women cannot win. They are criticized for adopting the masculine model of management, but they are also likely to be criticized for displaying an overtly feminine approach, which may be perceived as weakness by others or, in its extreme form, as betrayal of other women. It is difficult to know what is more irritating to other women: a woman manager operating within the masculine model or one who flutters her eyelashes.

Meehan here suggests that 'feminine' approaches to managing others, especially if they are pronounced, may be interpreted by others, not least other women, as inappropriate for the cut and thrust of organizational life, the tough realities of the global marketplace. We know already that at least one of the feminine in management theorists, Beverley Alimo-Metcalfe, concurs with this, although she sees such judgements as misguided in the face of the particular economic challenges that we currently face. However, Meehan then develops the point to claim that women managers who adopt exaggeratedly feminine styles may be despised by female colleagues *in particular* for trading on their sexuality at work. Likewise, Paula Nicolson (1996: 124) claims that 'Women who achieve at work frequently are seen as having "used" their sexuality, while men are seen as being "natural" or as having been "used" by the woman'.

An apposite example of Nicolson's claim is the controversy surrounding the apparent honeytrap laid for former Cabinet Minister David Blunkett by estate agent Sally Anderson. Having been introduced to Blunkett in upmarket London nightclub Annabel's, Anderson later hired PR agent Max Clifford to assist in selling her 'kiss and tell' story of their alleged affair to the British tabloid press. Blunkett hotly denied their relationship and – despite an earlier resignation following accusations that he had illegitimately arranged a visa for a former lover's nanny, and his return to a ministerial post in May 2005 – remained in office (Hinsliff 2005). Or at least he did until resigning for a second time, just weeks later, over his failure 'to seek the counsel of the advisory committee on business appointments over his directorship of DNA Bioscience' (Wintour 2005). The widespread media use of 'honeytrap' to describe the tactics used by Anderson to supposedly lure Blunkett into their liaison indicates the belief that her feminine 'wiles' were the MP's downfall – and of course assessments like these imply prevailing processes of 'feminization' which construct women as inescapably and irrevocably feminine and the feminine as damaging, even pathological, in organizational contexts.

Equally, however, as Meehan also recognizes, women face problems in adopting a more masculine approach to management. Epithets like the 'Iron Lady' as applied to Margaret Thatcher, underlining her cool, emotionless demeanour and unerring ability to make the toughest of decisions, but at the same time intended as a criticism of these qualities in a woman, demonstrate how discomfiting it can be for others to see women transgressing the gender boundary. Such vilification is also more recently evident in the widespread sniping at Katie Hopkins, who in June 2007 became the first contestant to quit the BBC's popular business competition/reality television series *The Apprentice*. Competitors here battle it out for a six-figure salary position with well-known British entrepreneur Sir Alan Sugar's firm Amstrad. Hopkins, who had already caused a media splash due to tabloid photographs documenting her affair with a married man as well as her liaison with a fellow contestant, was subsequently sacked from her £90,000 a year job as a brand consultant for the Met Office for bringing her employer into disrepute. Meanwhile she had also been subjected to what Gareth McLean (2007) describes as 'dubious – and, were it real life, surely illegal – interviews, in which [only] the female contestants were grilled about their family situations and childcare arrangements' by Sugar. Ironically, mother of two Hopkins decided to leave the show only minutes after being told she had qualified for the final due to worries about moving her children from Devon to London should she win. But Lisa Jardine *(Guardian* 2007) suggests it is:

> No wonder [Hopkins] wobbled and decided to stand down from the final – under that kind of pressure I would have done so too. If we were to take it seriously (which I hope we will not), [this] show set back the cause of equality in the workplace and, in particular, senior women's employment prospects by about 20 years.

However, it is the media demonization of Hopkins' behaviour during the competition which is most significant for our purposes here. She has been described, amongst other things, as a 'peak-time schemer' (Lawson 2007); a 'bed-hopping, acid tongued alpha female' (Conlan 2007); embodying a 'nauseating and unsophisticated model of "feminism"' and mistaking 'unkindness for strength' *(Guardian* 2007, Williams); 'the most terrifying, unpredictable screen villain since Sadako from the movie *Ring* (Brooker 2007) having a tendency to 'depressing', flirting and 'transparently bitchy put-downs' *(Guardian* 2007, Pool); and being 'an entirely self-created being, a triumph of mind over matter, duplicity over emotion, a cold, hard surface, reflecting back whatever she thinks her audience is looking for' *(Guardian* 2007, Cochrane). Most of these comments were, it should be noted, made by other women. But those who rallied to Hopkins' defence point out that her apparently ruthless and stop-at-nothing behaviour during the series would more than likely be called 'business acumen' in a man *(Guardian* 2007, Jardine). And Deborah Hargreaves *(Guardian* 2007) goes further:

> Many profess to be shocked by Katie's naked ambition. But is that because it is so unusual in a woman? I believe that many women do not get to the top because they are far too nice. Nice is good in one's personal life, but nice people tend to get shafted in business. It is interesting to note that out of the three women running FTSE 100 businesses, two of them – Marjorie Scardino at the publishing group Pearson and Cynthia Carroll at the mining giant Anglo American – are from the US, where it is more acceptable for women to show their go-getting side.

Carlene Boucher (1997: 154) agrees that women managers face a double bind. She quotes one of her respondents as saying that 'influencing' as a style of management is, she feels, 'more condoned for women' than the direct (and masculine) approach of simply telling someone to do something. Boucher goes on to suggest that a woman who 'tells' as opposed to 'selling' may well attract derogatory nicknames like 'bossy boots' – a term which, she also remarks, would never be used to describe a man. Mari Teigen (1999: 97) echoes Boucher's point in her analysis of the case of a woman who failed to secure an administrative position at the Norwegian Directorate of the Coast, and was rejected because she was defined as 'domineering and arrogant'. However, as Teigen also points out, 'If we think about gender differences in terms of binary oppositions, identical behaviour from a decisive and self-confident man might appear as dominating and arrogant coming from a woman.' Mats Alvesson and Yvonne Due Billing (1997: 183) agree that any deviation on the part of women managers from the transformational style often leads to unfair evaluations of their performance, and Tomlinson et al. point to these sorts of judgements being made about women managers by their *female* colleagues, quoting, for example, a store manager who says that 'there is a tendency among some women [managers] to over-react, try to be too hard and too severe to prove that they're not a weak-kneed woman' (1997: 222). Relatedly, Judy Wajcman (1998), in a study of companies that had been recognized as having exemplary equal opportunities policies, found that despite this those policies could not reach to the heart of such prejudices, and that women wanting to achieve corporate success were forced to 'manage like a man' or suffer the consequences.

A picture therefore emerges of female managers continually having to work to prove their 'gender competence' (Gherardi 1995: 135–6), whereby they are permitted to achieve at work, so long as they also and simultaneously do all the things and have all the feelings that 'proper' women do and have – wanting and having husbands and children, sustaining close and intimate relationships with others, seeking to placate and persuade as opposed to asserting themselves and so on. The massive global success of the Fox Television series *Ally McBeal* and Helen Fielding's *Bridget Jones* novels (both of which have been made into successful films) neatly demonstrates what modern Western society expects of its 'career women', and can be at least partly explained by Ally's and Bridget's combining workplace ability and hankerings for hearth and home (Brewis 2004). The connections made between gender and management style by the feminine in management literature in particular can be seen only to reinforce such problematic stereotypes.

It is also worth reminding ourselves that the same literature tends to claim that women's 'special' approach derives from the division of domestic labour and the consequent socialization of women to be nurturing, caring and comforting so that they are later able to care adequately for children and run welcoming and functional homes. A celebration of the skills that result from such socialization runs perilously close to reinforcing the patriarchal positioning of women as *properly* in charge in the private sphere. We should remind ourselves as well that expectations of women with regard to domestic labour already make it difficult for them to accede to and succeed in management, given the challenges of combining organizational demands with a full load of household duties. Moreover, women managers could end up being exploited as peacemakers or as troubleshooters, being called upon to resolve conflicts, make cuts and carry out dismissals, as a result of the assumed connection between their gendered socialization and their particular repertoire of management skills. Finally, it is also true to say that women can be caring and loving parents at home and demanding, transactional managers at work, which blows the key assumption behind most gender in management claims out of the theoretical water (Alvesson and Billing 2000: 149–50, 151, 153–4). To summarize, in asserting women's 'preference' for a transformational approach, commentators like Rosener fail to question the gender divide and thus end up being complicit with it. Indeed, as long as they continue to label women's managerial behaviour as typically different from men's, they reinforce the assumed connection between women and femininity and thus continue to ensure that women who do not conform will always be subject to assessments which derogate them. As Alvesson and Billing argue, 'In this way "knowledge" of female managers creates its own truth effects – it does not so much mirror as produce socially constructed "reality"' (Alvesson and Billing 1997: 146; also see Alvesson and Billing 2000: 150–1). As an alternative to this kind of argument, we would argue that any analysis of gender and managerial work must take into account not only the orientation to work that gender socialization *outside* the organization might produce, but also how the experience of work *in itself* produces and maintains particular forms of gender identity. Relatedly, we would contend that gender identity is much more dynamic and much less rooted in biological sex than the analyses provided by the gender in management school might imply. That is, we would argue that the process of becoming gendered continues *and changes* through life. How then does this process happen in the organization? How are our subjective experiences of gender informed and moulded by what happens in our workplaces? The final part of our discussion in this chapter, which deals with the gendering management perspective, seeks to answer these questions.

CASE EXAMPLE   Breaking through the glass ceiling? (1)

Clare Francis, 37, a rising star in the City, is in the 'marzipan layer', described as the layer beneath the icing. The 'icing' is made up of executive directors and board members.

A mother of two children, aged two and four, she is managing director and head of financial markets sales at Lloyds TSB. She looks after a global team of 120 people and a range of customers from multinational corporations to retail and private clients, advising them, from a risk management perspective, on interest rates, hedging, foreign exchange and balance sheet management.

'I went to the London Business School and worked in Asia and America early on. If you have the will to succeed, you can. If you are the only woman in a meeting with a client, you will be remembered', she said.

She gets up at 4.45 a.m. to commute 65 miles into London and returns home at 8.30 p.m., 'but I can do flexible working on one or two days. I have things like the latest Blackberry and can plug into the office from home.'

She attributes her success in part to a supportive husband, Jamie. 'He has his own property company so works from home quite a lot. We decided to settle near our parents so we have a great support network.'

Her advice is: 'If you don't succeed at first, try and try again. I am one of four sisters and come from a competitive background – I do think competitive sport helps.'

'The opportunities for women now are enormous. In my peer group, the head of structuring is a woman; the head of strategy is a woman. Above me, the head of corporate banking is a woman and in the senior management team, there are three women – one is head of risk, one is head of the retail bank, and one is finance director.'

Source: http://www.telegraph.co.uk/news/main.jhtml;jsessionid=AA3ZKUCXS0BU
5QFIQMGSFGGAVCBQWIV0?xml=/news/2007/01/05/nwomen105.xml

> **CASE EXAMPLE** Breaking through the glass ceiling? (2)
>
> Barbara Thomas Judge, the first woman chairman of the UK Atomic Energy Authority, wanted to be an actress but her mother was having none of it.
>
> 'She told me "we are having no starving actresses in this house. If you want to act, do it in front of a jury and become a lawyer"', says Lady Judge.
>
> A dual citizen of Britain and the USA, she was born Barbara Thomas and educated at New York University law school.
>
> In 1978 she became partner in a law firm and 'lightning struck' when she was appointed by President Carter to the powerful US Securities and Exchange Commission, the youngest person, and only the second woman, to serve on the Commission, the equivalent of the Financial Services Authority.
>
> When her then husband moved to Hong Kong, a friend advised her to work for a British rather than an American bank there, and she became a board member of the merchant bank Samuel Montagu & Co.
>
> Now living in Britain, she holds numerous senior positions including deputy chairman of Friends Provident.
>
> Her advice to girls is to study hard – 'people always go back to "What A-levels did you get? Did you get a First Class degree?" – and to graduate in something like law, medicine or accountancy. Women should also help other women. Men have been helping each other get on for years.'
>
> Lady Judge, 60, who remarried three years ago, acknowledges she has made sacrifices. 'I only had one child (a son, Lloyd, now 23). I would have liked to have more, but I deferred motherhood until I was 36.'
>
> She also works long hours. 'I get up at 5.30 a.m. and I always have a breakfast meeting. I get home at 7 p.m.'
>
> *Source*: http://www.telegraph.co.uk/news/main.jhtml;jsessionid=AA3ZKUCXS0BU5QFIQMGSFGGAVCBQWIV0?xml=/news/2007/01/05/nwomen105.xml

Gendering management

This approach has it that not only is one's identity as male or female, masculine or feminine, something separate from one's biological sex, but that the development of one's sense of oneself as gendered is the powerful result of discourse. Masculinity and femininity in this analysis are clusters of textual roles created by the operations of contemporary discourse around gender difference, roles which individuals must strive to live up to. The discourse of gender difference therefore shapes and delimits the possibilities open to us as men and women (Butler 1990, 1998, 2004; Brewis et al. 1997: 1277). Most men, it is true, never reach the fantasized ideal of masculinity, the kind of image popular heroes like actors George Clooney and Brad Pitt or sportsmen Zinedine Zidane and Lleyton Hewitt project, just as few women look like model Giselle Bundchen, actresses Cameron Diaz and Scarlett Johansson or singer Kylie Minogue.

As Pat Nivins (quoted in Bornstein 1998: 23) argues:

being a woman (or a man for that matter) is a lot like being an Aryan superman – a myth. Gender is a continuum with very few people at either extreme, and everybody else in the middle. At some point you just have enough characteristics of one or the other where society sees you as being of a particular gender.

Deborah Kerfoot (2000: 238) agrees that it is crucial to recognize the difference between real women/men as individuals, and 'Woman'/'Man' as a discursive category. However, it is also true to say that such images of the Real Man and the Real Woman, of the Perfect Genders, and the degree to which they are valued, certainly inspire ordinary people to work towards them; in fact Kate Bornstein (1998: 41) argues that it is precisely the impossibility of these standards that means most of us continue to be motivated to achieve them. As a result, they may be experienced as oppressive, for example through anorexia or bulimia nervosa, or the condition known as body dysmorphic disorder. Moreover, the fact that actors, sports stars and singers are rarely anything much like their images does not matter – the images may not be real, but they have effects in the real world, on real men and women. Bornstein's (2006) most recent work extends this concern into exploring ways of preventing suicides resulting from experiences of being 'different' – which has always, according to Bornstein, in reality encompassed most of us (Bornstein 1995).

This suggests that we as human individuals come to know who we are through being exposed to particular interpretations of what it is to be human, in this case, either male or female, masculine or feminine. Because we are expected to be either/or, we create and reinforce these stereotypes in our everyday acts and interactions with others. Moreover, gender identity here is not the *inevitable* product of biological sex: as Mats Alvesson and Yvonne Due Billing have it, 'there is not an automatic relationship between body, specific processes of social construction and a set of characteristics/orientations' (1997: 218). How we understand ourselves and how we work to present those selves to the world may in fact be the diametric opposite of our physiological sex. There is considerable evidence, for example, that women managers labour to distract their colleagues from their female bodies, in order to emphasize that they are just as capable of the masculine behaviours and demeanour which we have already identified as desirable in the modern organization. Formal kinds of office dress such as suits and blouses, which avoid any hint of sexuality and lend their wearer a professional, almost asexual image are an example of this labour (Brewis et al. 1997: 1287–8; Brewis 1999: 90–1; Brewis and Sinclair 2000: 200).

Indeed, we could even argue that sex itself is less a matter of biological reality than of social construction, given the medical profession's insistence on labelling even newborns with the most ambiguous of sex organs as boys *or* girls (O'Donovan 1985; Fausto-Sterling 2000). Even in nature, gender can be changeable (see Exhibit 8.6). And as Kate Bornstein (1995, 1998: 26) asks: 'who says that penises are male and vulvas are female?' She also points out that, although many cultures across the globe give babies a fixed and immutable gender at birth, dependent on the presence or absence of a penis, some allow or even encourage gender changes later in life (1998: 28). An example of the latter case would be the general acceptance (although not absolute tolerance) extended to *katoey* (biological males who display some degree of transgendered behaviour) in Thailand. Stephen Linstead and Alison Pullen

279

(2006b) observe that as many as *five* genders have been recorded operating in social systems globally. Nonetheless, we would also acknowledge that the powerful discursive connection between sexed body and gender identity (Kerfoot 1999: 186; Whitehead and Moodley 1999: 2; Alvesson and Billing 2000: 146) means that it is men who are more likely to identify with the masculine and women with the feminine.

Exhibit 8.6

Clownfish change size and sex to move up the ranks

What the movie *Finding Nemo* doesn't tell you about clownfish is that they're all transsexuals. In a study published in the journal *Nature,* evolutionary biologist Peter Buston and colleagues report that clownfish in Papua New Guinea reefs can change their sex at will for social reasons. Clownfish live in strict hierarchical communities. Each neighbourhood is dominated by a top-ranking female breeder. Her male partner is next, followed by up to four progressively smaller, non-breeding fish. When the dominant female dies, her mate changes sex and becomes female. The top-ranking non-breeder becomes a sexually active male, and all the other fish shift up a rank. Clownfish also appear to regulate their size in order to remain part of the group. Each fish keeps its body mass 20 per cent smaller than the fish directly above it in social rank, probably to avoid conflict. Fish who disrespectfully outgrow their rank are rejected by the clan.

Source: Extract from an adaptation by Katherine Redding and Kathleen M. Wong from a press release from the California Academy of Sciences 31 June 2003.

The upshot of this analysis, though, is that women may strive to project a masculine identity just as men tend to. Masculinity therefore is *not* what men do and what they are without thinking much about it: men have problems being men, and they certainly do not have exclusive property rights on masculinity (Kerfoot and Knights 1993: 660; Kerfoot 1999: 186). Neither is being male definitive or exhaustive of all that men are or can be (Kerfoot and Knights 1996: 85). The masculine subject is, rather, 'that person who invests a sense of being in masculine discourses; those languages, practices and symbols that speak to stereotypical ways of being a man, and which are subsequently dominant or hegemonic in various sites across the social field' (Kerfoot and Knights 1999: 201).

Masculine values

As implied in our discussions of the transactional management style, the prevailing discursive form of contemporary Western masculinity revolves around being rational, objective, sure of oneself, logical, decisive, unemotional, tough and competitive. This masculinity centres on control. It means being explicit and assertive, saying what you think and speaking your mind plainly; being outer-focused, possibly aggressive; valuing work, sports and organized activities; being action-oriented, liking to get things done, a doer; being analytical or calculating about situations, rather than intuitive, relying on hunches or gut feelings; being dualistic, or tending to see things as black or white, either/or; preferring quantitative solutions which involve numbers to qualitative ones which involve opinion; linear thinking (for example X causes Y, making predictive connections) rather than lateral thinking (making unusual connections, being creative); being rationalist, valuing reason more than emotion or playfulness; being reductionist, liking to reduce things to their simplest terms and principles, rather than relishing subtle differences; being materialist, with a constant eye on resources, costs and benefits; being constantly aware of one's position in a hierarchy, engaging in one-upmanship with colleagues, striving to maintain the upper hand and protect oneself from challenges; and isolating oneself from others and rejecting dependence on them (Hines 1992: 328; Tannen 1993: 24–5, cited in Nicolson 1996: 146; Stobbe 2005). Not all men will exhibit all, or even most, of these features of masculinity, because the whole taken together is a stereotype, but it is one which still resonates powerfully in Western society, even at the level of myth.

Nonetheless, there is a hidden fear at the heart of this version of masculinity. In taking a position in the world which emphasizes being active and assertive over others rather than yielding, listening and being gentle, men reject intimate relations and achieve social status and esteem by means which glorify force – in war or sport – or by force expressed as power in business and politics. Men then typically have difficulty handling their feelings because feelings make them vulnerable and womanly. Emotion is dangerous because it is impossible to fully control. Only certain feelings, like anger, which may be channelled towards competitive organizational goals, may be legitimately expressed (Reynolds 1992). Moreover, because masculinity revolves around control, sustaining this way of being in the world compels those who subscribe to it to look for constant reassurance *that they are actually in control*. Any evidence of weakness is simultaneously evidence of personal failure. And because social relations are far from being predictable or stable, control is only rendered all the more desirable for being impossible to attain/maintain. Consequently, those who seek to be masculine find their identities continually threatened; the masculine, far from being a seat of contentment and complacency, is a particularly worrisome place; an identity on which one must work continually to gain, assert and retain control (Hines 1992; Kerfoot and Knights 1993, 1996; Kerfoot 1999, 2000).

Despite its anxiety-generating tendencies, striving to identify with this form of masculinity is nonetheless likely to make the individual a successful organizational participant, someone deemed suitable to manage others, because modern management itself is largely a masculine activity. As Kerfoot (2000: 241–2) points out, employment security and material success, as well as the 'psychic kick' of sensations of mastery, are therefore two good reasons why people continue to work at being masculine, even though it is fraught with never-ending challenges. That is, masculinity is as beguiling as it is anxiety making. Men and women who aim towards success at work, or who already belong to the ranks of management, are therefore likely to be particularly driven to identify with masculinity, or, as regards the women at least, to achieve an acceptable balance of masculine and feminine attributes. Nor is it just managers who prize it as the organizational gold standard. Deborah Shepherd and Judith Pringle (2004), for example, suggest on the basis of their research at a New Zealand IT manufacturing company that a cultural change initiative was strongly resisted by *'people at all levels* devising strategies for subverting, ignoring or undermining the change initiatives. This resistance manifests itself in various communications exchanges, jokes and non-compliant behaviours.' (emphasis added).

On closer examination, the cultural initiative, had it been successful, would have shifted the organization from a very masculine culture (prizing individualism and competition) to a much more feminine one (valuing teamwork, diversity and a focus on customers). As Shepherd and Pringle suggest:

> While using gender as an analytical tool carries with it the risk of rigid or literal application of masculine and feminine as dichotomous categories, these dimensions do provide a useful and powerful analysis for understanding the layers of micro resistance to organizational change. (2004: 173)

Gendered norms such as these extend beyond management as practice to management *education,* at least according to Amanda Sinclair. She comments on her students' expectation 'that business school teachers would be tough, dominant males who knew it all, either from their research but more often from their extensive experiences consulting to industry'. This led, in the early days of her academic career at least, to her trying to ape 'the aggression, and intellectual and physical dominance of the classroom that I observed in the "most successful" of my colleagues'. Although she describes her attempts in this regard as unsuccessful, Sinclair goes on to aver that:

> the lure of belonging is an aphrodisiac for men and the women who find themselves accepted by the group, and it encourages a high level of conformity, as we have seen in the complicit silence against bad practice in boardrooms in Australia and the United States. (2005: 6)

In other words, and to emphasize the point, women just as much as men might be 'seduced by a masculinist way of being' (Whitehead 1999: 27) and the organizational advantages it seems to offer, which at the very least derive from not standing out against a masculinist backdrop (also see Sheppard 1989; McDowell and Court 1994; Collinson and Hearn 1996; Brewis et al. 1997; Collinson and Collinson 1997; Kerfoot and Knights 1998; Kerfoot 1999, 2000; Alvesson and Billing 2000).

Masculine modern management, then, as we have seen, requires its incumbents to remain in control, of themselves, others and the environment, by virtue of level-headed decision making, undertaken without anger, emotion or bias. Such management is therefore, as Ian Lennie (2000: 130–5) claims, predicated on a Cartesian separation of mind and body, on metaphorical disembodiment, within which the manager knows the world through detached, objective, cerebral observation and is therefore able to change it, by virtue of directing others' bodies in the execution of particular kinds of labour. As he argues, the management 'order' understands 'the sensual world as manageable, in the sense that it stands waiting to be shaped by the vision of a knowing subject' (Lennie 2000: 134). Being able to exercise managerial prerogative, carrying out the 'right to manage' others in contemporary organizations, also depends on instrumental control, on sustaining output through imposing targets that are quantifiable and often highly abstract, but which carry penalties if not achieved and are coercively policed, through the threat of discipline or dismissal, for example (Kerfoot and Knights 1996: 90). Managers therefore need to demonstrate their ability to take command, to show that they are capable of 'being "on top of" things ... to appear always in control of situations, even where circumstances dictate that this could not possibly be the case' (Kerfoot 2000: 232).

The successful 'alpha male' is, for many feminist writers, the unacceptable masculine that is to be avoided. But as Flett (2008) argues, if only for the reason that business is still dominated by males, the alpha male is a phenomenon to be understood and dealt with, rather than simply rejected or imitated. Fleet's argument is that women in business sabotage their own success by either voluntarily giving up their power to men, or by attacking each other in 'trying to get on the guy's team'. Indeed Flett argues that the 'greatest enemy to women in business is women in business', and that 'managing like a man' is not the same as knowing how men manage and how to deal with it. Although Fleet's book is not based on academic research, it is both based on business experience and extensive work done with women in top management roles developing strategy, and makes some insightful practical observations that often square with theory. Indeed, while there has been academic work on the different ways in which men and women communicate, Flett identifies the kind of problems that can ensue when the communication involves the ego-sensitivities of the alpha male to perceived advice, feedback or criticism (see Exhibit 8.7)

EXHIBIT 8.7

Common communication

What women say	Problems with alpha males What the alpha male hears
'I wish that meeting had finished on time.'	'You suck at running meetings.'
'I'm surprised that client didn't come in.'	'You can't pull the trigger effectively.'
'I'd like a rise because I've been here a year.'	'I should get more money because I've stuck it out, not because I'm worth more this year.'
'Why can't this team just get along?'	'You are really poor at managing people.'
'You should go and talk to Ben.'	'You don't know how to do your job, manage your people, or control situations, so I need to point them out for you.'
'I'd like to help you on something.'	'You suck and need someone to pull your head out of your ass.'
'Your wife must be a very strong woman.'	'You are a piece of shit who is lucky to have a woman.'
'I think we need to pay more attention to the clients.'	'You are asleep at the wheel and sinking this ship.'
'You are setting unrealistic expectations.'	'You are completely screwed in the head.'

Source: Adapted from Christopher V. Flett (2008) *What Men Don't Tell Women about Business: Opening Up the Heavily Guarded Alpha Male Playbook* Hoboken, NJ: John Wiley, p. 75.

Unsurprisingly, those who identify as feminine (arguably mainly women, although this category can include those men who either choose not to or cannot perform masculinity) are uncomfortable with or marginalized by management's masculinity. They find its competitiveness, bureaucratic impersonality, emotional coldness and lack of intimacy alien. They struggle with what Nickie Charles (2002: 43) describes as the:

> informal networks in which power is located ... the cultural processes within the workplace which maintain a situation in which men who are white, middle class, and heterosexual predominate in positions of power ... the actions of gendered social actors which maintain gender divisions of paid work.

This may result in these individuals distancing themselves from the content and the context of their work, appearing detached and uncommitted, valuing home, friends and family above their job; but at the very least it will translate into a constant sense of dissonance at work, a feeling of not fitting into the organizational environment (Kerfoot 1999: 188). Indeed there is empirical evidence to the effect that even women who have reached the organizational peak may opt out. Judi Marshall (1995), for example, talks of how her middle and senior management respondents paused to assess their careers, which for many then led to a period of unemployment as a result of their disassociation from the male organizational cultures in which they were employed. In a similar vein, Michelle Martinez (1997) quotes Judy Rosener's (1997) claim that 'Most women [managers] don't want to fit into a male-dominated company mold', as well as citing research data from the US consultancy Catalyst which suggest that 'The women [managers, all of whom had quit their jobs] ... surveyed were either moving to companies who provided a more level playing field, or starting their own businesses'. In fact Catalyst (1998) have produced a manual which they suggest will enable organizations to retain their female human resource, based on 'best practices from the corporate leaders'. Organizations cited include Motorola, Deloitte and Touche, IBM, Avon, American Airlines, McDonald's and Texas Instruments.

Another category of 'female escapee' is the woman achiever who gives up work because she finds juggling work and domestic commitments impossible, and wants to put her family first. Former barrister Naomi Rose, for example, who has a school-age daughter and a baby son, gave up her job when she realized that her devotion to her children far exceeded any commitment to her clients, and that hiring someone suitable to care for them while she worked would in fact cost as much as she was earning. As Maureen Freely points out, Naomi is also a woman who was 'raised to think that all able-bodied adults were meant to work and that work was the only route to a secure and dignified life' (1999: 1). In a similar vein, Brenda Barnes, former president/ chief executive of Pepsi-Cola North America, left her £ 1 million plus a year position so that she could spend more time with her three offspring. As she herself puts it:

> After years of hectic travel, dinner meetings, missing children's birthday parties and even living in separate cities from my husband as we both pursued careers, I decided I had made enough trade-offs for Pepsi. Now I need to give my family more time. I want to be like any other housewife. (quoted in Gordon 1997: 7)

These women, then, are rejecting the liberal feminist discourse that Christina Hughes (2002) refers to as 'Women have made it', wherein the successful 'performance' of femininity (like masculinity) hinges on achievements in the world of work, as opposed to the more traditional grounds of motherhood and putting their families first (Nicolson 1996: 10; Jamieson 2000 [1998]: 218). As Hughes also points out, this 'making it' requires that women experience high levels of job satisfaction, put in long hours at the office and pursue promotion opportunities assiduously – she also notes that women such as these are much less likely to be mothers (2002: 40 – also see Brewis 2005: 1830–1).

However, it isn't just women who 'bail out' – consider, for example, Daniel Petrie, former vice-president of Microsoft. Petrie was very attracted in the first instance to working for Bill Gates, despite the lengthy working days required. Many employees slept at the office or worked around the clock; at the very least a 12–hour day was expected. However tiring the work was, Petrie also states that he wanted to be a part of the energy and buzz which such high levels of commitment engendered. Nonetheless, he hadn't worked at Redmond Campus (the Microsoft HQ in Seattle) very long when the work started to take its toll. The trigger was the birth of his first child, but the feelings got worse when Petrie's sister was killed in a car accident. He started to absent himself from meetings held at unsocial hours, and told his staff to go home when he felt they had worked too hard or for too long. The upshot was that Petrie quit his job and went home to Australia to build a lifestyle which allowed for a shorter working week and more time with his kids – despite the disbelief of his Microsoft colleagues, who couldn't believe what he was giving up (Swan 1996).

British men who followed Petrie's lead include Danny O'Neill, who left his CEOship at the Britannic insurance group after only seven weeks in favour of more time with his children, and Richard Girling, RM software firm's former chief executive, who quit shortly after O'Neill in order to 'catch up on life' (quoted in Frith 2003). Then there is Alan Milburn, who left his job as Health Secretary because, as he explained in his resignation letter to Tony Blair:

> I have found it increasingly difficult to balance having a young family in the Northeast with the demands of being a cabinet minister ... I have already missed a good bit of my children growing up and I don't want to miss any more ... (quoted in Waugh 2003)

Milburn's decision came as a particular blow to Blair as he was very committed to the latter's New Labour endeavours and extremely loyal to his party leader.[7] In this regard we can also consider data from the pressure group Fathers Direct that suggest that 'only one in five men is happy with the time spent at work, compared with 35 per cent 10 years ago' (Frith 2003), as well as findings indicating that fathers tend to work longer hours than their childless counterparts, such that, for example, a third of fathers but less than 25 per cent of non-fathers work a 50 hour plus week. One explanation for this is that both men and women are having children later – at 'the time at which their jobs become most demanding' (Frith 2003). Also relevant are the claims made by Ning Tang and Christine Cousins, who suggest of both the UK and the Netherlands that 'it is men, and especially fathers, who report high levels of conflict between work and family life ... the inability to reconcile [the two] ... is related to their long working hours, especially in the UK' (2005: 542).

The crucial point here is that modern work environments encourage and nurture traditionally masculine ways of relating to self and behaving. However, organizations are not the only social site where this takes place, and masculinity is not uniform. Amanda Sinclair (1998: 61, citing Maddock and Parkin 1993: 76, and Collinson and Hearn 1994), for example, lists the various kinds of masculine managerial subcultures that may exist in modern organizations:

- traditional authoritarianism (maintained via bullying and a culture of fear)
- gentleman's club (protectionism, paternalism, based on the assumption that men are born to rule)
- entrepreneurialism (task-oriented, a workaholic culture)
- informalism (schoolboyish, 'larky', attached to sporting and sexual rituals)
- careerism (values expertise and bureaucratic career progression)
- gender-blind (everyone, regardless of gender, is 'one of the boys')
- feminist pretenders (supportive of equality but the onus is on women to make the necessary changes, that is, take the responsibility for developing equality)
- smart macho (highly competitive, driven by performance, discriminates against those who cannot work at the desired pace or who question the competitive ethos).

Neither is masculinity static. Deborah Kerfoot (1999, 2000; also see Kerfoot and Knights 1999) asserts that demands on managers are changing as organizations become increasingly concerned with flexibility and quality in order to ensure responsiveness to customers and therefore continued profitability in a highly charged business environment. Kerfoot argues that managers now find themselves responsible for getting the best out of their staff, fully exploiting the creativity and potential of their organization's human resource and extracting the optimum levels of productivity and service, as opposed to simply seeing workers as a 'necessary evil' (Kerfoot 1999: 191). She suggests that managers now have to 'communicate with, rather than dictate to, subordinates. This in a manner that demands more sophisticated means of control and direction than through the traditional impersonal hierarchical chain of command' (2000: 232). That is, Kerfoot has it that a certain 'feminization' of management is taking place within which managers must display both 'social skills' and 'emotional awareness', and build at least a degree of intimacy with their staff. This, she also claims, creates difficulties for managers because intimacy of any kind equates to a certain vulnerability, a revealing of aspects of oneself that self-estranged forms of masculinity insist are hidden away. Secondly, developing relationships with staff is both time-consuming and unpredictable in terms of quantifiable outcomes, and therefore 'troubling to masculinity' for these reasons (Kerfoot 1999: 194).

Robyn Thomas and Annette Davies (2005), in their analysis of the ways in which individual managers (both male and female) interpret and respond to the discourse of New Public Management (NPM),[8] also identify a potential conflict in the gendered expectations associated with emerging managerial regimes. They quote respondents' suggestions that in the police service, for example, there was simultaneously a masculinist emphasis on 'time-space commitment', evidenced by visibility, 'being available', working long hours as a 'badge of pride' and 'living on the job', as set against 'the promotion of so-called feminine leadership skills, such as counselling, coaching and support … This means being more "tolerant", showing mutual respect and valuing equal opportunities'. As Thomas and Davies comment, the managers they spoke to reacted to this in various and multi-faceted ways. Kate, a civilian manager, for instance, discusses how she has now adapted her working week since becoming a mother, as she refuses to privilege her career over her family. She comments that it is easier for her as a civilian to do this than for a male senior officer who, as a single parent, on one occasion wanted to leave work at 5 p.m. to care for his sick child, but did not feel able to do so. Thus Kate draws here on the more feminized aspects of the NPM discourse to resist 'the competitive masculinized subject position' (Thomas and Davies 2005: 693) which it also constructs – although she simultaneously accepts that this might come at the price of career advancement. We can see similarly contradictory and shifting identity practices in Caroline Essers and Yvonne Benschop's (2007) study of female Moroccan and Turkish entrepreneurs in the Netherlands. Here, for example, these five respondents seek to balance the discursive expectations they face as migrant women against those of being a successful entrepreneur by denouncing 'their femininity in business negotiations' and relocating it 'to interactions with clients that call for warmth and friendliness'. Thus they juggle their gender identities to resolve the conflict between their gendered ethnicities and their roles as businesspeople in a Western context.

Perhaps, then, as Kerfoot and Knights (1999) suggest, new forms of management are challenging dominant forms of masculinity. Do those identifying with 'old' masculinity – controlling, detached, impersonal, hierarchical – risk having their carefully honed traits and behaviours deemed unproductive in current organizational environments, even to the extent that these men and women lose their jobs? Can we speculate that:

> an unintended consequence of such [new management] practices would lead to a fundamental questioning of masculinity in management, organization and subjectivity? Does such critical reflection on the business of management itself [hold] the key to creating the conditions within which an alternative means of managing can emerge – one that is grounded in non-instrumental modes of relating to others? (Kerfoot and Knights 1999: 212)

In fact we would argue that such changes in management techniques and approaches can be seen very differently; the required shift towards a more open and engaged form of communication on the part of managers could be understood as a colonization of the feminine with the result of reinforcing the edifice of masculinism. This may well make management/masculinity easier to perform in the sense that it becomes less anxious and less obsessed with controlling its 'trying on' of feminine intimacy. As Arthur Brittan has it, 'hegemonic masculinity is able to defuse crisis tendencies in the gender order by using counter and oppositional discourse for its own purposes' (1989: 187).

The above analysis supports the view that masculinity is historical *in itself*, existing in different forms in different times, in different cultures and in different locations within the same culture (also see Connell 1995; Alvesson and Billing 2000; White-head 2004). However, while organizational masculinity itself might shift in emphasis, or exist in multiple forms in the same cultural site, or even in multiple forms in the same organization, this is unlikely to mean that men relinquish any of their privilege; although what is also clear is that the requirement to do masculine behaviour, of whatever sort, is a social challenge, not a natural expression of the essence of being male (Whitehead 2002, 2004 and see Exhibit 8.8). In the workplace, behaving in this way in order to succeed as a 'manager' is *problematic:* the demands of masculine management are potentially damaging, not just to male (and female) managers themselves, but also to their staff, colleagues, customers, families and the community at large. In the first edition of *Rethinking Organisational Behaviour*, Norman Jackson and Pippa Carter (2000: 197; also see Hales 2001: 70–1) offer an especially evocative example of the ways in which an emphasis on quantifiability, neutrality and the bottom line require almost inhuman responses to very human problems. They cite the case of a flaw in the Ford Pinto which meant that in certain conditions the fuel tank would rupture, the vehicle catch fire and the occupants burn to death, or at the very least sustain serious injuries. Ford decided it was *more efficient* simply to pay out on the resultant insurance claims than to work on redesigning the car, or even call in the existing model for repair. Would, ask Jackson and Carter, the victims and their families have agreed with this assessment of the best way to proceed?

EXHIBIT **8.8**

What kind of a man is your man-ager?

1.	ACHILLES	Sophisticate. Charming but flawed.
2.	ADONIS	Bodily obsessed, may sport a fake tan.
3.	ALPHA MALE	Extremely competitive, lives for the next deal.
4.	BACKPACKER	Sexy but dangerous: relationship day-tripper.
5.	CHAMELEMAN	Adaptable, smooth, urbane, attractive – but never the man you think he is.
6.	CLUB MAN	Blazers, old school ties, football shirts. Into male bonding.
7.	COOL POSER	Very fashion-conscious.
8.	CORPORATE MAN	Relishes security; a follower – not a leader. And also faithful.
9.	GADGETMAN	Techno-freak, poor eyesight. Insular and socially inept.
10.	JEFFREY	Social animal in a world of half-truths. Compelling character.
11.	JESTER	Loves laughter and an audience but prone to melancholy.
12.	LIBMAN	Pro-feminist male; politically correct, very well read.
13.	MANCHILD	Ageing stud: rich tastes, little dignity.
14.	MR ANGRY	Moody, aggressive but doesn't see his actions as damaging.
15.	MURDOCH	Napoleonic self-belief, usually justified. Ruthless, untiring.
16.	NEANDERTHAL	Anti-feminist with outdated views on relationships.
17.	PREACHER	Fundamentalist views. Single-minded, fervent and intense.
18.	RISKER	Optimistic and overdrawn at the bank. Likes to push his luck.
19.	ROMANCER	Calculating seducer. Dislikes women but pursues them.
20.	ROTTWEILER	Lager drinker who loves his mates and his country.
21.	SIGMUND	Lots of inner angst, low self-esteem but reliable and caring.

22.	TEDDY BEAR	Sensitive, vulnerable and a good listener – but not sexy.
23.	TRAIN SPOTTER	Middle-aged, plenty of brown cardigans and obsessed with data collection.
24.	UNIFORM MAN	Emotionally insecure. Rigid, brittle temperament.
25.	WALLFLOWER	Unambitious couch potato with predictable behaviour.
26.	(JOHN) WAYNE	Heroic, unchanging, loyal and steadfast.
27.	ZEBEDEE	Floundering and confused. Needs nurturing. Unreflective but busy.

Source: Based on Stephen Whitehead (2004) *The Many Faces of Men: The Definitive Guide to the Male Species*, London: Arrow.

In contrast to arguments discussed above, and the diversity approach in particular, our emphasis here is therefore much less on the connection between gender and management as a route to business efficiency. We are interested in the fact that, in the quest to become a 'real manager', people may come to depersonalize others, turn them into objects and resources rather than see them as fellow human beings. At the same time, sacrificing a whole range of one's own experience causes managers to become desensitized, further diminishing their capacities to empathize with and care about others, even themselves, suppressing 'a range of emotions, needs, and possibilities, such as nurturing, receptivity, empathy, and compassion ... because they might restrict [the] ability and desire to control [them]selves or dominate [other] human beings' (Kaufman 1994: 148). Macho managers who are hard on their employees are often even harder on themselves, and this self-sacrifice is another important element of masculine experience (Donaldson 1991). At the end of this process of stifling emotion, thwarting impulses, suppressing spontaneity for the sake of control, concealing true feelings and intentions – the process of *self*-discipline -managers come to regard their selves as just another resource, just another commodity to be 'downsized' if necessary (Jackall 1988). Management is predicated on particular forms of masculine identity work which limit the range of possibilities for managerial subjects to interact with others, and thus make for alienation and self-estrangement, but which simultaneously devalue other, more engaged forms of interaction (Kerfoot and Knights 1996; Kerfoot 1999, 2000). Thus managers may do things, but they do not necessarily feel that it was them*selves* who acted – they often see themselves as playing a role. Similarly, they may endure a great deal of stress as a result of the alienating and disembodying effects of the management role, becoming unable to assess the effects that the labour of management is having on their physical and emotional well-being. It may be others who have to inform such an individual of the damage that he or she is sustaining as a result (Lennie 2000: 135–6).

Furthermore, as Mike Donaldson (1991: 21–2) sees it, this form of masculinity turns on the man sacrificing himself for his family through submitting himself to the challenges of the working day, so that even though the role of breadwinner affords him a certain level of power, it is not without its costs. Indeed, there are data which suggest that fatherhood can impel men to spend *more* time at work for the sake of the child: new fathers feel driven to work *harder and longer* in order to provide better for their progeny, especially if the child is a boy (Kettle 2000). It may also be that men (and women) build their reputations as managers by spending as much time at work as possible. The Thomas and Davies data cited above certainly bear this out, as do David Collinson and Margaret Collinson (1997) quoting another male senior manager who jokes about making 'guest appearances at home' and his female colleague who works a 70-hour week and has a full-time live-in nanny for her children. In a similar vein, research carried out at Edinburgh University suggests that high-flying men, who view a 10-hour working day as normal, spend as little as 15 minutes a day with their children. Many, suggests this study, 'are enslaved by an office culture that regards pleas of wanting to spend more time with their children as professional vulnerability' (Harlow 1999: 5).

Indeed former British Prime Minister Tony Blair, a self-identified 'family man', was emphatic that he would not be taking leave following the birth of his fourth child. Blair in fact insisted until immediately after the birth that he would simply be scaling down his workload, because being prime minister was not the kind of job that one could simply abandon in order to spend more time with new arrival Leo (born May 2000) and his mother Cherie. This was in spite of Cherie's previous public announcement that she was very impressed by the decision of Finnish Prime Minister Paavo Lipponen to take six days off following the birth of his second child in March 2000, and that she expected her husband to follow suit. In the event, it was announced three days after Leo's birth that Deputy Prime Minister John Prescott would take over Blair's duties temporarily while the family decamped to Chequers, although Blair still remained in overall charge of the country (Jones 2000; Jones and Barwick 2000; Ward and Black 2000).

Blair, though, was far from alone amongst his party in finding that the demands of his job potentially compromised his home life. Stephen Whitehead (1999: 22) quotes one of Blair's female MPs on her obsession with her work:

> Politics takes over and dominates your life. It shapes the rest of your life and time with the family ... politics imposes tremendous sacrifices in people's families. The sacrifice is mainly made by our partners and children ... I'm conscious that in pursuing politics in the way I have done I haven't spent time with the family.

Feminine values

In the light of the above, the question we must now ask is: Would feminine values provide an alternative to the dominance of masculine identities in workplaces? Ruth Hines says yes, feminine values should be reintroduced into organizations to balance out the values of controlling, competitive, aggressive masculinity. She claims that the existing imbalance is damaging to personal survival, growth and wholeness, psychologically, physically and spiritually. This argument says that what is at stake is not just the suppression of *women,* individually or as a group, but the suppression of ways of thinking, feeling and acting that are considered *feminine*. These possibilities for thinking, feeling and acting become unavailable to women *or men* (Hines 1992: 314–15, 317). The wide-ranging taboo on the feminine at work is seen to be problematic because organizational subjects come to relate to themselves and others in highly restricted and restrictive ways. They can neither be fully themselves nor fully *human*. A better balance of organizational values would therefore ensure a healthier workplace. Carol Frenier (1996) concurs. Writing from a perspective informed by the psychology of Jung, Frenier asserts that we all have masculine and feminine aspects to our characters, whether we are male or female. She goes on to claim that an injection of feminine values into modern organizations, to complement the existing emphasis on the masculine, will make our progress towards genuinely sustainable lifestyles (a goal she sees as particularly important) more straightforward. Frenier claims that the feminine turns on dialogue, reflection and the development of community, the better to challenge some of the maxims we organize by, for example 'growth is the name of the game'. Her theme is one of encouraging not only our continued well-being but also our commercial success.

Lisa Zanetti (2006), while taking a much less managerialist angle on the subject than Frenier, 'addresses the undercurrents of discomfort, unease and even fear that surround the presence of women in the workplace' from a perspective similarly informed by Jungian depth psychology. One of her arguments turns on Jung's 'anima' and 'animus', which are his:

> conception of our relationships with the opposite sex ... The anima represents the feminine side of male, and the animus is the masculine side of females. A fully developed personality allows these complementary aspects to be expressed in consciousness and behaviour ... [but] in Western culture, the anima and animus are often repressed or underdeveloped. (Zanetti 2006: 98)

Of course the irony, as Frenier and Zanetti both point out, is that femininity is undervalued in the Western organization: thus women who aspire to career success will often permit their animus full rein. And '[w]hen women stand up for themselves [in this way] ... they often constellate their male colleagues' devouring mother complexes' (Zanetti 2006: 113), so ensuring the persistence of discursive constructions of achieving women as 'career bitches', 'ball-breakers' and so on (also see Sinclair 2005: 3, 4). Carlene Boucher (1997) on the other hand suggests that the women managers she spoke to about leadership sought to actively 'reject the stereotypical (male) values of a leader (emotional distance, objectivity, unconditional confidence, and so on) and develop a clear sense of their own values'. This, she argues, *tempers* 'some of the more potentially self-destructive aspects of this social construction of leadership' (Boucher 1997: 155) through an emphasis on connectedness and relatedness (with oneself and others), integrity and honesty.

The kind of argument presented by Hines, Frenier, Boucher and Zanetti does not *necessarily* privilege the feminine *over* the masculine but, rather, catalogues the problems which an *im*balance of values can generate in the organization. It claims that organizations should be informed by a consideration of what they presently do not welcome, the values of the feminine, or at least by a critical examination of the masculine character of modern organizational values/managerial practice and its consequences. As Mats Alvesson and Yvonne Due Billing (2000: 149) suggest, although there are undoubtedly problems with some of the available constructions of feminine values, as well as with certain suggestions about how they can benefit organizations, as we have already established in our discussion of the gender in management literature, feminine leadership could 'be seen as a constructive counterfoil to prevailing or older ideas about leadership, a counterfoil making it easier for a number of females – and progressive men – to identify with leadership and get some guidelines and legitimation'. They continue by pointing out that men and women who manage using the *range* of gendered behaviours may well be more effective because of their ability to care and share *as well as* to direct and control.

However, the problem with the 'imbalance of values' position is that in some of its forms it remains attached to its liberal feminist origins. It tends to be written in a paradoxical combination of demands for political action and gentle new age spirituality: the idea of 'balance' in particular implies inertia. As a view of gender, this is, as we have implied above, too *static*. Gender emerges and changes in a *dynamic* between a variety of features and forms of masculinity and femininity, which grow alongside each other. Indeed Kate Bornstein (1998: 8–9) argues that our gender identity might change hour by hour, minute by minute, even second by second:

> In response to each interaction we have with a new or different person, we subtly shift the *kind* of man or woman, boy or girl, or whatever gender we're being at the moment. We're usually not the same *kind* of man or woman with our lover as we are with our boss or a parent. When we're introduced for the first time to someone we find attractive, we shift into being a different *kind* of man or woman than we are with our childhood friends. We all change our genders.

This argument is not new. In the 1850s Engels remarked that within the working class the men were the bourgeoisie and the women the proletariat, in an internal relation of domination in which the oppressed *supported* the oppressors (Campbell 1984). Beatrix Campbell provides a detailed discussion of how this relationship continued to work in the north of England during the depression of the early 1980s. As she points out, in establishing such relations detail is everything. Ongoing studies of the organizational micropractices by which gendered subjectivity is shaped, the actual relations of power, knowledge and gender in talk, myth, image and action, need to be produced as a matter of course if we are to understand better how gendered identity emerges, is changed by and itself affects management practice over time.

Moreover, we should perhaps point out that, even in those studies which do not seek to assert the superiority of femininity over masculinity, there is perhaps a tendency at best to downplay what masculine values have to offer us in organizational terms. Straightforward derogation of masculinity, and a call for a feminization of organizations (as evident in much of the gender in management literature), is problematic, not least because it argues for a reversal of the relations between the norm and the margins, such that the feminine moves to centre stage and the masculine takes over her inferior position (Brewis et al. 1997: 1294–7). But even where this does not happen, there is a notable absence of analysis which acknowledges that masculine ways of doing things in organizations have afforded us considerable benefit over time: for example how masculinity is integral to scientific, economic and technological progress, how masculinity gets things done because it is task-focused and how *beneficial* forms of production and development (for example medical innovations) can be attributed to masculine behaviours and orientations (Alvesson and Billing 1997: 202). Furthermore, if we accept the proposition that most capitalistic organizations are instrumentally driven, being premised upon an efficient use of resources and a strong orientation to results which may at times necessitate cost cutting and an exploitation of available labour, then perhaps the idealized feminine is not in practice 'fully transferable to all or most [existing] organizations'; that it may in fact be of most relevance in '"family-like" organizational contexts' such as nurseries, rest homes, daycare centres and their ilk (Alvesson and Billing 2000: 150).

Conclusion

In sum, then, 'gendering management' identifies the ways in which gender and management actually interact. It does not focus on management as a process which needs to result in organizational effectiveness (at least not the kind of effectiveness which many commentaries take as their benchmark, where enhancement of the bottom line appears as the be-all and end-all), nor does it measure its value in accordance with its contribution to that process. Rather, it suggests that the most interesting and socially valuable material that can be gained from a study of management is a focus on how and why it happens in the way that it does. For some commentators in recent years, 'gender' needs to be thought differently. Calás and Smircich (2006) argue that it cannot be extricated from wider textures of difference that include race, ethnicity and class and extend globally. Ely and Padavic (2007) argue similarly that gender is systemic, but cannot be extricated from other identity systems that entail disparities of power and equality, and Joan Acker (2006) coins the term 'inequality regimes' to describe particular and localized intersecting patterns of discrimination. Taking the argument further, Judith Butler (2004) and Judith Lorber (2005) argue that gender as a concept has become too restricting, and that the next tasks are 'ungendering' or 'degendering'. Linstead and Pullen (2006a, 2006b, 2008) argue that this amounts to a recognition of the fluidity of gender. Yet regardless of the theoretical significance of these arguments, in the specific context of management practice, the concept of gender has continued importance and draws our attention to persistent political inequalities that, despite three decades of discussion and attempted change, have not been overturned.

Finally, to return to our set of opening questions. By now you should be able to come up with some answers to these for yourself, so, rather than answer them for you, we will finish with a guide to where we discuss the issues in the text.

Answers to questions about gender

1. What is expected of managers in modern Western organizations? What should be expected? How does this relate to gender? The feminine in management approach; Masculine values.
2. To what extent has management theory made room for gender? Classical management theory; Human relations theory; Maslow's hierarchy of needs; Later management theories; Gender in management; The feminine in management approach; Gender globalization; Gendering management; Masculine values; Feminine values.
3. Is gender a profit issue or a moral issue? Liberal feminism; Radical feminism; Diversity; Masculine values.

4. Are you more likely to attain a management position if you are male? Liberal feminism.

5. Are men and women concentrated in different occupations? Liberal feminism.

6. What is positive discrimination? Liberal feminism.

7. Are women equal to or different from men? Liberal feminism. Radical feminism.

8. Is globalization creating more opportunities for women or perpetuating their subordination? Gender globalization.

9. Does being male or female make a difference to the way you manage? Gender in management; Assessing the gender in management argument; Gendering management; Masculine values.

10. Do men experience gender-related problems too? Masculine values.

11. Would a 'feminization' of organizations represent a desirable alternative? Feminine values.

12. What is the relationship between gender and management? Gender and management – the whole chapter.

And one final question. Thinking back to the case of Chris Stefano in Chapter 1, what gender is Chris? We deliberately did not give any clues, but you probably gave Chris a gender anyway. Thinking about how you came to ascribe to Chris the gender you did might give some clues as to your own potential gender bias.

REVISITING THE CASE STUDY

So, having discussed gender and management in theory at some length, let us try to apply some of our ideas in practice by returning to our case study questions. The case is fictionalized, but is drawn from our research – the problems of Matthew and Julie are real ones.

1. What are your impressions of TransCorp as an organization?

To begin with, it seems from the case that TransCorp is an organization which expects its employees to work long hours – Matthew, as deputy production manager, routinely works at least a 12-hour day, and his staff are also expected to work beyond the confines of 9 to 5 if the organization requires it. TransCorp's culture also appears to emphasize a very impersonal mode of interaction – staff are expected to leave their personal feelings at home. This is evident in the symbolism of Matthew's office, a shrine to efficiency and lack of distraction. TransCorp is also an organization which values hard-headedness, logic and the bottom line in decision making. Matthew is relieved that he does not have to make the difficult choice as to who will work during the summer shutdown, but he is expected to come up with a staffing plan to cover that period, which focuses on minimum cost and maximum output and seemingly pays little attention to the effects on the staff involved (and indeed those who aren't involved). Finally, it seems that TransCorp does not value its staff sufficiently to listen carefully to their opinions and needs. The layout of Matthew's office, with its desk positioned to provide both a physical vantage point (others can't sneak up on him) and a symbolic barrier between himself and visitors, is testimony to this. As is, perhaps more evocatively, David's insistence that the production staff are simply 'goofing off' when they fail to turn up on time for an earlier-than-usual shift start.

2. What does the description of Matthew's day tell you about what it means and how it feels to manage in TransCorp? What do you think is expected of managers in this organization?

TransCorp can be seen as a very masculine organization, conforming to Ruth Hines' (1992: 328) description of the prevailing form of Western masculinity as 'hard, dry, impersonal, objective, explicit, outer-focused, action-oriented, analytic, dualistic, quantitative, linear, rationalist, reductionist and materialist'. Its culture emphasizes formal rationality, which is instrumental, calculative and directed at the efficient achievement of goals, at the expense of substantive rationality, which has more to do with reflecting on goals themselves, assessing whether or not these goals, if achieved, will lead to fulfilment and satisfaction for those involved. This is evident, as we might anticipate, in what TransCorp requires from its managers. Matthew is expected to keep his staff in line, to control them (David's insistence that he talks to the latecomers on the early shift); to appear formally dressed at all times (having to put his jacket back on to visit the shop floor); to put organizational targets above the needs of his team (reiterating the requirement for them to start their shift early to meet a particular deadline); and to approach his managerial work with the bottom line always in mind (the 'radical' plan required for the shutdown).

3. Given Matthew's feelings about his work, does it seem to suit his preferred managerial style?

It is clear that Matthew resents having to be one of the boys, or at least having to align himself with the prevailing definition of masculinity/management at TransCorp. One might surmise from his objection to having to work long hours, behave in a dictatorial manner with his staff and suppress emotion in dealing with others that his personal preference might lean more towards what Judy Rosener (1990) and others call a transformational leadership style: encouraging staff participation in goal setting; relating to staff as equals; interacting with and leading staff by virtue of his personal qualities rather than his managerial position; having some measure of intimacy with his staff; and being sensitive to the effect his actions have on his staff and others in the organization. So we might suggest that Matthew's image of himself as a manager conflicts, at least to some extent, with what TransCorp actually requires of him and, furthermore, that he perhaps resists the discourse of masculinity which prevails in the wider society. It seems that he does not necessarily conceive of himself as masculine in terms of being rational, objective, sure of himself, logical, decisive, aggressive and competitive, nor yet does he fear the expression of emotion. Thus to a degree Matthew is the kind of man that Silvia

Gherardi (1995) acknowledges as (ideally) preferring to work within a more democratic organizational framework and manage in a more democratic way, like the majority of male managers surveyed by the British Institute of Management (Vine 1997). He therefore subverts either/or assumptions about the gender framework.

4. What does this suggest about Matthew's view of himself as a manager and/or as a man?

However, Matthew also identifies with the prevailing managerial discourse at TransCorp because, it is implied, he will not make the grade at work if he does not – and we know from Deborah Kerfoot's (2000) and Amanda Sinclair's (2005) work that making the grade in this kind of management affords not only employment security and material success, but also the thrill associated with feelings of mastery. Matthew has not, therefore, rejected the masculine identity that life in TransCorp creates, sustains and reinforces, to the extent that he finds himself marginalized by it or he has to opt out, as Judi Marshall (1995), Judy Rosener (1997) and Deborah Kerfoot (1999) suggest might happen to those who find such values alien. He does find his work exciting and challenging, and also satisfying (although at the same time he resents it for what it forces him to do). Thus Matthew has not reached the stage where his 'experience of managerial ... work is one of dislocation, and a continual sense of being at odds with [his] environment and the working practices that surround [him]' (Kerfoot 1999: 188). It is arguably this ambiguity in his life as a manager and as a man which creates specific problems for him. He obviously finds his work stressful and entirely too demanding at times. He does not eat properly during the day, he wakes up tired and goes to bed exhausted. He anticipates with anxiety any confrontations during the day, like the one with the personnel on the morning shift, and any negative consequences of the decisions he makes, like his plan for the summer shutdown. However, he is not sufficiently disaffected to withdraw from TransCorp, as is made clear when he reacts angrily to Sarah's request for him to come home early and look after their children. This in itself reveals an enduring commitment to TransCorp on Matthew's part – he mutters to himself that he is struggling to keep it all together at work, in a crucial period for the company.

5. What are the consequences of Matthew's behaviour as a manager:

(a) for him as an individual?
(b) for his staff?
(c) for Sarah and his children?

(a) What does managing mean for Matthew, working within an organization which values a particular kind of masculinity as being the most appropriate way to interact with others and relate to oneself and one's managerial work? As we have seen, this form of masculinity is not necessarily one to which Matthew himself fully aspires, which causes him not inconsiderable difficulty, but, at the same time, he is also able to lose himself in it, to the extent that he does not always acknowledge the impact that this identification has on him as an individual. His constant fatigue is just one of the ways in which managing takes its toll, although he also berates himself for not having arrived at work earlier on the day with which the case study deals, and he goes to bed that night having set the alarm for 5.30 a.m. the following morning. As Ian Lennie (2000) points out, it may well be others who bring to a manager's attention just how much damage they are doing to themselves through their constant efforts to 'play the organizational game'. Managing, then, is partly a trap, yet it is also rewarding and frequently exciting – it represents a paradox.

(b) Matthew's approach to management, conforming as it does to the prevailing culture at TransCorp, also has ramifications for his staff, as he is rendered unable to listen to their complaints or suggestions, and instead exercises managerial pre-rogative in any situation of conflict. He is disengaged from their concerns and only permits himself to care about them in his more depressed moments. That is, Matthew for the most part has to suppress any tendencies to empathize with and feel compassion for his staff. His managerial labour means that he must be largely dismissive of their needs (Kaufman 1994; Kerfoot and Knights 1996; Kerfoot 1999, 2000), except on the odd occasion where, for example, he relates to them having to work longer hours than usual, or feels concern for those who will be denied overtime for working the summer shutdown.

(c) Finally, Matthew spends very little time at home with his family, which Sarah clearly resents, and of which he himself is dimly aware. However, one might surmise that he also has a nagging sense that he is doing the right thing for his family by acting as the breadwinner (which might be argued to be a compo-nent of the prevailing form of masculinity, as Mike Donaldson (1991) has sug-gested), and therefore perhaps fails to realize what he may be doing to them by allowing work to take over his life. Certainly, as David Collinson and Margaret Collinson (1997), John Harlow (1999), Stephen Whitehead (1999), Martin Ket-tle (2000) and Christina Hughes (2002) all point out, it is by no means unusual for men (and women) in senior positions to work extremely long hours, even when they have young children.

6. Julie tells Matthew that she is disgusted by the comment that David makes about her legs. What other problems might you expect a female manager in TransCorp to encounter?

Expectations of managers at TransCorp mean that women within the organiza-tion are also subject to the demands of masculinity if they aspire to success, as Stephen Whitehead (1999) and others suggest is commonly the case. Indeed, Julie complains to Matthew that she is expected to walk, talk and behave like a man by TransCorp in order to prove herself as a manager. However, Julie's other com-plaint is that TransCorp also expects her to retain some measure of femininity. For example she says that her colleagues 'look at me like I've just landed from Mars if I turn up in trousers'. This bears testimony to the particular problems experienced by women managers, or by those women who aspire to managerial positions, in organizations like TransCorp. On the one hand, they have to relate to themselves and behave in a very masculine way, which may be difficult because of the par-ticular way that women are socialized to be feminine within modern Western cul-tures (Rosener 1990, 1997; Alimo-Metcalfe 1995; Helgesen 1995). On the other hand, they must not appear to be too masculine, as they will be punished in equal measure if they step too far beyond their prescribed societal gender role, that is, femininity, which Deborah Kerfoot and David Knights (1996: 87) describe as 'not instrumentally attached to securing itself through projects and goals, and ... more engaged with, rather than detached from, the world'. The balance can be difficult to achieve, as researchers such as Deborah Sheppard (1989), Silvia Gherardi (1995), Mats Alvesson and Yvonne Due Billing (1997, 2000), Carlene Boucher (1997), Frances Tomlinson et al. (1997), Diane Meehan (1999), Mari Teigen (1999), Robyn Thomas and Annette Davies (2005) and Amanda Sinclair (2005) have suggested, and Julie's disgust at David's sexism is evocative of this. The advantage that men like Matthew have over women like Julie, then, as implied by Stephen Whitehead and Roy Moodley (1999), Deborah Kerfoot (1999) and Mats Alvesson and Yvonne Due Billing (2000), is that the strong cultural link between biology and gender behaviour makes it more acceptable for male managers to identify with the masculine discourse of management than it is for female managers.

In short, we can see from the case that management is a process and a set of practices which can be usefully understood by reference to discourses of gender difference. Any exploration and analysis of gender in this context, as we suggested earlier, provides examples of the ways in which it intersects with, informs and is informed by managerial behaviour. In particular, this suggests that the predominance of masculinist discourses of management in organizations bears examination in terms of the particular challenges and demands that it presents for real managerial subjects. It would, however, be foolish, not to say inaccurate, to overestimate the power of gender as an organizing principle of management work; it is important to remember the potential perils of gender oversensitivity, as well as the need to acknowledge the other differences which 'criss-cross' our gender identities and render generalizations on the basis of 'all men' or 'all women' virtually impossible. While a consideration of the interaction between gender and management is a fruitful one through which to arrive at an understanding of what it means and how it feels to manage, there is also room for applying a similar analysis to issues of ethnicity, class, (dis)ability and the limitless other features of diversity (an inequality) which form important components of our relationship with ourselves as individuals and as managers. Recalling one of the major objectives of this book, what is important is that these things about which we tend to make assumptions are subjected to critical thinking. This is the only way in which we can guard against blindness – gender blindness, race blindness, disability blindness – in all its forms. We can then challenge suppression where it is found, and as a result we can learn, personally and organizationally, so as to be able to manage with our eyes wide open.

References

Acker, J. (2006) 'Inequality regimes: Gender, class, and race in organizations', *Gender & Society*, 20(4): 441–64.
Alimo-Metcalfe, B. (1995) 'An investigation of female and male constructs of leadership and empowerment', *Women in Management Review*, 10(2): 3–8.

Alvesson, M. and Billing, Y.D. (1997) *Understanding Gender and Organizations*, London: Sage.

Alvesson, M. and Billing, Y.D. (2000) 'Questioning the notion of feminine leadership: A critical perspective on the gender labelling of leadership', *Gender, Work and Organization*, 7(3): 144–57.

Anker, R. (1997) 'Theories of occupational segregation by sex: An overview', *International Labour Review*, 136(3): 315–37.

Arredondo, P. (1996) *Successful Diversity Management Initiatives*, Thousand Oaks, CA: Sage.

ArtsProfessional (2006) 'Salary survey: Discrimination writ large', 132(23 October): 11. Available at: http:// www.artsprofessional.co.uk (accessed 12 June 2007).

Bologh, R. (1990) *Love or Greatness: Max Weber and Masculine Thinking – A Feminist Inquiry*, London: Unwin Hyman.

Bornstein, K. (1995) *Gender Outlaw: On Men, Women and the Rest of Us*, New York: Vintage.

Bornstein, K. (1998) *My Gender Workbook: How to Become A Real Man, A Real Woman, The Real You, or Something Else Entirely*, New York: Routledge.

Bornstein, K. (2006) *Hello Cruel World: 101 Alternatives to Suicide*, New York: Seven Stories Press.

Bouchei, C. (1997) 'How women socially construct leadership in organizations: A study using memory work', *Gender, Work and Organization*, 4(3): 149–58.

Braverman, H. (1974) *Labour and Monopoly Capital: The Degradation of Work in the Twentieth Century*, New York: Monthly Review Press.

Brewis, J. (1999) 'How does it feel? Women managers, embodiment and changing public sector cultures', in Whitehead, S. and Moodley, R. (eds), *Transforming Management: Gendering Change in the Public Sector*, London: UCL Press, 84–106.

Brewis, J. (2004) 'Sex and not the city? The aspirations of the thirty-something working woman', *Urban Studies*, 41(9): 1821–38.

Brewis, J. (2005) 'Signing my life away? Researching sex and organization', *Organization* 12(4): 493–510.

Brewis, J. and Linstead, S. (2000) *Sex, Work and Sex Work: Eroticizing Organization*, London: Routledge.

Brewis, J. and Sinclair, J. (2000) 'Exploring embodiment: Women, biology and work', in Hassard, J., Holliday, R. and Willmott, H. (eds) *Body and Organization*, London: Sage, 192–214.

Brewis, J., Hampton, M. and Linstead, S. (1997) 'Unpacking Priscilla: Subjectivity and identity in the organisation of gendered appearance', *Human Relations*, 50(10): 1275–304.

Brewis, J., Linstead, S., Boje, D. and O'Shea, T. (2006) 'The passion of organizing: A critical introduction to new approaches to motivation', in Brewis, J., Linstead, S., Boje, D. and O'Shea, T. (eds) *The Passion of Organizing*, Malmö, Sweden: Liber AB, 13–31.

Bristow, J. (2002) 'Maybe I do', in Fox, C. (ed.) *Maybe I Do: Marriage and Commitment in Singleton Society*, London: Academy of Ideas, 14–31.

Brittan, A. (1989) *Masculinity and Power*, Oxford: Blackwell.

Brooker, C. (2007) 'Charlie Brooker's screen burn', *Guardian*, 9 June. Available at: http://www. guardian.co.uk (accessed 14 June 2007).

Brown, C. and Jones, L. (2004) 'The gender structure of the nursing hierarchy: The role of human capital', *Gender, Work and Organization*, 11(1): 1–25.

Brown, H. (1992) *Women Organising*, London: Routledge.

Burrell, G. (1997) *Pandemonium: Towards a Retro-Organisation Theory*, London: Sage.

Butler, J. (1990) *Gender Trouble*, London: Routledge.

Butler, J. (1998) *Bodies that Matter: On the Discursive Limits of Sex*, London: Routledge.

Butler, J. (2004) *Undoing Gender*, London: Routledge.

Calás, M. and Smircich, L. (1995) 'Dangerous liaisons: The "feminine-in-management" meets "globalization"', in Frost, P., Mitchell, V. and Nord, W. (eds) *Managerial Reality*, New York: HarperCollins, 164–80.

Calás, M. and Smircich, L. (2004) 'Revisiting "dangerous liaisons": Or does the "feminine-in-management" still meet "globalization"', in Frost, P., Nord, W. and Krefting, L. (eds) *Managerial and Organizational Reality: Stories of Life and Work*, Upper Saddle River NJ: Pearson Prentice Hall, 467–81.

Calás, M. and Smircich, L. (2006) 'From the "woman's point of view" ten years later: Towards a feminist organization studies', in Clegg, S., Hardy, C., Lawrence, T. and Nord, W. (eds) *Handbook of Organization Studies*, London: Sage, 284–346.

Campbell, B. (1984) *Wigan Pier Revisited: Poverty and Politics in the Eighties,* London: Virago.

Catalyst (1998) *Advancing Women in Business – The Catalyst Guide: Best Practices from the Corporate Leaders,* San Francisco, CA: Jossey-Bass.

Charles, N. (2002) *Gender in Modern Britain,* Oxford: Oxford University Press.

Chodorow, N. (1989) *Feminism and Psychoanalytic Theory,* New Haven, CT: Yale University Press.

Cliff, J.E., Langton, N. and Aldrich, H.E. (2005) 'Walking the talk? Gendered rhetoric vs. action in small firms', *Organization Studies,* 26(1): 63–91.

Collinson, D.L. and Collinson, M. (1997) '"Delayering managers": Time–space surveillance and its gendered effects', *Organization,* 4(3): 375–407.

Collinson, D.L. and Hearn, J. (1994) 'Naming men as men: Implications for work, organization and management', *Gender, Work and Organization* 1(1): 2–22.

Collinson, D.L. and Hearn, J. (eds) (1996) *Men as Managers, Managers as Men: Critical Perspectives on Men, Masculinities and Management,* London: Sage.

Conlan, T. (2007) 'The week', *Observer,* 10 June. Available at: http://www.guardian.co.uk (accessed 14 June 2007).

Connell, R.W. (1995) *Masculinities,* Sydney, NSW: Allen & Unwin.

Crompton, R. (1997) 'Women, employment and feminism in the Czech Republic', *Gender, Work and Organization* 4(3): 137–48.

Cullen, D. (1994) 'Feminism, management and self-actualization', *Gender, Work and Organization* 1(3): 123–37.

Cullen, D. (1997) 'Maslow, monkeys and motivation theory', *Organisation* 4(3): 355–73.

Cunningham, R., Lord, A. and Delaney, L. (1999) '"Next Steps"' for equality? The impact of organizational change on opportunities for women in the Civil Service', *Gender, Work and Organization,* 6(2): 67–78.

Daly, M. (1984a) *Gyn/Ecology: The Metaethics of Radical Feminism,* London: The Women's Press.

Daly, M. (1984b) *Pure Lust: Elemental Feminist Philosophy,* London: The Women's Press.

Davidson, M.J. (1997) *The Black and Ethnic Minority Woman Manager: Cracking the Concrete Ceiling,* London: Paul Chapman.

Davidson, M.J. and Cooper, C.L. (1992) *Shattering the Glass Ceiling: The Woman Manager,* London: Paul Chapman.

Donaldson, M. (1991) *Time of Our Lives: Labour and Love in the Working Class,* Sydney, NSW: Allen & Unwin.

Eagly, A.H. and Johnson, B.T. (1990) 'Gender and leadership style: A meta-analysis', *Psychological Bulletin,* 108(2): 233–56.

Elliott, J. (2003) 'Young mothers say they want to stay at home', *Sunday Times,* 6 March, p. 23.

Elliott, J. and Chittenden, M. (2003) 'Women "choose to have lower pay than men"', *Sunday Times, 6* April, p. 25.

Ely, R. and Padavic, I. (2007) 'A feminist analysis of organizational research on sex differences', *Academy of Management Review,* 32(4): 1121–43.

Enloe, C. (1990) *Bananas, Bases and Beaches: Making Feminist Sense of International Politics,* London: Pandora.

Enloe, C. (1993) *The Morning After: Sexual Politics at the End of the Cold War,* Berkeley, CA: University of California Press.

Equal Opportunities Commission (2006) *Facts About Women & Men in Great Britain 2006,* Manchester: Equal Opportunities Commission.

Equal Opportunities Commission (2007) *Sex and Power: Who Runs Britain? 2007,* Manchester: Equal Opportunities Commission.

Essers, C. and Benschop, Y. (2007) 'Enterprising identities: Female entrepreneurs of Moroccan or Turkish origin in the Netherlands', *Organization Studies,* 28(1): 49–69.

Everingham, C., Stevenson, D. and Warner-Smith, P. (2007) '"Things are getting better all the time?" Challenging the narrative of women's progress from a generational perspective', *Gender, Work and Organization,* 41(3): 419–37.

Fagenson, E.A. (1993) 'Diversity in management: Introduction and the importance of women in management' in Fagenson, E.A. (ed.) *Women in Management: Trends, Issues and Challenges in Managerial Diversity,* London: Sage.

Fausto-Sterling, A. (2000) *Sexing the Body: Gender Politics and the Construction of Sexuality*, New York: Basic Books.

Fayol, H. (1949 [1916]) *General and Industrial Administration* (translated by C. Storrs), London: Sir Isaac Pitman.

Fiedler, F. (1967) *A Theory of Leadership Effectiveness*, New York: McGraw-Hill.

Fiedler, F. (1974) 'The contingency model – new directions for leadership utilization', *Journal of Contemporary Business*, 3: 65–79.

Fletcher, J.K. (2003 [2002]) 'The greatly exaggerated demise of heroic leadership: Gender, power, and the myth of the female advantage', in Ely, R.J., Foldy, E.G., Scully, M.A. and the Center for Gender in Organizations, Simmons School of Management (eds), *Reader in Gender, Work and Organization*, Malden, MA: Blackwell, 204–10.

Flett, C.V. (2008) *What Men Don't Tell Women About Business: Opening Up the Heavily Guarded Alpha Male Playbook*, Hoboken, NJ: John Wiley.

Forster, N. (1999) Another "glass ceiling"? The experiences of women professionals and managers on international assignments', *Gender, Work and Organization*, 6(2): 79–90.

Fransson, S. and Thörnqvist, C. (2006) 'Some notes on workplace equality renewal in the Swedish labour market', *Gender, Work and Organization*, 13(6): 606–20.

Freely, M. (1999) 'Nice work if you can get it', *Observer* (Review section), 4 July, pp. 1–2.

Frenier, C. (1996) *Business and the Feminine Principle: The Untapped Resource*, Oxford: Butterworth Heinemann.

Friedan, B. (1963) *The Feminine Mystique*, New York: Dell.

Frith, M. (2003) 'Brain drain: The men who won't let jobs deprive them of fatherhood', *Independent*, 14 June. Available at: http://www.independent.co.uk (accessed 19 June 2007).

Gastelaars, M. (2002) 'How do statistical aggregates work? About the individual and organizational effects of general classifications', in Czarniawska, B. and Hopfl, H. (eds) *Casting the Other: The Production and Maintenance of Inequalities in Work Organizations*, London: Routledge, pp. 7–22.

Gherardi, S. (1995) *Gender, Symbolism and Organisational Cultures*, London: Sage.

Gilbreth, F.B. (1911) *Motion Study*, New York: Van Nostrand.

Gillespie, R. (1991) *Manufacturing Knowledge: A History of the Hawthorne Experiments*, Cambridge: Cambridge University Press.

Gilligan, C. (1982) *In a Different Voice*, Cambridge, MA: Harvard University Press.

Gordon, G. (1997) 'I gave up £1m a year for my three babies', *Daily Express*, 25 September, p. 7.

Goss, D. (1994) *Principles of Human Resource Management*, London: Routledge.

Grey, C. (1995) 'Review article: Gender as a grid of intelligibility', *Gender, Work and Organization*, 2(1): 46–50.

Grice, A. (2004) 'Milburn agrees election role as Blair faces down Brown', *Independent, 9* September. Available at: http://www.independent.co.uk (accessed 19 June 2007).

Griffin, S. (1980) *Woman and Nature: The Roaring Inside Her*, New York: Harper & Row.

Grimshaw, D. and Rubery, J. (2007) *Undervaluing Women's Work*, Working Paper Series (53), Manchester: Equal Opportunities Commission.

Guardian (2007) 'All fired up', 8 June. It incorporates: Cochrane, K.; Hargreaves, D.; Jardine, L.; Pool, H.; Williams, Z. Available at: http://www.guardian.co.uk (accessed 14 June 2007).

Hales, C. (2001) *Managing Through Organization: The Management Process, Forms of Organization and the Work of Managers* (2nd edn), London: Thomson Learning Business Press.

Harlow, J. (1999) 'Men give 15 minutes a day to children', *Sunday Times*, 23 May, p. 5.

Harvard Business Review (1991) 'Debate: Ways men and women lead', January–February pp. 151–60. It incorporates: Cohen, A.R. (p. 158); Epstein, C.F. (pp. 150–1); Goldberg, C.R. (p. 160); Mansbridge, J. (pp. 154–6).

Hayward, H. (1992) 'Management: Theory and practice', in Fulop, L. with Frith, F. and Hayward, H. (eds) *Management for Australian Business: A Critical Text*, Melbourne, VIC: Macmillan, pp. 186–212.

Hearn, J. and Parkin, W (1994) 'Sexuality, gender and organisations: Acknowledging complex contentions', British Sociological Association Annual Conference, 'Sexualities in Social Context', 28–31 March, University of Central Lancashire, Preston, UK.

Helgesen, S. (1995) *The Female Advantage: Women's Ways of Leadership*, New York: Currency/ Doubleday.

Hersey, P. and Blanchard, K.H. (1996) *Management of Organizational Behavior: Utilizing Human Resources*, Englewood Cliffs, NJ: Prentice Hall.

Hines, R. (1992) Accounting: Filling the negative space', *Accounting, Organizations and Society*, 17(3): 314–41.

Hinsliff, G. (2005) 'Blunkett accused of falling for "honeytrap"', *Observer, 9* October. Available at: http://www.guardian.co.uk (accessed 19 June 2007).

Hite, L.M. (2007) 'Hispanic women managers and professionals: Reflections on life and work', *Gender, Work and Organization*, 14(1): 20–36.

Hochschild, A.R. (2003 [2000]) 'The nanny chain', in Ely, R.J., Foldy, E.G., Scully, M.A. and the Center for Gender in Organizations, Simmons School of Management (eds), *Reader in Gender, Work and Organization*, Malden, MA: Blackwell, pp. 401–7.

Hodgkinson, M. (2007) 'McEnroe backs Wimbledon's sexual equality', *Telegraph.co.uk*, 22 February. Available at: http://www.telegraph.co.uk (accessed 12 June 2007).

Holtermann, S. (1995) 'The costs and benefits to British employers of measures to promote equality of opportunity', *Gender, Work and Organization*, 2(3): 102–12.

House, R.J. (1971) 'A path-goal theory of leader effectiveness', *Administrative Science Quarterly*, 16: 321–38.

Hughes, C. (2002) *Women's Contemporary Lives: Within and Beyond the Mirror*, London and New York: Routledge.

Jackall, R. (1988) *Moral Mazes*, Oxford: Oxford University Press.

Jackson, N. and Carter, P. (2000) *Rethinking Organisational Behaviour*, Harlow: Financial Times/ Prentice Hall.

Jamieson, L. (2002 [1998]) 'The couple: Intimate and equal?', in Jordan, T. and Pile, S. (eds) *Social Change*, Oxford: Blackwell, pp. 216–22.

Jones, G. (2000) 'Blair will not take full birth leave', *Electronic Telegraph*, 15 May, issue 1816. Available at: http://www.telegraph.co.uk (accessed 4 August 2000).

Jones, G. and Barwick, S. (2000) 'Leo takes a firm grip on power', *Electronic Telegraph*, 23 May, issue 1824. Available at: http://www.telegraph.co.uk (accessed 4 August 2000).

Joshi, H., Makepeace, G. and Dolton, P. (2007) 'More or less unequal? Evidence on the pay of men and women from the British Birth Cohort Studies', *Gender, Work and Organization*, 14(1): 37–55.

Kandola, R. and Fullerton, J. (1998) *Managing the Mosaic: Diversity in Action* (2nd edn), London: Institute of Personnel and Development.

Kaplan, E.A. (1992) *Motherhood and Representation: The Mother in Popular Culture and Melo-drama*, New York: Routledge.

Kasten, K. (1972) 'Toward a psychology of being: A masculine mystique', *Journal of Humanistic Psychology*, 12(2): 23–4.

Kaufman, M. (1994) 'Men, feminism, and men's contradictory experiences of power', in Brod, H. and Kaufman, M. (eds) *Theorizing Masculinities*, Thousand Oaks, CA: Sage, pp. 142–63.

Kerfoot, D. (1999) 'The organization of intimacy: Managerialism, masculinity and the masculine subject', in Whitehead, S. and Moodley, R. (eds) *Transforming Management: Gendering Change in the Public Sector*, London: UCL Press, pp. 184–99.

Kerfoot, D. (2000) 'Body work: Estrangement, disembodiment and the organizational "other"', in Hassard, J., Holliday, R. and Willmott, H. (eds) *Body and Organization*, London: Sage, pp. 230–46.

Kerfoot, D. and Knights, D. (1993) 'Management, masculinity and manipulation: From paternalism to corporate strategy in financial services', *Journal of Management Studies*, 30(4): 659–77.

Kerfoot, D. and Knights, D. (1996) '"The best is yet to come?"': The quest for embodiment in managerial work', in Collinson, D.L. and Hearn, J. (eds) *Men as Managers, Managers as Men: Critical Perspectives on Men, Masculinities and Managements*, London: Sage, pp. 78–98.

Kerfoot, D. and Knights, D. (1998) 'Managing managerialism in contemporary organizational life: A "man"agerial project', *Organization*, 5(1): 7–26.

Kerfoot, D. and Knights, D. (1999) '"Man" management: Ironies of modern management in an "old" university', in Whitehead, S. and Moodley, R. (eds) *Transforming Management: Gendering Change in the Public Sector,* London: UCL Press, pp. 200–13.

Kettle, M. (2000) 'Blair "defies dad's instincts"', *Guardian Unlimited,* 17 June. Available at: http://www.guardian. co.uk (accessed 4 August 2000).

Kugelberg, C. (2006) 'Constructing the deviant other: Mothering and fathering at the workplace', *Gender, Work and Organization,* 13(2): 152–73.

Lawson, M. (2007) 'Sugar and a touch of tabloid spice', *Guardian,* 14 June. Available at: http://www.guardian.co.uk (accessed 14 June 2007).

Lennie, I. (2000) 'Embodying management', in Hassard, J., Holliday, R. and Willmott, H. (eds) *Body and Organization,* London: Sage, pp. 130–46.

Linstead, S.A. (2000) 'Gender blindness or gender suppression? A comment on Fiona Wilson's research note', *Organization Studies,* 21(1): 1–7.

Linstead, S.A and Pullen, A. (2006a) 'Fluid identities and ungendering the future', in Pullen, A. and Linstead, S. (eds) *Organization and Identity,* London: Routledge.

Linstead, S.A and Pullen, A. (2006b) 'Gender as multiplicity: Desire, displacement, difference and dispersion', *Human Relations,* 59(9): 1287–310.

Linstead S.A. and Pullen, A. (2008) 'Ungendering organization', in Barry, D. and Hansen, II. (eds) *Handbook of New and Emerging Approaches in Organization Studies,* London: Sage.

Lorber, J. (2005) *Breaking the Bowls: Degendering and Feminist Change,* New York: W.W. Norton.

Lorbiecki, A. and Jack, G. (2000) 'Critical turns in the evolution of diversity management', British Journal of Management, Special Issue, 11(s1): S17–31.

Lowry, R. (ed.) (1982) *The Journals of Abraham Maslow,* Brattleboro, VT: Lewis Publishing.

McCloskey, D.N. (2000) *Crossing: A Memoir,* Chicago: University of Chicago Press.

McDowell, L. (2001) 'Changing cultures of work: Employment, gender, and lifestyle', in Morley D. and Robins, K. (eds) *British Cultural Studies: Geography, Nationality, and Identity,* Oxford: Oxford University Press, pp. 343–60.

McDowell, L. and Court, G. (1994) 'Performing work: Bodily representations in merchant banks', *Environment and Planning D: Society and Space,* 12: 727–50.

McLean, G. (2007) 'Watch this', *Guardian,* 13 June. Available at: http://www.guardian.co.uk (accessed 14 June 2007).

McNeil, M. (1987) 'Being reasonable feminists', in McNeil, M. (ed.) *Gender and Expertise,* London: Free Association Books, pp 13–61.

Maddock, S. and Parkin, S. (1993) 'Gender cultures: Women's choices and strategies at work', *Women in Management Review,* 8(2): 3–9.

Marshall, J. (1995) *Women Managers Moving On: Exploring Career and Life Choices,* London: Routledge.

Martinez, M. (1997) 'Prepared for the future: Training women for corporate leadership', *HRMagazine,* April. Available at: http://www.shrm.org/hrmagazine/articles/0497cov.htm (accessed 7 February 1998).

Maslow, A. (1939) 'Dominance personality and social behaviour in women', *Journal of Social Psychology,* 10(1): 3–39.

Maslow, A. (1954) *Motivation and Personality,* New York: Harper.

Matteson, M.T. and Ivancevich, J.M. (eds) (1989) *Management and Organizational Behavior Classics,* Homewood, IL: BPI, Irwin.

Mayo, E. (1945) *The Social Problems of an Industrial Civilization,* Boston, MA: Division of Research, Graduate School of Business Administration, Harvard University.

Mayo, E. (1960 [1933]) *The Human Problems of an Industrial Civilization,* New York: Viking Press.

Meehan, D. (1999) 'The under-representation of women managers in higher education: Are there issues other than style?', in Whitehead, S. and Moodley, R. (eds) *Transforming Management: Gendering Change in the Public Sector,* London: UCL Press, pp. 33–49.

Metro (2007) 'Black women excluded from power', 10 June. Available at http://www.metro.co.uk/news/article.html?in_article_id=52426&in_page_id=34(accessed 11 June 2007).

Ministry of Defence (n.d., *c.*2001) *The Wider Employment of Women in Ground Combat,* unpublished MoD document.

Mortlake, G. (2007) 'No thanks necessary for getting you girls the big moolah', *Observer*, 25 February. Available at: http://www.guardian.co.uk (accessed 12 June 2007).

Nicolson, P. (1996) *Gender, Power and Organisation: A Psychological Perspective*, London: Routledge.

Nyland, C. (1989) *Reduced Worktime and the Management of Production*, Cambridge: Cambridge University Press.

Nyland, C. (2000) 'An early account of scientific management as applied to women's work, with a comment by Frederick W. Taylor', *Journal of Management History*, 6(6): 248–71.

O'Donovan, K. (1985) *Sexual Divisions in Law*, London: Weidenfeld & Nicolson.

Oerton, S. (1996) 'Sexualizing the organization, lesbianizing the women: Gender, sexuality and flat organizations', *Gender, Work and Organization*, 3(1): 26–37.

Parker, B. (1998) *Globalization and Business Practice: Managing Across Boundaries*, London: Sage.

Quelch, J. (2000) 'Meet Britain's real rulers: The first men of the Footsie', *Independent on Sunday*, 5 March. Available at: http://www.independent.co.uk/www (accessed 28 July 2000).

Reynolds, L. (1992) 'Translate fury into action', *Management Review* 81(3): 36–8.

Roethlisberger, F.J. and Dickson, W. (1939) *Management and the Worker: An Account of a Research Program, Conducted by the Western Electric Company, Hawthorne Works, Chicago*, Cambridge, MA: Harvard University Press.

Roper, M. (2001) 'Masculinity and the biographical meanings of management theory: Lyndall Urwick and the making of scientific management in inter-war Britain', *Gender, Work and Organization* 8(2): 182–204.

Rosener, J.B. (1990) 'Ways women lead', *Harvard Business Review* (November–December): 119–25.

Rosener, J.B. (1997) *America's Competitive Secret: Women Managers*, Oxford: Oxford University Press.

Rutherford, S. (2001) 'Any difference? An analysis of gender and management styles in a large airline', *Gender Work and Organization* 8(3): 326–45.

Shepherd, D.M. and Pringle, J.K. (2004) 'Resistance to organizational culture change: A gendered analysis', in Mills, A.J., Thomas, R. and Helms-Mills, J. (eds) *Identity Politics at Work: Resisting Gender, Gendering Resistance*, London and New York: Routledge, pp. 160–76.

Sheppard, D.L. (1989) 'Organisations, power and sexuality: The image and self-image of women managers', in Hearn, J., Sheppard, D.L., Tancred-Sheriff, P. and Burrell, G. (eds) *The Sexuality of Organisation*, London: Sage, pp. 139–57.

Sinclair, A. (1998) *Doing Leadership Differently: Gender, Power and Sexuality in a Changing Business Culture*, Melbourne, VIC: Melbourne University Press.

Sinclair, A. (2005) 'Journey around leadership', *Melbourne Business School Working Paper*, 10 March. Available at: http://www.mbs.edu/index.cfm?objectid=E13C6AE6–BB7B-8DCE-3624BD265AB37182 (accessed 16 July 2007).

Sloan Management Review (1995) 'CEO thought summit', 36(3): 13–21.

Solonas, V. (1983) *SCUM Manifesto*, AIM/Phoenix Press.

Stenning, A. and Hardy, J. (2005) 'Public sector reform and women's work in Poland: "Working for juice, coffee and cheap cosmetics!"', *Gender, Work and Organization*, 12(6): 503–26.

Stobbe, L. (2005) 'Doing machismo: Legitimating speech acts as a selection discourse', *Gender Work and Organization* 12(2): 105–23.

Swan, N. (1996) 'Interview with Daniel Petrie', *Radio National* (Australia), 26 September.

Tang, N. and Cousins, C. (2005) 'Working time, gender and family: An East–West European comparison', *Gender, Work and Organization*, 12(6): 527–50.

Tannen, D. (1993) *You Just Don't Understand: Women and Men in Conversation*, London: Virago.

Taylor, F.W. (1947 [1911]) *Scientific Management*, New York: Harper & Row.

Teigen, M. (1999) 'Documenting discrimination: A study of recruitment cases brought to the Norwegian Gender Equality Ombudsman', *Gender, Work and Organization*, 6(2): 91–105.

Thomas, D.A. and Ely, R.J. (1996) 'Making differences matter: A new paradigm for managing diversity', *Harvard Business Review*, (September–October): 79–90.

Thomas, R.R. Jr (1990) 'From affirmative action to affirming diversity', *Harvard Business Review*, (March–April): 107–17.

Thomas, R.R. Jr (1991) *Beyond Race and Gender: Unleashing the Power of Your Workforce by Managing Diversity*, New York: AMACOM.

Thomas, R. and Davies, A. (2005) 'Theorizing the micro-politics of resistance: New Public Management and managerial identities in the UK public services', *Organization Studies,* 26(5): 683–706.

Tienari, J. (1999) 'The first wave washed up on shore: Reform, feminization and gender segregation', *Gender, Work and Organization* 6(1): 1–19.

Tomlinson, F., Brockbank, A. and Traves, J. (1997) 'The "feminization" of management? Issues of "sameness" and "difference" in the roles and experiences of female and male retail managers', *Gender, Work and Organization* 4(4): 218–29.

Towards the Commission for Equality and Human Rights. Available at: http://www.cehr.org. uk/ (accessed 12 June 2007).

Trahair, R.C.S. (1984) *The Humanist Temper: The Life and Work of Elton Mayo,* New Brunswick, NJ: Transaction Books.

Urwick, L. (1969 [1937]) 'Organization as a technical problem', in Gulick, L. and Urwick, L. (eds) *Papers on the Science of Administration,* New York: Augustus M. Kelley, pp. 49–88.

Vincent, P. (1998) 'She'll be right mate', *Sydney Morning Herald,* 2F, Saturday, 5 September, p. 1 (Employment Section).

Vine, P. (1997) 'Battling the myth of superwoman', *British Journal of Administrative Management,* November–December: 12–13.

Wajcman, J. (1998) *Managing Like a Man: Women and Men in Corporate Management,* University Park, PA: Penn State University Press.

Walby, S. (1997) *Gender Transformations,* London: Routledge.

Walby, S. (2007) *Gender (In)equality and the Future of Work,* Working Paper Series (55), Manchester: Equal Opportunities Commission.

Ward, L. and Black, I. (2000) 'The big question: Will this woman's husband take paternity leave?', *Guardian,* 24 March, p. 3.

Waugh, P. (2003) 'Milburn quits for the "one shot in life" to be with his children', *The Independent,* 13 June. Available at: http://www.independent.co.uk (accessed 19 June 2007).

Weiss, R. (1997) 'Evolving view of chimp communities: Dominant females' reproductive success suggests new hierarchy model', *The Washington Post,* 8 August, p. A03.

White, J. (1995) 'Leading in their own ways: Women chief executives in local government', in Itzin, C. and Newman, J. (eds) *Gender, Culture and Organizational Change: Putting Theory into Practice,* London: Routledge, 193–210.

Whitehead, S. (1999) 'New women, new Labour? Gendered transformations in the House', in Whitehead, S. and Moodley, R. (eds) *Transforming Managers: Gendering Change in the Public Sector,* London: UCL Press, pp. 19–32.

Whitehead, S. (2002) *Men and Masculinities: Key Themes and New Directions,* Cambridge: Polity.

Whitehead, S. (2004) *The Many Faces of Men: The Definitive Guide to the Male Species,* London: Arrow.

Whitehead, S. and Moodley, R. (1999) 'Introduction: Locating personal and political transformations', in Whitehead, S. and Moodley, R. (eds) *Transforming Managers: Gendering Change in the Public Sector,* London: UCL Press, pp. 1–15.

Williams, C.L. (1995) *Still A Man's World: Men Who Do 'Women's Work',* Berkeley, CA: University of California Press.

Wilson, F.M. (1996) 'Research note: Organisation theory: Blind and deaf to gender?', *Organisation Studies,* 17(5): 825–42.

Wilson, F.M. (2003) *Organisational Behaviour and Gender,* Aldershot: Ashgate.

Wintour, P. (2005) 'Epiphany after second meeting at No. 10', *Guardian,* 3 November. Available at: http://www.guardian.co.uk (accessed 19 June 2007).

Wollstonecraft, M. (1970 [1792]) *A Vindication of the Rights of Woman* (2nd edn), Farnborough: Gregg.

Woodward, R. and Winter, P. (2006) 'Gender and the limits to diversity in the contemporary British Army', *Gender, Work and Organization,* 13(1): 45–67.

Zanetti, L.A. (2006) 'Fear of the female body in organizational contexts', in Brewis, J., Linstead, S., Boje, D. and O'Shea, T. (eds) *The Passion of Organizing,* Malmö, Sweden: Liber AB, pp. 93–116.

Notes

1. As of 1 October 2007, the remit of the Equal Opportunities Commission, which deals with sex discrimination and gender inequality in England, Scotland and Wales, was brought together with that of the Commission for Racial Equality and the Disability Rights Commission under the aegis of a new public body, the Commission for Equality and Human Rights. The CEHR has been set up to 'take on all of the powers of the existing Commissions as well as new powers to enforce legislation more effectively and promote equality for all' (Towards the Commission for Equality and Human Rights accessed 12 June 2007). Another relevant recent change in British statutory arrangements around gender and employment is the implementation of the Gender Equality Duty in April 2007. This Jenny Watson, then chair of the EOC, describes as 'the biggest change to sex equality legislation since the Sex Discrimination Act', given that it constitutes 'an obligation on all public bodies to promote gender equality and eliminate discrimination' (Equal Opportunities Commission 2006: 2).
2. These data and their implications are also discussed in Brewis (2004: 1830).
3. Compare this to the equivalent figure in 1950, of just 15 per cent.
4. Although as already noted there are problems associated with a disproportionate uptake of measures such as these by women.
5. Interestingly this is reminiscent of the arguments made by Sylvia Walby (2007) regarding gendered futures in employment, as discussed earlier. As you will recall, Walby's optimistic version of the future rests at least in part on this pipeline stereotype becoming actuality – although her considered opinion seems to be that this is unlikely.
6. A germane example is the study by Jennifer Cliff, Nancy Langton and Howard Aldrich (2005) of 229 Canadian small-business owners. Cliff et al.'s respondents *articulate* a gender-specific way of managing, but – and importantly – this is not played out in practice. They suggest this 'may help explain the persistent belief that a leader's sex leaves an identifiable imprint on organizational characteristics'. Instead, and 'Rather than conforming to the archetypically masculine model of organizing, both male and female owners manage their firms with a mix of masculine and feminine approaches.' (p. 63).
7. Milburn however returned to the Cabinet just 14 months later, in September 2004, as Chancellor of the Duchy of Lancaster and therefore a key player in determining future Labour Party policy. Indeed '[i]n negotiations with Mr Blair, Mr Milburn demanded a "proper job" which would give him control over the Labour manifesto.' (Grice 2004).
8. NPM, broadly understood, refers to developments in the public sector in Western Europe over the past three decades or so which have seen it become much more marketized and managerialized – bringing it, in short, closer to the private sector in ethos.

CHAPTER 9

Emotion work

KEY CONCEPTS

emotion

emotional labour

feelings

emotional dissonance

emotional display

surface acting

deep acting

customer service

coping strategies

employee well-being

alienation

emotional exhaustion

gender and emotional labour

CHAPTER AIM

To explore the growth of 'emotional labour' in contemporary work organisations and assess its significance for the employees involved.

LEARNING OUTCOMES

After reading and thinking about the material in this chapter, you will be able to:

1. Define what is meant by emotional labour.

2. Demonstrate knowledge of the factors that have brought about the expansion of emotional labour and the reasons for the increased importance attributed to it by management.

3. Explain the ways in which employees learn and experience emotional labour.

4. Assess employee reactions to emotional labour.

5. Identify how managers seek to manage this aspect of employee behaviour.

6. Evaluate research on the consequences of emotional labour for employee health and well-being.

7. Recognise wider implications of the growth of emotional labour, in particular for the position of women in the labour force.

Introduction

While it has become commonplace to distinguish between jobs involving mainly phys-ical tasks and ones that primarily call for mental performance (utilising knowledge and information), a growing proportion of the workforce are also engaged in what can be termed the performance of 'emotion' work. For those employed as airline cabin crew, call centre staff, rescue workers, debt collectors, tour guides, supermarket checkout operators, waiters, bank staff, beauty therapists, healthcare employees and in a host of other occupations, the management of their own – and other people's – emotions represents a key aspect of their job.

In most service occupations involving direct contact with the public (either face-to-face or voice-to-voice), the way in which employees deliver that service has come to represent an increasingly important aspect of the service itself. In some contexts of course, the significance of social interaction as a vital component of service pro-vision has long been recognised. In the restaurant industry, for example, the diner's experience depends not only on the quality of the food consumed but also on the ambience created in the restaurant, which invariably hinges on the disposition and demeanour of the staff waiting on the tables. Thus, as well as performing tasks such as providing information and advice about the menu, taking down orders accu-rately, and serving and clearing away the meals carefully and efficiently, waiters and waitresses are expected to behave in a manner which contributes to a positive and welcoming atmosphere, irrespective of the pressures they are under or the way they are responded to by their customers. Or, as one waiter succinctly put it, 'I always smile at them … that's part of my uniform' (quoted in Hall, 1993: 460).

In this way, the 'service and its mode of delivery are inextricably combined' (Filby, 1992: 37); or put differently, 'the emotional style of offering the service is part of the service itself' (Hochschild, 1983: 5). It is clear, however, that in recent years, the range of activities involving emotion work has expanded. Thus, for most supermar-ket checkout operators, for example, it is no longer sufficient to charge up the goods speedily and handle cash, cheques and credit cards accurately; this has also to be a service performed 'with a smile', a friendly greeting, eye contact and a cheery fare-well. Moreover, these requirements apply whatever the circumstances:

> The worst thing is that you are on the till trying to go as fast as you can and you can hear them [the customers] moaning that you are slow … there are times that I just want to look up and say shut up but you have to be busy and keep smiling.
> (supermarket checkout operator, quoted in Ogbonna and Wilkinson, 1990: 12)

Similarly, on an airline flight, the expectation is that cabin crew will always display an air of reassurance, even if they fear otherwise:

> Even though I'm a very honest person, I have learned not to allow my face to mirror my alarm or my fright. I feel very protective of my passengers. Above all, I don't want them to be frightened. If we were going down, if we were going to make a ditching in the water, the chances of our surviving are slim, even though we [the flight attendants] know exactly what to do. But I think I would

probably – and I think I can say this for most of my fellow flight attendants – be able to keep them from being too worried about it.

(Delta Airlines flight attendant quoted in Hochschild, 1983: 107)

So too, in the High Street banks, management now attach greater importance to the warmth and friendliness of the cashier. As the extract in Excerpt 9.1 relating to a customer service questionnaire distributed by a leading UK bank illustrates, these are aspects of employee behaviour that are now increasingly monitored by their employers.

As social actors we all learn through processes of socialisation in families, schools and elsewhere how to control and 'manage' emotions in different contexts. Many children, for example, are taught not to be overwhelmed by adversity, but rather to persevere by 'putting on a brave face' or 'grinning and bearing it': that is to say, create an emotional 'mask' behind which real feelings can be hidden. Similarly, in most work situations, individuals are required to suppress some emotions and often to display others. Doctors are taught to control their emotions towards pain and death, to remain neutral and detached. Similarly, people in authority may regard it as prudent to maintain an emotional distance between themselves and their subordinates, so as to avoid compromising their ability to exercise discipline over those under them. Likewise, those at lower levels within organisations may continue to 'show respect' for those higher up the hierarchy, even if they regard those at more senior levels as incompetent. Thus, in many situations in both work and non-work life, gaps occur between expressed and felt emotions, or what Snyder (1987: 1) refers to as 'the public appearances and private realities of the self'.

Excerpt 9.1

When serving you today

Barclays bank is one of many companies that uses customer surveys to monitor response not only to banking services, but also to the nature and style of service delivery. The Barclays surveys are distributed twice a year and comprise ten questions relating to a service interaction just completed.

The survey is headed 'When serving you today, how was I at ...'. Each of the ten questions has an 11-point response scale, the ends of which are anchored by the words 'Poor' and 'Exceptional'.

Three questions seek responses to the employee's competence in relation to banking services: 'demonstrating knowledge of our products and services', 'sorting out any problems or concerns' and 'offering advice'. Four questions seek customer judgements on the efficiency of the employee during the interaction: 'making an effort to serve you quickly, 'carrying out everything competently', 'explaining things clearly' and 'listening attentively'. Three questions are designed to monitor the emotional style of the interaction, ratings being sought for the quality of 'acknowledging/greeting you', 'appearing pleased to see you' and 'making you feel I treated you as an individual'.

Each survey form is individually numbered and is therefore traceable back to individual bank branches and employees.

Our particular interest in this chapter lies in those jobs where employees are explicitly required to adopt particular sets of 'emotion rules' which define – often in considerable detail – which emotions they must publicly display, and which to suppress, in the performance of their job. Although, implicitly or explicitly, such rules have long represented important elements in many occupations, the coincidence of three developments in recent years makes this aspect of work behaviour particularly worthy of closer attention at this time.

- It is only comparatively recently that researchers have paid specific and detailed attention to emotional aspects of work performance and their wider significance: most of the studies in this area have been published since 1980.
- There has been a substantial increase over the last two decades in the proportion of jobs in which employees are 'customer facing', that is, in direct contact with customers of different kinds. In large part, this growth reflects the expansion of the service sector. In addition, a significant proportion of manufacturing jobs (such as in sales and purchasing) rely heavily on contact with customers and outside suppliers.
- There has been greatly increased recognition given to 'customer service' as a vital aspect of competitiveness; this recognition in turn has increased the importance attaching to the emotional performance by employees in direct contact with customers.

The meanings attached by management to customer relations (so-called 'customer care') are examined later in the chapter. So too are the experiences of, and implications for, those delivering that 'care'. Before this, however, it is necessary first to consider briefly what different writers on this subject mean by terms such as emotion and emotional labour.

Learning outcome 1: Define what is meant by emotional labour

Emotion and emotional labour

Defining emotional labour

Puzzling over what constitutes an emotion has a long pedigree. As Rafaeli and Sutton (1989: 4) comment, though it was more than a century ago that writers such as Charles Darwin and William James wrote on the subject of emotion, those currently seeking to define and interpret human emotions remain baffled by a number of unanswered and seemingly intractable questions. The subject of human emotion, just like the range of emotions a person can express, is a very wide one, and it would delay us unduly to explore the many social, psychological and biological avenues of emotion. It is sufficient for the present discussion to note the widespread agreement among those writing on emotions in the workplace that emotions centrally concern an individual's feelings. A notable book on the subject, *Emotion in Organizations,* for example, described itself as 'a book about feelings' (Fineman, 1993: 1; see also Fineman, 2000), while other contributions to this area of study similarly make reference in their titles and subtitles to 'feelings' (James, 1989) 'human feeling' (Hochschild, 1983) and 'real feelings' (Van Maanen and Kunda, 1989).

Even when we narrow the focus to emotions or feelings expressed in the workplace, however, it remains apparent that the topic is still a potentially enormous one, not least because work represents an important part of social existence, and encapsulates the range of human feelings – the loves, hatreds, fears, compassions, frustrations, joys, guilt and envies – that develop over time wherever any social group interacts. In addition, large areas of research, for instance in relation to job satisfaction and motivation, are concerned with exploring the feelings people have about work. So, in the discussion that follows, the principal focus is narrowed to address those (increasingly common) situations where service employees are required, as part of their job contract, to display specific sets of emotions (by verbal and/or non-verbal means) with the aim, in turn, of inducing particular feelings and responses among those for whom the service is being provided. This can be summed up as *emotional labour*. Hochschild (1983: 7) coined this term to refer to 'the management of feeling to create a publicly observable facial and bodily display' (see Table 9.1). This form of labour, like physical labour, is purchased by employers for a wage; its precise performance can be specified in sets of rules, and its adherence monitored by different forms of supervision and control. Subsequent writers in this area have sought to develop Hochschild's pioneering work. Writers such as Wharton and Erickson (1993), Morris and Feldman (1996), Abiala (1999) and Bolton and Boyd (2003), for example, emphasise that emotional labour is not a uniform activity, but varies in both type and intensity: a variability which must be taken into account when assessing the consequences of performing this type of work (see below). The definitions used by writers such as Ashforth and Humphrey (1993: 90) and Morris and Feldman (1996: 987) concentrate attention more on behaviour, rather than (in Hochschild's definition) any presumed management of feelings underlying behaviour.

Exercise 9.1

What do you *think?*
Read the list of definitions of emotional labour in Table 9.1 and for each one, give an example of a job or occupation where the definition might apply. You should try to give examples other than those already mentioned in the chapter so far.

A number of writers such as Mann (1999: 353) and Lewig and Dollard (2003) see the dissonance, or gap, between real and displayed emotions as the core characteristic, or core problematic, of emotional labour. James (1989), on the other hand, defines emotional labour in a slightly different way, in terms of the work involved in dealing with other people's emotions – the sort of labour, for example, widely performed in hospitals and hospices, where James conducted her research.

This emotional labour task of managing other people's emotions is also well illustrated in Lively's (2002) study of legal assistants in the United States. In her interviews, the assistants make many references to the difficult task of dealing with

Table 9.1 Some definitions of emotional labour

Author	Definition
Hochschild (1983)	'the management of feeling to create a publicly observable facial and bodily display'
Ashforth and Humphrey (1993)	'the display of expected emotions'
Morris and Feldman (1996)	'the act of expressing organizationally desired emotions during service transactions'
Mann (1999)	[the discrepancy between] 'the emotional demeanor that an individual displays because it is considered appropriate, and the emotions that are genuinely felt but that would be inappropriate to display'
James (1989)	'labour involved in dealing with other people's feelings'
Pugliesi (1999)	distinguishes between 'self-focused' emotional labour (centred on the management of one's own feelings) and 'other-focused' emotional labour (directed towards the management of the feelings of others).

emotionally distraught clients, particularly those dealing with issues of divorce or bankruptcy. As two of her respondents comment:

> You're dealing with people in their most emotional state of all times – only death, in an individual's life, is probably equally as emotional as divorce.
>
> (Lively, 2002: 208)

> Bankruptcy ... is a very emotional procedure for the people involved .... Generally, by the time a client comes to see us to file a bankruptcy, they probably should have come to see us 6 months or a year ago. They probably have waited too long [and] they are just completely blown away with people collecting from them and threats of repossessions ... it's a very emotional situation.
>
> (Lively, 2002: 209)

On closer inspection, it is evident that these definitional positions are in practice closely related. In Hochschild's approach, for example, the employee's emotional display is specifically designed to induce a particular set of feelings (for example, the 'satisfied customer') in the recipient of the labour. Correspondingly, for the nurses in James' study, and the legal workers in Lively's account, one of the main ways in which patients'/clients' grief, anger and anxiety is dealt with is by the nurses and the legal assistants regulating their own emotions.

To sum up

In placing different emphases on the performer or recipient of emotional labour, the various definitions act to underline the essentially *interactive* nature of this form of labour. It is work performed by employees in direct contact with others (customers, patients, clients) in which the response of those 'others' has a direct bearing on the experience of employees performing emotional labour, and on the attitudes of employers as to how that labour should be performed.

Real versus displayed emotions

The foregoing discussion raises a key issue: what lies at the heart of emotional labour is not necessarily the expression of real emotions, but *displayed* emotions, which may or may not be truly felt. As the supermarket employee quoted earlier commented, the checkout operators have to smile – and the smile must look authentic – whether or not they feel positively disposed towards the customer. Where employees are required as part of their job to demonstrate feelings they might not share, they are performing emotional labour in the sense that the work role involves aspects not unlike those of an actor – for example, adopting the role and the script of the 'happy worker', pleased to be of service (no matter how the customer responds). This has become an influential metaphor not lost on the employee, as demonstrated by the Cathay Pacific flight attendant who commented: 'We say we are all entertainers now because everyone is on stage' (quoted by Linstead, 1995: 198).

A number of sociologists and psychologists have considered social life, including life within work organisations, from a performance or 'dramaturgical' perspective (see for example Goffman, 1969, 1971; Höpfl, 2002; Mangham and Overington, 1987). This perspective envisages social life as a series of scripted performances in which people act out parts which are consistent with the 'selves' that they wish to present. Individuals are viewed as performing different scripts in different social situations. Goffman (1969: 183) refers to 'the arts of impression management' in relation to how individuals present themselves to the outside world, how different circumstances elicit different performances from the 'actors' involved, and how people 'self-monitor' their performances and adjust these as conditions alter. (See also Snyder, 1987, for a discussion of self-monitoring.)

The metaphor of the theatre and its component terms such as actor, performance, role, script and being 'on' and 'off' stage, can usefully be applied to an analysis of emotional labour, and the display rules of emotional conduct (Höpfl, 2002). At the same time, from a dramaturgical perspective, emotional labour can be seen as a variant of what already occurs in most other social contexts. In jobs requiring emotional labour, employees perform a particular emotion script, just as in other settings individuals perform other emotional displays, some of which are likely to be as inauthentic as those indicated by the checkout operator quoted earlier, who is required to smile even at rude customers. The key difference between these work and other settings, however, lies in the fact that those employees performing emotional labour are *required* to follow what Ekman (1973) and Ashforth and Humphrey (1993: 89) term the 'display rules', as part of their job. Discretion and choice over the nature of displayed feelings is removed or reduced, and the emotional performance forms part of the effort–wage bargain in the same way that physical performance does. As discussed later, for some critics of emotional labour (such as Hochschild, 1983) the problem is that some jobs require employees to undertake 'unacceptable' levels of emotional display, with potentially detrimental effects on the individuals involved. Before examining the effects of emotional labour, however, and the way people learn, experience and cope with this form of labour, it is necessary to consider in a little more detail the factors behind the increase in this aspect of work.

> **To sum up**
>
> Emotional labour entails the performance of certain emotions in line with display rules established by management.

Learning outcome 2: Demonstrate knowledge of the factors that have brought about the expansion of emotional labour and the reasons for the increased importance attributed to it by management

The expansion of emotional labour

The growth in service activities

The degree to which advanced industrial economies have experienced a shift in industrial structure was highlighted, with a diminishing proportion of the total workforce engaged in the primary and secondary sectors, and a growing proportion located in the tertiary, service sector. While an important aspect of service activity involves commercial organisations providing services for one another (for example, management consultancy, specialised maintenance work and office cleaning), the growth in the service sector has been particularly notable in the area of personal services – the range of services available to the individual citizen. Few of these services are unique to the recent period. What is evident, however, is a growth in consumer choice, either as a result of the multiplication of similar services (such as a proliferation of leisure facilities, financial institutions or different restaurants in a particular locality) or because of the extension of existing services, in part as a result of advances in technology (for example, travel agents equipped with computer reservation systems enabling them to provide a much extended service, or libraries with access to much greater information via electronic storage systems).

The growth of services to individuals can be categorised in various ways. Lynch (1992), for example, identifies an expansion in:

* financial services (including banks, building societies and insurance companies)
* travel services (e.g. coach, rail and air services, together with related activities such as car hire)
* leisure services (e.g. hotels, restaurants, cinemas, theatres, pubs, clubs, sporting facilities)
* provisioning services (different types of retail outlets)
* communication services (e.g. telephone, media)
* convenience services (e.g. hairdressing, travel agents).

In addition, in the public (and increasingly, the privatised) sector there has been a growth in competition in, for example:

* educational services
* health and welfare services
* environmental services.

Increased emphasis on customer service

This expansion in service activities alone would probably have been sufficient to raise awareness of the significance of how employees interact with customers. However, a major reason why attention has come to focus so strongly on the nature of that interaction reflects not only the fact that such interactions have become more numerous, but that they are also occurring in an increasingly competitive environment, and that the *significance* of those interactions on the customer's overall judgement of the service has increasingly been recognised by management and, as a result, given greater emphasis. The increased competitiveness reflects both a general growth in service choices (for example, different leisure services competing for the customer's free time: should we take the kids to a theme park, the zoo, the swimming pool or the cinema today?) and also the multiplication of very similar services within a particular locality (shall we take the kids to eat at McDonald's or Burger King?).

One effect of this growth of very similar services (and this multiplication is as evident in financial services, air travel, supermarkets and a range of other activities as in the fast food industry) is a tendency to even out many of the differences in price and elements of the service 'product': overall the burgers are very similar, as are the guest rooms in the different hotel chains, the airline seats and the various products offered by different estate agents, banks, travel agents and supermarkets.

In such an environment, where the actual services being offered for sale are little differentiated, increased significance becomes attached not to the physical nature of the service being offered, but to its *psychological* nature. The facilities at different banks, for example, may be almost identical, but in which one do the customers feel that they have been 'treated' the best? In this situation, the aim of any particular service provider comes to centre on making customers feel more positively disposed to that service, such that they return to that particular service provider (be it a shop, restaurant, airline, or hotel) when a repeat service is sought. It is this psychological element that is of particular significance in the recent expansion of emotional labour.

The goal of securing a favourable psychological response from the customer has given rise to a much greater emphasis on customer service or 'customer care'. Notions of customer care have long existed of course, embodied in such maxims as 'service with a smile' and 'the customer is always right'. But the growth of a more articulated and extensive customer care philosophy can be traced to the growing importance attributed to customer relations within the 'excellence' movement (Peters and Waterman, 1982; Peters and Austin, 1985) and the spread into the service sector of ideas such as Total Quality Management and 'continuous improvement', originally formulated within manufacturing contexts (Deming 1982; Juran, 1979).

In part, customer care involves simply the efficient delivery of a service – a high quality product, delivered on time and to specification. However, with the duplication of very similar services, customer care manuals have also come to emphasise additional means of securing customer satisfaction. For example, the following comment, by a management writer on the psychology of customer care (Lynch, 1992: 29) is implicit in much of the thinking behind customer care:

> Any action which increases the self-esteem of the customer will raise the level of satisfaction .... Conveying in a sincere manner the message 'You are better than you think you are' is a powerful tool for any service provider.

Thus, boosting the customer's self-esteem is seen to be an important aspect of customer care. There are various ways of achieving this esteem or status enhancement; Lynch (1992), for example, cites the importance of using the customer's name. Indeed, the whole manner in which an employee may be required to deliver a service (smiling, gaining eye contact, giving a friendly greeting) can contribute to putting customers at their ease, showing deference to them, making them feel special, even sexually attractive (Hall, 1993; Linstead, 1995; Wood, 2000). In some situations, attributing status to the customers, and thereby potentially raising their self-esteem, is expressed in ways other than establishing 'friendly' relations. The undertaker's staff, for example, demonstrate a sensitivity to (and thus acknowledge the status of) the bereaved's feelings by performing their duties in a solemn way (at least while in sight of the bereaved). The waiter at a very high-class restaurant may also acknowledge a customer's status by being unobtrusive (though remaining attentive and efficient), thereby acknowledging the customer's right to privacy and his/her status as someone with the ability to eat at such an expensive restaurant (Hall, 1993). In a family-friendly restaurant (such as TGI Friday's), on the other hand, status is still attributed to the customer, but in the form of the waiter creating a more openly friendly relationship (see Excerpt 9.2).

Excerpt 9.2

Performing service at TGI Friday's

In an analysis of empowerment at TGI Friday's, Lashley (1999) reveals how the waiting staff are required to manage their behaviour to reflect the variation in the customers throughout the day. For example, at lunchtime, business customers predominate, in the afternoon there are more families and in the early evening there are mainly couples. Each group will require a different approach, and in this way the staff are performing emotion work.

As Lashley (1999: 797) explains,

'Dub-Dubs', as the waiting staff are called, have to advise customers on the menu and how best to structure their meal. They also have to identify the customer's service requirements and deliver what is needed. In some case, 'having a good laugh with the customers is needed', in others, they need to leave the guests to their own devices, or create the necessary celebratory atmosphere to match with a birthday or other party occasion. At other times they have to entertain restive children. Employee performance requires, therefore, more than the traditional acts of greeting, seating and serving customers. Employees have to be able to provide both the behaviours and the emotional displays, to match with customer wants and feelings.

Exercise 9.2

What do you think?

The argument in this part of the discussion has been that customers are increasingly influenced by the quality of the emotional labour that is performed on them. Given that we are all customers, it is useful to ask ourselves how important emotional labour is to us. And more specifically, how much it influences our patterns of purchasing goods and services.

1. How aware are you of the emotional labour that customer contact staff are performing on you? (Provide specific examples.)
2. Do you think the amount of emotional labour that you experience is increasing? In what ways?
3. How important is it to you that people who are delivering a service to you perform emotional labour as part of that service – is it more important to you in some settings (for example, a restaurant) than others (such as a supermarket)?
4. If it is more important to you in some settings than others, why is this the case?

What these various aspects of customer care underline is that in a context of intensifying competition, *how* a service is delivered has come to be defined as central to overall organisational success. As a result, those staff in direct contact with the customer, either face-to-face or voice-to-voice, have become increasingly recognised as key representatives of the service organisation. Customer-facing staff are situated in crucial 'boundary-spanning' positions which link the organisation to external individuals or groups. One chief executive of a major airline sums up these interactions between organisational members and customers as key 'moments of truth', on which the latter form lasting judgements about the organisation as a whole (Carlzon, 1987).

To sum up

Management have come to pay much greater attention to the manner in which employees perform their interactions with customers. In some settings, highly detailed rules and 'scripts' have been established, specifying which emotions must be displayed, and which suppressed; these display rules are monitored and backed up by sanctions (and less frequently, rewards) in an attempt to secure full compliance. However, the fact that systems of punishment and reward exist at all indicates that compliance with the rules of emotional display remains problematic in many organisations. As the next section examines, in practice many employees experience difficulties (as well as satisfactions) in performing this aspect of their job, and resort to various strategies to cope with the exacting demands of emotional labour.

Learning outcome 3: Explain the ways in which employees learn and experience emotional labour

Experiencing emotional labour

Selection and training for emotional labour

While various situations exist where employees are required to present feelings that are solemn (undertakers), disapproving (debt collectors) or even hostile (nightclub bouncers or police interrogators), most consideration has been given to the more common contexts where employees' emotional performance is designed to induce or reinforce positive feelings within the customer. In each of these contexts, the required emotional performance typically involves 'a complex combination of facial expression, body language, spoken words and tone of voice' (Rafaeli and Sutton, 1987: 33). This combination is secured primarily through the processes of selection, training and monitoring of employee behaviour.

Nonverbal elements form an important part of many jobs involving emotional labour, and can be prominent criteria in selection decisions. At Disneyland, for example, the (mainly young) people recruited to work in the park are chosen partly on the basis of their ability to exhibit a fresh, clean-cut, honest appearance – the nonverbal embodiment in fact of the values traditionally espoused in Walt Disney films (Van Maanen and Kunda, 1989). Airline companies too emphasise nonverbal aspects of the work of customer-contact staff, including the importance of a high standard of personal grooming, covering such aspects as weight regulation, uniform, and even colour of eye-shadow (Hochschild, 1983; Williams, 1988).

Similarly, at most supermarkets, checkout operators are expected to conform to particular patterns of nonverbal behaviour even when not serving. For example, one checkout operator, Denise (name changed), commented in an interview with the authors that at her store not only were the checkouts constantly monitored by closed-circuit television equipment but supervisors regularly patrolled behind the checkouts, preventing any of the operators from turning round to talk to fellow operators by whispering the command 'FF', which meant 'Face the front'. Denise and her colleagues were required not only to 'FF', but also to sit straight at all times; they were strictly forbidden, for example, from putting their elbows on the counter in front of them to relax their backs.

Nonverbal rules of emotional display play an important part in many service organisations, but it is the verbal rules that have increasingly been emphasised in a growing number of settings involving direct contact with customers. In some contexts, employees receive little or no guidance on the 'correct' verbal behaviour. Seymour and Sandiford (2005), for example, show how in small workplaces such as pubs, emotion skills tend to be picked up through experience. In other settings, however, the prescribed verbal repertoire is passed on through detailed training and instruction. At her supermarket, for example, Denise has been instructed to greet the customer, smile and make eye contact, and when the customer pays by cheque or credit card, read the customer's name and return the card using his or her name ('Thank you, Mrs Smith/Mr Jones').

This verbal display of friendliness and deference represents an increasingly common feature not only in supermarkets (Ogbonna and Wilkinson, 1990) but also in other areas of retailing and service activities involving the public. Those entering the space ride at Disneyland, for example, are met with the words 'Welcome voyager' by the ride operator (Van Maanen and Kunda, 1989). At McDonald's, counter and window crews are trained in highly routinised scripts, which include a number of verbal and nonverbal emotional labour elements (smiling, being cheerful, polite at all times, and so on) (Leidner, 1991). These scripts are not only designed to create a particular 'tone' for the interaction and a particular 'end' (a sale and customer satisfaction), but their high level of routinisation also allows for dealing with a high volume of customers with a minimum of delay.

Exercise 9.3

What do you think?

Think about any job you have had that involved a degree of emotional labour. This might have been working for example in a bar, a restaurant, a supermarket, a shop, in a crèche or as a holiday rep.

1. Overall, did you find the emotional labour part of the job enjoyable or not enjoyable?
2. What were the enjoyable aspects of the emotional labour?
3. What were the aspects that were not enjoyable?

Both verbal and nonverbal emotional labour is prominent in the work of waiters and waitresses (see for example Hall, 1993; Mars and Nicod, 1984; Spradley and Mann, 1975). Those waiting at tables are expected to perform a number of physical tasks, but in addition, a warm, friendly and deferential manner is widely seen by employers as a key element in creating a positive ambience. For the waiters and waitresses, there is an additional, instrumental reason for performing their emotional labour effectively, as a significant part of their income derives from tips. Studies have shown that those who smile more do better at attracting larger tips than those who do not (Tidd and Lockard, 1978, cited in Rafaeli and Sutton, 1987). Further, one study found that tips to waitresses were higher where the waitress had made physical contact with the (male) customers by, for example, a fleeting touch of the hand when returning change, or touching the customer's shoulder (Crusco and Wetzel, 1984). Such studies appear to underline further the significance of the service provider boosting the customer's self-esteem by making them feel attractive. This boosting of self-esteem, and the financial implications of doing so effectively, are even more pronounced in parts of the nightclub industry, as the case in Excerpt 9.3 illustrates.

Excerpt 9.3

Fantasy labour in the fantasy factory – strippers and lap dancers

Several researchers in the United States have studied the labour of dancers working in strip clubs – a setting which Wood (2000) recently termed the 'Fantasy factory'. These studies provide insights into particularly charged venues where emotional labour is undertaken. The studies also reinforce a number of the points made elsewhere in the chapter, particularly relating to the requirement of the dancers to display some emotions and suppress others, the financial inducements attaching to the 'counterfeiting of intimacy' (Foote, 1954; Boles and Garbin, 1974), and the fact that this is a setting overwhelmingly where women (literally) perform emotional labour for consumption by men, with potential consequences for the status of each.

In some clubs studied, the strippers performed their stage act for tips, these being secured in important part by the women making frequent eye contact with individuals which 'made a customer feel as if a dancer were specially interested in him' (Ronai and Ellis, 1989: 277). In addition, following the staged routines in some of the clubs, the women offered personal dances ('table' or 'lap' dances) to individuals for additional payment. These table dances represent a key source of income for the women, and in efforts to secure them, a variety of emotional labour activities are undertaken.

The essence of these is to make the (usually male) customer feel particularly important, sexy and desirable, which in turn leads the man to buy additional dances. Many of the dancers interviewed by Ronai and Ellis (1989) and Wood (2000) comment that the sexually charged looks, actions and phrases which make up this 'seduction rhetoric' need to appear genuine – to buy dancers, many individual customers had to feel that the women had 'dropped the routine' and were genuinely interested in, and attracted by, the customer. 'The smile must be convincing. The eye contact must be engaging … to make believable their attention and interest in the customers' (Wood, 2000: 24, 28). This is especially the case for regular customers, who can represent an important source of income (and presents, etc.) for individual dancers, but who are also very well placed to judge whether the verbal and nonverbal behaviour of 'their' dancer is repetitive or phoney (Ronai and Ellis, 1989: 287).

As well as expressing 'genuine' emotions, at the same time in conversations with the customers the dancers were required to suppress other emotions (like being bored or unattracted to the individual) as well as other aspects of their life. This was particularly the case if they were married and had children – attributes which potentially 'jeopardised his [the customer's] ability to see her as a sexy, sensual, and most important, available, woman' (Wood, 2000: 10–11).

'If I tell him I'm married and have a child, he's not going to think I'm sexy anymore. Men come in to see sexy, erotic, women who they think are party girls. Motherhood they can get at home' (dancer quoted in Wood, 2000: 16).

Further, emotional labour plays an important part in regulating customer emotions and controlling the interaction, making sure that customers know (and remain within) the limits of the interaction in what is, potentially, a risky situation for the worker.

Results of these encounters include an economic exchange (money paid in return for a dance provided). In common with several other arenas of emotional labour, however, the exchange is also a psychological one, more to the benefit of the male customer. 'Strippers increase the status of men through labor aimed at creating a designated impression for the men themselves – the impression of being interesting, sexy and desirable' (Wood, 2000: 15). The emotional costs of stripping, in terms of stigmatisation, rejection by customers, offensive behaviour as well as physical assaults, can be considerable. As Ronai and Ellis (1989: 296) sum it up, 'Stripping, as a service occupation, pays well, but costs dearly.'

It is the airline industry, however, that gave rise to one of the groundbreaking studies of emotional labour (Hochschild, 1979, 1983), and this has since been followed by further studies of emotional labour among airline cabin crew (Bolton and Boyd, 2003). In her study of Delta Airlines flight attendants (elsewhere often referred to as cabin crew, formerly as air hostesses or stewardesses), Hochschild explored the development, performance and consequences of emotional labour. Selection and training are shown to play particularly important roles in inculcating particular 'feeling rules' into the recruits. Selection criteria, for example, included both non-verbal and verbal aspects. Not only were physical attributes and overall appearance taken into account in the selection process for flight attendants, so too was the ability to 'project a warm personality' and display enthusiasm, friendliness and sociability (Hochschild, 1983: 97). However, while the selection process is used to identify those who have the predisposition to perform emotional labour effectively, Hochschild emphasises the training sessions as the place where the flight attendants are given more precise instruction on how to perform their role. As well as training in the technical aspects of their job (such as what procedures to follow in an emergency), instruction is also given on the emotional aspects of the work. At its simplest, the training affirms the importance of smiling:

> Now girls, I want you to go out there and really *smile*. Your smile is your biggest *asset*. I want you to go out there and use it. Smile. *Really* smile. Really *lay it on*.
>
> (Pilot speaking at a Delta Airlines Training Centre, quoted in Hochschild, 1983: 4, emphasis in original)

The employee's smile and accompanying pleasant and helpful manner are given considerable emphasis. Flight attendants are encouraged to think of passengers as 'guests in their own home', for whom no request is too much trouble (ibid: 105). The cabin crew member's smile is designed not only to convey a welcome (in the way the supermarket operator's smile and restaurant worker's smile endeavours to do), but also to project a confidence and a reassurance that the company in general, and the plane in particular, can be trusted with the customer's life (ibid: 4). The emphasis in the training is on fully identifying with the role, in order to generate a more 'sincere' or 'genuine' smile – 'smiling from the inside' – rather than a false-looking smile (see also Bolton and Boyd, 2003: 301).

It is one thing to be able to smile at friendly, considerate and appreciative customers, but another to smile under pressure, such as the bar worker, waitress or checkout operator faced with large numbers of customers, or service workers in general faced with offensive individuals. It is in these problematic circumstances that management also require compliance with display rules. It seeks to achieve this partly by encouraging employees to interpret the situation differently, to suppress any feelings of anger or frustration, and to respond in the manner prescribed by management.

The problem of dealing with difficult customers arises particularly in studies of call centre staff (see for example, Callaghan and Thompson, 2002; Korczynski, 2003; Taylor and Tyler, 2000). In their study of telephone sales agents, for example, Taylor and Tyler (2000: 84) describe how the (mainly female) agents are trained not to get angry with offensive (often male) customers. As one trainer commented:

> If a man's having a go at you ... he might even be embarrassing you ... don't get ruffled, you've got to keep your cool. Remember that you are trying to offer him something and get him to pay for the privilege. He can really talk to you how he wants. Your job is to deal with it ... *just take a few deep breaths and let your irritation cool down* ... think to yourself he's not worth it. (emphasis in original)

This example matches closely aspects of the emotion training of the Delta flight attendants described by Hochschild (1983), in particular the instructions on how to respond positively to awkward, angry or offensive customers ('irates' as they are known in Delta). A key training device for dealing with such passengers was to reconceptualise them as people with a problem, who needed sympathy and understanding. Thus, employees were encouraged to think that perhaps the passenger who was drinking too much and being offensive was doing so to mask a fear of flying (or a stressful job, sadness at being away from home, or whatever). Underlying this training is the requirement for attendants to respond positively to such passengers, reflecting the fact that they may be frequent flyers and thus important sources of revenue to the company. Thus, the attendants are required to 'think sales' (ibid: 108), no matter how irksome or rude the passenger is being.

Different ways of doing emotional labour

It is evident from the studies undertaken that workers perform a variety of forms of emotional labour and do so in different ways. Hochschild (1983) for example, distinguishes between those who engage in 'surface' acting and those who perform 'deep' acting. Surface acting involves a behavioural compliance with the display rules (facial expression, verbal comments, and so on) without any attempt being made to internalise these rules: the emotions are feigned or faked. Deep acting, on the other hand, involves employees internalising their role more thoroughly in an attempt to 'experience' the required emotions. Selection procedures and training programmes such as the ones described by Hochschild are designed to elicit deep acting – that, by developing a set of inner feelings (towards the company, the customer and the attendant's work role), the outward behaviour would follow as a matter of course.

Exercise 9.4

What do you think?
Surface and deep acting are two ways of performing emotional labour, and have different implications for how employees approach and perform their work role.

1. What are the advantages and disadvantages of each approach?
2. Overall, if you had to recommend to someone how they should handle their emotional labour, would you advocate a surface-acting or a deep-acting approach? Why do you say this?

Ashforth and Humphrey (1993: 94) have subsequently pointed out that these two 'routes' to emotional labour should be supplemented by a third, which takes into account the situation where the expected emotional display is fully consistent with an individual's own inner feelings (see also Ashforth and Tomiuk, 2000). In such cases, there is no need for the worker to 'act' at all, since the emotion is in harmony with

Excerpt 9.4

Acting natural

Deep acting of the type described by Hochschild has also been encouraged in more recent years by managers encouraging employees to behave 'naturally' rather than simply stick to a rigid prescribed script. In efforts to create a more 'genuine' interaction, an increasing number of organisations are giving employees the freedom to 'be themselves', to be 'more natural' and 'more authentic' in their interactions with customers.

Rosenthal, Hill and Peccei (1997), for example, report a study of a major UK food retailer which in the mid-1990s moved away from highly scripted forms of service as part of a 'Service excellence' initiative. These researchers found that many employees preferred being able to be more 'natural' in their dealings with customers, compared with the previous need to adhere to pre-set company scripts (ibid: 493).

However, as Taylor (1998: 92) points out in a study of telephone sales staff, in practice the degree of empowerment within this 'emotional autonomy' is very partial. Management at the telephone sales organisation sought a 'naturalness' from employees only in so far as the expression of positive dispositions by staff helped build up a rapport with customers. To put it another way, acting natural was fine in the eyes of management as long as it served the organisation's objectives – to increase sales and improve customer service. The emotional autonomy did not extend to empowering employees to tell rude customers just where to get off.

what the individual would have naturally displayed as part of his/her own identity. In such situations there is no emotional dissonance – that is, no incongruence or gap between felt emotions and displayed emotions (or put differently, between feeling and action) (Lewig and Dollard, 2003). An example is a nurse who has entered that occupation to fulfil a strong desire to care for people who are ill. Other examples in the emotional labour literature include youth shelter workers who identify very closely with the plight of the young people seeking refuge in the shelter (Karabanow, 1999) and highly enthusiastic employees attached to 'high-commitment' organisations such as The Body Shop (Martin, Knopoff and Beckman, 1998).

To sum up

Emotional labour involves both extensive verbal and nonverbal behaviour. Both of these form important elements in the selection and training programmes for various occupations. Emotional labour may be performed through surface or deep acting, or in circumstances where the employee so fully identifies with the job that no 'acting' is involved at all.

However, even those who identify fully with their job will have their off-days and occasional bad moods. At those times they – like their counterparts who identify with their job less strongly – will be required to manage their emotions to hide their true feelings.

Learning outcome 4: Assess employee reactions to emotional labour

---

Reactions to emotional labour

Problematic circumstances for performing emotional labour

For many employees, for much of the time, performing emotional labour is unproblematic. Smiling at customers often elicits a smile in return, and the creation of a friendly interaction. As the flight attendant in Excerpt 9.5 comments, 'It's great to come off a flight on a high, you've made the passengers happy and receptive to you. As you're saying Goodbye you're getting a response, eye contact, thank you's' (Williams, 2003: 532 and Excerpt 9.5). As Korczynski (2003: 57) comments, customers can be 'a key source of meaning and pleasure in service jobs', representing an important source of job satisfaction (see for example Lewig and Dollard, 2003: 328–9). Likewise, among services such as hairdressing and beauty therapy, researchers have noted the presence of 'genuine feeling' between worker and clients and a 'reciprocity' in the relationships between employees and customers (Furman, 1997; Sharma and Black, 2001).

Excerpt 9.5

Emotional labour over Australia

In a study of almost 3000 flight attendants in Australia, Claire Williams (2003) highlights both the pleasurable and the problematic aspects of emotional labour among this occupational group.

Overall, a higher proportion of the flight attendants found the emotional labour aspects of their job stressful (44 per cent) than a source of satisfaction (34 per cent) (the remainder seeing this aspect of their job as neither stressful nor satisfying). However, further analysis of the comments that the flight attendants made indicated that, for many, emotional labour was a source of both satisfaction and stress. As one put it:

> It's great to come off a flight on a high, you've made the passengers happy and receptive to you. As you're saying Goodbye, you're getting a response, eye contact, thank you's, hope to see you next flight! Then there are days when you're happy and friendly and they just don't want to acknowledge your presence or nothing you can do will help solve their problem. You are verbally abused and left standing red faced with a plastic smile crumbling on your face.

Interestingly, a common explanation among those who found emotional labour a great source of satisfaction was the way that encouraging and forcing themselves to look more cheerful actually made them feel better. They also noted a sense of achievement derived from overcoming difficulties at work.

Williams also reports several examples of sexual harassment among her sample, particularly from members of sports teams and businessmen (though also from flight crew and other members of the cabin crew). Overall, almost four out of five

---

(79 per cent) of women flight attendants (and 61 per cent of male flight attendants) reported that they had to deal with verbal sexual harassment in their jobs, with other instances of physical sexual harassment.

An important factor in the impact of harassment on the attendants was how management dealt with harassment: whether they were supportive towards the flight attendants or whether they maintained a bias in favour of the customer. Emotional labour was much more likely to be reported as satisfying where the flight attendants felt valued by the airline companies – not only in relation to support over sexual harassment instances, but also other employee issues such as health and safety concerns.

Williams concludes that the organisational context – in particular the nature of management attitudes and behaviour towards their employees – acts as a mediating influence on how emotional labour is experienced at work.

Source: Williams (2003).

Further, as just noted, there will be those service employees who are very positively disposed to their work, and to smile while doing it is wholly consistent with their general feelings towards the job and the customer. In these latter cases, there is little or no dissonance or 'gap' between the individual's felt and expressed emotions at work: expectation and actuality are closely aligned. In Sharpe's (2005) study of adventure guides, the emotional labour performed, despite the lengthy time periods involved, was also found to be largely unproblematic (see Excerpt 9.6 for a more detailed account of this study). For Sharpe, a key factor in this is her perception of all individuals incorporating many versions of the 'self' (rather than as Hochschild tended to emphasise, the existence of 'one true self'). Because of this, the employees of the trekking firm are seen as capable of performing the emotional labour of the guide role – in ways that involved acting differently (more outgoing, extrovert, and so on) to when they were away from the job – without this causing any particular difficulties. We return to this point again later.

Excerpt 9.6

The emotional labour of adventure guides
As Erin Sharpe (2005) points out, emotional labour figures prominently in the work of adventure guides. Though far removed from the work contexts of most groups discussed in the literature on emotional labour, the emotional labour component of the guide's job is considerable. Further, it is an interaction between employee and customer that goes on for days, and in close proximity.

The author reports a study of 'Wanderlust', an outdoor adventure company specialising in canoe and kayak trips in North and Central America and Australia. Data were collected from participation on eight Wanderlust trips.

The company emphasised the importance of guides handling their emotions in three particular aspects of the job. First, the company put particular emphasis on safety, and as part of this, guides adopted an emotional demeanour that underlined their status as a safe and competent guide, remaining calm in dangerous or risky conditions. As one guide told the author of the study: 'An emotion I don't want to manifest is fear ... it can lead to chaos and loss of control .... I don't want people to lose confidence in my ability when I'm scared. So you have to develop a certain amount of control of your fear and your emotions' (Sharpe, 2005: 37–8).

The second area of emotional labour for the guides was in generating fun among the groups they were leading. Guides were responsible for making the trips enjoyable, and this entailed telling jokes, smiling and laughing a lot, being energetic, upbeat, outgoing and 'generally working to maintain a fun-loving attitude'. This was clearly much easier for the extrovert than the more introvert guides. As one guide put it:

> For me, doing a trip is almost like putting on a show, and keeping that attitude is tough .... It's like I step on a stage and a different persona comes over me. Most of the people who have seen me on trail consider me a huge extrovert, when I'm actually a borderline introvert. It takes an extra effort for me to be that person.
>
> (Sharpe, 2005: 39)

The third aspect of the guides' emotional labour was seen to be encouraging a sense of community. For the guides this meant that socialising and getting to know the participants was part of their job responsibilities, including befriending those who had difficulties mixing with the rest of the group.

The guides noted various ways of coping with the emotional demands, including finding ways to physically remove themselves for periods of time (using pretexts such as organising equipment and checking the weather radio).

Overall, the study shows that maintaining the required persona could be emotionally exhausting. However, unlike Hochschild's (1983) discussion of emotional labour among flight attendants, Sharpe found no sense of the guides being estranged from their 'real' selves. The author interprets and discusses this in terms of a picture of the self as made up of multiple selves rather than 'one true self'. So while guides were required to act differently than they would do at home, they did not consider these actions as fake, but rather that their 'guide persona' was one of many versions of their self. Thus the author argues that the study shows that while emotional labour may be demanding and can be exhausting, giving rise to various coping strategies, nevertheless it does not necessarily involve any alienation from a true self.

Source: Sharpe (2005).

Other circumstances can arise, however, where the performance of emotional labour becomes much more problematic for the individual. One relates to the overall *amount* of emotional labour demanded by the job, especially where the emotional display is required over long periods of time. Cabin crew members aboard intercontinental flights, for example, not only work long duty times, but also suffer from additional fatigue as a result of jet lag and interrupted sleep patterns. The strain of prolonged emotional display, particularly where customers are being difficult or offensive (see also below), is illustrated in the following extract from Hochschild (1983: 127):

A young businessman said to a flight attendant, 'Why aren't you smiling?' She put her tray back on the food cart, looked him in the eye and said, 'I'll tell you what. You smile first, then I'll smile.' The businessman smiled at her. 'Good', she replied. 'Now freeze and hold that for fifteen hours.'

A second problematic circumstance is where the dissonance between felt and displayed emotions is particularly acute. As Lewig and Dollard (2003: 379) demonstrate in their study of call centre workers in South Australia, emotional dissonance exacerbates the level of emotional exhaustion that employees experience (see also Grandey, 2003). High levels of dissonance may arise if the required emotional display is considered inappropriate by the worker performing the task. The supermarket employee Denise quoted earlier, for example, expressed considerable difficulty with using the customer's name when handling cheques or credit cards. To Denise, a shy self-effacing woman, this seemed 'too forward, too familiar' in a situation where she was not acquainted with the individual whose name she was required to use; the result was a continuing unease and embarrassment.

A commonly reported situation of emotional dissonance is where employees are required to maintain a particular emotional display towards customers who are being rude or offensive. Examples of objectionable behaviour are evidenced in many studies of emotional labour, and occur in all settings from the supermarket checkout, the hospital and the restaurant, to the aircraft cabin, the call centre and the nightclub. Instances range from verbal abuse to physical assault. In Lewig and Dollard's (2003) call centre study, the aspect of work that employees considered to be the most stressful (for example, more than meeting performance targets) was having to deal with angry and abusive customers. The impact of such abuse can be very considerable. Korczynski (2003: 64), for example, quotes a manager at a banking call centre in Australia as saying 'staff will feel dejected for the rest of the day after one abusive phone call'.

To handle these sort of problematic situations, and generally to reduce the stresses of the emotional aspects of the job, it is clear that performers of this kind of labour adopt a variety of coping strategies. Before turning to these, however, we briefly examine the monitoring of emotional labour by management.

Learning outcome 5: Identify how managers seek to manage this aspect of employee behaviour

---

Monitoring emotional labour

It is one thing for management to issue sets of guidelines and instructions and run training programmes and refresher courses to perfect and sustain various forms of emotional labour; it is another, however, to be confident that once trained, employees will carry out the emotional labour as specified at all times. What managers seek is that the prescribed emotional labour is conducted 'authentically'. In this they are reflecting the findings of studies such as Grandey and colleagues (2005), that have demonstrated the contribution to customer satisfaction of 'display authenticity' – the latter resulting either from genuinely authentic behaviour or an apparent authenticity that is the outcome of skilled impression management.

That managers recognise the tendency for employees to lapse in their emotional display is reflected in the practices adopted to monitor and modify employee behaviour: disciplining those falling short of the prescribed norms and (less frequently) rewarding unusually high performers. Many of the studies of emotional labour highlight particular supervisory practices, often covertly conducted, to check employee behaviour. Airlines, for example, regularly use 'ghost riders' to check on how employees perform their roles; similarly, supermarkets employ 'mystery shoppers' (people hired by the company and disguised as customers) to monitor performance of checkout operators. At Disneyland, supervisors secrete themselves around the park to check on the behaviour of workers while remaining unobserved themselves (Van Maanen and Kunda, 1989).

Telephone call centre supervisors routinely listen in to calls, and these may be taped for use in appraisal meetings with employees (Taylor, 1998: 93; Taylor and Tyler, 2000: 83; see also Callaghan and Thompson, 2002). In their survey of 55 call centres in Scotland, Taylor and Bain (1999: 106) identified nine measures used by management in a majority of centres to monitor employee performance. These included quantitative measures such as length of calls and time between calls. However, the most common measure of all – present in more than four out of five call centres – was the monitoring of employee 'politeness towards customer'.

In addition to these various monitoring methods, a growing number of services regularly issue 'customer service' questionnaires (like the banking illustration given earlier) to gain information about the demeanour and emotional style of the employee. Excerpt 9.7 gives another example of such a questionnaire used in the UK – this time involving the performance of postal delivery workers.

Excerpt 9.7

Assessing performance in Royal Mail

Royal Mail distributes questionnaires to customers to measure the service provided by local delivery offices. Various questions ask about time of deliveries, condition of mail received, extent to which letters are delivered to the wrong address, and so on.

In addition, several questions seek information about the postman's/postwoman's demeanour, appearance and emotional style. Not only the questions, but also the response scales used provide insight into employer expectations of postal employees. These questions and response choices include:

1. Does your postman/postwoman show respect for your property and the neighbourhood?
   - shows very little respect
   - shows some respect but could be more careful
   - always shows respect.
2. Which best describes your postman/postwoman's appearance?
   - often looks a bit scruffy
   - usually reasonably tidy
   - always neat and smart.
3. How friendly is your postman/postwoman?
   - never seems cheerful or acknowledges me
   - acknowledges me, but only if I greet him/her
   - acknowledges me, but doesn't always seem cheerful
   - always seems cheerful and acknowledges me.

> The questionnaire includes the address and postcode of the household completing it, thus allowing identification of individual delivery offices, postal delivery rounds – and specific postal employees.

Emotional labour coping strategies

Despite this level of surveillance, however, it is clear that those required to perform very frequent repetitions of an emotional display and/or perform emotional labour over long periods adopt various coping strategies, both in response to the general pressures and to handle particular situations such as angry or offensive customers. At their simplest these strategies involve employees retiring to places, such as a rest room or canteen ('off-stage' areas where customers are not present) where they can 'let off steam'. Here, employees can express their anger or frustration in ways which are denied them when performing their job.

> We do get some very difficult customers ... when you get too angry you just go into the [back] office and have a good swear at them and you come out smiling.
> (supermarket employee, quoted by Ogbonna and Wilkinson, 1990: 12)

This 'off-stage' area may be as simple as the space created by employees turning their back on the customer – and the opportunity this provides for gestures such as face-pulling or eye-rolling that indicate to other employees a dropping of the emotional mask. In studies of emotional labour, such strategies are reported in a wide variety of contexts from High Street retail stores (Martin, Knopoff and Beckman, 1998: 450) to strip clubs (Wood, 2000: 25) and guided treks (Sharpe, 2005 and Excerpt 9.6). As well as 'letting off steam', one of the additional benefits of these off-stage behaviours is that they may reinforce the degree of co-worker solidarity: a solidarity or collective response which both Karabanow (1999) and Korczynski (2003) identify as an important factor in coping with jobs with high emotional labour demands.

Other strategies for coping with rude customers include engaging in covert activity which at the same time maintains the mask of emotional display: for example, the waiter who adulterates the offensive customer's food in some way, or the sales assistant who manages to look in all directions except at the loud customer who is demanding his or her attention. Disneyland ride operators deploy a number of covert activities in response to their situation, and particularly when confronted by offensive customers; these can include the 'break-up-the-party' ploy of separating pairs into different rides (despite there being room for both on the same ride), the 'seat-belt squeeze' in which customers are over-tightened into their seats, and other variants of inflicting physical discomfort (Van Maanen and Kunda, 1989: 67).

Call centre employees also report a variety of covert methods for dealing with rude or offensive customers. These include limiting the amount of information provided and responding in a tone of voice which, while officially conforming to the rules, in practice allows employees to restrict their required emotional display. One operator in a telecommunications centre described this in the following way:

> Some customers are just a pain in the arse and they treat you like dirt. But I've worked out a way of saying things that puts them in their place. If you choose

your words carefully, there's no way they can pull you in and dig you up for what you've said.

(quoted in Taylor and Bain, 1999: 113)

A telephone sales agent in the study by Taylor and Tyler (2000: 89) makes a similar point:

If I don't like someone... it's difficult to explain but I will be efficient with them, giving them what they want and no more, but I will not be really friendly .... I sometimes have a really monotone voice, sounding a bit cold .... I will not laugh at their jokes, for example.

Resistance in call centres is also facilitated by experienced employees being able to tell when their calls are being monitored by supervisors (ibid: 89). This allows for more overt coping strategies such as disconnecting offensive calls.

A more general defence mechanism for coping with the demands of emotional labour is referred to in several studies by phrases such as 'switching off', 'switching to automatic' or 'going robot'. Filby (1992: 39) for example, refers to emotional labourers' ability to 'switch onto autopilot'. These various expressions refer to behaviour involving a continued outward adherence to the basic emotional performance, but an inward escape from the pressures of the job. Many performers of emotional labour, for example, are expected to smile as though they mean it ('smile from the inside') so that customers believe in its authenticity or sincerity and do not see it as simply part of an act. To switch into automatic may involve limiting this expression of 'sincerity'. Employees may have only limited scope for adopting this strategy, however, if 'sincerity' is also monitored. British Airways passengers arriving at London Heathrow, for example, are regularly canvassed about the service they have just received: did the check-in staff at the departure airport use the passenger's name; did they look them in the eye and smile; and did the smile seem genuine or forced – on a scale of one to four (Blyton and Turnbull, 1998: 69)?

There are also other coping strategies and ways individual employees protest against the pressure of display rules. Hochschild (1983), for example, notes the use of 'slow-downs' among flight attendants and the way some employees enact minor infringements of uniform and appearance codes as a way of not being fully submissive to management instruction. Likewise, Hampson and Junor (2005) note examples of customer service workers siding with customers in ways that may run contrary to management instruction. Overall, what such actions, protests and coping strategies indicate is that, in some cases at least, employees experience difficulties in continually performing their role as laid down in training manuals and management instruction.

To sum up

Emotional labour becomes problematic under certain circumstances. Reflecting this, management have established extensive means to monitor employee compliance with particular sets of display rules. Despite this surveillance, employees adopt various strategies to cope with excessive emotional labour.

Some commentators argue that in more extreme cases, the demands for emotional labour have consequences for the workers involved which go significantly beyond the (relatively) minor irritations of the rude customer. It is to a discussion of these consequences that we now turn, in particular the physical and psychological health implications of performing emotional labour, and the argument that emotional labour has particular implications for women's position in the labour force.

Learning outcome 6: Evaluate research on the consequences of emotional labour for employee health and well-being

---

Some wider implications of emotional labour

Emotional labour and employee well-being

In principle, just as emotional labour may be a source of job satisfaction for those who gain fulfilment from the work they perform, it is also potentially as significant a source of job dissatisfaction and alienation as other forms of labour. Indeed, for some writers on this subject, any alienation arising from emotional labour could be particularly acute, since the nature of the task carries the potential for individuals to become self-estranged – detached from their own 'real' feelings – which in turn might threaten their sense of their own identity. Further, where the expressed emotions are not felt, this gap between real and displayed feelings may cause the individual to feel false and create a sense of strain. Various writers have drawn attention to this 'falseness' potentially leading to poor self-esteem, depression, cynicism and alienation from work (Ashforth and Humphrey, 1993: 97).

It is this emotional dissonance within which emotional labourers have been described as 'suffer[ing] from a sense of being false, mechanical, no longer a whole integrated self' (Ferguson, 1984: 54, cited in Mumby and Putnam, 1992: 472). Prolonged requirement to conform to emotional display rules, or where these rules require an intensive display of an emotion script, could also contribute to 'emotion overload', particularly where women have to perform a 'second shift' of emotion management in their domestic sphere, once their first shift of emotional labour is completed (Hochschild, 1989; Wharton and Erickson, 1993).

But while in principle there is a potential for emotional labour to be dissatisfying or alienating, is this the case in practice? Overall, the evidence on this question remains somewhat inconclusive, though a number of studies in recent years have added significantly to our knowledge in this area.

In her initial study of flight attendants, Hochschild (1983) highlighted a number of negative aspects of the job, leading to 'an estrangement between self and feeling and between self and display'. Hochschild identifies such problems as 'feeling phony', with the flight attendants being unable to express genuine feelings or identify their own needs – inabilities which, for some, resulted in problems of establishing and maintaining close relationships in their private lives.

In reviewing Hochschild's work, however, Wouters (1989) argues that the costs of emotional labour should not obscure more positive aspects. For Wouters, the distinction between true and displayed feelings is not as hard and fast as Hochschild implies, for individuals perform all sorts of emotional scripts, outside as well as inside the workplace – a multiplicity which undermines any distinction between the 'displayed' feelings in emotional labour and 'true' feelings expressed elsewhere (see also discussion in Excerpt 9.6). Wouters (1989: 116) also argues that the costs of emotional labour must be offset against the positive side of such jobs, including the pleasure that many derive from serving customers and receiving from them a positive response in return. This argument reiterates the point made earlier: that there are individuals who strongly identify with their work role, and for whom their job and the emotional display rules entailed in that job are fully consistent with their personal values and identity. Indeed, for some employees it is this 'fit' between personal values and job demands that has attracted them into the job in the first place. For such individuals, the performance of the tasks is likely to enhance, rather than reduce, psychological well-being (Ashforth and Humphrey, 1993: 100–1).

Exercise 9.5

What do you think?

Hochschild and Wouters clearly disagree on how we should view emotional labour. For Hochschild, emotional labour is a potentially major problem, while for Wouters, any difficulties entailed in this type of labour are more than offset by the positive aspects of jobs such as those of flight attendants.

Which of these arguments do you think is the more convincing, and why?

In recent years, a number of more quantitative studies have been conducted to measure the effects of emotional labour on employees' health and well-being – notably the impact on job satisfaction, stress levels, degree of 'emotional exhaustion' (or 'burnout') and various physical symptoms. Again, however, these studies do not all point in the same direction, though certain general patterns are identifiable. Among the factors which may militate against a more consistent picture are:

- A lack of a standard measure of emotional labour (some studies for example simply measure the presence of emotional labour, while others concentrate on the gap between real and displayed emotions as the core measure of emotional labour).
- The diverse range of occupations studied. Among others, these include debt collectors, military recruiting staff, nurses, hairdressers, chauffeurs, travel guides, university employees, shop assistants, waiters, banking staff and survey research workers: a range which incorporates a wide variety in the type and extent of emotional labour demands.
- The potential importance of organisational and managerial context; for example the extent to which managers enforce particular emotion rules, and support (or fail to support) staff who are being subjected to abuse of one form or another from customers.

Several studies identify possible health problems related to emotional labour. In her study of university employees in the United States, for example, Pugliesi (1999) found emotional labour was associated with increased perceptions of job stress, decreased job satisfaction and lower levels of overall worker well-being. Morris and Feldman (1997) similarly found an association between one aspect of emotional labour – the degree of emotional dissonance – and the extent of 'emotional exhaustion' among over 500 respondents drawn from nursing, recruiting and debt-collecting organisations in the United States. Mann (1999) too found a relationship between reported degree of emotional dissonance and higher stress levels among respondents in 12 UK companies, while Lewig and Dollard (2003) report a similar correlation between emotional dissonance and emotional exhaustion.

While Pugliesi found emotional labour to be associated with higher stress and lower well-being regardless of other job factors, a number of other studies have highlighted the importance of certain conditions under which emotional labour has a more marked effect for the people involved. For example, in their study of workers involved in a survey research organisation in the United States, Schaubroeck and Jones (2000) found that overall, emotional labour was associated with the presence of a number of health symptoms. However, this association was mainly present among individuals who reported low levels of job involvement and a low level of identification with the organisation. As the authors conclude, this finding suggests that 'emotional labour is most unhealthful when one's emotional expressions on the job are not an authentic representation of one's personal beliefs'.

In an earlier study, Wharton (1993) also identified the importance of particular job factors in moderating any effects of emotional labour on employees. In a study of over 600 banking and health service employees (almost two-thirds of whom were judged to hold jobs which required emotional labour), Wharton found no simple relationship between emotional labour and variables such as the degree of 'emotional exhaustion': as a whole, workers performing emotional labour were no more likely to suffer from emotional exhaustion than others. There was also no evidence of the expected relationship between emotional labour and job satisfaction (indeed, those performing jobs involving emotional labour were slightly more satisfied overall than those performing other jobs). What the study found, however, was that people performing emotional labour were less likely to experience emotional exhaustion if they had greater autonomy over how they carried out their work.

To sum up

Despite the variation in results between individual studies, at present the balance of available evidence indicates that, in certain circumstances at least, emotional labour is associated with stress, emotional exhaustion and a lower level of general well-being. This is more likely to be the case where demands for emotional labour are high and/or where emotional dissonance is marked. The latter is likely to be greater among those who identify least with their job or with the organisation they work for. Those with very restricted degrees of control over how they perform their jobs may also find performing emotional labour to be a more negative experience than those with higher levels of job autonomy.

Learning outcome 7: Recognise wider implications of the growth of emotional labour, in particular for the position of women in the labour force

The gender implications of emotional labour

As well as its potential for creating feelings of alienation and emotional exhaustion, several commentators have pointed to possible negative implications of emotional labour for women's position in the labour force: in particular, that it reinforces certain gender stereotypes which in the past have been detrimental to women (see for example Hochschild, 1983; James, 1989; Mumby and Putnam, 1992). Three aspects of emotional labour are central to this argument:

- The distribution of emotional labour reflects a gender imbalance: the majority of those doing emotional labour for a living are women. Hochschild (1983), for example, estimates that twice as many women as men occupy jobs that require emotional labour. Moreover, even in single occupations employing both men and women, a number of studies have identified an expectation that the women employees will perform more emotional labour than their male counterparts (Morris and Feldman, 1996: 997; Taylor and Tyler, 2000).
- Most people performing emotional labour occupy relatively low positions within work hierarchies, with emotional labour rarely being ascribed the status of a skill. Thus, just as women in general are located disproportionately within lower levels of occupational hierarchies, they are similarly disproportionately represented among those lower-status jobs requiring emotional labour. For some (see for example Ashforth and Humphrey, 1995; Domagalski, 1999; James, 1989) this reflects the status of 'rationalism' within contemporary capitalism, and also the customary association of rationality and masculinity (Pringle, 1989). In combination, these create a contrast between jobs that are seen to be highly 'rational' and as a result are afforded high status (and are disproportionately occupied by men), and jobs that are more 'emotional' and are accorded much lower status (and are filled disproportionately by women).
- In hospitals, for example, it is the rational skills of the (mainly male) doctors and hospital managers that are accredited the highest status and rewards, while the emotional well-being of the patient – a key ingredient in their return to full health – is borne largely by the (mainly female) nurses and auxiliaries, and tends to be unrecognised and much more poorly rewarded (James, 1989). This tendency to attribute status to some jobs rather than others is related to the issue of the social construction of skill.
- The main emotions displayed in emotional labour – in particular those involving a display of caring – act to reinforce gender stereotypes, and in particular that 'caring' is an emotion that is more 'natural' in women. Women are widely seen to be not only naturally more caring than men, but also more emotional than men, and more used to dealing with other people's feelings, as part of their domestic caring role. Various studies, for example, have indicated that women are the primary providers of emotional support for their partners and children (see discussion in Wharton and Erickson, 1993: 469).

   Critics of emotional labour argue that, as a result of this greater responsibility for emotion management in the domestic sphere, this comes to be viewed as a 'natural' ability in women, or a 'talent' which they have, rather than a skill which has to be acquired. The effect is for management to treat emotional labour as an extension of this natural talent, not a learned skill – with the effect that it is not accorded the status of a skill. It leads management to select women rather than men for many jobs involving emotional labour: see, for example Leidner (1991) on the distribution of work tasks in McDonald's, and Taylor and Tyler (2000) on the selection of candidates for telephone sales positions.

Thus, just as the skills employed (disproportionately by women) in the domestic sphere tend to be under-recognised, so too the performance of emotional labour skills in the paid work sphere also tends to go under-recognised and under-rewarded. Filby (1992) correctly points out that it would be misleading to argue that all emotional labour deserves 'skilled' status: indeed, 'much emotion work ... is untutored and probably poor' (Filby, 1992: 39). Nevertheless, as the foregoing discussion has illustrated, in a number of different contexts, emotional labour is learned through considerable training, and is performed in far from straightforward circumstances.

An extension of this argument of reinforcing stereotypes is that many front-line service jobs entail the performance of tasks as deferential servants – on aircraft, in hotels and in restaurants and night clubs, for example. It may be argued that, since the majority of emotional labour jobs are performed by women, this potentially acts to reinforce an image of women as servants – an image already emphasised by the unpaid and problematic status of domestic activities. This is particularly pertinent to those settings comprising mainly women performing emotional labour for a largely male customer group; it is mostly men, for example, who fly business class on airlines, eat business lunches, stay at hotels on sales conferences and visit certain types of nightclub. Further, as well as the nurturing and servant roles, some emotional labour jobs also involve women workers emphasising other aspects of their 'feminine' qualities, in particular applying their sexuality as a way of 'keeping the customers happy'.

As Hochschild (1983: 182) describes, flight attendants are required to play these different roles simultaneously: 'those of the supportive mother and those of the sexually desirable mate', manifesting themselves in 'both "motherly" behavior and a "sexy" look'. Similarly, Linstead (1995: 196) argues that through the nature of their advertising, airlines 'make no secret of their wish to entice a predominantly male clientele on board in the lucrative first and business sectors with gently erotic evocations'. In general, this message may be more subtle now than in the 1970s – when airlines used such advertising slogans as 'I'm Cheryl, fly me' (quoted in Lessor, 1984: 42) and 'We really move our tails for you to make your every wish come true' (quoted in Hochschild, 1983: 93) – but the message remains, nevertheless.

Sexuality is similarly present in other settings of emotional labour. Filby (1992), for example, in his study of women working in betting shops, notes the sexual banter between cashiers and (mostly male) customers, which forms part of the employees' task of building customer relations and customer loyalty to that branch.

Likewise, Hall (1993) notes the existence of the 'obligatory job flirt' which occurs in many restaurants, again as part of a broader management requirement to 'keep the customer happy'. This mix of emotional labour and sexuality reaches its apogee in the strip clubs described by Wood (2000) and others, where much of the income-generating activity for the women dancers is predicated on their ability to flirt and raise the sexual self-esteem of their (overwhelmingly male) customers.

However, the arguments over women and emotional labour are not as clear-cut as some of these critics have suggested. For example, as noted above, it is not necessarily the case that women performing emotional labour experience a negative reaction. Indeed, Wharton (1993) in her study found that women performing emotional labour were significantly more satisfied than their male counterparts engaged in similar types of work. As a result of patterns of socialisation, for example, 'women may be better equipped than men for the interpersonal demands of frontline service work and thus experience those jobs more positively than their male counterparts' (Wharton, 1993: 225). Further, in the longer term, other factors may act in favour of changing the position of women performing emotional labour. The growth of jobs requiring emotional labour is resulting in more men needing to manage their emotions as part of the job. As the number of both women and men performing emotional labour rises, this may affect the way emotional labour is delivered, particularly where the clientele is becoming less male-dominated. Linstead (1995: 196) notes, for example, the acknowledged need among airline companies to shift the nature of emotional labour in business and first class to attract the growing market in female business travellers.

Further, as the emphasis on effective service increases, employees and groups such as trade unions will potentially be able to use this recognised importance as a lever for improving the status and rewards pertaining to those performing these types of jobs – indeed, at least one writer (Foegen, 1988) has called for workers performing emotional labour to receive separate 'hypocrisy pay' as a recognition of the task involved. More generally, trade unions in Britain have made significant inroads into areas such as call centres: in the survey of call centres by Taylor and Bain (1999: 113–14), more than half had a union or staff association, with unions not only negotiating standard items such as pay, holidays, hours and overtime payments, but also raising such concerns as job stress and levels of employee monitoring and surveillance.

Taking this point further, emotional display does not render women powerless. Indeed, in certain circumstances the 'emotion' could be used as a source of power. Linstead (1995), for example, writing on a strike among Cathay Pacific (CP) flight attendants, points to the attendants' explicit use of emotional display as a means of attracting media attention and public support. The 'perfumed picket line' as it was dubbed by one of the Hong Kong newspapers, gained much more coverage than the CP 'managers in suits'. While the attendants did not win the strike (not least because management was successful in hiring outside crews to operate a reduced service), the flight attendants nevertheless indicated their potential power in 'turn[ing] the seductive skills which company training had developed into an effective weapon to mobilize public opinion' (Linstead, 1995: 190).

To sum up

Several writers have highlighted gender implications of emotional labour, and particularly the way that emotional labour can act to reinforce gender stereotypes in the workplace. The arguments in this area do not all point in the same direction, however, indicating the need for greater clarity regarding the particular contexts and conditions under which emotional labour acts to the detriment of women's status in the labour market.

Conclusion

Analysing the growth and implications of emotional labour underscores a number of broader developments and issues in contemporary industrial society. It is a growth borne out of not only the expansion of the services available to the general public, but also the competition between those services and the identification of customer relations as a key to business success in a competitive environment. Though long established in various areas of employment, a required emotional display and self-management of feelings have become part of an increasing number of jobs. There is every indication too, that this aspect of work will grow further in coming years, as a public increasingly used to a high level of 'customer care' raises its baseline expectation of what constitutes an appropriate level of that 'care' in an ever-widening range of services.

As well as reflecting a growth of, and increased competition between, service providers, and the greater significance attached to customers, emotional labour also underscores certain other issues raised elsewhere in the book. Most notably, emotional labour is an aspect of work that to date has been performed predominantly by women, often while occupying comparatively low positions within their work organisations. It is an aspect of women's work which has also typically been accorded relatively little status. Hence, just as women in general have not typically been the beneficiaries of how the notion of skill has been socially constructed, in a similar way, emotional labour has not been accorded prestige or skilled status. Rather, the performing of emotional labour has tended to be seen as something that women are 'naturally' good at – an innate talent rather than an acquired skill.

At the same time, as has been noted, it is important not to adopt too simplistic a view of emotional labour. It is an aspect of work that varies considerably in its nature and degree. Its impact on employees will depend on the character of the individuals involved, and some will be far more predisposed to the requirements of emotional labour than others. Further, for many, emotional labour represents a relatively minor part of their job, not unpleasant and often helping to create a more friendly working environment: smiling at others often elicits a smile in return. It is in those cases where emotional labour expectations are excessive that it becomes problematic, potentially giving rise to feelings of alienation, dissonance and emotional exhaustion. Yet, even in these situations it is clear that workers employ various coping strategies to mitigate the excesses of emotional labour.

References

Abiala, K. (1999) 'Customer orientation and sales situations: variations in interactive service work', *Acta Sociologica*, 42 (3): 207–22.

Ashforth, B. and Humphrey, R. (1993) 'Emotional labour in service roles: the influence of identity', *Academy of Management Review*, 18 (1): 88–115.

Ashforth, B. and Humphrey, R. (1995) 'Emotion in the work place: a reappraisal', *Human Relations*, 48 (2): 97–125.

Ashforth, B. E. and Tomiuk, M. (2000) 'Emotional labour and authenticity: views from service agents', in S. Fineman (ed.), *Emotion in Organizations*, 2nd edn, London: Sage: 184–203.

Blyton, P. and Turnbull, P. (1998) *The Dynamics of Employee Relations*, 2nd edn, Basingstoke: Macmillan.

Boles, J. and Garbin, A. P. (1974) 'The strip club and stripper–customer patterns of interaction', *Sociology and Social Research*, 58 (1): 136–44.

Bolton, S. C. and Boyd, C. (2003) 'Trolley dolly or skilled emotion manager? Moving on from Hochschild's managed heart', *Work, Employment & Society*, 17 (2): 289–308.

Callaghan, G. and Thompson, P. (2002) 'We recruit attitude: the selection and shaping of routine call centre labour', *Journal of Management Studies*, 39 (2): 233–54.

Carlzon, J. (1987) *Moments of Truth*, New York: Harper and Row.

Crusco, A. H. and Wetzel, C. G. (1984) 'The Midas touch: the effects of interpersonal touch on restaurant tipping', *Personality and Social Psychology Bulletin*, 10 (4): 512–17.

Deming, W. E. (1982) *Quality, Productivity and Competitive Position*, Cambridge, Mass.: MIT Press.

Domagalski, T. A. (1999) 'Emotion in organizations: main currents', *Human Relations*, 52 (6): 833–52.

Ekman, P. (1973) 'Cross culture studies of facial expression', in P. Ekman (ed.), *Darwin and Facial Expression*, New York: Academic Press: 169–222.

Ferguson, K. (1984) *The Feminist Case Against Bureaucracy*, Philadelphia: Temple University Press.

Filby, M. P. (1992) '"The figures, the personality and the bums": service work and sexuality', *Work, Employment and Society*, 6 (1): 23–42.

Fineman, S. (ed.) (1993) *Emotion in Organizations*, London: Sage.

Fineman, S. (2000) *Emotion in Organizations*, 2nd edn, London: Sage.

Foegen, J. H. (1988) 'Hypocrisy pay', *Employee Responsibilities and Rights Journal*, 1 (1): 85–7.

Foote, N. N. (1954) 'Sex as play', *Social Problems*, 1: 159–63.

Furman, F. K. (1997) *Facing the Mirror: Older Women and Beauty Shop Culture*, London: Routledge.

Goffman, E. (1969) *The Presentation of Self in Everyday Life*, London: Allen Lane.

Goffman, E. (1971) *Relations in Public*, New York: Basic Books.

Grandey, A. A. (2003) 'When "the show must go on": surface acting and deep acting as determinants of emotional exhaustion and peer-rated service delivery' *Academy of Management Journal*, 46 (1): 86–96.

Grandey, A. A., Fisk, G. M., Mattila, A. S., Jansen, K. J. and Sideman, L. A. (2005) 'Is "service with a smile" enough? Authenticity of positive displays during service encounters', *Organizational Behavior and Human Decision Processes*, 96: 38–55.

Hall, E. (1993) 'Smiling, deferring and flirting: doing gender by giving good service', *Work and Occupations*, 20 (4): 452–71.

Hampson, I. and Junor, A. (2005) 'Invisible work, invisible skills: interactive customer service as articulation work', *New Technology, Work and Employment*, 20 (2): 166–81.

Hochschild, A. R. (1979) 'Emotion work, feeling rules and social structure', *American Journal of Sociology*, 85 (3): 551–75.

Hochschild, A. R. (1983) *The Managed Heart: Commercialization of Human Feeling*, Berkeley: University of California Press.

Hochschild, A. R. (1989) *The Second Shift: Working Patterns and the Revolution at Home*, Berkeley: University of California Press.

Höpfl, H. (2002) 'Playing the part: reflections on aspects of mere performance in the customer–client relationship', *Journal of Management Studies*, 39 (2): 255–67.

James, N. (1989) 'Emotional labour: skill and work in the social regulation of feelings', *Sociological Review*, 37 (1): 15–42.

Juran, J. M. (1979) *Quality Control Handbook*, New York: McGraw-Hill.

Karabanow, J. (1999) 'When caring is not enough: emotional labor and youth shelter workers', *Social Service Review*, 73 (3): 340–57.

Korczynski, M. (2003) 'Communities of coping: collective emotional labour in service work', *Organization*, 10 (1): 55–79.

Lashley, C. (1999) 'Empowerment through involvement: a case study of TGI Friday's restaurants', *Personnel Review*, 29 (6): 791–811.

Leidner, R. (1991) 'Serving hamburgers and selling insurance: gender, work and identity in interactive service jobs', *Gender and Society*, 5 (2): 154–77.

Lessor, R. (1984) 'Social movements, the occupational arena and changes in career consciousness: the case of women flight attendants', *Journal of Occupational Behaviour*, 5: 37–51.

Lewig, K. A. and Dollard, M. F. (2003) 'Emotional dissonance, emotional exhaustion and job satisfaction in call centre workers', *European Journal of Work and Organizational Psychology,* 12 (4): 366–92.

Linstead, S. (1995) 'Averting the gaze: gender and power on the perfumed picket line', *Gender, Work and Organization,* 2 (4): 190–206.

Lively, K. J. (2002) 'Client contact and emotional labor: upsetting the balance and evening the field, *Work and Occupations,* 29 (2): 198–225.

Lynch, J. J. (1992) *The Psychology of Customer Care,* London: Macmillan.

Mangham, I. L. and Overington, M. A. (1987) *Organizations as Theatre,* Chichester: Wiley.

Mann, S. (1999) 'Emotion at work: to what extent are we expressing, suppressing or faking it?', *European Journal of Work and Organizational Psychology,* 8 (3): 347–69.

Mars, G. and Nicod, M. (1984) *The World of Waiters,* Boston, Mass.: Allen and Unwin.

Martin, J., Knopoff, K. and Beckman, C. (1998) 'An alternative to bureaucratic impersonality: bounded emotionality at The Body Shop', *Administrative Science Quarterly,* 43: 429–69.

Morris, J. A. and Feldman, D. C. (1996) 'The dimensions, antecedents and consequences of emotional labor', *Academy of Management Review,* 21 (4): 986–1010.

Morris, J. A. and Feldman, D. C. (1997) 'Managing emotions in the workplace', *Journal of Managerial Issues,* 9 (3): 257–74.

Mumby, D. and Putnam, L. (1992) 'The politics of emotion: a feminist reading of bounded rationality', *Academy of Management Review,* 17 (3): 465–86.

Ogbonna, E. and Wilkinson, B. (1990) 'Corporate strategy and corporate culture: the view from the checkout', *Personnel Review,* 19 (4): 9–15.

Peters, T. and Austin, N. (1985) *A Passion for Excellence,* New York: Random House.

Peters, T. and Waterman, R. H. (1982) *In Search of Excellence,* New York: Harper and Row.

Pringle, R. (1989) 'Bureaucracy, rationality and sexuality: the case of secretaries', in J. Hearn, D. L. Sheppard, P. Tancred-Sheriff and G. Burrell (eds), *The Sexuality of Organization,* London: Sage: 158–77.

Pugliesi, K. (1999) 'The consequences of emotional labor: effects on work stress, job satisfaction and well-being', *Motivation and Emotion,* 23 (2): 125–54.

Rafaeli, A. and Sutton, R. I. (1987) 'Expression of emotion as part of the work role', *Academy of Management Review,* 12 (1): 23–37.

Rafaeli, A. and Sutton, R. I. (1989) 'The expression of emotion in organizational life', in L. L. Cummings and B. M. Staw (eds), *Research in Organizational Behaviour,* Greenwich, Conn.: JAI Press: 1–42.

Ronai, C. R. and Ellis, C. (1989) 'Turn-ons for money: interactional strategies of the table dancer', *Journal of Contemporary Ethnography,* 18 (3): 271–98.

Rosenthal, P., Hill, S. and Peccei, R. (1997) 'Checking out service: evaluating excellence, HRM and TQM in retailing', *Work, Employment and Society,* 11 (3): 481–503.

Schaubroeck, J. and Jones, J. R. (2000) 'Antecedents of workplace emotional labor dimensions and moderators of their effects on physical symptoms', *Journal of Organizational Behavior,* 21: 163–83.

Seymour, D. and Sandiford, P. (2005) 'Learning emotion rules in service organizations: socialization and training in the UK public-house sector', *Work, Employment and Society,* 19 (3): 547–64.

Sharma, U. and Black, P. (2001) 'Look good, feel better: beauty therapy as emotional labour', *Sociology,* 35 (4): 913–31.

Sharpe, E. K. (2005) '"Going above and beyond": the emotional labour of adventure guides', *Journal of Leisure Research,* 37 (1): 29–50.

Snyder, M. (1987) *Public Appearances, Private Realities,* New York: Freeman.

Spradley, J. P. and Mann, B. J. (1975) *The Cocktail Waitress: Women's Work in a Man's World,* New York: Wiley.

Taylor, P. and Bain, P. (1999) '"An assembly line in the head": work and employee relations in the call centre', *Industrial Relations Journal,* 30 (2): 101–17.

Taylor, S. (1998) 'Emotional labour and the new workplace', in P. Thompson and C. Warhurst (eds), *Workplaces of the Future,* Basingstoke: Macmillan: 84–103.

Taylor, S. and Tyler, M. (2000) 'Emotional labour and sexual difference in the airline industry', *Work, Employment and Society,* 14 (1): 77–95.

Tidd, K. L. and Lockard, J. S. (1978) 'Monetary significance of the affiliative smile', *Bulletin of the Psychonomic Society,* 11: 344–6.

Van Maanen, J. and Kunda, G. (1989) '"Real feelings": emotional expression and organizational culture' in L. L. Cummings and B. M. Staw (eds), *Research in Organizational Behaviour,* Greenwich, Conn.: JAI Press: 43–103.

Wharton, A. (1993) 'The affective consequences of service work: managing emotions on the job', *Work and Occupations,* 20 (2): 205–32.

Wharton, A. and Erickson, R. (1993) 'Managing emotions on the job and at home: understanding the consequences of multiple emotional roles', *Academy of Management Review,* 18 (3): 457–86.

Williams, C. (1988) *Blue, White and Pink Collar Workers in Australia,* Sydney: Allen and Unwin.

Williams, C. (2003) 'Sky service: the demands of emotional labour in the airline industry', *Gender, Work and Organization,* 10 (5): 513–50.

Wood, E. A. (2000) 'Working in the fantasy factory: the attention hypothesis and the enacting of masculine power in strip clubs', *Journal of Contemporary Ethnography,* 29 (1): 5–31.

Wouters, C. (1989) 'The sociology of emotions and flight attendants: Hochschild's managed heart', *Theory, Culture and Society,* 6: 95–123.

CHAPTER 10

Identity work

Social organization is both means and bar to control. The concrete physical and biological settings in which actions occur are crucial. It is thus the outcomes and contentions among identities which is what cumulates into social organisation. (Harrison, 1992: 16)

Explanations of identity

The mainstream agenda in OB can be shown to refer to common and basic processes through which individuals develop identities. Through these processes, notably learning, perception and socialisation, the individual is seen to develop a distinctive personality and patterns of motivation. There are many useful things to learn from examining that journey, but as an account of the development of subjectivity and identity within an organisational context, it has distinct limitations. It fails adequately to understand individual identity as a social reality through which we transact with our environment. Hence we deal with objective reality through a subjective construction which interprets and shapes our whole world in terms of what we value about ourselves. Our focus on subjective identity lies in this process, because as individuals we guide our actions according to what will in our view best defend, enhance or substantiate our identities. As Knights and Willmott (1985) argued, each of us is effectively engaged in securing for ourselves identities which provide both a sense of personal stability and a basis for directing our activity. Identity in this light is a tool which we use to present ourselves in – and possibly transform ourselves into – images appropriate to our social, cultural and work context.

Unless one takes personality and identity as being entirely a genetically determined phenomenon, there can be little doubt that an individual's identity is to a great extent determined by social contexts and pressures. In researching differential socio-emotional development in male and female children, Lewis found that as early as biological influences can be distinguished, there are parallel differences in the treatment of the two sexes by adults and other children (M. Lewis, 1975). Thus though biological influences undoubtedly have some effects on personality in the same way that they have an influence on hair colour and general bodily characteristics, these effects cannot be easily differentiated from social or environmental influences.

According to Weigert *et al.* (1986: 31) 'identity is a definition that transforms a mere biological individual into a human person. It is a definition that emerges from and is sustained by the cultural meanings of social relationships activated in interaction.' To extend the above example, if someone dyes or changes their hairstyle, they have taken steps to place a self-directed social construction on the body they were born with. They are taking for themselves an identity produced out of what they select as attractive or appropriate out of the social values, expectations and fashions of their time. The tradition of sociological social psychology represented by Weigert and other writers tries to avoid the contradictions which have existed between notions of personal and social identity. They take the view that identity is a social product which is both bestowed on individuals by others and appropriated by individuals for themselves. It takes the form of a *typified self,* in that it is any of a number of self-produced categorisations out of what is available to the individual within the various situations in which they participate.

If the focus is shifted from personal to social identity, it is possible to see that we are constantly representing our subjective selves to the others in our social environment. In the way we dress, speak and behave we present a changing image of who we are to those with whom we interact: our identity is, in this sense, a negotiated construction. Depending on whom we are dealing with at the time, we can present an image which is intended both to appear appropriate to the situation and to appear consistent with the expectations of the other. Using a Symbolic Interactionist framework, Erving Goffman (1971) explored this conception of self within a dramaturgical metaphor: representation of social identity being a performance analogous to that of an actor. The image presented is not necessarily the 'real' self of the person, but is a situationally appropriate image sustained both by the 'actor' and by those observing and/or interacting with the performer. The others involved collaborate with the actor to enable him or her to present a consistent performance and hence a social identity consistent within the situation. The students in a lecture theatre, for example, collaborate with the lecturer to maintain an image of authority for the latter and of subordination for themselves, even though they may in no way consider themselves socially or intellectually inferior to the lecturer. They simply exercise *tact* in order to continue participating in the production of a performance which fits the perceived rules of the situation.

The interface between social and personal identity lies in this act of interpersonal negotiation. A social identity does not simply spring fully formed from the demands of the situation, but requires effort and practice from the individual and appropriate feedback from others. Thus the contexts from which we are able to construct a unique subjective identity for ourselves consist mainly of 'rationalised' performances, and we construct our personal identity out of the strategies and responses we devise to deal with the situations we encounter. The problems which many people find in discovering their 'own' identity may in part arise from the consequences of trying to be consistent over time and from the wide range of images they have had to present to survive in a complex and changing social environment.

The idea that we each possess a core identity which relates to what we value about ourselves is examined in the social learning conception of identity (Miller, 1963).

As a source of meaning, identity links us to others in the social structure through perceived similarities and processes of identification. As definition identity sets us apart from others, it is the basis of social comparison in that it shows us the things and people with whom our particular set of personal meanings debar us from identifying. Personal, subjective identity consists of the meanings and images we have found accurately to represent us in the past. Social identity, where it is different to the former, consists of the negotiated position between our personal identity and the meanings and images demanded of us in our current social context.

This leads us to a final aspect of identity as a linking concept between differing levels of explanation. We gain identities through interaction and association with others, but the major source of these interactions and associations is not other individuals in themselves but the social and cultural groupings to which we belong. These groups provide us with points of reference and comparison out of which we can define ourselves. Social groupings are in turn defined in terms of the social structure within which they exist. Through this route identity is directly moulded by social structure. For this reason, Miller (1963) saw identity as the foundation of the links between social structure and personality and fundamental as such to the explanation of socialisation, motivation and psychological conflict. Our personal transactions with social structures are conducted for the most part through the organisations we belong to, work for and with which we have to deal. Organisations attempt to socialise people into their particular workplace cultures. Management attempts to influence individual motivation to its advantage. The amelioration of the psychological, interpersonal and group conflicts engendered by these activities is a major rationale for the involvement of social and behavioural scientists in organisations.

Redefining the agenda

To understand more adequately the individual's development towards becoming a participant in organisations who is active, yet acted upon, we also need further to redefine some of the issues and agenda. For example, because so much of OB takes the structures, workings and goals of organisational life for granted, it underestimates the degree to which the environment restricts sources of meaning for secure identities and imposes costs on individuals. The resources which an individual can bring to an *identity project* will depend on their *situational power* in the organisation. Admittedly, this situational power does not depend simply on a person's place in an organisational hierarchy. An individual's perception of their own situational power, whether at an interpersonal, group or organisational level, will also condition how secure they feel. Thus a shopfloor worker can construct an identity just as, or even more, secure as that of someone with more position power. These identities are also not necessarily situation specific: they can provide meaning and support outside the context within which they were constructed, though there are of course limits. The 'organisation man', secure in his or her identification with organisational goals and objectives, may generalise associated attitudes and behaviours to situations where such an identity may be inappropriate.

Nevertheless, the attitudes, behaviours, and abilities through which our identities are externally communicated will reflect the constraints placed on us at work and the standards and values of the dominant organisational cultures with which we are in contact. The individual and group identities we eventually secure will be favourable, neutral or antagonistic to organisations on the basis of the climate and context in which they are constructed in, mediated by our experiential base and the standards of comparison this gives us.

The treatment of identity in mainstream psychology also tends to neglect contextual issues because it treats identity in the same fashion as we tend to do in everyday life, as inherent in the person. Breakwell (1987: 95) argues that psychologists 'tend to treat identity as the origin of action', and use it as a 'motivational variable'. In contrast, we have to see identity as the outcome of interaction within particular material contexts which act as constraints on available sources of meaning and on the process of identity construction.

The central limiting factor on available sources of meaning is the context of *fragmented* and *commodified* work. Labour is reduced to abstract capacities which serve the ends of production rather than those of the person; as in the appropriation by work organisations of the *use-time* available to individuals for developing and pursuing their own capacities, abilities and interests (Seve, 1978). Subjectively, this reduction of the relations between people and things to their value in a system of exchange both increase feelings of powerlessness and decreases feelings of personal responsibility. In an externally controlled environment, the most individuals can often hope for is to maintain or increase their situational power and material resources. Our relationships with, and our attribution of motives to, others are reduced to their instrumental function in the process of, 'accumulation without regard to need' (Wexler, 1983: 122). Socio-psychological models of motivation continually reflect this, as in the rational calculations of personal advantage we are assumed to make in exchange and equity theory or the assessments of personal power in Lee and Lawrence's 'political model' of motivation.

The instrumentality of relationships also extends into the definition of gender identities in the workplace. Hearn and Parkin (1987) identify the *desexualised* nature of work organisations as reinforcing patriarchy and sexism. Instrumentality in the continuing forms of fragmented, Taylorised work relations defines masculinity and reproduces organisational work as a male concern:

> The workman is, potentially at least, nothing more than the doer of the task, without feelings and emotions. The ideal workman would appear to almost lose physical presence, or be a mere disembodied bearer of role, in effect part of a machine system. (Hearn and Parkin, 1987: 19)

Women workers are in general separated from the dominantly male culture of organisations and feminine gender identity is suppressed or at best marginalised. Women managers especially are often required to exhibit what is almost a male gender identity in work and are often viewed as exceptions to women in general. Hearn and Parkin (1987: 108) cite as an example the lack of appropriate female role models in management on which to base standards and the subsequent development of the 'image' or clothing consultant to advise women in particular on what is termed 'executive' or 'power' dressing. Likewise domestic labour is not viewed as 'real' work in the fashion that paid work is, the identity construct of 'worker' being reserved for the latter. Women's labour in organisations can often be an extension of domestic labour, as in the example of bosses' secretaries who act as, 'office wives, protecting their charges from unnecessary interference and strain, making tea, buying presents, even cleaning their bosses' false teeth', (1987: 92).

Sexual, and racial, discrimination in labour markets is reinforced by stereotypical categorisations of women and black workers which portrays them as 'naturally' inferior in various abilities or only suited to certain types of work. Notions such as women being better suited than men to boring, repetitive tasks serve to legitimise restricted access to labour markets. Black workers in particular can be discriminated against in the recruitment and selection process on the basis of a stereotyped lack of acceptability in white workplace cultures. Jenkins (R. Jenkins, 1986) notes that the causes of racism are often attributed to those who are discriminated against; 'managers do, in the main, see black workers as posing problems for their organisations. These problems were typically seen to be created by black workers, not by white racism' (1986: 114).

Predominantly white, male management, whose workplace identities would be expected to be closely aligned with organisational goals, would not be expected to view problems as created by their own racism or by racism institutionalised into workplace cultures. Rather, they would be seen to reside in those who demonstrably deviate from the cultural standards they have come to see as 'natural'. White workers are viewed as individuals, whereas black workers are perceived as groups characterised by often contradictory stereotypes: 'if you've got a problem with one of them, you've got a problem with all of them, whereas with the whites, you're just dealing with an individual' (R. Jenkins, 1986: 99). Of course, the fact that people tend to fall back on the resources of group identity in the face of discrimination and consequent situational powerlessness, is wholly understandable. The unfortunate effect is that it simply acts to reinforce stereotypes. Falling back on group identity is also a perceived problem with white workers, especially when that identity is crystallised in trade union activity. But this type of resistance is at least seen as acceptable in the sense that its source is a competing power structure, which is also likely to be seen as part of the same socio-cultural framework, and thus their actions are legitimised, though disapproved of.

It is important to recognise that any form of organisational domination does not only or primarily occur through overt coercion such as threats to job security. Consent has to be mobilised because domination by coercion is often 'inefficient': it requires constant reinforcement of coercive pressures and extensive monitoring of reactions to them. Domination of the individual through self-limitation and constraint is far more effective. This is engendered through individual assimilation of, and accommodation to, dominant workplace cultures and ideologies. At its most visible level, this process can be seen in the internalisation of the norms and accepted standards of behaviour in work-groups which occurs in organisational socialisation and in the construction of the 'concertive controls' proposed by J. R. Barker. If consent is not present, the pressures to shape ourselves in appropriate images may not be perceived as legitimate and may actively promote resistance. In Westwood's (1984) account of the lives of women at 'Stitchco' the women participated in a patriarchal labour process which from the management view was 'harmonious' in its appeals to both common progressive goals and paternalistic values. The women, however, had a 'clear understanding that there were sides in industry and that these sides maintained an uneasy truce which was easily broken' (1984: 25). Westwood argues that the, 'deprivation, pain and waste that black and white working-class women live with on a daily basis', can be, 'a spur to action rather than defeat'. As such, domination becomes the source of an identity project which empowers their creativity and resourcefulness, sisterhood being the focus of a resistance which does more than enable their survival in a hostile environment.

When we attempt to construct an identity that offers us a degree of protection from uncertainty (Knights and Willmott, 1985) we often find ourselves in competition with others for sources of meaning. This may take the form of access to and 'possession' of material resources for living and the symbols on which we place value. In order to maintain an identity we attempt to control our environment and those in it and to resist those pressures which act to define our identities for us. The sense of individual meaning we gain from identity gives us a basis to resist external manipulation, but at the same time places us in competition with those in a similar position to ourselves who could aid us in our resistance. Thus we could both resist the attempts to shape our identities made by groups in organisations, and yet use our positional or situational power in those groups to enhance our identities at the expense of others. The separation that this achieves acts to blind us to the fact that an organisation is a structure of *interdependence* and the success of systems of control depends upon our compliance with managerial demands. By neglecting the context in which we compete for sources of meaning we can become estranged from one of the major sources available to us, the collective identity and power of those with similar interests.

We have already recognised that, in terms of identity construction, the contextual issues raised above are not necessarily simply sources of constraint. They may for some individuals be the very factors which allow them to secure identity. The worker with worries over job security may find meaning in defining themselves in line with nationalist or traditionalist sentiments which can give expression to their fears through hostility to 'immigrant' workers or women who should remain at home. Similarly hostility and resistance to organisational goals and practices may arise out of the conditions of exploitation, domination and alienation which renders others submissive. It would appear that identities are constructed out of whatever meanings are readily available and are constrained only by the individual's ability to sustain them. Thus the construction of identity is a continuous process which has to be understood in the context of the workplace, where it is maintained and reproduced on a daily basis.

Organisations and identities

If our society is characterised by the involvement of individuals in organisational structures, then organisations are characterised by their attempts to *control the performance and behaviour* of the individuals of whom they consist. It is this rule-bound control of individual behaviour which distinguishes organisational behaviour from other forms of social organisation. Home and family life, for example, are undoubtedly organised, and controls and sanctions are placed on the behaviour of family members. But this control is in no sense as systematic as that existing in even a small commercial organisation. On this basis, for work organisations of any type to maintain their present forms of authority, hierarchy and control it becomes necessary to produce some kind of change in the types of regulation to which employees will consent – this was the main theme of Chapter 10. There is, of course, a great amount of prior socialisation for work contained in our experience of schooling and this is presently being extended in the kinds of job training to 'fit' youth better for work. This, however, merely serves to illustrate that organisations depend on being able to mould people into the kind of workers they need.

However, organisations do not simply transform individual identities at work by some form of brainwashing; nor do they simply depend on individuals recognition of economic necessity to ensure their consent to the control of their performance in their work. The concept of 'economic man' is not adequate to the explanation of how a worker's consent to change and rationalise his or her working practices can be obtained. The rules and procedures used to control work-related behaviour will often conflict with the individual's attempt to secure a stable and favourable identity. Unless, that is, people can manage to construct for themselves a workable identity out of the very rules which constrain them. Alternatives can include becoming an 'organisation man'; setting themselves up in opposition to their employers; or distancing themselves from the whole affair and concentrating their lives on external interests. Whatever the tactics employed by individuals as mechanisms for survival and coping, they may in time transform themselves into an image that functions in a way that is useful to the organisation for which they work. Even the deviant or militant worker is useful in this sense in terms of providing an image of what the 'good ' employee should not be, and in providing a focus for the attribution of blame.

Identity becomes not only the basis of individual involvement in organisations but also the basis for manipulation by them. This is achieved through a negotiated transaction between organisational strategies of control and individual strategies for securing identity. The consequences of this negotiation are not always positive for the organisations concerned. We all to some extent cope in a creative fashion with the constraints of work or unemployment. Strategies used to survive can become powerful tools for extending our own abilities and capacities. Those who try to manipulate our behaviour must face the fact that they are attempting to interfere with the self-perceptions and judgements that actually make us what we are. If manipulation is perceived as going too far, it may do no more than to encourage employee identities more resistant to organisational control.

Identity work and situational power

Subjective experience in organisations consists of lived relationships bounded by social, organisational and work-group cultures in the context of structural and ideological constraints. These form the three basic contexts within which individual identity is continually reproduced. Lived relationships are the subjective arena of identity construction. Even though our subjective 'now' is informed by our past experience and moulded by the pressures brought to bear on us, we still act as if we are independent and self-directed entities. Thus our everyday existence can continue as if it largely bypasses the influence of cultural and structural constraints on our behaviour.

Social, organisational and work-group cultures are the arenas in which 'fitting behaviour' is moulded and regulated and in which we perform 'identity work' (Goffman, 1971; Cohen and Taylor, 1978). Just as our perceptions of the world are simplified by the use of stereotypical categories, the activities we carry out in the workplace are simplified by the use of stereotyped categories of behaviour. This process of constructing and enacting scripts we shall refer to as '*scenariotyping*'. These various cultural contexts also represent the medium of communication and translation of structural contexts to everyday existence. These are the limiting factors on identity construction in work and social life. They act to define possible sources of meaning and activity in hierarchical organisations and also provide the contextual limitations on what is acceptable practice for those who study, design and intervene in organisations.

Individual and group concerns with job security, status, promotion, conflict and satisfaction, can be characterised under a number of related categories. Included are the prediction and control of reality; coping with uncertainty; retaining autonomy and discretion; and maintaining or enhancing individual assessments of situational power. For the individual these represent the tensions created by trying to maintain and monitor the *strategies* through which we enact behaviours. A secure identity, or at least an identity which is not too severely threatened, forms both a bulwark against threats and provides personal standards for social comparison and action. The ability to control the various categories of individual and group concerns can also represent sources and reflections of organisational or situational power. The strategies utilised by individuals and groups to secure or appropriate identity will seek to control sources of power and meaning. As a consequence, identity construction may threaten the organisation of work (Weigert, 1986, Knights and Willmott, 1985, Breakwell, 1987).

Organisations, in trying to reduce uncertainty, are willing to allow room for the maintenance of worker identities in so far as they make the control of behaviour and production processes more effective. In implementing the introduction of CNC, machine tools firms such as Westland Helicopters have allowed an element of manual input from operators on the basis that human intervention is necessary in automated processes because they are not absolutely error-free (Corbett, 1985a). Such decisions allow operators to exert some levels of skill and discretion within labour processes with increasing tendencies towards deskilling. Thus alongside gains in the reduction of uncertainty in the production process there may also be benefits to the organisation in reducing the level of threat to skilled identities implied by automation.

The greater the effort put into attempts to define employee's work life, the greater the use of undefined areas by workers to develop 'informal workgroup cultures'. Cultures of this type can provide workers with a degree of autonomy and a basis for active resistance. By the same token, membership of subcultural groups in organisations may provide the benefits to threatened identities which they do for subcultures in wider society: 'the threatened can regain self-esteem, generate positive distinctiveness and promote continuity', (Breakwell, 1986: 141). Although Breakwell argues that societal subcultures have virtually no impact on power structures, they are, she maintains, the focus of possible social concerns and the associated 'moral panics' (Cohen, 1973) which identify them as being 'scheduled for control'.

This is not to say, of course, that managers never recognise this tendency and take steps to short-circuit the development of informal groups which may, in time, become hostile to organisational goals. Drago and McDonough (1984: 67) quote a management planning document from the General Food's Topeka plant where they were initiating a controlled participation experiment; 'No power groups will exist within the organisation that create an anti-management posture'. In trying to predict and control reality, for most of us it is our subjective concepts and values that are most amenable to change, as we cannot on our own hope to change the structural framework that surrounds us in the organisations within which we work. Even for those with the power to change the form of, and processes within, organisations there is still no absolute security of position or certainty that their actions will produce results fully in line with their goals. Thus, in coping with the uncertainties of organisational life, most individuals are forced either into a strategy of accommodation which necessitates a gradual redefinition of self and subjective reality, or a strategy of assimilation which requires these to be subjected to the superordinate goals of the group.

Putting the pressure on

All people working in organisations face pressures to mould their identities to fit normative expectations. According to Kunda (1992: 11), 'under normative control, membership is founded not only on the behavioural or economic transaction . . . but, more crucially, on an experiential transaction'. Although the expectations which arise originate within the interactions, goals, strategies or policies of the various individuals and groups in an organisation, in subjective terms they can also appear to originate in the organisation itself. In the OB literature expectations are mainly dealt with through the notion of *role:* the roles we wish to play ourselves, the roles others wish or expect us to play and the roles demanded of us from our relations with work organisations. The total number of *role expectations* which impinge on any individual is referred to as a *role-set,* and can comprise of contradictory demands from workmates, supervisors, management, customers or clients and from home or social life. The role expectations are not separate and neutral consequences of status, position or skill. Rather, they are specific and interdependent products of a social organisation of work which itself depends for effective production on the internalisation of role demands. The divisions of labour which result in fragmented work are likewise dependant on *role specialisation* being perceived as a natural social order.

Role control

Salaman (1979: 133–6) raises the possibility that variations in role discretion and role expectations may be linked to strategic decisions on the forms of control exercised over different categories of workers. Professional employees face contradictory expectations arising from their peers, their external professional associations and from the organisation itself. These have to be handled by the individual and managed by the organisation. Direct control by managers over professionals, involving rule-bound job definitions and tightly regulated behaviour, may conflict with the latters' values and socialisation. A more effective form of control can be achieved through a focus on their role as a professional, performing their organisational duties to the satisfaction and benefit of their masters or clients.

In contrast to the forms of control appropriate to professionals, 'Role type control is less commonly employed with workers because senior members of organisations (and, possibly, the workers themselves) see the workers as being in conflict with the goals and reward system of the enterprise' (Salaman, 1979: 136). The moulding of worker's attitudes and behaviour can be identified with, 'adjusting one's perspectives on what one will be able to achieve' (Frese, 1982: 210). Since such 'adjustments' necessitate at least some internalisation and legitimation of structures of regulation, it may be expected that role-type control would be possible at most levels of organisations. But of course not everyone in an organisation 'knows their place' or is resigned to power-lessness and helplessness. The informal socialisation of workers, or 'learning the ropes', will consist largely of learning the shortcuts around, and resistance to, organisational controls. Such knowledge and its associated activities confer at least some small sense of personal autonomy, meaning and hence identity to workers. Consequently direct controls, combined with elements of technical and bureaucratic control where possible or appropriate, are more often employed by management at lower levels of organisations.

Socialisation within work is not necessarily directed at the technical aspects for other grades. When examining the socialisation of skilled manual workers into their workplace identities, Penn argues that such socialisation is more directed at: 'instruction into the appropriate actions of the trade' (1986: 4). Such instruction and the identities it produces are aimed at generating scripts for interaction in the workplace. They deal with: 'Norms and procedures held to be appropriate for dealing with three groupings found in the workplace: fellow workers, other workers and management' (1986: 4).

This process builds on *anticipatory socialisation* into work in the home and at school, in that apprentices require a commitment to deferred gratification and continued learning after the end of formal schooling. Hence there is a form of pre-selection for skilled manual work in that those who have previously internalised appropriate forms of meaning are preferred: 'a certain degree of seriousness and moral uprightness is required by a sponsor who already works in a firm' (1986: 4). In contrast, 'tearaways' who define their identities as inimical to authority and those who seek immediate extrinsic gratification in work are not wanted (Willis, 1977). Organisations, then, try to get the right kind of material to mould into the images they require.

The types of assessment techniques used in recruitment and selection procedures also reflect differential concerns; this time with the personality dimension of identity. The study by Hollway (1984) cited in the section on personality, shows that the assessment of managers, and hence the forms of control used over them, are related to the 'fit' of their personalities into dominant organisational cultures. When reviewing organisational recruitment procedures in the British Army and Ford UK, Salaman (1979) also notes that this 'fit' is shown by the candidates' willingness to demonstrate an 'appropriate' range of attitudes.

In this sense, roles are scenariotyped scripts which are themselves as essential to the labour process as the working practices, labour and machinery through which they are played out. Attempts to increase worker 'participation' can thus be seen not only as efforts to place individual goals more in line with organisational goals, but as attempts to produce role-based control of workers. The aim is to produce workers who will themselves initiate the enactment of the correct scripts, rather than having to be directed to do so. This produces savings for the organisation in terms of the amounts of direct supervision necessary and in terms of the number of supervisors needed. There is currently a parallel emphasis on the operational skills 'content' seen as necessary to make management education more responsive to the 'needs' of business. The management trainee is assumed to have the necessary role commitment and motivation to consent to organisational control structures. Thus 'education' becomes a process of exposing the trainee to the 'skills', techniques and attitudes which will be required of them and then teaching them how to recognise the appropriate contingencies in which particular scripts should be enacted.

Role stress

The psychological pressures on individuals have been well-documented, not in terms of pressures to mould identity, but in terms of the intrapsychic conflicts they can produce. Interpersonal conflicts and conflicts between role expectations are seen as causative factors in producing anxiety and stress. An example of the conflicts which fulfilling a role may induce is seen in Hochschild's (1983) notion of *emotional labour*. Hochschild characterises emotional labour as, 'a covert resource, like money or knowledge, or physical labour, which companies need to make the job done' (1993: xii). This was originally identified in occupations where individuals have to manage their emotions in order to serve the commercial purposes of the enterprise. Recent writings on emotional labour (see Fineman, 1993) have extended such notions to the full range of behaviour in work organisations. Using flight attendants and bill collectors, Hochschild (1983) showed how people are constrained to maintain emotions in their work – friendliness for the stewardess; suspension of trust and sympathy for the debt-collector – which relate only to the requirements of the job. This requirement extends beyond individuals and includes collective emotional labour:

> It is not simply individuals who manage their feelings in order to do a job; whole organisations have entered the game. The emotion management that keeps the smile on Delta Airlines competes with the emotion management that keeps the same smile on United and TWA. (Hochschild, 1983: 185–6).

In such situations, where management attempts to mould the social identities of individuals and groups into images consonant with commercial demands, people often become estranged from their own feelings. As an interdependent process, emotional labour requires both the collaboration of the client and the adjustment of personal feelings to accommodate the client's demands. For the emotional labourer identification with the job itself can lead to difficulties in making constant adjustments to situations and considerable socio-emotional costs may be incurred.

Work in the 'caring' professions requires that people identify closely with their work and that they exercise self-control over their role-based work. The responses people make when they cannot take the demands that their work places on them are examined in the section below on individual responses to pressures on identity.

The problem with role-based stress as an explanatory concept is that it has the effect of portraying the process as natural and individually-based, instead of as a product of the historically produced conditions of work. In his study of responses to the pressure of work in 'Towerco', Sturdy (1987) notes that management are aware of the negative effects that such pressures have on employee morale and yet would not want to completely remove backlogs of work as it would portray their sections as overstaffed and on occasion would leave people with little or nothing to do.

The anxieties and pressures of work at Powerco led to the practice of 'shifting' in the employees, where people, even in conditions where motivation and commitment might not be expected, indulged in 'unceasing effort beyond what would be expected from even the most committed worker' (1987: 35). Their compulsion to keep ahead of the work and not let backlogs build up, to relieve pressure by getting work 'shifted', extended to refusing breaks and feeling frustrated rather than relieved when interruptions such as computer breakdowns stopped the work. Though partially based in the desire to increase security in work, shifting, according to Sturdy acts, for the individual not only as a relief for the helplessness they feel, but as a mechanism which obscures the experience of subordination itself. By using shifting to cope with the pressure of work, the individual co-operates with the structures of workplace control to produce a sense of identity which offers some level of autonomy and responsibility. At the same time, shifting paradoxically increases the pressures employees feel as both management and themselves come to depend on the gains stemming from their increased productivity. Identities can, then, be reactively moulded as a response to situational stress factors and in directions which reproduce the experience of subordination and domination in work.

Stress control?

The role of the organisation in producing unhealthy systems and conditions of work is in danger of being ignored. In its place we get systems of stress 'management' reinforcing the self-attribution of stress and anxiety as personal problems to be coped with rather than structural issues to be contested. In order for such programmes to succeed, they have to change both attitudes and cultural factors in the workplace and become part of managerial strategies for moulding the identities of workers. The Control Data Corporation places great emphasis on group sessions where, 'eventually group members learn to help one another to sustain the changes in their behaviour, and they practice various techniques and strategies to avoid failure' (McKenna, 1987: 402). The feeling that a person can cope with adverse situations can both be a source of meaning and danger to them in, for example, working in difficult and dangerous occupations, such as construction or agricultural work. The result would be to divorce a person's view of their working conditions from their desire for personal safety to the extent that they take unnecessary risks or adhere to dangerous practices.

The ability to deal with and to some extent actually relish a high-pressure working environment is seen as a valued characteristic in managers. The person who is able to cope with the conflicting demands of a managerial position is encouraged to view this capacity as a personality trait which indicates their suitability as a leader. Through such a process it is no surprise that organisational elites come to view themselves as those most fit to lead and survive in the given environment. Such legitimations, though active in the securing of managerial identities, are not necessarily part of any conscious conspiracy of control or domination. They may simply be the habitual response managers have learned in order to cope with various situations where their identities are threatened. Domination and control would thus be outcomes of the scripts managers use in their daily activities, these outcomes requiring from managers, some level of self-justification which ideologies can supply.

It does appear that material on the moulding of identities in organisations tends to focus on professional, skilled and managerial workers. However, such concepts as emotional labour and the utility of 'wellness programmes' would indicate that organisations may routinely attempt to mould the identities of all levels of employees. Aichholzer and Schienstock (1985) examine opportunities for maintaining identities in the face of the intensification of control surrounding the introduction of new technologies. Such intensification is seen in 'tighter binding of human actions with machine processes, an increasing transparency of the labour process as a whole, a rising vertical integration and extension of technological control to white collar work' (1985: 20). They also note a number of apparent 'counter-tendencies' to increased control. These include the reintegration of fragmented work-roles, the revaluing of 'marginal' human functions in work and an emphasis on problemsolving activities. Aichholzer and Schienstock argue that these counter-tendencies in effect pressurise workers to internalise controls in order to soften the new problems of control raised by new forms of technology and work organisation and that this questions the 'maintenance of individual and collective identities in the modern labour process' (1985: 81).

It is, however, possible to identify aspects of the analysis of the shaping of work around technologies which do offer redefinition of psychological pressures and stresses in directions which integrate notions of psychological well-being and growth into the design of work. In particular, the identification of dimensions (see Figure 10.1) through which the degree of flexibility and discretion available to employees can be analysed offers insights into how workers can have inputs to the process of shaping their work-related behaviours, objectives and environment (Rauner et al., 1988: 55–7).

- *Time structure* – time pressures imposed and possibility of individual or group planning use of time themselves.
- *Space for movement* – degree of formalisation versus choice governing movement of workers within and between job functions.
- *Social relations* – degree of formalisation versus informal possibilities in workplace interactions and organisational communications.
- *Responsibility and control flexibility* – scope and degree of responsibility available to workers and possibilities for self-management and control.

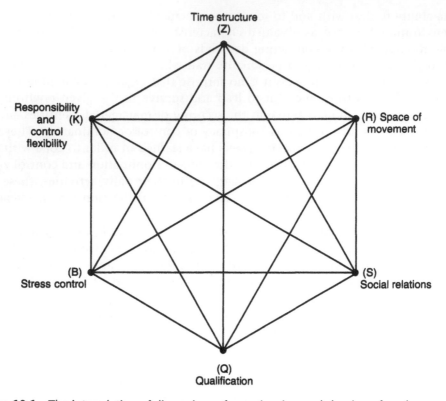

Figure 10.1 The interrelation of dimensions of experiencing and shaping of work

Source: F. Rauner, R. Rasmussen and J. M. Corbett, 'The Social Shaping of Technology and Work: Human Centred CIM Systems', *Artificial Intelligence and Society*, vol. 2 (1980) 56.

- *Qualification* – range of functional abilities related to task and work processes, and possibilities of learning and personality development.
- *Stress control* – degree of control over physical and psychological pressures resulting from work organisation and human-machine interactions.

All six dimensions are to be viewed through their relations to the others. This allows analysis of, in the first instance, the extent to which a labour process permits 'humane' work, and in the second of the dimensions along which increased flexibility and discretion would most benefit psychological well-being. These six interrelated dimensions should enable both more precise determinations of the restrictiveness inherent in a labour process and a focus which emphasises the necessity of designs which enable subjective as well as operational flexibility, thus allowing room for the constructive use of subjective variables in analysing individual experience.

Responses to pressures on identity

The production of scenariotyped behaviours and the ideological formulations which justify them enables people, collectively or individually, to enact their own situational power and resist controls. This does not, however, explain why individuals and groups try to resist organisational controls. Resistance is in itself both a source of meaning and a pressure on identity. This is founded on the perception by individuals of contradictions between the goals, ideologies, approved identities and required behaviours which are exhibited in organisational settings. Leonard (1984: 116–18) identifies four sources of pressures leading to resistance, avoidance and dissent; which provide a useful framework for discussion and reaction.

- *Contradictory consciousness* This arises from competing ideologies based on the material interests of groups and classes. Because dominant ideologies partly clash with people's actual experiences of everyday life, they can never have more than an imperfect influence on identities. Leonard cites class, gender and ethnic struggles as examples of the conflicts which produce psychological disturbances in individuals and can produce acts of deviance, but at the same time still result in a general submission to the demands of the dominant order. These acts of deviance may be directed towards material gains, individual protest or to fulfil particular values not acceptable to the social order. There may be important consequences for organisations in the form of theft, industrial sabotage, or other 'destructive' actions.
- *Unconscious resistance* Leonard represents this partly in Freudian terms as the struggle of id against ego and superego. The individual attempts not to repress or bury those impulses which 'are unacceptable or inconvenient to dominant social forces' (1984: 117). However, impulses to act against the social order may be renounced and buried in the unconscious because the obstacles to action are too great or perceived situational power is too little. Anxiety and frustration are the likely results of everyday unconscious resistance, though at its extreme, internal conflicts could result in forms of mental disorder. Leonard identifies tendencies to neurotic and psychotic illness with social class position. In organisational terms neurotic reactions could be characterised as consistent with the frustrations caused by conflicts around the role-based control and supervisory responsibilities of professional and managerial classes (Kets De Vries and Miller, 1984, have noted neurotic syndromes in managers of failing firms). Psychotic reactions, characterised as escapes into alternative realities, are associated with the working classes. In a parallel concept, the Hungarian psychologist, Laszlo Garai (see Eros, 1974), refers to individuals having recourse to 'fictive satisfactions', when the specifically human 'need' for self-realisation and non-alienated activity is blocked. These can take the form of destructive impulses, cynicism or the ritual affirmation of helplessness, all of which are likely to be perceived as unmotivated or individually deviant.
- *The development of individual capacities* This arises from the attempt to avoid the dehumanising effects of alienated labour. It may lead to the development of personal activities either within work or outside it, which are directed at benefits for the individual rather than the organisation. Outside work they may develop artistic, literary, craft or sporting skills (these also being fictive satisfactions) which 're-humanise' their lives; making active and identity-enhancing use of their time, rather than merely recuperating from work. Within the workplace people can develop capacities from the exploration and development of their skills which

extends beyond what is demanded by wage labour. Wilkinson (1983b) provides an example of CNC machine tool operators, some of whom effectively redefined the technology which had deskilled them and brought some interest back into their work by teaching themselves to programme the computers and to edit computer tapes.

However, just as is the world of fashion or popular music, where people's creative and autonomous control over their own image and expression are eventually incorporated into commercial products, the smart company will incorporate the efforts of individuals to indulge in non-alienated activity into the organisation of the labour process. In the world of the work organisation the 'revolt into style' may be transformed into the instrumental rewards of the suggestion box.

- *Participation in collective action*   This 'contains contradictions between hope and despair, optimism and depression, depending on the balance of political forces at any given time' (Leonard, 1984: 118). Capacities are further developed through joining informal coalitions to pursue some more or less specified goal, or becoming formally involved in unions, professional and other associations. The immediate benefit is in an enhancement of situational power through collective strength. Leonard sees benefits in collective resistance, in that it counters individualistic impulses and moves towards altruistic activity which attempts to transform social relations into forms beneficial to the individual and group. It also raises consciousness about forms of change that are available, associated with a redefinition of self that can counter subordination.

These forms are neither exhaustive, nor mutually exclusive. Nor does it necessarily follow that resistance is inevitable, even though it may be structured into the forms and processes of organisations. Where there are no overt conflicts, it is possibly easier for individuals to accept managerial definitions of reality, to become 'organisation people' and to gain meaning from their appointed role. For the purpose of clarity, our further examination of responses to pressures, and threats to identity, is divided into responses at individual and group levels. It must be remembered, however, that these responses are interdependent processes, which can be conceptually separated, but which are all part of the cycle of organisational control and resistance.

Individual responses

In securing and maintaining a stable and meaningful identity, an individual is faced with the difficulty of presenting consistent images to the other people with whom must deal. The pressure engendered by the necessity to perform both organisationally and interpersonally derived roles involves a continuous process of identity management to maintain situational fit or appropriateness. As long as this does not threaten core identity, people can follow the scripts they learn from others in order to fulfil their various role expectations. When threat does arise, they are left with the choice to submit or resist: both involve possibly substantial redefinitions of the identities they have secured.

The management of identities has been explored in work such as that of Goffman (1961) on *impression management*. The individual, like an actor on stage, attempts to maintain a consistent and believable performance for their audience – those who have a significant influence over the role they play. When used in this sense, identity is malleable and instrumentally defined. However active and manipulative such identities are, they are still dependant on the collaboration of others not to interfere with the performance. We know that the performance of an actor is not real. But, according to Goffman, we exercise 'tact' to allow the performance to proceed, as in the case of a management 'pep-talk'.

The management of impressions is one example of the process of identity work referred to earlier. Kunda's study of Tech' (1992, ch. 5) provides numerous and excellent examples of forms of identity work (also see Van Maanen, 1992 on the linkage of identity work to discourses of masculinity). These include routine *identity displays* of behaviours which either embrace or distance the worker from organisational roles, and *artifactual displays,* for example, of signs and posters, in personal workspaces which supply the image of 'a strong individual surviving in a hard, competitive, often irrational world'. Both types of display are seen as dramatic performances which balance the display of the successful organisational self with an image of ability to organisational concerns giving oneself some space for manoeuvre. But such performance may break down in the context of threats and constraints in the work environment, and we may be forced to respond with impressions and performance which are 'out of character' for the expected role. Kunda characterises these as *enlargement dramas,* where in formal or informal circumstances the routine order of role-playing is allowed to break down temporarily and the individual is allowed to enlarge upon the self she generally presents, exhibiting attitudes or capabilities beyond her required role. Such dramas are often associated with temporary or marginal members of organisations. Similarly, individuals may experience difficulty in coping with situations where their projected images are not adequate to achieving some measure of control or meaning. For example, *Hochschild*, in examining the supervision of emotional labour, cites the reaction of a flight attendant whose, paycheque had been mishandled, 'I can't take this all day and then come back here and take it from you! You know I get paid to take it from the passengers, but I don't get paid to take it from you' (1983: 18).

The scenariotyped behaviours demanded of those Hochschild examines can, like those demanded of people in the caring professions, conflict with the levels of commitment involved in their work. Such constrained responses can have serious consequences for mental health and social relationships. In order to respond to conflicts between commitment and capacity to act, people may *burnout.* Storlie (1979) argues that this occurs where the individual confronts an intractable reality which cannot be changed, so that the only effective response is to change themselves: the end result being that they continue to 'go through the motions', but remove any emotional or identity investment they had in their work. This acts as a defence mechanism against the stresses that may result from the conflicts between their own tendencies and their role demands. Emotional labour can thus lead the individual into a removal of emotion, labour being reduced to mere activity. This may have some benefits to the employer, but for the employee such numbing of emotional response leads to a loss of a central source of meaning for them, (see Kunda, 1992: 198–204, for an extended discussion).

The identity work we perform depends to a great deal on our ability to utilise and manage the scripts available to us. Conversely, we need to break free of the habituated scripts we use to *'make out'* when the conditions under which we employ them become untenable. Opportunities to secure new or enhanced meanings, symbols, capacities and goods are as much pressures on our identities as are threats to them. The types of opportunity we will respond to will depend upon the current identities and strategies we employ, our perceived power and ability to take them and our expectations concerning what benefits we can hope to obtain. Breaking free from established patterns of identity work can therefore be difficult, as Sloan's (1987) study of sales work illustrates. The salesmen had invested a great deal in a conception of professional identity which could legitimate the arduous work and their manipulative relations with customers. Professionals did not need unions. There was also a gendered dimension whereby masculinity was central to the identity; 'A little alcohol and a lot of imagination reproduced a culture in which reps were not only professional salesmen, but were also professional lovers' (1987: 31); the 'heroic' males of Insco are apparently not alone!

All of the above are responses to the identity concerns of individuals. It is difficult to locate them in a framework which is solely based on different categories of resistance or dissent. The relatively unconscious coping strategies identified by Roy can be seen as responses to identity concerns, but are essentially strategies of accommodation rather than resistance. Typical forms of individual response to pressure contain a combination of coping strategies, instrumentally derived tactics and accommodation to the dominant culture, as well as different types of resistance. As far as the individual is concerned, they are making-out in the best fashion possible in the given circumstances, the form of response being determined in subjective terms by what appears to work. As long as there are available scripts which satisfy goals and identity concerns, there are no real bars to an individual fitting into whatever forms of work and survival they have access to.

Such strategies or responses could in one sense be said never entirely to fail. With the capacity to redefine meanings and manage impressions, human beings are capable of creating their own self-fulfilling prophecies, shifting the ground on which they stand to justify both success and failure. We not only manage the impressions we give to others, but those we produce of ourselves. Central to this are self-attributed judgements which justify our actions in terms of our current identity concerns and environmental influences.

In counterpoint to strategies which lead to extremely negative consequences for the individual, there are forms of making-out which can lead more unambiguously to social recognition, approval and self-justified identities. Recognition as a leader in an organisation is one such form. Pressure to define identity in line with the assumed leadership qualities would in turn lead to behaviours and self-perceptions supportive in subjective terms. The failure of others to recognise an individual as a leader, or attempts to undermine their leadership, might lead to perceived contradictions with their self-justified role. These could be handled by more autocratic attempts at control, justified by attributions of deviant characteristics to those causing the disturbance. Conversely, if strategies to cope with the situation fail and put the identity of the ostensible leader at risk, he could distance himself from the role on the basis that dealing with such people was impossible or not worth the effort.

The strategies suggested in the example above are two of those that Knights and Willmott (1985) identify as being used by individuals secure identities and reduce anxiety. These are described as *domination* and *distancing*. In organisations, a strategy of domination would involve those with power over the distribution and possession of scarce resources using it to give themselves the illusion of independence and security. It is partially an illusion, because such reliance acts to obscure the interdependence of social relations. Managers or others can then ignore the fact that their power is dependant on the compliance of their subordinates.

Compliance in this sense is related to Rotter's (1972) notion of internal and external *loci of control* People who feel that they are externally controlled may also put themselves into a state of *'learned helplessness'* where the tendency to comply becomes part of the way they define themselves (Seligman, 1975). To subordinates, however, compliance may simply be their way of making-out and avoiding 'identity damaging disciplinary controls' (Knights and Willmott, 1985: 25). Strategies which employ the, 'cynical distancing of self from the activities and social relations within which individuals are immediately involved' (1985: 27) reinforce individualism and subordination.

Distancing is also one of the main forms of identity work identified by Cohen and Taylor (1978). Unlike Knights and Willmott, their focus is not on power and interdependence, but rather on 'escape attempts' from, or resistance to, the mundanity and unpleasantness of everyday life – in other words, on subjectively making-out. However, the strategies they see as employed in identity work can still have relevance to the understanding of how making-out is incorporated into the social relations of production. Cohen and Taylor start out at the level of the 'regularities which we happily accept as part of life' (1978: 26). These regularities are not necessarily tedious behavioural repetition, but are scripts to which we unreflexively accommodate as a method of managing the 'paramount reality' of our objective world. Scripts in this sense are more than the 'mindless' behaviour posited by Langer or the 'sensorimotor' activity posited by Hacker and Volpert.

The habitual dependence on scripts referred to by Cohen and Taylor can be a defence against uncertainty and provide meaning through its very regularity. However, our capacity for self-reflection allows us to create a 'zone for self' or 'identity domain' (1978: 32), which enables us to distance ourselves from those who appear to be committed to the scripts which they live by. The capacity to be self-reflexive can effectively remove the need actually to do anything about the conditions of our existence, because we critically separate ourselves from them in our thoughts At the same time, we often deprecate those we see as not having our own level of critical self-awareness, defining them as something less than ourselves. The paradox here is the likelihood that our fellow workers are having the same thoughts as and about ourselves. But they do not see our thoughts, only our regulated actions and routine behavioural displays.

A concomitant capacity which self-reflexiveness endows us with is the release of the *escape into fantasy*, where we can alter the conditions of our life to our own satisfaction. This form of escape is akin to the strategy of unconscious resistance identified by Leonard. Leonard's identification of these escapes with position in the organisational hierarchy can now be understood, in that fantasy is free. Cohen and Taylor also note socially institutionalised routes of escape which are seen as legitimate self-expression, and where 'assertions of meaninglessness of the activity are virtually taboo' (1978: 95). These *activity enclaves* give us free areas in our lives, where, in the terminology of Seve and Leonard, we can develop 'personal concrete capacities'. Such socially approved escapes from work or the lack of it include hobbies, games, sports, holidays, and the attractions of mass culture.

On the other hand, there are less socially approved activity enclaves which more resemble Garai's fictive satisfactions, in that they are often socially viewed as self-obsessive or destructive. 'Preoccupations' with sex, gambling, drugs and even dependence on therapy are examples of this form of escape. They are, however, only different from other forms in terms of the social, legal and historical contexts in which they are carried out. Again, self-reflexiveness carries its own internal contradictions. Distancing ourselves from the roles we play is, in the end, another limited and passive strategy which tends to confirm existing organisational structures and separates the individual from the possibilities inherent in social relations.

Finally, to escape from this vicious spiral of making-out through reconstruction of identity concerns, Cohen and Taylor identify the strategy of *self-conscious reinvestment*. The individual becomes recommitted to aspects of the very regularities – language, rituals, clothes – from which they are escaping. Within work organisations this represents the return to the fold, making something of one's life or the rescue of career. All of these means of psychic escape can be utilised to further managerial control, either by employee's dependence on the financial and social supports necessary to pursue them or, in the case of reinvestment, the cleaving back to the very structures of control themselves. For those who run organisations, the problem is to monitor the identity work of employees to ensure that they do not overstep the bounds of the acceptable. For the employee, the problem is to discover the appropriate mode of escape, enjoyment and making-out for the subjective and objective conditions pertaining at the time.

Group responses

Individuals use groups actively to transform their personal and social identities. For example, the reflexiveness involved in the raising of consciousness of disadvantage in social groups can be the spur for responses to pressures which direct the use of groups as technologies of action. Thus interest groups can actively promote not only the material interests of members but also their development of positive identities as mechanisms for making-out. The patriarchal nature of power relations in organisations is currently being contested throughout industry, commerce and the professions by women's groups which rely on their own systems of *networking* to counter the male cliques who generally control their destinies. Such networks provide both a forum for ideas and information and work to heighten awareness of the position of women in organisations. Their capacity for social transformation will be dependant not only on the extent and nature of the contacts they can build up but also on the extent to which they can empower women to develop strong individual and group identities. On this basis they are often more than promotional or defensive interest groups, in that they act to foster the recognition and self-development of the capacities of all women. 'Our purpose is to help women to develop their potential – not to foster élitism' (North-West Women into Management, 1987). The use of networking by managers in the social construction of leadership, negotiation and teamworking is discussed in some depth by Hosking and Morley (1991: Part 3).

The recognition of group identity by members and those outside group boundaries, will be a major determinant of the kinds of responses groups will make to threats to their identity. The better defined the identity of a group, the greater the value of the group to its members as a source of social support, comparison and evaluation. The more effective these processes are, the greater the range of external pressures which can be perceived as affecting the group; and thus the more likely that some kind of collective response will be demanded. Likewise, the stronger the identity of a particular group, the more the likelihood of other competing groups perceiving them and their actions as sources of threat, and thus the more likely that competitors will take action which once more demands some form of response.

An important factor is the extent to which group identity is constructed around a coherent set of values, common instrumental strategies for maximising extrinsic rewards or the needs and desires of group members for affiliation and interaction. This is most visible in the contestation over control of the labour process between management and workers. But that conflict is also manifested within intergroup relations. Thompson and Bannon (1985) show that the instrumental and anti-authoritarian attitudes of the better paid 'high-flying' groups caused friction not only with management, but with lowly rewarded and traditional craft work-groups. Each group identity was strengthened by the conflict and the prime target of resentment was more often other work-groups, rather than management. Individual identities can, of course, suffer in intergroup struggles, but this is a measure of the extent to which group membership provides powerful means of resisting pressures from outside. The pressure to conform can outweigh the pressure to secure oneself against uncertainty and damage. Brown confirms the above example, arguing that intergroup conflict acts to strengthen group and intra-group identities and when groups do resist management: 'the psychological satisfactions an individual may gain from his group membership may be more potent than the rewards (or threats) the management can hold ouf (H. Brown, 1980: 167). For management the problem of how to disrupt, short-circuit or redirect group identities is central for securing organisation goals, mobilising consent, exerting influence and promoting 'motivation' and organisationally directed goals. The types of response made are examined in the next section.

Even when there is only a tacit, unacknowledged sense of group identity, the stereotyped judgements of power-holders about particular groups may lead them to form sub-cultural units. They are likely to be based around resistance to managerial activities rather than in a coherent ideology of their own. Individual cohesion within such a group may be low and resistance may not be co-ordinated in any sense. It may not even be visible as such, but manifested in jokes at the expense of superiors, general stubbornness and lack of co-operation (Nichols and Beynon, 1977). At this level, pressure on individual identity may be no more than disapproval at not joining in or, at worst, definition as being somehow different. Over time, the benefits – in terms of access to sources of meaning – of belonging to such a group may coalesce it into a true subculture with the ability to protect members against threats to identity.

Much of the informal organisational processes, including subcultural groupings, are generated within the free areas which groups and their members carve out for themselves within labour processes. Whether formally or informally constituted, such groups have to in some fashion reduce the possible internal tensions which might develop out of any contradictory goals and identity concerns of their members. The internal dynamics of groups have been seen largely to consist of role-based mechanisms and processes directed at the maintenance of the group. According to Breakwell, 'group dynamics are the most frequent sources of threats to identity. These threats need not be personalised: they are directed at the individual as a group member, a cipher in a social category, not as a personality' (1986: 128). The detailed operation of such processes will be group-specific; but, like the actions of individuals, it will be orientated towards identity securing strategies. Just as the construction of individual identities depends in part on competition with others for sources of meaning, the production of group identities depends on gaining access to symbols and resources or behaviour patterns which serve to distinguish the group from others.

At the extremes of group response to pressures on identity are traditional forms of industrial action and attempts at 'self-management'. The first could be seen in accounts by skilled workers involved in the 1987 British Telecom strike. A persistent theme was that the background to the action was as much in a 'gut reaction' to the way in which management attitudes and behaviour represented an attack on their self-perceptions and identities as skilled workers; as it was about pay and conditions. Pressure of this sort on individual identities can be the triggering factor which alerts workers to the possibilities and benefits which Leonard identifies in collective action. In this sense, the rhetorical focus on empowerment through the self-management of personal development in current HRM strategies and organisational learning initiatives will always run the risk of actually engendering resistance.

Self-management as a strategy for making-out ranges from the individual setting up in business to 'be your own boss', to large-scale worker cooperatives. The use of group and intergroup self-management as a strategy could be seen as evidence of Garai's hypothesised need for non-alienated activity to motivate people towards transformations of work in the direction of self-control. Such efforts would act initially to reinforce the interdependence of productive relations and reinforce the security of previously constructed workplace identities, such as the craft pride of workers in the Triumph Meriden co-operative in the 1970s. However, attempts to secure autonomy and self-direction may simply be part of strategies to defend existing work against movements of capital, no matter how alienating. Unless the financial and management processes under which co-operatives operate are constructed differently from conventional businesses, the only extra source of meaning available in such work may be a collective identity and a set of common goals.

Self-management, though, is not restricted to the total direction of a business with which a sole trader or co-operative must contend. It can just as readily be a tactic within overall struggles to achieve control of the portions of the labour process. In attempting to control the speed of a production line or the throughput of work in a particular department, a group is actively trying to manage its environment. Parallel for professional groups are the 'collective mobility projects' (Armstrong, 1984). Claims on access to decision-making power by professional groups such as accountants, engineers and personnel specialists rest in part on their ability to restrict sources of meaning to members, and to use specialised knowledge to downgrade the competence of other groups.

In the above sense, any form of resistance to external control, by groups or individuals, is a type of strategy for increasing the scope of self-management. It could thus be seen as a basic response, at different levels of the organisation, to constraints embodied in the work situation. Describing such action as resistance runs the risk of being a purely ideological judgement based on the damage done to existing structures of power and reward. But dominant groups do have their own needs for autonomy, discretion and non-alienated activity. It is therefore probable that they will define other people's self-management as a threat to their identities and produce regulatory responses. The activities of managerial groups in this area are the focus of the next section.

Management: from response to regulation

The form and content of control processes are influenced by the responses of managerial groups to pressures on the identities produced in their role as agents of capital. Mobilising their consent to expose themselves to the threats and pressures of management roles has its own particular place in the labour process. It also underpins the mobilisation of consent of production workers to comply with that supervision. Resistance and contestation by other individuals and groups are threats to managerial identities which are only somewhat ameliorated by the situational power they wield. Managers have been reported often to feel frustrated and ineffectual in their workplace roles and that they have little control over the strategic policies which determine their activities. This will depend of course on the position and situational power of the managers involved, but does point to the fact that managerial work has its own levels of alienation and partialisation. If this is so, then dominant organisational groups will also expend effort and devise strategies to secure and defend their identities. Hochschild (1993: xi), for example, notes that managers are involved in emotional labour in regulating not only their own feelings but those of others.

Effective managerial identity work can utilise worker resistance and associated damage to productivity and profitability as an ideological justification for managers' own strategies to enhance identity. By being perceived by peers and superiors as being capable leaders who are able to contain, regulate or negate disturbances to the efficient flow of work, managers are able to secure sources of meaning which in turn reinforce their ideological supports.

The fashion for reorganising production processes into semi-autonomous work-groups provided examples of the way in which interventions by management act both to secure managerial identities and short-circuit potential worker resistance. Such work-groups give employees some latitude of decision-making over operational matters and integrate different levels of production-related skills into more flexible working on more 'natural' units of work, turning production-line assembly into a semblance of unit or small-batch production. Wall *et al.* (1986), in a long-term study of autonomous work-groups, identified the justifications underlying their implementation as being in their assumed effects in increasing intrinsic motivation to work, enhancing employee satisfaction, improving group performance and reducing labour turnover; as well as suggested increases in organisational commitment and improvements in mental health.

The results of this study indicated that 'employees clearly appreciated the autonomous work system. On balance managers did too, though clearly there were costs in terms of personal stress arising from the difficulties involved in managing and maintaining the system' (1986: 298). Of the assumed effects, only intrinsic job satisfaction and productivity were significantly increased, along with reported perceptions of increased autonomy. Labour turnover actually increased through increased dismissals of those who could not or would not fit in with the new systems. The increased productivity was not due to employees working any harder. If anything, their individual productivity was lower in comparison to those working on more traditional lines. Improvements largely flowed from reduced indirect labour costs, due to decreases in the need for direct supervision of the work-groups. This organisational benefit can be seen as a gain at the expense of increased managerial effort, with greater responsibilities being generated in monitoring and managing the new system.

Although suffering increased stress, the fact that managers thought the effort worthwhile indicates that associated productivity benefits provide enough possibilities for enhanced situational meaning to offset personal costs. When such a system becomes established, it is also possible that managers may also gain from new sources of meaning. As they are directly responsible for co-ordinating teams of workers who are more satisfied in their work, it is likely to enhance self-perceptions of managerial effectiveness; though this potential is limited by possible conflicts with existing managerial ideologies, as we shall point out below. Increased intrinsic worker satisfaction is also a potential source of meaning to managers, because greater intrinsic satisfaction may reduce the scope for contradictory consciousness arising in workers. If this leads to short-circuiting of potential resistance in employees, then managerial identities are further secured.

However, in one of the most widely studied implementations of autonomous working, conflicts with ideological conceptions of managerial control were seen to interfere with the factors which made such systems of work more effective. In a case study based on this material, the experimental assembly of trucks within an autonomous work-group system in the Volvo company between 1974 and 1976, Bladder and Shimmin (1984: 117–19) note that workers finishing their daily quota of work were allowed some relaxation around their work station. Senior managers, however, saw this relaxation as 'slack' which could be taken up and controlled by increasing work quotas. This obviously produced demoralisation in the workforce. Allowing slack time is contrary to the managerial conception of how productivity is to be maximised, even though it may be one of the major factors which produces the sense of autonomy for workers which allows the system to succeed. An enhanced source of workplace meaning for one group appears in this case to be an unacceptable threat to the processes of control which supply meaning to another group. This example illustrates the point that the ideological underpinnings which control systems provide for managerial identities may, in some circumstances, be more central to them than the control outcomes in increased profit. In this sense, strategies of control, regulation and discipline become part of the instrumental transformations of social reality which managerial groups set as the goals of their own identity work.

Strategic choices about organisational design can, however, be reinforced by a level of indoctrination into the dominant organisational goals. Such indoctrination may be a primary level of response to the attempts of members to secure a measure of autonomy and discretion within their work and to create free areas where they can develop their own identities and capacities. Lynn (1966) argues that the behaviours of even 'democratic leaders' can approximate to the principles of 'brainwashing'. Prescriptions to maintain warm and friendly relations with subordinates go hand-in-hand with maintaining a social distance between themselves and the group.

> We see here the dual role of the brainwasher: the aloofness corresponds to the threatener role, the friendliness to the protector role. The authoritarian leader is only playing the threatener role and misses out on the friendliness. Vice versa with the *laissez-faire* leader. It is the brainwashing, democratic leader who plays both roles who is the most effective. (1966: 270)

Such indoctrination can take place within both formal and informal socialisation, and function to reinforce self-control, rather than self-management. The study of bakery salesmen by Ditton (1974) showed how the salesmen were trained to cheat their customers in order not to lose out themselves when they ended up short in their takings. Supervisors both tacitly and overtly encouraged this activity as it short-circuited possible conflicts with workers, such as those that could be caused by the firm trying to recoup losses from the drivers' pay. The socialisation process also worked to weed out salesmen who would not or could not collaborate in theft and to legitimise it to others as the only real means for making-out in the job. Hence there was no objection to them making a little for themselves on top of balancing their books. Comments from a sales manager, such as 'They're not real salesmen if they can't make a bob or two on the side, are they?' (1974: 36), indicate that the ability to steal was linked to job competence, the same manager being noted for encouraging valued salesmen to, 'use fiddled cash personally'.

This socialisation into theft was of course only sanctioned by management to the extent that salesmen did not begin to steal from their employers as well as their customers. Mars (1983) has claimed that fiddling can increase job satisfaction, and raise work rates and productivity by making the process of work more interesting and binding those involved together. It can be used by management as a reward, as in Ditton's example, as long as they 'turn a blind eye', or can still be used as a method of 'cracking the whip'.

> The final irony for management is that they lose control of the fiddle that they themselves have started. The workforce then seize it, and use its unofficial and unsanctioned ability to increase their wages (especially in times of national restraint) as a basic condition of employment. (Ditton, 1974: 36)

The strategies and identity work of managerial groups are likewise incorporated into organisational processes through the ideological legitimations which supply positive self-attributions. Organisational ideologies play a crucial role in underpinning identities, particularly those of management. Salaman (1979: 199–212) locates five.

Structuralism presents organisational processes as outcomes of politically neutral principles of management and achievement based on merit, with, 'managers operating as referees of a variety of competing demands and pressures'. Markets complement internal hierarchies as functionally necessary principles. The ideology of achievement within structuralism links it to the approach of *psychologism,* where organisational performance is the responsibility and outcome of individual behaviour. People are resources, and where their qualities, abilities and goals are not in line with neutral structures, they must be moulded to fit. Conflicts of interest are avoided through the rational application of objective and neutral procedures for assessment and feedback. *Consensualism* presents the specialised division of labour and differentiated rewards as a necessary precondition of the achievement of overall organisational goals benefiting all members. The organisation survives by virtue of consensus, whilst conflict is due to the pathological personalities and behaviours of individuals or to inadequate communications. *Welfareism* focuses on integrating the commitment of employees through concern for their well-being and happiness. The emphasis is on 'personal relations at work, on less onerous and oppressive forms of control, on more relaxed supervisory methods, on some changes even in the organisation of work'. *Legalism* presents the social relations of production as being determined by the binding contractual agreements between the parties involved in the enterprise. Conflict is handled through negotiation and appeals to the obligations, rights and duties of participants. The contract implies consent to direction of effort by those who are assigned 'the right to manage'.

Whether or not such ideologies in practice act as coherent guiding principles of organisations, they do present some common themes – notably the neutrality of managerial practices, the rational and consensus-based form of organisations and the emphasis on individual responsibility for exhibiting appropriate behaviours and identities. If internalised by employees, they have the effect of reducing uncertainty for dominant groupings and thus to increase their situational power in securing strategic identities. They risk failure in the light of the contradictory consciousness raised by perceived conflicts between espoused values and actual practice. Knights and Collinson give the example of a US-owned firm in Britain that directed its communicative efforts through a house magazine that:

> simply exacerbated the 'them and us' attitudes since the harmonious and efficient image of Slavs depicted by it conflicted dramatically with the experience of shop floor workers. The shop floor was insulted by what it saw as the deceptive 'propaganda' in the magazine. (1987: 9)

Ideologies of this sort survive in part because dominant groupings have the power to shape cultural meanings on the workplace; and also because they can call on the expertise of their peers and outside professionals to justify them or supply the technologies of regulation to make them applicable to changing circumstances.

Organisational Development is a good example of the importance of managerial identity to strategic interventions in the organisation of work. 'Technologies' employed in OD interventions include team reviews, sensitivity training, performance counselling and the redesign of jobs. They largely depend on *social facilitation* effects for their operation – in other words, on pressures brought to bear on individuals through the effects of social comparison processes, group norms and the perceptions of expected rewards. An important aim is the achievement of a 'best fit' between the policy goals of the organisation and the workplace identities of both employees and those which manage them. The latter is important successful in that interventions have to convince the managerial client that they have bought the right strategy (Evden, 1986). Any doubts, or sophisticated ideas such as failure being a valuable learning experience, undermines the positive identities such interventions can reinforce.

The utility of managerial education outside – though sponsored by – organisations, could also be said to be based on reinforcing the ideological identity work required of managers. A secure cultural identity is an important factor in reducing employee uncertainty and thus organisational cohesiveness. The content of managerial education is effectively directed at making concrete the notion that systematic control over complex and variable processes is possible. The reduction of uncertainty provided by the ideas themselves, backed up by the demonstration of techniques which purport to provide reliable diagnostic and control procedures, acts as a powerful enabling factor in the maintenance of ideological structures. The expected payoffs for the employee in both financial terms and in terms of career mobility are thus bought through a process of personal identity work. This increases the employee's self-perceived competence at handling the contingent uncertainties of organisational life with the concomitant organisational gains of increased effort and commitment in overcoming goal barriers.

Conclusion

Identity work is conscious and unconscious, individual and collective, competitive and collaborative. It is the vehicle of our self-expression and enactment and at the same time binds us to systems of ideological self-legitimation through which we accede to systems of control, both internal and external. The networks we access and the roles we are expected to take on in the workplace provide the scripts, our interactions and negotiations with others the arena in which we act them out. It appears that what we strive towards in producing consistent role performances and in maintaining a secure identity is a situation where we do not have to negotiate who and what we are with others, where our concerns, actions and status are automatically legitimate. In this sense, identity work is the medium through which we express power over ourselves, others and situations.

We buy into systems of control in order to increase our situational power and at the same time we resist pressures to make us completely controlled by our role and the demands of others. In many ways identity work is the primary work of organising, if not of organisations themselves. As such, it must also be the primary work of those who structure the processes of organising towards corporate ends. The appeal of management, beyond the extrinsic rewards, must be that to some extent just being a manager automatically affirms and protects identity. This would of course be at the expense of diminishing the manager's capacity to resist the role demands the position confers. Manager as communicators of role demands have in effect committed themselves to controlling the identity work of others, which in turn commits them to one or another form of response to such pressures, which in turn. . .

It is through identity work that the condition of being a subject and of being subject gains substance for managers and workers alike and the negotiation and pursuit of identity concerns and projects are the drama of everyday organisational experience. As we have seen, the psychological processes which underwrite that drama cannot give an adequate account of it in purely mechanistic terms, but neither can interpretative or structural accounts afford to ignore the influence those processes have on us in our journey to becoming fully-fledged participants in the modern work organisation.

References

Aichholzer, G. and G. Schienstock (1985) 'Labour in Conflict: Between Capital Interests and the Maintenance of Identity', paper for *20th Annual Meeting of the Canadian Sociology and Anthropology Association,* University of Montreal.

Armstrong, P. (1984) 'Competition between the Organizational Professions and the Evolution of Management Control Strategies', in K. Thompson (ed.) *Work, Employment and Unemployment,* Milton Keynes: Open University Press.

Breakwell, G. M. (1986) *Coping with Threatened Identities,* London: Methuen.

Breakwell, G.M. (1987) 'Identity', in, H. Beloff and A.M. Colman (1987) *Psychology Survey 1987,* Leicester: British Psychological Society.

Brown, H. (1980) 'Work Groups', in G. Salaman and K. Thompson, (eds) *People andOrganizations,* Harlow: Longman.

Cohen, Stanley (1973) *Folk Devils and Moral Panics,* London: Paladin.

Cohen, Stanley and L. Taylor (1978) *Escape Attempts: The Theory and Practice of Resistance to Everyday Life,* Harmondsworth: Pelican.

Corbett, J.M. (1985a) The Design of MachineTool Technology and Work: Technical Science and Technical Choice', unpublished draft, Sheffield, MRC/ESRC Social and Applied Psychology Unit.

Ditton, J. (1974) 'The Fiddling Salesman: Connivance at Corruption', *New Society,* 28 Nov.

Drago, R. and T. McDonough (1984) 'Capitalist Shopfloor Initiatives, Restructuring and Organising in the '80s', *Review of Radical Political Economics,* vol. 716, no. 4: 52–77.

Eros, F. (1974) 'Review of L. Garai's Personality Dynamics and Social Existence', *European Journal of Social Psychology,* vol. 4, no. 3: 369–79.

Fineman, S. (ed.) (1993) *Emotion in Organizations,* London: Sage.

Frese, M. (1982) 'Occupational Socialisation and Psychological Development: An Underdeveloped Research Perspective in Industrial Psychology', *Journal of Occupational Psychology,* 55: 209–24.

Goffman, E. (1961) *Asylums,* New York: Doubleday.

Goffman, E. (1971) *The Presentation of Self in Everyday Life,* Harmondsworth: Pelican.

Harrison, E. and M. Marchington (1992) 'Corporate Culture and Management Control: Understanding Customer Care', *Paper to Employment Research Unit Annual Conference,* Cardiff Business School, Sep.

Hearn, J. and W. Parkin (1987) *Sex at Work: the Power and Paradox of Organization Sexuality,* Brighton: Wheatsheaf.

Hochschild, A. R. (1983) *The Managed Heart: Commercialisation of Human Feeling,* London: University of California Press.

Hochschild, A. R. (1993) Preface to: Fineman, S. (ed.) *Emotion in Organizations,* London: Sage.

Hollway, W. (1984) 'Fitting Work: Psychological Assessment in Organizations', in J. Henriques *et al, Changing the Subject: Psychology, Social Regulation and Subjectivity,* Londo: Methuen.

Hosking, D. and I. Morley (1991) *A Social Psychology of Organising: People, processes and Contexts,* Hemel Hempstead: Harvester Wheatsheaf.

Jenkins, R. (1986) *Racism and Recruitment: Managers, Organisations and Equal Opportunties in the Labour market,* Cambridge: Cambridge University Press.

Kets de Vries, M. R. F. and D. Miller (1984) *The Neurotic Organisation: Diagnosing and Changing Counterproductive Styles of Management,* San Francisco: Jossey-Bass.

Knights, D. and D. Collinson (1987) 'Shop Floor Culture and the Problem of Managerial Control', in J. McGoldrick (ed.) *Business Case File in Behavioural Science,* London: Van Nostrand.

Knights, D. and H. Willmott (1985) 'Power and Identity in Theory and Practice', *Sociological Review,* vol. 33, no. 1: 22–46.

Kunda, G. (1992) *Engineering Culture: Control and Commitment in a High Tech Corporation,* Philadelphia: Temple University Press.

Leonard, P. (1984) *Personality and Ideology: Towards a Materialist Understanding of the Individual,* London: Macmillan.

Lewis, M. (1975) 'Early Sex Differences in the Human: Studies of Socioemotional Development', *Archives of Sexual Behaviour,* vol. 4, no. 4: 329–35.

Lynn, R. (1966) 'Brainwashing Techniques in Leadership and Childrearing', *British Journal of Social and Clinical Psychology,* 5: 270–3

Mars, G. (1983) *Cheats at Work: An Anthology of Workplace Crime,* London: Unwin.

McKenna, E. (1987) *Psychology in Business: Theory and Applications,* London: Lawrence Erlbaum Associates.

Miller, D.R. (1963) The Study of Social Relationships: Situations, Identities and Social Interaction', in S. Koch (ed.) *Psychology: a Study of a Science,* vol. 5, New York: McGraw-Hill.

Nichols, T. and Beynon, H. (1977) *Living With Capitalism,* London: Routledge & Kegan Paul.

North-West Women Into Management (1987) Newletter, Manchester, Jun.

Penn, R. (1986) 'Socialisation into Skilled Identities: an Analysis of a Neglected Phenomenon', paper to 4th International Labour Process Conference, Aston.

Rauner, F., L. Rasmussen and M. Corbett (1988) The Social Shaping of Technology and Work: Human Centred CIM Systems/ *Artificial Intelligence and Society,* vol. 2: 47–61.

Rotter, J.B. (1972) 'Generalised Expectancies for Internal versus External Control of Reinforcement', in J. B. Rotter *et al.* (ed) *Applications of a Social Learning Theory of Personality,* New York: Holt, Rinehart & Winston.

Salaman, G. (1979) *Work Organizations: Resistance and Control,* London: Longman.

Seligman, M. E. P. (1975) *Helplessness,* San Francisco: Freeman.

Seve, L. (1978) *Man in Marxist Theory and the Psychology of Personality,* Sussex: Harvester Press.

Sloan, M. (1987) 'Culture and Control at Salesco: a Participant Observation Study', unpublished BA Dissertation, Lancashire Polytechnic.

Sturdy, A. (1987) 'Coping with the Pressure of Work', paper presented to 5th International Labour Process Conference, UMIST.

Thompson, P. and E. Bannon (1985) *Working the System: The Shop Floor and New Technology,* London: Pluto.

Wall, T. D., N. J. Kemp, P. R. Jackson and C. W. Clegg (1986) 'Outcomes of Autonomous Workgroups: A Long-Term Field Experiment', *Academy of Management Journal.*

Weigert, A.J., J. Smith Teitge and D.W. Teitge (1986) *Society and Identity: Towards a Sociological Psychology,* New York: Cambridge University Press.

Westwood, S. (1984) *All Day, Every Day: Factory and Family in the Making of Women's Lives,* London: Pluto.

Wexler, P. (1983) *Critical Social Psychology,* Boston: Routledge & Kegan Paul.

Wilkinson, B. (1983b) 'Technical Change and Work Organization', *Industrial Relations Journal,* vol. 14, no. 2: Summer.

Willis, P. (1977) *Learning to Labour,* Farnborough: Saxon House.

CHAPTER 11

Reassessing identity: the relevance of identity research for analysing employment relations

Robyn Thomas and Annette Davies

Introduction

Questions of identity arise with increasing regularity in the media, policy and academic debates. Gendered identities, cultural identities, national identities, racial identities, online identity, identity theft . . . it seems that identity has never received as much attention. This concern over identity is equally apparent in the study of work organizations, where identity, and the related concepts of subjectivity, identification, dis-identification, identity work, organizational identities and occupational identities, pepper contemporary debates in the literature. Despite this fascination with identity in studies on work organizations, however, a brief scan of the more influential academic journals in employment relations and the sociology of work reveals only a few articles, over the past decade, that principally focus on the dynamic relations of power and individual identity within the employment relationship.[1] We aim to show in this chapter that concerns over how we construct our identities within – and through – work should form a prominent analytical concern in contemporary debates on employment relations.

Of course, a concern over the self, seen as a coherent and autonomous entity, has been an enduring concern in the sociology of work, dating back to Durkheim and Marx with their critiques over the damage to the individual from capitalist relations of production. Where identity has been of interest, in both functionalist and radical structuralist approaches to the study of work, it has been understood as being a unified and essentialized[2] – a fixed phenomenon. From a functionalist perspective, for example, the importance of an individual's identity has been the focus of attention for as long as the field has existed, where the concern has been to encourage individuals to define themselves in relation to the organization, so as to achieve greater congruence between individual and organization's identity, thus enhancing commitment, loyalty, motivation and job satisfaction (Haslam et al., 2003). In radical structuralist analysis, conversely, the worker's identity is viewed as an expression of

class relations. Individuals are viewed as the 'personification of economic categories' (Marx, 1976: 92), where agency is structurally determined by the location in
the sphere of production. In Marxian analysis, work provided the principal source
of identity and the relationship between the two was seen as key to understanding
social solidarity, power and historical change (Leidner, 2006).

Contemporary theorizing on identities, however, has tended to take constructionist, particularly poststructuralist approaches to the concept, where identity is
understood as contested and contingent. The conceptualization of identity has thus
shifted to a more processual understanding; identity is something that is crafted
on an ongoing basis, in interaction with social–linguistic and institutionalized patterns of being and knowing. This suggests that identities are much more pluralistic,
complex, contradictory and fluid than has been traditionally conceived (Collinson, 2003). Appreciating identities in this manner also raises attention to enduring
debates within the study of work organizations on the role of agency and structure,
where the dynamics of identity construction and contestation can be understood
as surface manifestations of deeper expressions of the agency–structure relationship
(Ybema et al., 2009). Identity can be usefully conceptualized as a dynamic struggle
between various subject positions within discourse,[3] vying for our attention and our
active human agency. Thus individuals are situated in social contexts that both constrain and sustain identity (Thomas, 2009). As Ybema et al. (2009: 307) conclude,
the self–other dynamic of identity construction 'can be seen to refract the agency-
structure dialectic *in action*, for it shows in plain words how selves and sociality are
mutually implicated and mutually co-constructed' (emphasis in the original).

The paucity of studies in the sociology of work and employment relations that
focus directly on personal identities as a focus for political struggle in the workplace
can be partly explained by the considerable antipathy, ambivalence, even strong
animosity among some scholars towards poststructuralist conceptualizations of
identity, power and agency, with identity research being equated with 'political conservatism, individualism and/or failure to consider resistance' (McCabe, 2007: 244).
When identity is discussed, especially within the more traditional employment relations literature, considerable attention is given to a narrow range of collective social
identities that are occupational, union or class based. This narrow focus is beginning
to be criticized from within the discipline, with emphasis being given to identities
formed outside of the workplace or to the complex intersections between multiple
and competing identities (Briskin, 2008; Holgate et al., 2006; Piore and Safford,
2006). Despite this, however, the empirical and analytical promise of a poststructuralist understanding of individual identity remains underappreciated. This chapter
aims to address this neglect drawing attention to some of the ways in which post-
structuralist approaches to identity might inform the analysis of work organizations.

The chapter is structured as follows. First, we locate our argument within the
context of contemporary configurations of capitalism, drawing from debates that
suggest that questions over identities have become more prominent, prescient and
pressing than for the previous generation. We consider the implications of this for
current employment relations in Western socio-economic contexts. Following this,
the main body of the chapter, in making a case for taking an 'identities-turn' in
employment relations, draws attention to the ways that employees, in responding to management interventions, critically reflect on their selves, as members of

different collectives, and in the context of particular constraints on their subjectivity. In doing so, we draw on empirical research that explores the reform agenda in 'modernizing' the UK public services and the experiences of social work professionals–managers. Finally, in the discussion section, we critically explore and address the ambivalence and hostility by some scholars over the 'identities-turn' in studies of work organizations, focusing on debates over agency, structure and political adequacy.

Identity uncertainty

A widely-held belief among academic commentators, the media and the public at large is that we are facing a new configuration of capitalistic relations, termed variously as 'new capitalism' (Sennett, 2006); a 'new spirit of capitalism' (Boltanski and Chiapellio, 2006); 'casino capitalism' (Strange, 1986); 'liquid modernity' (Bauman, 2004), 'reflexive modernisation' (Beck et al., 1994) and the 'network society' (Castells, 1996). With different emphasis and interests, the theoretical skeleton common to these accounts is that the dynamic of capitalism is facing significant and intensified change, marked by increases in the speed of movement of people and capital across national borders, together with changes in production and consumption. The consequences for individuals are greater experiences of turbulence in our lives, where many traditional 'identity anchors', the established structures in our working lives, places and forms of work and communities, that inform us who we are and who we might be, are increasingly being undermined.

Emphasizing both the constraints on and possibilities for identity, Bauman's (2004) 'liquid modernity' thesis, for example, argues that the collapse of many of the stable pillars of society has left us more questioning and anxious about our selves. Greater choices of identities (offering new spaces for being) and demands to be certain identities (with the potential for oppression) arise from the ambivalence and ambiguity of the concept in contemporary society. This suggests the need for greater mental identity-maintenance work, or 'identity work', that is reflexive reordering of an understanding of self, stimulated by heightened anxiety, uncertainty, unfamiliarity and insecurity over who we are and who we might be. In some contexts, individuals are pressured to undertake almost constant reinvention. Thus we see pressures to become 'future oriented' selves (Sennett, 2006), discarding temporary 'cloakroom identities' (Bauman, 2004) on an ongoing basis.

While labour force statistics from both the UK and US throw doubt over the transformation of work and the emergence of a new employment relations characterized by insecurity (Doogan, 2009), and there is a significant debate within the academic literature over the nature and extent of change (du Gay, 2007; Webb, 2006), this discourse of 'new capitalism' can be seen to represent a persuasive and powerful ideological reference within society, which has material effects on employment relations. In other words, despite labour force statistics pointing to the contrary (Doogan, 2009), the discourse of new capitalism has powerful effects, stimulating heightened feelings of insecurity, anxiety and uncertainty over self-identity. As Grey (2009) observes, the power effects of the discourse of fast capital direct us to act upon it in ways that makes its effects, to a certain extent, a self-fulfilling prophesy.

Furthermore, the discourse of new capitalism extends to the workplace. Opportunistic cost-cutting through restructuring organizations, downsizing, de-layering, contracting out, off-shoring and other methods of 'corporate liposuction' (Burrell, 1997) have delivered greater pressures, an intensification of work and greater uncertainty over job security, while attempting to maintain low costs, high quality and customer service. This has resulted in the need to put greater efforts into encouraging identification with the organization, where a climate of downsizing and delayering fosters cynicism and detachment among the survivors (Thomas and Dunkerley, 1999). The demands of global financial markets and mobile capital (Froud et al., 2006) have also contributed to the relentless consumption of management fads, change and restructuring programmes and mergers and rationalizations to achieve short-term gains in share value in an insatiable beauty contest to financial communities (Froud et al., 2006; Webb, 2006). The changing composition of the workforce, with the greater concentration of professional, technical and managerial workers, requiring higher levels of discretion and tacit skills, calls out for control strategies that facilitate self-autonomy and flexibility. Attempts to encourage employees to identify with the organization take on greater urgency as workforces become more geographically dispersed, mobile and diverse, requiring strategies to engender feelings of coherence among workers connected via virtual offices. Together, these changes suggest that identities have become a location for struggle in contemporary work organizations.

Within the public sector, the discourse of change has been embraced, with neo-liberalist calculative rationality driving endless change initiatives over the past two decades under the reform agenda of New Public Management (NPM), 'marketisation' and 'governance' (Ferlie et al., 2007; Thomas and Davies, 2005a; Webb, 2006). Although there are debates concerning the coherence and impact of this reform agenda (Clarke et al., 2000; McLaughlin et al., 2002), the period has been marked by a panoply of initiatives directed at improving cost-effectiveness, efficiency and performance in public service organizations. In pursuing these aims there has been the adoption of a range of management practices such as the use of performance indicators and targets, strong attempts to engender a 'customer' focus, decentralization and increased individualization of the employment relationship (Farnham et al., 2003; Horton, 2003; Truss, 2008). This programme of ideological and cost-driven changes can be seen as being targeted directly at public service professionals' understanding of professional service, and collective, professional and personal self-understandings, suggesting that questions of identity are at the epicentre of political struggles in public services employment relations.

In this chapter we direct our focus on an area of the public services that has faced considerable challenge over the past few decades, that of social work. We present empirical material drawn from part of a wider study on restructuring and change in the UK public services, commencing in 2001 and involving professionals–managers from three sectors: education, police and social services (Davies and Thomas, 2008; Thomas and Davies, 2005a, b). The social workers presented in the analysis are employed in two English local authorities and are located at the middle management level. These professional social workers and 'team leaders' are positioned at the focal point of struggles over meanings of professional practices and identities in the context of wider changes in the public services. There has been reluctance in the past to consider managers as subjects of capitalist relations of production within employment relations. More often they are narrowly conceived as the architects of control and the agents of capital (Willmott, 1997). However, there are studies that have focused on a managerial labour process, and the dynamics of control and resistance among this group (Alvesson and Willmott, 1996; Gottfried, 1994; LaNuez and Jermier, 1994; Thomas and Dunkerley, 1999; Willmott, 1997). It is notable that middle managers, in both the public and private sectors, have been under considerable attack from the discourses of change over the past two decades (Ehrenreich, 2006; Heckscher, 1995; Thomas and Dunkerley, 1999; Thomas and Linstead, 2002). Ehrenreich's (2006) documentation of a 'white collar underclass' of jobless former middle managers in the US, and Sennett's (1998) detailed analysis of the material consequences of the identity crisis of middle management from flexible capitalism, are both illustrative of a range of studies that highlight the declining status, power, career prospects and control for this group in contemporary capitalist economies.

For social work middle managers, legislation and executive powers have both attempted to impose change agendas such that a once professionally regulated service is now increasingly subject to external regulation and output controls (Jones, 1999; Lawler and Hearn, 1995). As with other parts of the public services, social work reform has been directed at cost control, performance monitoring and the marketization of services (Ackroyd et al., 2007; Farnham and Horton, 1996; Pollitt, 1993). The NHS and Community Care Act (1990) intensified the pressures to implement more explicit management systems into social service departments. A mixed economy of welfare was introduced breaking up the monopoly of service provision by local authorities, now recast as enablers (Farrell and Morris, 2003; Harris, 1998). Significantly, underlying all these changes, the need to cut the public spending budget has been as much a driver for change as policy-initiated change. Thus the emphasis on effective service delivery is entwined with economic measures of performance. For example, in one of the local authorities involved in the research presented in this chapter, budgets had been reduced by £10 million over a 3-year period with the concomitant pressure to cut staff numbers.

The consequences of declining resources, efficiency measures and frequent changes to policy and practice for social work professionals have been profound. This has led to frequent suggestions that we are now witnessing a crisis in social work, pointing to evidence of change fatigue, stress and frustration, rising levels of long-term sickness and absenteeism, declining job satisfaction and increased questioning over long-term career commitment among the profession (Carey, 2003; Dominelli, 1996; Jones, 2001). Problems with recruitment and retention are extreme, with one in seven social worker posts remaining unfilled. Unison, the union representing 40,000 social workers, has described the recruitment crisis as a 'ticking time bomb' (Mulholland, 2009).

'There's a kind of party line': identity control at work

Thus, emerging configurations of capitalist relations have had profound effects on organizing, with new patterns of employment relations, a changing composition and character of the workforce and a move towards more flexible, fragmented and individualized forms of work. These developments are themselves located in the dominant discourse of neo-liberalism, of consumption, consumerism, calculative rationality and individualism. They suggest that for individuals in work organizations, identity is increasingly problematic: open to challenge and scrutiny. It is in relation to this that there has been considerable interest in the role of change discourses in targeting an individual's sense of self. It is the heightened feelings of insecurity and vulnerability, together with the loss of traditional identity anchors such as class, community and religion, that render individuals more open to the appeals of corporate identifications (Alvesson and Willmott, 2002).

There has been considerable interest during the past couple of decades over managerial attempts at regulating, even prescribing, the self-identities of employees, so as to align the individual's self-conceptions with organizationally inspired discourses (Alvesson and Willmott, 2002; Alvesson et al., 2008; Casey, 1995; Kunda, 1992; McCabe, 2007; Musson and Duberley, 2007) with the aim of increasing levels of commitment and flexibility, as part of the rewriting of the wage–effort bargain. Contemporary discourses of empowerment, leadership, teamworking, customer orientation and so on are aimed at capturing the 'hearts and minds' (Deetz, 1992) of the employee. Thus identity colonization is a critical element in the lexicon of control strategies available to management. Identity control can be understood as part of normative control in the organization, defined as the 'more or less intentional effects of social practices upon processes of identity construction and reconstruction' to produce the 'appropriate individual' (Alvesson and Willmott, 2002: 629). Attempts at identity control are more likely to be successful if the management discourses resonate with, or complement, other salient sources of identification for the individual, or if they are seen to satisfy a feeling of uncertainty or incompleteness in the individual's identity make-up.

Attempts to regulate the identities of public service professionals within the discourses of reform are clearly identifiable (du Gay, 1996; Halford and Leonard, 1999; Llewellyn, 2004; Meyer and Hammerschmid, 2006). Specifically, a range of 'disciplinary technologies'[4] have been targeted at a public service professional cadre seen to be out of line with the subject position promoted in the neo-liberalist discourse. The UK public services were depicted by the New Right architects of reform to be run by self-interested and largely unmanaged professionals who had been able to exercise considerable control over service delivery (Ackroyd et al., 2007). Consequently, on the back of this discourse, concerted efforts by successive governments over the past few decades have been made to reign in professional autonomy, to establish greater control over the nature and form of service delivery and to make public service professionals more accountable for their performance. Consequently, there has been a marked rise in initiatives to encourage and cajole public service professionals to recast their professional identities away from notions of welfarism and professional discretion, and towards entrepreneurial, competitive and individualist understandings (Clarke and Newman, 1997; du Gay, 2007, 1996; Townley, 1993b). This has meant that across the public services there have been struggles over the meaning of performance, public service work, professional and personal identities.

For social workers, the reform agenda has presented profound challenges over the meaning and practice of social work (Farrell and Morris, 2003; Jones, 1999). There has been a marked increase in techniques of individual accountability, particularly through forms of codifying, calculating and standardizing decision-making and care practice, with the proliferation of rules, procedures and checklists (Ackroyd et al., 2007). The language of customer rights has been promoted over professional discretion and direction, seen as a direct challenge to professional control (Smith, 2001). The day-to-day activities of middle-raking social workers have been increasingly configured around line management duties, budget management and contract negotiation (Causer and Exworthy, 1999). These bureaucratic controls interface with normative controls (e.g. identity and cultural) (Alvesson and Kärreman, 2004), such that they operate also at the symbolic level, prescribing a managerial, entrepreneurial and competitively individualized social worker identity.

Attempts at fundamental reforms of social worker practice thus involve challenging and redirecting deeply-held understandings on what it means to be a social worker. The extent to which the reform agenda over the past two decades has resulted in institutionalizing new understandings and forms of identification over social work performance is open to question. From our research in two social work case study local authorities, however, attempts at identity regulation and the struggles around the meanings of professional practice were very apparent.[5] For example, Sebastian, a services manager reflects on the increased accountability and value-for-money targets, along with a new more explicitly managerial identity. He comments on this change:

> ... now having to be much more of a separate manager and not so much managing the professional, having to manage the professional work of the teams, but also *at the same time* meeting targets. And those targets weren't there before. So that's the difference. We used to manage the service, we ran the services as well as we could, now as well as managing the services *we've also got to meet targets* ... So whereas what we were doing was the best job we could do to help people get into employment we've also now got to *prove that*, prove that we've actually saved the money.

Others referred to the ways that the social worker professional identity was being reconstructed to be more dispassionate, bureaucratized and obedient. Rob, a manager in children services, explains the increased pressures he experiences, arising largely from having to keep up with new compliance procedures, together with a wide range of other bureaucratic tasks that he is now expected to perform:

> The amount of knowledge that we're meant to have as a front line practitioner in this job, plus the amount of management things that we're doing in terms of looking at effectiveness and things like that ... I mean I've got a whole row of procedure manuals over there, and I can't possibly know the entire contents of that procedures manual, you know, because the social work manual is three inches thick and there's a health and safety manual too that we're now accountable for.

Greater accountability and increased responsibility for a large number of tasks have gone hand-in-hand with attempts to curtail levels of professional trust and discretion. As Joe, a team manager working with disabled children, stated:

> I mean it's almost like you need less and less bright people doing social work because actually what you don't want them to do is to kind of really think too much

about the wider issues, the wider aspects of what they're doing, what you want them to do really is to do what they're told.

We also see how these social work professional–managers are struggling to maintain their understandings of professional practice in the face of severe resource constraints and demands to be more dispassionate. Sally, a team manager with disabled children, stated:

> I think there's certain professional standards and I think probably the most important one is when we come to, sort of, funding issues and what resources we've got. And there's a kind of a party line about what we can and can't do which is very difficult for me because I'd like to give everything to everybody. I mean particularly when you work with families with disabled children who are under immense stress and have had some very traumatic and difficult lives and you actually, your heart goes out to them and you actually want to do as much as you possibly can . . . And that's really, really difficult and sometimes, you know, it grates a bit and you feel that you can't provide those things for people.

An overwhelming message from the research participants was that there was an explicit attempt to promote a more ruthless, calculative and target-oriented managerial identity that complemented the climate of strong performance, cost-consciousness and individual accountability: 'it's everyone for themselves', 'a dog eat dog culture', that there had to be 'zero defects' and, from one participant, the observation that 'they will crucify you if something goes wrong'.

The scale and nature of change has led a number of critical scholars to argue that we are witnessing de-professionalization within social services, with an increasingly fragmented and commodified profession being controlled by externally imposed compliance procedures, resulting in the demise of the 'autonomous reflective practitioner' (Ackroyd et al., 2007; Dominelli, 1996). Following Ferlie et al.'s (1996) classification of 'winners' and 'losers' in public service restructuring, Farrell and Morris (2003: 142) also suggest a de-professionalization thesis; this arising from the 'burdens of greater legislation, increased accountability, surveillance and financial pressures'. However, despite these unquestionable demands for change, what we also observe, in studying the way these public service professionals respond to the discourses and disciplinary technologies of change, is that the de-professionalization thesis is too broad-brush and sweeping, failing to capture and appreciate the complexities of change as it is played out in practice. Crucially, however, we also argue here that the de-professionalization thesis under-appreciates the agency of social work professionals.

'I am what I am': agency, dis-identification and the crafting of selves

Management discourses are not the only, or necessarily most salient, source of identity for individuals, nor are employees passive consumers of management discourses. The subject 'is not hailed in a passive sense' (Benwell and Stokoe, 2006: 32) by disciplinary discourses but is *actively engaged*, investing in some subject positions, while reflexively resisting, renegotiating and re-crafting others. Therefore, attempts by management to produce the 'appropriate individual' can be understood as part of the processes of identity struggle, that is, a dynamic and ongoing interaction between managerial-inspired discourses and personal and collective identities. Drawing from theoretical insights from political philosophies of activism of feminism(s) (Butler, 1992; Weedon, 1987), post-colonialism (Bhabha, 1994; Said, 1979; Spivak, 1987) and queer theory (Sedgwick, 1990, 1999), identity can be understood as both a target of control and a source of resistance within employment relations (Kondo, 1990; Meyerson and Scully, 1995; Thomas and Davies, 2005a; Thomas et al., 2004). While the contested nature of change is recognized in studies on changing employment relations in the workplace (Arrowsmith et al., 2003; Edwards, 1986), an analysis of identities, as a key focus of such contestation, remains under-explored.

In studies on work organizations, there has been a focus on *dis-identification*, why and how individuals are compelled to resist attempts at identity regulation at the level of the individual subject. Studies on dis-identification have focused on how individuals pitch their understandings of themselves in opposition to the identity positions offered or prescribed in work organizations. Such research emphasizes the complexities and ambiguities around the dynamics of identity construction, highlighting how power can create and constrain identities (Kondo, 1990). Dis-identification is thus a key element in the processes of crafting *who we are* (Holmer-Nadesan, 1996; Sveningsson and Alvesson, 2003; Thomas and Davies, 2005a; Thomas and Linstead, 2002), with identity being understood as the temporary reflexive understanding gained from a complex interweaving of identification and dis-identification, emphasizing the dynamics of agency and discourses, in context (Kondo, 1990; Thomas and Davies, 2005a). The critical focus therefore, in advocating an 'identities-turn' in employment relations, is that it affords in-depth insights into the ways that employees, in responding to management interventions, consider who they are, as members of different collectives, and in the context of particular constraints on their subjectivity.

Thus, returning to our case on social work professional–managers, this complexity around the interrelationship of identity construction and contestation is apparent. The social workers involved in the research are seen to be dis-identifying and identifying with salient discourses as they struggle to craft their identities and to construct an understanding of social work practice. These struggles, in turn, reflect – and are located within – a wider matrix of discourses. An understanding of social worker agency and struggle, at this level of analysis, can offer greater nuance and appreciation of the dynamics of micro-political resistance. Such insights, we argue, may be overlooked with more broad-brush portrayals of de-professionalization and a professional cadre experiencing psychological withdrawal. Rather, through processes of dis-identification, social workers, in a critical engagement with the new social worker subject position promoted in the neo-liberal discourse of reform, can be seen to be reinterpreting and rewriting attempts at transforming the meanings of professionalism and practice. This can be illustrated with Dave's reflections. Dave is the head of a unit for young offenders. He highlights how he constantly questions and challenges the attempts to re-craft understandings of social work care and what it means to be a social worker. Drawing on an identity constructed around images of professional care, Dave illustrates how this provides him with a critical platform from which to challenge the many ways in which the service is being reduced to a series of 'boxes to be ticked'. So, despite the fact that he is *swamped by paperwork*, he often refuses to privilege such tasks as a priority as they clash with his fundamental understanding of himself as a social worker in delivering *care*, an understanding that is grounded in his ethical and strongly emotional constructions of being a public service professional. As he comments, new requests for recording and accounting for daily work are 'a complete waste of time' and 'totally pointless'. Joe, another team manager, likewise, highlights the daily struggles over the meanings of service, drawing attention to the conflict between a caring and cost-conscious subjectivity:

> These are the areas where I kick against, if you like. Where you're being asked, because of some sort of policy or some sort of head counting, that I consider to be bad practice – or they could do things in a better way, which is a better service to disabled children and their families.

Other social work managers also highlighted the myriads of ways in which they refused to take on what was seen to be a finance-driven, single-minded, calculative managerial subjectivity. However, in their refusal of this subjectivity we see how this subjectivity is rewritten to incorporate notions of professional discretion. Margaret, a team leader in elderly services, while recognizing some of the benefits of being more accountable, was actively challenging the new disempowered social worker subject position, drawing on a professionally empowered identity to shape her sense of self and performance priorities:

> I think accountability is, should be there . . . So in 1997 the split was implemented and I became provider only and that makes my accountability to someone else, rather than to myself, so that makes sense. But it means we, instead of someone coming to me like used to happen saying 'could we give Mrs X some extra help, she's poorly today', I have to go through a system of sending a piece of paper to a care manager to explain why I think Mrs X needs some extra help. And if they decide not to action it then I'm left waiting and Mrs Smith's left waiting because I can't spend their money. I can't take the risk and say 'I'm going to put it in anyway'. Though, saying that – I do! We send a bit of paper saying in the meantime, 'awaiting your reply, I am supporting this' . . . we've decided that we would loosen procedures up a bit and benefit the service user – and ourselves really.

Dis-identification also arises from a subjectivity of 'the caring and supportive colleague'. We also see how these managers, in dealing with demands to work harder and suffering from long working hours and increased pressure from higher caseloads and fewer staff, are attempting to redefine the meaning of the service they can provide. Frances, a team manager in adult care, is candid about what she can and cannot achieve in performing her role and draws on a collegial and caring subject position in the way she manages her team and appraises their performance. She comments: 'I tell the staff that all time. I say "Look, you know, don't let yourself feel responsible" '.

These social work professional–managers clearly demonstrate a strong emotional attachment and investment in their work, especially in an occupational identity underpinned by the discourse of client (and colleague) care and public service.

Attempts at reconfiguring meanings and identities around a calculative and codi-
fied way of being and acting have had mixed success, given the clash between these
new meanings and individual social work professional–managers' preferred interests
(Weedon, 1987). These 'caring' professionals have invested considerable energy in
identifying with a social work profession and social service institution that has traditionally celebrated welfare provision and care unfettered in principle by questions
of cost, and determined by the discretion of the ethically oriented practitioner. This
forms a relatively enduring and appealing identity for many social workers. Judy,
for example, is adamant when she says: '*I am what I am, I'm a caring person*'. Other
research has also emphasized how a caring and service identity remains 'surprisingly
robust' (Morgan et al., 2000) in social work, with attempts to instil new meanings
of calculative rationality being viewed as 'insensitive, inappropriate and vulgar'
(Carey, 2003: 133). This ethical and caring identity serves as a powerful resource
that some of the social workers in our study drew on in challenging and destabilizing these new meanings. However, this is not the only identity resource drawn
on by the social workers in challenging attempts to conjoin social workers' sense of
their self with the neo-liberalist discourse. Mary, a team manager in adult services,
for example, draws on professional expertise and discretion in asserting her identity
as a skilled and knowledgeable professional–manager:

> I'm experienced and knowledgeable and professional in my job and this job can-
> not be reduced to tick boxes, which in any case aren't about the quality of service,
> they're just about covering your back.

So, shifting the spotlight of analysis to the micro-political highlights that under-
neath the few expressions of overt antagonism to managerialism is a persistent
struggle over attempts to rewrite the meanings of effective service. It is the 'pas-
sionate attachment' (Butler, 1997) and the considerable and ongoing investment
in alternative identity positions that provide both the site of this struggle and the
source of its resistance.

Discussion: the relevance of identity research

In this chapter, we draw on poststructuralist theorizing on identity to argue for a
more nuanced understanding of individual agency in the changing context of
employment relations. In this discussion section, we wish to return to our observations raised at the start of the chapter over the neglect of individual identity within
the discipline. Burrell (2006) wryly observes, the 'meteorite' of postmodernist thinking left a very small crater in employment relations and, further, where there has
been any impact on debates by the ideas promoted in these 'Parisian fashions', the
'response teams swept into action'. (Burrell, 2006: 175). Certainly, poststructuralist-
influenced approaches to appreciating the interrelations between power relations
and identity at work have had little take up among researchers in the sociology of
work and employment relations literature. What is more, there has been ambivalence at best and more often explicit hostility, by some critical scholars towards work
that has focused on individual identities at work (Martinez Lucio and Stewart, 1997;

Thompson and Ackroyd, 1995). The nature of this criticism is twofold: that such approaches promote an individualized understanding of the worker at the expense of collective identities; and that it is politically inadequate, offering an etiolated notion of agency and resistance and thereby removing the base from which to analyse and challenge the dynamics of employment relations. Drawing on our own research and others that have examined the dynamics of identity construction and contestation at work, we will now consider this critique and conclude by highlighting some of the analytical promise offered by focusing on the dynamics of power, identities and agency in contemporary debates on work organizations and employment relations.

McCabe (2007) notes the strong suspicion in critical realist critiques that a focus on the individual equates to a promotion of individualism. The accusation is that the 'celebration of the individual' leads to an individualistic and myopic focus, with a concomitant failure to appreciate the wider structures of power that shape the actual identities that are available to individuals in organizations and who is able to occupy them, within historical and cultural contexts, and material relations (Fairclough, 2005; Thompson, 2005). This reflects a mistaken conflation of individualism with identity. Further it is also suggested that it is only through collective activity that increased control in workplaces can be challenged and an emphasis on identity reduces the opportunities for the more informed to be able to transform the social world in ways that eliminates such restrictions (Bain and Taylor, 2000). For example, Blyton and Turnbull (1998: 9) are keen to emphasize that it is the 'collective aspects of relations between workforce and management that we take as our focal point'.

Focusing on the individual does not suggest that we are ignoring or discounting wider structures (dominant and deep-seated discourses), power relations, agency, material conditions nor historical development (McCabe, 2007). Moreover, it is precisely the criticism of the individualistic tendencies of contemporary discourses of change and how these attempt to seduce and entice us into processes of individualization that provides the motivation to challenge and critique among those interested in subjectivity (Alvesson and Willmott, 2002; Bergström and Knights, 2006; Collinson, 2003; Hodgson, 2005; Holmer-Nadesan, 1996; McCabe, 2007; Meriliäinen et al., 2004; Thomas and Davies, 2005a).

In addition, an emphasis on subjectivity does not mean resorting to either determinism on the one hand or naïve humanism on the other. Ironically, it was attempts to bring back the 'missing subject' (Newton, 1998) in labour process theory, drawing insights from Foucault (1982), that can be seen as pivotal in putting issues of identity, subjectivity and the subject at the forefront of debates over control, agency and resistance at work (Knights and Willmott, 1989). In particular, labour process theory was viewed as being unable to fully appreciate how processes of individualization, fragmentation and intensification of work in contemporary capitalist employment relations had profound implications for self-identity (Casey, 1999; du Gay, 1996; Grey, 1994; Knights and Morgan, 1991; Sewell and Wilkinson, 1992; Willmott, 1993). However, appropriation of Foucault's (1977) ideas into the labour process debate, with the so-called manufacturing of subjectivity thesis, was viewed as being too deterministic, suggesting a 'docile body', a mere throughput for management-inspired discourses, with the impression being that the individual was more 'done to' than 'doing' (Newton, 1998). Consequently, battle lines have been drawn and theoretical positions defended, resulting in a polarized debate around questions of structure and agency in workplace power relations. These debates have centred on the problem of an *under socialized* or *over socialized* understanding of the subject, with both approaches resting on the assumption of a human being as a 'little world in himself' (Elias, 1968: 249, cited in du Gay, 2007: 24), that is, someone who is viewed as having insufficient or too much agency.

Of course, the issue of structure versus agency has long been debated within the study of work organizations (Reed, 2003). Rather than stalling in dualistic thinking over agency and structure, however, we argue that it is conceptually fruitful to focus on the mutual cohabitation of the self and the social, whereby identity can be usefully conceived of as arising from the *interactions* between forms of identity regulation (located in often deeply entrenched discourses) and human agency, rather than one or other being an overriding influence (Bergström and Knights, 2006). Such an approach usefully locates the individual in social and temporal contexts that both constrain and sustain identity construction.

Thus, in the example of social work professional–managers presented in this chapter, there is an active engagement – a struggle – over the discourses that both constrain and sustain identities. Changes in the employment relationship for social work professionals have contributed to increased pressure of work, greater accountability, demands for a diverse range of managerial skills, longer working hours, greater insecurity and stress. However, the impact of these changes cannot be viewed in a deterministic way. Rather, the effect is to provide the context of struggle, manipulation and mediation by these public service professionals. Given their equivocal positions as both recipients and bearers of control (Willmott, 1997), these middle-raking social work professionals can be regarded as 'central political actors' (Laine and Vaara, 2007) whose agency can be targeted at challenging and reinterpreting meanings within the ideological project of new public management. As Laine and Varra argue (2007: 53) 'they can act as agents creating new discursive and social practices'. This is where challenge becomes meaningful for them: in engaging in the struggle around meanings, they can have considerable effects in further destabilizing the discourses of change.

The focus of this research was on the way that individuals exercise power in positioning themselves in a dynamic relationship with the discourses of change. In exerting their influence, these individuals drew on the collective occupational identity of the social work professional or public service manager, although no reference was made to any union-based identity or to collective action in response to the pressures of change. While it could be argued that a collective response may provide a more powerful means of transforming behavioural norms (McNay, 2000), the emphasis within this chapter has been on the way that individual identity performances also have important, albeit more subtle, effects in shifting and transforming meanings and understandings within work organizations.

Thus, we can see how, by focusing on the struggle around identities, in the analysis of changing employment relations, we are able to present an alternative critique of power–knowledge relations in organizations, gaining insights into how and why individuals challenge the meanings within discourses, rendering them less robust and unified. Taking a micro-political approach (Thomas and Davies, 2005a), we have shown how social work professionals are able to subvert, resist and re-inscribe attempts to re-craft their identities and the meanings of effective performance that are prescribed within the reform agenda. We see how they exercise power in the ways they position themselves when faced with tensions within their employment relationship. Through a process of challenging and (re)constructing meanings within social work practice, they exploit the contradictions within the discourses of change, drawing on different meanings around public service, managerial efficiency, personal survival and support for front-line staff. This detailed understanding of the ways that employees respond to change, focusing on identity work in dynamic interaction with the power of subjectivizing forces, provides an important account of human agency in the employment relationship. As Jermier et al. (1994) note, power relations in employment relations occur in more complex ways than can be understood in simple all or nothing polarized categories: 'most employees in advanced capitalist societies are neither class-conscious revolutionaries nor passive docile automatons' (Jermier et al., 1994: 9). Such neat bounded categories bear little reflection on our lived experiences. We need to appreciate that questions of 'who we are?' dynamically interact with 'who our organization wants us to be?' and that responses to such questions are many and varied. Therefore, a detailed understanding of the dynamics of control and agency in analysing work and employment relations is crucial.

Notes

1. We reviewed the following journals for the period 1999–2009: Sociology; The Sociological Review; Work, Employment and Society; British Journal of Industrial Relations; European Journal of Industrial Relations; Industrial Relations; Industrial Relations Journal and Employee Relations. For each journal we searched abstracts and key words for the terms 'identity' and/or 'subjectivity'. Overall, very little attention was given to individual identity, although collective identity was a strong focus in the articles. In addition, where individual identity was of concern, this was in the sociology of work journals rather than those more directly focused on industrial/employment relations.
2. Essentialism here refers to the assumption that all those identifying, or being identified, with a particular social category (e.g. gender) display common characteristics and have a common existence.
3. We take a critical understanding of discourses, whereby they are seen not only to constitute meanings of terms and practices, but also they engender personal identities. Discourses are thus 'historically and culturally variable ways of specifying knowledge and truth' (Meriläinen et al., 2004). Discourses thus 'do not identify objects, they constitute them and in the practice of doing so conceal their own invention' (Foucault, 1972: 49).
4. A Foucauldian term, disciplinary technologies are targeted at producing a 'docile body' necessary for the smooth operation of capitalism (Foucault, 1977). For example, HRM can be seen as a comprising a set of disciplinary technologies by which individuals come to know themselves, through a range of techniques designed to label, classify, delineate, rank and elicit self-confessions (Townley, 1993a).
5. In this research, we view the interview as an arena for critical reflexive engagement between the interviewer and interviewee, with the interview texts being constructed collectively by both parties. Taking a constructionist approach, where meaning is constituted in language and social action, our presentation of material in this chapter represents our constructions of the social workers' constructions of their struggles around identities, power and agency (Thomas and Linstead, 2002).

References

Ackroyd, S., Kirkpatrick, I. and Walker, R. M. (2007) 'Public management reform in the UK and its consequences for professional organization: a comparative analysis', *Public Administration*, 85, 1: 9–26.

Alvesson, M., Ashcraft, A. and Thomas, R. (2008) 'Identity matters', *Organization*, 15, 1: 5–28.

Alvesson, M. and Kärreman, D. (2004) 'Interfaces of control. Technocratic and socio-ideological control in a global management consultancy firm', *Accounting, Organizations and Society*, 29: 423–44.

Alvesson, M. and Willmott, H. (2002) 'Identity regulation as organizational control: producing the appropriate individual', *Journal of Management Studies*, 39, 5: 619–44.

Alvesson, M. and Willmott, H. (1996) *Making Sense of Management: A Critical Introduction*. London: Sage.

Arrowsmith, J., Gilman, M. W., Edwards, P. and Monder, R. (2003) 'The impact of the national minimum wage in small firms', *British Journal of Industrial Relations*, 41, 3. 435–56.

Bain, P. and Taylor, P. (2000) 'Entrapped by the "electronic panoptican"? Worker resistance in the call centre', *New Technology, Work and Employment*, 15, 1: 2–18.

Bauman, Z. (2004) *Identity*. Cambridge: Polity Press.

Beck, U., Giddens, A. and Lash, S. (1994) *Reflexive Modernisation: Politics, Tradition and Aesthetics in the Modern Social Order*. Stanford, CA: Stanford University Press.

Benwell, B. and Stokoe, E. (2006) *Discourse and Identity*. Edinburgh: Edinburgh University Press.

Bergström, O. and Knights, D. (2006) 'Organizational discourse and subjectivity: subjectification during processes of recruitment', *Human Relations*, 59, 3: 351–77.

Bhabha, H. (1994) *The Location of Culture*. London: Routledge.

Blyton, P. and Turnbull, P. (1998) *Dynamics of Employee Relations*. Second Edition. Basingstoke: Macmillan.

Boltanski, L. and Chiapello, E. (2007) *The New Spirit of Capitalism*. London: Verso.

Briskin, L. (2008) 'Cross-constituency organizing in Canadian unions', *British Journal of Industrial Relations*, 46, 2: 221–47.

Burrell, G. (1997) *Pandemonium: Towards a Retro-Organization Theory*. London: Sage.

Burrell, G. (2006) 'Foucauldian and postmodern thought and the analysis of work', in M. Korczynski, R. Hodson and P. Edwards (eds) *Social Theory at Work*. Oxford: Oxford University Press.

Butler, J. (1997) *The Psychic Life of Power*. Stanford: Standford University Press.

Butler, J. (1992) 'Contingent foundations: feminism and the question of "postmodernism"', in J. Butler, and J. W. Scott (eds) *Feminists Theorize the Political*. London: Routledge.

Carey, M. (2003) 'Anatomy of a care manager', *Work, Employment and Society*, 17, 1: 121–35.

Casey, C. (1995) *Work, Self and Society: After Industrialism*. London: Routledge.

Casey, C. (1999) ' "Come, join our family": discipline and integration in corporate organizational culture', *Human Relations*, 52, 2: 155–78.

Castells, M. (1996) *The Rise of the Network Society*. Oxford: Blackwell.

Causer, G. and Exworthy, M. (1999) 'Professionals as managers across the public sector', in M. Exworthy, and S. Halford (eds) *Professionals and the New Managerialism in the Public Sector*. Milton Keynes: OU Press.

Clarke, J. and Newman, J. (1997) *The Managerial State*. London: Sage.

Clarke, J., Gerwitz, S. and McLaughlin, E. (2000) 'Reinventing the welfare state', in J. Clarke, S. Gerwitz and E. McLaughlin (eds) *New Managerialism, New Welfare?* London: Sage.

Collinson, D. (2003) 'Identities and insecurities: selves at work', *Organization*, 10: 527–47.

Davies, A. and Thomas, R. (2008) 'Dixon of Dock Green got shot! Policing identity work and organizational change', *Public Administration*, 86: 627–42.

Deetz, S. (1992) *Democracy in an Age of Corporate Colonization*. Albany NY: Albany State University of New York Press.

Dominelli, L. (1996) 'Deprofessionalising social work: anti-oppressive practice, competencies and postmodernism', *British Journal of Social Work*, 26, 2: 153–75.

Doogan, K. (2009) *New Capitalism? The Transformation of Work*. London: Polity Press.

du Gay, P. (1996) *Consumption and Identity at Work*. London: Sage.

du Gay, P. (2007) *Organizing Identity*. London: Sage.

Edwards, P. (1986) *Conflict at Work*. Oxford: Blackwell.

Ehrenreich, B. (2006) *Bait and Switch: The Futile Pursuit of the Corporate Dream*. London: Granta Books.

Elias, N. (1968) *The Civilizing Process, Vol. 1*. Oxford: Basil Blackwell.

Fairclough, N. (2005) 'Critical discourse analysis, organizational discourse, and organizational change', *Organization Studies*, 26: 915–39.

Farnham, D. and Horton, S. (1996) *Managing People in the Public Services*. Hampshire: Macmillan.

Farnham, D., Horton, S. and White, G. (2003) 'Organisational change and staff participation and involvement in Britain's public services', *International Journal of Publics Sector Management*, 16, 6: 434–45.

Farrell, C. and Morris, J. (2003) 'The "neo-bureaucratic state": professionals, managers and professional managers in schools, general practices and social work', *Organization*, 10, 1: 129–56.

Ferlie, E., Ashburner, L., Fitzgerald, L. and Pettigrew, A. (1996) *The New Public Management in Action*. Oxford: Oxford University Press.

Ferlie, E., Lynn, L. E. Jr. and Pollitt, C. (2007) Introductory Remarks, in E. Ferlie, L. E. Lynn Jr. and C. Pollitt (eds) *The Oxford Handbook of Public Management*. Oxford: Oxford University Press.

Foucault, M. (1972) *The Archaeology of Knowledge & The Discourse on Language*. New York: Pantheon Books/Tavistock.

Foucault, M. (1977) *Discipline and Punish: The Birth of the Prison*. London: Allen Lane.

Foucault, M. (1982) 'The subject and power', in H. L. Drefus and P. Rabinow (eds) *Beyond Structuralism and Hermeneutics*. Brighton: Harvester.

Froud, J., Sukhdev, J., Leaver, A. and Williams, K. (2006) *Financialization and Strategy: Narrative and Numbers*. Abingdon, Oxon: Routledge.

Gottfried, H. (1994) 'Learning the score: the duality of control and everyday resistance in the temporary help service industry', in John M. Jermier, David Knights, and Walter R. Nord (eds) *Resistance and Power in Organizations*. 102–27, London: Routledge.

Grey, C. (1994) 'Career as a project of self and labour process discipline', *Sociology*, 28, 2: 479–97.

Grey, C. (2009) *A Very Short, Fairly Interesting and Reasonably Cheap Book about Organizations* (second edition). London: Sage.

Halford, S. and Leonard, P. (1999) 'New Identities? Professionalism, managerialism and the construction of self', in M. Exworthy and S. Halford (eds) *Professionals and the New Managerialism in the Public Sector*. Buckingham: Open University Press.

Harris, J. (1998) 'Scientific management, bureau professionalism, new managerialism: the labour process of state social work', *British Journal of Social Work*, 28: 839–62.

Haslam, S. A., Eggins, R. A. and Reynolds, K. J. (2003) 'The ASPIRe model: actualizing social and personal identity resources to enhance organisational outcomes', *Journal of Organisational and Occupational Psychology*, 76: 83–113.

Heckscher, C. (1995) *White Collar Blues*. New York: Basic Books.

Hodgson, D. E. (2005) 'Putting on a professional performance': performativity, subversion and project management', *Organization*, 12, 1: 51–68.

Holgate, J., Hebson, G. and McBride, A. (2006) 'Why gender and "difference" matters: a critical appraisal of industrial relations research', *Industrial Relations Journal*, 37, 4: 310–28.

Holmer-Nadesan, M. (1996) 'Organizational identity and space of action', *Organization Studies*, 17, 1: 49–81.

Horton, S. (2003) 'Participation and involvement: the democratisation of new public management, *International Journal of Public Sector Management*, 16, 6: 403–11.

Jermier, J. M., Knights, D. and Nord, W. R. (1994) 'Introduction', in J. M. Jermier, D. Knights, and W. R. Nord (eds) *Resistance and Power in Organizations*. London: Routledge.

Jones, C. (1999) 'Social work: regulation and managerialism', in M. Exworthy and S. Halford (eds) *Professionals and the New Managerialism in the Public Sector*. Milton Keynes: OU Press.

Jones, C. (2001) 'Voices from the front line: state social workers and new labour', *British Journal of Social Work*, 31: 547–62.

Knights, D. and Willmott, H. (1989) 'Power and subjectivity at work', *Sociology*, 23: 535–58.

Knights, D. and Morgan, G. (1991) 'Corporate strategy, organisations and subjectivity: a critique', *Organization Studies*, 12: 251–73.

Kondo, D. (1990) *Crafting Selves: Power, Gender and Discourses of Identity in a Japanese Workplace*. Chicago: University of Chicago Press.

Kunda, G. (1992) *Engineering Culture. Control and Commitment in a High-Tech Corporation*. Philadelphia: Temple University Press.

Laine, P-M. and Vaara, E. (2007) 'Struggling over subjectivity: a discursive analysis of strategic development in an engineering group', *Human Relations*, 60, 1: 29–58.

LaNuez, D. and. Jermier, J. M. (1994) 'Sabotage by managers and technocrats: neglected patterns of resistance at work', in John M. Jermier, David Knights and Walter R. Nord (eds) *Resistance and Power in Organizations*. 219–51, London: Routledge.

Lawler, J. and Hearn, J. (1995) 'UK public service organizations: the rise of managerialism and the impact of change on social services departments', *International Journal of Public Sector Management*, 8, 4: 7–16.

Leidner, R. (2006) 'Identity and work', in M. Korczynski, R. Hodson and P. Edwards (eds) *Social Theory at Work*. Oxford: Oxford University Press.

Llewellyn, N. (2004) 'In search of modernization: the negotiation of social identity in organizational reform', *Organization Studies*, 25, 6: 947–68.

Martinez Lucio, M. and Stewart, P. (1997) 'The paradox of contemporary labour process theory: the rediscovery of labour and the disappearance of collectivism', *Capital and Class*, 62: 49–77.

Marx, K. (1976) *Capital: A Critique of Political Economy*. Harmondsworth: Penguin.

McCabe, D. (2007) 'Individualization at work? subjectivity, teamworking and anti-unionism', *Organization*, 14, 2: 243–66.

McLaughlin, K., Osborne, S. P. and Ferlie, E. (2002) (eds) *New Public Management: Current Trends and Future Prospects*. London: Routledge.

McNay, L. (2000) *Gender and Agency: Reconfiguring the Subject in Feminist and Social Theory*. Cambridge: Polity.

Meriliänen, S., Tienari, J., Thomas, R. and Davies, A. (2004) 'Management consultant talk: a cross-cultural comparison of normalising discourse and resistance', *Organization*, 11, 2: 539–64.

Meyer, R. and Hammerschmid, G. (2006) 'Public management reform: an identity project', *Public Policy and Administration*, 21, 1: 99–115.

Meyerson, D. E. and Scully, M. A. (1995) 'Tempered radicalism and the politics of ambivalence and change', *Organization Science*, 6, 5: 585–600.

Morgan, P., Allington, N. and Heery, E. (2000) 'Employment insecurity in the public services', in E. Heery and J. Salmon (eds) *The Insecure Workforce*. London: Routledge.

Mulholland, H. (2009) 'Tories warn of social work recruitment crisis', *Guardian Newspaper*, Guardian.co.uk, Tuesday 3rd February 2009.

Musson, G. and Duberley, J. (2007) 'Change, change or be exchanged: the discourse of participation and the manufacture of identity', *Journal of Management Studies*, 44, 1: 143–64.

Newton, T. (1998) 'Theorizing subjectivity in organizations: the failure of foucauldian studies', *Organization Studies*, 19, 3: 415–47.

Piore, M. J. and Safford, S. (2006) 'Changing regimes of workplace governance, shifting axes of social mobilization, and the challenge to industrial relations theory', *Industrial Relations*, 45, 3: 299–325.

Pollitt, C. (1993) *Managerialism and the Public Services*. Oxford: Blackwell.

Reed, M. (2003) 'The agency/structure dilemma in organization theory: open doors and brick walls, in H. Tsoukas and C. Knudsen (eds) *The Oxford Handbook of Organization Theory: Meta-Theoretical Perspectives*. Oxford: Oxford University Press.

Said, E. (1979) *Orientalism*. London: Routledge.

Sedgwick, E. K. (1990) *Epistemologies of the Closet*. Berkley, CA: University of California Press.

Sedgwick, E. K. (1999) *A Dialogue on Love*. New York: Beacon Press.

Sennett, R. (1998) *The Corrosion of Character*. New York: Norton.

Sennett, R. (2006) *The Culture of the New Capitalism*. New Haven: Yale University Press.

Sewell, G. and Wilkinson, B. (1992) 'Someone to watch over me: surveillance, discipline and the just-in-time labour process', *Sociology*, 26, 2: 271–91.

Smith, C. (2001) 'Trust and confidence: possibilities for social work in high modernity', *British Journal of Social Work*, 31, 2: 287–316.

Spivak, G. C. (1987) *In Other Worlds: Essays in Cultural Politics*. New York: Methuen.

Strange, S. (1986) *Casino Capitalism*. Oxford: Blackwell.

Sveningsson, S. and Alvesson, M. (2003) 'Managing managerial identities: organizational fragmentation, discourse and identity struggle', *Human Relations*, 56 (10): 1163–93.

Thomas, R. and Dunkerley, D. (1999) 'Careering downwards? middle management in the downsized organization', *British Journal of Management*, 10, 2: 157–69.

Thomas, R. and Linstead, A. (2002) 'Losing the plot? middle managers and identity', *Organization*, 9, 1: 71–93.

Thomas, R., Mills, A. J. and Helms-Mills, J. (2004) 'Introduction: resisting gender, gendering resistance', in R. Thomas, A. J. Mills and J. Helms-Mills (eds) *Identity Politics at Work*. London: Routledge.

Thomas, R. and Davies, A. (2005a) 'Theorising the micro-politics of resistance: discourses of change and professional identities in the UK public services', *Organization Studies*, 26, 5: 683–706.

Thomas, R. and Davies, A. (2005b) 'What have the feminists done for us? feminist theory and organizational resistance', *Organization*, 12, 5: 711–40.

Thomas, R. (2009) 'Critical studies on identities: mapping the Terrain', in M. Alvesson, T. Bridgman and H. Willmott (eds) *The Oxford Handbook of Critical Management Studies*. 166–85, Oxford: Oxford University Press.

Thompson, P. and Ackroyd, S. (1995) 'All quiet on the workplace front? a critique of recent trends in british industrial sociology', *Sociology*, 29, 4: 615–33.

Thompson, P. (2005) 'Brands, boundaries and bandwagons: a critical reflection on critical management studies', in C. Grey and H. Willmott (eds) *Critical Management Studies: A Reader*. Oxford: Oxford University Press.

Townley, B. (1993a) 'Foucault, power/knowledge, and its relevance for human resource management', *Academy of Management Review*, 18, 3: 518–45.

Townley, B. (1993b) 'Performance appraisal and the emergence of management', *Journal of Management Studies*, 30, 2: 221–38.

Truss, C. (2008) 'Continuity and change: The role of the HR function in the modern pubic sector', *Public Administration*, 86, 4: 1071–88.

Webb, J. (2006) *Organisations, Identities and the Self*. Basingstoke: Palgrave.

Weedon, C. (1987) *Feminist Practice and Poststructuralist Theory*. Oxford: Blackwell.

Willmott, H. (1993) 'Strength is ignorance; slavery is freedom: managing culture in modern organizations', *Journal of Management Studies*, 30, 4: 515–52.

Willmott, H. (1997) 'Rethinking management and managerial work: capitalism, control and subjectivity', *Human Relations*, 50, 11: 1329–59.

Ybema, S., Keenoy, T., Oswick, C., Beverungen, A., Ellis, N. and Sabelis, I. (2009) 'Articulating identities', *Human Relations*, 62, 3: 299–322.

Index